MW01049307

NFPA® 99

Health Care Facilities Code

2024 Edition

This edition of NFPA 99, *Health Care Facilities Code*, was prepared by the Technical Committees on Electrical Systems, Fundamentals of Health Care Facilities, Health Care Emergency Management and Security, Hyperbaric and Hypobaric Facilities, Mechanical Systems, Medical Equipment, and Piping Systems, released by the Correlating Committee on Health Care Facilities and acted on by the NFPA membership during the 2023 NFPA Technical Meeting held June 22. It was issued by the Standards Council on August 25, 2023, with an effective date of September 14, 2023, and supersedes all previous editions.

This document has been amended by one or more Tentative Interim Amendments (TIAs) and/or Errata. See "Codes & Standards" at www.nfpa.org for more information.

This edition of NFPA 99 was approved as an American National Standard on September 14, 2023.

Origin and Development of NFPA 99

The idea for this document grew as the number of documents under the original NFPA Committee on Hospitals grew. By the end of 1980, there existed 12 documents on a variety of subjects, 11 directly addressing fire-related problems in and about health care facilities. These documents covered health care emergency preparedness, inhalation anesthetics, respiratory therapy, laboratories in health-related institutions, hyperbaric facilities, hypobaric facilities, inhalation anesthetics in ambulatory care facilities, home use of respiratory therapy, medical–surgical vacuum systems in hospitals, essential electrical systems (EES) for health care facilities, safe use of electricity in patient care areas of health care facilities, and safe use of high-frequency electricity in health care facilities.

A history on the documents that covered these topics are in the "Origin and Development of NFPA 99" in the 1984 edition of NFPA 99. What was then the Health Care Facilities Correlating Committee reviewed the matter beginning in late 1979 and concluded that combining all the documents under its jurisdiction would be beneficial to those who used those documents for the following reasons:

(1) The referenced documents were revised independently. Combining the documents into one would place them on the same revision cycle.
(2) It would place in one unit many documents that referenced each other.
(3) It would be an easier and more complete reference for the various users of the document (e.g., hospital engineers, medical personnel, designers and architects, various enforcing authorities).

In January 1982, a compilation of the latest edition of each of the 12 documents under the jurisdiction of the correlating committee was published as NFPA 99, *Health Care Facilities Code*. The document was formally adopted at the 1983 Fall Meeting.

The 1984 edition included technical, administrative, and organizational changes.

For the 1987 edition, the third and final step in the process of combining the previous individual documents took place — that of integrating the content of these individual documents into a cohesive document. Technical changes were made, and NFPA 56F, *Standard on Nonflammable Medical Piped Gas Systems*, was incorporated into the document.

The 1990 edition implemented structural changes and added some modifiers to make it easier to determine where requirements apply. Technical changes included correlation with NFPA *101®*, *Life Safety Code®*, changes for compressed medical air systems on the use of gas-powered medical devices operating at a gauge pressure of 1379 kPa (200 psi) and piped gas systems in general, clarification that patient care areas and wet locations are mutually exclusive, and additional guidance on the effects of a disaster on staff.

For the 1993 edition, further efforts made the document more user friendly (e.g., placing all "recommended" guidance either in notes or in the appendix). Significant technical changes included adding requirements and recommendations to further prevent or minimize fires in operating rooms. There were also major changes to requirements for installing, testing, inspecting, verifying, and maintaining nonflammable medical piped gas systems. New sections on dental compressed air and dental vacuum requirements were added.

Changes to the 1996 edition made the document easier to use; for example, Chapters 3 and 4 were restructured so that all requirements for a Type 1, Type 2, or Type 3 essential electrical system, or a Level 1, Level 2, Level 3, or Level 4 piped gas or vacuum system, were in one section. Other technical changes included moving requirements on flammable anesthetizing locations and the use of flammable inhalation anesthetics to a new Appendix 2. Guidance on emergency preparedness was moved to a new mandatory chapter. A new chapter on home health care was added. Requirements for storage rooms containing gas cylinders and containers totaling less than 85 m³ (3000 ft³) were also added.

For the 1999 edition, some significant technical and structural changes were made. Chapters on ambulatory health care centers, clinics, and medical/dental offices were replaced completely by a new Chapter 13 covering health facilities other than hospitals, nursing homes, and limited care facilities as defined in the document. A new chapter on freestanding birthing centers was added.

The 2002 edition included format and technical revisions in accordance with the 2000 edition of the *Manual of Style for NFPA Technical Committee Documents.* Occupancy Chapters 13 through 21 stated what was required, while Chapters 4 through 12 prescribed how those requirements were to be achieved.

The changes made to the 2005 edition were mainly for clarity and were editorial in nature. A centralized computer was allowed to be used in lieu of one of the master alarms for medical gas and vacuum systems. Stainless steel tubing was added as an approved material for vacuum systems.

The 2012 edition went through a major revision. NFPA 99 was changed from a standard to a code to reflect how the document was used and adopted and to indicate how health care is delivered. The risk to a patient does not change for a given procedure; if the procedure is performed in a doctor's office versus a hospital, the risk remains the same. Therefore, NFPA 99 eliminated the occupancy chapters and transitioned to a risk-based approach. The new Chapter 4 outlined the parameters for this approach. The code reflected the risk to the patient in defined categories of risk.

Chapter 5 went through editorial changes in the 2012 edition as well, with the addition of new material on the testing and maintenance of gas and vacuum systems. In addition, the administrative details for the care, maintenance, and handling of cylinders were moved to chapters under the responsibility of the new Technical Committee on Medical Equipment, formed by the combination of the Technical Committee on Gas Delivery Equipment and the Technical Committee on Electrical Equipment. Several new chapters were added on information technology and communications systems; plumbing; heating, ventilation, and air conditioning; security management; and features of fire protection. Many of these systems, not previously addressed by NFPA 99, are important systems and protection features in health care. The hyperbaric chapter also had minor changes for clarity.

The 2015 edition of NFPA 99 built on the major changes of the 2012 edition. The way risk categories are defined was revised to be more inclusive so that categories could then be applied to equipment and activities rather than to chapters that deal with systems. The requirements for Category 3 medical gas and vacuum systems, while originally aimed specifically for dental applications, were expanded to include the possibility that other gases might fall under Category 3 based on the facility's risk assessment.

The Technical Committee on Electrical Systems continued the task of correlating requirements with Chapter 6 and *NFPA 70, National Electrical Code.* They removed the requirements for Level 3 EES, determining that the requirements in *NFPA 70* that apply to all buildings would provide the necessary level of safety if there was not a need for a Level 1 or Level 2 EES. Each of the technical committees made a concerted effort to specifically identify how each chapter was to apply to existing buildings or installations and to list the sections that applied.

The 2018 edition of the code featured numerous technical changes and requirements for new technologies and materials. Some major or noteworthy changes were as follows:

(1) The requirements addressing the risk assessment in Chapter 4 were revised to clarify the responsibility for conducting a risk assessment and determining risk categories. It further stressed, through annex language, that determining risk should be a collaborative effort.
(2) Chapter 5 included requirements that allow for the use of oxygen concentrators as central supply sources for piped systems.
(3) Corrugated medical tubing was made a permitted material for medical gas and vacuum systems.
(4) Chapter 6 was restructured in a more logical manner, grouping related requirements and allowing for the deletion of duplicated requirements for different types of EES.
(5) Chapter 7 included requirements for wireless phone and paging integration and for clinical information systems.

(6) Chapter 14 compiled all of the requirements for inspection, testing, and maintenance for hyperbaric facilities into one section.
(7) A new Chapter 15 was added to the code. After several editions of trying to work the requirements for dental systems into Chapter 5, a decision was made to create a chapter dedicated to the application of piped gas and vacuum systems for these systems that do not always readily fall under the requirements for medical gas and vacuum as addressed in Chapter 5.

The 2021 edition of NFPA 99 introduced several substantial changes to the code. Some of the most notable changes were as follows:

(1) The scope was changed to include hyperbaric chambers for veterinary care.
(2) New guidance described what to do when clinical spaces are converted to nonclinical spaces regarding medical gas inlets and outlets.
(3) The term *responsible facility authority* was introduced into the code with requirements for responsibilities and qualifications.
(4) Existing language in Chapter 5 on cryogenic fluid central supply systems was replaced with extracts from NFPA 55, which covers that topic.
(5) A new section on health care microgrids was added to Chapter 6.
(6) Requirements for electrical equipment site acceptance testing and electrical preventative maintenance were added to Chapter 6.
(7) Procedures for removing flammable liquid–soaked materials from the operating room were altered to require those materials to be removed only from the patient care vicinity.
(8) Requirements for the fire protection of heliports was added to Chapter 16 by referencing NFPA 418.

Key revisions for the 2024 edition of NFPA 99 are as follows:

(1) A definition for *nonessential electrical loads* has been added to Chapter 3.
(2) The following changes have been made to Chapter 5:

   (a) A reference to ASSE/IAPMO/ANSI 6060, *Professional Qualifications Standard for Medical Gas Systems Designers,* has been added.
   (b) Maximum allowable quantity (MAQ) limits for medical gas and cryogenic fluid central supply systems in health care facilities have been added.
   (c) Requirements for medical gas and vacuum system auxiliary connections to facilitate emergency preparedness, maintenance, and supplementation have been added.
   (d) Pressure-drop calculations and limits have been added to medical gas piping system design requirements.
   (e) A new section on the withdrawal of cryogenic liquids from containers for use in liquid form has been added.
(3) The following changes have been made to Chapter 6:

   (a) The term *electrical preventive maintenance (EPM)* has been revised to *electrical maintenance program (EMP)* for correlation with the 2023 edition of NFPA 70B.
   (b) Terminology related to power sources for essential electrical systems (EESs) has been revised to remove the unnecessary words "alternate" and "normal" and to clarify that power sources other than utility sources and engine generators can be used to supply the EES.
   (c) Requirements for performance, maintenance, and testing of the life safety branch of the EES have been added.
   (d) A requirement mandating a bypass-isolation switch for health care facilities in which a single transfer switch is permitted has been added.
(4) Emergency management requirements in Chapter 12 have been revised to address exercises, events, and incidents.
(5) Hyperbaric chamber pressure relief requirements and hyperbaric chamber primary and secondary fire suppression options have been added to Chapter 14.
(6) Revisions to dental gas and vacuum system requirements in Chapter 15 have been made for consistency with Chapter 5, where applicable.

Correlating Committee on Health Care Facilities

Sharon S. Gilyeat, *Chair*
Koffel Associates, Inc., MD [SE]

Chad E. Beebe, ASHE - AHA, WA [U]

Bruce D. Brooks, BrooksBright, VA [SE]
Rep. American Institute of Architects

Gordon D. Burrill, Teegor Consulting Inc., Canada [U]
Rep. Canadian Healthcare Engineering Society

David A. Dagenais, Partners/Wentworth-Douglass Hospital, NH [U]
Rep. NFPA Health Care Section

Keith Ferrari, Linde/Praxair, NC [M]

Robert M. Gagnon, Gagnon Engineering, MD [SE]

Robert Hijazi, Dearborn, MI [M]
Rep. Association for the Advancement of Medical Instrumentation

Chad Kennedy, Schneider Electric, SC [M]

Maria B. Marks, Siemens Industry, Inc., MD [M]

Denise L. Pappas, Keltron Corporation, MA [M]
Rep. National Electrical Manufacturers Association

Eric R. Rosenbaum, JENSEN HUGHES, MD [SE]

Robert Sontag, State of Colorado, CO [E]
Rep. Fire Marshal's Association of Colorado

Joseph H. Versteeg, Versteeg Associates, CT [E]
Rep. DNV Health Care Inc.

Alternates

H. Shane Ashby, West Tennessee Healthcare, TN [U]
(Voting Alt.)

Vincent Della Croce, Siemens, FL [M]
(Alt. to Maria B. Marks)

William E. Koffel, Koffel Associates, Inc., MD [SE]
(Alt. to Sharon S. Gilyeat)

James S. Peterkin, TLC Engineering, FL [U]
(Alt. to Chad E. Beebe)

Rodger Reiswig, Johnson Controls, VA [M]
(Alt. to Denise L. Pappas)

Nonvoting

Richard C. Barry, Healogics, FL [SE]
Rep. TC on Hyperbaric and Hypobaric Facilities

Michael A. Crowley, Coffman Engineers, Inc., GA [SE]
Rep. TC on Piping Systems

Jason D'Antona, Partners Healthcare, MA [U]
Rep. TC on Electrical Systems

Marvin J. Fischer, Monroe Township, NJ [O]
(Member Emeritus)

Gregory E. Harrington, NFPA Staff Liaison

Nicholas E. Gabriele, JENSEN HUGHES, CT [SE]
Rep. TC on Health Care Emergency Management & Security

Pamela Gwynn, UL LLC, NC [RT]
Rep. TC on Medical Equipment

James K. Lathrop, Koffel Associates, Inc., CT [SE]
Rep. TC on Fundamentals

Michael P. Sheerin, TLC Engineering for Architecture, FL [SE]
Rep. TC on Mechanical Systems

This list represents the membership at the time the Committee was balloted on the final text of this edition. Since that time, changes in the membership may have occurred. A key to classifications is found at the back of the document.

NOTE: Membership on a committee shall not in and of itself constitute an endorsement of the Association or any document developed by the committee on which the member serves.

Committee Scope: This Committee shall have primary responsibility for documents that contain criteria for safeguarding patients and health care personnel in the delivery of health care services within health care facilities: a) from fire, explosion, electrical, and related hazards resulting either from the use of anesthetic agents, medical gas equipment, electrical apparatus, and high frequency electricity, or from internal or external incidents that disrupt normal patient care; b) from fire and explosion hazards; c) in connection with the use of hyperbaric and hypobaric facilities for medical purposes; d) through performance, maintenance and testing criteria for electrical systems, both normal and essential; and e) through performance, maintenance and testing, and installation criteria: (1) for vacuum systems for medical or surgical purposes, and (2) for medical gas systems; and f) through performance, maintenance and testing of plumbing, heating, cooling, and ventilating in health care facilities.

Technical Committee on Electrical Systems

Jason D'Antona, *Chair*
Partners Healthcare, MA [U]

Gary A. Beckstrand, Utah Electrical JATC, UT [L]
    Rep. International Brotherhood of Electrical Workers

Krista McDonald Biason, HGA Architects and Engineers, MN [SE]

David M. Campbell, AFC Cable Systems, Inc., MA [M]
    Rep. The Aluminum Association, Inc.

H. David Chandler, Newcomb & Boyd, GA [SE]
    Rep. NFPA Health Care Section

Nancy W. Chilton, Schneider Electric, NC [M]

Dan Chisholm, Jr., Motor and Generator Institute/MGI Systems, Inc., FL [IM]

Richard L. Day, Michigan State Fire Marshal's Office, MI [E]

Vincent Della Croce, Siemens, FL [M]

Jan Ehrenwerth, Yale University, CT [C]
    Rep. American Society of Anesthesiologists

Steven A. Elliott, US Department of Veterans Affairs, NV [U]
    Rep. US Department of Veterans Affairs

Chris M. Finen, Eaton Corporation, TN [M]

Pamela Gwynn, UL LLC, NC [RT]

Leif Hoegberg, Electrical Reliability Services, CA [IM]
    Rep. InterNational Electrical Testing Association

Stephen M. Lipster, SNAG Consulting, SC [SE]

Thomas J. Parrish, Telgian Corporation, MI [SE]

Kevin T. Porter, Encore Wire Corporation, TX [M]
    Rep. National Electrical Manufacturers Association

Don Rabel, Mid-West Electric Company, TX [IM]
    Rep. National Electrical Contractors Association

Vincent M. Rea, TLC Engineering for Architecture, FL [SE]

Mike Rink, University of Rochester Medical Center, NY [U]

Brian E. Rock, Hubbell Incorporated, CT [M]

Steve R. Sappington, Caterpillar Inc., GA [M]

Michael L. Savage, Sr., Marion County Building Safety, FL [E]

Kevin A. Scarlett, Washington State Department of Health, WA [E]

John Schutte, Mortenson Construction, TX [IM]

Ronald M. Smidt, Atrium Health, NC [U]
    Rep. American Society for Healthcare Engineering

Walter N. Vernon, IV, Mazzetti, CA [SE]

Leonard W. White, Salas O'Brien/ Stanford White Associates
Consulting Engineers, Inc., NC [SE]

David A. Williams, Delta Charter Township, MI [E]
    Rep. International Association of Electrical Inspectors

Robert Wolff, BRE Engineers, NC [SE]

Alternates

Jesse Avery, Mazzetti, CA [SE]
    (Alt. to Walter N. Vernon, IV)

Chad E. Beebe, ASHE - AHA, WA [U]
    (Alt. to Ronald M. Smidt)

Dan Chisholm, Sr., MGI Systems, Inc., FL [IM]
    (Alt. to Dan Chisholm, Jr.)

John Quentin Cowans, Siemens, GA [M]
    (Alt. to Vincent Della Croce)

David A. Dagenais, Partners/Wentworth-Douglass Hospital, NH [U]
    (Alt. to Jason D'Antona)

Herbert H. Daugherty, Electric Generating Systems Association, FL [M]
    (Voting Alt.)

Matthew B. Eason, Newcomb & Boyd, GA [SE]
    (Alt. to H. David Chandler)

Paul David Evers, UL LLC, FL [RT]
    (Alt. to Pamela Gwynn)

Lauris V. Freidenfelds, Telgian Engineering & Consulting, IL [SE]
    (Alt. to Thomas J. Parrish)

Larry Geyer, Quality Electric Inc., ID [IM]
    (Alt. to Don Rabel)

Chad Kennedy, Schneider Electric, SC [M]
    (Alt. to Nancy W. Chilton)

David S. Linder, Hubbell Incorporated, CT [M]
    (Alt. to Brian E. Rock)

David C. Lyons, University of Rochester, NY [C]
    (Alt. to Jan Ehrenwerth)

Terrance L. McKinch, Signal Energy Constructors, MI [IM]
    (Alt. to John Schutte)

Taw North, TLC Engineering for Architecture, FL [SE]
    (Alt. to Vincent M. Rea)

John L. Williams, Washington State Department of Health, WA [E]
    (Alt. to Kevin A. Scarlett)

Jeffrey S. Sargent, NFPA Staff Liaison

This list represents the membership at the time the Committee was balloted on the final text of this edition. Since that time, changes in the membership may have occurred. A key to classifications is found at the back of the document.

NOTE: Membership on a committee shall not in and of itself constitute an endorsement of the Association or any document developed by the committee on which the member serves.

Committee Scope: This Committee shall have primary responsibility for documents or portions of documents covering the minimum requirements for performance, testing, maintenance, operations, and failure management of electrical systems, low voltage systems, wireless technologies, informatics, and telemedicine to safeguard patients, staff, and visitors within health care facilities based on established risk categories.

Technical Committee on Fundamentals of Health Care Facilities

James K. Lathrop, *Chair*
Koffel Associates, Inc., CT [SE]

Bruce L. Abell, US Army Corps of Engineers, VA [U]

Gary A. Beckstrand, Utah Electrical JATC, UT [L]
Rep. International Brotherhood of Electrical Workers

Bruce D. Brooks, BrooksBright, VA [SE]
Rep. American Institute of Architects

Gordon D. Burrill, Teegor Consulting Inc., Canada [U]
Rep. Canadian Healthcare Engineering Society

Michael A. Crowley, Coffman Engineers, Inc., GA [SE]

Roger N. Dahozy, US Department of Health & Human Services, AZ [E]

Richard L. Day, Michigan State Fire Marshal's Office, MI [E]

Carl J. Ferlitch, Jr., Chubb Group of Insurance Companies, PA [I]

Amy L. Flower, Fire Protection & Code Consultants, IN [SE]

Shaine M. Grogan, JENSEN HUGHES, MA [SE]

Leah Hummel, American Society for Healthcare Engineering (ASHE), ND [U]

David P. Klein, US Department of Veterans Affairs, DC [U]

Maria B. Marks, Siemens Industry, Inc., MD [M]
Rep. Automatic Fire Alarm Association, Inc.

Bret M. Martin, CNA Insurance, NC [I]

Michele Mucia, Carrier Automated Logic Corporation, IL [M]

James S. Peterkin, TLC Engineering, FL [SE]

Milosh T. Puchovsky, Worcester Polytechnic Institute, MA [SE]

Pamela Reno, Telgian, OH [SE]

Dennis L. Schmitt, Illinois Department of Public Health (IDPH), IL [E]

Joe Scibetta, BuildingReports, GA [M]

Robert Sontag, State of Colorado, CO [E]

Michael C. Stone, National Electrical Manufacturers Association, CA [M]

John L. Williams, Washington State Department of Health, WA [E]

Alternates

Joshua Brackett, Baptist Health, AR [U]
(Alt. to Leah Hummel)

Michael James Brennan, RSCC Wire and Cable LLC., IL [M]
(Alt. to Michael C. Stone)

Shane M. Clary, Bay Alarm Company, CA [M]
(Alt. to Maria B. Marks)

Allison C. Ellis, Koffel Associates, Inc., MD [SE]
(Alt. to James K. Lathrop)

Peter Leszczak, US Department of Veterans Affairs, CT [U]
(Alt. to David P. Klein)

Kevin A. Scarlett, Washington State Department of Health, WA [E]
(Alt. to John L. Williams)

Justin A. Schwartz, US Army Corps of Engineers, VA [U]
(Alt. to Bruce L. Abell)

Gregory E. Harrington, NFPA Staff Liaison

This list represents the membership at the time the Committee was balloted on the final text of this edition. Since that time, changes in the membership may have occurred. A key to classifications is found at the back of the document.

NOTE: Membership on a committee shall not in and of itself constitute an endorsement of the Association or any document developed by the committee on which the member serves.

Committee Scope: This Committee shall have primary responsibility for documents or portions of documents on the scope, application, and intended use of documents under the Health Care Facilities Project, including reference standards, performance, the protection from fire and explosion hazards, protection of special hazards, establishing criteria for levels of health care services based on risk, as well as definitions not assigned to other committees in the Health Care Facilities Project.

Technical Committee on Health Care Emergency Management and Security

Nicholas E. Gabriele, *Chair*
JENSEN HUGHES, CT [SE]

Robert M. Becker, Incident Management Solutions, Inc., NY [SE]

Pete Brewster, US Department of Veterans Affairs, WV [U]

David A. Dagenais, Partners/Wentworth-Douglass Hospital, NH [U]

Sharon S. Gilyeat, Koffel Associates, Inc., MD [SE]

Kenneth J. Hebert, The Joint Commission, IL [E]

Susan B. McLaughlin, MSL Health Care Partners, IL [U]
Rep. American Society for Healthcare Engineering

Joseph McNulty, Baltimore City Fire Department, MD [E]

James L. Paturas, Yale New Haven Health System, CT [U]

Jack Poole, Poole Fire Protection, Inc., KS [SE]

Pamela Reno, Telgian, OH [SE]

Patrick C. Rhinehart, Northside Hospital, GA [U]

Kevin A. Scarlett, Washington State Department of Health, WA [E]

James P. Simpson, Electrical Training Alliance, MN [L]
Rep. International Brotherhood of Electrical Workers

Jerry Spickler, Johnson Controls, OH [M]

Michael D. Widdekind, Zurich Services Corporation, MD [I]

Alternates

Chad E. Beebe, ASHE - AHA, WA [U]
(Alt. to Susan B. McLaughlin)

Myron Lee Draper, Koffel Associates, Inc., MD [SE]
(Alt. to Sharon S. Gilyeat)

Zachary Goldfarb, Incident Management Solutions, Inc., NY [SE]
(Alt. to Robert M. Becker)

Michael Jenkins, Johnson Controls, CO [M]
(Alt. to Jerry Spickler)

Andrew D. Mcguire, JENSEN HUGHES, CT [SE]
(Alt. to Nicholas E. Gabriele)

Valerie Miller, Zurich North America, PA [I]
(Alt. to Michael D. Widdekind)

John Pelazza, Yale New Haven Health System, CT [U]
(Alt. to James L. Paturas)

Eric Reed, Poole Fire Protection, Inc., KS [SE]
(Alt. to Jack Poole)

Nonvoting

Reginald D. Jackson, US Department of Labor, DC [E]

Camille Levy, NFPA Staff Liaison

This list represents the membership at the time the Committee was balloted on the final text of this edition. Since that time, changes in the membership may have occurred. A key to classifications is found at the back of the document.

NOTE: Membership on a committee shall not in and of itself constitute an endorsement of the Association or any document developed by the committee on which the member serves.

Committee Scope: This Committee shall have primary responsibility for documents or portions of documents covering the framework for emergency management and security of health care facilities proportionate to the risk of the patient and health care staff. This Committee shall have primary responsibility for the elements of planning over a continuum from minor incidences to catastrophic events, including: management controls, mitigation practices, incident response, continuity of services, recovery, stored capacity, staff training, and program evaluation based on established risk categories.

Technical Committee on Hyperbaric and Hypobaric Facilities

Richard C. Barry, *Chair*
Healogics, FL [SE]

James Edwin Bell, Fink Engineering, UT [M]

Chae Bliss, Aviv Clinic, FL [U]

W. Robert Bryant, Perry Baromedical Corporation, TX [M]

Francois Burman, Divers Alert Network, NC [SE]

Chris M. Campbell, Sandy Springs Fire, GA [E]

Lisa Carr, Christiana Care Health Services, DE [U]

Mario Caruso, Hyperbaric Consulting LLC, FL [SE]

David Charash, Dive Medicine And Hyperbaric Consultants, CT [SE]

Mark Chipps, Life Support Technologies Group Inc., NY [U]

David Lindsie Cone, University of South Carolina: Prisma Health Richland, SC [SE]

Jay Duchnick, University of California San Diego, CA [SE]

Keith Ferrari, Linde/Praxair, NC [M]

Adrian Garay, HYPERBARIC MODULAR SYSTEMS, Inc., CA [M]

Kevin P. Gardner, Aurora St. Luke's Hospital, WI [U]

Derall Garrett, Undersea Hyperbaric Medical Society (UHMS), FL [U]

Jacquline Hocking, Cutiscare, LLC, OR [U]

Leah Hummel, American Society for Healthcare Engineering (ASHE), ND [U]

Barry E. Newton, WHA International, Inc., NM [SE]

Dennis Noskin, H2M Architects+ Engineers/ Dennis Noskin Architects, NY [SE]

Coleen Ramos, Phoenix Fire Department, AZ [E]

Robert B. Sheffield, International ATMO, Inc., TX [U]

John M. Skinner, Medical Equipment Technology, Inc., GA [IM]

Deepak Talati, Sechrist Industries, Inc., CA [M]

Shaun Wallace, Altitude Control Technologies, CA [U]

John L. Williams, Washington State Department of Health, WA [E]

Alternates

Justin Callard, Hyperbaric Technicians & Nurses Association Inc., Australia [C]
(Voting Alt.)

Paul Mario Caruso, Hyperbaric Consulting LLC, FL [SE]
(Alt. to Mario Caruso)

Gwenael Chiffoleau, WHA International, NM [SE]
(Alt. to Barry E. Newton)

Kevin I. Posey, International ATMO, Inc., TX [U]
(Alt. to Robert B. Sheffield)

Kevin A. Scarlett, Washington State Department of Health, WA [E]
(Alt. to John L. Williams)

Nonvoting

Wilbur T. Workman, Undersea & Hyperbaric Medical Society, TX [O]
Rep. Undersea & Hyperbaric Medical Society
(Member Emeritus)

Gregory E. Harrington, NFPA Staff Liaison

This list represents the membership at the time the Committee was balloted on the final text of this edition. Since that time, changes in the membership may have occurred. A key to classifications is found at the back of the document.

NOTE: Membership on a committee shall not in and of itself constitute an endorsement of the Association or any document developed by the committee on which the member serves.

Committee Scope: This Committee shall have primary responsibility for documents or portions of documents covering the construction, installation, testing, performance, and maintenance of hyperbaric and hypobaric facilities for safeguarding staff and occupants of chambers.

Technical Committee on Mechanical Systems

Michael P. Sheerin, *Chair*
TLC Engineering for Architecture, FL [SE]

Chad E. Beebe, ASHE - AHA, WA [U]

Christopher Bernecker, H. T. Lyons, Inc., PA [IM]

Gordon D. Burrill, Teegor Consulting Inc., Canada [U]
Rep. Canadian Healthcare Engineering Society

Yingying Cui, New York City Department of Buildings, NY [E]

Luke Cummings, Mayo Clinic, MN [U]

Raj Daswani, Arup, CA [SE]

Keith Ferrari, Linde/Praxair, NC [M]

Jonathan Hartsell, Rodgers, NC [IM]

Sean Hutchinson, Siemens- Building Technologies, NJ [M]

Roger W. Lautz, Affiliated Engineers, Inc., WI [SE]

Cary J. Norberg, National Energy Management Institute Committee (NEMIC), VA [IM]

Allan D. Volz, OSF HealthCare System, IL [U]

Scott Walter Wenger, UA Local 400, WI [L]
Rep. United Assn. of Journeymen & Apprentices of the Plumbing & Pipe Fitting Industry

Alternates

Johnnie Michael Norris, Denver Plumbers JATC, CO [L]
(Alt. to Scott Walter Wenger)

Camille Levy, NFPA Staff Liaison

This list represents the membership at the time the Committee was balloted on the final text of this edition. Since that time, changes in the membership may have occurred. A key to classifications is found at the back of the document.

NOTE: Membership on a committee shall not in and of itself constitute an endorsement of the Association or any document developed by the committee on which the member serves.

Committee Scope: This committee shall have primary responsibility for documents or portions of documents covering the performance, operations, testing, and maintenance, for air quality, temperature, humidity, critical space pressure relationships, water and waste water, and their associated systems based on established risk categories.

Technical Committee on Medical Equipment

Pamela Gwynn, *Chair*
UL LLC, NC [RT]
Rep. UL LLC

Chad E. Beebe, ASHE - AHA, WA [U]
Lisa Carr, Christiana Care Health Services, DE [U]
Charles Connor, Karmanos Cancer Institute, MI [U]
Shelly Louise Crisler, Department Of Veterans Affairs, MO [U]
David A. Dagenais, Partners/Wentworth-Douglass Hospital, NH [U]
  Rep. NFPA Health Care Section
Keith Ferrari, Linde/Praxair, NC [M]
  Rep. Compressed Gas Association
Alan Lipschultz, HealthCare Technology Consulting LLC, MD [M]
  Rep. Association for the Advancement of Medical Instrumentation

David C. Lyons, University of Rochester, NY [C]
  Rep. American Society of Anesthesiologists
Shane Robertson, Busch Vacuum Solutions, AL [M]
Brian E. Rock, Hubbell Incorporated, CT [M]
Lawrence S. Sandler, Bonita Springs, FL [SE]
Kevin A. Scarlett, Washington State Department of Health, WA [E]
Robert M. Sutter, B&R Compliance Associates, FL [SE]
Varun Verma, Philips Healthcare, OH [M]

Alternates

Gary L. Bean, Air Products & Chemicals, Inc., GA [M]
  (Alt. to Keith Ferrari)
Paul David Evers, UL LLC, FL [RT]
  (Alt. to Pamela Gwynn)

Robert Hijazi, Dearborn, MI [M]
  (Alt. to Alan Lipschultz)

Gregory E. Harrington, NFPA Staff Liaison

This list represents the membership at the time the Committee was balloted on the final text of this edition. Since that time, changes in the membership may have occurred. A key to classifications is found at the back of the document.

NOTE: Membership on a committee shall not in and of itself constitute an endorsement of the Association or any document developed by the committee on which the member serves.

Committee Scope: This committee shall have primary responsibility for documents or portions of documents covering the maintenance, performance, and testing of electrical medical equipment and portable patient-related gas equipment for the purpose of safeguarding patients and health care personnel within patient care areas of health care facilities from the hazards of fire, explosion, electricity, nonionizing radiation, heat, and electrical interference based on established risk categories.

Technical Committee on Piping Systems

Michael A. Crowley, *Chair*
Coffman Engineers, Inc., GA [SE]

Mark W. Allen, Beacon Medaes- Consultant, SC [M]

Grant A. Anderson, Bard, Rao & Athanas Consulting Engineers, LLC, MA [SE]

Chad E. Beebe, ASHE - AHA, WA [U]
   Rep. American Society for Healthcare Engineering

David Braidich, US Army Corps of Engineers, VA [U]

Mark David Carter, National Institutes Of Health, MD [U]

Dana A. Colombo, PIPE/National ITC Corporation, LA [L]

Marc Dodson, C-Scan Technologies, Inc., AZ [SE]

Keith Ferrari, Linde/Praxair, NC [M]
   Rep. Compressed Gas Association

Mark T. Franklin, Sherman Engineering Company, PA [M]

Andrew Fuchs, Local 137, IL [L]

Neil Gagné, Wm. G. Frank Medical Gas Testing & Consulting, LLC, NH [SE]

Ed Golla, TRI/Air Testing, TX [RT]

John C. Gregory, WSP USA, AZ [SE]

Scott Hamilton, ASSE International, IL [U]
   Rep. International Association of Plumbing & Mechanical Officials

Daniel Patrick Kelly, Bon Secours Charity Health System, NY [U]

James K. Lathrop, Koffel Associates, Inc., CT [SE]

Edward A. Litvin, US Department of Veterans Affairs, DC [U]
   Rep. US Department of Veterans Affairs

Anthony Lowe, Allied Hospital Systems, MD [IM]

James L. Lucas, Tri-Tech Medical Inc., OH [M]

David C. Lyons, University of Rochester, NY [C]
   Rep. American Society of Anesthesiologists

Bret M. Martin, CNA Insurance, NC [I]

Jeffery F. McBride, Red Lion Medgas Consultants, Inc., DE [SE]

Douglas Miller, Local 190, MI [L]

Kevin A. Scarlett, Washington State Department of Health, WA [E]

Elizabeth A. "Betsy" Shapiro, American Dental Association, IL [U]
   Rep. American Dental Association

E. Daniel Shoemaker, Accutron Inc., AZ [M]

Ronald M. Smidt, Atrium Health, NC [U]
   Rep. NFPA Health Care Section

Allan D. Volz, OSF HealthCare System, IL [U]

Jonathan C. Willard, Acute Medical Gas Services, NH [SE]

Jonathan Wong, Coastal Pediatric Dental, VA [U]

Alternates

Gary L. Bean, Air Products & Chemicals, Inc., GA [M]
   (Alt. to Keith Ferrari)

Mathis W. Carlson, Meditrac, IN [M]
   (Alt. to E. Daniel Shoemaker)

Bob Carpenter, Viega, LLC., CO [M]
   (Voting Alt.)

Gary Currence, Allied Hospital Systems, MD [IM]
   (Alt. to Anthony Lowe)

David A. Dagenais, Partners/Wentworth-Douglass Hospital, NH [U]
   (Alt. to Chad E. Beebe)

Robert G. Loeb, University of Arizona, AZ [C]
   (Alt. to David C. Lyons)

Edward J. Lyczko, The Cleveland Clinic, OH [U]
   (Alt. to Daniel Patrick Kelly)

John Mullen, International Association of Plumbing & Mechanical Officials (IAPMO), NC [U]
   (Alt. to Scott Hamilton)

Johnnie Michael Norris, Denver Plumbers JATC, CO [L]
   (Alt. to Douglas Miller)

Sunil Parikh, Tri-Tech Medical, Inc., OH [M]
   (Alt. to James L. Lucas)

Vincent Rizzo, US Department of Veterans Affairs, DC [U]
   (Alt. to Edward A. Litvin)

Paul Rumbos, Major Medical Hospital Services, Inc., NJ [SE]
   (Alt. to Jonathan C. Willard)

Sharon Stanford, American Dental Association, IL [U]
   (Alt. to Elizabeth A. "Betsy" Shapiro)

Daniel Richard Sullivan, BeaconMedaes, SC [M]
   (Alt. to Mark W. Allen)

John L. Williams, Washington State Department of Health, WA [E]
   (Alt. to Kevin A. Scarlett)

Gregory E. Harrington, NFPA Staff Liaison

This list represents the membership at the time the Committee was balloted on the final text of this edition. Since that time, changes in the membership may have occurred. A key to classifications is found at the back of the document.

NOTE: Membership on a committee shall not in and of itself constitute an endorsement of the Association or any document developed by the committee on which the member serves.

Committee Scope: This Committee shall have primary responsibility for documents or portions of documents covering the performance, maintenance, installation, and testing of medical and dental related gas piping systems and medical and dental related vacuum piping systems based on established risk categories.

Contents

Chapter 1	**Administration**	**99– 14**
1.1	Scope.	**99– 14**
1.2	Purpose.	**99– 15**
1.3	Application.	**99– 15**
1.4	Equivalency.	**99– 15**
1.5	Units.	**99– 15**
1.6	Code Adoption Requirements.	**99– 15**
Chapter 2	**Referenced Publications**	**99– 15**
2.1	General.	**99– 15**
2.2	NFPA Publications.	**99– 16**
2.3	Other Publications.	**99– 16**
2.4	References for Extracts in Mandatory Sections.	**99– 18**
Chapter 3	**Definitions**	**99– 19**
3.1	General.	**99– 19**
3.2	NFPA Official Definitions.	**99– 19**
3.3	General Definitions.	**99– 19**
3.4	BICSI Definitions.	**99– 27**
Chapter 4	**Fundamentals**	**99– 28**
4.1	Risk Categories.	**99– 28**
4.2	Risk Assessment.	**99– 28**
4.3	Application.	**99– 28**
4.4	Materials.	**99– 28**
Chapter 5	**Gas and Vacuum Systems**	**99– 29**
5.1	Category 1 Piped Gas and Vacuum Systems.	**99– 29**
5.2	Category 2 Piped Gas and Vacuum Systems.	**99– 74**
5.3	Category 3 Piped Gas and Vacuum Systems.	**99– 75**
5.4	Liquid Withdrawal and Piping.	**99– 76**
Chapter 6	**Electrical Systems**	**99– 78**
6.1	Applicability.	**99– 78**
6.2	Nature of Hazards.	**99– 78**
6.3	General.	**99– 78**
6.4	Category 1 Spaces.	**99– 83**
6.5	Category 2 Spaces.	**99– 83**
6.6	Category 3 and 4 Spaces.	**99– 83**
6.7	Essential Electrical Systems.	**99– 83**
6.8	Site Acceptance Testing.	**99– 93**
6.9	Electrical Maintenance Program (EMP).	**99– 93**
6.10	Health Care Microgrids.	**99– 94**
6.11	Classification of Emergency Power Supply Systems (EPSSs).	**99– 95**
Chapter 7	**Information Technology and Communications Systems**	**99– 96**
7.1	Applicability.	**99– 96**
7.2	Reserved.	**99– 96**
7.3	Category 1 Systems.	**99– 96**
7.4	Category 2 Systems.	**99– 100**
7.5	Category 3 Systems.	**99– 100**
Chapter 8	**Plumbing**	**99– 101**
8.1	Applicability.	**99– 101**
8.2	System Category Criteria.	**99– 101**
8.3	General Requirements.	**99– 101**
8.4	Category 1. (Reserved)	**99– 101**
8.5	Category 2. (Reserved)	**99– 101**
8.6	Category 3. (Reserved)	**99– 101**
Chapter 9	**Heating, Ventilation, and Air Conditioning (HVAC)**	**99– 102**
9.1	Applicability.	**99– 102**
9.2	System Category Criteria.	**99– 102**
9.3	General.	**99– 102**
9.4	Category 1. (Reserved)	**99– 103**
9.5	Category 2. (Reserved)	**99– 103**
9.6	Category 3. (Reserved)	**99– 103**
Chapter 10	**Electrical Equipment**	**99– 104**
10.1	Applicability.	**99– 104**
10.2	Performance Criteria for Patient Care–Related Electrical Appliances and Equipment.	**99– 104**
10.3	Testing Requirements — Patient Care–Related Electrical Appliances and Equipment.	**99– 105**
10.4	Nonpatient Electrical Appliances and Equipment.	**99– 106**
10.5	Administration.	**99– 106**
Chapter 11	**Gas Equipment**	**99– 110**
11.1	Applicability.	**99– 110**
11.2	Portable Cylinder and Container Source.	**99– 110**
11.3	Cylinder and Container Storage Requirements.	**99– 110**
11.4	Performance Criteria and Testing.	**99– 112**
11.5	Administration.	**99– 112**
11.6	Operation and Management of Cylinders.	**99– 114**
11.7	Liquid Oxygen Equipment.	**99– 115**
Chapter 12	**Emergency Management**	**99– 117**
12.1	Applicability.	**99– 117**
12.2	Responsibilities.	**99– 117**
12.3	Emergency Management Categories.	**99– 117**
12.4	General.	**99– 117**
12.5	Emergency Management Category 1 and Emergency Management Category 2 Requirements.	**99– 117**
Chapter 13	**Security Management**	**99– 122**
13.1	Applicability.	**99– 122**
13.2	Security Management Plan.	**99– 122**
13.3	Security Vulnerability Assessment (SVA).	**99– 122**
13.4	Responsible Person.	**99– 122**
13.5	Security-Sensitive Areas.	**99– 122**
13.6	Access and Egress Security Measures.	**99– 123**
13.7	Media Control.	**99– 123**
13.8	Crowd Control.	**99– 123**
13.9	Access Control Equipment.	**99– 123**
13.10	Employment Practices.	**99– 123**
13.11	Security Operations.	**99– 123**
13.12	Program Evaluation.	**99– 124**
Chapter 14	**Hyperbaric Facilities**	**99– 124**
14.1	Scope.	**99– 124**
14.2	Construction and Equipment.	**99– 124**
14.3	Administration and Maintenance.	**99– 134**
Chapter 15	**Dental Gas and Vacuum Systems**	**99– 138**
15.1	Applicability.	**99– 138**
15.2	Nature of Hazards of Gas and Vacuum Systems.	**99– 138**
15.3	Category 1 Dental Gas and Vacuum Systems.	**99– 138**
15.4	Category 2 Dental Gas and Vacuum Systems.	**99– 143**
15.5	Category 3 Dental Gas and Vacuum Systems.	**99– 157**
Chapter 16	**Features of Fire Protection**	**99– 162**
16.1	Applicability.	**99– 162**
16.2	Construction and Compartmentation.	**99– 162**
16.3	Special Hazard Protection for Flammable Liquids and Gases.	**99– 162**
16.4	Laboratories.	**99– 162**
16.5	Utilities.	**99– 162**
16.6	Waste Chutes, Incinerators, and Linen Chutes.	**99– 162**

99-13

16.7 Fire Detection, Alarm, and Communications Systems. 99–163
16.8 Heliports. 99–164
16.9 Automatic Sprinklers and Other Extinguishing Equipment. 99–164
16.10 Manual Extinguishing Equipment. 99–164
16.11 Compact Storage. 99–164
16.12 Compact Mobile Storage. 99–164
16.13 Maintenance and Testing. 99–164
16.14 Fire Loss Prevention in Operating Rooms. 99–164

Annex A   Explanatory Material 99–166
Annex B   Additional Explanatory Notes 99–224
Annex C   Sample Ordinance Adopting NFPA 99 99–242
Annex D   Informational References 99–243
Index   99–248

NFPA 99

Health Care Facilities Code

2024 Edition

IMPORTANT NOTE: This NFPA document is made available for use subject to important notices and legal disclaimers. These notices and disclaimers appear in all publications containing this document and may be found under the heading "Important Notices and Disclaimers Concerning NFPA Standards." They can also be viewed at www.nfpa.org/disclaimers or obtained on request from NFPA.

UPDATES, ALERTS, AND FUTURE EDITIONS: New editions of NFPA codes, standards, recommended practices, and guides (i.e., NFPA Standards) are released on scheduled revision cycles. This edition may be superseded by a later one, or it may be amended outside of its scheduled revision cycle through the issuance of Tentative Interim Amendments (TIAs). An official NFPA Standard at any point in time consists of the current edition of the document, together with all TIAs and Errata in effect. To verify that this document is the current edition or to determine if it has been amended by TIAs or Errata, please consult the National Fire Codes® Subscription Service or the "List of NFPA Codes & Standards" at www.nfpa.org/docinfo. In addition to TIAs and Errata, the document information pages also include the option to sign up for alerts for individual documents and to be involved in the development of the next edition.

NOTICE: An asterisk (*) following the number or letter designating a paragraph indicates that explanatory material on the paragraph can be found in Annex A.

A reference in brackets [ ] following a section or paragraph indicates material that has been extracted from another NFPA document. Extracted text may be edited for consistency and style and may include the revision of internal paragraph references and other references as appropriate. Requests for interpretations or revisions of extracted text shall be sent to the technical committee responsible for the source document.

Information on referenced and extracted publications can be found in Chapter 2 and Annex D.

Chapter 1   Administration

1.1 Scope.

1.1.1 The scope of this code is to establish minimum criteria as follows in 1.1.2 through 1.1.14.

1.1.2 Fundamentals. Chapter 4 establishes criteria for levels of health care services or systems based on risk to the patients, staff, or visitors in health care facilities.

1.1.3 Gas and Vacuum Systems.

1.1.3.1 Chapter 5 covers the performance, maintenance, installation, and testing of the following:

(1) Nonflammable medical gas systems with operating pressures below a gauge pressure of 2068 kPa (300 psi)
(2) Vacuum systems in health care facilities
(3) Waste anesthetic gas disposal (WAGD) systems, also referred to as scavenging
(4) Manufactured assemblies that are intended for connection to the medical gas, vacuum, or WAGD systems (also referred to as scavenging)

1.1.3.2 Requirements for portable compressed gas systems are covered in Chapter 11.

1.1.3.3 Requirements for piped gas and vacuum systems in hyperbaric facilities are covered in Chapter 14.

1.1.3.4 Requirements for piped dental gas and vacuum systems are covered in Chapter 15.

1.1.4 Electrical Systems.

1.1.4.1 Chapter 6 covers the performance, maintenance, and testing of electrical systems (both normal and essential) in health care facilities.

Δ **1.1.4.2** The following areas are not addressed in this code, but are addressed in other NFPA documents:

(1) Specific requirements for wiring and installation of electrical systems and components thereof are covered in *NFPA 70*.
(2) Requirements for illumination and identification of means of egress in health care facilities are covered in NFPA *101*.
(3) Requirements for installation, testing, and maintenance of fire protection signaling systems are covered in *NFPA 72*.
(4) Requirements for installation of fire pumps are covered in NFPA 20, except that the alternate power source is permitted to be the essential electrical system.
(5) Requirements for installation of stationary engines and gas turbines are covered in NFPA 37.

1.1.5 Information Technology and Communications Systems. Chapter 7 covers the performance, maintenance, and testing of information technology and communications systems in health care facilities.

1.1.6 Plumbing. Chapter 8 covers the performance, maintenance, and testing of plumbing systems in health care facilities.

1.1.7 HVAC Systems. Chapter 9 covers the performance, maintenance, and testing of heating, cooling, and ventilating in health care facilities.

1.1.8 Electrical Equipment. Chapter 10 covers the performance, maintenance, and testing of electrical equipment in health care facilities.

1.1.9 Gas Equipment. Chapter 11 covers the performance, maintenance, and testing of gas equipment in health care facilities.

1.1.10* Emergency Management. Chapter 12 establishes criteria for emergency management in the development of a program for effective disaster preparedness, response, mitigation, and recovery in health care facilities.

1.1.11 Security Management. Chapter 13 establishes criteria for security management, including management controls, mitigation practices, staff training, and program evaluation in health care facilities.

1.1.12* Hyperbaric Facilities. Chapter 14 establishes criteria for design and operation of hyperbaric chambers and facilities. Chapter 14 covers electrical, fire, pressure, and gas hazards associated with hyperbaric facilities that are used, or intended to be used, for medical and experimental procedures at gauge pressures from 0 kPa to 690 kPa (0 psi to 100 psi).

1.1.13 Dental Gas and Vacuum System. Chapter 15 covers the performance, maintenance, and testing of dental gas and vacuum systems in health care facilities.

1.1.14 Features of Fire Protection. Chapter 16 covers the performance, maintenance, and testing of fire protection equipment in health care facilities.

1.2 Purpose. The purpose of this code is to provide minimum requirements for the installation, inspection, testing, maintenance, performance, and safe practices for facilities, material, equipment, and appliances.

1.3 Application.

1.3.1 This code shall apply to all health care facilities other than home care and veterinary care, except as required by 1.3.1.1.

1.3.1.1 Hyperbaric chambers for veterinary care shall be in accordance with the requirements of Chapter 14.

1.3.1.2 This code is intended for use by those persons involved in the design, construction, inspection, and operation of health care facilities and in the design, manufacture, and testing of appliances and equipment used in patient care rooms of health care facilities.

Δ **1.3.1.3*** Facilities that employ systems, equipment, or appliances that are subject to regulation by this code shall not be required to be subject to any other provisions of this code unless so directed by the scope of the individual chapter(s) of this code or as directed by the authority having jurisdiction's adoption of this code.

1.3.2 Construction and equipment requirements shall be applied only to new construction and new equipment, except as modified in individual chapters.

1.3.2.1 Only the altered, renovated, or modernized portion of an existing system or individual component shall be required to meet the installation and equipment requirements stated in this code.

1.3.2.2 If the alteration, renovation, or modernization adversely impacts the existing performance requirements of a system or component, additional upgrading shall be required.

Δ **1.3.2.3** Continued use of an existing system that is noncompliant with the requirements of this code shall be permitted unless the authority having jurisdiction has determined that such use poses a distinct hazard to life.

1.3.2.4 Reducing safety features in existing systems shall not be permitted where such is required for new construction or equipment.

1.3.3 Policies.

1.3.3.1 The health care organization shall ensure that policies are established and maintained that permit the attending medical professional to supersede the requirements of this code in order to satisfy the emergency needs of any patient.

1.3.3.2 Each application of the provisions of 1.3.3.1, where this code's requirements are superseded to satisfy the emergency needs of a patient, shall be clearly documented and reviewed with the intent of meeting similar future needs within the requirements of this code.

1.3.4 Patient Care Spaces.

1.3.4.1 The health care facility's governing body or its designee shall establish the following areas in accordance with the type of patient care anticipated *(see 3.3.146, Patient Care Space)*:

(1) Category 1 spaces
(2) Category 2 spaces
(3) Category 3 spaces
(4) Category 4 spaces

1.3.4.2 Anesthesia. It shall be the responsibility of the health care facility's governing body to designate all anesthetizing locations.

1.3.4.3 Wet Procedure Locations. It shall be the responsibility of the health care facility's governing body to designate wet procedure locations.

1.4 Equivalency.

1.4.1 Nothing in this code is intended to prevent the use of systems, methods, or devices of equivalent or superior quality, strength, fire resistance, effectiveness, durability, and safety to those prescribed by this code. Technical documentation shall be submitted to the authority having jurisdiction to demonstrate equivalency. The system, method, or device shall be approved for the intended purpose by the authority having jurisdiction.

1.4.2 Alternative systems, methods, or devices approved as equivalent by the authority having jurisdiction shall be recognized as being in compliance with this code.

1.4.3 The authority having jurisdiction shall be permitted to grant exceptions to this code.

1.5* **Units.** Primary units will be trade units, and secondary units will be the conversion.

1.6 Code Adoption Requirements.

1.6.1 The effective date of application of any provision of this code is not determined by the National Fire Protection Association. All questions related to applicability shall be directed to the authority having jurisdiction.

1.6.2 Enforcement. This code shall be administered and enforced by the authority having jurisdiction. *(See Annex C for a sample wording for enabling legislation.)*

Chapter 2   Referenced Publications

Δ **2.1*** **General.** The documents referenced in this chapter, or portions of such documents, are referenced within this code and shall be considered part of the requirements of this code, and the following shall also apply:

(1) Documents referenced in this chapter, or portion of such documents, shall only be applicable to the extent called for within other chapters of this code.
(2) Where the requirements of a referenced code or standard differ from the requirements of this code, the requirements of this code shall govern.
(3) Existing buildings or installations that do not comply with the provisions of the codes or standards referenced in this chapter shall be permitted to be continued in service, provided that the lack of conformity with these documents does not present a serious hazard to the occupants

as determined by the authority having jurisdiction. [*101*:2.1]

Δ **2.2 NFPA Publications.** National Fire Protection Association, 1 Batterymarch Park, Quincy, MA 02169-7471.

NFPA 10, *Standard for Portable Fire Extinguishers,* 2022 edition.

NFPA 13, *Standard for the Installation of Sprinkler Systems,* 2022 edition.

NFPA 14, *Standard for the Installation of Standpipe and Hose Systems,* 2024 edition.

NFPA 20, *Standard for the Installation of Stationary Pumps for Fire Protection,* 2022 edition.

NFPA 25, *Standard for the Inspection, Testing, and Maintenance of Water-Based Fire Protection Systems,* 2023 edition.

NFPA 30, *Flammable and Combustible Liquids Code,* 2024 edition.

NFPA 31, *Standard for the Installation of Oil-Burning Equipment,* 2020 edition.

NFPA 37, *Standard for the Installation and Use of Stationary Combustion Engines and Gas Turbines,* 2021 edition.

NFPA 45, *Standard on Fire Protection for Laboratories Using Chemicals,* 2024 edition.

NFPA 54, *National Fuel Gas Code,* 2024 edition.

NFPA 55, *Compressed Gases and Cryogenic Fluids Code,* 2023 edition.

NFPA 58, *Liquefied Petroleum Gas Code,* 2024 edition.

NFPA 70®, *National Electrical Code®,* 2023 edition.

NFPA 72®, *National Fire Alarm and Signaling Code®,* 2022 edition.

NFPA 82, *Standard on Incinerators and Waste and Linen Handling Systems and Equipment,* 2019 edition.

NFPA 90A, *Standard for the Installation of Air-Conditioning and Ventilating Systems,* 2024 edition.

NFPA 91, *Standard for Exhaust Systems for Air Conveying of Vapors, Gases, Mists, and Particulate Solids,* 2020 edition.

NFPA 96, *Standard for Ventilation Control and Fire Protection of Commercial Cooking Operations,* 2024 edition.

NFPA *101®, Life Safety Code®,* 2024 edition.

NFPA 110, *Standard for Emergency and Standby Power Systems,* 2022 edition.

NFPA 111, *Standard on Stored Electrical Energy Emergency and Standby Power Systems,* 2022 edition.

NFPA 170, *Standard for Fire Safety and Emergency Symbols,* 2021 edition.

NFPA 211, *Standard for Chimneys, Fireplaces, Vents, and Solid Fuel–Burning Appliances,* 2024 edition.

NFPA 259, *Standard Test Method for Potential Heat of Building Materials,* 2023 edition.

NFPA 260, *Standard Methods of Tests and Classification System for Cigarette Ignition Resistance of Components of Upholstered Furniture,* 2024 edition.

NFPA 261, *Standard Method of Test for Determining Resistance of Mock-Up Upholstered Furniture Material Assemblies to Ignition by Smoldering Cigarettes,* 2023 edition.

NFPA 286, *Standard Methods of Fire Tests for Evaluating Contribution of Wall and Ceiling Interior Finish to Room Fire Growth,* 2024 edition.

NFPA 400, *Hazardous Materials Code,* 2022 edition.

NFPA 418, *Standard for Heliports,* 2021 edition.

NFPA 495, *Explosive Materials Code,* 2023 edition.

NFPA 701, *Standard Methods of Fire Tests for Flame Propagation of Textiles and Films,* 2023 edition.

NFPA 750, *Standard on Water Mist Fire Protection Systems,* 2023 edition.

NFPA 2001, *Standard on Clean Agent Fire Extinguishing Systems,* 2022 edition.

NFPA 5000®, Building Construction and Safety Code®, 2024 edition.

2.3 Other Publications.

2.3.1 AAMI Publications. Association for the Advancement of Medical Instrumentation, 901 N. Glebe Road, Suite 300, Arlington, VA 22203.

ANSI/AAMI ES60601-1, *Medical electrical equipment — Part 1: General requirements for basic safety and essential performance,* 2005, revised 2012.

2.3.2 ANSI Publications. American National Standards Institute, Inc., 25 West 43rd Street, 4th Floor, New York, NY 10036.

ANSI B57.1, *Compressed Gas Cylinder Valve Outlet and Inlet Connections,* 1965.

ANSI Z136.3, *American National Standard for Safe Use of Lasers in Health Care,* 2018.

2.3.3 ASHRAE Publications. American Society of Heating, Refrigerating and Air Conditioning Engineers, Inc., 180 Technology Parkway NW, Peachtree Corners, GA 30092.

ASHRAE 90.1, *Energy Standard for Buildings Except Low-Rise Residential Buildings,* 2019.

ASHRAE 170, *Ventilation of Health Care Facilities,* 2021, Addenda c, d, e, f, g, and h.

2.3.4 ASME Publications. The American Society of Mechanical Engineers, Two Park Avenue, New York, NY 10016-5990.

ASME A17.1/CSA B44, *Safety Code for Elevators and Escalators,* 2019.

ASME A17.3, *Safety Code for Existing Elevators and Escalators,* 2020.

ASME B1.20.1, *Pipe Threads, General Purpose, Inch,* 2013, reaffirmed 2018.

ASME B16.22, *Wrought Copper and Copper Alloy Solder-Joint Pressure Fittings,* 2021.

ASME B16.26, *Cast Copper Alloy Fittings for Flared Copper Tubes,* 2018.

ANSI/ASME B16.50, *Wrought Copper and Copper Alloy Braze-Joint Pressure Fittings,* 2021.

ASME B31.3, *Process Piping,* 2020.

ASME B40.100, *Pressure Gauges and Gauge Attachments,* 2013.

ASME PVHO-1, *Safety Standard for Pressure Vessels for Human Occupancy,* 2019.

Boiler and Pressure Vessel Code, 2021.

2.3.5 ASSE Publications. ASSE International, 18927 Hickory Creek Drive, Suite 220, Mokena, IL 60448.

ASSE/IAPMO/ANSI 6010, *Professional Qualifications Standard for Medical Gas Systems Installers,* 2021.

Shaded text = Revisions.   Δ = Text deletions and figure/table revisions.   • = Section deletions.   *N* = New material.

ASSE/IAPMO/ANSI 6015, *Professional Qualifications Standard for Bulk Medical Gas/Cryogenic Fluid Central Supply Systems Installers*, 2021.

ASSE/IAPMO/ANSI 6020, *Professional Qualifications Standard for Medical Gas Systems Inspectors*, 2021.

ASSE/IAPMO/ANSI 6030, *Professional Qualifications Standard for Medical Gas Systems Verifiers*, 2021.

ASSE/IAPMO/ANSI 6035, *Professional Qualifications Standard for Bulk Medical Gas/Cryogenic Fluid Central Supply Systems Verifiers*, 2021.

ASSE/IAPMO/ANSI 6040, *Professional Qualifications Standard for Medical Gas Systems Maintenance Personnel*, 2021.

ASSE/IAPMO/ANSI 6060, *Professional Qualifications Standard for Medical Gas Systems Designers*, 2021.

2.3.6 ASTM Publications. ASTM International, 100 Barr Harbor Drive, P.O. Box C700, West Conshohocken, PA 19428-2959.

ASTM A269/A269M, *Standard Specification for Seamless and Welded Austenitic Stainless Steel Tubing for General Service*, 2015a, reapproved 2019.

ASTM A312/A312M, *Standard Specification for Seamless, Welded, and Heavily Cold Worked Austenitic Stainless Steel Pipes*, 2022.

ASTM B32, *Standard Specification for Solder Metal*, 2020.

ASTM B88, *Standard Specification for Seamless Copper Water Tube*, 2020.

ASTM B103/B103M, *Standard Specification for Phosphor Bronze Plate, Sheet, Strip, and Rolled Bar*, 2019.

ASTM B280, *Standard Specification for Seamless Copper Tube for Air Conditioning and Refrigeration Field Service*, 2020.

ASTM B819, *Standard Specification for Seamless Copper Tube for Medical Gas Systems*, 2019.

ASTM B828, *Standard Practice for Making Capillary Joints by Soldering of Copper and Copper Alloy Tube and Fittings*, 2016.

ASTM D5/D5M, *Standard Test Method for Penetration of Bituminous Materials*, 2020.

ASTM D1785, *Standard Specification for Poly(Vinyl Chloride) (PVC) Plastic Pipe, Schedules 40, 80, and 120*, 2021a.

ASTM D2466, *Standard Specification for Poly(Vinyl Chloride) (PVC) Plastic Pipe Fittings, Schedule 40*, 2021.

ASTM D2467, *Standard Specification for Poly(Vinyl Chloride) (PVC) Plastic Pipe Fittings, Schedule 80*, 2020.

ASTM D2665, *Standard Specification for Poly(Vinyl Chloride) (PVC) Plastic Drain, Waste, and Vent Pipe and Fittings*, 2020.

ASTM D2672, *Standard Specification for Joints for IPS PVC Pipe Using Solvent Cement*, 2020e1.

ASTM D2846/D2846M, *Standard Specification for Chlorinated Poly(Vinyl Chloride) (CPVC) Plastic Hot- and Cold-Water Distribution Systems*, 2019a.

ASTM D4359, *Standard Test Method for Determining Whether a Material Is a Liquid or a Solid*, 1990, reapproved 2019.

ASTM E84, *Standard Test Method for Surface Burning Characteristics of Building Materials*, 2022.

ASTM E136, *Standard Test Method for Assessing Combustibility of Materials Using a Vertical Tube Furnace at 750°C*, 2019a.

ASTM E1537, *Standard Test Method for Fire Testing of Upholstered Furniture*, 2022.

ASTM E1590, *Standard Test Method for Fire Testing of Mattresses*, 2022.

ASTM E2652, *Standard Test Method for Assessing Combustibility of Materials Using a Tube Furnace with a Cone-shaped Airflow Stabilizer, at 750°C*, 2018.

ASTM E2965, *Standard Test Method for Determination of Low Levels of Heat Release Rate for Materials and Products Using an Oxygen Consumption Calorimeter*, 2022.

ASTM F438, *Standard Specification for Socket-Type Chlorinated Poly(Vinyl Chloride) (CPVC) Plastic Pipe Fittings, Schedule 40*, 2017.

ASTM F439, *Standard Specification for Chlorinated Poly (Vinyl Chloride) (CPVC) Plastic Pipe Fittings, Schedule 80*, 2019.

ASTM F441/F441M, *Standard Specification for Chlorinated Poly(Vinyl Chloride) (CPVC) Plastic Pipe, Schedules 40 and 80*, 2020.

ASTM F493, *Standard Specification for Solvent Cements for Chlorinated Poly(Vinyl Chloride) (CPVC) Plastic Pipe and Fittings*, 2020.

2.3.7 AWS Publications. American Welding Society, 8669 NW 36 Street, #130, Miami, FL 33166-6672.

ANSI/AWS A5.8M/A5.8, *Specification for Filler Metals for Brazing and Braze Welding*, 2019.

AWS B2.2/B2.2M, *Specification for Brazing Procedure and Performance Qualification*, 2016.

Δ **2.3.8 BICSI Publications.** BICSI, 8610 Hidden River Parkway, Tampa, FL 33637.

The BICSI Information Transport Systems (ITS) Dictionary, 3rd edition, 2005.

2.3.9 CDA Publications. Copper Development Association Inc., 7918 Jones Branch Dr., Suite 300, McLean, VA 22102.

Copper Tube Handbook, 2020.

Δ **2.3.10 CGA Publications.** Compressed Gas Association, 8484 Westpark Drive, Suite 220, McLean, VA 22102.

CGA C-7, *Guide to Classification and Labeling of Compressed Gases*, 2020.

CGA G-4, *Oxygen*, 2015, reaffirmed 2020.

CGA G-4.1, *Cleaning Equipment for Oxygen Service*, 2018.

CGA G-6.1, *Standard for Insulated Liquid Carbon Dioxide Systems at Consumer Sites*, 2013.

CGA G-6.5, *Standard for Small Stationary Insulated Carbon Dioxide Supply Systems*, 2022.

CGA G-8.1, *Standard for Nitrous Oxide Systems at Customer Sites*, 2013, reaffirmed 2018.

CGA M-1, *Standard for Medical Gas Supply Systems at Health Care Facilities*, 2018.

CGA P-2.5, *Standard for Transfilling of High Pressure Gaseous Oxygen Used for Respiration*, 2018.

CGA P-2.6, *Standard for Transfilling of Liquid Oxygen Used for Respiration*, 2018.

CGA P-18, *Standard for Bulk Inert Gas Systems*, 2020.

CGA V-1, *Standard for Compressed Gas Cylinder Valve Outlet and Inlet Connections* (ANSI B57.1), 2021.

CGA V-5, *Standard for Diameter Index Safety System (Noninterchangeable Low Pressure Connections for Medical Gas Applications)*, 2019.

CGA V-6, *Standard Bulk Refrigerated Liquid Transfer Connections*, 2021.

2.3.11 CSA Group Publications. CSA Group, 178 Rexdale Blvd., Etobicoke, ON M9W 1R3, Canada.

CSA C22.2 No. 0.3, *Test Methods for Electrical Wires and Cables*, 2009, reaffirmed 2019.

2.3.12 FGI Publications. Facility Guidelines Institute, 9750 Fall Ridge Trail, St. Louis, MO 63127.

Guidelines for Design and Construction of Hospitals, 2022.

Guidelines for Design and Construction of Outpatient Facilities, 2022.

Guidelines for Design and Construction of Residential Health, Care, and Support Facilities, 2022.

2.3.13 ISA Publications. International Society of Automation, 67 T.W. Alexander Drive, P.O. Box 12277, Research Triangle Park, NC 27709.

ANSI/ISA S-7.0.01, *Quality Standard for Instrument Air*, 1996.

N 2.3.14 ISO Publications. International Organization for Standardization, ISO Central Secretariat, BIBC II, Chemin de Blandonnet 8, CP 401, 1214 Vernier, Geneva, Switzerland.

ISO 724, *ISO general-purpose metric screw threads — Basic dimensions*, 1993.

Δ 2.3.15 MSS Publications. Manufacturers Standardization Society of the Valve and Fittings Industry, Inc., 127 Park Street NE, Vienna, VA 22180.

MSS SP-58, *Pipe Hangers and Supports — Materials, Design, Manufacture, Selection, Application, and Installation*, 2018.

2.3.16 State of California Publications. State of California, Department of Consumer Affairs, 3485 Orange Grove Avenue, North Highlands, CA 95660-5595.

California Technical Bulletin 117, *Requirements, Test Procedure and Apparatus for Testing the Flame Retardance of Resilient Filling Materials Used in Upholstered Furniture*, 2000.

California Technical Bulletin 129, *Flammability Test Procedure for Mattresses for Use in Public Buildings*, 1992.

California Technical Bulletin 133, *Flammability Test Procedure for Seating Furniture for Use in Public Occupancies*, 1991.

2.3.17 TC Publications. Transport Canada, 330 Sparks Street, Ottawa, ON K1A 0N5, Canada.

Transportation of Dangerous Goods Regulations.

2.3.18 TIA Publications. Telecommunications Industry Association, 1310 North Courthouse Road, Suite 890, Arlington, VA 22201.

TIA/EIA 568-B, *Commercial Building Telecommunications Cabling Standard*, 2012.

TIA/EIA 606-B, *Administration Standard for Commercial Telecommunications Infrastructure*, 2009.

Δ 2.3.19 UL Publications. Underwriters Laboratories Inc., 333 Pfingsten Road, Northbrook, IL 60062-2096.

UL 723, *Test for Surface Burning Characteristics of Building Materials*, 2018.

UL 1069, *Hospital Signaling and Nurse Call Equipment*, 2007, revised 2022.

UL 1685, *Vertical-Tray Fire-Propagation and Smoke-Release Test for Electrical and Optical-Fiber Cables*, 2015, revised 2020.

Δ 2.3.20 US Government Publications. US Government Publishing Office, 732 North Capitol Street, NW, Washington, DC 20401.

DOE-STD-3020, *Specification for HEPA Filters Used by DOE Contractors*, Department of Energy, 2015.

Title 16, Code of Federal Regulations, Part 1632, "Standard for the Flammability of Mattresses and Mattress Pads (FF 4-72)."

Title 21, Code of Federal Regulations, Part 210, "Current Good Manufacturing Practice in Manufacturing, Processing, Packing, or Holding of Drugs — General."

Title 21, Code of Federal Regulations, Part 211, "Current Good Manufacturing Practice for Finished Pharmaceuticals."

Title 21, United States Code, Chapter 9, "Federal Food, Drug, and Cosmetic Act."

2.3.21 USP Publications. US Pharmacopeia, 12601 Twinbrook Parkway, Rockville, MD 20852-1790.

Monograph: Oxygen USP.

Monograph: Oxygen USP 93.

2.3.22 Other Publications.

Merriam-Webster's Collegiate Dictionary, 11th edition, Merriam-Webster, Inc., Springfield, MA, 2020.

2.4 References for Extracts in Mandatory Sections.

NFPA 10, *Standard for Portable Fire Extinguishers*, 2022 edition.
NFPA 13, *Standard for the Installation of Sprinkler Systems*, 2022 edition.
NFPA 30, *Flammable and Combustible Liquids Code*, 2024 edition.
NFPA 55, *Compressed Gases and Cryogenic Fluids Code*, 2023 edition.
NFPA 70®, *National Electrical Code®*, 2023 edition.
NFPA 70B, *Standard for Electrical Equipment Maintenance*, 2023 edition.
NFPA 99B, *Standard for Hypobaric Facilities*, 2024 edition.
NFPA 101®, *Life Safety Code®*, 2024 edition.
NFPA 110, *Standard for Emergency and Standby Power Systems*, 2022 edition.

NFPA 2500, *Standard for Operations and Training for Technical Search and Rescue Incidents and Life Safety Rope and Equipment for Emergency Services,* 2022 edition.

NFPA 5000®, *Building Construction and Safety Code®,* 2024 edition.

Chapter 3 Definitions

3.1 General. The definitions contained in this chapter shall apply to the terms used in this code. Where terms are not defined in this chapter or within another chapter, they shall be defined using their ordinarily accepted meanings within the context in which they are used. *Merriam-Webster's Collegiate Dictionary,* 11th edition, shall be the source for the ordinarily accepted meaning.

3.2 NFPA Official Definitions.

3.2.1* Approved. Acceptable to the authority having jurisdiction.

3.2.2* Authority Having Jurisdiction (AHJ). An organization, office, or individual responsible for enforcing the requirements of a code or standard, or for approving equipment, materials, an installation, or a procedure.

3.2.3* Code. A standard that is an extensive compilation of provisions covering broad subject matter or that is suitable for adoption into law independently of other codes and standards.

3.2.4 Guide. An NFPA standard that is advisory or informative in nature and that contains only nonmandatory provisions. A guide may contain mandatory statements such as when a guide can be used, but the NFPA standard as a whole is not suitable for adoption into law.

3.2.5 Labeled. Equipment or materials to which has been attached a label, symbol, or other identifying mark of an organization that is acceptable to the authority having jurisdiction and concerned with product evaluation, that maintains periodic inspection of production of labeled equipment or materials, and by whose labeling the manufacturer indicates compliance with appropriate standards or performance in a specified manner.

3.2.6* Listed. Equipment, materials, or services included in a list published by an organization that is acceptable to the authority having jurisdiction and concerned with evaluation of products or services, that maintains periodic inspection of production of listed equipment or materials or periodic evaluation of services, and whose listing states that either the equipment, material, or service meets appropriate designated standards or has been tested and found suitable for a specified purpose.

3.2.7 Shall. Indicates a mandatory requirement.

3.2.8 Should. Indicates a recommendation or that which is advised but not required.

3.2.9 Standard. An NFPA standard, the main text of which contains only mandatory provisions using the word "shall" to indicate requirements and that is in a form generally suitable for mandatory reference by another standard or code or for adoption into law. Nonmandatory provisions are not to be considered a part of the requirements of a standard and shall be located in an appendix, annex, footnote, informational note, or other means as permitted in the NFPA manuals of style. When used in a generic sense, such as in the phrases "standards development process" or "standards development activities," the term "standards" includes all NFPA standards, including codes, standards, recommended practices, and guides.

3.3 General Definitions.

3.3.1 Adiabatic Heating. The heating of a gas caused by its compression. (HYP)

3.3.2 Aerosol. An intimate mixture of a liquid or a solid in a gas; the liquid or solid, called the dispersed phase, is uniformly distributed in a finely divided state throughout the gas, which is the continuous phase or dispersing medium. (MED)

3.3.3 Alarm System. (PIP)

3.3.3.1 *Area Alarm System.* A warning system within an area of use that provides continuous visible and audible surveillance of Category 1 and Category 2 medical gas and vacuum systems. (PIP)

3.3.3.2 *Category 3 Alarm System.* A warning system within an area of use that provides continuous visible and audible surveillance of Category 3 medical gas systems. (PIP)

3.3.3.3 *Local Alarm System.* A warning system that provides continuous visible and audible surveillance of medical gas and vacuum system source equipment at the equipment site. (PIP)

3.3.3.4 *Master Alarm System.* A warning system that monitors the operation and condition of the source of supply, the reserve source (if any), and the pressure in the main lines of each medical gas and vacuum piping system. (PIP)

3.3.4 Ambulatory Health Care Occupancy. An occupancy used to provide services or treatment simultaneously to four or more patients that provides, on an outpatient basis, one or more of the following: (1) treatment for patients that renders the patients incapable of taking action for self-preservation under emergency conditions without the assistance of others; (2) anesthesia that renders the patients incapable of taking action for self-preservation under emergency conditions without the assistance of others; (3) treatment for patients who, due to the nature of their injury or illness, are incapable of taking action for self-preservation under emergency conditions without the assistance of others. [*101*, 2024] (FUN)

3.3.5 Ampacity. The maximum current, in amperes, that a conductor can carry continuously under the conditions of use without exceeding its temperature rating. [**70,** 2023] (ELS)

3.3.6 Anesthetic. As used in this code, applies to any inhalational agent used to produce sedation, analgesia, or general anesthesia. (MED)

N **3.3.7 Anesthetizing Location.** Any location where moderate sedation, deep sedation, or general anesthesia is intended to be administered. (PIP)

3.3.8 Appliance. Utilization equipment, generally other than industrial, normally built in standardized sizes or types, that is installed or connected as a unit to perform one or more functions. (MED)

3.3.9 Applicable Code. The building code, fire code, or NFPA *101* adopted by the jurisdiction, or NFPA *101* where no such code has been adopted by the jurisdiction. (FUN)

3.3.10* Applicator. A means of applying high-frequency energy to a patient other than by an electrically conductive connection. (MED)

3.3.11 Area of Administration. Any point within a room within 4.3 m (15 ft) of oxygen equipment or an enclosure containing or intended to contain an oxygen-enriched atmosphere. (MED)

3.3.12* Atmosphere. The pressure exerted by, and gaseous composition of, an environment. (HYP)

    3.3.12.1 *Atmosphere Absolute (ATA).* The pressure of the earth's atmosphere, 760.0 mmHg, 101.325 kPa, or 14.7 psia. Two ATA = two atmospheres. *(See also 3.3.12, Atmosphere.)* (HYP)

    3.3.12.2* *Atmosphere of Increased Burning Rate.* Any atmosphere containing a percentage of oxygen or oxygen and nitrous oxide greater than the quotient of 23.45 divided by the square root of the total pressure in atmospheres. (HYP)

    3.3.12.3 *Chamber Atmosphere.* The environment inside a chamber. (HYP)

3.3.13 Automatic. Providing a function without the necessity of human intervention. (ELS)

N **3.3.14 Auxiliary Source Connection.** A backup connection for a source medical gas system that serves a facility during equipment replacement or in an emergency. (PIP)

3.3.15 Bathroom. An area including a sink with one or more of the following: a toilet, a urinal, a tub, a shower, a bidet, or similar plumbing fixtures. [**70,** 2023] (FUN)

3.3.16 Battery-Powered Lighting Units. Individual unit equipment for backup illumination consisting of a rechargeable battery, battery-charging means, provisions for one or more lamps mounted on the equipment, or with terminals for remote lamps, or both, and relaying device arranged to energize the lamps automatically upon failure of the supply to the unit equipment. [**70,** 2023] (ELS)

3.3.17 Bends. Decompression sickness; caisson worker's disease. (HYP)

3.3.18 Branch Circuit. (Branch-Circuit) The circuit conductors between the final overcurrent device protecting the circuit and the outlet(s). [**70,** 2023] (ELS)

3.3.19 Branch Line. See 3.3.152, Piping. (PIP)

3.3.20 Bulk System. An assembly of equipment for supplying compressed gas (consisting of, but not limited to, storage containers, pressure regulators, pressure relief devices, vaporizers, manifolds, and interconnecting piping) that terminates where the gas, at service pressure, first enters the main line. The storage containers are either stationary or movable and include unconnected reserves on hand at the site, and the source gas is stored as a compressed gas or cryogenic fluid. (PIP)

    3.3.20.1 *Bulk Inert Gas System.* A bulk system with a storage capacity of more than 566 m^3 [20,000 ft^3 (scf)] of inert gas. (PIP)

Δ   **3.3.20.2** *Bulk Nitrous Oxide System.* A bulk system with a storage capacity of more than 1452 kg (3200 lb) [approxi-

mately 793 m^3 (28,000 ft^3) at normal temperature and pressure] of nitrous oxide. (PIP)

    3.3.20.3* *Bulk Oxygen System.* A bulk system with a storage capacity of more than 566 m^3 (20,000 ft^3) at normal temperature and pressure of oxygen. (PIP)

3.3.21* Central Supply System. The complete source of supply for a medical gas or vacuum system or a medical support gas system. (PIP)

3.3.22 Clean Agent. Electrically non-conducting, volatile, or gaseous fire extinguishant that does not leave a residue upon evaporation. [**10,** 2022] (FUN)

3.3.23* Clinical IT Network. An information technology video, voice, and data communication network that is dedicated for shared use by medical devices, nurse call, clinical information systems, patient-critical applications, and clinical wireless communication equipment. (ELS)

3.3.24 Combustible. Capable of undergoing combustion. (MED)

3.3.25* Combustible Liquid. Any liquid that was a closed-cup flash point at or above 37.8°C (100°F). Combustible liquids are classified as follows: (a) Class II liquid. Any liquid that has a flash point at or above 37.8°C (100°F) and below 60°C (140°F); (b) Class IIIA liquid. Any liquid that has a flash point at or above 60°C (140°F) and below 93°C (200°F); (c) Class IIIB liquid. Any liquid that has a flash point at or above 93°C (200°F). (FUN)

3.3.26* Combustion. A chemical process of oxidation that occurs at a rate fast enough to produce heat and usually light in the form of either a glow or flame. [**5000,** 2024] (HYP)

3.3.27 Compact Storage. Storage on solid shelves not exceeding 0.9 m (36 in.) in total depth, arranged as part of a compact storage module, with no more than 0.76 m (30 in.) between shelves vertically and with no internal vertical flue spaces other than those between individual shelving sections. [**13,** 2022] (FUN)

3.3.28* Compressed Medical Gases (CMG). Any liquefied or vaporized gas alone or in combination with other gases that is classified as a drug. [**55,** 2023] (PIP)

3.3.29 Container. A low-pressure, vacuum-insulated vessel containing gases in liquid form. (MED)

    3.3.29.1 *Liquid Oxygen Base Reservoir Container.* A container used for liquid oxygen not exceeding 60 L (15.8 gal) specifically designed for use as a medical device as defined by 21 USC 9, "Federal Food, Drug, and Cosmetic Act," that is intended to deliver gaseous oxygen for therapeutic use, transfilling, or both. (MED)

    3.3.29.2 *Liquid Oxygen Portable Container.* A container used for liquid oxygen not exceeding 1.5 L (0.396 gal) specifically designed for use as a medical device as defined by 21 USC 9, "Federal Food, Drug, and Cosmetic Act," that is intended for portable therapeutic use and to be filled from its companion base unit, which is a liquid oxygen base reservoir container. (MED)

3.3.30 Critical Branch. A system of feeders and branch circuits supplying power for task illumination, fixed equipment, select receptacles, and select power circuits serving areas and functions related to patient care that are automatically connected to alternate power sources by one or more transfer switches during interruption of the normal power source. (ELS)

3.3.31 Critical Equipment. That equipment essential to the safety of the occupants of the facility. (HYP)

3.3.32 Cryogenic Fluid Central Supply System. An assembly of equipment for supplying compressed gas, including, but not limited to, a stationary tank(s) that is permanently installed through anchoring to a foundation, pressure regulators, pressure relief devices, vaporizers, manifolds, and interconnecting piping that is designed to be filled at the health care facility with a cryogenic fluid and that terminates at the source valve. (PIP)

3.3.32.1 *Bulk Nitrous Oxide Central Supply System.* A central supply system with a storage capacity of more than 1452 kg (3200 lb) [i.e., approximately 793 m³ (28,000 ft³) at normal temperature and pressure] of nitrous oxide. (PIP)

3.3.33 Cylinder. A supply tank containing high-pressure gases or gas mixtures at pressures that can be in excess of 13.8 kPa gauge (2000 psi gauge). (MED)

N **3.3.34 Debrief.** A forum for planners, facilitators, controllers, and evaluators to review and provide feedback after an exercise is held. (HES)

3.3.35 Decompression Sickness. A syndrome due to evolved gas in the tissues resulting from a reduction in ambient pressure. (HYP)

3.3.36* Defend in Place. The operational response to an emergency in a building, in which the initial action does not involve evacuation of the building occupants. (FUN)

3.3.37 Demand Check. A paired set of fittings that permit gas flow when correctly mated but interrupt flow when separated. (PIP)

3.3.38 Dental Air. Compressed gas to drive dental devices, supplied by compressed air systems, pressurized cylinders of air, or nitrogen. (PIP)

3.3.39 Dental Office. A building or part thereof in which the following occur: (1) examinations and minor treatments/procedures performed under the continuous supervision of a dental professional; (2) use of limited to minimal sedation and treatment or procedures that do not render the patient incapable of self-preservation under emergency conditions; and (3) no overnight stays for patients or 24-hour operations. (PIP)

3.3.40 Dental Vacuum/Scavenging. A system used in dentistry for oral evacuation and nitrous oxide/oxygen scavenging. (PIP)

N **3.3.41 Dental-Surgical Vacuum.** A method that provides drainage, aspiration, and suction to remove body fluids from patients during dental treatment. (PIP)

3.3.42 Detonation. An exothermic reaction wherein the reaction propagates through the unreacted material at a rate exceeding the velocity of sound, hence the explosive noise. (MED)

3.3.43* Direct Electrical Pathway to the Heart. An externalized conductive pathway, insulated except at its ends, one end of which is in direct contact with heart muscle while the other is outside the body and is accessible for inadvertent or intentional contact with grounded objects or energized, ground-referenced sources. (MED)

3.3.44* Disaster. Within the context of this code, any unusual occurrence or unforeseen situation that seriously overtaxes or threatens to seriously overtax the routine capabilities of a health care facility. (HES)

3.3.45 D.I.S.S. Connector. A system of noninterchangeable medical gas and vacuum connectors complying with CGA V-5, *Standard for Diameter Index Safety System (Noninterchangeable Low Pressure Connections for Medical Gas Applications).* (PIP)

3.3.46* Double-Insulated Appliances. Appliances where the primary means of protection against electrical shock is not grounding. The primary means is by the use of combinations of insulation and separation spacings in accordance with an approved standard. (MED)

3.3.47 Electrical Life Support Equipment. Electrically powered equipment whose continuous operation is necessary to maintain a patient's life. (ELS)

Δ **3.3.48* Electrical Maintenance Program (EMP).** A managed program of inspecting, testing, monitoring, analyzing, and servicing electrical systems and equipment with the purpose of maintaining safe operations and production by reducing or eliminating system interruptions and equipment failures. [**70B, 2023**] (ELS)

3.3.49 Electrode. An electrically conductive connection to a patient. (MED)

3.3.50 Emergency Management. The act of developing procedures and plans to create effective preparedness, mitigation, response, and recovery during a disaster affecting a health care facility. (HES)

3.3.51 Emergency Oxygen Supply Connection (EOSC). An assembly of equipment that permits a gas supplier to make a temporary connection to supply oxygen to a building that has had its normal source of oxygen interrupted. (PIP)

3.3.52 Equipment Branch. A system of feeders and branch circuits arranged for delayed, automatic, or manual connection to the alternate power source and that serves primarily 3-phase power equipment. (ELS)

3.3.53 Equipment Grounding Bus. A grounding terminal bus in the feeder circuit of the branch circuit distribution panel that serves a particular area. (MED)

3.3.54* Essential Electrical System. A distribution system designed to ensure continuity of electrical power to designated areas and functions of a health care facility upon loss of one of the on-site or off-site sources with reliability and capacity sufficient to provide effective facility operation consistent with the facility's emergency operations plan. (ELS)

3.3.55 Evacuation — Waste Gas. See 3.3.194, Waste Anesthetic Gas Disposal (WAGD). (PIP)

N **3.3.56 Exercise.** An instrument to train for, assess, practice, and improve performance in prevention, protection, response, and recovery capabilities in a risk-free environment. (HES)

3.3.57 Exposed Conductive Surfaces. Those surfaces that are capable of carrying electric current and that are unprotected,

Shaded text = Revisions. Δ = Text deletions and figure/table revisions. • = Section deletions. *N* = New material.

2024 Edition

uninsulated, unenclosed, or unguarded, permitting personal contact. (ELS)

3.3.58* Facility Fire Plan. A plan developed by the health care facility to describe the actions to be taken during a fire emergency. (FUN)

3.3.59 Fault Current. A current in an accidental connection between an energized and a grounded or other conductive element resulting from a failure of insulation, spacing, or containment of conductors. (ELS)

3.3.60 Feeder. All circuit conductors between the service equipment, the source of a separately derived system, or other power supply source and the final branch-circuit overcurrent device. (ELS)

3.3.61* FGI Guidelines. A collection of documents that includes the following: (1) *Guidelines for Design and Construction of Hospitals;* (2) *Guidelines for Design and Construction of Outpatient Facilities;* and (3) *Guidelines for Design and Construction of Residential Health, Care, and Support Facilities.* (FUN)

3.3.62* Flammable. A combustible that is capable of easily being ignited and rapidly consumed by fire. (FUN)

3.3.63 Flammable Gas. Any substance that exists in the gaseous state at normal atmospheric temperature and pressure and is capable of being ignited and burned when mixed with proper proportion of air, oxygen, or other oxidizers. (HYP)

3.3.64 Flammable Liquid. A liquid that has a closed-cup flash point that is below 37.8°C (100°F) and a maximum vapor pressure of 2068 mmHg (40 psi absolute) at 37.8°C (100°F). (FUN)

3.3.65* Flash Point. The minimum temperature at which a liquid or a solid emits vapor sufficient to form an ignitable mixture with air near the surface of the liquid or the solid. (FUN)

3.3.66 Flow-Control Valve. A valve, usually a needle valve, that precisely controls flow of gas. (MED)

3.3.67* Flowmeter. A device for measuring volumetric flow rates of gases and liquids. (MED)

3.3.68* Frequency. The number of oscillations, per unit time, of a particular current or voltage waveform. The unit of frequency is the hertz. (MED)

3.3.69* Fume Hood. An enclosure designed to draw air inward by means of mechanical ventilation. (ELS)

3.3.70* General Anesthesia and Levels of Sedation/Analgesia.

3.3.70.1 *General Anesthesia.* A drug-induced loss of consciousness during which patients are not arousable, even by painful stimulation. The ability to independently maintain ventilatory function is often impaired. Patients often require assistance in maintaining a patent airway, and positive-pressure ventilation may be required because of depressed spontaneous ventilation or drug-induced depression of neuromuscular function. Cardiovascular function may be impaired. (PIP)

3.3.70.2 *Deep Sedation/Analgesia.* A drug-induced depression of consciousness during which patients cannot be easily aroused but respond purposefully following repeated or painful stimulation. The ability to independently maintain ventilatory function may be impaired. Patients may require assistance in maintaining a patent airway, and spontaneous ventilation may be inadequate. Cardiovascular function is usually maintained. (PIP)

3.3.70.3 *Moderate Sedation/Analgesia (Conscious Sedation).* A drug-induced depression of consciousness during which patients respond purposefully to verbal commands, either alone or accompanied by light tactile stimulation. No interventions are required to maintain a patient airway, and spontaneous ventilation is adequate. Cardiovascular function is usually maintained. (PIP)

3.3.70.4 *Minimal Sedation (Anxiolysis).* A drug-induced state during which patients respond normally to verbal commands. Although cognitive function and coordination may be impaired, ventilatory and cardiovascular functions are unaffected. (PIP)

3.3.71* Ground-Fault Circuit Interrupter (GFCI). A device intended for the protection of personnel that functions to de-energize a circuit or portion thereof within an established period of time when a ground-fault current exceeds the values established for a Class A device. [70, 2023] (ELS)

3.3.72 Grounding. See 3.3.73, Grounding System. (ELS)

3.3.73* Grounding System. A system of conductors that provides a low-impedance return path for leakage and fault currents. (ELS)

3.3.74 Hazard Current. For a given set of connections in an isolated power system, the total current that would flow through a low impedance if it were connected between either isolated conductor and ground. (ELS)

3.3.74.1 *Fault Hazard Current.* The hazard current of a given isolated power system with all devices connected except the line isolation monitor. (ELS)

3.3.74.2 *Monitor Hazard Current.* The hazard current of the line isolation monitor alone. (ELS)

3.3.74.3 *Total Hazard Current.* The hazard current of a given isolated system with all devices, including the line isolation monitor, connected. (ELS)

3.3.75* Health Care Facilities. Buildings, portions of buildings, or mobile enclosures in which human medical, dental, psychiatric, nursing, obstetrical, or surgical care is provided. (FUN)

3.3.76* Health Care Facility's Governing Body. The person or persons who have the overall legal responsibility for the operation of a health care facility. (FUN)

3.3.77* Health Care Microgrid. A group of interconnected loads and distributed energy resources within clearly defined boundaries that acts as a single controllable entity with respect to the utility. (ELS)

3.3.78 Health Care Microgrid Control System. A system including health care microgrid control functions that can manage itself, operate autonomously, and connect to and disconnect from the utility for the exchange of power and the supply of ancillary services. (ELS)

Δ **3.3.79* Home Care.** Medical services or equipment provided in noncommercial, residential settings that purposely facilitate the provision of medical or custodial care. (FUN)

3.3.80 Hospital. A building or portion thereof used on a 24-hour basis for the medical, psychiatric, obstetrical, or surgical care of four or more inpatients. [*101*, 2024] (FUN)

3.3.81 Humidifier. A device used for adding water vapor to inspired gas. (MED)

3.3.82 Hyperbaric Facility. Building, structure, or space used to house hyperbaric chambers and auxiliary service equipment for medical applications and procedures at pressures above normal atmospheric pressure. (HYP)

3.3.83* Hyperbaric Operations. Procedures conducted on the patient receiving hyperbaric treatment. (HYP)

3.3.84 Hyperbaric Stand-Alone Oxygen System. The oxygen system is entirely separate from the hospital's Category 1 Oxygen System or is a freestanding hyperbaric facility. (HYP)

3.3.85 Hypobaric Facility. Building, structure, or space used to house hypobaric chambers and auxiliary service equipment for medical applications and procedures at pressures below atmospheric pressure. (HYP)

3.3.86 Hypoxia. A state of inadequate oxygenation of the blood and tissue sufficient to cause impairment of function. [**99B**, 2024] (HYP)

3.3.87 Immediate Restoration of Service. Automatic restoration of operation with an interruption of not more than 10 seconds. (ELS)

3.3.88* Impedance. Impedance is the ratio of the voltage drop across a circuit element to the current flowing through the same circuit element. The unit of impedance is the ohm. (MED)

N **3.3.89 Incident.** An occurrence or event, regardless of cause, that requires an emergency response to protect life or property. (HES)

△ **3.3.90 Incident Command System (ICS).** The combination of facilities, equipment, personnel, procedures, and communications operating within a common organizational structure that has responsibility for the management of assigned resources to effectively accomplish stated objectives pertaining to an incident or training exercise. [**2500**, 2022] (HES)

3.3.91* Instrument Air. A medical support gas that falls under the general requirements for medical gases. Medical air and instrument air are distinct systems for mutually exclusive applications. (PIP)

3.3.92 Intermittent Positive-Pressure Breathing (IPPB). Ventilation of the lungs by application of intermittent positive pressure to the airway. (MED)

3.3.93* Intrinsically Safe. As applied to equipment and wiring, equipment and wiring that are incapable of releasing sufficient electrical energy under normal or abnormal conditions to cause ignition of a specific hazardous atmospheric mixture. (HYP)

3.3.94 Invasive Procedure. Any procedure that penetrates the protective surfaces of a patient's body (i.e., skin, mucous membrane, cornea) and that is performed with an aseptic field (procedural site). [Not included in this category are placement of peripheral intravenous needles or catheters used to administer fluids and/or medications, gastrointestinal endoscopies (i.e., sigmoidoscopies), insertion of urethral catheters, and other similar procedures.] (ELS)

3.3.95 Isolated Patient Lead. A patient lead whose impedance to ground or to a power line is sufficiently high that connecting the lead to ground, or to either conductor of the power line, results in current flow below a hazardous limit in the lead. (MED)

3.3.96* Isolated Power System (IPS). A system comprising an isolation transformer or its equivalent, a line isolation monitor, and its ungrounded circuit conductors. (ELS)

3.3.97 Isolation Transformer. A transformer of the multiple-winding type, with the primary and secondary windings physically separated, that inductively couples its ungrounded secondary winding to the grounded feeder system that energizes its primary winding. (ELS)

3.3.98* Laboratory. A building, space, room, or group of rooms intended to serve activities involving procedures for investigation, diagnosis, or treatment in which flammable, combustible, or oxidizing materials are to be used. (FUN)

3.3.99 Leak Detectant. For purposes of this standard, a reagent, a solution, or an electronic or mechanical device suitable for the detection or visualization of escaping gas. (PIP)

3.3.100 Life Safety Branch. A system of feeders and branch circuits supplying power for lighting, receptacles, and equipment essential for life safety that is automatically connected to alternate power sources by one or more transfer switches during interruption of the normal power source. (ELS)

3.3.101* Limited-Combustible (Material). See 4.4.2. (FUN)

3.3.102 Line Isolation Monitor. A test instrument designed to continually check the balanced and unbalanced impedance from each line of an isolated circuit to ground and equipped with a built-in test circuit to exercise the alarm without adding to the leakage current hazard. (ELS)

3.3.103* Liquid. Any material that (1) has a fluidity greater than that of 300 penetration asphalt when tested in accordance with ASTM D5/D5M, *Standard Test Method for Penetration of Bituminous Materials*, or (2) is a viscous substance for which a specific melting point cannot be determined but that is determined to be a liquid in accordance with ASTM D4359, *Standard Test Method for Determining Whether a Material is a Liquid or a Solid*. [**30**, 2024] (FUN)

3.3.104* Local Signal. A visible indication of the operating status of equipment. (PIP)

3.3.105 mA. Milliampere. (FUN)

3.3.106 Manifold. A device for connecting the outlets of one or more gas cylinders to the central piping system for that specific gas. (PIP)

3.3.107* Manufactured Assembly. A factory-assembled product designed for aesthetics or convenience that contains medical gas or vacuum outlets, including their primary valves, piping, or other devices related to medical gases. (PIP)

N **3.3.108 Manufactured Rough-In Assembly.** A factory-assembled product designed for aesthetics or convenience that contains only the secondary valves of medical gas or vacuum outlets, piping, or other devices related to medical gases. (PIP)

3.3.109 Mask. A device that fits over the mouth and nose (oronasal) or nose (nasal) used to administer gases to a patient. (MED)

3.3.110* Medical Air. For purposes of this code, medical air is air supplied from cylinders, bulk containers, or medical air compressors or reconstituted from oxygen USP and oil-free, dry nitrogen NF. (PIP)

3.3.110.1 *Proportioning System for Medical Air USP.* A central supply that produces medical air (USP) reconstituted from oxygen USP and nitrogen NF by means of a mixer or blender. (PIP)

3.3.111 Medical Air Compressor. A compressor that is designed to exclude oil from the air stream and compression chamber and that does not under normal operating conditions or any single fault add any toxic or flammable contaminants to the compressed air. (PIP)

3.3.112 Medical Gas. A patient medical gas or medical support gas. *(See also 3.3.150, Patient Medical Gas, and 3.3.115, Medical Support Gas.)* (PIP)

3.3.113 Medical Gas System. An assembly of equipment and piping for the distribution of nonflammable medical gases such as oxygen, nitrous oxide, compressed air, carbon dioxide, and helium. (PIP)

3.3.114* Medical Office. A building or part thereof in which the following occur: (1) examinations and minor treatments/procedures performed under the continuous supervision of a medical professional; (2) the use of limited to minimal sedation and treatment or procedures that do not render the patient incapable of self-preservation under emergency conditions; and (3) no overnight stays for patients or 24-hour operations. (FUN)

3.3.115 Medical Support Gas. Nitrogen or instrument air used for any medical support purpose (e.g., to remove excess moisture from instruments before further processing, or to operate medical–surgical tools, air-driven booms, pendants, or similar applications) and, if appropriate to the procedures, used in laboratories and are not respired as part of any treatment. Medical support gas falls under the general requirements for medical gases. (PIP)

3.3.116 Medical–Surgical Vacuum. A method used to provide a source of drainage, aspiration, and suction in order to remove body fluids from patients. (PIP)

3.3.117 Medical–Surgical Vacuum System. An assembly of central vacuum–producing equipment and a network of piping for patient suction in medical, medical–surgical, and waste anesthetic gas disposal (WAGD) applications. (PIP)

3.3.118 Multiple Treatment Facility. A diagnostic or treatment complex under a single management comprising a number of single treatment facilities, which can be accessed one from the other without exiting the facility (i.e., does not involve widely separated locations or separate distinct practices). (FUN)

3.3.119 mV. Millivolt. (FUN)

3.3.120 Nasal Cannula. Device consisting of two short tubes to be inserted into the nostrils to administer oxygen or other therapeutic gases. (MED)

3.3.121 Nebulizer. A device used for producing an aerosol of water and/or medication within inspired gas supply. (MED)

3.3.122 Negative Pressure. Pressure less than atmospheric. (MED)

3.3.123 Nitrogen. An element that, at atmospheric temperatures and pressures, exists as a clear, colorless, and tasteless gas; it comprises approximately four-fifths of the earth's atmosphere. (MED)

3.3.123.1 *Nitrogen NF.* Nitrogen complying as a minimum with nitrogen NF. (PIP)

3.3.124 Nitrogen Narcosis. A condition resembling alcoholic inebriation, which results from breathing nitrogen in the air under significant pressure. (HYP)

3.3.125 Nitrous Oxide. An inorganic compound, one of the oxides of nitrogen. It exists as a gas at atmospheric pressure and temperature, possesses a sweetish smell, and is used for inducing anesthesia when inhaled. The oxygen in the compound will be released under conditions of combustion, creating an oxygen-enriched atmosphere. (MED)

3.3.126 Noncombustible (Material). See 4.4.1. (FUN)

N **3.3.127 Nonessential Electrical Loads.** Those electrical loads of a health care facility that do not require multiple power sources. (ELS)

3.3.128 Nonflammable. Not readily capable of burning with a flame and not liable to ignite and burn when exposed to flame. (FUN)

3.3.129 Nonflammable Anesthetic Agent. Refers to those inhalation agents that, because of their vapor pressure at 37°C (98.6°F) and at atmospheric pressure, cannot attain flammable concentrations when mixed with air, oxygen, or mixtures of oxygen and nitrous oxide. (MED)

3.3.130* Nonflammable Medical Gas System. See 3.3.113, Medical Gas System, and Chapter 5. (PIP)

3.3.131 Nonmedical Compressed Air. Air that is used for purposes other than patient care or medical devices that provide direct patient care. (MEC)

3.3.132 Nursing Home. A building or portion of a building used on a 24-hour basis for the housing and nursing care of four or more persons who, because of mental or physical incapacity, might be unable to provide for their own needs and safety without the assistance of another person. [*101,* 2024] (FUN)

3.3.133 Opportunity for Improvement. An identified gap or shortfall with the potential to raise something to a more desirable or outstanding quality or condition. (HES)

3.3.134* Oxidizing Gas. A gas that supports combustion. (HYP)

3.3.135* Oxygen. A chemical element that, at normal atmospheric temperatures and pressures, exists as a colorless, odorless, and tasteless gas and comprises about 21 percent by volume of the earth's atmosphere. (MED)

3.3.135.1 *Gaseous Oxygen.* A colorless, odorless, tasteless, and nontoxic gas, comprising about 21 percent of normal air by volume, that is about 10 percent heavier than air; also the physical state of the element at atmospheric temperature and pressure. (MED)

3.3.135.2* *Liquid Oxygen.* Exists at cryogenic temperature, approximately −184.4°C (−300°F) at atmospheric pressure. It retains all of the properties of gaseous oxygen, but, in addition, when allowed to warm to room temperature at atmospheric pressure, it will evaporate and expand to fill a volume 860 times its liquid volume. (MED)

3.3.136 Oxygen Concentrator Unit. An engineered assembly of components that operate to raise the concentration of oxygen, providing oxygen as a drug product. (PIP)

3.3.137* Oxygen Delivery Equipment. Any device used to transport and deliver an oxygen-enriched atmosphere to a patient. (MED)

3.3.138* Oxygen Hood. A device encapsulating a patient's head and used for a purpose similar to that of a mask. *(See also 3.3.109, Mask.)* (HYP)

3.3.139 Oxygen 93 USP. Oxygen complying with Oxygen USP 93 Monograph. (PIP)

3.3.140* Oxygen Toxicity (Hyperbaric). Physical impairment resulting from breathing gaseous mixtures containing oxygen-enriched atmospheres at elevated partial pressures for extended periods of time. (HYP)

3.3.141 Oxygen USP. Oxygen complying with Oxygen USP Monograph. (PIP)

3.3.142 Oxygen-Enriched Atmosphere (OEA). For the purposes of this code, an atmosphere in which the concentration of oxygen exceeds 23.5 percent by volume. (HYP)

3.3.143 Patient Bed Location. The location of a patient sleeping bed, or the bed or procedure table of a Category 1 space. (ELS)

3.3.144 Patient Care–Related Electrical Equipment. Electrical equipment appliance that is intended to be used for diagnostic, therapeutic, or monitoring purposes in a patient care vicinity. (MED)

3.3.145* Patient Care Space. Any space of a health care facility wherein patients are intended to be examined or treated. (FUN)

3.3.145.1 *Category 1 Space.* Space in which failure of equipment or a system is likely to cause major injury or death of patients, staff, or visitors. (FUN)

3.3.145.2 *Category 2 Space.* Space in which failure of equipment or a system is likely to cause minor injury to patients, staff, or visitors. (FUN)

3.3.145.3 *Category 3 Space.* Space in which the failure of equipment or a system is not likely to cause injury to patients, staff, or visitors but can cause discomfort. (FUN)

3.3.145.4 *Category 4 Space.* Space in which failure of equipment or a system is not likely to have a physical impact on patient care. (FUN)

3.3.146 Patient Care Vicinity. A space, within a location intended for the examination and treatment of patients, extending 1.8 m (6 ft) beyond the normal location of the bed, chair, table, treadmill, or other device that supports the patient during examination and treatment and extending vertically to 2.3 m (7 ft 6 in.) above the floor. (MED)

3.3.147 Patient Equipment Grounding Point. A jack or terminal that serves as the collection point for redundant grounding of electric appliances serving a patient care vicinity or for grounding other items in order to eliminate electromagnetic interference problems. (MED)

3.3.148* Patient Lead. Any deliberate electrical connection that can carry current between an appliance and a patient. (MED)

3.3.149 Patient Medical Gas. Piped gases such as oxygen, nitrous oxide, helium, carbon dioxide, and medical air that are used in the application of human respiration and the calibration of medical devices used for human respiration. (PIP)

3.3.150 Piped Distribution System. A pipeline network assembly of equipment that starts at and includes the source valve, warning systems (master, area, local alarms), bulk gas system signal actuating switch wiring, interconnecting piping, and all other components up to and including the station outlets/inlets. (PIP)

3.3.151 Piping. The tubing or conduit of the system. The three general classes of piping are main lines, risers, and branch (lateral) lines. (PIP)

3.3.151.1 *Branch (Lateral) Lines.* Those sections or portions of the piping system that serve a room or group of rooms on the same story of the facility. (PIP)

3.3.151.2 *Main Lines.* The piping that connects the source (pumps, receivers, etc.) to the risers or branches, or both. (PIP)

3.3.151.3 *Risers.* The vertical pipes connecting the system main line(s) with the branch lines on the various levels of the facility. (PIP)

N **3.3.152 Planned Event.** A planned, nonemergency assembly that brings a group of people together in one or more locations for a limited period of time for a particular activity. (HES)

3.3.153 Plug (Attachment Plug, Cap). A device that, by insertion in a receptacle, establishes connection between the conductors of the attached flexible cord and the conductors connected permanently to the receptacle. (MED)

3.3.154 Plume (Medical). The smoke by-product consisting of vapors, smoke, and particulate debris produced during the thermal destruction of tissue by energy-based devices such as lasers, electrosurgical generators, and broadband light sources. (MEC)

Δ **3.3.155 Power Sources.** A system of one or more off-site or one or more on-site power generation or storage components intended to provide power to nonessential electrical loads and the essential electrical system. (ELS)

3.3.156 Pressure.

3.3.156.1 *Absolute Pressure.* The total pressure in a system with reference to zero pressure. (HYP)

3.3.156.2 *Ambient Pressure.* Refers to total pressure of the environment referenced. (HYP)

3.3.156.3 *Gauge Pressure.* Refers to total pressure above (or below) atmospheric. (HYP)

3.3.156.4 *High Pressure.* A pressure exceeding 1.38 kPa (200 psi) gauge (215 psia). (MED)

3.3.156.5* *Operating Pressure.* The pressure that a particular piping system is set to operate at. (PIP)

3.3.156.6* *Partial Pressure.* The pressure, in absolute units, exerted by a particular gas in a gas mixture. (HYP)

3.3.156.7 *Positive Pressure.* Pressure greater than ambient atmospheric. (MED)

3.3.156.8 *Working Pressure (Rated).* The maximum rated operating pressure for a pipe, tube, or vessel based on its material, its allowable stress in tension, its outside diameter and wall thickness, the operating temperature, the joining method, and industry safety factors. (PIP)

3.3.157* Pressure-Reducing Regulator. A device that automatically reduces gas under high pressure to a usable lower working pressure. (MED)

3.3.158 Procedure Room. Where the proceduralist is using instrumentation that requires constant observation and control. (MED)

3.3.159* Producer. The machine(s) or device(s) that generate the flow and suction required for vacuum, WAGD, and plume evacuation systems to operate. (PIP)

3.3.160 psia. Pounds per square inch absolute, a unit of pressure measurement with zero pressure as the base or reference pressure. (HYP)

3.3.161* psig. Pounds per square inch gauge, a unit of pressure measurement with atmospheric pressure as the base or reference pressure. (HYP)

3.3.162 Qualified Person. A person who, by possession of a recognized degree, certificate, professional standing, or skill, and who, by knowledge, training, and experience, has demonstrated the ability to perform the work. (HYP)

3.3.163 Reactance. The component of impedance contributed by inductance or capacitance. The unit of reactance is the ohm. (MED)

Δ **3.3.164* Receptacle.** A contact device installed at the outlet for the connection of an attachment plug, or for the direct connection of electrical utilization equipment designed to mate with the corresponding contact device. A single receptacle is a single contact device with no other contact device on the same yoke or strap. A multiple receptacle is two or more contact devices on the same yoke or strap. [70, 2023] (ELS)

3.3.165 Reference Grounding Point. The ground bus of the panelboard or isolated power system panel supplying the patient care room. (MED)

3.3.166 Relocatable Power Tap (RPT). A device for indoor use consisting of an attachment plug on one end of a flexible cord and three or more receptacles on the opposite end. *(See 10.2.3.6.)* (MED)

3.3.167* Remote. A Level 3 source of supply that is accessed by exiting the single or multiple treatment facility. (PIP)

3.3.168 Reserve Supply. Where existing, that portion of the supply equipment that automatically supplies the system in the event of failure of the operating supply. The reserve supply only functions in an emergency and not as a normal operating procedure. (PIP)

3.3.169 Risk Categories. (FUN)

3.3.169.1 *Category 1.* Activities, systems, or equipment whose failure is likely to cause major injury or death to patients, staff, or visitors. (FUN)

3.3.169.2 *Category 2.* Activities, systems, or equipment whose failure is likely to cause minor injury to patients, staff, or visitors. (FUN)

3.3.169.3 *Category 3.* Activities, systems, or equipment whose failure is not likely to cause injury to patients, staff, or visitors but can cause discomfort. (FUN)

3.3.169.4 *Category 4.* Activities, systems, or equipment whose failure would have no impact on patient care. (FUN)

3.3.170 Scavenging. Evacuation of exhaled mixtures of oxygen and nitrous oxide. (PIP)

3.3.171 Selected Receptacles. A minimal number of receptacles selected by the health care facility's governing body as necessary to provide essential patient care and facility services during loss of normal power. (ELS)

3.3.172 Self-Extinguishing. A characteristic of a material such that, once the source of ignition is removed, the flame is quickly extinguished without the fuel or oxidizer being exhausted. (HYP)

3.3.173 Semipermanent Connection. A noninterchangeable connection, usually a D.I.S.S. connector, which is the termination of the pipeline and that is intended to be detached only for service. It is not the point at which the user makes connections or disconnections. (PIP)

3.3.174 Service Inlet. The pneumatic terminus of a Level 3 piped vacuum system. (PIP)

3.3.175 Service Outlet. The pneumatic terminus of a piped gas system for other than critical, continuous duty, nonflammable medical life support–type gases such as oxygen, nitrous oxide, or medical air. (PIP)

3.3.176* Single Treatment Facility. A diagnostic or treatment complex under a single management comprising a number of use points, but confined to a single contiguous group of use points (i.e., does not involve widely separated locations or separate distinct practices). (PIP)

3.3.177* Site of Intentional Expulsion. All points within 0.3 m (1 ft) of a point at which an oxygen-enriched atmosphere is intentionally vented to the atmosphere. (MED)

N **3.3.178 Sleep Lab.** A specialized center where sleep studies are administered to diagnose common sleep disorders that is equipped with a sleeping area, monitoring equipment, and a separate observation area for the medical professionals monitoring the patient during sleep. (PIP)

3.3.179 Space. A portion of the health care facility designated by the health care facility's governing body that serves a specific purpose. (FUN)

3.3.180 Standard Cubic Feet per Minute (SCFM). Volumetric flow rate of gas in units of standard cubic feet per minute. (PIP)

3.3.181 Station Inlet. An inlet point in a piped medical/surgical vacuum distribution system at which the user makes connections and disconnections. (PIP)

3.3.182 Station Outlet. An outlet point in a piped medical gas distribution system at which the user makes connections and disconnections. (PIP)

3.3.183 Supply Source. Those portions of the central supply system that act as a self-contained supply. (PIP)

3.3.183.1 *Operating Supply.* The portion of the central supply system that is supplying the piping system at the time of observation. (PIP)

3.3.183.2 *Primary Supply.* The portion of the central supply system that is the default supply for the piping system. (PIP)

3.3.183.3 *Reserve Supply.* Where provided, the portion of the central supply system that will supply the piping system when the primary and secondary supplies are exhausted or are not operative. (PIP)

3.3.183.4 *Secondary Supply.* Where provided, the portion of the central supply system that will supply the piping system when the primary supply is exhausted or is not operative. (PIP)

3.3.184* Surface-Mounted Medical Gas Rail Systems. A surface-mounted gas delivery system intended to provide ready access for two or more gases through a common delivery system to provide multiple gas station outlet locations within a single patient room or Category 1 Space. (PIP)

3.3.185 Task Illumination. Provisions for the minimum lighting required to carry out necessary tasks in the areas described in Chapter 6, including safe access to supplies and equipment and access to exits. (ELS)

3.3.186 Terminal. The end of a flexible hose or tubing used in a manufactured assembly where the user is intended to make connection and disconnection. (PIP)

3.3.187 Touch Current. Leakage current flowing from the enclosure or from parts thereof, excluding patient connections, accessible to any operator or patient in normal use, through an external path other than the protective grounding (earth) conductor to earth or to another part of the enclosure. (MED)

3.3.188 Transfilling. The process of transferring a medical gas in gaseous or liquid state from one container or cylinder to another container or cylinder. (MED)

3.3.189 Tube.

3.3.189.1* *Endotracheal Tube.* A tube for insertion through the mouth or nose into the upper portion of the trachea (windpipe). (MED)

3.3.190 Use Point. A location with any number of station outlets and inlets arranged for access by a practitioner during treatment of a patient. (PIP)

3.3.191 Vaporizer. A heat exchange unit designed to convert cryogenic liquid into the gaseous state. (PIP)

3.3.192 Ventilation. The mechanical or natural movement of air. (MEC)

3.3.193 Waste Anesthetic Gas Disposal (WAGD). The process of capturing and carrying away gases vented from the patient breathing circuit during the normal operation of gas anesthesia or analgesia equipment. (PIP)

3.3.194 Waste Water. (MEC)

3.3.194.1 *Black Waste Water.* Grossly contaminated and contain pathogenic, toxigenic, or other harmful agents. (MEC)

3.3.194.2 *Clear Waste Water.* Originates from a sanitary water source and does not pose substantial risk from dermal, ingestion, or inhalation exposure. (MEC)

3.3.194.3 *Gray Waste Water.* Contains significant contamination and has the potential to cause discomfort or sickness if contacted or consumed by humans. Can contain potentially unsafe levels of microorganisms or nutrients for microorganisms, as well as other organic or inorganic matter (chemical or biological). (MEC)

3.3.195* Wet Procedure Locations. The area in a patient care space where a procedure is performed that is normally subject to wet conditions while patients are present, including standing fluids on the floor or drenching of the work area, either of which condition is intimate to the patient or staff. (FUN)

3.4 BICSI Definitions. These terms are defined in *The BICSI Information Transport Systems (ITS) Dictionary.*

3.4.1 Telecommunications Entrance Facility (EF). An entrance to a building for both public and private network service cables that includes the building entrance point and the entrance room or space at the point of demarcation between campus or utility service and building interior distribution of communications systems. (ELS)

3.4.2 Telecommunications Equipment Room (TER). An environmentally controlled centralized space for telecommunications equipment, typically including main or intermediate cross-connect equipment and cabling. (ELS)

3.4.3 Telecommunications Room (TR). An enclosed architectural space for housing telecommunications equipment, cable terminations, and cross-connect cabling, serving a floor or an area of a floor. (ELS)

Chapter 4 Fundamentals

4.1* Risk Categories. All activities, as well as systems or equipment that are new or altered, shall be designed to meet Category 1 through Category 4 requirements, as detailed in this code.

4.1.1* Category 1. Activities, systems, or equipment whose failure is likely to cause major injury or death of patients, staff, or visitors shall be designed to meet Category 1 requirements, as detailed in this code.

4.1.2* Category 2. Activities, systems, or equipment whose failure is likely to cause minor injury of patients, staff, or visitors shall be designed to meet Category 2 requirements, as detailed in this code.

4.1.3 Category 3. Activities, systems, or equipment whose failure is not likely to cause injury to patients, staff, or visitors, but can cause discomfort, shall be designed to meet Category 3 requirements, as detailed in this code.

4.1.4 Category 4. Activities, systems, or equipment whose failure would have no impact on patient care shall be designed to meet Category 4 requirements, as detailed in this code.

Δ **4.1.5*** Activities, systems, and equipment shall be permitted to be designed to a higher risk category.

4.2* Risk Assessment.

4.2.1 The health care facility's governing body shall establish the processes and operations that are planned for the health care facility.

4.2.1.1 The governing body shall conduct risk assessments and shall determine risk categories based on the character of the processes and operations conducted in the health care facility.

4.2.2* Risk categories shall be classified by the health care facility's governing body by following and documenting a defined risk assessment procedure.

4.2.2.1 Where required by the authority having jurisdiction, the risk assessment shall be provided to the authority having jurisdiction for review based on the character of the processes and operations conducted in the health care facility.

4.2.3 A documented risk assessment shall not be required where Category 1 is selected.

4.3 Application. The Category definitions in Chapter 4 shall apply to Chapters 5 through 11, 14, and 15, except as modified in those chapters.

4.4 Materials.

4.4.1* Noncombustible Material.

4.4.1.1 A material that complies with any of the following shall be considered a noncombustible material:

(1) A material that, in the form in which it is used and under the conditions anticipated, will not ignite, burn, support combustion, or release flammable vapors when subjected to fire or heat

(2) A material that is reported as passing ASTM E136, *Standard Test Method for Assessing Combustibility of Materials Using a Vertical Tube Furnace at 750°C*

(3) A material that is reported as complying with the pass/fail criteria of ASTM E136 when tested in accordance with the test method and procedure in ASTM E2652, *Standard Test Method for Assessing Combustibility of Materials Using a Tube Furnace with a Cone-shaped Airflow Stabilizer, at 750°C*

4.4.1.2 Where the term *limited-combustible* is used in this code, it shall also include the term *noncombustible*. [**5000:**7.1.4.1.2]

4.4.2* Limited-Combustible Material. A material shall be considered a limited-combustible material where one of the following is met:

(1) The conditions of 4.4.2.1 and 4.4.2.2, and the conditions of either 4.4.2.3 or 4.4.2.4, shall be met.

(2) The conditions of 4.4.2.6 shall be met.

4.4.2.1 The material shall not comply with the requirements for noncombustible material in accordance with 4.4.1.

4.4.2.2 The material, in the form in which it is used, shall exhibit a potential heat value not exceeding 3500 Btu/lb (8141 kJ/kg) where tested in accordance with NFPA 259.

Δ **4.4.2.3** The material shall have the structural base of a noncombustible material with a surfacing not exceeding a thickness of $\frac{1}{8}$ in. (3.2 mm) where the surfacing exhibits a flame spread index not greater than 50 when tested in accordance with ASTM E84, *Standard Test Method for Surface Burning Characteristics of Building Materials*, or UL 723, *Test for Surface Burning Characteristics of Building Materials*.

Δ **4.4.2.4** The material shall be composed of materials that, in the form and thickness used, exhibit neither a flame spread index greater than 25 nor evidence of continued progressive combustion when tested in accordance with ASTM E84, *Standard Test Method for Surface Burning Characteristics of Building Materials*, or UL 723, *Test for Surface Burning Characteristics of Building Materials*, and shall be of such composition that all surfaces that would be exposed by cutting through the material on any plane would exhibit neither a flame spread index greater than 25 nor exhibit evidence of continued progressive combustion when tested in accordance with ASTM E84 or UL 723.

4.4.2.5 Materials shall be considered limited-combustible materials where tested in accordance with ASTM E2965, *Standard Test Method for Determination of Low Levels of Heat Release Rate for Materials and Products Using an Oxygen Consumption Calorimeter*, at an incident heat flux of 75 kW/m^2 for a 20-minute exposure and both of the following conditions are met:

(1) The peak heat release rate shall not exceed 150 kW/m^2 for longer than 10 seconds.

(2) The total heat released shall not exceed 8 MJ/m^2.

4.4.2.6 Where the term *limited-combustible* is used in this *Code*, it shall also include the term *noncombustible*. [**5000:**7.1.4.2.6]

Chapter 5   Gas and Vacuum Systems

5.1 Category 1 Piped Gas and Vacuum Systems.

5.1.1* Applicability.

5.1.1.1* These requirements shall apply to health care facilities that require Category 1 systems as referenced in Chapter 4.

5.1.1.2* Where the terms *medical gas* or *medical support gas* occur, the provisions shall apply to all piped systems for oxygen, nitrous oxide, medical air, carbon dioxide, helium, nitrogen, instrument air, and mixtures thereof. Wherever the name of a specific gas service occurs, the provision shall apply only to that gas.

5.1.1.3* An existing system that is not in strict compliance with the provisions of this code shall be permitted to be continued in use, unless the authority having jurisdiction has determined that such use constitutes a distinct hazard to life.

N 5.1.1.4 This chapter shall apply to new health care facilities as specified by Section 1.3 unless otherwise specified by 5.1.1.6.

5.1.1.5 The following sections of this chapter shall apply to the operation, management, and maintenance of Category 1 medical gas and vacuum systems in both new and existing facilities:

(1)   5.1.2
(2)   5.1.3.1
(3)   5.1.3.2
(4)   5.1.3.3.4
(5)   5.1.3.6.2
(6)   5.1.3.6.3.10(A)(2)
(7)   5.1.3.7.6(A)(2)
(8)   5.1.3.8.4.1(2)
(9)   5.1.14

5.1.1.6 Category 1 systems shall be permitted to serve spaces identified as Category 1, Category 2, or Category 3.

5.1.2 Nature of Hazards of Gas and Vacuum Systems. Potential fire and explosion hazards associated with positive pressure gas central piping systems and medical–surgical vacuum systems shall be considered in the design, installation, testing, operation, and maintenance of these systems.

5.1.3* Category 1 Sources.

5.1.3.1 Central Supply System Identification and Labeling.

Δ 5.1.3.1.1* Cylinders, containers, and tanks shall be designed, fabricated, tested, and marked (i.e., stamped) in accordance with Department of Transportation (DOT) regulations, Transport Canada's (TC) *Transportation of Dangerous Goods Regulations,* or the ASME *Boiler and Pressure Vessel Code.* [55:7.1.5.1]

5.1.3.1.2* Cylinder contents shall be identified by attached labels or stencils naming the contents in accordance with the mandatory requirements of CGA C-7, *Guide to Classification and Labeling of Compressed Gases.*

5.1.3.1.3 Liquid containers shall have additional product identification visible from all directions with a minimum of 51 mm (2 in.) high letters such as a 360-degree wraparound tape for medical liquid containers.

5.1.3.1.4 Cryogenic liquid containers shall be provided with gas-specific outlet connections in accordance with the mandatory requirements of CGA V-5, *Standard for Diameter Index Safety System (Noninterchangeable Low Pressure Connections for Medical Gas Applications),* or CGA V-1, *Standard for Compressed Gas Cylinder Valve Outlet and Inlet Connections.*

5.1.3.1.5 Cylinder and cryogenic liquid container outlet connections shall be affixed in such a manner as to be integral to the valve(s), unremovable with ordinary tools, or so designed as to render the attachment point unusable when removed.

5.1.3.1.6 The contents of cylinders and cryogenic liquid containers shall be verified prior to use.

5.1.3.1.7 Labels shall not be defaced, altered, or removed, and connecting fittings shall not be modified.

5.1.3.1.8 Source locations containing positive-pressure gases other than oxygen and medical air shall be provided with signage located on or immediately adjacent to the door that is visible upon entering the space as follows:

Positive-Pressure Gases
NO Smoking or Open Flame
Room May Have Insufficient Oxygen
Open Door and Allow Room to Ventilate Before Entering

5.1.3.1.8.1 Existing signage that is not in strict compliance with the requirements of this code shall be permitted to be continued in use unless the authority having jurisdiction has determined that such use constitutes a distinct hazard to life.

5.1.3.1.9 Source locations containing only oxygen or medical air shall be provided with signage located on or immediately adjacent to the door that is visible upon entering the space as follows:

Medical Gases
NO Smoking or Open Flame

5.1.3.1.9.1 Existing signage that is not in strict compliance with the requirements of this code shall be permitted to be continued in use unless the authority having jurisdiction has determined that such use constitutes a distinct hazard to life.

N 5.1.3.1.10 In health care facilities where smoking is prohibited, signs required by 5.1.3.1.8 and 5.1.3.1.9 shall be permitted to omit the reference to smoking.

5.1.3.2 Central Supply System Operations.

5.1.3.2.1 The use of adapters or conversion fittings to adapt one gas-specific fitting to another shall be prohibited.

5.1.3.2.2 Cylinders and containers shall be handled in strict accordance with 11.6.2.

5.1.3.2.3 Only gas cylinders, reusable shipping containers, and their accessories shall be permitted to be stored in rooms containing central supply systems or gas cylinders.

5.1.3.2.4 No flammable materials, cylinders containing flammable gases, or containers containing flammable liquids shall be stored in rooms with gas cylinders.

5.1.3.2.5* If cylinders are wrapped when received, the wrappers shall be removed prior to storage.

5.1.3.2.6 Cylinders without correct markings or whose markings and gas-specific fittings do not match shall not be used.

5.1.3.2.7 Cryogenic liquid storage units intended to supply gas to the facility shall not be used to transfill other liquid storage vessels.

5.1.3.2.8 Care shall be exercised when handling cylinders that have been exposed to freezing temperatures or containers that contain cryogenic liquids to prevent injury to the skin.

5.1.3.2.9 Cylinders containing compressed gases and containers for volatile liquids shall be kept away from radiators, steam piping, and like sources of heat.

5.1.3.2.10 When cylinder valve protection caps are supplied, they shall be secured tightly in place unless the cylinder is connected for use.

5.1.3.2.11 Cylinders in use and in storage shall be prevented from reaching temperatures in excess of 52°C (125°F).

5.1.3.2.12 Central supply systems for nitrous oxide and carbon dioxide using cylinders or portable containers shall be prevented from reaching temperatures lower than the recommendations of the central supply system's manufacturer, but shall never be lower than –7°C (20°F) or greater than 52°C (125°F).

5.1.3.3* Central Supply System Locations.

5.1.3.3.1 General. Central supply systems shall be located to meet the criteria in 5.1.3.3.1 through 5.1.3.3.1.10.

5.1.3.3.1.1 Any of the following central supply systems shall be permitted to be located together in the same outdoor enclosure:

(1) Manifolds for gas cylinders *(see 5.1.3.5.10)*
(2) Manifolds for cryogenic liquid containers *(see 5.1.3.5.11)*
(3) Cryogenic fluid central supply *(see 5.1.3.10)*
(4)* Individual components on the oxygen side of concentrator sources *(see 5.1.3.9)*

5.1.3.3.1.2 Any of the following systems shall be permitted to be located together in the same indoor enclosure:

(1) Manifolds for gas cylinders *(see 5.1.3.5.10)*
(2) Manifolds for cryogenic liquid containers *(see 5.1.3.5.11)*
(3) In-building emergency reserves *(see 5.1.3.5.13)*
(4) Instrument air standby headers *(see 5.1.13.3.7.6)*
(5)* Individual components on the oxygen side of concentrator sources *(see 5.1.3.9)*

5.1.3.3.1.3 Any of the following central supply systems shall be permitted to be located together in the same room:

(1) Medical air central supply compressor supply sources *(see 5.1.3.6.3)*
(2) Medical–surgical vacuum central supply sources *(see 5.1.3.7)*
(3) Waste anesthetic gas disposal (WAGD) central supply sources *(see 5.1.3.8)*
(4) Instrument air compressor central supply sources *(see 5.1.13.3.7)*
(5) Any other compressor, vacuum pump, or electrically powered machinery
(6)* Compressors, dryers, and air receivers used to supply oxygen concentrators *(see 5.1.3.9)*
(7) Concentrator units with air and oxygen sides in an integral unit *(see 5.1.3.9)*

5.1.3.3.1.4 Any central supply system listed under 5.1.3.3.1.3 shall not be located in the same room with any central supply system listed under 5.1.3.3.1.1 or 5.1.3.3.1.2, except instrument air reserve headers complying with 5.1.3.2.11 and 5.1.13.3.7.6 shall be permitted to be in the same room as an instrument air compressor.

Δ 5.1.3.3.1.5 Indoor locations for oxygen, nitrous oxide, and mixtures of these gases shall not communicate with the following:

(1) Areas involved in critical patient care
(2) Anesthetizing locations
(3) Locations storing flammables
(4) Rooms containing open electrical contacts or transformers
(5) Storage tanks for flammable or combustible liquids
(6) Engines
(7) Kitchens
(8) Areas with open flames

5.1.3.3.1.6* Cryogenic fluid central supply systems for oxygen shall comply with NFPA 55.

5.1.3.3.1.7 Bulk nitrous oxide central supply systems shall comply with NFPA 55 and with the mandatory requirements of CGA G-8.1, *Standard for Nitrous Oxide Systems at Customer Sites.*

5.1.3.3.1.8 Central supply systems for carbon dioxide using permanently installed containers with product capacities greater than 454 kg (1000 lb) shall comply with NFPA 55 and with the mandatory requirements of CGA G-6.1, *Standard for Insulated Liquid Carbon Dioxide Systems at Consumer Sites.*

5.1.3.3.1.9 Central supply systems for carbon dioxide using permanently installed containers with product capacities of 454 kg (1000 lb) or less shall comply with NFPA 55 and with the mandatory requirements of CGA G-6.5, *Standard for Small Stationary Insulated Carbon Dioxide Supply Systems.*

Δ 5.1.3.3.1.10* Cryogenic fluid central supply systems for inert gases shall comply with NFPA 55 and with the mandatory requirements of CGA P-18, *Standard for Bulk Inert Gas Systems.*

5.1.3.3.2* Design and Construction.

N 5.1.3.3.2.1 Medical gas and vacuum systems shall be designed by one of the following:

(1) A party technically competent and experienced in the field of medical gas and vacuum system design and meeting the requirements of ASSE/IAPMO/ANSI 6060, *Professional Qualifications Standard for Medical Gas System Designers*
(2) A party deemed technically competent through other qualification(s) deemed sufficient by the health care facility's governing body

5.1.3.3.2.2 Locations for central supply systems other than cryogenic fluid central supply systems and motor-driven equipment and locations for the storage of positive-pressure gases shall meet the following requirements:

(1) The location shall be constructed with access to move cylinders, equipment, and so forth in and out of the location on hand trucks complying with the requirements of 11.4.3.1.1.
(2) The location shall be provided with lockable doors or gates or otherwise able to be secured.
(3) If outdoors, the location shall be well drained and provided with an enclosure (e.g., wall or fencing) constructed of noncombustible materials.

(4) If outdoors, cylinders and containers shall be protected from prolonged contact with soil.

(5) If indoors, the location shall have interior finishes of noncombustible or limited-combustible materials.

(6)* If indoors, rooms containing oxygen, nitrous oxide, or other oxidizers shall be separated from the rest of the building by walls and floors having a 1-hour fire resistance rating with doors and other opening protectives having a ¾-hour fire protection rating.

(7)* The location shall comply with *NFPA 70* for ordinary locations.

(8)* Fuel-fired equipment shall not be located in the room.

(9) If the location requires heat, the maximum allowable temperature of the in-room heating element shall be 130°C (266°F).

(10) The location shall be provided with racks, chains, or other fastenings to secure all cylinders from falling, whether connected, unconnected, full, or empty.

(11)* The location shall be supplied with electrical power compliant with the requirements for essential electrical systems as described in Chapter 6.

(12) The location shall have racks, shelves, and supports, where provided, constructed of noncombustible materials or limited-combustible materials.

(13) The location shall protect electrical devices from physical damage.

(14)* The location shall allow access by delivery vehicles and management of cylinders.

(15) The location shall be designed to meet the operational requirements of 5.1.3.2 regarding room temperature.

N 5.1.3.3.2.3 Locations for motor-driven central supply systems shall meet the following requirements:

(1) They shall be constructed with access to move equipment and so forth in and out of the location as necessary.

(2) They shall be provided with lockable doors or gates or otherwise able to be secured.

(3) They shall comply with *NFPA 70* for ordinary locations.

(4) The maximum allowable temperature of the room shall be in accordance with the manufacturer's recommendations.

(5) They shall be supplied with electrical power compliant with the requirements for essential electrical systems as described in Chapter 6.

5.1.3.3.2.4 Design and construction of locations for cryogenic fluid central supply systems shall comply with 5.1.3.10.

N 5.1.3.3.2.5* The total quantity of medical gases connected to or in storage for central supply systems shall comply with Table 5.1.3.3.2.5 for each enclosure or room.

N 5.1.3.3.2.6 Storage of portable patient care gas equipment shall comply with Chapter 11.

N 5.1.3.3.2.7* The limits for the maximum allowable quantities listed in Table 5.1.3.3.2.5 shall be permitted to be exceeded where documented by an approved risk assessment by the health care facility's governing body.

5.1.3.3.3 Ventilation.

5.1.3.3.3.1 Ventilation for Indoor Locations. Central supply system locations, medical gas storage rooms, and transfilling room ventilation shall comply with 9.3.6.

N Table 5.1.3.3.2.5 Storage Quantities for Medical Gas and Cryogenic Fluid Central Supply Systems in Health Care Facilities

Gas	Maximum Allowable Quantity, Connected and in Storage		
	Outdoor Enclosures[a]	Indoor Nonsprinklered[b]	Indoor Sprinklered[c]
Oxygen and nitrous oxide[d]	No limit	283 m³ (10,000 ft³)	566 m³ (20,000 ft³)
Carbon dioxide, helium, medical air, and nitrogen	No limit		

[a]Outdoor enclosure constructed and ventilated in accordance with this code and NFPA 55.
[b]Indoor structure constructed in accordance with 5.1.3.3.2 and ventilated in accordance with 9.3.6.
[c]Indoor structure constructed in accordance with 5.1.3.3.2, ventilated in accordance with 9.3.6, and provided with an approved, automatic sprinkler system in accordance with NFPA 13.
[d]Sum of all oxidizing gases within a room.

5.1.3.3.3.2 Venting of Relief Valves. Indoor supply systems shall have all relief valves vented per 5.1.3.5.6.1(4) through 5.1.3.5.6.1(9).

5.1.3.3.3.3 Ventilation for Motor-Driven Equipment. The following source locations shall be ventilated to prevent accumulation of heat:

(1) Medical air central supply systems sources *(see 5.1.3.6)*

(2) Medical–surgical vacuum central supply systems sources *(see 5.1.3.7)*

(3) Waste anesthetic gas disposal (WAGD) central supply systems sources *(see 5.1.3.8.1)*

(4) Instrument air central supply systems sources *(see 5.1.13.3.7)*

5.1.3.3.3.4 Ventilation for Outdoor Locations.

(1) Outdoor locations surrounded by impermeable walls, except fire barrier walls, shall have protected ventilation openings located at the base of each wall to allow free circulation of air within the enclosure.

(2) Walls that are shared with other enclosures or with buildings shall be permitted to not have openings.

(3) The fire barrier wall shall not have openings or penetrations, except conduit or piping shall be permitted, provided that the penetration is protected with a firestop system in accordance with the building code.

5.1.3.3.4 Storage.

5.1.3.3.4.1 Full or empty medical gas cylinders, when not connected, shall be stored in locations complying with 5.1.3.3.2 through 5.1.3.3.3 and shall be permitted to be in the same rooms or enclosures as their respective central supply systems. Approved existing installations shall be permitted to be continued in service.

5.1.3.3.4.2* Cylinders, whether full or empty, shall not be stored in enclosures containing motor-driven machinery, with

the exception of cylinders intended for instrument air reserve headers complying with 5.1.13.3.7.6, which shall be permitted to be placed in the same location containing an instrument air compressor when it is the only motor-driven machinery located within the room. Only cylinders intended for instrument air reserve headers complying with 5.1.13.3.7.6 shall be permitted to be stored in enclosures containing instrument air compressors.

5.1.3.4 Control Equipment. For control equipment, as specified in 5.1.3.5.5, 5.1.3.5.6, and 5.1.3.5.7, that is physically remote from the supply system, the control equipment shall be installed within a secure enclosure to prevent unauthorized access in accordance with 5.1.3.3.2.2(2).

5.1.3.4.1 The enclosure shall provide enough space to perform maintenance and repair.

5.1.3.4.2 The location of the enclosure for control equipment other than for medical air shall not communicate with combustible or flammable materials.

5.1.3.5* Central Supply Systems. Central supply systems shall be permitted to consist of the following:

(1) Cylinder manifolds for gas cylinders in accordance with 5.1.3.5.10
(2) Manifolds for cryogenic liquid containers in accordance with 5.1.3.5.11
(3) Cryogenic fluid central supply systems in accordance with 5.1.3.10
(4) Medical air compressor systems in accordance with 5.1.3.6
(5) Medical–surgical vacuum producers in accordance with 5.1.3.7
(6) WAGD producers in accordance with 5.1.3.8
(7) Instrument air compressor systems in accordance with 5.1.13.3.7
(8) Proportioning systems for medical air USP in accordance with 5.1.3.6.3.14
(9) Oxygen central supply systems using concentrators in accordance with 5.1.3.9

5.1.3.5.1 General. Central supply systems shall be obtained from a supplier or manufacturer familiar with their proper construction and use and installed in accordance with the manufacturer's instructions.

Δ **5.1.3.5.2 Permitted Locations for Medical Gases.** Central supply systems for oxygen, medical air, nitrous oxide, carbon dioxide, and all other patient medical gases shall be piped only to medical gas outlets complying with 5.1.5, into areas where the gases will be used under the direction of licensed medical professionals for purposes congruent with the following:

(1) Direct respiration by patients
(2) Clinical application of the gas to a patient, such as the use of an insufflator to inject carbon dioxide into patient body cavities during laparoscopic surgery and carbon dioxide used to purge heart-lung machine blood flow ways
(3) Medical device applications directly related to respiration
(4) Power for medical devices used directly on patients
(5) Calibration of medical devices intended for 5.1.3.5.2(1) through 5.1.3.5.2(4)
(6) Simulation centers for the education, training, and assessment of health care professionals

5.1.3.5.3 Medical Support Gases. Central supply systems for medical support gases shall not be piped to, or used for, any purpose except medical support application.

5.1.3.5.4* Materials. Materials used in central supply systems shall meet the following requirements:

(1) In those portions of systems intended to handle oxygen at gauge pressures greater than 3000 kPa (435 psi), interconnecting hose shall contain no polymeric materials.
(2) In those portions of systems intended to handle oxygen or nitrous oxide at gauge pressures of less than 3000 kPa (435 psi), construction shall be compatible with oxygen under the temperatures and pressures to which the components can be exposed in the containment and use of oxygen, nitrous oxide, mixtures of these gases, or mixtures containing more than 23.5 percent oxygen.
(3) If potentially exposed to cryogenic temperatures, materials shall be designed for low temperature service.
(4) If intended for outdoor installation, materials shall be installed in accordance with the manufacturer's requirements.

5.1.3.5.5 Controls for Line Pressure.

5.1.3.5.5.1* All positive-pressure supply systems shall be provided with means to control the final line pressure at the source with all the following characteristics:

(1) Able to maintain stable pressures within the limits of Table 5.1.11
(2) Each control mechanism able to flow 100 percent of the peak calculated demand
(3) Redundant, such that each component of the control mechanism can be isolated for service or replacement while maintaining normal operation
(4) Protected against overpressure (see 5.1.3.5.6)
(5) Be constructed of materials deemed suitable by the manufacturer

5.1.3.5.5.2 The line pressure regulators required under 5.1.3.5.5.1, where used for cryogenic fluid central supply systems, shall be of a balanced design.

5.1.3.5.6 Relief Valves.

Δ **5.1.3.5.6.1** All pressure relief valves shall meet the following requirements:

(1) They shall be of brass, bronze, or stainless steel construction.
(2) They shall be designed for the specific gas service.
(3) They shall have a relief pressure setting not higher than the maximum allowable working pressure (MAWP) of the component with the lowest working pressure rating in the portion of the system being protected.
(4) They shall be vented to the outside of the building, except that relief valves for compressed air systems having less than 84,950 L (3000 ft³) at STP shall be permitted to be diffused locally by means that will not restrict the flow.
(5) They shall have a vent discharge line that is not smaller than the size of the relief valve outlet or 20 mm (NPS ¾), whichever is larger.
(6) Where two or more relief valves discharge into a common vent line, the internal cross-sectional area of the common line shall be not less than the aggregate cross-sectional area of all relief valve vent discharge lines served.

(7) They shall discharge to open air such that escaping gas does not impinge on personnel, equipment, or adjacent structures or enter into enclosed spaces.

(8) They shall have the discharge terminal turned down and screened to prevent the entry of rain, snow, or vermin.

(9) They shall be designed in accordance with ASME B31.3, *Process Piping.*

5.1.3.5.6.2 Pressure relief valves for cryogenic fluid central supply systems shall be in accordance with 5.1.3.10.10.

5.1.3.5.6.3 When vented to outdoors, materials and construction for relief valve discharge lines shall be the same as required for positive-pressure gas distribution. *(See 5.1.10.1.)*

5.1.3.5.6.4 Central supply systems for positive-pressure gases shall include one or more relief valves, all meeting the following requirements:

(1) They shall be located between each final line regulator and the source valve.

(2) They shall have a relief setting that is 50 percent above the normal system operating pressure, as indicated in Table 5.1.11.

5.1.3.5.6.5 When vented outside, relief valve vent lines shall be labeled in accordance with 5.1.11.1 in any manner that will distinguish them from the medical gas pipeline.

5.1.3.5.7 Multiple Pressures. Where a single central supply system supplies separate piped distribution networks operating at different pressures, each piped distribution network shall comply with 5.1.3.5.5 for pressure controls, 5.1.3.5.6 for relief valves, 5.1.4.2 for the source valve, and 5.1.9.2.4(7) for the master alarm.

5.1.3.5.8 Local Signals.

5.1.3.5.8.1 The following central supply systems shall have local signals located at the source equipment:

(1) Manifolds for gas cylinders without reserve supply *(see 5.1.3.5.10)*

(2) Manifolds for gas cylinders with reserve supply

(3) Manifolds for cryogenic liquid containers *(see 5.1.3.5.11)*

(4) Cryogenic fluid central supply systems *(see 5.1.3.10)*

(5) In-building emergency reserves *(see 5.1.3.5.13)*

(6) Instrument air headers *(see 5.1.13.3.7.6)*

5.1.3.5.8.2 The local signals shall meet the following requirements:

(1) Provision of visual indication only

(2) Labeling for the service and condition being monitored

(3) If intended for outdoor installation, be installed per manufacturer's requirements

5.1.3.5.9* Headers. In central supply systems using cylinders containing either gas or liquid, each header shall include the following:

(1)* Cylinder connections in the number required for the header's application

(2) Cylinder lead for each cylinder constructed of materials complying with 5.1.3.5.4 and provided with end fittings permanently attached to the cylinder lead complying with the mandatory requirements of CGA V-1, *Standard for Compressed Gas Cylinder Valve Outlet and Inlet Connections* (ANSI B57.1)

(3) Filter of a material complying with 5.1.3.5.4 to prevent the intrusion of debris into the manifold controls

(4) Header shutoff valve downstream of the nearest cylinder connection, but upstream of the point at which the header connects to the central supply system

(5) Pressure indicator indicating the pressure of header contents

(6) Check valve to prevent backflow into the header and to allow service to the header

(7) If intended for gas cylinder service, a check valve at each connection for the cylinder lead in 5.1.3.5.9(2) to prevent loss of gas in the event of damage to the cylinder lead or operation of an individual cylinder relief valve

(8) If intended for gas cylinder service, a pressure regulator to reduce the cylinder pressure to an intermediate pressure to allow the proper operation of the primary and secondary headers

(9) If intended for service with cryogenic liquid containers, a pressure relief valve

(10) Vent valves, if fitted on a header, vented outside of the building per 5.1.3.5.6.1(5) through 5.1.3.5.6.1(9) and 5.1.3.5.6.3

5.1.3.5.10* Manifolds for Gas Cylinders.

5.1.3.5.10.1 The manifolds in this category shall be located in accordance with 5.1.3.3.1 and shall meet the following:

(1) If located outdoors, they shall be installed in an enclosure used only for this purpose and sited to comply with minimum distance requirements in Table 5.1.3.5.11.1.

(2) If located indoors, they shall be installed within a room used only for enclosure of such manifolds.

5.1.3.5.10.2 The manifold locations for this category shall be constructed in accordance with 5.1.3.3.2.

5.1.3.5.10.3 The manifolds in this category shall have their primary and secondary headers located in the same enclosure.

5.1.3.5.10.4 The manifolds in this category shall consist of the following:

(1) Two equal headers in accordance with 5.1.3.5.9, each with a sufficient number of gas cylinder connections for one average day's supply, but not fewer than two connections, and with the headers connected to the final line pressure regulator assembly in such a manner that either header can supply the system

(2) Vent valves, if fitted on a header, vented outside of the building per 5.1.3.5.6.1(5) through 5.1.3.5.6.1(9) and 5.1.3.5.6.3

(3) Intermediate relief valve(s), piped to the outside in accordance with 5.1.3.5.6.1(5) through 5.1.3.5.6.1(9), that protects the piping between the header pressure regulator and the line pressure regulator assembly, and protects the line pressure regulators from overpressure in the event of a header regulator failure

5.1.3.5.10.5 The manifolds in this category shall include an automatic means of alternating the two headers to accomplish the following in normal operation:

(1) One header is the primary and the other is the secondary, with either being capable of either role.

(2) When the primary header is supplying the system, the secondary header is prevented from supplying the system.

(3) When the primary header is depleted, the secondary header automatically begins to supply the system.

5.1.3.5.10.6 The manifolds in this category shall have a local signal that visibly indicates the operating status of the equipment and shall activate an indicator at all master alarm panels when or at a predetermined set point before the secondary header begins to supply the system, indicating changeover has occurred or is about to occur.

5.1.3.5.10.7 If manifolds are located out of doors, they shall be installed per the manufacturer's requirements.

5.1.3.5.11* Manifolds for Cryogenic Liquid Containers.

Δ **5.1.3.5.11.1** Manifolds for cryogenic liquid containers shall be located in accordance with 5.1.3.3.1 and the following:

(1) If located outdoors, they shall be installed in an enclosure used only for the enclosure of such containers and sited to comply with minimum distance requirements in Table 5.1.3.5.11.1.

(2) If located indoors, they shall be installed within a room used only for the enclosure of such containers.

5.1.3.5.11.2 The manifolds in this category shall have their primary and secondary headers located in the same enclosure.

5.1.3.5.11.3 The reserve header shall be permitted to be located in the same enclosure as the primary and secondary headers or in another enclosure compliant with 5.1.3.5.11.1.

5.1.3.5.11.4 The manifolds in this category shall consist of the following:

(1) Two equal headers in accordance with 5.1.3.5.9, each having sufficient internal or external vaporization capacity to meet the required peak flow rate and each having sufficient number of liquid container connections for one average day's supply, and with the headers connected to the final line pressure regulator assembly in such a manner that either header can supply the system

(2) Reserve header in accordance with 5.1.3.5.9 having sufficient number of gas cylinder connections for one average day's supply, but not fewer than three connections, and connected downstream of the primary/secondary headers and upstream of the final line pressure regulators

(3) Pressure relief installed downstream of the connection of the reserve header and upstream of the final line pressure regulating assembly and set at 50 percent above the nominal inlet pressure

(4) If provided with one liquid container header (primary), one gas cylinder header (secondary), and a reserve gas cylinder header (a hybrid arrangement), a secondary gas cylinder supply having equal capacity to meet the required peak flow rate of the primary header, and a reserve gas cylinder header in accordance with 5.1.3.5.9 having sufficient number of gas cylinder connections for one average day's supply, but not fewer than three connections

5.1.3.5.11.5 The manifolds in this category shall include an automatic means of controlling the three headers to accomplish the following during normal operation:

(1) If provided with two liquid container headers, one cryogenic liquid header shall be the primary and the other shall be the secondary, with either being capable of either role.

(2) If provided with one liquid container header and one gas cylinder header (a hybrid arrangement), the liquid container header is the primary and the gas cylinder header is the secondary.

(3) When the primary header is supplying the system, the secondary header is prevented from supplying the system.

(4) When the primary header is depleted, the secondary header automatically begins to supply the system.

5.1.3.5.11.6 The manifolds in this category shall be equipped with a means to conserve the gas produced by evaporation of the cryogenic liquid in the secondary header (when so provided). This mechanism shall discharge the conserved gas into the system upstream of the final line regulator assembly.

5.1.3.5.11.7 The manifolds in this category shall include a manual or automatic means to place either header into the role of primary header and the other into the role of secondary header, except where a liquid/gas hybrid manifold is employed.

5.1.3.5.11.8 The manifolds in this category shall include a means to automatically activate the reserve header if for any reason the primary and secondary headers cannot supply the system.

5.1.3.5.11.9 The manifolds in this category shall have a local signal that visibly indicates the operating status of the equipment and activates an indicator at all master alarms under the following conditions:

(1) When or at a predetermined set point before the secondary header begins to supply the system, indicating changeover

(2) Where a hybrid arrangement is employed, when or at a predetermined set point before the secondary (cylinder) header contents fall to one average day's supply, indicating secondary low

(3) When or at a predetermined set point before the reserve header begins to supply the system, indicating reserve is in use

(4) When or at a predetermined set point before the reserve header contents fall to one average day's supply, indicating reserve low

5.1.3.5.12* Emergency Oxygen Supply Connection (EOSC). Emergency oxygen supply connections (EOSCs) shall be installed to allow connection of a temporary auxiliary source of

Δ **Table 5.1.3.5.11.1 Minimum Separation Distance Between Portable Cryogenic Containers and Exposures**

	Minimum Distance	
Exposure	ft	m
(1) Building exits	10	3.1
(2) Wall openings	1	0.3
(3) Air intakes	10	3.1
(4) Property lines	5	1.5
(5) Room or area exits	3	0.9
(6) Combustible materials, (e.g., paper, leaves, weeds, dry grass, debris)	15	4.5
(7) Incompatible hazardous materials	20	6.1

[55:Table 8.6.3]

supply for emergency or maintenance situations where either of the following conditions exist:

(1) The bulk liquid system or cryogenic fluid central supply system is outside of and remote from the building that the oxygen supply serves, and there is no connected in-building oxygen reserve sufficient for one average day's supply. *(See 5.1.3.5.13 for requirements for such reserves.)*

(2) Multiple freestanding buildings are served from a single oxygen source such that damage to the interconnecting oxygen line could result in one or more buildings losing oxygen supply, in which case each building is required to be provided with a separate emergency connection.

5.1.3.5.12.1 EOSCs shall be located as follows:

(1) Located on the exterior of the building being served in a location accessible by emergency supply vehicles at all times in all weather conditions

(2) Connected to the main supply line immediately downstream of the main shutoff valve

5.1.3.5.12.2 EOSCs shall consist of the following:

(1) Physical protection to prevent unauthorized tampering

(2) Female DN (NPS) inlet for connection of the emergency oxygen source that is sized for 100 percent of the system demand at the emergency source gas pressure

(3) Manual shutoff valve to isolate the EOSC when not in use

(4) Two check valves, one downstream of the EOSC and one downstream of the main line shutoff valve, with both upstream from the tee connection for the two pipelines

(5) Relief valve sized to protect the downstream piping system and related equipment from exposure to pressures in excess of 50 percent higher than normal line pressure

(6) Any valves necessary to allow connection of an emergency supply of oxygen and isolation of the piping to the normal source of supply

(7) Minimum of 1 m (3 ft) of clearance around the EOSC for connection of temporary auxiliary source

(8)* Four alarm connection points installed to both master alarm panels to allow the temporary supply to be monitored while in use

5.1.3.5.13 In-Building Emergency Reserves (IBERs).

5.1.3.5.13.1 IBERs shall not be used as substitutes for the bulk gas reserve system that is required in 5.1.3.10.3.4.

5.1.3.5.13.2 When an IBER is provided inside the building as a substitute for the EOSC or for other purposes, it shall be located in accordance with 5.1.3.3 as follows:

(1) In a room or enclosure constructed per 5.1.3.3.2

(2) In a room or enclosure ventilated per 5.1.3.3.3

5.1.3.5.13.3 IBERs shall consist of either of the following:

(1) Gas cylinder header per 5.1.3.5.9 with sufficient cylinder connections to provide for at least one average day's supply with the appropriate number of connections being determined after consideration of the delivery schedule, the proximity of the facility to alternate supplies, and the facility's emergency plan

(2) Manifold for gas cylinders complying with 5.1.3.5.10

5.1.3.5.13.4 IBERs shall include a check valve in the main line placed on the distribution system side of the ordinary source's main line valve to prevent flow of gas from the emergency reserve to the ordinary source.

5.1.3.5.13.5 IBERs shall have a local signal that visibly indicates the operating status of the equipment and an alarm at all master alarms when or just before the reserve begins to serve the system.

N **5.1.3.5.14* Auxiliary Connections.** All medical gas and vacuum systems shall be provided with a point of access for connection of a temporary or supplemental source of supply complying with 5.1.3.5.14.1 through 5.1.3.5.14.5.

N **5.1.3.5.14.1** The auxiliary connection shall be located in the main line, on the patient side of the source valve, as determined by the responsible facility authority.

N **5.1.3.5.14.2** The auxiliary connection shall be the same size as the main line but not required to be larger than DN50 (NPS 2 in.).

N **5.1.3.5.14.3** The auxiliary connection shall consist of a tee, valve, and removable plugged or capped connection point.

N **5.1.3.5.14.4** The valve and connection point shall be labeled in accordance with 5.1.11.

N **5.1.3.5.14.5** The valve shall be secured in accordance with 5.1.4.1.2.

5.1.3.6* Category 1 Medical Air Central Supply Systems.

5.1.3.6.1* Quality of Medical Air. Medical air shall be required to have the following characteristics:

(1) It shall be supplied from cylinders, bulk containers, or medical air compressor sources, or it shall be reconstituted from oxygen USP and oil-free, dry nitrogen NF.

(2) It shall meet the requirements of medical air USP.

(3) It shall have no detectable liquid hydrocarbons.

(4) It shall have less than 25 ppm gaseous hydrocarbons.

(5) It shall have equal to or less than 1 mg/m^3 (6.85×10^{-7} lb/yd^3) of permanent particulates sized 1 micron or larger in the air at normal atmospheric pressure.

5.1.3.6.2* Uses of Medical Air. Medical air sources shall be connected to the medical air distribution system only and shall be used only for air in the application of human respiration, in the calibration of medical devices for respiratory application, and in simulation centers for the education, training, and assessment of health care professionals in accordance with 5.1.3.5.2.

5.1.3.6.3* Medical Air Compressor Supply Sources.

5.1.3.6.3.1 Location. Medical air compressor systems shall be located per 5.1.3.3 as follows:

(1) Indoors in a dedicated mechanical equipment area, adequately ventilated and with any required utilities (e.g., electricity, drains, lighting)

(2) In a room ventilated per 5.1.3.3.3.3

(3) For air-cooled equipment, in a room designed to maintain the ambient temperature range as recommended by the manufacturer

Δ **5.1.3.6.3.2 Required Components.** Medical air compressor systems shall consist of the following:

(1) Components complying with 5.1.3.6.3.4 through 5.1.3.6.3.8, arranged per 5.1.3.6.3.9

(2) Automatic means to prevent backflow from all on-cycle compressors through all off-cycle compressors

(3) Manual shutoff valve to isolate each compressor from the centrally piped system and from other compressors for maintenance or repair without loss of pressure in the system

(4) Intake filter–muffler(s) of the dry type

(5) Pressure relief valve(s) set at 50 percent above line pressure

(6) Piping and components between the compressor and the source shutoff valve that do not contribute to contaminant levels

(7) Except as defined in 5.1.3.6.3.2(1) through 5.1.3.6.3.2(6), materials and devices used between the medical air intake and the medical air source valve that are of any design or construction appropriate for the service as determined by the manufacturer

5.1.3.6.3.3 Air Drying Equipment. Medical air compressor systems shall preclude the condensation of water vapor in the piping distribution system by air drying equipment.

5.1.3.6.3.4 Compressors for Medical Air.

(A)* Compressors for medical air shall be designed to prevent the introduction of contaminants or liquid into the pipeline by any of the following methods:

(1) Elimination of oil anywhere in the compressor (e.g., liquid ring and permanently sealed bearing compressors)

(2) Reciprocating compressors provided with a separation of the oil-containing section from the compression chamber by at least two seals creating an area open to atmosphere that allows the following:

    (a) Direct and unobstructed visual inspection of the interconnecting shaft through vent and inspection openings no smaller than 1.5 shaft diameters in size

    (b) Confirmation by the facility operators of proper seal operation by direct visual inspection through the above-shaft opening, without disassembly of the compressor (e.g., extended head compressors with an atmospheric vent between the compression chamber and the crankcase)

(3) Rotating element compressors provided with a compression chamber free of oil that provide the following:

    (a) Separation of each oil-containing section from the compression chamber by at least one seal having atmospheric vents on each side with the vent closest to the oil-containing section supplied with a gravity drain to atmosphere

    (b) Unobstructed visualization of the atmospheric vent(s), closest to each oil-containing section, that is accessible for inspection without disassembling the compressor

    (c) Entry of the rotating shaft into each compression chamber at a point that is above atmospheric pressure

    (d) Confirmation by the facility operators of proper seal operation by direct visual inspection of the atmospheric vents

(B) For liquid ring compressors, service water and seal water shall be treated to control waterborne pathogens and chlorine from hyperchlorination from entering the medical air.

(C) Liquid ring compressors shall comply with the following:

(1) Service water and seal water of a quality recommended by the compressor manufacturer shall be used.

(2) Reserve medical air standby headers or a backup compressor shall be installed.

(3) When installed, the header shall comply with 5.1.3.5.9.

(4) When installed, the number of attached cylinders shall be sufficient for 1 hour normal operation.

(D) Compressors shall be constructed of materials deemed suitable by the manufacturer.

(E) Antivibration mountings shall be installed for compressors as required by equipment dynamics or location and in accordance with the manufacturer's recommendations.

(F) Flexible connectors shall connect the air compressors with their intake and outlet piping.

5.1.3.6.3.5 Aftercoolers.

(A) Aftercoolers, where required, shall be provided with individual condensate traps.

(B) The receiver shall not be used as an aftercooler or aftercooler trap.

(C) Aftercoolers shall be constructed of materials deemed suitable by the manufacturer.

(D) Antivibration mountings shall be installed for aftercoolers as required by equipment dynamics or location and in accordance with the manufacturer's recommendations.

5.1.3.6.3.6 Medical Air Receivers. Receivers for medical air shall meet the following requirements:

(1) They shall be made of corrosion-resistant materials or otherwise be made corrosion resistant.

(2) They shall comply with Section VIII, "Unfired Pressure Vessels," of the ASME *Boiler and Pressure Vessel Code.*

(3) They shall be equipped with a pressure relief valve, automatic drain, manual drain, sight glass, and pressure indicator.

(4) They shall be of a capacity sufficient to prevent the compressors from short-cycling.

5.1.3.6.3.7 Medical Air Dryers. Medical air dryers, where required, shall meet the following requirements:

(1) Be designed to provide air at a maximum dew point that is below the frost point [0°C (32°F)] at 345 kPa to 380 kPa (50 psi to 55 psi) at any level of demand

(2) Be sized for 100 percent of the system peak calculated demand at design conditions

(3) Be constructed of materials deemed suitable by the manufacturer

(4) Be provided with antivibration mountings installed as required by equipment dynamics or location and in accordance with the manufacturer's recommendations

(5)* Be provided with a sample port downstream of each dryer for maintenance

5.1.3.6.3.8 Medical Air Filters. Medical air filters shall meet the following requirements:

(1) Be appropriate for the intake air conditions

(2) Be located upstream (source side) of the final line regulators

(3) Be sized for 100 percent of the system peak calculated demand at design conditions and be rated for a minimum of 98 percent efficiency at 1 micron or greater

(4) Be equipped with a continuous visual indicator showing the status of the filter element life

(5) Be constructed of materials deemed suitable by the manufacturer

5.1.3.6.3.9 Piping Arrangement and Redundancies.

(A) Component arrangement shall be as follows:

(1) Components shall be arranged to allow service and a continuous supply of medical air in the event of a single fault failure.

(2) Component arrangement shall be permitted to vary as required by the technology(ies) employed, provided that an equal level of operating redundancy and medical air quality is maintained.

(B) Medical air compressors shall be sufficient to serve the peak calculated demand with the largest single compressor out of service. In no case shall there be fewer than two compressors.

(C) When aftercoolers are provided, they shall be arranged to meet either one of the following:

(1) Arranged as a duplex or multiplex set, sized to serve the peak calculated demand with the largest single aftercooler out of service, and provided with valves adequate, to isolate any single aftercooler from the system without shutting down supply of medical air

(2) Arranged one per compressor, sized to handle the output of that compressor, and valved as appropriate to allow repair or replacement with that compressor out of service but without shutting down supply of medical air

(D)* A medical air receiver(s) shall be provided with proper valves to allow the flow of compressed air to enter and exit out of separate receiver ports during normal operation and allow the receiver to be bypassed during service without shutting down the supply of medical air.

(E) Dryers, filters, and regulators shall be at least duplexed, with each component sized to serve the peak calculated demand with the largest of each component out of service.

(F)* Dryers, filters, and regulators shall be provided with manual valves upstream and manual valves or check valves downstream to allow service to the components without shutting down the system in either one of the following ways:

(1) They shall be installed for each component, upstream and downstream of each component, allowing each to be individually isolated.

(2) They shall be installed upstream (source side) and downstream of components in series so as to create redundant parallel branches of components.

(G) A three-way valve (three-port), indexed to flow, full port shall be permitted to be used to isolate one branch or component for the purposes of 5.1.3.6.3.9(C), 5.1.3.6.3.9(D), 5.1.3.6.3.9(E), and 5.1.3.6.3.9(F).

(H) Under normal operation, only one aftercooler shall be open to airflow with the other aftercooler valved off.

(I) Under normal operation, only one dryer–filter(s)–regulator sequence shall be open to airflow with the other sequence valved off.

(J) If the relief valve required in 5.1.3.6.3.2(5) and 5.1.3.6.3.6(3) can be isolated from the system by the valve arrangement used to comply with 5.1.3.6.3.9(F), then a redundant relief valve(s) shall be installed in the parallel sequence.

(K) A DN8 (NPS ¼) valved sample port shall be provided downstream of the final line pressure regulators, dew point monitor, and carbon monoxide monitor and upstream of the source shutoff valve to allow for sampling of the medical air.

(L) Medical air source systems shall be provided with a source valve per 5.1.4.2.

(M) Where medical air piping systems at different operating pressures are required, the piping shall separate after the filters but shall be provided with separate line regulators, dew point monitors, relief valves, and source shutoff valves.

5.1.3.6.3.10* Electrical Power and Control.

(A) Medical air source systems shall be controlled to ensure continuous supply of medical air at pressures consistent with Table 5.1.11 under all conditions of system use as follows:

(1) Automatic activation of compressor(s) as necessary to supply the demand.

(2) Managing the operation to equalize wear on all compressors. Where this equalization is achieved manually, the facility staff shall arrange a schedule for manual alternation.

(B) Controls shall provide the following functions:

(1) Where medical air source systems having two or more compressors employ any electrical circuit device that upon failure could prevent supply of medical air, the controls shall be provided with an automatically activated alternative method for ensuring supply (e.g., redundant component(s), an alternate electrical supply path, or other equivalent method).

(2) Control circuits shall be arranged in such a manner that isolation of one compressor or component from the system (e.g., for maintenance or repair) does not interrupt the operation of other compressor(s) or component(s).

(3) Automatic restart function shall be included, such that the supply of medical air will resume normally after power interruption without manual intervention.

(C) Each compressor motor shall be provided with electrical components including, but not limited to, the following:

(1) Dedicated disconnect switch installed in the electrical circuit ahead of each motor starter

(2) Motor starting device

(3) Overload protection

(D) Medical air compressor system controls shall be provided with electrical systems including, at a minimum:

(1) Built-in disconnect means shall be included to allow appropriate operation of multiple compressor systems and protect service personnel from exposure to live voltages.

(2) Control circuits shall be arranged so that failure of any component of the control circuit, or shutdown of one compressor (e.g., for service), does not interrupt automatic operation of the standby compressor.

(3) An automatic restart function shall be included, such that the compressor(s) will restart after power interruption without manual intervention.

(4) Where components are common to more than one control circuit (e.g., autodrains) the common device shall be provided with electrical protection to prevent loss of the control circuits(s) in the event of short circuit in the device.

(E) Electrical installation and wiring shall conform to the requirements of *NFPA 70*.

(F) Emergency electrical service for the compressors shall conform to the requirements of the essential electrical system as described in Chapter 6.

5.1.3.6.3.11 Compressor Intake.

(A) The medical air compressors shall draw their air from a source of clean air.

(B) The medical air intake shall be located a minimum of 7.6 m (25 ft) from ventilating system exhausts, fuel storage vents, combustion vents, plumbing vents, vacuum and WAGD discharges, or areas that can collect vehicular exhausts or other noxious fumes.

(C) The medical air intake shall be located a minimum of 6 m (20 ft) above ground level.

(D) The medical air intake shall be located a minimum of 3.0 m (10 ft) from any door, window, or other opening in the building.

(E) If an air source equal to or better than outside air (e.g., air already filtered for use in operating room ventilating systems) is available, it shall be permitted to be used for the medical air compressors with the following provisions:

(1) This alternate source of supply air shall be available on a continuous 24-hour-per-day, 7-day-per-week basis.
(2) Ventilating systems having fans with motors or drive belts located in the airstream shall not be used as a source of medical air intake.

(F) Compressor intake piping shall be permitted to be made of materials and use a joining technique as permitted under 5.1.10.2 and 5.1.10.3.

(G) Air intakes for separate compressors shall be permitted to be joined together to one common intake where the following conditions are met:

(1) The common intake is sized to minimize back pressure in accordance with the manufacturer's recommendations.
(2) Each compressor can be isolated by manual or check valve, blind flange, or tube cap to prevent open inlet piping when the compressor(s) is removed for service from the consequent backflow of room air into the other compressor(s).

(H) The end of the intake shall be turned down and screened or otherwise be protected against the entry of vermin, debris, or precipitation by screening fabricated or composed of a noncorroding material.

(I) Medical air intake shall be labeled in accordance with 5.1.11.1 with any method that would distinguish it as a medical air intake.

5.1.3.6.3.12 Operating Alarms and Local Signals. Medical air systems shall be monitored for conditions that can affect air quality during use or in the event of failure, based on the type of compressor(s) used in the system.

(A) A local alarm complying with 5.1.9.5 shall be provided for the medical air compressor source.

(B) Where liquid ring air compressors, compressors having water-cooled heads, or water-cooled aftercoolers are used, air receivers shall be equipped with a high water level sensor that shuts down the compressor system and activates a local alarm indicator. *[See 5.1.9.5.3(8).]*

(C) Where liquid ring compressors are used, each compressor shall have a liquid level sensor in each air–water separator that, when the liquid level is above the design level, shuts down its compressor and activates a local alarm indicator. *[See 5.1.9.5.3(9).]*

(D) Where nonliquid ring compressors compliant with 5.1.3.6.3.4(A)(1) are used, the air temperature at the immediate outlet of each compressor cylinder shall be monitored by a high-temperature sensor that shuts down that compressor and activates a local alarm indicator *[see 5.1.9.5.3(10)]*. The temperature setting shall be as recommended by the compressor manufacturer.

(E) Where compressors compliant with 5.1.3.6.3.4(A)(2) and 5.1.3.6.3.4(A)(3) are used, the following requirements shall apply:

(1) The air temperature at the immediate outlet of each compressor chamber shall be monitored by a high-temperature sensor that shuts down that compressor and activates a local alarm indicator *(see 5.1.9.5.3)*, the temperature setting shall be as recommended by the compressor manufacturer.
(2) Coalescing filters with element change indicator shall be provided.
(3) Charcoal absorber shall be provided.
(4) Gaseous hydrocarbons shall be monitored on a quarterly basis.

(F) When the capacity of the medical air system not in use is less than the equivalent capacity of one compressor, a local alarm shall activate *[see 5.1.9.5.3(1)]*. This signal shall require manual reset.

5.1.3.6.3.13 Medical Air Quality Monitoring. Medical air quality shall be monitored downstream of the medical air regulators and upstream of the piping system as follows:

(1) Dew point shall be monitored and shall activate a local alarm and all master alarms when the dew point at system delivery pressure exceeds +2°C (+35°F).
(2) Carbon monoxide shall be monitored and shall activate a local alarm when the CO level exceeds 10 ppm. *[See 5.1.9.5.3(2).]*
(3) Dew point and carbon monoxide monitors shall activate their individual monitor's signal at the alarm panels where their signals are required when their power is lost.

5.1.3.6.3.14 Category 1 Medical Air Proportioning Supply Sources.

(A) General.

(1)* Medical air reconstituted from oxygen USP and nitrogen NF, produced using a proportioning system(s), shall be required to meet the following:

    (a) The quality of medical air shall be in accordance with 5.1.3.6.1.

(b) The system shall be capable of supplying this quality of medical air, in accordance with 5.1.3.6.1, over the entire range of flow.

(c) The system shall produce medical air with an oxygen content of 19.5 percent to 23.5 percent.

(2) The medical air proportioning system shall operate automatically.

(3) The mixture shall be analyzed continuously, and a recording capability shall be provided (e.g., via data port).

(4) The analyzing system specified in 5.1.3.6.3.14(A)(3) shall be a dedicated and independent analyzer used to control the medical air proportioning system.

(5) If the mixture goes out of specification, an alarm shall be activated automatically, the primary medical air proportioning system shall be disconnected, and the reserve supply shall be activated.

(6) The system shall be arranged such that manual intervention is necessary to correct the composition of the mixture before reconnecting the medical air proportioning system to the health care facility pipeline system.

(7) If dedicated sources of oxygen USP and nitrogen NF supply the medical air proportioning system, reserve sources for the oxygen and nitrogen shall not be required.

(8) If dedicated sources of oxygen USP and nitrogen NF supply the medical air proportioning system, they shall not be used as the reserves for oxygen and nitrogen systems supplying the pipelines of the health care facility.

(9)* If the sources of oxygen USP and nitrogen NF that supply the medical air proportioning system are the same sources that supply the health care facility, engineering controls shall be provided to prevent cross contamination of oxygen and nitrogen supply lines, as provided in 5.1.3.5.7.

(10) A risk analysis and approval from the authority having jurisdiction shall be required.

(B) Location. The medical air proportioning system shall be located per 5.1.3.3 as follows:

(1) The medical air proportioning system's supply of oxygen USP and nitrogen NF shall be located per 5.1.3.3 and NFPA 55, as applicable.

(2) The mixing device and controls, analyzers, and receivers shall be located indoors within a room or area per 5.1.3.3.1.

(3) The indoor location shall include atmospheric monitoring for oxygen concentration.

(4) The indoor location shall be constructed with all required utilities (e.g., electricity, drains, lighting) per *NFPA 5000*.

(5) The indoor location shall be ventilated and heated per Chapter 9 and the manufacturer's recommendations.

(C) Required Components. The medical air proportioning system shall consist of the following:

(1) Supply of oxygen USP and supply of nitrogen NF as follows:

(a) The supply lines shall be filtered to remove particulate entering the proportioning system.

(b) The minimum safe supply gas temperature and recommended local signal shall be specified by the medical air proportioning system manufacturer.

(2) Mixing device with analyzers and engineering controls per manufacturer's recommendations to include, as a minimum, the following:

(a) At least two oxygen analyzers capable of independently monitoring oxygen concentration

(b) Mechanism where each analyzer based upon nonconforming oxygen concentration is capable, directly or via other medical air proportioning system controls, of automatically shutting off the supply from the medical air proportioning system to the medical air piped distribution system and activating the reserve supply

(c) Mechanism where each analyzer, based upon nonconforming oxygen concentration, is capable, directly or via other proportioning system controls, of automatically shutting off the supply of oxygen and nitrogen to the proportioning system and activating the reserve supply

(d) Provision for manual resetting of the proportioning system after detection of nonconforming oxygen concentration and subsequent shutdown once conforming oxygen concentration is established, in order to re-establish flow to the medical air piping system

(e) Means of verifying the performance of the analyzers by reference to an air standard, with known traceable oxygen content

(3) Minimum of one recorder for recording the medical air proportioning system performance and air quality for a period of not less than 24 hours

(4) Continuous analysis of the mixture and a recording capability provided (e.g., via a data port)

(5) Mechanism for isolating the primary medical air proportioning system from the reserve supply and the medical air piping distribution system by employing sequential valves for redundancy

(6) Capability of the reserve supply to automatically activate if the primary supply is isolated

(7) Reserve supply of medical air USP sized, at minimum, for one average day's supply and consisting of one of the following:

(a) Additional medical air proportioning unit with a dedicated supply of oxygen USP and nitrogen NF

(b) Medical air compressor system per 5.1.3.6.3, with the exception of the allowance of a simplex medical air compressor system

(c) Medical air cylinder manifold per 5.1.3.5.10

(8) Receiver fitted with a pressure relief valve and pressure gauge as follows:

(a) The receiver shall be constructed of corrosion-resistant materials.

(b) The receiver, relief valves, and pressure gauges shall comply with ASME *Boiler and Pressure Vessel Code* and manufacturer's recommendations.

(9)* Warning systems per 5.1.9, including a local signal and master alarm that indicates nonconforming oxygen concentration per manufacturer's recommendations

(10) Final line pressure regulators complying with 5.1.3.5.5

(11) Pressure relief complying with 5.1.3.5.6

(12) Local signals complying with 5.1.3.5.8.2

5.1.3.7* Medical–Surgical Vacuum Central Supply Systems.

5.1.3.7.1 Medical–Surgical Vacuum Central Sources. Medical–surgical vacuum central supply systems shall be located per 5.1.3.3 as follows:

(1) Indoors in a dedicated mechanical equipment area, adequately ventilated and with any required utilities
(2) In a room ventilated per 5.1.3.3.3.3
(3) For air-cooled equipment, in a room designed to maintain the ambient temperature range as recommended by the equipment manufacturer

5.1.3.7.1.1 Medical–surgical vacuum central supply systems shall consist of the following:

(1) Two or more vacuum pumps sufficient to serve the peak calculated demand with the largest single vacuum pump out of service
(2) Automatic means to prevent backflow from any on-cycle vacuum pumps through any off-cycle vacuum pumps
(3) Shutoff valve or other isolation means to isolate each vacuum pump from the centrally piped system and other vacuum pumps for maintenance or repair without loss of vacuum in the system
(4) Vacuum receiver
(5) Piping between the vacuum pump(s), discharge(s), receiver(s), and vacuum source shutoff valve in accordance with 5.1.10.2, except brass, galvanized, or black steel pipe, which is permitted to be used as recommended by the manufacturer
(6) Except as defined in 5.1.3.7.1.1(1) through 5.1.3.7.1.1(5), materials and devices used between the medical vacuum exhaust and the medical vacuum source that are permitted to be of any design or construction appropriate for the service as determined by the manufacturer
(7) Vacuum filtration per 5.1.3.7.4

5.1.3.7.2 Vacuum Pumps.

5.1.3.7.2.1 Vacuum pumps shall be constructed of materials deemed suitable by the manufacturer.

5.1.3.7.2.2 Antivibration mountings shall be installed for vacuum pumps as required by equipment dynamics or location and in accordance with the manufacturer's recommendations.

5.1.3.7.2.3 Flexible connectors shall connect the vacuum pumps with their intake and outlet piping.

5.1.3.7.2.4 For liquid ring vacuum pumps, seal water shall be of a quality recommended by the vacuum pump manufacturer.

5.1.3.7.3 Vacuum Receivers. Receivers for vacuum shall meet the following requirements:

(1) They shall be made of materials deemed suitable by the manufacturer.
(2) They shall comply with Section VIII, "Unfired Pressure Vessels," of the ASME *Boiler and Pressure Vessel Code.*
(3) They shall be capable of withstanding a gauge pressure of 415 kPa (60 psi) and 760 mm (30 in.) gauge HgV.
(4) They shall be equipped with a manual drain.
(5) They shall be of a capacity based on the technology of the pumps.

5.1.3.7.4 Vacuum Filtration. Central supply systems for vacuum other than liquid ring pumps shall be provided with inlet filtration with the following characteristics:

(1) Filtration shall be at least duplex to allow one filter to be exchanged without impairing the vacuum system.
(2) Filtration shall be located on the patient side of the vacuum producer.
(3) Filters shall be efficient to 0.3 μm and 99.97 percent HEPA or better in accordance with DOE-STD-3020, *Specification for HEPA Filters Used by DOE Contractors.*
(4) Filtration shall be sized for 100 percent of the peak calculated demand while one filter or filter bundle is isolated.
(5) Grouping multiple filters into bundles to achieve the required capacities shall be permitted.
(6) The system shall be provided with isolation valves on the source side of each filter or filter bundle and isolation valves on the patient side of each filter or filter bundle, permitting the filters to be isolated without shutting off flow to the central supply system.
(7) A means shall be available to allow the user to observe any accumulations of liquids.
(8) A vacuum relief petcock shall be provided to allow vacuum to be relieved in the filter canister during filter replacement.
(9) Filter elements and canisters shall be permitted to be constructed of materials as deemed suitable by the manufacturer.
(10) In normal operation, one filter or filter bundle shall be isolated from the system to be available for service should a blockage in the operating filter occur or rotation of the filters be desired after filter element exchange.

5.1.3.7.5 Piping Arrangement and Redundancies.

5.1.3.7.5.1 Piping arrangement shall be as follows:

(1) Piping shall be arranged to allow service and a continuous supply of medical–surgical vacuum in the event of a single fault failure.
(2) Piping arrangement shall be permitted to vary based on the technology(ies) employed, provided that an equal level of operating redundancy is maintained.
(3) Where only one set of vacuum pumps is available for a combined medical–surgical vacuum system and an analysis, a research, or a teaching laboratory vacuum system, such laboratories shall be connected separately from the medical–surgical system directly to the receiver tank through its own isolation valve and fluid trap located at the receiver, and between the isolation valve and fluid trap, a scrubber shall be permitted to be installed.

5.1.3.7.5.2 The medical–surgical vacuum receiver(s) shall be serviceable without shutting down the medical–surgical vacuum system by any method to ensure continuation of service to the facility's medical–surgical pipeline distribution system.

5.1.3.7.5.3 Medical–surgical vacuum central supply systems shall be provided with a source shutoff valve per 5.1.4.2.

5.1.3.7.6 Electrical Power and Control.

(A) Medical vacuum source systems shall be controlled to ensure continuous supply of suction at pressures consistent with Table 5.1.11 under all conditions of system use as follows:

(1) Automatic activation of pump(s) as necessary to supply the demand.

(2) Managing the operation to equalize wear on all pumps. Where this equalization is achieved manually, the facility staff shall arrange a schedule for manual alternation.

(B) Controls shall provide the following functions:

(1) Where medical vacuum source systems having two or more pumps employ any electrical circuit device that upon failure could prevent supply of medical vacuum, the controls shall be provided with an automatically activated alternative method for ensuring supply (e.g., redundant component(s), an alternate electrical supply path, or other equivalent method).

(2) Control circuits shall be arranged in such a manner that isolation of one pump or component from the system (e.g., for maintenance or repair) does not interrupt the operation of other pump(s) or component(s).

(3) An automatic restart function shall be included, such that the supply of medical vacuum will resume normally after power interruption without manual intervention.

(C) Each pump motor shall be provided with electrical components including, but not limited to:

(1) Dedicated disconnect switch installed in the electrical circuit ahead of each motor starter

(2) Motor starting device

(3) Overload protection

(D) Vacuum source system controls shall be provided with electrical systems including, at a minimum:

(1) Control circuits shall be arranged so that failure of any component of the control circuit, or shutdown of one pump (e.g., for service), does not interrupt automatic operation of the standby pump.

(2) Controls shall be provided with built-in disconnect means to allow appropriate operation of multiple pump systems and protect service personnel from exposure to live voltages.

(3) Where components are common to more than one control circuit, the common device shall be provided with electrical protection to prevent loss of the control circuits(s) in the event of short circuit in the device.

(4) An automatic restart function shall be included, such that the pump(s) will restart after power interruption without manual intervention.

(E) Electrical installation and wiring shall conform to the requirements of *NFPA 70*.

(F) Emergency electrical service for the pumps shall conform to the requirements of the essential electrical system as described in Chapter 6.

5.1.3.7.7 Medical–Surgical Vacuum Exhaust.

5.1.3.7.7.1 The medical–surgical vacuum pumps shall exhaust in a manner and location that minimizes the hazards of noise and contamination to the facility and its environment.

5.1.3.7.7.2 The exhaust shall be located as follows:

(1) Outdoors

(2) At least 7.5 m (25 ft) from any door, window, air intake, or other openings in buildings or places of public assembly

(3) At a level different from air intakes

(4) Where prevailing winds, adjacent buildings, topography, or other influences will not divert the exhaust into occupied areas or prevent dispersion of the exhaust

5.1.3.7.7.3 The end of the exhaust shall be turned down and screened or otherwise be protected against the entry of vermin, debris, or precipitation by screening fabricated or composed of a noncorroding material.

5.1.3.7.7.4 Vacuum exhaust shall be labeled in accordance with 5.1.11.1 with any method that would distinguish it as a vacuum exhaust.

5.1.3.7.7.5 The exhaust shall be free of dips and loops that might trap condensate or oil or provided with a drip leg and valved drain at the bottom of the low point.

5.1.3.7.7.6 Vacuum exhausts from multiple pumps shall be permitted to be joined together to one common exhaust where the following conditions are met:

(1) The common exhaust is sized to minimize back pressure in accordance with the pump manufacturer's recommendations.

(2) Each pump can be isolated by manual or check valve, blind flange, or tube cap to prevent open exhaust piping when the pump(s) is removed for service from consequent flow of exhaust air into the room.

5.1.3.7.7.7 Vacuum exhaust piping shall be permitted to be made of materials and use a joining technique as permitted under 5.1.10.2 and 5.1.10.3.

5.1.3.7.8 Operating Alarms. When the capacity of the medical vacuum supply system not in use is less than the equivalent capacity of one pump, a local alarm shall activate *[see 5.1.9.5.3(4)]*. This signal shall require manual reset.

5.1.3.8* Waste Anesthetic Gas Disposal (WAGD) Central Supply Systems.

5.1.3.8.1* Supply Sources. WAGD supply sources shall be chosen in consultation with the medical staff having knowledge of the requirements to determine the type of system, number and placement of terminals, and other required safety and operating devices.

5.1.3.8.1.1 WAGD shall be permitted to be produced through the medical–surgical vacuum source, by a dedicated producer, or by venturi.

5.1.3.8.1.2 If WAGD is produced by the medical–surgical vacuum source, the following shall apply:

(1) The medical–surgical vacuum source shall comply with 5.1.3.7.

(2) The total concentration of oxygen shall be maintained below 23.6 percent unless one of the following conditions is met:

    (a) The vacuum pump complies with 5.1.3.8.2.1.

    (b) The combined medical–surgical vacuum/WAGD system is monitored for oxygen and an alarm will initiate at all master alarm panels if the oxygen concentration exceeds 23.6 percent.

(3) The medical–surgical vacuum source shall be sized to accommodate the additional volume.

5.1.3.8.1.3 If WAGD is produced by a dedicated WAGD producer with a total power equal to or greater than 1 horsepower in total (both producers), the following shall apply:

(1) The WAGD source shall be located in accordance with 5.1.3.3.
(2) The WAGD source shall be located indoors in a dedicated mechanical equipment area with any required utilities.
(3) The WAGD source shall be ventilated per 5.1.3.3.3.3.
(4) For air-cooled equipment, the WAGD source shall be located to maintain the ambient temperature range as recommended by the manufacturer.
(5) The WAGD producers shall comply with 5.1.3.8.2.

5.1.3.8.1.4 If WAGD is produced by a dedicated WAGD producer with a total power less than 1 horsepower in total (both producers), the following shall apply:

(1) The WAGD source shall be permitted to be located near the inlet(s) served.
(2) For air-cooled equipment, the WAGD source shall be located to maintain the ambient temperature range as recommended by the manufacturer.

5.1.3.8.1.5 For liquid ring pumps in WAGD service, seal water shall be of a quality as recommended by the pump manufacturer.

5.1.3.8.1.6 The WAGD source shall consist of the following:

(1) Two or more WAGD producers sufficient to serve the peak calculated demand with the largest single WAGD producer out of service
(2) Automatic means to prevent backflow from any on-cycle WAGD producers through any off-cycle WAGD producers
(3) Shutoff valve to isolate each WAGD producer from the centrally piped system and other WAGD producers for maintenance or repair without loss of WAGD in the system
(4) Piping between the WAGD producers and the source shutoff valve compliant with 5.1.10.2, as recommended by the manufacturer
(5) Antivibration mountings installed for WAGD producers as required by equipment dynamics or location and in accordance with the manufacturer's recommendations
(6) Flexible connectors interconnecting the producers with their intake and outlet piping as required by equipment dynamics or location and in accordance with the WAGD producer manufacturer's recommendations

5.1.3.8.1.7 If WAGD is produced by a venturi, the following shall apply:

(1) The venturi shall not be user-adjustable (i.e., require the use of special tools).
(2) The venturi shall be driven using water, inert gas, instrument air, or other dedicated air source.
(3) Medical air shall not be used to power the venturi.

5.1.3.8.2 WAGD Producers.

5.1.3.8.2.1 Vacuum pumps dedicated for WAGD service shall be as follows:

(1) Compliant with 5.1.3.7.2
(2) Designed of materials and using lubricants and sealants that are inert in the presence of oxygen, nitrous oxide, and halogenated anesthetics

5.1.3.8.2.2 Vacuum producers (e.g., fans or blowers) designed for operation at vacuums below 130 mm (5 in.) HgV shall be as follows:

(1) Permitted to be made of any materials determined by the manufacturer as suitable for the service
(2) Provided with antivibration mountings as required by equipment dynamics or location and in accordance with the manufacturer's recommendation
(3) Connected with their intake and outlet piping through flexible connections
(4) Used only for WAGD service and not employed for other services
(5) Interconnected via piping, ductwork, and so forth, made of materials determined by the manufacturer as suitable to the service

5.1.3.8.3 WAGD Alarms.

5.1.3.8.3.1 When the WAGD system is served by a central source(s), a local alarm complying with 5.1.9.5 shall be provided for the WAGD source.

5.1.3.8.3.2 Where WAGD source systems have two or more producers, and the capacity of the WAGD system not in use is less than the equivalent capacity of one producer, a local alarm shall activate *[see 5.1.9.5.3(5)]*. This signal shall require manual reset.

5.1.3.8.4 Electrical Power and Control.

5.1.3.8.4.1 WAGD source systems shall be controlled to ensure continuous flow under all conditions of system use as follows:

(1) Automatic activation of producer(s) as necessary to supply the demand.
(2) Managing the operation to equalize wear on all producers. Where this equalization is achieved manually, the facility staff shall arrange a schedule for manual alternation.

5.1.3.8.4.2 Controls shall provide the following functions:

(1) Where WAGD source systems having two or more producers employ any electrical circuit device which upon failure could stop the WAGD, the controls shall be provided with an automatically activated alternative method for ensuring supply (i.e., redundant component(s), an alternate electrical supply path or other equivalent method).
(2) Control circuits shall be arranged in such a manner that isolation of one producer or component from the system (e.g., for maintenance or repair) does not interrupt the operation of other pump(s) or component(s).
(3) An automatic restart function shall be included, such that the supply of WAGD will resume normally after power interruption without manual intervention.

5.1.3.8.4.3 Each producer motor shall be provided with electrical components including, but not limited to, the following:

(1) Dedicated disconnect switch installed in the electrical circuit ahead of each motor starter
(2) Motor starting device
(3) Overload protection

5.1.3.8.4.4 WAGD source system controls shall be provided with electrical systems including at least:

(1) Control circuits shall be arranged so that failure of any component of the control circuit, or shutdown of one

producer (e.g., for service) does not interrupt automatic operation of the standby producer.

(2) Controls shall be provided with built in disconnect means to allow appropriate operation of multiple producer systems and protect service personnel from exposure to live voltages.

(3) Where components are common to more than one control circuit, the common device shall be provided with electrical protection to prevent loss of the control circuits(s) in the event of short circuit in the device.

(4) An automatic restart function shall be included, such that the pump(s) will restart after power interruption without manual intervention.

5.1.3.8.4.5 Electrical installation and wiring shall conform to the requirements of *NFPA 70*.

5.1.3.8.4.6 Emergency electrical service for the producers shall conform to the requirements of the essential electrical system as described in Chapter 6.

Δ 5.1.3.8.5 WAGD Exhaust. WAGD producers shall exhaust in compliance with 5.1.3.7.7 unless otherwise permitted by one of the following:

(1) Producers under 1 hp and venturi producers shall be permitted to exhaust individually in a manner that will allow for dispersion of the exhaust gases and not allow the exhaust gas to reenter the building through openable windows, nearby intakes, or other openings.

(2) Anesthetic gas recovery (AGR) and anesthetic gas destruction systems shall be permitted to be installed in the WAGD exhaust piping if the AGR and anesthetic gas destruction systems can be bypassed without compromising the flow of exhaust when required.

5.1.3.9* Oxygen Central Supply Systems Using Concentrators. Any oxygen central supply system that includes one or more oxygen concentrator supply systems shall comply with 5.1.3.9.1 through 5.1.3.9.5.

5.1.3.9.1* Oxygen Concentrator Supply Units.

5.1.3.9.1.1 Oxygen concentrator supply units for use with medical gas pipelines shall produce oxygen meeting the requirements of Oxygen 93 USP or Oxygen USP.

5.1.3.9.1.2 Output shall have less than or equal to 1 mg/m³ $(1.685 \times 10^{-6}$ lb/yd³) of permanent particulates sized 1 micron or larger at normal atmospheric pressure.

5.1.3.9.1.3 Materials of construction on the air side of the oxygen concentrator unit shall be suitable for the service as determined by the manufacturer.

5.1.3.9.1.4 Materials of construction on the oxygen side of the oxygen concentrator unit shall comply with 5.1.3.5.4.

5.1.3.9.1.5 The components that make up the oxygen concentrator unit shall be as follows:

(1) The manufacturer of the concentrator unit shall be permitted to use such components and arrangement of such components as needed to produce oxygen complying with 5.1.3.9.1.1 in the quantity as required by the facility, except where otherwise specifically defined in this code.

(2) Air receivers and oxygen accumulators, where used, shall comply with Section VIII, "Unfired Pressure Vessels," of

the ASME *Boiler and Pressure Vessels Code* and be provided with overpressure relief valves.

5.1.3.9.1.6 The supply air to the concentrator(s) shall be of a quality to ensure the oxygen concentrator unit can produce oxygen complying with 5.1.3.9.1.1 and shall not be subject to normally anticipated contamination (e.g., vehicle or other exhausts, gas leakage, discharge from vents, flooding).

5.1.3.9.1.7 The oxygen concentrator supply unit and any associated electrical equipment shall be provided with, at a minimum, the following electrical components:

(1) Either a disconnect switch for each major electrical component or a single disconnect that deactivates all electrical components in the concentrator unit

(2) Motor-starting devices with overload protection for any component with an electrical motor over 2 hp

5.1.3.9.1.8 A vent valve shall be provided as follows:

(1) Located on the source side of the concentrator outlet isolation valve to permit the operation of the oxygen concentrator unit for validation, calibration, and testing while the unit is isolated from the pipeline system

(2) Sized to allow for at least 25 percent of the oxygen concentrator unit flow

(3) Vented to a location compliant with 5.1.3.3.3.2

5.1.3.9.1.9 A DN8 (NPS ¼) valved sample port shall be provided near the oxygen concentration monitor sensor connection for sampling of the gas from the oxygen concentrator unit.

5.1.3.9.1.10 At least one 0.1 micron filter suitable for oxygen service shall be provided at the outlet of the oxygen concentrator supply unit.

5.1.3.9.1.11 A check valve shall be provided at the outlet of the oxygen concentrator supply unit to prevent backflow into the oxygen concentrator supply unit and to allow service to the unit.

5.1.3.9.1.12 An outlet valve shall be provided to isolate all components of the oxygen concentrator from the pipeline with the following characteristics:

(1) The valve shall have both manual and automatic actuation with visual indication of open or closed.

(2) The valve shall close automatically whenever the oxygen concentrator unit is not producing oxygen of a concentration equal to that in 5.1.3.9.1.1.

(3) Continuing operation of the oxygen concentrator supply unit through the vent mode shall be permitted with the isolating valve closed.

(4) The isolating valve, when automatically closed due to low concentration, shall require manual reset to ensure the oxygen concentrator supply unit is examined prior to return to service.

(5) Closing the isolating valve, whether automatically or manually, shall activate an alarm signal at the master alarms *(see 5.1.9.2)* indicating that the oxygen concentrator supply unit is disconnected.

Δ 5.1.3.9.1.13 The oxygen concentrator supply source shall be provided with an oxygen concentration monitor with the following characteristics:

(1) The monitor shall be capable of monitoring 99 percent oxygen concentration with 1 percent accuracy.

(2) The monitor shall continuously display the oxygen concentration and activate the local alarm and master alarms in accordance with 5.1.3.9.5 when a concentration lower than 91 percent is observed.

(3) The monitor shall continuously display the oxygen concentration.

(4) The monitor shall be permitted to be inserted into the pipeline without a demand check.

5.1.3.9.2 Location. An oxygen central supply system using a concentrator(s) shall be located in accordance with 5.1.3.3 and as follows:

(1) Indoors in a dedicated mechanical equipment area, ventilated, and with any required utilities (e.g., electricity, drains, lighting).

(2)* In a room ventilated in accordance with 5.1.3.3.3.3.

(3) For air cooled equipment, in a room designed to maintain the ambient temperature range as recommended by the manufacturer.

(4) A room containing an oxygen central supply system using a concentrator(s) that does not have the concentrator purge gas vented to the outside shall be equipped with oxygen depletion monitors with alarm indicators at the entrance(s) that will indicate ambient oxygen levels in the room below 19.5 percent.

(5)* Individual elements of the oxygen central supply system using a concentrator(s) shall be permitted to be located in separate rooms or enclosures as necessary to meet 5.1.3.9.2(1) through 5.1.3.9.2(4).

Δ **5.1.3.9.3 Arrangement and Redundancies.** An oxygen central supply system using a concentrator(s) shall be permitted to consist of two or three supply sources, as follows:

(1) If two supply sources are provided, the following shall apply:

   (a) One source shall be an oxygen concentrator supply source.

   (b) The second source shall be a cylinder header complying with 5.1.3.5.9 with sufficient cylinder connections for one average day's supply.

   (c) Containers shall not be used as a supply source.

(2) If three supply sources are provided, the following shall apply:

   (a) Each source shall be capable of independently supplying the full system demand in the event of the unavailability of one or both of the other sources.

   (b) Each source shall be permitted to be either of the following:

      i. An oxygen concentrator supply source complying with 5.1.3.9.1

      ii. A cylinder header complying with 5.1.3.5.9 with sufficient cylinder connections for one average day's supply

   (c) Containers shall not be used as a supply source.

(3) Use of oxygen concentrator supply systems as all three sources shall only be permitted after a documented risk analysis by the governing authority of the health care facility indicates an understanding of the inherent risks and defines how those risks will be mitigated.

(4) An isolation valve and automatic check valve shall be provided to isolate each of the three sources from the others and from the pipeline. The valves in 5.1.3.5.9(4),

5.1.3.5.9(6), 5.1.3.9.1.11, and 5.1.3.9.1.12 shall be permitted to be used for this purpose.

(5) Each of the three supply sources shall be provided with a pressure relief valve complying with 5.1.3.5.6 on the source side of its respective isolating valve.

(6) The three supply sources shall join to the pipeline systems through control arrangements with at least the following characteristics:

   (a) The control arrangements shall be able to maintain stable pressures within the limits of Table 5.1.11.

   (b) The control arrangements shall be able to flow 100 percent of the peak calculated demand.

   (c) The control arrangements shall be redundant, such that each component of the control mechanism can be isolated for service or replacement while maintaining normal operation.

   (d) The cascade of sources shall comply with 5.1.3.9.4.

   (e) The system shall be protected against overpressure (*see 5.1.3.5.6*).

(7) A pressure relief valve shall be provided in the common line between the sources and the line pressure controls.

(8) A source valve in accordance with 5.1.4.2 shall be provided on the patient side of the line pressure controls.

(9) A gauge and switch or sensor shall be located between the three sources and the line pressure controls to monitor the pressure feeding the line pressure controls.

(10) An oxygen concentration monitor, sampling the gas on the patient side of the line pressure controls and on the source side of the source valve, shall be provided with the following characteristics:

   (a) The monitor shall be capable of monitoring 99 percent oxygen concentration with ±1.0 percent accuracy.

   (b) The monitor shall be attached to the pipeline through a demand check in accordance with 5.1.8.2.3.

   (c) The monitor shall continuously display the oxygen concentration and activate the local alarm and master alarms when an oxygen concentration lower than 91 percent is observed.

(11) A DN8 (NPS ¼) valved sample port shall be provided on the patient side of the line pressure controls and source side of the source valve for sampling the oxygen.

(12) An auxiliary source connection complying with 5.1.4.10 shall be provided.

(13) Electrical installation and wiring shall conform to the requirements of *NFPA 70*.

(14) Emergency electrical service for all components of the oxygen supply system shall conform to the requirements of the essential electrical system as described in Chapter 6.

5.1.3.9.4 Operating Controls. An oxygen central supply system using a concentrator(s) shall include means to provide the following functions:

(1) Selection of an appropriate primary supply source. When the primary supply source is in operation and oxygen quality is suitable, the secondary and reserve supply sources shall be prevented from supplying the system.

(2) Automatic activation of the secondary supply source shall be available if the primary supply source is not able to maintain pressure or concentration of oxygen.

(3) Automatic activation of the reserve supply source shall be available if the primary and secondary supply source are not able to maintain supply pressure or concentration of oxygen.

(4) Where two or more concentrator supply sources are included in the system, the oxygen concentrator supply sources shall be permitted to rotate as the primary supply source.

(5) Automatic operation such that the supply of gas will continue through interruption of the main electrical source.

(6) The oxygen concentrator supply source(s) in the system shall be capable of automatically returning to normal operation following a power interruption. If required by the technology, it shall be permitted to isolate the concentrator supply source(s) using the automatic valve(s) to restore normal oxygen concentration prior to reconnecting the oxygen concentrator supply source to the system by opening the automatic valve. The valve can be actuated automatically for this purpose as an exception to 5.1.3.9.1.12(4).

5.1.3.9.5 Operating Alarms and Local Signals.

5.1.3.9.5.1 For each oxygen concentrator supply source in the system, the supply source's concentration monitor *(see 5.1.3.9.1.13)* shall be able to perform the following:

(1) Indicate low oxygen concentration when a concentration lower than 91 percent is observed
(2) Activate a local alarm *(see 5.1.9.5)*
(3) Activate an alarm signal at the master alarm *(see 5.1.9.2)* indicating that the oxygen concentration from that supply source is low
(4) Activate the automatic isolating valve for that oxygen concentrator supply source *(see 5.1.3.9.1.12)* to prevent supply from that oxygen concentrator supply source
(5) Close the automatic isolating valve for that oxygen concentrator supply source *(see 5.1.3.9.1.12)*, which activates an alarm signal at the master alarm *(see 5.1.9.2)* indicating that the oxygen concentrator supply source is disconnected

5.1.3.9.5.2 For the entire oxygen central supply system, the system concentration monitor *[see 5.1.3.9.3(10)]* shall be able to perform the following:

(1) Indicate low oxygen concentration when a concentration lower than 91 percent is observed
(2) Activate a local alarm *(see 5.1.9.5)*
(3) Activate an alarm signal at the master alarm *(see 5.1.9.2)* indicating the oxygen concentration is low

5.1.3.9.5.3 For each header source *(see 5.1.3.5.9)* in the supply system, local signals and alarms shall be provided as follows:

(1) A pressure gauge for delivery pressure
(2) A means to activate an alarm signal at the master alarm *(see 5.1.9.2)* indicating the oxygen cylinders are in use
(3) A means to activate an alarm signal at the master alarm *(see 5.1.9.2)* indicating the content of the oxygen cylinder header is reduced below one average day's supply

5.1.3.9.5.4 An oxygen central supply system using a concentrator(s) shall be provided with operating alarms as follows:

(1) *Change of Source.* An operating alarm shall be provided as follows:

(a) If the supply source in use fails to supply the system and is changed in accordance with 5.1.3.9.4(2) or 5.1.3.9.4(3), a local alarm and a signal at the master alarm shall be activated, indicating an oxygen supply change has occurred.
(b) The signal in 5.1.3.9.5.4(1)(a) shall not be activated if the system has rotated sources in accordance with 5.1.3.9.4(6).

(2) *Internal Pressure Low.* A local alarm and a signal at the master alarm shall be activated when or just before the pressure falls below the pressure required to drive the calculated required flow rate through the line pressure controls indicating the oxygen supply internal pressure is low *[see 5.1.3.9.3(9) for sensor location]*.

5.1.3.10* Cryogenic Fluid Central Supply Systems.

5.1.3.10.1 General.

5.1.3.10.1.1* The storage, use, and handling of cryogenic fluid central supply systems that deliver compressed medical gases (CMGs) to health care facilities shall be in accordance with the requirements of this section. [**55**:17.1.1]

5.1.3.10.1.2 Applicability.

(A) The source valve shall be the line separating the applicability between NFPA 55 and this code. [**55**:17.1.2.1]

(B) Cryogenic fluid central supply system installations up to, but not including, the source valve shall be covered by NFPA 55. [**55**:17.1.2.2]

(C) The source valve and all downstream piping and components, including wiring to storage system alarms, shall be covered by this code. [**55**:17.1.2.3]

5.1.3.10.2 Cryogenic Fluid Central Supply Systems Installation.

5.1.3.10.2.1 Cryogenic fluid central supply systems shall be installed by personnel qualified in accordance with CGA M-1, *Standard for Medical Gas Supply Systems at Health Care Facilities*, or ASSE/IAPMO/ANSI 6015, *[Professional Qualifications Standard for] Bulk Medical Gas/Cryogenic Fluid Central Supply Systems Installers*. [**55**:17.2.1]

N 5.1.3.10.2.2 Initial inspection and testing of the cryogenic fluid central supply system shall be conducted by a party technically competent and experienced in the field of cryogenic fluid systems and that meets the requirements of ASSE/IAPMO/ANSI 6035, *[Professional Qualifications Standard for] Bulk Medical Gas/Cryogenic Fluid Central Supply Systems Verifiers*, in accordance with this code and the requirements of CGA M-1, *Standard for Medical Gas Supply Systems at Health Care Facilities*. [**55**:17.2.2]

5.1.3.10.2.3 Cryogenic fluid central supply systems shall be installed in compliance with the Food and Drug Administration (FDA) Current Good Manufacturing Practices per 21 CFR 210 and 21 CFR 211. [**55**:17.2.3]

5.1.3.10.2.4 Cryogenic fluid central supply systems shall be installed in accordance with CGA M-1, *Standard for Medical Gas Supply Systems at Health Care Facilities*. [**55**:17.2.4]

5.1.3.10.2.5 Cryogenic fluid central supply systems shall have a minimum work space clearance of 3 ft (1 m) around the storage container, vaporizer(s), and cabinet opening or front side of the pressure-regulating manifold for system maintenance and operation. [**55**:17.2.5]

Δ **5.1.3.10.2.6** Inert cryogenic fluid central supply systems shall be sited in accordance with Chapter 8 of NFPA 55 and CGA P-18, *Standard for Bulk Inert Gas Systems.* [**55**:17.2.6]

5.1.3.10.2.7 Oxygen cryogenic fluid central supply systems shall be sited in accordance with Chapters 8 and 9 of NFPA 55, as applicable, and CGA M-1, *Standard for Medical Gas Supply Systems at Health Care Facilities.* [**55**:17.2.7]

5.1.3.10.2.8 Carbon dioxide refrigerated liquid central supply systems shall be sited in accordance with Chapter 13 of NFPA 55 and CGA G-6.1, *Standard for Insulated Liquid Carbon Dioxide Systems at Consumer Sites.* [**55**:17.2.8]

5.1.3.10.2.9 Nitrous oxide refrigerated liquid central supply systems shall be sited in accordance with Chapter 16 of NFPA 55 and CGA G-8.1, *Standard for Nitrous Oxide Systems at Customer Sites.* [**55**:17.2.9]

N **5.1.3.10.2.10** Outdoor bulk cryogenic liquid systems shall have at least two means of egress provided from any enclosure. [**55**:17.2.10]

N **5.1.3.10.2.11** Outdoor bulk cryogenic liquid systems shall be in accordance with CGA M-1, *Standard for Medical Gas Supply Systems at Health Care Facilities.* [**55**:17.2.10.1]

5.1.3.10.3 Cryogenic Fluid Central Supply Systems Operation.

5.1.3.10.3.1 The following components of the cryogenic fluid central supply system shall be accessible and visible to delivery personnel during filling operations:

(1) Fill connection
(2) Top and bottom fill valves
(3) Hose purge valve
(4) Vent valve
(5) Full trycock valve
(6) Liquid level indicator
(7) Tank pressure indicator

[**55**:17.3.1]

5.1.3.10.3.2 Cryogenic fluid central supply systems shall consist of the following:

(1) One or more main supply vessel, with capacity determined after consideration of the customer usage requirements, delivery schedules, proximity of the facility to alternative supplies, and the emergency plan
(2) A contents gauge on every main vessel
(3) A reserve supply sized for greater than an average day's supply, with the size of vessel or number of cylinders determined after consideration of delivery schedules, proximity of the facility to alternative supplies, and the emergency plan
(4) At least two main vessel relief valves and rupture discs installed downstream of a three-way (i.e., three-port) valve
(5) A check valve located in the primary supply piping upstream of the intersection with a secondary supply or reserve supply

[**55**:17.3.2]

5.1.3.10.3.3 Reserve CMG supply systems consisting of either a second cryogenic fluid source or a compressed gas source shall include the following:

(1) Where the reserve source is a compressed gas source, the reserve shall be equipped with the following:

(a) A cylinder manifold having not less than three gas cylinder connections or as otherwise required for an average of one day's gas supply
(b) A pressure switch to monitor the pressure in the cylinder manifold

(2) Where the reserve source is a second cryogenic fluid vessel, the reserve tank shall be equipped with the following:

(a) An actuating switch or sensor to monitor the internal tank pressure
(b) A contents gauge to monitor the liquid level

(3) Where the reserve source is either a cryogenic fluid or compressed gas source, a check valve shall be provided to prevent backflow into the reserve system.

[**55**:17.3.3]

5.1.3.10.3.4 Bulk cryogenic liquid sources shall include automatic means to provide the following functions:

(1) When the main supply is supplying the system, the reserve supply shall be prevented from supplying the system until the main supply is reduced to a level at or below the reserve activation pressure.
(2) When the main supply cannot supply the system, the reserve supply shall automatically begin to supply the system.
(3) Where there is more than one main supply vessel, the system shall operate as follows for primary, secondary, and reserve operation:

(a) If provided with two liquid container headers, one cryogenic liquid header shall be the primary and the other shall be the secondary, with either being capable of either role.
(b) If provided with one liquid container header and one gas cylinder header (i.e., a hybrid arrangement), the liquid container header shall be the primary and the gas cylinder header shall be the secondary.
(c) When the primary header is supplying the system, the secondary header shall be prevented from supplying the system.
(d) When the primary header is depleted, the secondary header shall automatically begin to supply the system.

(4) Where there are two or more cryogenic vessels, they shall be permitted to alternate (e.g., on a timed basis) in the roles of primary, secondary, and reserve, provided that an operating cascade (i.e., primary–secondary–reserve) is maintained at all times.
(5) Where a cryogenic vessel is used as the reserve, the reserve vessel shall include a means to conserve the gas produced by evaporation of the cryogenic liquid in the reserve vessel and to discharge the gas into the line upstream of the final line regulator assembly.

[**55**:17.3.4]

5.1.3.10.4 Main Supply System. The main supply vessel for a cryogenic fluid central supply system shall be a cryogenic storage tank. [**55**:17.4]

5.1.3.10.5 Reserve Supply System.

5.1.3.10.5.1 A CMG reserve supply system shall consist of either of the following:

(1) A secondary cryogenic vessel
(2) A high-pressure compressed gas source

[**55**:17.5.1]

5.1.3.10.5.2 A cryogenic source reserve supply shall have a switch or sensor to monitor the tank pressure. [**55**:17.5.2]

5.1.3.10.5.3 A compressed gas reserve supply shall meet the following requirements:

(1) It shall be manifolded with no fewer than three gas cylinders.
(2) It shall have a pressure switch or sensor to monitor the contents using manifold pressure.
(3) It shall have a check valve to prevent backflow into the system.
(4) It shall have a check valve at each connection on the cylinder header to minimize loss of gas from the reserve system.

[**55**:17.5.3]

5.1.3.10.6 Cryogenic Fill System. Cryogenic fluid central supply systems shall include a fill mechanism consisting of the following components:

(1) A nonremovable product-specific fill connection in compliance with CGA V-6, *Standard Bulk Refrigerated Liquid Transfer Connections*
(2) A means to cap and secure the fill connection inlet
(3) A check valve to prevent product backflow from the fill inlet
(4) A fill hose purge valve
(5) Supports that hold the fill piping off the ground
(6) A secure connection between the bulk tank and the fill piping
(7) Supports, as necessary, to hold the fill line in position during all operations associated with the filling procedure

[**55**:17.6]

5.1.3.10.7 Vaporizers.

5.1.3.10.7.1 Vaporizers used to convert cryogenic CMG to a gaseous state shall meet the following requirements:

(1) Vaporizers shall be permitted to operate by either ambient heat transfer or external thermal source (e.g., electric heater, hot water, steam).
(2) Vaporizers using a heat source other than ambient air shall be protected in the event of a loss of the energy source.

[**55**:17.7.1]

5.1.3.10.7.2 Vaporizers shall be designed to provide capacity for the customer's use under the following conditions:

(1) Customer's average and peak flows
(2) Local conditions (e.g., structures that obstruct air circulation or sunlight)
(3) Seasonal conditions (e.g., freeze periods)

[**55**:17.7.2]

5.1.3.10.7.3 A system design that uses switching vaporizers shall meet all of the following requirements:

(1) Valves shall be permitted to be manual or automatic.
(2) Valves and piping shall allow an operating vaporizer or an operating section of a vaporizer to be switched to a nonoperating condition for deicing.
(3) The system design shall provide continuous flow of CMG to the health care facility during vaporizer switchover.
(4) The system design shall provide continuous flow of CMG to the health care facility if vaporizer switchover fails.

[**55**:17.7.3]

5.1.3.10.7.4 Where a vaporizer uses an external thermal source, the flow of the CMG shall be unaffected by the loss of the external thermal source by one of the following methods:

(1) Reserve ambient heat transfer vaporizers sized for at least one day's average supply and piped so that the flow of the CMG is unaffected by flow stoppage through the external thermal source vaporizer
(2) A noncryogenic source capable of providing at least one day's average supply

[**55**:17.7.4]

5.1.3.10.7.5 Where vaporizers are used in the reserve system, they shall be as follows:

(1) Sized by the supplier to provide a source of vaporized CMG from the reserve bulk liquid storage vessel during times when the reserve system is operational
(2) Able to provide a flow rate equal to at least that of the main system vaporizer(s); however, the duration of flow might be different
(3) Indirectly heated by ambient air

[**55**:17.7.5]

5.1.3.10.7.6 Low-temperature protection systems that interrupt or reduce flow shall not be used on the reserve system of cryogenic fluid central supply systems. [**55**:17.7.6]

5.1.3.10.8 High-Pressure Manifolds.

5.1.3.10.8.1 Manifold assemblies shall be fit for service and shall have supports that are independent of the cylinders. [**55**:17.8.1]

5.1.3.10.8.2 Cylinders on the manifold shall be secured against falling. [**55**:17.8.2]

5.1.3.10.8.3* Cylinders on the manifold shall have the same service pressure rating or the filled pressure of each cylinder shall not exceed the service pressure rating of the lowest rated cylinder on the manifold. [**55**:17.8.3]

5.1.3.10.9 Pressure Control Devices. The final pressure control device assembly or assemblies shall not be fabricated on-site. [**55**:17.9]

5.1.3.10.10 Pressure Relief Devices.

5.1.3.10.10.1 Pressure relief devices (PRDs) shall meet the following requirements:

(1) PRDs shall have a relief pressure setting not higher than the maximum allowable working pressure (MAWP) of the component with the lowest working pressure rating in the portion of the system being protected.
(2) PRDs shall be of brass or bronze construction.
(3) PRDs shall be designed for the specific gas service.
(4) PRDs shall have the discharge protected to prevent the entry of rain or snow.

(5) PRDs shall be designed in accordance with ASME B31.3, *Process Piping*.

[**55**:17.10.1]

5.1.3.10.10.2 PRDs shall have an identifier that contains the date of manufacture or test. [**55**:17.10.2]

5.1.3.10.10.3 The final line pressure relief valves shall be approved by a nationally recognized organization and shall have a relief capacity greater than or equal to the maximum throughput of the final line regulator. [**55**:17.10.3]

(A) The pressure relief valve shall be set at 50 percent above the normal working pressure, but no higher than the MAWP, of the health care facility pipeline. [**55**:17.10.3.1]

(B) The relief valve information shall be permanently identified either on the nameplate of the relief valve or on a permanently attached metal tag. [**55**:17.10.3.2]

5.1.3.10.11 Tubing and Valves.

5.1.3.10.11.1 New, hard-drawn Type K or L copper tube shall be used for all process piping. [**55**:17.11.1]

(A) Tubing shall comply with ASTM B819, *Standard Specification for Seamless Copper Tube for Medical Gas Systems.* [**55**:17.11.1.1]

(B) Tubing shall be capped and bear the marking OXY or MEDICAL or be otherwise packaged and labeled to indicate it is clean for oxygen service according to the supplier's policy. [**55**:17.11.1.2]

5.1.3.10.11.2 Copper Tubing.

(A) Instrumentation tubing shall be constructed of annealed copper tubing or seamless stainless steel tubing. [**55**:17.11.2.1]

(B) Copper tubing shall comply with ASTM B88, *Standard Specification for Seamless Copper Water Tube.* [**55**:17.11.2.2]

5.1.3.10.11.3 Valves of quick-open or quarter-turn designs, such as ball or plug valves, shall not be permitted in the portion of an oxygen piping system operating above 435 psi [3000 kPa]. [**55**:17.11.3]

5.1.3.10.11.4 Alternate Materials.

(A)* Alternate materials of construction for piping, tubing, valves, and instruments shall be permitted for installation at the request of the health care facility or the supplier. [**55**:17.11.4.1]

(B) Technical documentation of alternate materials shall be submitted to the health care facility QA representative to demonstrate equivalency. [**55**:17.11.4.2]

5.1.3.10.12* Alarms. The cryogenic fluid central supply system shall have a local signal that visibly indicates the operating status of the equipment and an indicator at all master alarms under the following conditions:

(1) When, or at a predetermined set point before, the main supply reaches an average day's supply, indicating low contents
(2) When, or at a predetermined set point before, the reserve supply begins to supply the system, indicating reserve is in use
(3) When, or at a predetermined set point before, the reserve supply contents fall to one day's average supply, indicating low reserve

(4) If the reserve is a cryogenic vessel, when, or at a predetermined set point before, the reserve internal pressure falls too low for the reserve to operate properly, indicating reserve failure
(5) Where there is more than one main supply vessel, when, or at a predetermined set point before, the secondary vessel begins to supply the system, indicating changeover

[**55**:17.12]

5.1.4* Valves.

5.1.4.1 General.

5.1.4.1.1 Gas and Vacuum Shutoff Valves. Shutoff valves shall be provided to isolate sections or portions of the piped distribution system for maintenance, repair, emergencies, or planned future expansion needs and to facilitate periodic testing.

5.1.4.1.2 Security. All valves, except valves in zone valve box assemblies, shall be secured by any of the following means:

(1) Located in secured areas
(2) Locked or latched in their operating position
(3) Located above ceilings, but remaining accessible and not obstructed

5.1.4.1.3 Labeling. All valves shall be labeled as to gas supplied and the area(s) controlled, in accordance with 5.1.11.2.

5.1.4.1.4 Accessibility.

(A) Zone valves shall be installed in valve boxes with removable covers large enough to allow manual operation of valves.

(B) Zone valves for use in certain areas, such as psychiatric or pediatric areas, shall be permitted to be secured with the approval of the authority having jurisdiction to prevent inappropriate access.

5.1.4.1.5 Flammable Gases. Valves for nonflammable medical gases shall not be installed with valves for flammable gases in the same zone valve box assembly with flammable gases.

5.1.4.1.6 Valve Types. New or replacement valves shall be permitted to be of any type as long as they meet the following conditions:

(1) They have a minimum Cv factor in accordance with either Table 5.1.4.1.6(a) or Table 5.1.4.1.6(b).
(2) They use a quarter turn to off.
(3) They are constructed of materials suitable for the service.
(4) They are provided with copper tube extensions by the manufacturer for brazing or with corrugated medical tubing (CMT) fittings.
(5) They indicate to the operator if the valve is open or closed.
(6) They permit in-line serviceability.
(7) They are cleaned for oxygen service by the manufacturer if used for any positive-pressure service.
(8) They have threaded purge ports on the patient side and the source side.
(9) They have a minimum working pressure equal to or greater than the relief valve protecting the piping system on which the valve is installed for any positive-pressure service.

(10) Seals necessary for the operation of the valve and prevention of leaks comply with 5.1.3.5.4 and are replaceable.

5.1.4.2 Source Valve.

5.1.4.2.1 A shutoff valve shall be placed at the immediate connection of each central supply system to the piped distribution system to allow the entire central supply system, including all accessory devices (e.g., air dryers, final line regulators), to be isolated from the facility.

5.1.4.2.2 The source valve shall be located in the immediate vicinity of the central supply system.

5.1.4.3* Main Line Valve.

5.1.4.3.1 A shutoff valve shall be provided in the main supply line inside of the buildings being served, except where one or more of the following conditions exist:

(1) The source and source valve are located inside the building served.
(2) The source system is physically mounted to the wall of the building served, and the pipeline enters the building in the immediate vicinity of the source valve.

5.1.4.3.2 The main line valve shall be located on the facility side of the source valve and outside of the source room, the enclosure, or where the main line first enters the building.

5.1.4.4 Riser Valve. Each riser supplied from the main line shall be provided with a shutoff valve in the riser adjacent to the main line.

△ Table 5.1.4.1.6(a) Positive-Pressure Gases

Valve Size (in.)	Minimum Cv (full open)
½	17
¾	31
1	60
1¼	110
1½	169
2	357
2½	390
3	912
4	1837

Table 5.1.4.1.6(b) Vacuum and WAGD

Valve Size (in.)	Minimum Cv (full open)
½	17
¾	31
1	60
1¼	110
1½	169
2	357
2½	196
3	302
4	600
5	1022
6	1579
8	3136

5.1.4.5 Service Valves.

5.1.4.5.1 Service valves shall be installed to allow servicing or modification of lateral branch piping from a main or riser without shutting down the entire main, riser, or facility.

5.1.4.5.2 Only one service valve shall be required for each branch off of a riser, regardless of how many zone valve boxes are installed on that lateral.

5.1.4.5.3 Service valves shall be placed in the branch piping prior to any zone valve box assembly on that branch.

5.1.4.6 Zone Valves.

5.1.4.6.1 All station outlets/inlets shall be supplied through a zone valve, which shall be placed as follows:

(1) It is installed so that a wall intervenes between the valve and the outlets/inlets that it controls.
(2)* It is readily operable from a standing position.
(3)* It is installed where it is visible and accessible at all times.
(4) It is not installed where it can be hidden from plain view, such as behind normally open or normally closed doors.
(5) It is not installed in a room with the station outlets/inlets that it controls.
(6) It is not installed in rooms, areas, or closets that can be closed or locked.

△ **5.1.4.6.2*** A zone valve in each medical gas and vacuum line shall be provided for each Category 1 space and be located as follows:

(1) In patient care spaces that are not anesthetizing locations, they shall be installed immediately outside the area or zone being controlled.
(2) In anesthetizing locations, they shall be installed immediately outside each room.

5.1.4.6.3 Piping on the patient side of zone valves shall be arranged to provide the following:

(1) Shutting off the supply of medical gas or vacuum to one zone will not affect the supply of medical gas or vacuum to another zone or the rest of the system.
(2) Service will only be to outlets/inlets located on that same story.
(3) All gas delivery columns, hose reels, ceiling tracks, control panels, pendants, booms, or other special installations are located on the patient side of the zone valve.

5.1.4.6.4 A pressure/vacuum indicator shall be provided on the station outlet/inlet side of each zone valve.

5.1.4.7 In-Line Shutoff Valves. Optional in-line valves shall be permitted to be installed to isolate or shut off piping for servicing of individual rooms or areas.

5.1.4.8 Valves for Future Connections.

5.1.4.8.1 Future connection valves shall be labeled as to gas content.

5.1.4.8.2 Downstream piping shall be closed with a brazed cap with tubing allowance for cutting and rebrazing.

5.1.4.9 In-Line Check Valves. New or replacement check valves shall be as follows:

(1) They shall be of brass or bronze construction.
(2) They shall have brazed extensions.
(3) They shall have in-line serviceability.

(4) They shall not have threaded connections.
(5) They shall have threaded purge points of ⅛ in. NPT.
(6) They shall be sized to have a maximum velocity which does not exceed the manufacturer's recommendations.

5.1.4.10 Auxiliary Source Connection. All cryogenic fluid central supply systems shall be provided with an auxiliary source connection point of the same size as the main line, which shall be located immediately on the patient side of the source valve.

5.1.4.10.1 The connection shall consist of a tee, a valve, and a removable plug or cap.

5.1.4.10.2 The auxiliary source connection valve shall be normally closed and secured.

5.1.5* Station Outlets/Inlets.

5.1.5.1 Each station outlet/inlet for medical gases or vacuums shall be gas-specific, whether the outlet/inlet is threaded or is a noninterchangeable quick coupler.

5.1.5.2 Each station outlet shall consist of a primary and a secondary valve (or assembly).

5.1.5.3 Each station inlet shall consist of a primary valve (or assembly) and shall be permitted to include a secondary valve (or assembly).

5.1.5.4 The secondary valve (or assembly) shall close automatically to stop the flow of gas (or vacuum, if provided) when the primary valve (or assembly) is removed.

5.1.5.5 Each outlet/inlet shall be legibly identified in accordance with 5.1.11.3.

5.1.5.6 Threaded outlets/inlets shall be noninterchangeable connections complying with the mandatory requirements of CGA V-5, *Standard for Diameter Index Safety System (Noninterchangeable Low Pressure Connections for Medical Gas Applications).*

5.1.5.7 Each station outlet/inlet, including those mounted in columns, hose reels, ceiling tracks, or other special installations, shall be designed so that parts or components that are required to be gas-specific for compliance with 5.1.5.1 and 5.1.5.9 cannot be interchanged between the station outlet/inlet for different gases.

5.1.5.8 The use of common parts in outlets/inlets, such as springs, O-rings, fasteners, seals, and shutoff poppets, shall be permitted.

5.1.5.9 Components of a vacuum station inlet necessary for the maintenance of vacuum specificity shall be legibly marked to identify them as components or parts of a vacuum or suction system.

5.1.5.10 Components of inlets not specific to a vacuum shall not be required to be marked.

5.1.5.11 Factory-installed copper inlet tubes on station outlets extending no further than 205 mm (8 in.) from the body of the terminal shall be not less than DN8 (NPS ¼) (⅜ in. O.D.) size, with 8 mm (0.3 in.) minimum inside diameter.

Δ **5.1.5.12** Factory-installed outlet tubes on station inlets extending no further than 205 mm (8 in.) from the body of the terminal shall be not less than DN10 (NPS ⅜) (½ in. O.D.) size, with 10 mm (0.4 in.) minimum inside diameter.

5.1.5.13 Station outlets/inlets shall be permitted to be recessed or otherwise protected from damage.

5.1.5.14 When multiple wall outlets/inlets are installed, they shall be spaced to allow the simultaneous use of adjacent outlets/inlets with any of the various types of therapy equipment.

5.1.5.15 Station outlets in systems having nonstandard operating pressures shall meet the following additional requirements:

(1) They shall be gas-specific.
(2) They shall be pressure-specific where a single gas is piped at more than one operating pressure [e.g., a station outlet for oxygen at 550 kPa (80 psi) shall not accept an adapter for oxygen at 345 kPa (50 psi)].
(3) If operated at a pressure in excess of 550 kPa (80 psi), they shall be either D.I.S.S. connectors or comply with 5.1.5.15(4).
(4) If operated at a gauge pressure between 1380 kPa and 2070 kPa (200 psi and 300 psi), the station outlet shall be designed so as to prevent the removal of the adapter until the pressure has been relieved to prevent the adapter injuring the user or others when removed from the outlet.

5.1.5.16 WAGD networks shall provide a WAGD inlet in all locations where nitrous oxide or halogenated anesthetic gas is intended to be administered.

5.1.5.16.1 Station inlets for WAGD service shall have the following additional characteristics:

(1) They shall not be interchangeable with any other systems, including medical–surgical vacuum.
(2) Components necessary for the maintenance of WAGD specificity shall be legibly marked to identify them as components of a WAGD inlet.
(3) They shall be of a type appropriate for the flow and vacuum level required by the facility's gas anesthetic machines.
(4) They shall be located to avoid physical damage to the inlet.

5.1.5.17 Where installed in a down-facing position, such as in a ceiling or ceiling column, station outlets/inlets shall be D.I.S.S. connectors.

5.1.6* Manufactured Assemblies.

Δ **5.1.6.1** Manufactured assemblies and manufactured rough-in assemblies shall be tested by the manufacturer prior to arrival at the installation site in accordance with the following:

(1) Initial blowdown test in accordance with 5.1.12.2.2
(2) Initial pressure test in accordance with 5.1.12.2.3
(3) Piping purge test in accordance with 5.1.12.2.5

N **5.1.6.2** Manufactured assemblies shall be tested by the manufacturer prior to arrival at the installation site in accordance with the following:

(1) Standing pressure test in accordance with 5.1.12.2.6 or 5.1.12.2.7, except as permitted by 5.1.6.3
(2) Operational pressure test in accordance with 5.1.12.4.10, except that the test gas is permitted to be in accordance with the manufacturer's process requirements

5.1.6.3 The leakage from a completed manufactured assembly shall not exceed 0.006 cm³/sec (0.00037 in.³/sec) when tested at 20 percent above operating pressure for pressure pipelines and shall not exceed 0.002 cm³/sec (0.00012 in.³/sec) for vacuum and WAGD systems when started at 635 mm (25 in.) HgV.

5.1.6.4 The manufacturer of the assembly shall provide documentation certifying the performance and successful completion of the tests required in 5.1.6.1.

5.1.6.5 Manufactured assemblies employing flexible hose shall use hose and flexible connectors with a minimum burst gauge pressure of 6895 kPa (1000 psi).

5.1.6.6 The manufacturer of the assembly shall provide documentation certifying that the flexible hose assembly has a minimum burst gauge pressure of 6895 kPa (1000 psi).

Δ **5.1.6.7** Components of manufactured assemblies shall have a flame spread index of not greater than 200 when tested in accordance with ASTM E84, *Standard Test Method for Surface Burning Characteristics of Building Materials,* or UL 723, *Test for Surface Burning Characteristics of Building Materials,* or shall comply with the requirements for heat release in accordance with NFPA 286 as described in Section 10.2 of NFPA *101.*

5.1.6.8 Manufactured assemblies employing flexible hose or tubing shall be attached to the pipelines using station outlets/inlets.

5.1.6.9 Manufactured assemblies employing hose or flexible connectors, where the station outlet/inlet attached to the piping is not fully and immediately accessible (i.e., cannot be manipulated without the removal of panels, doors, and so forth), shall have station outlets/inlets with the following additional characteristics:

(1) They shall be gas-specific connections with positive locking mechanisms that ensure the connector is firmly seated and cannot detach without intentional actuation of the release (e.g., D.I.S.S. connectors).
(2) In pressure gases, they shall be permitted to omit the secondary valve (or assembly) required in 5.1.5.2.
(3) In vacuum and WAGD, they shall be permitted to omit both primary and secondary valves (or assemblies) for minimum restriction to flow.
(4) They shall be provided with a second terminal at which the user connects and disconnects that complies with 5.1.5.

5.1.6.10 Hose or flexible connectors employed in manufactured assemblies shall be labeled by stenciling or adhesive markers that identify the patient medical gas, the medical support gas, or the vacuum system and include the following:

(1) Name of the gas or vacuum system or the chemical symbol in accordance with Table 5.1.11
(2) Gas or vacuum system color code in accordance with Table 5.1.11
(3) Where positive-pressure piping systems operate at pressures other than the standard gauge pressure in Table 5.1.11, the operating pressure in addition to the name of the gas
(4) Recommended or required replacement date based on manufacture date

5.1.6.11 Station outlets/inlets installed in manufactured assemblies connected to the pipeline by brazing shall comply with 5.1.5.

5.1.6.12 The installation of manufactured assemblies shall be tested in accordance with 5.1.12.

5.1.7* Surface-Mounted Medical Gas Rails (MGR).

5.1.7.1 Medical gas rail (MGR) assemblies shall be permitted to be installed where multiple uses of medical gases and vacuum at a single patient location are required or anticipated.

5.1.7.2 MGR assemblies shall be entirely visible in the room, not passing into or through walls, partitions, and so forth.

5.1.7.3 MGR assemblies shall be made of materials with a melting point of at least 538°C (1000°F).

5.1.7.4 MGR assemblies shall be cleaned per 5.1.10.1.1.

5.1.7.5 Station outlets or inlets shall not be placed on the ends of MGR assemblies.

5.1.7.6 Openings for station outlets/inlets in the MGR shall be gas-specific.

5.1.7.7 Openings in the MGR not occupied by station outlets/inlets (e.g., for future use) shall be capped or plugged so that a special tool is required for removal (i.e., cannot be removed by a wrench, pliers, a screwdriver, or other common tool).

5.1.7.8 MGR assemblies shall connect to the pipeline through fittings that are brazed to the pipeline.

5.1.7.9 Where the pipeline and the MGR assembly are of dissimilar metals, the connections shall be plated or otherwise protected from interaction between the metals.

5.1.7.10 The installation of the MGR shall be tested in accordance with 5.1.12.

5.1.8 Pressure and Vacuum Indicators.

5.1.8.1 General.

5.1.8.1.1 Pressure indicators and manometers for medical gas piping systems shall be cleaned for oxygen service.

5.1.8.1.2 Gauges shall comply with ASME B40.100, *Pressure Gauges and Gauge Attachments.*

5.1.8.1.3* The scale range of positive pressure analog indicators shall be such that the normal operating pressure is within the middle third of the total range [e.g., an indicator of 0 to 2070 kPa (0 to 300 psi) would have a lower third of 0 to 690 kPa (0 to 100 psig), a middle third of 690 kPa to 1380 kPa (100 psig to 200 psig), and a top third of 1380 kPa to 2070 kPa (200 psig to 300 psig)].

5.1.8.1.4 The accuracy of digital indicators shall be ±5 percent of the operating pressure at which they are used.

5.1.8.1.5 The scale range of vacuum indicators shall be 0 to 760 mm (0 to 30 in.) gauge HgV. Indicators with a normal range display shall indicate normal only above 300 mm (12 in.) gauge HgV.

5.1.8.1.6 Indicators adjacent to master alarm actuators and area alarms shall be labeled to identify the name of, or chemical symbol for, the particular piping system that they monitor.

N **5.1.8.1.7** Pressure and vacuum indicators used for testing shall be in accordance with 5.1.12.1.14.

5.1.8.2 Locations.

5.1.8.2.1 Pressure/vacuum indicators shall be readable from a standing position.

5.1.8.2.2 Pressure/vacuum indicators shall be provided at the following locations, as a minimum:

(1) Adjacent to the alarm-initiating device for source main line pressure and vacuum alarms in the master alarm system

(2) At or in area alarm panels to indicate the pressure/vacuum at the alarm-activating device for each system that is monitored by the panel

(3) On the station outlet/inlet side of zone valves

5.1.8.2.3 All pressure-sensing devices and main line pressure gauges downstream of the source valves shall be provided with a gas-specific demand check fitting to facilitate service testing or replacement.

5.1.8.2.3.1 Gas-specific demand check fittings shall not be required on zone valve pressure indicators.

5.1.8.2.4 Demand check fittings shall be provided for all monitors.

5.1.9 Category 1 Warning Systems.

5.1.9.1 General. All master, area, and local alarm systems used for medical gas and vacuum systems shall include the following:

(1) Separate visual indicators for each condition monitored, except as permitted in 5.1.9.2.4(10) for local alarms that are displayed on master alarm panels

(2) Visual indicators that remain in alarm until the situation that has caused the alarm is resolved

(3) Cancelable audible indication of each alarm condition that produces a sound with a minimum level of 80 dBA at 0.92 m (3 ft)

(4) Means to indicate a lamp or LED failure and audible failure

(5) Visual and audible indication that the communication with an alarm-initiating device is disconnected

(6) Labeling of each indicator, indicating the condition monitored

(7) Labeling of each alarm panel for its area of surveillance

(8) Reinitiating of the audible signal if another alarm condition occurs while the audible alarm is silenced

(9) Power for master alarms, area alarms, sensors, and switches from the life safety branch of the essential electrical system as described in Chapter 6

(10) Power for local alarms, dew point sensors, and carbon monoxide sensors permitted to be from the same essential electrical branch as is used to power the air compressor system

(11) Where used for communications, wiring from switches or sensors that is supervised or protected as required by 517.30(C)(3) of *NFPA 70* for life safety and critical branches circuits in which protection is any of the following types:

  (a) Conduit
  (b) Free air
  (c) Wire
  (d) Cable tray
  (e) Raceways

(12) Communication devices that do not use electrical wiring for signal transmission and are supervised such that failure of communication initiates an alarm

(13) Assurance by the responsible authority of the facility that the labeling of alarms, where room numbers or designations are used, is accurate and up-to-date

(14) Provisions for automatic restart after a power loss of 10 seconds (e.g., during generator start-up) without giving false signals or requiring manual reset

(15) Alarm switches/sensors installed so as to be removable and accessible for service and testing

5.1.9.2 Master Alarms. A master alarm system shall be provided to monitor the operation and condition of the source of supply, the reserve source (if any), and the pressure in the main lines of each medical gas and vacuum piping system.

5.1.9.2.1 The master alarm system shall consist of two or more alarm panels located in at least two separate locations, as follows:

(1) One master alarm panel shall be located in the office or work space of the on-site individual responsible for the maintenance of the medical gas and vacuum piping systems.

(2) In order to ensure continuous surveillance of the medical gas and vacuum systems while the facility is in operation, the second master alarm panel shall be located in an area of continuous observation (e.g., the telephone switchboard, security office, or other continuously staffed location).

5.1.9.2.2 A centralized computer system shall be permitted to be substituted for one of the master alarms required in 5.1.9.2.1 if the computer system complies with 5.1.9.3.

5.1.9.2.3 The master alarm panels required in 5.1.9.2.1 shall communicate directly to the alarm-initiating devices that they monitor.

5.1.9.2.3.1 If communication is achieved by wires, the following shall apply:

(A) Each of the two mandatory alarms shall be wired independently to the initiating device(s) for each signal.

(B) The wiring between each mandatory alarm(s) and the initiating device(s) shall not utilize common conductors that, if interrupted, would disable more than one signal.

(C) Each set of wires (in whatever number as required by the alarm) shall run to the initiating device(s) without interruption other than in-line splices necessary to complete the necessary length of wire.

(D) Where initiating devices are remote from the building and the wiring is to run underground in compliance with *NFPA 70*, the following exceptions shall be permitted to be used:

(1) Wiring from the initiating device and through the underground section shall be permitted to be run to a junction box located where the wiring first enters the building.

(2) A single set of wires complying with 5.1.9.2.3.1(B) and 5.1.9.2.3.1(C) for each signal shall be permitted to connect the initiating device and the junction box.

(3) Between the junction box and the two mandatory alarm panels, wiring shall comply with 5.1.9.2.3.1(A) through 5.1.9.2.3.1(C), 5.1.9.2.3.4, and 5.1.9.2.3.5 in all respects.

5.1.9.2.3.2 If communication is achieved by means other than wires, the following shall apply:

(A) Each of the mandatory alarms shall communicate independently to the initiating device(s) for each signal.

(B) The means of communication between each mandatory alarm(s) and the initiating device(s) shall not utilize a common communication device that, if interrupted, would disable the signal from another initiating device(s).

5.1.9.2.3.3 A single initiating device shall be permitted to actuate multiple master alarms.

5.1.9.2.3.4 The mandatory master alarm panels shall not be arranged such that failure of either panel would disable any signal on the other panel.

5.1.9.2.3.5 Where a relay is required to ensure correct operation of an initiating device, the control power for the relay shall not be such that disabling any master alarm panel would disable the relay.

5.1.9.2.3.6 Master alarm signals shall not be relayed from one master alarm panel to another.

5.1.9.2.3.7 Where multi-pole alarm relays are used to isolate the alarm-initiating signals to master alarm panels, the control power source for the relays shall be independent of any of the master alarm panels.

5.1.9.2.3.8 Multiple master alarms shall be permitted to monitor a single initiating device.

Δ **5.1.9.2.4** Master alarm panels for medical gas and vacuum systems shall each include the following signals:

(1) Alarm indication when or just before changeover occurs in a medical gas system that is supplied by a manifold or other alternating-type bulk system that has, as a part of its normal operation, a changeover from one portion of the operating supply to another

(2) Alarm indication for a cryogenic fluid central supply system when the main supply reaches one average day's supply, indicating low contents

(3) Alarm indication when or just before changeover to the reserve supply occurs in a medical gas system that consists of one or more units that continuously supply the piping system while another unit remains as the reserve supply and operates only in an emergency

(4) Alarm indication for cylinder reserve pressure low when the content of a cylinder reserve header is reduced below one average day's supply

(5) For cryogenic fluid central supply systems, alarm indication when or at a predetermined set point before the reserve supply contents fall to one average day's supply, indicating low reserve

(6) Where a cryogenic liquid storage unit is used as a reserve for a cryogenic fluid central supply system, alarm indication when the gas pressure available in the reserve unit is below that required for the medical gas system to function

(7) Alarm indication when the pressure in the main line of each separate medical gas system increases 20 percent from the normal operating pressure

(8) Alarm indication when the pressure in the main line of each separate medical gas system decreases 20 percent from the normal operating pressure

(9) Alarm indication when the medical–surgical vacuum pressure in the main line of each vacuum system drops to or below 300 mm (12 in.) gauge HgV

(10) Single alarm indication from the local alarm panel(s) as described in 5.1.3.6.3.12 and 5.1.9.5.3 to indicate when one or more of the conditions being monitored at a site is in alarm

(11) Medical air dew point high alarm from each compressor site to indicate when the line pressure dew point is greater than +2°C (+35°F)

(12) WAGD low alarm when the WAGD vacuum level or flow is below effective operating limits

(13) Instrument air dew point high alarm from each compressor site to indicate when the line pressure dew point is greater than −30°C (−22°F)

(14) Alarm indication if the primary or reserve production stops on a proportioning system

(15) When oxygen is supplied from an oxygen central supply system using concentrators (see 5.1.3.9), the following signals:

(a) For each concentrator supply source used in the oxygen central supply system, alarm indication that oxygen concentration from that oxygen concentrator supply source is below 91 percent

(b) For each oxygen concentrator supply source used in the oxygen central supply system, alarm indication that the isolating valve for that oxygen concentrator supply source is closed and the supply source is isolated

(c) For each cylinder header used as a source, alarm indication that the header is in use

(d) For each cylinder header used as a source, alarm indication that the cylinder contents are below one average day's supply

(e) If the supply source in use changes because of a failure to appropriately supply the system, alarm indication that an unexpected oxygen supply change has occurred

(f) Alarm indication that the pressure in the common line on the source side of the line pressure controls is low

(g) Alarm indication that the oxygen concentration from the central supply system is below 91 percent

(16) For combined medical-surgical vacuum/WAGD systems that are monitored for oxygen concentration, an alarm indication when the concentration of oxygen exceeds 23.6 percent

5.1.9.2.5 The alarm indications required in 5.1.9.2.4(7) and 5.1.9.2.4(9) shall originate from sensors installed in the main lines immediately downstream (on the patient or use side) of the source valves. Where it is necessary to install a main line valve in addition to a source valve (see 5.1.4.3), the sensors shall be located downstream (on the patient or use side) of the main valve.

5.1.9.3 Master Alarms by Computer Systems. Computer systems used as substitute master alarms as required by 5.1.9.2.1(2) shall have the mechanical and electrical characteristics described in 5.1.9.3.1 and the programming characteristics described in 5.1.9.3.2.

5.1.9.3.1 Computer systems used to substitute for alarms shall have the following mechanical and electrical characteristics:

(1) The computer system shall be in continuous uninterrupted operation and provided with power supplies as needed to ensure such reliability.
(2) The computer system shall be continuously attended by responsible individuals or shall provide remote signaling of responsible parties (e.g., through pagers, telephone autodialers, or other such means).
(3) Where computer systems rely on signal interface devices (e.g., electronic interfaces, other alarm panels, 4 mA to 20 mA cards), such interfaces shall be supervised such that failure of the device(s) shall initiate an alarm(s).
(4) If the computer system does not power the signaling switches/sensors from the same power supply required in 5.1.9.3.1(1), the power supply for the signaling switches/sensors shall be powered from the life safety branch of the essential electrical system as described in Chapter 6.
(5) Computer systems shall be permitted to communicate directly to the sensors/switches in 5.1.9.2.3 in the same manner as an alarm panel if operation of another alarm panel(s) is not impaired.
(6) Communication from the computer system to the signaling switches or sensors shall be supervised such that failure of communication shall initiate an alarm.
(7) Computer systems shall be provided with an audio alert per 5.1.9.1(3), except the audio alert shall be permitted to be only as loud as needed to alert the system operator.
(8) The facility shall ensure compliance with 5.1.9.1(13).

5.1.9.3.2 The operating program for computer systems used to substitute for alarms shall include the following:

(1) The medical gas alarm shall be allocated the priority of a life safety signal.
(2) A medical gas alarm signal shall interrupt any other activity of a lesser priority to run the alarm algorithm(s).
(3) The alarm algorithm shall include activation of an audible alert, activation of any remote signaling protocol, and display of the specific condition in alarm.
(4) The alarm algorithm shall provide for compliance with 5.1.9.1(1) through 5.1.9.1(5), and 5.1.9.1(8).

Δ 5.1.9.4* Area Alarms. Area alarm panels shall be provided to monitor all medical gas, medical–surgical vacuum, and piped WAGD systems supplying the following:

(1) Anesthetizing locations
(2)* Category 1 spaces

5.1.9.4.1* Area alarms shall be located at a nurse's station or other similar location that will provide for surveillance.

5.1.9.4.2 Area alarm panels for medical gas systems shall have separate visual indicators for an alarm condition when either of the following occurs:

(1) The pressure in the main line of each separate medical gas system increases 20 percent from the normal operating pressure.
(2) The pressure in the main line of each separate medical gas system decreases 20 percent from the normal operating pressure.

5.1.9.4.3 Area alarm panels for medical–surgical vacuum systems shall indicate if the vacuum in the area drops to or below 300 mm (12 in.) gauge HgV.

5.1.9.4.4* Alarm sensors for area alarms shall be located as follows:

(1)* Category 1 spaces, other than anesthetizing locations addressed in 5.1.9.4.4(2), shall have the alarm sensors installed on the patient or use side of each of the individual zone valves.
(2)* Anesthetizing locations, including those that are part of a group of anesthetizing locations, shall have the sensors installed in either of the following locations:
   (a) On the source side of each group of anesthetizing location zone valves on the same branch line
   (b) On the patient or use side of each of the individual zone valves

5.1.9.4.5 One area alarm panel shall be acceptable to monitor multiple rooms located within an immediate vicinity meeting the requirements of 5.1.9.4.4(2).

5.1.9.4.6 Area alarm panels for medical gas systems shall provide visual and audible indication in the event a mismatch occurs between the transducer(s) and its associated circuit board(s).

5.1.9.5* Local Alarms. Local alarms shall be installed to monitor the function of the air compressor system(s), medical–surgical vacuum pump system(s), WAGD systems, instrument air systems, and proportioning systems.

5.1.9.5.1 The signals referenced in 5.1.9.5.3 shall be permitted to be located as follows:

(1) On or in the control panel(s) for the central supply system or supply source being monitored
(2) Within a monitoring device (e.g., dew point monitor or carbon monoxide monitor)
(3) On a separate alarm panel(s)

5.1.9.5.2 If there is more than one central supply system, for a specific gas or vacuum pipeline or more than one central supply system and pipeline for the same gas in the building, then it shall be necessary for each location to have separate local alarms per 5.1.9.5.3 and signals at the master panels per 5.1.9.2.4.

5.1.9.5.3 The following functions shall be monitored at each local alarm site:

(1) Low medical air reserve capacity, to indicate when the medical air source is operating under a demand that could not be managed if one compressor ceased to operate
(2) High carbon monoxide level, to indicate when the carbon monoxide level in the medical air system is 10 ppm or higher
(3) Medical air dew point high, to indicate when the line pressure dew point is greater than +2°C (+35°F)
(4) Low medical vacuum reserve capacity, to indicate when the medical vacuum source is operating under a demand that could not be managed if one pump ceased to operate
(5) Low WAGD reserve capacity, to indicate when the WAGD source is operating under a demand that could not be managed if one producer ceased to operate
(6) Instrument air dew point high, to indicate when the line pressure dew point is greater than −30°C (−22°F)
(7) Low instrument air reserve capacity, if instrument air is provided by a source with more than one compressor, to

indicate when the instrument air source is operating under a demand that could not be managed if one compressor ceased to operate

(8) For compressor systems using liquid ring compressors or compressors with water-cooled components, high water in the receiver tank, to indicate when the water level in the receiver tank has reached a level determined to be detrimental to the operation of the system

(9) For compressor systems using liquid ring compressors, high water in the separator

(10) For compressor systems using other than liquid ring compressors, high discharge air temperature

(11) Proportioning systems high/low indicator when the oxygen concentration is outside the 19.5 percent to 23.5 percent oxygen range

(12) Proportion systems reserve system in operation

(13) When oxygen is supplied from an oxygen central supply system using concentrators (see 5.1.3.9), the following signals shall be provided at the system's local alarm site(s):

(a) For each cylinder header used as a source, an alarm indication that the header is in use

(b) For each cylinder header used as a source, an alarm indication that the cylinder contents are below one average day's supply

(c) If the source in use changes because of a failure to appropriately supply the system, an alarm indication indicating an unexpected oxygen supply change has occurred

(d) An alarm indication that the pressure in the common line on the source side of the line pressure controls is low

(e) An alarm indication that the oxygen concentration from the supply system is below 91 percent

5.1.10 Category 1 Distribution.

5.1.10.1 Piping Materials for Field-Installed Positive Pressure Medical Gas Systems.

5.1.10.1.1 Tubes, valves, fittings, station outlets, and other piping components in medical gas systems shall have been cleaned for oxygen service by the manufacturer prior to installation in accordance with the mandatory requirements of CGA G-4.1, *Cleaning Equipment for Oxygen Service*, except that fittings shall be permitted to be cleaned by a supplier or agency other than the manufacturer.

5.1.10.1.2 Each length of tube shall be delivered plugged or capped by the manufacturer and kept sealed until prepared for installation.

5.1.10.1.3 Fittings, valves, and other components shall be delivered sealed and labeled and kept sealed until prepared for installation.

5.1.10.1.4* Tubes shall be one of the following:

(1) Hard-drawn seamless copper in accordance with ASTM B819, *Standard Specification for Seamless Copper Tube for Medical Gas Systems*, medical gas tube, Type L, except Type K shall be used where operating pressures are above a gauge pressure of 1275 kPa (185 psi) and the pipe sizes are larger than DN80 [NPS 3 (3⅛ in. O.D.)].

(2)* Listed corrugated medical tubing (CMT) fabricated from copper alloy No. 51000 strip, meeting ASTM B103/B103M, *Standard Specification for Phosphor Bronze Plate,*

Sheet, Strip, and Rolled Bar, with a design margin of 3.5, externally coated with a nonmetallic sheath marked with the manufacturer's marking. The listing shall include testing to demonstrate that CMT systems can be consistently gas-purged with results equivalent to comparable medical gas copper tubing.

5.1.10.1.5 CMT shall have a flame spread index of 25 or less and a smoke developed index of 50 or less as determined by ASTM E84, *Standard Test Method for Surface Burning Characteristics of Building Materials.*

5.1.10.1.6 CMT shall be identified by the manufacturer as suitable for oxygen service at a minimum of every 0.92 m (3 ft).

5.1.10.1.7 ASTM B819, *Standard Specification for Seamless Copper Tube for Medical Gas Systems*, medical gas tube shall be identified by the manufacturer's markings "OXY," "MED," "OXY/MED," "OXY/ACR," or "ACR/MED" in blue (Type L) or green (Type K).

5.1.10.1.8 The installer shall furnish documentation certifying that all installed piping materials comply with the requirements of 5.1.10.1.1.

5.1.10.2 Piping Materials for Field-Installed Medical–Surgical Vacuum and WAGD Systems.

5.1.10.2.1 Tubes for Vacuum and WAGD Systems at Vacuums Greater than 125 mm (5 in.) HgV. Piping for vacuum and WAGD systems at vacuums greater than 125 mm (5 in.) HgV shall be constructed of any of the following:

(1) Hard-drawn seamless copper tube in accordance with the following:

(a) ASTM B88, *Standard Specification for Seamless Copper Water Tube*, copper tube (Type K, Type L, or Type M)

(b) ASTM B280, *Standard Specification for Seamless Copper Tube for Air Conditioning and Refrigeration Field Service*, copper ACR tube

(c) ASTM B819, *Standard Specification for Seamless Copper Tube for Medical Gas Systems*, copper medical gas tubing (Type K or Type L)

(2) Stainless steel tube in accordance with the following:

(a) ASTM A269/A269M, *Standard Specification for Seamless and Welded Austenitic Stainless Steel Tubing for General Service*, TP304L or 316L

(b) ASTM A312/A312M, *Standard Specification for Seamless, Welded, and Heavily Cold Worked Austenitic Stainless Steel Pipes*, TP304L or 316L

(c) A312 TP 304L/316L, Sch. 5S pipe, and A403 WP304L/316L, Sch. 5S fittings

(3) CMT meeting the requirements of 5.1.10.1.4(2)

5.1.10.2.2 Vacuum and WAGD Tube Marking Where Required.

Δ **5.1.10.2.2.1** Copper tubing for vacuum or WAGD service that is installed along with any medical gas tubing shall, prior to installation, be prominently labeled or otherwise identified to preclude using materials or installation procedures in the medical gas system that are not suitable for oxygen service.

Δ **5.1.10.2.2.2** If medical gas tube in accordance with ASTM B819, *Standard Specification for Seamless Copper Tube for Medical Gas Systems*, or CMT in accordance with 5.1.10.1.4(2), 5.1.10.1.5, and 5.1.10.1.6 is used for vacuum or WAGD piping, special marking in accordance with 5.1.10.2.2.1 shall not be required.

Δ **5.1.10.2.3 Piping Materials for Field-Installed WAGD.** Piping for WAGD systems operated at no greater than 130 mm (5 in.) HgV shall be constructed of either of the following:

(1) Any materials complying with 5.1.10.2.1
(2) Any noncorroding tube or ductwork suitable to the vacuum level

Δ **5.1.10.2.3.1** WAGD system piping that is joined to the vacuum piping shall be connected at a minimum distance of 1.5 m (5 ft) from any vacuum inlet.

5.1.10.2.3.2* Systems complying with 5.1.10.2.3.1 shall be labeled as indicated in 5.1.11 for both WAGD and vacuum.

5.1.10.3 Joints.

Δ **5.1.10.3.1*** Positive pressure patient gas systems, medical support gas systems, vacuum systems, and WAGD systems constructed of hard-drawn seamless copper or stainless steel tubing shall have all turns, offsets, and other changes in direction made using fittings or techniques appropriate to any of the following acceptable joining methods:

(1) Brazing, as described in 5.1.10.4
(2) Welding, as described in 5.1.10.5
(3) Memory metal fittings, as described in 5.1.10.6
(4) Axially swaged fittings, as described in 5.1.10.7
(5) Threaded, as described in 5.1.10.8

5.1.10.3.2 Positive pressure patient gas systems, medical support gas systems, vacuum systems, and WAGD systems constructed of CMT shall have turns, offsets, and other changes in direction made by bending the tubing up to the minimum bend radius or by fittings in accordance with 5.1.10.3.1.

5.1.10.3.3 Vacuum systems and WAGD systems fabricated from copper tubing shall be permitted to have branch connections made using mechanically formed, drilled, and extruded tee-branch connections that are formed in accordance with the tool manufacturer's instructions. Such branch connections shall be joined by brazing, as described in 5.1.10.4.

5.1.10.3.4 Branch connections made using mechanically formed, drilled, and extruded tee-branch connections shall be prohibited in CMT systems.

5.1.10.3.5 WAGD systems designed for operation below 130 mm (5 in.) HgV shall be permitted to be joined using any method that will result in a leak-free network when tested per 5.1.12.4.2.

5.1.10.4 Brazed Joints.

5.1.10.4.1 General Requirements.

5.1.10.4.1.1 Fittings shall be wrought copper capillary fittings complying with ASME B16.22, *Wrought Copper and Copper Alloy Solder-Joint Pressure Fittings*, or brazed fittings complying with ANSI/ASME B16.50, *Wrought Copper and Copper Alloy Braze-Joint Pressure Fittings*.

5.1.10.4.1.2 Cast copper alloy fittings shall not be permitted.

5.1.10.4.1.3 Brazed joints shall be made using a brazing alloy that exhibits a melting temperature in excess of 538°C (1000°F) to retain the integrity of the piping system in the event of fire exposure.

5.1.10.4.1.4 Brazed tube joints shall be the socket type.

5.1.10.4.1.5 Filler metals shall bond with and be metallurgically compatible with the base metals being joined.

5.1.10.4.1.6 Filler metals shall comply with ANSI/AWS A5.8M/A5.8, *Specification for Filler Metals for Brazing and Braze Welding*.

5.1.10.4.1.7 Copper-to-copper joints shall be brazed using a copper–phosphorus or copper–phosphorus–silver brazing filler metal (BCuP series) without flux.

5.1.10.4.1.8 Brazing performed between cryogenic fluid central supply system vessels and their vaporizers (i.e., subject to cryogenic exposure) shall be permitted to be brazed using BAg brazing alloy with flux by a brazer qualified to the mandatory requirements of CGA M-1, *Standard for Medical Gas Supply Systems at Health Care Facilities*.

5.1.10.4.1.9 Joints to be brazed in place shall be accessible for necessary preparation, assembly, heating, filler application, cooling, cleaning, and inspection.

5.1.10.4.1.10 Braze joints shall be continuously purged with nitrogen NF.

5.1.10.4.2 Cutting Tube Ends.

5.1.10.4.2.1 Tube ends shall be cut square using a sharp tubing cutter to avoid deforming the tube.

5.1.10.4.2.2 The cutting wheels on tubing cutters shall be free from grease, oil, or other lubricant not suitable for oxygen service.

5.1.10.4.2.3 The cut ends of the tube shall be rolled smooth or deburred with a sharp, clean deburring tool, taking care to prevent chips from entering the tube.

5.1.10.4.3 Cleaning Joints for Brazing.

5.1.10.4.3.1 The interior surfaces of tubes, fittings, and other components that are cleaned for oxygen service shall be stored and handled to avoid contamination prior to assembly and brazing.

5.1.10.4.3.2 The exterior surfaces of tube ends shall be cleaned prior to brazing to remove any surface oxides.

5.1.10.4.3.3 When cleaning the exterior surfaces of tube ends, no matter shall be allowed to enter the tube.

5.1.10.4.3.4 If the interior surfaces of fitting sockets become contaminated prior to brazing, they shall be recleaned for oxygen in accordance with 5.1.10.4.3.10 and be cleaned for brazing with a clean, oil-free, stainless steel or brass wire brush.

5.1.10.4.3.5 Clean, nonshedding, abrasive pads shall be used to clean the exterior surfaces of the tube ends.

5.1.10.4.3.6 The use of steel wool or sand cloth shall be prohibited.

5.1.10.4.3.7 The cleaning process shall not result in grooving of the surfaces to be joined.

5.1.10.4.3.8 After being abraded, the surfaces shall be wiped using a clean, lint-free white cloth.

5.1.10.4.3.9 Tubes, fittings, valves, and other components shall be visually examined internally before being joined to verify that they have not become contaminated for oxygen service and that they are free of obstructions or debris.

5.1.10.4.3.10 The interior surfaces of tube ends, fittings, and other components that were cleaned for oxygen service by the manufacturer, but that became contaminated prior to being installed, shall be permitted to be recleaned on-site by the installer by thoroughly scrubbing the interior surfaces with a clean, hot water–alkaline solution, such as sodium carbonate or trisodium phosphate, using a solution of 450 g (1 lb) of sodium carbonate or trisodium phosphate to 11 L (3 gal) of potable water, and thoroughly rinsing them with clean, hot, potable water.

5.1.10.4.3.11 Other aqueous cleaning solutions shall be permitted to be used for on-site recleaning permitted in 5.1.10.4.3.10, provided that they are in accordance with the mandatory requirements of CGA G-4.1, *Cleaning Equipment for Oxygen Service.*

5.1.10.4.3.12 Material that has become contaminated internally and is not clean for oxygen service shall not be installed.

5.1.10.4.3.13 Joints shall be brazed within 8 hours after the surfaces are cleaned for brazing.

5.1.10.4.4 Brazing Dissimilar Metals.

5.1.10.4.4.1 Flux shall only be used when brazing dissimilar metals, such as copper and bronze or brass, using a silver (BAg series) brazing filler metal.

5.1.10.4.4.2 Surfaces shall be cleaned for brazing in accordance with 5.1.10.4.3.

5.1.10.4.4.3 Flux shall be applied sparingly to minimize contamination of the inside of the tube with flux.

5.1.10.4.4.4 The flux shall be applied and worked over the cleaned surfaces to be brazed using a stiff bristle brush to ensure complete coverage and wetting of the surfaces with flux.

5.1.10.4.4.5 Where possible, short sections of copper tube shall be brazed onto the noncopper component, and the interior of the subassembly shall be cleaned of flux prior to installation in the piping system.

5.1.10.4.4.6 On joints DN20 (NPS ¾) (⅞ in. O.D.) size and smaller, flux-coated brazing rods shall be permitted to be used in lieu of applying flux to the surfaces being joined.

5.1.10.4.5* Nitrogen Purge.

5.1.10.4.5.1 When brazing, joints shall be continuously purged with oil-free, dry nitrogen NF to prevent the formation of copper oxide on the inside surfaces of the joint.

5.1.10.4.5.2 The source of the purge gas shall be monitored, and the installer shall be audibly alerted when the source content is low.

5.1.10.4.5.3 The purge gas flow rate shall be controlled by the use of a pressure regulator and flowmeter, or combination thereof.

5.1.10.4.5.4 Pressure regulators alone shall not be used to control purge gas flow rates.

5.1.10.4.5.5 In order to ensure that all ambient air has been removed from the pipeline prior to brazing, an oxygen analyzer shall be used to verify the effectiveness of the purge. The oxygen analyzer shall read below 1 percent oxygen concentration before brazing begins.

5.1.10.4.5.6 During and after installation, openings in the piping system shall be kept sealed to maintain a nitrogen atmosphere within the piping to prevent debris or other contaminants from entering the system.

5.1.10.4.5.7 While a joint is being brazed, a discharge opening shall be provided on the opposite side of the joint from where the purge gas is being introduced.

5.1.10.4.5.8 The flow of purge gas shall be maintained until the joint is cool to the touch.

5.1.10.4.5.9 After the joint has cooled, the purge discharge opening shall be sealed to prevent contamination of the inside of the tube and maintain the nitrogen atmosphere within the piping system.

5.1.10.4.5.10 The final brazed connection of new piping to an existing pipeline containing the system gas shall be permitted to be made without the use of a nitrogen purge.

5.1.10.4.5.11 After a final brazed connection in a positive pressure medical gas pipeline is made without a nitrogen purge, an outlet in the immediate downstream zone of the affected portion(s) of both the new and existing piping shall be tested in accordance with the final tie-in test in 5.1.12.4.9.

5.1.10.4.5.12* When using the autogenous orbital welding process, joints shall be continuously purged inside and outside with inert gas(es) in accordance with the qualified welding procedure.

5.1.10.4.6 Assembling and Heating Brazed Joints.

5.1.10.4.6.1 Tube ends shall be inserted into the socket, either fully or to a mechanically limited depth that is not less than the minimum cup depth (overlap) specified by ANSI/ASME B16.50, *Wrought Copper and Copper Alloy Braze-Joint Pressure Fittings.*

5.1.10.4.6.2 Where flux is permitted, the joint shall be heated slowly until the flux has liquefied.

5.1.10.4.6.3 After flux is liquefied, or where flux is not permitted to be used, the joint shall be heated quickly to the brazing temperature, taking care not to overheat the joint.

5.1.10.4.6.4 Techniques for heating the joint, applying the brazing filler metal, and making horizontal, vertical, and large-diameter joints shall be as stated in sections on applying heat and brazing and horizontal and vertical joints in Chapter VII, "Brazed Joints," in the CDA *Copper Tube Handbook.*

5.1.10.4.7 Inspection of Brazed Joints.

5.1.10.4.7.1 After brazing, the outside of all joints shall be cleaned by washing with water and a wire brush to remove any residue and allow clear visual inspection of the joint.

5.1.10.4.7.2 Where flux has been used, the wash water shall be hot.

5.1.10.4.7.3 Each brazed joint shall be visually inspected after cleaning the outside surfaces.

5.1.10.4.7.4 Joints exhibiting the following conditions shall not be permitted:

(1) Flux or flux residue (when flux or flux-coated BAg series rods are used with dissimilar metals)
(2) Base metal melting or erosion
(3) Unmelted filler metal
(4) Failure of the filler metal to be clearly visible all the way around the joint at the interface between the socket and the tube
(5) Cracks in the tube or component
(6) Cracks in the braze filler metal
(7) Failure of the joint to hold the test pressure under the installer-performed initial pressure test *(see 5.1.12.2.3)* and standing pressure test *(see 5.1.12.2.6 or 5.1.12.2.7)*

5.1.10.4.7.5 Brazed joints that are identified as defective under the conditions of 5.1.10.4.7.4(2) or 5.1.10.4.7.4(5) shall be replaced.

5.1.10.4.7.6 Brazed joints that are identified as defective under the conditions of 5.1.10.4.7.4(1), 5.1.10.4.7.4(3), 5.1.10.4.7.4(4), 5.1.10.4.7.4(6), or 5.1.10.4.7.4(7) shall be permitted to be repaired, except that no joint shall be reheated more than once before being replaced.

5.1.10.5 Welded Joints.

5.1.10.5.1 Gas Tungsten Arc Welding (GTAW) for Copper and Stainless Tube.

5.1.10.5.1.1 Welded joints for medical gas and medical–surgical vacuum systems shall be permitted to be made using a gas tungsten arc welding (GTAW) autogenous orbital procedure.

5.1.10.5.1.2 The GTAW autogenous orbital procedure and the welder qualification procedure shall be qualified in accordance with Section IX, "Welding and Brazing Qualifications," of the ASME *Boiler and Pressure Vessel Code.*

5.1.10.5.1.3 Welder qualification procedures shall include a bend test and a tensile test in accordance with Section IX, "Welding and Brazing Qualifications," of the ASME *Boiler and Pressure Vessel Code* on each tube size diameter.

5.1.10.5.1.4 Each welder shall qualify to a welding procedure specification (WPS) for each tube diameter.

5.1.10.5.1.5* GTAW autogenous orbital welded joints shall be purged during welding with a commercially available mixture of 75 percent helium (±5 percent) and 25 percent argon (±5 percent).

5.1.10.5.1.6 The shield gas shall be as required in 5.1.10.5.1.5.

5.1.10.5.1.7 Test coupons shall be welded and inspected, as a minimum, at start of work and every 4 hours thereafter, or when the machine is idle for more than 30 minutes, and at the end of the work period.

5.1.10.5.1.8 Test coupons shall be inspected on the I.D. and O.D. by a qualified quality control inspector.

5.1.10.5.1.9 Test coupons shall also be welded at change of operator, weld head, welding power supply, or gas source.

5.1.10.5.1.10 All production welds shall be visually inspected on the O.D. by the operator, and any obvious weld failures shall be cut out and re-welded.

5.1.10.5.2 Welding for Stainless Tube.

5.1.10.5.2.1 Stainless tube shall be welded using metal inert gas (MIG) welding, tungsten inert gas (TIG) welding, or other welding techniques suited to joining stainless tube.

5.1.10.5.2.2 Welders shall be qualified to Section IX, "Welding and Brazing Qualifications," of the ASME *Boiler and Pressure Vessel Code.*

5.1.10.6 Memory Metal Fittings.

5.1.10.6.1 Memory metal fittings having a temperature rating not less than 538°C (1000°F) and a pressure rating not less than 2070 kPa (300 psi) shall be permitted to be used to join copper or stainless steel tube.

5.1.10.6.2 Memory metal fittings shall be installed by qualified technicians in accordance with the manufacturer's instructions.

5.1.10.7 Axially Swaged Fittings.

5.1.10.7.1 Axially swaged fittings providing metal-to-metal seals, suitable for service at 2070 kPa (300 psig) and able to withstand a temperature of 538°C (1000°F) and that, when complete, are permanent and nonseparable, shall be permitted to be used to join copper or stainless steel tube.

5.1.10.7.2 Axially swaged fittings shall be installed by qualified technicians in accordance with the manufacturer's instructions.

5.1.10.8 Threaded Fittings. Threaded fittings shall meet the following criteria:

(1) They shall be limited to connections for pressure and vacuum indicators, alarm devices, gas-specific demand check fittings, and source equipment on the source side of the source valve.
(2) They shall be tapered pipe threads complying with ASME B1.20.1, *Pipe Threads, General Purpose, Inch.*
(3)* They shall be made up with polytetrafluoroethylene (PTFE) tape or other thread sealant recommended for oxygen service, with sealant applied to the male threads only and care taken to ensure sealant does not enter the pipe.

5.1.10.9 Special Fittings.

5.1.10.9.1 Listed or approved metallic gas tube fittings that, when made up, provide a permanent joint having the mechanical, thermal, and sealing integrity of a brazed joint shall be permitted to be used.

Δ **5.1.10.9.2* Fittings with Internal Seals.** Fittings with internal seals shall be permitted where they meet all of the following requirements:

(1) The fittings shall be brass, bronze, or copper.
(2) All materials used shall comply with 5.1.3.5.4.
(3) Internal seals, insulators, and other polymeric materials shall be limited only to those parts essential for sealing or creating the dielectric break.
(4) Internal seals, insulators, and other elastomeric materials shall be replaceable.
(5) The fittings shall be cleaned for oxygen when used for patient gases or medical support gases.
(6) The fittings shall be installed only where visible and accessible, allowing for testing and servicing.

5.1.10.10 Prohibited Joints. The following joints shall be prohibited throughout medical gas and vacuum distribution pipeline systems:

(1) Flared and compression-type connections, including connections to station outlets and inlets, alarm devices, and other components
(2) Other straight-threaded connections, including unions
(3) Pipe-crimping tools used to permanently stop the flow of medical gas and vacuum piping
(4) Removable and nonremovable push-fit fittings that employ a quick assembly push fit connector

5.1.10.11 Pipe Sizing and System Design.

5.1.10.11.1 Pipe Sizing.

N **5.1.10.11.1.1** The system designer shall size the piping such that calculated pressure or vacuum losses across the piping as designed do not exceed 10 percent of the intended operating pressure or vacuum at the source valve.

N **5.1.10.11.1.2** The pressure drop calculations required by 5.1.10.11.1.1 shall become part of the facility's permanent records.

Δ **5.1.10.11.1.3** The design and installation of piping shall meet the following requirements:

(1) Mains and branches supplying medical gas to more than a single terminal shall not be smaller than DN15 (NPS ½) (⅝ in. O.D.) size.
(2) Mains and branches supplying medical vacuum to more than a single terminal shall not be smaller than DN20 (NPS ¾) (⅞ in. O.D.) size.
(3) Mains and branches supplying WAGD or support gases to more than a single terminal shall not be smaller than DN15 (NPS ½) (⅝ in O.D.) size.
(4) Drops to individual terminals shall not be smaller than DN15 (NPS ½) (⅝ in. O.D.) size.
(5) Runouts to pressure sensing devices shall be permitted to be DN8 (NPS ¼) (⅜ in. O.D.) size.

5.1.10.11.2 Protection of Piping. Piping shall be protected against freezing, corrosion, and physical damage.

5.1.10.11.2.1 Piping exposed in corridors and other areas where subject to physical damage from the movement of carts, stretchers, portable equipment, or vehicles shall be protected.

5.1.10.11.2.2 Piping underground within buildings or embedded in concrete floors or walls shall be installed in a continuous conduit.

5.1.10.11.3 Location of Piping.

5.1.10.11.3.1 Piping risers shall be permitted to be installed in pipe shafts if protected from physical damage, effects of excessive heat, corrosion, or contact with oil.

5.1.10.11.3.2 Piping shall not be installed in kitchens, stairwells, elevator shafts, elevator machine rooms, areas with open flames, electrical service equipment over 600 volts, and areas prohibited under *NFPA 70* except for the following locations:

(1) Room locations for medical air compressor supply systems and medical–surgical vacuum pump supply systems
(2) Room locations for secondary distribution circuit panels and breakers having a maximum voltage rating of 600 volts

5.1.10.11.3.3 Medical gas piping shall be permitted to be installed in the same service trench or tunnel as fuel gas lines, fuel oil lines, electrical lines, steam lines, and similar utilities if the space is ventilated (naturally or mechanically) and the ambient temperature around the medical gas piping is limited to 54°C (130°F) maximum.

5.1.10.11.3.4 Medical gas piping shall not be located where subject to contact with oil, including a possible flooding area in the case of a major oil leak.

5.1.10.11.4 Pipe Support.

5.1.10.11.4.1 Piping shall be supported from the building structure.

5.1.10.11.4.2 Hangers and supports shall comply with and be installed in accordance with MSS SP-58, *Pipe Hangers and Supports — Materials, Design, Manufacture, Selection, Application, and Installation.*

5.1.10.11.4.3 Supports for copper tube shall be sized for copper tube.

5.1.10.11.4.4* Supports for CMT shall be in accordance with the CMT manufacturer's installation instructions.

Δ **5.1.10.11.4.5** In potentially damp locations, copper tube hangers or supports that are in contact with the tube shall be plastic-coated or otherwise electrically insulated from the tube by a material that will not absorb moisture.

5.1.10.11.4.6 Maximum support spacing shall be in accordance with Table 5.1.10.11.4.6.

5.1.10.11.4.7 Where required, medical gas and vacuum piping shall be seismically restrained against earthquakes in accordance with the applicable building code.

5.1.10.11.5 Underground Piping Outside of Buildings.

5.1.10.11.5.1 Buried piping outside of buildings shall be installed below the local level of frost penetration.

5.1.10.11.5.2 The installation procedure for underground piping shall protect the piping from physical damage while being backfilled.

Table 5.1.10.11.4.6 Maximum Pipe Support Spacing

Pipe Size	Hanger Spacing	
	mm	ft
DN8 (NPS ¼) (⅜ in. O.D.)	1520	5
DN10 (NPS ⅜) (½ in. O.D.)	1830	6
DN15 (NPS ½) (⅝ in. O.D.)	1830	6
DN20 (NPS ¾) (⅞ in. O.D.)	2130	7
DN25 (NPS 1) (1⅛ in. O.D.)	2440	8
DN32 (NPS 1¼) (1⅜ in. O.D.)	2740	9
DN40 (NPS 1½) (1⅝ in. O.D.) and larger	3050	10
Vertical risers, all sizes, every floor, but not to exceed	4570	15

5.1.10.11.5.3 If underground piping is protected by a conduit, cover, or other enclosure, the following requirements shall be met:

(1) Access shall be provided at the joints, prior to backfilling over them, for visual inspection and leak testing.
(2) The conduit, cover, or enclosure shall be self-draining and not retain groundwater in prolonged contact with the pipe.

5.1.10.11.5.4 Buried piping that will be subject to surface loads shall be buried at a depth that will protect the piping or its enclosure from excessive stresses.

5.1.10.11.5.5 The minimum backfilled cover above the top of the pipe or its enclosure for buried piping outside of buildings shall comply with the following requirements:

(1) Except as permitted by 5.1.10.11.5.5(2), it shall be 900 mm (36 in.).
(2) It shall be permitted to be reduced to 450 mm (18 in.) where there is no potential for damage from surface loads or surface conditions.

5.1.10.11.5.6 Trenches shall be excavated such that the pipe or its enclosure has firm, substantially continuous bearing on the bottom of the trench.

5.1.10.11.5.7 Backfill shall be clean, free from material that can damage the pipe, and compacted.

5.1.10.11.5.8 A continuous tape or marker placed immediately above the pipe or its enclosure shall clearly identify the pipeline by specific name.

Δ **5.1.10.11.5.9** A continuous warning means shall be provided above the pipeline at approximately one-half the depth of burial.

5.1.10.11.5.10 Where underground piping is installed through a wall sleeve, the outdoor end of the sleeve shall be sealed to prevent the entrance of groundwater into the building.

5.1.10.11.6 Hose and Flexible Connectors.

Δ **5.1.10.11.6.1** Metallic and nonmetallic hose and flexible connectors shall be no longer than necessary and not penetrate or be concealed in walls, floors, ceilings, or partitions.

N **5.1.10.11.6.2** Connections that are part of a manufactured assembly shall be permitted to be concealed above a ceiling in accordance with 5.1.6.9 where access is provided to the ceiling space for inspection and maintenance.

5.1.10.11.6.3 Metallic and nonmetallic flexible connectors shall have a minimum burst pressure, with a gauge pressure of 6895 kPa (1000 psi).

5.1.10.11.6.4 Metallic flexible joints shall be permitted in the pipeline where required for expansion joints, seismic protection, thermal expansion, or vibration control and meet the following requirements:

(1) For all wetted surfaces, made of bronze, copper, or stainless steel
(2) Cleaned at the factory for oxygen service and received on the job site with certification of cleanliness
(3) Suitable for service at 2070 kPa (300 psig) or above and able to withstand temperatures of 538°C (1000°F)

(4) Provided with brazing extensions to allow brazing into the pipeline in accordance with 5.1.10.4
(5) Supported with pipe hangers and supports as required for their additional weight

5.1.10.11.6.5 Metallic flexible joints in accordance with 5.1.10.11.6.4 shall be permitted to be concealed in walls, ceilings, or partitions.

5.1.10.11.7 Prohibited System Interconnections.

Δ **5.1.10.11.7.1** Two or more medical gas or vacuum piping systems shall not be interconnected for installation, testing, or any other reason except as permitted by 5.1.10.11.7.2.

5.1.10.11.7.2 Medical gas and vacuum systems with the same contents shall be permitted to be interconnected with an in-line valve installed between the systems.

5.1.10.11.7.3 Leak testing shall be accomplished by separately charging and testing each individual piping system.

5.1.10.11.8 Manufacturer's Instructions.

5.1.10.11.8.1 The installation of individual components shall comply with the manufacturer's instructions.

5.1.10.11.8.2 The manufacturer's instructions shall include directions and information deemed by the manufacturer to be adequate for attaining proper operation, testing, and maintenance of the medical gas and vacuum systems.

5.1.10.11.8.3 Copies of the manufacturer's instructions shall be left with the system owner.

5.1.10.11.9 Changes in System Use.

5.1.10.11.9.1 Where a positive pressure medical gas piping distribution system originally used or constructed for use at one pressure and for one gas is converted for operation at another pressure or for another gas, the requirements of 5.1.10 shall apply as if the system were new.

5.1.10.11.9.2 A vacuum system shall not be permitted to be converted for use as a gas system.

5.1.10.11.10 Qualification of Installers.

5.1.10.11.10.1 The installation of medical gas and vacuum systems shall be made by qualified, competent technicians who are experienced in performing such installations, including all personnel who actually install the piping system.

Δ **5.1.10.11.10.2** Installers of medical gas and vacuum piped distribution systems, all appurtenant piping supporting pump and compressor source systems, and appurtenant piping supporting source gas manifold systems not including permanently installed bulk source systems shall be certified in accordance with ASSE/IAPMO/ANSI 6010, *Professional Qualifications Standard for Medical Gas Systems Installers.*

5.1.10.11.10.3 CMT systems shall be installed by ASSE 6010–qualified installers using the CMT manufacturer's instructions.

5.1.10.11.10.4 Installers of medical gas and vacuum systems shall not use their certification to oversee installation by noncertified personnel.

5.1.10.11.10.5 Brazing shall be performed by individuals who are qualified in accordance with the provisions of 5.1.10.11.11.

5.1.10.11.10.6 Prior to any installation work, the installer of medical gas and vacuum piping shall provide and maintain documentation on the job site for the qualification of brazing procedures and individual brazers required by 5.1.10.11.11.

5.1.10.11.10.7 Health care organization personnel shall be permitted to install piping systems if all of the requirements of 5.1.10.11.10 are met during the installation.

5.1.10.11.11 Qualification of Brazing Procedures and Brazing.

5.1.10.11.11.1 Brazing procedures and brazer performance for the installation of medical gas and vacuum piping shall be qualified in accordance with either Section IX, "Welding and Brazing Qualifications," of the ASME *Boiler and Pressure Vessel Code*, or AWS B2.2/B2.2M, *Specification for Brazing Procedure and Performance Qualification*, both as modified by 5.1.10.11.11.2 through 5.1.10.11.11.5.

5.1.10.11.11.2 Brazers shall be qualified by visual examination of the test coupon followed by sectioning.

5.1.10.11.11.3 The brazing procedure specification shall address cleaning, joint clearance, overlap, internal purge gas, purge gas flow rate, and filler metal.

Δ **5.1.10.11.11.4** The brazing procedure qualification record and the brazer performance qualification record shall document filler metal used, base metals, cleaning, joint clearance, overlap, internal purge gas and flow rate during brazing of coupon, and absence of internal oxidation in the completed coupon.

5.1.10.11.11.5 Brazing procedures qualified by a technically competent group or agency shall be permitted under the following conditions:

(1) The brazing procedure specification and the procedure qualification records meet the requirements of this code.
(2) The employer obtains a copy of both the brazing procedure specification and the supporting qualification records from the group or agency and signs and dates these records, thereby accepting responsibility for the qualifications that were performed by the group or agency.
(3) The employer qualifies at least one brazer following each brazing procedure specification used.

Δ **5.1.10.11.11.6** An employer shall be permitted to accept the brazer qualification records of a previous employer under the following conditions:

(1) The brazer has been qualified following the same or an equivalent procedure that the new employer uses.
(2) The new employer obtains a copy of the brazer performance qualification test records from the previous employer and signs and dates these records, thereby accepting responsibility for the qualifications performed by the previous employer.

5.1.10.11.11.7 Performance qualifications of brazers shall remain in effect indefinitely, unless the brazer does not braze with the qualified procedure for a period exceeding 6 months or there is a specific reason to question the ability of the brazer.

5.1.10.11.12 Breaching or Penetrating Medical Gas Piping.

5.1.10.11.12.1 Positive pressure patient medical gas piping and medical support gas piping shall not be breached or penetrated by any means or process that will result in residual copper particles or other debris remaining in the piping or affect the oxygen-clean interior of the piping.

5.1.10.11.12.2 The breaching or penetrating process shall ensure that any debris created by the process remains contained within the work area.

5.1.11* Labeling, Identification, and Operating Pressure. Color and pressure requirements shall be in accordance with Table 5.1.11.

5.1.11.1 Pipe Labeling.

5.1.11.1.1 Piping shall be labeled by stenciling or adhesive markers that identify the patient medical gas, the medical support gas, or the vacuum system and include the following:

(1) Name of the gas or vacuum system or the chemical symbol per Table 5.1.11
(2) Gas or vacuum system color code per Table 5.1.11

5.1.11.1.2 Where positive-pressure gas piping systems operate at pressures other than the standard gauge pressure in Table 5.1.11, the operating pressure in addition to the name of the gas shall be labeled.

5.1.11.1.3 Where vacuum systems are used to serve WAGD systems in accordance with 5.1.10.2.3.1, piping in the immediate area of the WAGD system shall be labeled to indicate both systems.

5.1.11.1.4 Pipe labels shall be located as follows:

(1) At intervals of not more than 6.1 m (20 ft)
(2) At least once in or above every room
(3) On both sides of walls or partitions penetrated by the piping
(4) At least once in every story height traversed by risers

5.1.11.1.5 Medical gas piping shall not be painted.

5.1.11.1.6 Labeling of piping for compressor intakes, vacuum exhausts, and relief valve vent lines shall meet the requirements of 5.1.11.1.1 and state the specific function to distinguish them from the patient supply piping.

5.1.11.2 Shutoff Valves.

5.1.11.2.1 Shutoff valves shall be identified with the following:

(1) Name or chemical symbol for the specific medical gas or vacuum system
(2) Gas or vacuum system color code in accordance with Table 5.1.11
(3) Room or areas served
(4) Caution to not close or open the valve except in emergency

5.1.11.2.2 Where positive-pressure gas piping systems operate at pressures other than the standard gauge pressure of 345 kPa to 380 kPa (50 psi to 55 psi) or a gauge pressure of 1100 kPa to 1275 kPa (160 psi to 185 psi) for nitrogen or instrument air, the valve identification shall also include the nonstandard operating pressure.

5.1.11.2.3* Where vacuum systems are used to serve WAGD systems in accordance with 5.1.10.2.3.1, valves that are on the source side of the connection to the WAGD system shall be labeled to indicate both systems.

Δ Table 5.1.11 Standard Designation Colors and Operating Pressures for Gas and Vacuum Systems

Gas Service	Abbreviated Name	Colors (Background/Text)	Standard Gauge Pressure	
			kPa	psi
Medical air	Med air	Yellow/black	345–380	50–55
Carbon dioxide	CO_2	Gray/black or gray/white	345–380	50–55
Helium	He	Brown/white	345–380	50–55
Nitrogen	N_2	Black/white	0–2070	0–300
Nitrous oxide	N_2O	Blue/white	345–380	50–55
Oxygen	O_2	Green/white or white/green	345–380	50–55
Oxygen/carbon dioxide mixtures	$O_2/CO_2n\%$ (n = % of CO_2)	Green/white	345–380	50–55
Medical–surgical vacuum	Med vac	White/black	380 mm to 760 mm (15 in. to 30 in.) HgV	
Waste anesthetic gas disposal	WAGD	Violet/white	Varies with system type	
Medical–surgical vacuum/ WAGD combination	Med–surg/ WAGD	White/black and violet/white	380 mm to 760 mm (15 in. to 30 in.) HgV	
Other mixtures	Gas A%/Gas B%	Colors as above Major gas for background/minor gas for text	None	
Nonmedical air and dental air	—	Yellow and white diagonal stripe/black	None	
Nonmedical vacuum and dental vacuum	—	White and black diagonal stripe/black boxed	None	
Laboratory air	—	Yellow and white checkerboard/black	None	
Laboratory vacuum	—	White and black checkerboard/black boxed	None	
Instrument air	—	Red/white	0–2070	0–300

5.1.11.2.4 Source valves shall be labeled in substance as follows:

SOURCE VALVE
FOR THE (GAS/VACUUM NAME) SERVING (NAME OF THE AREA/BUILDING SERVED BY THE SOURCE VALVE).

5.1.11.2.5 Main line valves shall be labeled in substance as follows:

MAIN LINE VALVE FOR THE (GAS/VACUUM NAME) SERVING (NAME OF THE BUILDING).

5.1.11.2.6 The riser valve(s) shall be labeled in substance as follows:

RISER FOR THE (GAS/VACUUM NAME) SERVING (NAME OF THE AREA/BUILDING SERVED BY THE PARTICULAR RISER).

5.1.11.2.7 The service valve(s) shall be labeled in substance as follows:

SERVICE VALVE FOR THE (GAS/VACUUM NAME) SERVING (NAME OF THE AREA/BUILDING SERVED BY THE PARTICULAR VALVE).

5.1.11.2.8* Zone valve box assemblies shall be labeled with the rooms, areas, or spaces that they control as follows:

ZONE VALVES FOR THE (GAS/VACUUM NAME) SERVING (NAME OF ROOMS OR SPACES SERVED BY THE PARTICULAR VALVE).

Labeling shall either be visible from outside the zone valve box assembly through the cover or be replicated on the outside, but not affixed to the removable cover.

5.1.11.3 Station Outlets and Inlets.

5.1.11.3.1 Station outlets and inlets shall be identified as to the name or chemical symbol for the specific medical gas or vacuum provided and shall include the following:

(1) Name of the gas or vacuum system or the chemical symbol in accordance with Table 5.1.11
(2) Gas or vacuum system color code in accordance with Table 5.1.11

5.1.11.3.1.1 In sleep labs, where the outlet is downstream of a flow control device, the station outlet identification shall include a warning not to use the outlet for ventilating patients.

5.1.11.3.2 Where medical gas systems operate at pressures other than the standard gauge pressure of 345 kPa to 380 kPa (50 psi to 55 psi) or a gauge pressure of 1100 kPa to 1275 kPa (160 psi to 185 psi) for nitrogen, the station outlet identifica-

Shaded text = Revisions.   Δ = Text deletions and figure/table revisions.   • = Section deletions.   *N* = New material.

tion shall include the nonstandard operating pressure in addition to the name of the gas.

5.1.11.4 Alarm Panels.

5.1.11.4.1 Labeling of alarm panels for each indicator shall indicate the condition monitored and its area of surveillance.

5.1.11.4.2* Area alarm panels shall be identified with the following:

(1) Name or chemical symbol of the specific medical gas or vacuum system being monitored
(2) Gas or vacuum system color code, in accordance with Table 5.1.11, of the specific medical gas or vacuum system being monitored
(3) Area(s) monitored by the alarm panel

5.1.11.4.3 Where medical gas systems operate at pressures other than the standard gauge pressure of 345 kPa to 380 kPa (50 psi to 55 psi), or a gauge pressure of 1100 kPa to 1275 kPa (160 psi to 185 psi) for nitrogen or instrument air, the area alarm panel identification shall include the nonstandard operating pressure in addition to the name of the gas.

5.1.11.4.4 Where vacuum systems are used to serve WAGD systems per 5.1.10.2.3.1, an area alarm panel(s) monitoring the area in which the WAGD system is used shall be labeled to indicate both systems.

5.1.11.5 Source Equipment.

5.1.11.5.1 Source equipment shall be labeled or tagged to identify the patient medical gas, the medical support gas, or the vacuum system and include the following information:

(1) Name of the gas or vacuum system
(2) Gas or vacuum system color code
(3) Rooms, areas, or buildings served
(4) Emergency contact information for the department or individual responsible for maintaining the equipment

5.1.11.5.2 Where vacuum systems are used to serve WAGD systems in accordance with 5.1.10.2.3.1, labeling for the medical–surgical vacuum source shall indicate that it serves both systems.

5.1.12* Performance Criteria and Testing — Category 1 (Gases, Medical–Surgical Vacuum, and WAGD).

5.1.12.1 General.

5.1.12.1.1 Inspection and testing shall be performed on all new piped medical gas and vacuum systems, additions, renovations, temporary installations, or repaired systems to ensure, by a documented process and procedure, that all applicable provisions of this document have been adhered to and system integrity has been achieved or maintained.

5.1.12.1.2 Inspection and testing shall include all components of the system, or portions thereof, including, but not limited to, gas bulk source(s); manifolds; compressed air source systems (e.g., compressors, dryers, filters, regulators); source alarms and monitoring safeguards; master alarms; pipelines; isolation valves; area alarms; zone valves; and station inlets (vacuum) and outlets (pressure gases).

Δ **5.1.12.1.3*** All systems that are breached and all components that are subject to additions, renovations, or replacement shall be inspected and tested.

5.1.12.1.4 Systems shall be deemed breached at the point of pipeline intrusion by physical separation or by system component removal, replacement, or addition.

5.1.12.1.5 Breached portions of the systems subject to inspection and testing shall be confined to only the specific altered zone and components in the immediate zone or area that is located upstream for vacuum systems and downstream for pressure gases at the point or area of intrusion and any other areas affected by the breach.

5.1.12.1.6 The inspection and testing reports shall be submitted directly to the party that contracted for the testing, who shall submit the report through channels to the responsible facility authority and any others that are required.

5.1.12.1.7 Reports shall contain detailed listings of all findings and results.

5.1.12.1.8 The responsible facility authority shall review these inspection and testing records prior to the use of all systems to ensure that all findings and results of the inspection and testing have been successfully completed.

5.1.12.1.9 All documentation pertaining to inspections and testing shall be maintained on-site within the facility.

5.1.12.1.10 Before piping systems are initially put into use, the facility authority shall be responsible for ascertaining that the gas/vacuum delivered at the outlet/inlet is that shown on the outlet/inlet label and that the proper connecting fittings are installed for the specific gas/vacuum service.

N **5.1.12.1.11*** New medical gas and vacuum pipeline distribution systems shall not be connected to the existing in-use systems until the initial pressure test is successfully completed in accordance with 5.1.12.2.3.

5.1.12.1.12 Acceptance of the verifier's final report shall be permitted to satisfy the requirements in 5.1.12.1.10.

5.1.12.1.13 The removal of components within a source system for repair and reinstallation, or the replacement of components like for like, shall be treated as new work for the purposes of testing whenever such work involves cutting or brazing new piping, or both.

5.1.12.1.13.1 Where no piping is changed, functional testing shall be performed as follows:

(1) To verify the function of the replaced device
(2) To ensure no other equipment in the system has been adversely impacted

5.1.12.1.13.2 Where no piping is changed, in addition to tests of general function required by 5.1.12.1.13.1, testing shall be performed as follows:

(1) Pressure gas sources shall be tested for compliance with 5.1.12.4.14.2 as applicable to the equipment type.
(2) Medical air and instrument air sources shall be tested to 5.1.12.4.14.3.
(3) Vacuum and WAGD systems shall be tested to 5.1.12.4.14.6.
(4) Alarm systems shall be tested to 5.1.12.4.5.2 and 5.1.12.4.5.3.
(5) All affected components shall be tested as appropriate to that specific component (e.g., a replaced dew point monitor would be tested to 5.1.3.6.3.13).

5.1.12.1.14 The rated accuracy of pressure and vacuum indicators used for testing shall be 1 percent (full scale) or better.

5.1.12.2 Installer-Performed Tests.

5.1.12.2.1 General.

5.1.12.2.1.1 The tests required by 5.1.12.2 shall be performed and documented by the installer prior to the tests listed in 5.1.12.4.

5.1.12.2.1.2 The test gas shall be oil-free, dry nitrogen NF.

5.1.12.2.1.3 Where manufactured assemblies are to be installed, the tests required by 5.1.12.2 shall be performed as follows:

(1) After completion of the distribution piping, but before the standing pressure test
(2) Prior to installation of manufactured assemblies supplied through flexible hose or flexible tubing
(3) At all station outlets/inlets on installed manufactured assemblies supplied through copper tubing

5.1.12.2.2* Initial Piping Blowdown. Piping in medical gas and vacuum distribution systems shall be blown clear by means of oil-free, dry nitrogen NF after installation of the distribution piping but before installation of station outlet/inlet rough-in assemblies and other system components.

5.1.12.2.3 Initial Pressure Test.

5.1.12.2.3.1 Each section of the piping in medical gas and vacuum systems shall be pressure tested.

Δ **5.1.12.2.3.2** Initial pressure tests shall be conducted as follows:

(1) After blowdown of the distribution piping
(2) After installation of station outlet/inlet rough-in assemblies
(3)* Prior to the installation of components of the distribution piping system that would be damaged by the test pressure

5.1.12.2.3.3 The source shutoff valve shall remain closed during the tests specified in 5.1.12.2.3.

5.1.12.2.3.4 The test pressure for pressure gases and vacuum systems shall be 1.5 times the system operating pressure but not less than a gauge pressure of 1035 kPa (150 psi).

5.1.12.2.3.5* The test pressure shall be maintained until each joint has been examined for leakage by means of a leak detectant that is safe for use with oxygen and does not contain ammonia.

5.1.12.2.3.6 Leaks, if any, shall be located, repaired (if permitted), replaced (if required), and retested.

5.1.12.2.4 Initial Cross-Connection Test. It shall be determined that no cross-connections exist between the various medical gas and vacuum piping systems.

5.1.12.2.4.1 All piping systems shall be reduced to atmospheric pressure.

5.1.12.2.4.2 Sources of test gas shall be disconnected from all piping systems, except for the one system being tested.

5.1.12.2.4.3 The system under test shall be charged with oil-free, dry nitrogen NF to a gauge pressure of 345 kPa (50 psi).

5.1.12.2.4.4 After the installation of the individual faceplates with appropriate adapters matching outlet/inlet labels, each individual outlet/inlet in each installed medical gas and vacuum piping system shall be checked to determine that the test gas is being dispensed only from the piping system being tested.

5.1.12.2.4.5 The cross-connection test referenced in 5.1.12.2.4 shall be repeated for each installed medical gas and vacuum piping system.

5.1.12.2.4.6 The proper labeling and identification of system outlets/inlets shall be confirmed during these tests.

5.1.12.2.5 Initial Piping Purge Test. The outlets in each medical gas piping system shall be purged to remove any particulate matter from the distribution piping.

5.1.12.2.5.1 Using appropriate adapters, each outlet shall be purged with an intermittent high-volume flow of test gas until the purge produces no discoloration in a clean white cloth.

5.1.12.2.5.2 The purging required in 5.1.12.2.5.1 shall be started at the closest outlet/inlet to the zone valve and continue to the furthest outlet/inlet within the zone.

5.1.12.2.6 Standing Pressure Test for Positive Pressure Medical Gas Piping. After successful completion of the initial pressure tests under 5.1.12.2.3, medical gas distribution piping shall be subject to a standing pressure test.

5.1.12.2.6.1* Tests shall be conducted after the final installation of station outlet valve bodies, faceplates, and all other distribution system components.

5.1.12.2.6.2 The source valve shall be closed during this test.

5.1.12.2.6.3 The piping systems shall be subjected to a 24-hour standing pressure test using oil-free, dry nitrogen NF.

5.1.12.2.6.4 Test pressures shall be 20 percent above the normal system operating line pressure.

5.1.12.2.6.5* The leakage over the 24-hour test shall not exceed 0.5 percent of the starting pressure [e.g., 2 kPa (0.3 psi) starting at 415 kPa (60 psig)], except that attributed to specific changes in ambient temperature.

5.1.12.2.6.6 Leaks, if any, shall be located, repaired (if permitted) or replaced (if required), and retested.

5.1.12.2.6.7 The 24-hour standing pressure test of the positive-pressure system shall be witnessed by an ASSE 6020 inspector, an ASSE 6030 verifier, or the authority having jurisdiction or its designee. A form indicating that this test has been performed and witnessed shall be provided to the verifier at the start of the tests required in 5.1.12.4.

5.1.12.2.7 Standing Vacuum Test for Vacuum Piping. After successful completion of the initial pressure tests under 5.1.12.2.3, vacuum distribution piping shall be subjected to a standing vacuum test.

5.1.12.2.7.1 Tests shall be conducted after installation of all components of the vacuum system.

5.1.12.2.7.2 The piping systems shall be subjected to a 24-hour standing vacuum test.

5.1.12.2.7.3 Test pressure shall be between 300 mm (12 in.) HgV and full vacuum.

5.1.12.2.7.4 During the test, the source of test vacuum shall be disconnected from the piping system.

5.1.12.2.7.5* The leakage over the 24-hour test shall not exceed 0.5 percent of the starting pressure [e.g., 0.3 mm (0.125 in.) HgV starting at 635 mm (25 in.) HgV] except that attributed to specific changes in ambient temperature.

5.1.12.2.7.6 The 24-hour standing pressure test of the vacuum system shall be witnessed by the authority having jurisdiction or its designee. A form indicating that this test has been performed and witnessed shall be provided to the verifier at the start of the tests required in 5.1.12.4.

5.1.12.2.7.7 Leaks, if any, shall be located, repaired (if permitted) or replaced (if required), and retested.

5.1.12.3 System Inspection.

5.1.12.3.1 General.

5.1.12.3.1.1 System inspections shall be performed prior to concealing piping distribution systems in walls, ceilings, chases, trenches, underground, or otherwise hidden from view.

5.1.12.3.1.2 The test gas shall be nitrogen NF.

5.1.12.3.1.3 Inspections shall be conducted by a party technically competent and experienced in the field of medical gas and vacuum pipeline inspections and testing and meeting the requirements of ASSE/IAPMO/ANSI 6020, *Professional Qualifications Standard for Medical Gas Systems Inspectors*, or ASSE/IAPMO/ANSI 6030, *Professional Qualifications Standard for Medical Gas Systems Verifiers*.

5.1.12.3.1.4 Inspections shall be performed by a party other than the installing contractor.

5.1.12.3.1.5 Where systems have not been installed by in-house personnel, inspections shall be permitted by personnel of the organization who meet the requirements of 5.1.12.3.1.3.

5.1.12.3.2 Inspections.

5.1.12.3.2.1 The initial pressure tests performed by the installing contractor shall be witnessed by an ASSE 6020 inspector, an ASSE 6030 verifier, or the authority having jurisdiction or its designee. A form indicating that this test has been performed and witnessed shall be provided to the verifier at the start of the tests required in 5.1.12.4.

5.1.12.3.2.2 The presence and correctness of labeling and valve tagging required by this code for all concealed components and piping distribution systems shall be inspected.

5.1.12.4 System Verification.

5.1.12.4.1 General.

Δ **5.1.12.4.1.1** Verification tests shall be performed only after all tests required in 5.1.12.2 have been completed.

5.1.12.4.1.2 The test gas shall be oil-free, dry nitrogen NF or the system gas where permitted.

5.1.12.4.1.3 Testing shall be conducted by a party technically competent and experienced in the field of medical gas and vacuum pipeline testing and meeting the requirements of ASSE/IAPMO/ANSI 6030, *Professional Qualifications Standard for Medical Gas Systems Verifiers*, except as required by 5.1.12.4.1.4.

5.1.12.4.1.4 Testing of the cryogenic fluid central supply system shall be conducted by a party technically competent and experienced in the field of cryogenic fluid systems and meeting the requirements of ASSE/IAPMO/ANSI 6035, *Professional Qualifications Standard for Bulk Medical Gas/Cryogenic Fluid Central Supply Systems Verifiers*, in accordance with the mandatory requirements in CGA M-1, *Standard for Medical Gas Supply Systems at Health Care Facilities*.

5.1.12.4.1.5 Testing shall be performed by a party other than the installing contractor.

5.1.12.4.1.6 When systems have not been installed by in-house personnel, testing shall be permitted by personnel of that organization who meet the requirements of 5.1.12.4.1.3.

5.1.12.4.1.7 All tests required under 5.1.12.4 shall be performed after installation of any manufactured assemblies supplied through tubing or flexible hose.

5.1.12.4.1.8 Where there are multiple possible connection points for terminals, each possible position shall be tested independently.

5.1.12.4.1.9 The gas of system designation shall be permitted to be used for all tests, regardless of the size of the system, which include the following:

(1) Standing pressure *(see 5.1.12.4.2)*
(2) Cross-connection *(see 5.1.12.4.3)*
(3) Alarms *(see 5.1.12.4.5)*
(4) Piping purge *(see 5.1.12.4.6)*
(5) Piping particulates *(see 5.1.12.4.7)*

5.1.12.4.2* Standing Pressure Test. Piping systems shall be subjected to a 10-minute standing pressure test at operating line pressure using the following procedure:

(1) After the system is filled with nitrogen or source gas, the source valve and all zone valves shall be closed.
(2) The piping system shall show no decrease in pressure after 10 minutes.
(3) Any leaks found shall be located, repaired, and retested per 5.1.12.2.6.

5.1.12.4.3 Cross-Connection Test. After the closing of walls and completion of the requirements of 5.1.12.2, it shall be determined that no cross-connection of piping systems exists by either of the methods detailed in 5.1.12.4.3.1 or 5.1.12.4.3.2.

5.1.12.4.3.1 Individual Pressurization Method.

(A) All medical gas and vacuum piping systems shall be reduced to atmospheric pressure.

(B) All sources of test gas from all of the medical gas and vacuum systems, with the exception of the one system to be checked, shall be disconnected.

(C) The system being checked shall be pressurized to a gauge pressure of 345 kPa (50 psi).

(D) With adapters matching outlet labels, each individual station outlet/inlet of all medical gas and vacuum systems installed shall be checked to determine that test gas is being dispensed only from the outlets/inlets of the piping system being tested.

(E) The source of test gas shall be disconnected, and the system tested reduced to atmospheric pressure.

(F) Proceed to test each additional piping system until all medical gas and vacuum piping systems are free of cross-connections.

Shaded text = Revisions.   Δ = Text deletions and figure/table revisions.   • = Section deletions.   *N* = New material.

2024 Edition

5.1.12.4.3.2 Pressure Differential Method.

(A) The pressure in all medical gas systems shall be reduced to atmospheric.

(B) The test gas pressure in all medical gas piping systems shall be increased to the values indicated in Table 5.1.12.4.3.2(B), simultaneously maintaining these nominal pressures throughout the test.

(C) Systems with nonstandard operating pressures shall be tested at a gauge pressure of at least 70 kPa (10 psi) higher or lower than any other system being tested.

(D) Any vacuum systems shall be in operation so that these vacuum systems are tested at the same time the medical gas systems are tested.

(E) Following the adjustment of pressures in accordance with 5.1.12.4.3.2(B) and 5.1.12.4.3.2(C), each station outlet for each medical gas system shall be tested using the gas-specific connection for each system with test gauge attached to verify that the correct test pressure/vacuum is present at each outlet/inlet of each system as listed in Table 5.1.12.4.3.2(B).

(F) Each test gauge used in performing this test shall be calibrated with the pressure indicator used for the line pressure regulator used to provide the source pressure.

(G) Each station outlet shall be identified by label (and color marking, if used), and the pressure indicated on the test gauge shall be that listed in Table 5.1.12.4.3.2(B) for the system being tested.

5.1.12.4.4 Valve Test. Valves installed in each medical gas and vacuum piping system shall be tested to verify proper operation and rooms or areas of control.

5.1.12.4.4.1 Records shall be made listing the rooms or areas controlled by each valve for each gas.

5.1.12.4.4.2 The information shall be utilized to assist and verify the proper labeling of the valves.

5.1.12.4.5 Alarm Test.

5.1.12.4.5.1 General.

(A) All warning systems for each medical gas and vacuum system(s) shall be tested to ensure that all components function properly prior to placing the system in service.

Table 5.1.12.4.3.2(B) Alternate Test Pressures

Medical Gas	Pressure (Gauge)	Vacuum (HgV)
Gas mixtures	140 kPa (20 psi)	—
Nitrogen/ instrument air	210 kPa (30 psi)	—
Nitrous oxide	275 kPa (40 psi)	—
Oxygen	345 kPa (50 psi)	—
Medical air	415 kPa (60 psi)	—
Systems at nonstandard pressures	70 kPa (10 psi) greater or less than any other system	—
Vacuum	—	510 mm (20 in.) HgV
WAGD	—	380 mm (15 in.) HgV (if so designed)

(B) Permanent records of these tests shall be maintained.

(C) Warning systems that are part of an addition to an existing piping system shall be tested prior to the connection of the new piping to the existing system.

(D) Tests of warning systems for new installations (initial tests) shall be performed after the cross-connection testing *(see 5.1.12.4.3)*, but before purging the piping *(see 5.1.12.4.6)* and performing the remaining verification tests. *(See 5.1.12.4.7 through 5.1.12.4.14.)*

(E) Initial tests of warning systems that can be included in an addition or extension to an existing piping system shall be completed before connection of the addition to the existing system.

(F) Test gases for the initial tests shall be oil-free, dry nitrogen NF, the gas of system designation, or operating vacuum.

(G) Where computer systems are used as substitutes for a required alarm panel as permitted under 5.1.9.2.2, the computer system shall be included in the alarm tests as modified in 5.1.9.3.

5.1.12.4.5.2 Master Alarms.

(A) The master alarm system tests shall be performed for each of the medical gas and vacuum piping systems.

(B) Permanent records of these tests shall be maintained with those required under 5.1.12.1.7.

(C) The audible and noncancelable visual signals of 5.1.9.1 shall indicate if the pressure in the main line increases or decreases 20 percent from the normal operating pressure.

(D) The operation of all master alarm signals referenced in 5.1.9.2.4 shall be verified.

5.1.12.4.5.3 Area Alarms. The warning signals for all medical gas piping systems shall be tested to verify an alarm condition if the pressure in the piping system increases or decreases 20 percent from the normal operating pressure for positive-pressure gases, or when the vacuum system(s) drops below a gauge pressure of 300 mm (12 in.) HgV.

5.1.12.4.6 Piping Purge Test. In order to remove any traces of particulate matter deposited in the pipelines as a result of construction, a heavy, intermittent purging of the pipeline shall be done.

5.1.12.4.6.1 The appropriate adapter shall be obtained from the facility or manufacturer, and high purge rates of at least 225 Nl/min (8 SCFM) shall be put on each outlet.

5.1.12.4.6.2 After the purge is started, it shall be rapidly interrupted several times until the purge produces no discoloration in a white cloth loosely held over the adapter during the purge.

5.1.12.4.6.3 In order to avoid possible damage to the outlet and its components, this test shall not be conducted using any implement other than the proper adapter.

5.1.12.4.6.4* No pronounced or objectionable odor shall be discernible from any positive pressure outlet.

5.1.12.4.7 Piping Particulate Test. For each positive-pressure gas system, the cleanliness of the piping system shall be verified.

5.1.12.4.7.1 A minimum of 1000 L (35 ft^3) of gas shall be filtered through a clean, white 0.45 micron filter at a minimum flow rate of 100 Nl/min (3.5 SCFM).

5.1.12.4.7.2 Twenty-five percent of the zones shall be tested at the outlet most remote from the source.

5.1.12.4.7.3 The filter shall accrue no more than 0.001 g (1 mg) of matter from any outlet tested.

5.1.12.4.7.4 If any outlet fails this test, the most remote outlet in every zone shall be tested.

5.1.12.4.7.5 The test shall be performed with the use of oil-free, dry nitrogen NF.

5.1.12.4.8* Verifier Piping Purity Test. For each medical gas system, the purity of the piping system shall be verified in accordance with 5.1.12.4.8.

5.1.12.4.8.1 These tests shall be performed with oil-free, dry nitrogen NF or the system gas.

5.1.12.4.8.2 The outlet most remote from the source shall be tested for total nonmethane hydrocarbons and halogenated hydrocarbons and compared to the source gas.

5.1.12.4.8.3 If the system gas is used as the source gas, it shall be tested at the source equipment.

5.1.12.4.8.4 The difference between the two tests shall in no case exceed 5 ppm of total non-methane hydrocarbons.

5.1.12.4.8.5 The difference between the two tests shall in no case exceed 5 ppm halogenated hydrocarbons.

5.1.12.4.8.6 The moisture concentration of the outlet test shall not exceed 500 ppm or an equivalent pressure dew point of -12°C (10°F) at a gauge pressure of 345 kPa (50 psi).

5.1.12.4.9 Final Tie-In Test.

5.1.12.4.9.1 Prior to the connection of any work or any extension or addition to an existing piping system, the tests in 5.1.12.4.1 through 5.1.12.4.8 shall be successfully performed on the new work.

5.1.12.4.9.2 Each joint in the final connection between the new work and the existing system shall be leak-tested with the gas of system designation at the normal operating pressure by means of a leak detectant that is safe for use with oxygen and does not contain ammonia.

5.1.12.4.9.3 Vacuum joints shall be tested using an ultrasonic leak detector or other means that will allow detection of leaks in an active vacuum system.

5.1.12.4.9.4 For pressure gases, immediately after the final brazed connection is made and leak-tested, an outlet in the new piping and an outlet in the existing piping that are immediately downstream from the point or area of intrusion shall be purged in accordance with the applicable requirements of 5.1.12.4.6.

5.1.12.4.9.5 Before the new work is used for patient care, positive-pressure gases shall be tested for operational pressure and gas concentration in accordance with 5.1.12.4.10 and 5.1.12.4.11.

5.1.12.4.9.6 Permanent records of these tests shall be maintained in accordance with 5.1.14.7.

5.1.12.4.10 Operational Flow Pressure Drop Test. Operational flow pressure drop tests shall be performed at each station outlet/inlet or terminal where the user makes connections and disconnections.

5.1.12.4.10.1 Tests shall be performed with the gas of system designation or the operating vacuum.

5.1.12.4.10.2 All gas outlets with a gauge pressure of 345 kPa (50 psi), including, but not limited to, oxygen, nitrous oxide, medical air, and carbon dioxide, shall deliver 100 SLPM (3.5 SCFM) with a pressure drop of not more than 35 kPa (5 psi) and static pressure of 345 kPa to 380 kPa (50 psi to 55 psi).

5.1.12.4.10.3 Medical support gas outlets shall deliver 140 SLPM (5.0 SCFM) with a pressure drop of not more than 35 kPa (5 psi) gauge and static pressure of 1100 kPa to 1275 kPa (160 psi to 185 psi) gauge.

5.1.12.4.10.4 Medical–surgical vacuum inlets shall draw 85 Nl/min (3 SCFM) without reducing the vacuum pressure below 300 mm (12 in.) gauge HgV at any adjacent station inlet.

5.1.12.4.10.5 Oxygen and medical air outlets serving Category 1 spaces shall allow a transient flow rate of 170 SLPM (6 SCFM) for 3 seconds and a pressure drop of not more than 70 kPa (10 psi) gauge.

5.1.12.4.10.6* Where outlets are being fed with non-standard line pressure, volume, or gas content, for clinical reasons, they shall be labeled in accordance with 5.1.11.

5.1.12.4.11 Medical Gas Concentration Test. After purging each system with the gas of system designation, the following shall be performed:

(1) Each pressure gas source and outlet shall be analyzed for concentration of gas, by volume.
(2) Analysis shall be conducted with instruments designed to measure the specific gas dispensed.
(3)* Allowable concentrations shall be as indicated in Table 5.1.12.4.11.

5.1.12.4.12 Medical Air Purity Test for Compressor Sources.

5.1.12.4.12.1 The medical air source shall be analyzed for concentration of contaminants by volume prior to the source valve being opened.

5.1.12.4.12.2 A sample(s) shall be taken for the air system test at the system sample port.

5.1.12.4.12.3 The test results shall not exceed the parameters in Table 5.1.12.4.12.3.

Table 5.1.12.4.11 Gas Concentrations

Medical Gas	Concentration
Oxygen USP	≥99% oxygen
Oxygen 93 USP	≥90% oxygen ≤96%
Nitrous oxide USP	≥99% nitrous oxide
Nitrogen NF	≤1% oxygen or ≥99% nitrogen
Medical air USP	19.5%–23.5% oxygen
Other gases	Named gases by ±1%, or per specification

5.1.12.4.13 Labeling. The presence and correctness of labeling required by this code for all components (e.g., station outlets/inlets, shutoff valves, and alarm panels) shall be verified.

5.1.12.4.14 Source Equipment Verification.

5.1.12.4.14.1 General. Source equipment verification shall be performed following the installation of the interconnecting pipelines, accessories, and source equipment.

5.1.12.4.14.2 Gas Supply Sources.

(A) The system apparatus shall be tested for proper function, including the changeover from primary to secondary supply (with its changeover signal) and the operation of the reserve (with its reserve-in-use signal), before the system is put into service.

(B) If the system has an actuating switch and signal to monitor the contents of the reserve, its function shall be tested before the system is put into service.

(C) If the system has an actuating switch and signal to monitor the pressure of the reserve unit, its function shall be tested before the system is put into service.

(D) Testing of the bulk supply signal and the master signal panel installations shall be arranged with the owner or the organization responsible for the operation and maintenance of the supply system for the testing of the bulk supply signals to ensure proper identification and activation of the master signal panels so that the facility can monitor the status of that supply system.

(E) The tests required in 5.1.12.4.14.2(D) shall also be conducted when the storage units are changed or replaced.

5.1.12.4.14.3 Medical Air Compressor Systems.

(A) Tests of the medical air compressor system shall include the purity test for air quality, and the test of the alarm sensors after calibration and setup per the manufacturer's instructions, as well as reserve capacity controls.

(B) Tests shall be conducted at the sample port of the medical air system.

(C) The operation of the system control sensors, such as dew point, air temperature, and all other air quality monitoring sensors and controls, shall be checked for proper operation and function before the system is put into service.

(D) The quality of medical air as delivered by the compressor air supply shall be verified after installation of new components prior to use by patients.

(E) The air quality tests in 5.1.12.4.14.3(D) shall be conducted after the medical air source system has been operating

Table 5.1.12.4.12.3 Contaminant Parameters for Medical Air

Parameter	Limit Value
Pressure dew point	2°C (35°F)
Carbon monoxide	10 ppm
Carbon dioxide	500 ppm
Gaseous hydrocarbons	25 ppm (as methane)
Halogenated hydrocarbons	2 ppm

normally but with the source valve closed under a simulated load for an elapsed time of at least 12 hours.

(F) The aggregate run time on the compressors shall not be used to determine the elapsed time.

(G) Loading shall be simulated by continuously venting air at approximately 25 percent of the rated system capacity.

(H) A demand of approximately 25 percent of the rated compressor capacity shall be created to cause the compressors to cycle on and off continuously and the dryers to operate for the 12-hour period.

5.1.12.4.14.4 Oxygen Central Supply System Using Concentrators. The oxygen central supply system using concentrators shall be tested according to the following:

(1) The oxygen central supply system shall be tested for purity of the oxygen.
(2) Tests of the alarms after calibration and setup per the manufacturer's instructions shall be conducted as well as tests of the operational controls.
(3) Each concentrator supply system shall be operated with the supply system's isolating valve closed and the unit venting at a flow of 25 percent or more of nameplate capacity for an elapsed time of at least 12 hours prior to the tests in 5.1.12.4.14.4(4).
(4) The oxygen quality from each concentrator supply system shall be validated as follows:

    (a) The operation of all control sensors/switches and the oxygen monitor shall be checked for proper operation and function.
    (b) The quality of the oxygen shall be confirmed to meet the USP monograph appropriate for the technology in use.
    (c) The accuracy of the oxygen monitor shall be validated against oxygen of known concentration, and the monitor calibrated in accordance with the manufacturer's specifications.

(5) The central supply system shall be tested for correct operation of the cascade (i.e., primary — secondary — reserve). It shall be permitted to test source rotation for systems so constructed.
(6) The operation of all alarms [see 5.1.9.2.4(15) and 5.1.9.5.3(13)] shall be tested.
(7) The accuracy of the central system oxygen monitor shall be calibrated in accordance with the manufacturer's specifications.
(8) Tests in 5.1.12.4.14.4(3) to 5.1.12.4.14.4(5) shall be performed when any concentrator supply system has been opened to atmosphere (e.g., during service or replacement).

5.1.12.4.14.5 Proportioning Systems for Medical Air USP.

(A) The system apparatus shall be tested for proper function, including the changeover from primary to secondary (if applicable) and operation of the reserve, before the system is put into service.

(B) Tests shall include the purity of the air quality and test of the alarm sensors after calibration and setup per the manufacturer's instructions.

(C) Tests shall be conducted at the sample port of the proportioning system.

(D) The operation of the control sensors and all quality monitoring sensors and controls shall be checked for proper operation and function before the system is put into service.

5.1.12.4.14.6 Medical–Surgical Vacuum Systems. The proper functioning of the medical–surgical vacuum source system(s) shall be tested before it is put into service.

5.1.13 Category 1 Medical Support Gases.

5.1.13.1* Applicability.

5.1.13.1.1 Medical support gases consist of nitrogen NF or instrument air and are used primarily for powering equipment used in patient care procedures. Medical support gas applications require delivery at pressures, cleanliness, or purities specific to their intended function(s) (e.g., to operate medical–surgical tools). Medical support gases shall be permitted to be piped into areas intended for any medical support purpose and, if appropriate to the procedures, to be piped into laboratories.

5.1.13.1.2* Medical support gas sources shall be permitted to be used for many general utility uses.

5.1.13.1.3 Medical support gas systems shall not convey oxidizing gases other than air or gases intended for patient or staff respiration.

5.1.13.2 Nature of Hazards. Design, installation, and operation of medical support gas systems shall consider all hazards involved with any pressurized gas except those associated with oxidizing gases and hazards associated with the elevated pressures typical of these systems.

5.1.13.3 Medical Support Gas Central Supply Systems.

5.1.13.3.1 General. Medical support gas central supply systems shall be located to meet the requirements of 5.1.3.3.1 through 5.1.3.3.1.10.

5.1.13.3.2 Design and Construction.

5.1.13.3.2.1 Locations for medical support gas central supply systems, excluding cryogenic fluid central supply systems, and for the storage of positive-pressure gases shall meet the requirements of 5.1.3.3.2.

5.1.13.3.2.2 Design and construction of locations for cryogenic fluid central supply systems shall meet the requirements of 5.1.3.10.

5.1.13.3.3 Ventilation. Ventilation for medical support gas central supply systems shall meet the requirements of 5.1.3.3.3.

5.1.13.3.4 Storage. Storage for medical support gas central supply systems shall meet the requirements of 5.1.3.3.4.

5.1.13.3.5 Control Equipment. Control equipment for medical support gas central supply systems shall meet the requirements of 5.1.3.4.

5.1.13.3.6 Nitrogen NF Central Supply Systems. Nitrogen NF central supply systems shall be permitted to consist of the following:

(1) Manifolds for gas cylinders in accordance with 5.1.3.5.11
(2) Manifolds for cryogenic liquid containers in accordance with 5.1.3.10
(3) Cryogenic fluid central supply systems in accordance with 5.1.3.10

5.1.13.3.6.1 General.

(A) Nitrogen NF central supply systems shall be obtained from a supplier or manufacturer familiar with their proper construction and use.

(B) Nitrogen NF central supply systems shall be installed in accordance with the manufacturer's instructions.

5.1.13.3.6.2 Medical Support Gases. Nitrogen NF central supply systems for medical support gases shall not be piped to, or used for, any purpose except medical support application.

5.1.13.3.6.3 Materials. Materials used in nitrogen NF central supply systems shall meet the requirements of 5.1.3.5.4.

5.1.13.3.6.4 Controls for Line Pressure. Controls for line pressure used for nitrogen central supply systems shall meet the criteria in 5.1.3.5.5.

5.1.13.3.6.5 Relief Valves. Relief Valves used for nitrogen central supply systems shall meet the criteria in 5.1.3.5.6.

5.1.13.3.6.6 Multiple Pressures. Where a single nitrogen central supply system supplies separate piped distribution networks, operating at different pressures, each piped distribution network shall meet the criteria in 5.1.3.5.7.

5.1.13.3.6.7 Local Signals.

(A) The following nitrogen NF central supply systems shall have local signals located at the source equipment:

(1) Manifolds for gas cylinders without reserve supply *(see 5.1.3.5.11)*
(2) Manifolds for cryogenic liquid containers *(see 5.1.3.10)*
(3) Cryogenic fluid central supply systems *(see 5.1.3.10)*

(B) Local signals shall meet the requirements of 5.1.3.5.8.2.

5.1.13.3.6.8 Headers. In nitrogen NF central supply systems using cylinders containing either gas or liquid, each header shall meet the requirements of 5.1.3.5.9.

5.1.13.3.6.9 Nitrogen NF Manifolds for Gas Cylinders. Manifolds for gas cylinders shall be in accordance with 5.1.3.3.1 and shall meet the requirements of 5.1.3.5.11.

5.1.13.3.6.10 Nitrogen NF Manifolds for Cryogenic Liquid Containers. Manifolds for cryogenic liquid containers shall be in accordance with 5.1.3.3.1 and shall meet the requirements of 5.1.3.5.1.

5.1.13.3.6.11 Nitrogen NF Cryogenic Fluid Central Supply Systems. Cryogenic fluid central supply systems shall be in accordance with 5.1.3.3.1 and shall meet the requirements of 5.1.3.10.

5.1.13.3.7* Instrument Air Supply Systems.

5.1.13.3.7.1 Quality of Instrument Air. The quality of instrument air shall be as follows:

(1) Compliant with ANSI/ISA S-7.0.01, *Quality Standard for Instrument Air*
(2) Filtered to 0.01 micron
(3) Free of liquids (e.g., water, hydrocarbons, solvents)
(4) Free of hydrocarbon vapors
(5) Dry to a dew point of −40°C (−40°F)

5.1.13.3.7.2 Instrument air supply systems shall be located per 5.1.3.3 as follows:

(1) Indoors, in a dedicated mechanical equipment area that is adequately ventilated and with any required utilities
(2) In a room ventilated per 5.1.3.3.3.3
(3) For air-cooled equipment, in a room designed to maintain the ambient temperature range as recommended by the equipment manufacturer

5.1.13.3.7.3 Instrument air sources shall provide air with the following characteristics:

(1) A gauge pressure adequate for the intended line pressure and pressure controls (*see Table 5.1.11*)
(2) The quality of instrument air, as described in 5.1.13.3.7.1

5.1.13.3.7.4 Instrument air sources shall be of either of the following formats:

(1) At least two compressors
(2) One compressor and a standby header complying with 5.1.3.5.9

5.1.13.3.7.5 Instrument air compressors shall be permitted to be of any type capable of the output pressure needed for the intended line pressure (*see Table 5.1.11*), and of providing air meeting the definition of instrument air in 5.1.13.3.7.1.

5.1.13.3.7.6 Instrument Air Standby Headers. Where instrument air systems are provided with a standby header, the header shall meet the following requirements:

(1) It shall comply with 5.1.3.5.9, except that the number of attached cylinders shall be sufficient for 1 hour of normal operation.
(2) It shall use connectors as for medical air in the mandatory requirements of CGA V-1, *Standard for Compressed Gas Cylinder Valve Outlet and Inlet Connections* (ANSI B57.1).
(3) It shall enter the system upstream of the final line filters.
(4) It shall automatically serve the system in the event of a failure of the compressor.

5.1.13.3.7.7* Intake Air. Intake air for instrument air compressors shall be permitted to be drawn from outside, from ducted air, or from the equipment location.

Δ **5.1.13.3.7.8 Instrument Air Filters.** Instrument air sources shall be provided with filtration sized for 100 percent of the system peak calculated demand at design conditions and with the following elements and characteristics:

(1) Activated carbon filters located upstream (source side) of the final line filters
(2) Line filters located upstream (source side) of the final line regulators and downstream of the carbon filters rated for a minimum of 98 percent efficiency at 0.01 micron
(3) Equipped with a continuous visual indicator showing the status of the line filter element life
(4) Constructed of materials deemed suitable by the manufacturer
(5) Filters combining the functions in 5.1.13.3.7.8(1) to 5.1.13.3.7.8(4) in a single unit shall be permitted to be used

5.1.13.3.7.9 Instrument Air Accessories. Accessories used for instrument air sources shall comply with the following subparagraphs:

(1) For aftercoolers, 5.1.3.6.3.5
(2) For air receivers, 5.1.3.6.3.6

(3) For air dryers, 5.1.3.6.3.7 [except 5.1.3.6.3.7(1)]
(4) For required components, 5.1.3.6.3.2

5.1.13.3.7.10 Instrument Air Piping Arrangement and Redundancies. Instrument air sources shall comply with 5.1.3.6.3.9, except for the following:

(1) Systems employing a standby header shall be permitted to have simplex aftercoolers and dryers.
(2) Systems employing a standby header shall not require a three-valve receiver bypass.
(3) Standby headers, where provided, shall be isolated from the compressor by a check valve to prevent backflow through the compressor.

5.1.13.3.7.11 Instrument Air Monitoring and Alarms.

(A) Instrument air sources shall include the following alarms:

(1) A manual-reset local alarm that indicates when the capacity of the instrument air central supply system not in use is less than the equivalent capacity of one compressor
(2) Local alarm and alarms at all master alarm panels that activate when the dew point at system pressure exceeds −30°C (−22°F), indicating a high dew point

(B) For sources with standby headers, the following additional conditions shall activate a local alarm at the compressor site, a local signal at the header location, and alarms at all master alarm panels:

(1) Alarm that activates when or just before the reserve begins to supply the system, indicating reserve in use
(2) Alarm that activates when or just before the reserve falls below one average hour's supply, indicating reserve is low

5.1.13.3.7.12 Electrical Power and Control.

(A) Instrument air source systems with compressors shall be controlled to ensure continuous supply of air at pressures consistent with Table 5.1.11 under all conditions of system use as follows:

(1) Automatic activation of compressor(s) as necessary to supply the demand.
(2) If provided with more than one compressor, managing the operation to equalize wear on all compressors. Where this equalization is achieved manually, the facility staff shall arrange a schedule for manual alternation.

(B) Controls shall provide the following functions:

(1) Where instrument air source systems having two or more compressors employ any electrical circuit device that upon failure could prevent supply of air, the controls shall be provided with an automatically activated alternative method for ensuring supply (e.g., redundant component(s), an alternate electrical supply path, or other equivalent method).
(2) Control circuits shall be arranged in such a manner that isolation of one compressor or component from the system (e.g., for maintenance or repair) does not interrupt the operation of other compressor(s) or component(s).
(3) An automatic restart function shall be included, such that the supply of air will resume normally after power interruption without manual intervention.

(C) Each compressor motor shall be provided with electrical components including, but not limited to, the following:

(1) Dedicated disconnect switch installed in the electrical circuit ahead of each motor starter
(2) Motor starting device
(3) Overload protection

Δ **(D)** Instrument air compressor system controls shall be provided with electrical systems including, at a minimum, the following:

(1) Built-in disconnect means to allow appropriate operation of multiple compressor systems and protect service personnel from exposure to live voltages
(2) Control circuits arranged so that failure of any component of the control circuit, or shutdown of one compressor (e.g., for service), does not interrupt automatic operation of the standby compressor
(3) An automatic restart function such that the compressor(s) will restart after power interruption without manual intervention
(4) Where components are common to more than one control circuit (e.g., autodrains), a common device provided with electrical protection to prevent loss of the control circuits(s) in the event of short circuit in the device

(E) Electrical installation and wiring shall conform to the requirements of *NFPA 70*.

(F) Emergency electrical service for the compressors shall conform to the requirements of the essential electrical system, as described in Chapter 6.

5.1.13.4 Valves. Requirements for medical support gas valves shall be in accordance with 5.1.4.1.1 through 5.1.4.8.

5.1.13.5 Outlets. Requirements for medical support gas outlets shall be in accordance with 5.1.5.1, 5.1.5.2, 5.1.5.4 through 5.1.5.8, 5.1.5.11, and 5.1.5.13 through 5.1.5.15.

5.1.13.6 Manufactured Assemblies. Requirements for medical support gases in manufactured assemblies shall be in accordance with 5.1.6.1 through 5.1.6.12.

5.1.13.7 Pressure Indicators. Requirements for medical support gas pressure indicators shall be in accordance with 5.1.8.1.1 through 5.1.8.1.4, 5.1.8.1.6, and 5.1.8.2.

5.1.13.8 Line Pressure Control. Instrument air systems shall be provided with means to control line pressure at the source with at least the following characteristics:

(1) Able to maintain stable pressures within the limits of Table 5.1.11
(2) Able to flow 100 percent of the peak calculated demand
(3) Redundant, such that each component of the control mechanism can be isolated for service or replacement while maintaining normal operation
(4) Protected against overpressure *(see 5.1.3.5.6)*
(5) Be constructed of materials deemed suitable for the service by the manufacturer

5.1.13.9 Warning Systems.

5.1.13.9.1 General requirements for medical support gas warning systems shall be in accordance with 5.1.9.1.

5.1.13.9.2 Master alarm requirements for medical support gas shall be in accordance with 5.1.9.2.

5.1.13.9.3 Area alarm requirements for medical support gas shall be in accordance with 5.1.9.4.

5.1.13.9.4 Local alarm requirements for medical support gas shall be in accordance with 5.1.9.5.

5.1.13.10 Distribution. Requirements for medical support gas piping distribution shall be in accordance with 5.1.10.1, 5.1.10.3, 5.1.10.4, 5.1.10.4.1 through 5.1.10.4.6, 5.1.10.10, 5.1.10.10(1), 5.1.10.10(2), 5.1.10.10(3), and 5.1.10.11.

5.1.13.11 Labeling and Identification. Requirements for medical support gas labeling shall be in accordance with 5.1.11.1 through 5.1.11.4.

5.1.13.12 Performance Testing. Requirements for medical support gas performance testing shall be in accordance with 5.1.12, with the following exceptions:

(1) The piping purity test *(see 5.1.12.4.8)* shall be permitted to be omitted.
(2) The medical gas concentration test *(see 5.1.12.4.11)* shall be permitted to be omitted.

5.1.14* Category 1 Operation and Management.

5.1.14.1 Responsible Facility Authority.

5.1.14.1.1 General. Each health care facility shall designate one or more individuals to be the responsible facility authority with respect to the facility's medical gas and vacuum systems.

5.1.14.1.2 Responsibilities.

5.1.14.1.2.1 The responsible facility authority shall have primary responsibility for implementation of the piped medical gas and vacuum system requirements of this code for the health care facility, including all medical gas, support gas, medical vacuum, and WAGD systems.

5.1.14.1.2.2 The responsible facility authority shall be responsible for the following:

(1) Advising on Section 1.3 and the risk assessment in accordance with Section 4.2, as these apply to piped medical gas and vacuum systems, and the interpretations of Sections 5.1 through 5.3, as they apply to the facility
(2) Writing and upkeep of the portions of the health care facility's emergency plan that might affect or be affected by piped medical gas and vacuum quality, quantity, and continuity of supply
(3) Ensuring that the health care facility's emergency plan specifically addresses unusual or exceptional requirements necessary for patient and staff safety arising from elements of design or construction of the building
(4) Developing and enforcing permit-to-work rules pertaining to the piped medical gas and vacuum systems and equipment to maintain patient, staff, and visitor safety during repair, modification, or construction of those systems
(5) Evaluation and acceptance of the test reports required in accordance with 5.1.12
(6) Maintenance of the facility's records on piped medical gas and vacuum system installations and operations

5.1.14.1.3 Qualifications.

5.1.14.1.3.1 The person(s) designated as the responsible facility authority shall be qualified to interpret, implement, and advise on this Code.

5.1.14.1.3.2 Appropriate qualification shall be demonstrated by any of the following:

(1) Completion of an educational program acceptable to the health care facility's governing body and substantially equivalent or superior to either 5.1.14.1.3.2(2) or 5.1.14.1.3.2(3)

(2) Credentialing to the requirements of ASSE/IAPMO/ANSI 6010, *Professional Qualifications Standard for Medical Gas Systems Installers,* and technical competence on the specific equipment and design of that facility

(3) Credentialing to the requirements of ASSE/IAPMO/ANSI 6020, *Professional Qualifications Standard for Medical Gas Systems Inspectors,* and technical competence on the specific equipment and design of that facility

(4) Credentialing to the requirements of ASSE/IAPMO/ANSI 6030, *Professional Qualifications Standard for Medical Gas Systems Verifiers,* and technical competence on the specific equipment and design of that facility

(5) Credentialing to the requirements of ASSE/IAPMO/ANSI 6040, *Professional Qualifications Standard for Medical Gas Maintenance Personnel,* and technical competence on the specific equipment and design of that facility

5.1.14.2 Permit-to-Work System.

5.1.14.2.1* The responsible facility authority of the health care facility shall develop, maintain, and manage a permit-to-work system ensuring uninterrupted quality, quantity, and continuity of supply during all piped medical gas and vacuum system maintenance, repair, or construction work.

5.1.14.2.2 The responsible facility authority's plan shall include processes to assure at least the following:

(1) The affected medical staff and facility administration is appropriately in communication prior to any work on piped medical gas and vacuum systems

(2) Alternative supply or adjustments in patient care arrangements are in place prior to system interruption, including monitoring, as appropriate, of the work being performed and the alternate arrangements in use

(3) All work on piped medical gas and vacuum systems is performed by competent individuals holding appropriate qualifications for the work

(4)* Procedures for shutdown and restoration of medical gases are described, communicated, and observed by all persons working on or with the systems

(5) Safety procedures are in place and are observed for all persons involved in working on the systems

(6) This code is observed in the execution of maintenance, repair, or construction procedures

(7) The affected portions of the systems are correctly tested in accordance with 5.1.12 and 5.1.13 and demonstrated to be acceptable for patient use

5.1.14.3 Special Precautions — Patient Gas, Vacuum, WAGD, and Medical Support Gas Systems.

5.1.14.3.1* Piping systems shall not be used for the distribution of flammable anesthetic gases.

5.1.14.3.2 Piping systems shall not be used as a grounding electrode.

5.1.14.3.3* Liquid or debris shall not be introduced into the medical–surgical vacuum or WAGD systems for disposal.

5.1.14.3.4* The medical–surgical vacuum and WAGD systems shall not be used for nonmedical applications (e.g., vacuum steam condensate return).

5.1.14.3.5* When clinical spaces are converted to nonclinical spaces, medical gas inlets and outlets that are not accessible for maintenance and testing shall be either removed or decommissioned.

N **5.1.14.3.6*** Access to and, in case of an adverse event, protection of cylinder and container manifolds and cryogenic fluid central supply systems shall be considered in the emergency operations plan.

5.1.14.4 Maintenance of Medical Gas, Vacuum, WAGD, and Medical Support Gas Systems.

5.1.14.4.1* General. Health care facilities with installed medical gas, vacuum, WAGD, or medical support gas systems, or combinations thereof, shall develop and document periodic maintenance programs for these systems and their subcomponents as appropriate to the equipment installed.

5.1.14.4.2 Maintenance Programs.

5.1.14.4.2.1 Inventories. Inventories of medical gas, vacuum, WAGD, and medical support gas systems shall include at least all source subsystems, control valves, alarms, manufactured assemblies containing patient gases, and outlets.

5.1.14.4.2.2* Inspection Schedules. Scheduled inspections for equipment and procedures shall be established through the risk assessment of the facility and developed with consideration of the original equipment manufacturer recommendations and other recommendations as required by the authority having jurisdiction.

5.1.14.4.2.3 Inspection Procedures. The facility shall be permitted to use any inspection procedure(s) or testing methods established through its own risk assessment.

5.1.14.4.2.4 Maintenance Schedules. Scheduled maintenance for equipment and procedures shall be established through the risk assessment of the facility and developed with consideration of the original equipment manufacturer recommendations and other recommendations as required by the authority having jurisdiction.

5.1.14.4.2.5 Qualifications.

(A) Persons maintaining these systems shall be qualified to perform these operations.

(B) Appropriate qualification shall be demonstrated by any of the following:

(1) A documented training program acceptable to the health care facility by which such persons are employed or contracted to work with specific equipment as installed in that facility

(2) Credentialing to the requirements of ASSE/IAPMO/ANSI 6040, *Professional Qualifications Standard for Medical Gas Systems Maintenance Personnel,* and technically competent on the specific equipment as installed in that facility.

(3) Credentialing to the requirements of ASSE/IAPMO/ANSI 6030, *Professional Qualifications Standard for Medical Gas Systems Verifiers,* and technically competent on the specific equipment as installed in that facility.

5.1.14.4.3* Inspection and Testing Operations.

5.1.14.4.3.1 Manufactured Assemblies Employing Flexible Connection(s) Between the User Terminal and the Piping System.

(A) Nonstationary booms and articulating assemblies, other than head walls utilizing flexible connectors, shall be tested for leaks, per manufacturer's recommendations, every 18 months or at a duration as determined by a risk assessment.

(B) The system pressure to nonstationary booms and articulating arms shall be maintained at operating pressure until each joint has been examined for leakage by effective means of leak detection that is safe for use with oxygen.

(C) Safe working condition of the flexible assemblies shall be confirmed.

(D) D.I.S.S. connectors internal to the boom and assemblies shall be checked for leakage.

(E) Leaks, if any, shall be repaired (if permitted), or the components replaced (if required), and the equipment retested prior to placing the equipment back into service.

(F) Additional testing of nonstationary booms or articulating arms shall be performed at intervals defined by documented performance data.

5.1.14.5 Medical Gas and Vacuum Systems Information and Warning Signs.

5.1.14.5.1 The gas content of medical gas and vacuum piping systems shall be labeled in accordance with 5.1.11.1.

5.1.14.5.2 Labels for shutoff valves shall be in accordance with 5.1.11.2 and updated when modifications are made changing the areas served.

5.1.14.5.3 Station inlets and outlets shall be identified in accordance with 5.1.11.3.

5.1.14.5.4 Alarm panel labeling shall be in accordance with 5.1.11.4 and updated when modifications are made changing the areas served.

5.1.14.6 Source equipment labeling shall be in accordance with 5.1.11.5.

5.1.14.7 Medical Gas and Vacuum Systems Maintenance and Record Keeping.

5.1.14.7.1 Permanent records of all tests required by 5.1.12.4.1 through 5.1.12.4.14 shall be maintained in the organization's files.

5.1.14.7.2 The supplier of the cryogenic fluid central supply system shall, upon request, provide documentation of vaporizer(s) sizing criteria to the facility.

5.1.14.7.3 An annual review of cryogenic fluid central supply system capacity shall be conducted to ensure the source system has sufficient capacity.

5.1.14.7.4 Central supply systems for nonflammable medical gases shall conform to the following:

(1) They shall be inspected annually.
(2) They shall be maintained by a qualified representative of the equipment owner.

(3) A record of the annual inspection shall be available for review by the authority having jurisdiction.

5.1.14.7.5 A periodic testing procedure for nonflammable medical gas and vacuum and related alarm systems shall be implemented.

5.1.14.7.6 Whenever modifications are made that breach the pipeline, any necessary installer and verification test specified in 5.1.12 shall be conducted on the downstream portions of the medical gas piping system.

5.1.14.7.7 Procedures, as specified, shall be established for the following:

(1) Maintenance program for the medical air compressor supply system in accordance with the manufacturer's recommendations
(2) Facility testing and calibration procedure that ensures carbon monoxide monitors are calibrated at least annually or more often if recommended by the manufacturer
(3) Maintenance program for both the medical–surgical vacuum piping system and the secondary equipment attached to medical–surgical vacuum station inlets to ensure the continued good performance of the entire medical–surgical vacuum system
(4) Maintenance program for the WAGD system to ensure performance
(5) Facility testing and calibration procedure that ensures that oxygen concentration monitors are calibrated at least every three months, or more often if recommended by the manufacturer
(6) Where oxygen sources include concentrator units, maintenance programs for the oxygen concentrator units and all essential subcomponents

5.1.14.7.8 Audible and visual alarm indicators shall meet the following requirements:

(1) They shall be periodically tested to determine that they are functioning properly.
(2) Records of the test shall be maintained until the next test is performed.

5.1.14.7.9 Medical–surgical vacuum station inlet terminal performance, as required in 5.1.12.4.10.4, shall be tested as follows:

(1) On a regular preventive maintenance schedule as determined by the facility maintenance staff
(2) Based on flow of free air (Nl/min or SCFM) into a station inlet while simultaneously checking the vacuum level

5.1.14.7.10 Where oxygen central supply systems using concentrators are used and one or more of the three sources is a cylinder header, the facility shall establish procedures to ensure the facility is always provided with one average day's supply of oxygen meeting the supply system product purity specification in reserve, as follows:

(1) The facility shall establish a minimum cylinder pressure that will permit one average day's supply. That value will be included as part of the standard operating procedure for the oxygen supply system.
(2) The cylinders shall be inspected daily and any loss of pressure noted.
(3) When the cylinders are found to have lost pressure due to use or leakage and thus are below the preestablished pressure, the cylinders shall be exchanged.

5.1.14.7.11* Access to valves and alarms shall be made part of the standard operating procedures for the facility and shall include the following:

(1) No items are to be placed in front of or affixed to any alarm panel that would restrict the view or diminish the sound of the alarm.
(2) Valves in secured areas are to be specified as follows:
  (a)* The valve is visible from the intended operator's position.
  (b) The valve is operable with no more than ordinary aids, such as a ladder.
  (c) If the valve is provided with security hardware, such hardware is visible and readily removeable when needed.

5.2 Category 2 Piped Gas and Vacuum Systems.

5.2.1* Applicability.

5.2.1.1* These requirements shall apply to health care facilities that require Category 2 systems as referenced in Chapter 4.

5.2.1.2 The following subsections of this chapter shall apply to the operation, management, and maintenance of Category 2 medical gas and vacuum systems in both new and existing health care facilities:

(1) 5.1.3.6.2
(2) 5.1.10.11.7.1
(3) 5.2.3.1
(4) 5.2.3.2
(5) 5.2.3.3
(6) 5.2.3.5(2)
(7) 5.2.3.7(2)
(8) 5.2.3.8(2)
(9) 5.2.13
(10) 5.2.14

5.2.1.3 Category 2 systems shall be permitted to serve spaces identified as Category 2 or Category 3.

5.2.2 Nature of Hazards of Gas and Vacuum Systems. The requirement of 5.1.2 shall apply to the nature of hazards of gas and vacuum systems.

5.2.3 Sources.

5.2.3.1 Central Supply System Identification and Labeling. Category 2 systems shall comply with 5.1.3.1.

5.2.3.2 Central Supply Operations. Category 2 systems shall comply with 5.1.3.2.

5.2.3.3 Central Supply System Locations. Category 2 systems shall comply with 5.1.3.3.

5.2.3.4 Central Supply Systems. Category 2 systems shall comply with 5.1.3.5.

5.2.3.5 Medical Air Supply Systems. Category 2 systems shall comply with 5.1.3.6, except as follows:

(1) Medical air compressors, dryers, aftercoolers, filters, and regulators shall be permitted to be simplex.
(2) The facility staff shall develop their emergency plan to deal with the loss of medical air.

5.2.3.6 Oxygen supply systems using concentrators shall be permitted to consist of two sources, one of which shall be a cylinder header with sufficient cylinder connections for one average day's supply.

5.2.3.7 Medical–Surgical Vacuum. Category 2 systems shall comply with 5.1.3.7, except as follows:

(1) Medical–surgical vacuum systems shall be permitted to be simplex.
(2) The facility staff shall develop their emergency plan to deal with the loss of medical–surgical vacuum.

5.2.3.8 WAGD. Category 2 systems shall comply with 5.1.3.8, except as follows:

(1) Medical WAGD pumps shall be permitted to be simplex.
(2) The facility staff shall develop their emergency plan to deal with the loss of WAGD.

5.2.3.9 Instrument Air Supply Systems. Instrument air outlets in Category 2 spaces shall be supplied by any of the following:

(1) An instrument air central supply system in accordance with 5.1.13.3.7, excluding 5.1.13.3.7.4 (Category 2 systems are permitted to consist of a single compressor)
(2) A cylinder manifold in accordance with 5.1.3.5.10
(3) A cylinder header in accordance with 5.1.3.5.9, provided with a means for pressure control in accordance with 5.1.3.5.5.1, excluding 5.1.3.5.5.1(3) (the pressure control means for Category 2 systems are not required to be redundant)

5.2.4 Valves. Category 2 systems shall comply with 5.1.4.

5.2.5 Station Outlets and Inlets. Category 2 systems shall comply with 5.1.5.

5.2.6 Manufactured Assemblies. Category 2 systems shall comply with 5.1.6.

5.2.7 Surface-Mounted Medical Gas Rails. Category 2 systems shall comply with 5.1.7.

5.2.8 Pressure and Vacuum Indicators. Category 2 systems shall comply with 5.1.8.

5.2.9 Warning Systems. Warning systems associated with Category 2 systems shall provide the master, area, and local alarm functions of a Category 1 system as required in 5.1.9, except as follows:

(1) Warning systems shall be permitted to be a single alarm panel.
(2) The alarm panel shall be located in an area of continuous surveillance while the facility is in operation.
(3) Pressure and vacuum switches/sensors shall be mounted at the source equipment with a pressure indicator at the master alarm panel.

5.2.10 Distribution. Category 2 systems shall comply with 5.1.10.

5.2.11 Labeling and Identification. Category 2 systems shall comply with 5.1.11.

5.2.12 Performance Criteria and Testing — Gas, Medical–Surgical Vacuum, and WAGD. Category 2 systems shall comply with 5.1.12.

5.2.13 Medical Support Gases. Category 2 systems shall comply with 5.1.13.

5.2.14* Operation and Management. Category 2 systems shall comply with 5.1.14.

5.3 Category 3 Piped Gas and Vacuum Systems.

5.3.1* Applicability.

5.3.1.1* These requirements shall apply to health care facilities that require Category 3 systems as referenced in Chapter 4.

5.3.1.2 The following sections of this chapter shall apply to the operation, management, and maintenance of the medical gas and vacuum systems in both new and existing health care facilities:

(1) 5.1.3.6.2
(2) 5.1.10.11.7.1
(3) 5.3.3.1 through 5.3.3.3
(4) 5.3.3.6.1(2)
(5) 5.3.3.7(2)
(6) 5.3.3.8(2)
(7) 5.3.14

5.3.1.3 Category 3 systems shall be permitted to only serve spaces identified as Category 3.

5.3.2 Nature of Hazards of Gas and Vacuum Systems. The requirement of 5.1.2 shall apply to the nature of hazards of gas and vacuum systems.

5.3.3 Sources.

5.3.3.1 Central Supply System Identification and Labeling. Category 3 systems shall comply with 5.1.3.1.

5.3.3.2 Central Supply Operations.

5.3.3.2.1 Category 3 systems shall comply with the requirements of 5.1.3.2 except for emergency electrical service.

Δ **5.3.3.2.2** Emergency electrical service shall conform to the requirements of Section 6.6 and *NFPA 70*.

5.3.3.3 Central Supply System Locations. Category 3 systems shall comply with 5.1.3.3.

5.3.3.4 Control Equipment. Category 3 systems shall comply with 5.1.3.4.

5.3.3.5 Central Supply Systems. Category 3 central supply systems shall be permitted to consist of the following:

(1) Gas cylinder or cryogenic liquid container headers in accordance with 5.3.3.5.10
(2) Oxygen concentrator supply units in accordance with 5.3.3.5.11
(3) Cylinder manifolds for gas cylinders in accordance with 5.3.3.5.12
(4) Manifolds for cryogenic liquid containers in accordance with 5.3.3.5.13
(5) Cryogenic fluid central supply systems in accordance with 5.3.3.5.14
(6) Medical air compressor systems in accordance with 5.3.3.6
(7) Proportioning air systems in accordance with 5.3.3.6.2
(8) Medical-surgical vacuum systems in accordance with 5.3.3.7
(9) Waste anesthetic gas disposal systems (WAGDs) in accordance with 5.3.3.8
(10) Instrument air compressor systems in accordance with 5.3.3.9

5.3.3.5.1 General. Category 3 systems shall comply with 5.1.3.5.1.

5.3.3.5.2 Permitted Locations for Medical Gases. Category 3 systems shall comply with 5.1.3.5.2.

5.3.3.5.3 Support Gases. Category 3 systems shall comply with 5.1.3.5.3.

5.3.3.5.4 Materials. Category 3 systems shall comply with 5.1.3.5.4.

5.3.3.5.5 Controls for Line Pressure. With the exception of final line controls, which shall be permitted to be simplex, Category 3 systems shall comply with 5.1.3.5.

5.3.3.5.6 Relief Valves. Category 3 systems shall comply with 5.1.3.5.6.

5.3.3.5.7 Auxiliary Source Connection. Category 3 systems shall comply with 5.1.4.10.

5.3.3.5.8 Multiple Pressures. With the exception of each piped distribution network from the single central supply system, the control mechanism components of which shall be permitted to be simplex, Category 3 systems shall comply with 5.1.3.5.7.

5.3.3.5.9 Local Signals. Category 3 systems shall comply with 5.1.3.5.8.

5.3.3.5.10 Gas Cylinder or Cryogenic Liquid Container Header. Category 3 systems shall comply with 5.1.3.5 and 5.1.3.5.9, expect as follows:

(1) Gas cylinder or cryogenic liquid container headers shall be in accordance with 5.1.3.5.9, with sufficient cylinder connections to provide for at least one average day's supply, and with the appropriate number of connections determined only after consideration of the delivery schedule, the proximity of the facility to alternate supplies, and the facility's emergency plan.
(2) The header(s) shall have a local signal that visibly indicates the operating status of the equipment and complies with 5.1.3.5.8.
(3)* The facility staff shall develop an emergency plan to deal with the loss of the headers' medical gas.

Δ **5.3.3.5.11 Oxygen Central Supply Systems Using Concentrators.** Category 3 systems shall comply with 5.1.3.5, 5.1.3.9.1, and 5.1.3.9, except as follows:

(1) Oxygen supply systems using concentrators shall be permitted to consist of one source.
(2) The facility staff shall develop an emergency plan to deal with the loss of oxygen.
(3) Emergency electrical service shall conform to the requirements of Section 6.6 and *NFPA 70*.

5.3.3.5.12 Manifolds for Gas Cylinders. Category 3 systems shall comply with 5.1.3.5 and 5.1.3.5.10.

5.3.3.5.13 Manifolds for Cryogenic Liquid Containers. Category 3 systems shall comply with 5.1.3.5 and 5.1.3.5.11.

5.3.3.5.14 Cryogenic Fluid Central Supply Systems. Category 3 systems shall comply with 5.1.3.5 and 5.1.3.10.

5.3.3.6 Medical Air.

Δ **5.3.3.6.1 Medical Air Compressor Systems.** Category 3 systems shall comply with 5.1.3.5 and 5.1.3.6, except as follows:

(1) Medical air compressors, dryers, aftercoolers, filters, and regulators shall be permitted to be simplex.

(2) The facility staff shall develop an emergency plan to deal with the loss of medical air.

(3) Emergency electrical service shall conform to the requirements of Section 6.6 and *NFPA 70*.

5.3.3.6.2 Proportioning Air Systems. Category 3 systems shall comply with 5.1.3.5, 5.1.3.6, and 5.1.3.6.3.14.

Δ **5.3.3.7 Medical–Surgical Vacuum Systems.** Category 3 systems shall comply with 5.1.3.5 and 5.1.3.7, except as follows:

(1) Medical–surgical vacuum systems shall be permitted to be simplex.

(2) The facility staff shall develop an emergency plan to deal with the loss of medical–surgical vacuum.

(3) Emergency electrical service shall conform to the requirements of Section 6.6 and *NFPA 70*.

Δ **5.3.3.8 Waste Anesthetic Gas Disposal Systems (WAGDs).** Category 3 systems shall comply with 5.1.3.5 and 5.1.3.8, except as follows:

(1) Medical WAGD pumps shall be permitted to be simplex.

(2) The facility staff shall develop an emergency plan to deal with the loss of WAGD.

(3) Emergency electrical service shall conform to the requirements of Section 6.6 and *NFPA 70*.

Δ **5.3.3.9 Instrument Air Compressor Systems.** Category 3 systems shall comply with 5.1.3.5 and 5.1.13.3.7, except as follows:

(1) Instrument air compressor systems shall be permitted to be simplex with no standby header.

(2) The facility staff shall develop an emergency plan to deal with the loss of instrument air.

(3) Emergency electrical service shall conform to the requirements of Section 6.6 and *NFPA 70*.

5.3.4 Valves. Category 3 systems shall comply with 5.1.4.

5.3.5 Station Outlets and Inlets. Category 3 systems shall comply with 5.1.5.

5.3.6 Manufactured Assemblies. Category 3 systems shall comply with 5.1.6.

5.3.7 Surface-Mounted Medical Gas Rails. Category 3 systems shall comply with 5.1.7.

5.3.8 Pressure and Vacuum Indicators. Category 3 systems shall comply with 5.1.8.

5.3.9 Warning Systems. Warning systems associated with Category 3 systems shall provide the master, area, and local alarm functions of a Category 1 system as required in 5.1.9, except as follows:

(1) Warning systems shall be permitted to be a single alarm panel (i.e., a combination master/area alarm panel).

(2) The alarm panel shall be located in an area of continuous surveillance while the facility is in operation.

(3) Pressure and vacuum switches/sensors shall be mounted at the source equipment with a pressure indicator at the master alarm panel.

(4) Electrical power for warning systems shall be in accordance with Section 6.6 for Category 3 and Category 4 spaces.

5.3.10 Distribution. Category 3 systems shall comply with 5.1.10.

5.3.11 Labeling and Identification. Category 3 systems shall comply with 5.1.11.

5.3.12 Performance Criteria and Testing — Gas, Medical–Surgical Vacuum, and WAGD. Category 3 systems shall comply with 5.1.12.

5.3.13 Medical Support Gases. Category 3 systems shall comply with 5.1.13, except as follows:

(1) Instrument air compressor systems shall be permitted to be simplex with no standby header.

(2) The facility staff shall develop an emergency plan to deal with the loss of instrument air.

5.3.14 Operation and Management. Category 3 systems shall comply with 5.1.14.

N **5.4 Liquid Withdrawal and Piping.**

N **5.4.1* General.** This section shall apply to health care facilities that draw cryogenic liquids from containers for use in liquid form.

N **5.4.2 Containers.**

N **5.4.2.1** Containers used for cryogenic liquid systems shall comply with 5.1.3.

N **5.4.2.2** Container storage locations shall comply with 5.1.3.1.8, 5.1.3.1.9, 5.1.3.3.2, and 5.1.3.5.12.

N **5.4.2.3** Container operations shall comply with 5.1.3.1.6, 5.1.3.1.7, and 5.1.3.2.

N **5.4.3 Ventilation.** Locations holding containers for liquid withdrawal shall comply with the ventilation requirements of 5.1.3.3.3.1 or 5.1.3.3.3.4.

N **5.4.4 Materials.** Materials used with liquid withdrawal systems shall be compatible with the temperatures, pressures, and gases to which they could be exposed under normal use and under any conditions that can reasonably be anticipated in the event of a single fault in a protection device(s).

N **5.4.5 Relief Valves.**

N **5.4.5.1** Liquid withdrawal systems and devices shall be provided with pressure relief mechanisms wherever liquid can be trapped between two valves or control devices and where, due to low or intermittent flow, liquid could convert to gas.

N **5.4.5.2*** All pressure relief valves shall meet the following requirements:

(1) They shall be designed for the specific gas service.

(2) They shall be designed for service with cryogenic liquids.

(3) They shall have a relief pressure setting no higher than the maximum allowable working pressure (MAWP) of the component with the lowest working pressure rating in the portion of the system being protected.

(4) They shall be vented into a safe location with the understanding that they could discharge gas or liquid at cryogenic temperatures.

N 5.4.6 Manifolds for Cryogenic Liquid Withdrawal.

N 5.4.6.1 Manifolds for cryogenic liquid withdrawal shall be located in accordance with 5.1.3.3.1 and meet one of the following requirements:

(1) If located outdoors, they shall be installed in an enclosure used only for this purpose and sited to comply with the minimum distance requirements of Table 5.1.3.5.11.1.
(2) If located indoors, they shall be installed within a room used only for the enclosure of such manifolds.

N 5.4.6.2* Manifold locations for cryogenic liquid withdrawal shall comply with the following:

(1) The location shall be constructed in accordance with 5.1.3.3.2.
(2) Ventilation shall be sufficient to maintain manifold room oxygen levels between 19.5 and 23.5 percent.

N 5.4.6.3 Manifolds for cryogenic liquid withdrawal shall have their primary and secondary headers located in the same enclosure.

N 5.4.6.4 Manifolds for cryogenic liquid withdrawal shall meet the following requirements:

(1) They shall consist of two or more equal headers, each having sufficient capacity to meet the required peak flow rate and expected duration of supply.
(2) They shall consider the normal evaporation rate of the containers and piping.

N 5.4.6.5 Manifolds for cryogenic liquid withdrawal shall include an automatic means of controlling the two headers to accomplish the following during normal operation:

(1)* One cryogenic liquid header shall be the primary and the other, the secondary, with either being capable of either role.
(2) When the primary header is depleted, the secondary header shall automatically begin to supply the system.

N 5.4.6.6 Manifolds for cryogenic liquid withdrawal shall include a manual or automatic means to place either header into the role of primary header and the other into the role of secondary header.

N 5.4.6.7 Manifolds for cryogenic liquid withdrawal shall have a local signal(s) that visibly indicates the operating status of the container contents and the operating header.

N 5.4.6.8 Audible and visual alarms shall be provided to indicate the following conditions:

(1) Low contents of the containers
(2) When or at a predetermined set point before the secondary header begins to supply the system, indicating changeover has occurred or is about to occur

N 5.4.6.9 Piping.

N 5.4.6.9.1 Materials.

N 5.4.6.9.1.1 Piping materials for field-installed cryogenic liquid withdrawal systems shall be in accordance with the manufacturer's recommendations.

N 5.4.6.9.1.2 Valves and other control apparatus shall be suitable for cryogenic service.

N 5.4.6.9.1.3* Special purpose devices shall meet the following requirements:

(1) They shall be constructed of materials compatible with cryogenic service.
(2) They shall be placed such that they are visible for inspection, testing, and service.
(3) They shall be placed or guarded to prevent the development of any hazards when they operate.

N 5.4.6.9.1.4 Electrical devices and wiring placed in proximity to cryogenic fluid or potentially exposed to ice or condensate shall be protected for wet locations.

N 5.4.6.9.2 Installation. Piping for field-installed cryogenic liquid withdrawal systems shall be installed in accordance with the manufacturer's recommendations.

N 5.4.6.9.3 Insulation or Protection. All piping for field-installed cryogenic liquid withdrawal systems shall be insulated or protected to prevent inadvertent contact, icing, and condensation.

N 5.4.6.10 Testing. Piping for field-installed cryogenic liquid withdrawal systems shall be tested in accordance with the manufacturer's recommendations and include the following:

(1) Evaluation of relief valve locations and cracking pressures
(2) Leak tests at the higher of 1.5 times the expected normal operating pressure or the highest relief valve cracking pressure in the piping
(3) Insulation integrity
(4)* Other criteria as determined by the application

Chapter 6 Electrical Systems

6.1* Applicability.

6.1.1 Electrical Installation. Installation shall be in accordance with *NFPA 70*.

6.1.2 This chapter shall apply to new health care facilities as specified in Section 1.3.

6.1.3 The following paragraphs shall apply to new and existing health care facilities:

(1) 6.3.2.2.1
(2) 6.3.2.3.6(B)(2) and 6.3.2.3.6(B)(3)
(3) 6.3.2.3.8
(4) 6.3.2.6.8
(5) 6.3.2.8.2
(6) 6.3.3.2.5 through 6.3.3.2.7
(7) 6.3.3.3.3 and 6.3.3.3.4
(8) 6.3.4
(9) 6.7.1.2.7.2(H)
(10) 6.7.2.2.5(B)
(11) 6.7.2.2.6
(12) 6.7.4
(13) Section 6.8

6.1.4 The following paragraphs shall apply only to existing health care facilities:

(1) 6.3.2.5.1.3
(2) Section 6.9

6.2 Nature of Hazards.

6.2.1* Fire and Explosions.

6.2.2 Shock. (Reserved)

6.2.3 Thermal. (Reserved)

Δ **6.2.4 Location of Electrical System Components.**

6.2.4.1 Electrical system components shall be located to minimize interruptions caused by natural forces common to the area or natural disasters identified in the facility's emergency operations plan.

Δ **6.2.4.2** Installations of electrical sources shall be located to reduce possible interruption of electrical systems resulting from natural forces and to reduce possible disruption of electrical systems due to internal wiring and equipment failures.

6.2.4.3 Feeders and associated raceways serving essential electrical system transfer equipment shall be located such that physical separation is provided between each of the electrical system feeders to prevent possible simultaneous interruption.

6.3 General.

6.3.1 Sources. Each health care appliance requiring electrical power for operation shall be supplied by one or more power sources as required for the particular system.

6.3.1.1 Power/Utility Company. (Reserved)

6.3.1.2 On-Site Generator Set. (Reserved)

6.3.2 Distribution.

6.3.2.1* Distribution system arrangements shall be designed to minimize interruptions to the electrical systems due to internal failures by the use of equipment rated for the application.

6.3.2.2 Receptacles.

6.3.2.2.1* Types of Receptacles.

(A) Each receptacle shall provide at least one separate, grounding terminal capable of maintaining low-contact resistance with its mating plug, despite severe electrical and mechanical use of the receptacle. The grounding terminal of each receptacle shall be connected to the reference grounding point by means of an insulated copper equipment grounding conductor.

(B) Special receptacles, such as the following, shall be permitted:

(1) Four-pole units providing an extra pole for redundant grounding or ground continuity monitoring
(2) Locking-type receptacles

(C) All non-locking-type, 125-volt, 15- or 20-ampere single, duplex, or quadruplex type receptacles, or any combination thereof, located in operating rooms and at patient bed locations in Category 1 and Category 2 spaces shall be listed and identified as "hospital grade."

(D) Receptacles that are located within patient rooms, bathrooms, playrooms, and activity rooms of pediatric units or spaces with similar risk as determined by the health care facility's governing body by conducting a risk assessment, other than infant nurseries, shall be listed and identified as "tamper resistant" or shall employ a listed tamper-resistant cover.

6.3.2.2.2 Minimum Number of Receptacles. The number of receptacles shall be determined by the intended use of the spaces in accordance with 6.3.2.2.2(A) through 6.3.2.2.2(E).

(A) Receptacles Serving Patient Bed Locations in Category 2 Spaces. Each patient bed location shall be provided with a minimum of eight non-locking-type, 125-volt, 15- or 20-ampere receptacles, at least four of which shall be connected to either the normal branch circuit or a critical branch circuit supplied by a different transfer switch other than the receptacles at the same location. These receptacles shall be permitted to be of the single, duplex, or quadruplex type, or any combination thereof. Other receptacles (e.g., portable x-ray receptacles) serving special-purpose, cord-and-plug-connected equipment shall be permitted to be of the locking or non-locking-type.

(B) Receptacles Serving Patient Bed Locations in Category 1 Spaces Other than Operating Rooms. Each patient bed location shall be provided with a minimum of 14 non-locking-type, 125-volt, 15- or 20-ampere receptacles, at least seven of which shall be connected to either the normal branch circuit or a critical branch circuit supplied by a different transfer switch other than the receptacles at the same location. These receptacles shall be permitted to be of the single, duplex, or quadruplex type, or any combination thereof. Other receptacles (e.g., portable x-ray receptacles) serving special-purpose, cord-and-plug-connected equipment shall be permitted to be of the locking or non-locking-type.

(C) Receptacles in Operating Rooms. Each operating room shall be provided with a minimum of 36 125-volt, 15- or 20-ampere receptacles, at least 12 of which shall be connected to either the normal branch circuit or a critical branch circuit supplied by a different transfer switch other than the receptacles at the same location. They shall be permitted to be of the single, duplex, or quadruplex type, or any combination of the three. Other receptacles (e.g., portable x-ray receptacles) serving special-purpose, cord-and-plug-connected equipment shall be permitted to be of the locking or non-locking-type.

(D) Receptacles in Bathrooms or Toilet Rooms. Receptacles shall not be required in bathrooms or toilet rooms.

(E) Receptacles for Special Rooms. Receptacles shall not be required in rooms where medical requirements mandate otherwise (e.g., certain psychiatric, pediatric, or hydrotherapy rooms).

6.3.2.2.3 Polarity of Receptacles. Each receptacle shall be wired in accordance with *NFPA 70* to ensure correct polarity.

6.3.2.2.4 Other Services Receptacles. Receptacles provided for other services having different voltages, frequencies, or types on the same premises shall be of such design that attachment plugs and caps used in such receptacles cannot be connected to circuits of a different voltage, frequency, or type, but shall be interchangeable within each classification and rating required for two-wire, 125-V, single-phase ac service.

6.3.2.2.5* Use of Isolated Ground Receptacles.

(A) An isolated ground receptacle, if used, shall not defeat the purposes of the safety features of the grounding systems detailed in 6.3.2.5.1.

(B) An isolated ground receptacle shall not be installed within a patient care vicinity.

(C) Isolated grounding receptacles installed in branch circuits for patient care spaces shall be connected to an insulated equipment grounding conductor in accordance with 250.146(D) of *NFPA 70* in addition to the two equipment grounding conductor paths required in 6.3.2.5.1.4.

(D) The equipment grounding conductor installed for isolated grounding receptacles in patient care areas shall be clearly identified using green insulation with one or more yellow stripes along its entire length.

6.3.2.2.6 Special-Purpose Outlets. Branch circuits serving only special-purpose outlets or receptacles (e.g., portable x-ray receptacles) shall not be required to conform to the requirements of 6.4.3.

6.3.2.2.7* Clinical Laboratories. Outlets with two to four receptacles, or an equivalent multioutlet assembly, shall be installed every 0.5 m to 1.0 m (1.6 ft to 3.3 ft) in instrument usage areas, and either installation shall be at least 80 mm (3.15 in.) above the countertop.

6.3.2.3 Wet Procedure Locations.

6.3.2.3.1* Wet procedure locations shall be provided with special protection against electric shock.

6.3.2.3.2 This special protection shall be provided as follows:

(1) Power distribution system that inherently limits the possible ground-fault current due to a first fault to a low value, without interrupting the power supply
(2) Power distribution system in which the power supply is interrupted if the ground-fault current does, in fact, exceed the trip value of a Class A GFCI

6.3.2.3.3 Patient beds, toilets, bidets, and wash basins shall not be required to be considered wet procedure locations.

6.3.2.3.4* Operating rooms shall be considered to be a wet procedure location, unless a risk assessment conducted by the health care governing body determines otherwise.

6.3.2.3.5 If the risk assessment conducted by the health care facility's governing body, as defined in Chapter 3, determines that the operating room is not a wet procedure location, then the special protection of 6.3.2.3 shall not be required.

6.3.2.3.6 In existing construction, the requirements of 6.3.2.3.1 shall not be required when a written inspection procedure, acceptable to the authority having jurisdiction, is performed by a designated individual at the hospital to indicate that equipment grounding conductors for 120-V, single-phase, 15-A and 20-A receptacles; equipment connected by cord and plug; and fixed electrical equipment are installed and maintained in accordance with *NFPA 70*, the applicable performance requirements of this chapter, and Chapter 10 of this code.

(A) The procedure shall include electrical continuity tests of all required equipment, grounding conductors, and their connections.

(B) Fixed receptacles, equipment connected by cord and plug, and fixed electrical equipment shall be tested as follows:

(1) When first installed
(2) Where there is evidence of damage
(3) After any repairs

6.3.2.3.7 The use of an isolated power system (IPS) shall be permitted as a protective means capable of limiting ground-fault current without power interruption if the IPS complies with 6.3.2.9.

6.3.2.3.8* Operating rooms defined as wet procedure locations shall be protected by either isolated power or ground-fault circuit interrupters.

6.3.2.3.9 Where GFCI protection is used in an operating room, one of the following shall apply:

(1) Each receptacle shall be an individual GFCI device.
(2) Each receptacle shall be individually protected by a single GFCI device.

6.3.2.4* Circuits.

6.3.2.4.1 Normal branch circuits serving a patient bed location shall be supplied from not more than one normal branch-circuit distribution panel.

6.3.2.4.2 Branch circuits serving a patient bed location shall be permitted to be supplied from more than one critical branch-circuit distribution panel.

6.3.2.4.3 Only authorized personnel shall have access to overcurrent protective devices serving Category 1 and Category 2 spaces.

Δ **6.3.2.4.4** Overcurrent protective devices serving Category 1 and Category 2 spaces shall not be located in public access spaces.

6.3.2.4.5 Isolated power panels shall be permitted to be located in Category 1 spaces.

6.3.2.4.6 Low-voltage wiring shall comply with either of the following:

(1) Fixed systems of 30 V (dc or ac rms) or less shall be permitted to be ungrounded if the insulation between each ungrounded conductor and the primary circuit, which is supplied from a conventionally grounded distribution system, is the same protection as required for the primary voltage.

(2) A grounded low-voltage system shall be permitted if load currents are not carried on the equipment grounding conductors.

6.3.2.5 Grounding.

6.3.2.5.1 Grounding requirements shall comply with the requirements in 6.3.2.5.1.1 through 6.3.2.5.1.5.

△ **6.3.2.5.1.1 Equipment Grounding Circuitry Integrity.** Equipment grounding and bonding conductors and patient care vicinity grounding and bonding conductors shall be installed such that the continuity of the system cannot be interrupted nor the resistance raised above an acceptable level by the installation, removal, or replacement of any installed device or end use equipment.

6.3.2.5.1.2 Reliability of Grounding. The equipment grounding conductors shall conform to *NFPA 70*. Branch circuits serving electrical equipment within the patient care vicinity shall be provided with effective ground-fault current paths dual-fed by a wiring method that qualifies as an equipment grounding conductor and by an insulated copper equipment grounding conductor.

6.3.2.5.1.3 Separate Equipment Grounding Conductor. When existing construction does not have a separate equipment grounding conductor, the continued use of the system shall be permitted if it meets the performance requirements in 6.3.3.1.

6.3.2.5.1.4 Grounding of Receptacles and Fixed Electrical Equipment in Patient Care Spaces.

(A) Wiring Methods. All branch circuits serving patient care spaces shall be provided with an effective ground-fault current path by installation in a metal raceway system, or a cable having a metallic armor or sheath assembly. The metal raceway system, or metallic cable armor, or sheath assembly shall itself qualify as an equipment grounding conductor.

(B) Insulated Equipment Grounding Conductors and Insulated Equipment Bonding Jumpers. The following shall be directly connected to an insulated copper equipment grounding conductor that is clearly identified along its entire length by green insulation, with no yellow stripes, and installed with the branch circuit conductors in the wiring methods as provided in 6.3.2.5.1.4(A):

(1) The grounding terminals of all receptacles other than isolated ground receptacles.

(2) Where receptacles are mounted in metal receptacle outlet boxes, metal device boxes, or metal enclosures, the performance of the connection between the receptacle grounding terminal and the metal box or enclosure shall be equivalent to the performance provided by copper wire sized in accordance with 250.146 and Table 250.122 of *NFPA 70*, but no smaller than 12 AWG.

(3) All non-current-carrying conductive surfaces of fixed electrical equipment likely to become energized and subject to personal contact, operating at over 100 volts.

(4) Metal faceplates, which shall be connected to the equipment grounding conductor by means of a metal mounting screw(s) securing the faceplate to a grounded outlet box or grounded wiring device.

(5) Luminaires more than 2.3 m (7½ ft) above the floor and switches located outside of the patient care vicinity, which shall be permitted to be connected to an equipment grounding return path complying with 6.3.2.5.1.4(A) and 6.3.2.5.1.4(B).

6.3.2.5.1.5* Grounding Interconnects. In patient care spaces supplied by the normal distribution system and any branch of the essential electrical system, the grounding system of the normal distribution system and that of the essential electrical system shall be interconnected.

6.3.2.5.2 Patient Equipment Grounding Point. A patient equipment grounding point comprising one or more grounding terminals or jacks shall be permitted in an accessible location in the patient care vicinity.

6.3.2.5.3* Special Grounding in Patient Care Rooms. In addition to the grounding required to meet the performance requirements of 6.3.3.1, additional grounding shall be permitted where special circumstances so dictate.

6.3.2.6 Battery-Powered Lighting Units.

6.3.2.6.1 One or more battery-powered lighting units shall be provided within locations where deep sedation and general anesthesia is administered.

6.3.2.6.2 The lighting level of each unit shall be sufficient to terminate procedures intended to be performed within the operating room.

6.3.2.6.3 The sensor for units shall be wired to the unswitched portion of branch circuit(s) serving general lighting within the room.

6.3.2.6.4 The Level 1 or Level 2 EPS [emergency power supply] equipment location(s) shall be provided with battery-powered emergency lighting. This requirement shall not apply to units located outdoors in enclosures that do not include walk-in access. [**110:**7.3.1]

6.3.2.6.5 The emergency lighting charging system and the normal service room lighting shall be supplied from the load side of the transfer switch. [**110:**7.3.2]

6.3.2.6.6 The minimum average horizontal illumination provided by normal lighting sources in the separate building or room housing the EPS equipment for Level 1 shall be 32.3 lux (3.0 ft-candles) measured at the floor level, unless otherwise specified by a requirement recognized by the authority having jurisdiction. [**110:**7.3.3]

6.3.2.6.7 Units shall be capable of providing lighting for 1½ hours.

6.3.2.6.8 Units shall be tested monthly for 30 seconds, and annually for 30 minutes.

6.3.2.7 Other Non-Patient Care Areas. (Reserved)

6.3.2.8 Ground-Fault Protection.

△ **6.3.2.8.1 Ground-Fault Protection of Equipment (GFPE).**

N **6.3.2.8.1.1 Applicability.** The requirements of 6.3.2.8.1 shall apply to health care facilities housing Category 1 spaces or using life-support equipment and buildings that provide essential utilities or services for the operation of Category 1 spaces or electrical life-support equipment.

6.3.2.8.1.2 Disconnecting Means. Where ground-fault protection is provided for operation of the service or feeder disconnecting means in accordance with 517.17 of *NFPA 70*, an additional step of ground-fault protection shall be provided at the disconnecting means for the next level of feeders downstream toward the load.

6.3.2.8.1.3 Selectivity. GFPE for operation of the service and feeder disconnecting means shall be fully selective such that the downstream device and not the upstream device opens for downstream ground faults.

6.3.2.8.2 Ground-Fault Circuit-Interrupter (GFCI) Protection of Personnel. Ground-fault circuit interrupters (GFCIs) shall be listed.

6.3.2.9* Isolated Power Systems.

6.3.2.9.1 Isolation Transformer. An isolated power system shall not be required to be installed in any patient care space, except as specified in 6.3.2.3.

6.3.2.9.1.1 The isolation transformer shall be listed and approved for the purpose.

6.3.2.9.1.2 The primary winding shall be connected to a power source so that it is not energized with more than 600 V (nominal).

(A) If present, the neutral of the primary winding shall be grounded in an approved manner.

(B) If an electrostatic shield is present, it shall be connected to the reference grounding point.

6.3.2.9.1.3 Wiring of isolated power systems shall be in accordance with 517.160 of *NFPA 70*.

6.3.2.9.2 Impedance of Isolated Wiring.

6.3.2.9.2.1* The impedance (capacitive and resistive) to ground of either conductor of an isolated system shall exceed 200,000 ohms when installed. The installation at this point shall include receptacles but is not required to include lighting fixtures or components of fixtures. This value shall be determined by energizing the system and connecting a low-impedance ac milliammeter (0 to 1 mA scale) between the reference grounding point and either conductor in sequence. This test shall be permitted to be performed with the line isolation monitor (*see 6.3.2.9.3.1*) connected, provided that the connection between the line isolation monitor and the reference grounding point is open at the time of the test. After the test is made, the milliammeter shall be removed and the grounding connection of the line isolation monitor shall be restored. When the installation is completed, including permanently connected fixtures, the reading of the meter on the line isolation monitor, which corresponds to the unloaded line condition, shall be made. This meter reading shall be recorded as a reference for subsequent line impedance evaluation. This test shall be conducted with no phase conductors grounded.

6.3.2.9.2.2 An approved capacitance suppressor shall be permitted to be used to improve the impedance of the permanently installed isolated system; however, the resistive impedance to ground of each isolated conductor of the system shall be at least 1 megohm prior to the connection of the suppres-

sion equipment. Capacitance suppressors shall be installed so as to prevent inadvertent disconnection during normal use.

6.3.2.9.3 Line Isolation Monitor.

6.3.2.9.3.1* In addition to the usual control and protective devices, each isolated power system shall be provided with an approved, continually operating line isolation monitor that indicates possible leakage or fault currents from either isolated conductor to ground.

6.3.2.9.3.2 The monitor shall be designed such that a green signal lamp, conspicuously visible in the area where the line isolation monitor is utilized, remains lighted when the system is adequately isolated from ground; and an adjacent red signal lamp and an audible warning signal (remote if desired) shall be energized when the total hazard current (consisting of possible resistive and capacitive leakage currents) from either isolated conductor to ground reaches a threshold value of 5.0 mA under normal line voltage conditions. The line isolation monitor shall not alarm for a fault hazard current of less than 3.7 mA.

6.3.2.9.3.3* The line isolation monitor shall comply with either of the following:

(1) It shall have sufficient internal impedance such that, when properly connected to the isolated system, the maximum internal current that will flow through the line isolation monitor, when any point of the isolated system is grounded, shall be 1 mA.
(2) It shall be permitted to be of the low-impedance type such that the current through the line isolation monitor, when any point of the isolated system is grounded, will not exceed twice the alarm threshold value for a period not exceeding 5 milliseconds.

6.3.2.9.3.4* An ammeter connected to indicate the total hazard current of the system (contribution of the fault hazard current plus monitor hazard current) shall be mounted in a plainly visible place on the line isolation monitor with the "alarm on" zone (total hazard current = 5.0 mA) at approximately the center of the scale. A line isolation monitor shall be located in the operating room.

6.3.2.9.3.5 Means shall be provided for shutting off the audible alarm while leaving the red warning lamp activated. When the fault is corrected and the green signal lamp is reactivated, the audible alarm-silencing circuit shall reset automatically, or an audible or distinctive visual signal shall indicate that the audible alarm is silenced.

6.3.2.9.3.6 A reliable test switch shall be mounted on the line isolation monitor to test its capability to operate (i.e., cause the alarms to operate and the meter to indicate in the "alarm on" zone). This switch shall transfer the grounding connection of the line isolation monitor from the reference grounding point to a test impedance arrangement connected across the isolated line; the test impedance(s) shall be of the appropriate magnitude to produce a meter reading corresponding to the rated total hazard current at the nominal line voltage, or to a lesser alarm hazard current if the line isolation monitor is so rated. The operation of this switch shall break the grounding connection of the line isolation monitor to the reference grounding point before transferring this grounding connector to the test impedance(s), so that making this test will not add to the hazard of a system in actual use; nor will the test include the effect of the line-to-ground stray impedance of the system. The test switch shall be of a self-restoring type.

6.3.2.9.3.7 The line isolation monitor shall not generate energy of sufficient amplitude or frequency, as measured by a physiological monitor with a gain of at least 104 with a source impedance of 1000 ohms connected to the balanced differential input of the monitor, to create interference or artifact on human physiological signals. The output voltage from the amplifier shall not exceed 30 mV when the gain is 104. The impedance of 1000 ohms shall be connected to the ends of typical unshielded electrode leads that are a normal part of the cable assembly furnished with physiological monitors. A 60 Hz notch filter shall be used to reduce ambient interference, as is typical in physiological monitor design.

6.3.2.9.4 Identification of Conductors for Isolated (Ungrounded) Systems. The isolated conductors shall be identified in accordance with 517.160(A)(5) of *NFPA 70*.

6.3.3 Performance Criteria and Testing.

6.3.3.1 Grounding System in Patient Care Spaces.

6.3.3.1.1* Grounding System Testing. The effectiveness of the grounding system shall be determined by voltage measurements and impedance measurements.

6.3.3.1.1.1 For new construction, the effectiveness of the grounding system shall be evaluated before acceptance.

6.3.3.1.1.2 Small wall-mounted conductive surfaces not likely to become energized, such as surface-mounted towel and soap dispensers, mirrors, and so forth, shall not be required to be intentionally grounded or tested.

6.3.3.1.1.3 Large metal conductive surfaces not likely to become energized, such as windows, door frames, and drains, shall not be required to be intentionally grounded or periodically tested.

6.3.3.1.1.4* Whenever the electrical system has been altered or replaced, that portion of the system shall be tested.

6.3.3.1.2 Reference Point. The voltage and impedance measurements shall be taken with respect to a reference point, which shall be one of the following:

(1) Reference grounding point *(see Chapter 3)*
(2) Grounding point, in or near the room under test, that is electrically remote from receptacles (e.g., an all-metal cold-water pipe)
(3) Grounding contact of a receptacle that is powered from a different branch circuit from the receptacle under test.

6.3.3.1.3* Voltage Measurements.

6.3.3.1.3.1 The voltage measurements shall be made under no-fault conditions between a reference point and exposed fixed electrical equipment with conductive surfaces in a patient care vicinity.

6.3.3.1.3.2 The voltage measurements shall be made with an accuracy of ± 5 percent.

6.3.3.1.3.3 Voltage measurements for faceplates of wiring devices shall not be required.

6.3.3.1.4* Impedance Measurements. The impedance measurement shall be made with an accuracy of ± 5 percent.

6.3.3.1.4.1 For new construction, the impedance measurement shall be made between the reference point and the grounding contact of 10 percent of all receptacles within the patient care vicinity.

6.3.3.1.4.2 The impedance measurement shall be the ratio of voltage developed (either 60 Hz or dc) between the point under test and the reference point to the current applied between these two points.

6.3.3.1.5 Test Equipment. Electrical safety test instruments shall be tested periodically, but not less than annually, for acceptable performance.

6.3.3.1.5.1 Voltage measurements specified in 6.3.3.1.3 shall be made with an instrument having an input resistance of 1000 ohms ± 10 percent at frequencies of 1000 Hz or less.

6.3.3.1.5.2 The voltage across the terminals (or between any terminal and ground) of resistance-measuring instruments used in occupied patient care rooms shall not exceed 500 mV rms or 1.4 dc or peak to peak.

6.3.3.1.6 Criteria for Acceptability for New Construction.

6.3.3.1.6.1 The voltage limit shall be 20 mV.

6.3.3.1.6.2 The impedance limit shall be 0.2 ohm for systems containing isolated ground receptacles and 0.1 ohm for all others.

6.3.3.2 Receptacle Testing in Patient Care Spaces.

6.3.3.2.1 The physical integrity of each receptacle shall be confirmed by visual inspection.

6.3.3.2.2 The continuity of the grounding circuit in each electrical receptacle shall be verified.

6.3.3.2.3 Correct polarity of the hot and neutral connections in each electrical receptacle shall be confirmed.

6.3.3.2.4 The retention force of the grounding blade of each electrical receptacle (except locking-type receptacles) shall be not less than 115 g (4 oz).

6.3.3.2.5 Where hospital-grade receptacles are required at patient bed locations and in locations where deep sedation or general anesthesia is administered, testing shall be performed after initial installation, replacement, or servicing of the device.

6.3.3.2.6 Additional testing of receptacles in patient care spaces shall be performed at intervals defined by documented performance data.

6.3.3.2.7 Receptacles not listed as hospital-grade, at patient bed locations and in locations where deep sedation or general anesthesia is administered, shall be tested at intervals not exceeding 12 months.

6.3.3.3 Isolated Power Systems.

6.3.3.3.1 Patient Care Spaces. If installed, the isolated power system shall be tested in accordance with 6.3.3.3.2.

6.3.3.3.2 Line Isolation Monitor Tests. The line isolation monitor (LIM) circuit shall be tested after installation, and prior to being placed in service, by successively grounding each line of the energized distribution system through a resistor whose value is 200 × V (ohms), where V equals measured line voltage. The visual and audible alarms *(see 6.3.2.9.3.2)* shall be activated.

6.3.3.3.3 The LIM circuit shall be tested at intervals of not more than 1 month by actuating the LIM test switch *(see 6.3.2.9.3.6)*. For a LIM circuit with automated self-test and self-calibration capabilities, this test shall be performed at intervals of not more than 12 months. Actuation of the test switch shall activate both visual and audible alarm indicators.

6.3.3.3.4 After any repair or renovation to an electrical distribution system, the LIM circuit shall be tested in accordance with 6.3.3.3.2.

6.3.3.4 Ground-Fault Protection Testing. When equipment ground-fault protection is first installed, each level shall be performance-tested to ensure compliance with 6.3.2.8.

6.3.4 Administration of Electrical System.

6.3.4.1 Record Keeping.

6.3.4.1.1* A record shall be maintained of the tests required by this chapter and associated repairs or modification.

6.3.4.1.2 At a minimum, the record shall contain the date, the rooms or areas tested, and an indication of which items have met, or have failed to meet, the performance requirements of this chapter.

6.3.4.1.3 Isolated Power System (Where Installed). A permanent record shall be kept of the results of each of the tests.

6.4 Category 1 Spaces.

6.4.1 Category 1 spaces shall be served by an essential electrical system in accordance with 6.7.5.

6.4.2 Category 1 spaces shall not be served by an essential electrical system in accordance with 6.7.6.

6.4.3 Category 1 spaces shall be served by circuits from a critical branch panel(s) served from a single automatic transfer switch and a minimum of one circuit served by the normal power distribution system or by a system originating from a second critical branch automatic transfer switch.

6.4.4 An essential electrical system in accordance with 6.7.5 serving a Category 1 space shall be permitted to serve Category 2 spaces in the same facility.

6.5 Category 2 Spaces.

6.5.1 Category 2 spaces shall be served by a Type 1 or Type 2 EES.

6.5.2 Category 2 spaces served by a Type 1 or Type 2 EES shall be served by circuits from a branch panel(s) served from a single automatic transfer switch and a minimum of one circuit served by the normal power distribution system or by a system originating from a second automatic transfer switch.

6.6 Category 3 and 4 Spaces.

6.6.1 Category 3 or Category 4 spaces shall not be required to be served by an EES.

6.7* Essential Electrical Systems.

6.7.1 Sources.

6.7.1.1* Design Considerations. Essential electrical system loads shall be supplied by a minimum of two independent sources or sets of sources and sets of feeders designed to ensure sufficient reliability to provide effective facility operation consistent with the facility's emergency operations plan.

6.7.1.1.1 Current-sensing devices, phase and ground, shall be selected to minimize the extent of interruption to the electrical system due to abnormal current caused by overload or short circuits, or both.

Δ **6.7.1.1.2** The essential electrical system shall have a minimum of two independent power sources or sets of power sources.

N **6.7.1.1.2.1** At least one power source shall be on-site and sized to supply the entire essential electrical system.

N **6.7.1.1.2.2** The additional power source(s) shall be permitted to be either on-site or off-site.

6.7.1.2 General. Alternate power sources for essential electrical systems shall be designed to meet the requirements of such service.

6.7.1.2.1* Power Source. Type 1 and Type 2 essential electrical system power sources shall be classified as Type 10, Class X, Level 1 sources as defined in Table 6.11.1(a).

6.7.1.2.2 Use for Essential Electrical System.

Δ **6.7.1.2.2.1** The power source supplying the essential electrical system shall be either reserved exclusively for such service or used for other purposes of peak demand control, internal voltage control, load relief for the external utility, cogeneration, or other approved uses.

Δ **6.7.1.2.2.2*** Each independent source or sets of sources supplying the essential electrical system shall be designed to meet the maximum demand likely to be produced by the connected load and be consistent with the facility's emergency operations plan.

6.7.1.2.2.3*

(A) Sources supplying the essential electrical system shall be permitted to supply optional loads.

(B) Optional loads shall be served by their own transfer means, such that they will not be transferred onto the generating equipment if the transfer would overload the equipment and will be shed prior to a generating equipment overload.

6.7.1.2.2.4 Where optional loads include contiguous or same-site facilities not covered in this code, provisions shall be made to meet the requirements of NFPA *101* for emergency egress under load-shed conditions.

N **6.7.1.2.2.5 Temporary On-Site Power Source for Maintenance or Repair of the On-Site Power Source.**

N **(A)** If the essential electrical system relies on a single on-site power source that will be disabled for maintenance or repair, it shall include a permanent switching means to connect a portable or temporary on-site power source that is available for the duration of the maintenance or repair and that complies with the following requirements:

(1) The connection to the portable or temporary on-site power source shall not require modification of the permanent system wiring.
(2) Transfer of power to the portable or temporary on-site power source shall be in accordance with 6.7.2.1.3.
(3) The connection point for the portable or temporary on-site power source shall be marked with the phase rotation and system bonding requirements.
(4) Mechanical or electrical interlocking shall prevent inadvertent interconnection of power sources.

(5) The switching means shall include a contact point that annunciates at a location remote from the generator or at another facility monitoring system to indicate that the on-site power source is disconnected from the essential electrical system.

N **(B)** Using manual switching to switch from the on-site power source to the portable or temporary on-site power source and using the switching means for connection of a load bank shall be permitted.

N **(C)** The permanent switching means to connect a portable or temporary on-site power source for the duration of maintenance or repair shall not be required where any of the following conditions exists:

(1) All processes that rely on the essential electrical system source are capable of being disabled during maintenance or repair of the on-site power source.
(2) The building or structure is unoccupied and fire protection systems are fully functional and do not require an on-site power source.
(3) Other temporary on-site power sources can be substituted for the essential electrical system.

6.7.1.2.3 Location.

6.7.1.2.3.1 Indoor On-Site Power Source Installations. Indoor on-site power sources for Level 1 installations shall be installed in a room dedicated to such sources.

Δ **(A)** The on-site power sources room shall be separated from the rest of the building by construction with a minimum 2-hour fire resistance rating.

Δ **(B)** The on-site power source equipment shall be permitted to be installed in the room with the on-site power sources.

Δ **(C)** No other equipment, including architectural appurtenances, except those that serve the space shall be permitted in the room containing the on-site power sources.

6.7.1.2.3.2 Outdoor On-Site Power Source Installations.

(A) If the on-site power source is a generator, it shall comply with either of the following:

(1) The generator shall be installed in a suitable enclosure located outside the building and capable of resisting the entrance of snow or rain at a maximum wind velocity as required by local building codes.
(2) The generator shall be constructed such that it is capable of resisting the impacts of snow or rain.

Δ **(B)** Equipment serving a generator shall be permitted to be installed in the generator enclosure.

Δ **(C)** No other equipment, including architectural appurtenances, except those that serve the space shall be permitted in the generator enclosure.

Δ **6.7.1.2.3.3** On-site power source equipment for Level 1 systems shall not be installed in the same room as other power source service equipment where the service equipment is rated over 150 volts to ground and equal to or greater than 1000 amperes.

Δ **6.7.1.2.3.4** The rooms, enclosures, or separate buildings housing on-site power source equipment for Level 1 or Level 2 systems shall be designed and located to minimize damage from flooding, including that caused by the following:

(1) Firefighting
(2) Sewer water backup
(3) Other disasters or occurrences

Δ **6.7.1.2.3.5** Minimizing the possibility of damage resulting from interruptions of the on-site power source shall be a design consideration for that equipment.

Δ **6.7.1.2.3.6** Design considerations shall minimize the effect of the failure of one on-site power source on the continued operation of other units.

Δ **6.7.1.2.4* Capacity and Rating.** The essential electrical system source or sets of sources shall have the capacity and rating to meet the maximum demand likely to be produced by the connected load and be consistent with the facility's emergency operations plan.

Δ **6.7.1.2.5 Load Pickup.** The source or set of sources shall have the required capacity and response to pick up and carry the load within the time specified in Table 6.11.1(b) upon failure of the other source or set of sources.

6.7.1.2.6 Heating, Cooling, and Ventilating. Design of the heating, cooling, and ventilation system for the on-site power sources room shall provide for factors including, but not limited to, the following:

(1) Heat
(2) Cold
(3) Dust
(4) Humidity
(5) Snow and ice accumulations around housings
(6) Louvers
(7) Remote radiator fans, as applicable
(8) Prevailing winds blowing against radiator fan discharge air

6.7.1.2.7 Alarm Annunciator.

6.7.1.2.7.1 A remote annunciator that is storage battery–powered shall be provided to operate outside of the generating room in a location readily observed by operating personnel at a regular work station.

6.7.1.2.7.2 The annunciator shall be hard-wired to indicate alarm conditions of the on-site power source as indicated in 6.7.1.2.7.2(A) through 6.7.1.2.7.2(H).

(A) Individual visual signals shall indicate the following:

(1) When the on-site power source is operating to supply power to load
(2) When the battery charger is malfunctioning (if provided)

(B)* A remote, common audible alarm shall be provided as specified in 6.7.1.2.7.2(G). [**110**:5.6.6]

(C) Local annunciation and either facility or network remote annunciation shall be provided for a Level 1 on-site power source.

(D) For the purposes of defining the types of annunciation in 6.7.1.2.7.2(C), the following shall apply:

(1) Local annunciation is located on the equipment itself or within the same equipment room.
(2) Facility remote annunciation is located on site but not within the room where the equipment is located.
(3) Network remote annunciation is located off site. [**110**:5.6.6.3]

(E) An alarm-silencing means shall be provided, and the panel shall include repetitive alarm circuitry so that, after the audible alarm has been silenced, it reactivates after the fault condition has been cleared and has to be restored to its normal position to be silenced again. [**110:**5.6.6.4]

Δ **(F)** In lieu of the requirement in 6.7.1.2.7.2(E), a manual alarm-silencing means shall be permitted that silences the audible alarm after the occurrence of the alarm condition, provided such means do not inhibit any subsequent alarms from sounding the audible alarm again without further manual action. [**110:**5.6.6.5]

Δ **(G)** Individual alarm indication to annunciate any of the conditions listed in Table 6.7.1.3.8.2 shall have the following characteristics:

(1) Be battery powered
(2) Be visually indicated
(3) Have additional contacts or circuits for a common audible alarm that signals locally and remotely when any of the itemized conditions occurs
(4) Have switches to test the operation of all visual alarm indicators

(H)* The following shall apply to centralized computer systems:

(1) They shall not be used as a substitute for the alarm annunciator in 6.7.1.2.7.
(2) They shall be permitted to supplement the alarm annunciator in 6.7.1.2.7.

(I) Wireless transmission of the EPS data required by 6.7.1.3.8.2 and 6.7.1.3.8.3 shall be permitted.

6.7.1.3 Generator Set.

6.7.1.3.1 General. A single generator set that operates the essential electrical system shall be permitted to be part of the system supplying the other purposes as specified in 6.7.1.2.2.1, provided that any such use will not decrease the mean period between service overhauls to less than 3 years.

Δ **6.7.1.3.2 Location.** The generator equipment shall be installed in a location that permits ready accessibility and a minimum of 0.9 m (36 in.) from the skid rails' outermost point in the direction of access for inspection, repair, maintenance, cleaning, or replacement. This requirement shall not apply to units in outdoor housings.

Δ **6.7.1.3.3 Maintenance of Temperature.** The generator shall be heated as necessary to maintain the water jacket and battery temperature determined by the generator manufacturer for cold start and load acceptance for the type of system.

Δ **6.7.1.3.4* Heating, Cooling, and Ventilating.** With the generator running at rated load, ventilation airflow shall be provided to limit the maximum air temperature in the generator room or the enclosure housing the unit to the maximum ambient air temperature permitted by the generator manufacturer.

Δ **6.7.1.3.4.1** Consideration shall be given to all the heat emitted to the generator equipment room by the energy converter, uninsulated or insulated exhaust pipes, and other heat-producing equipment.

6.7.1.3.4.2* If required by the manufacturer, ventilation shall be supplied to the generator equipment.

Δ **(A)** For generators supplying Level 1 EPSS, ventilation air shall be supplied directly from a source outside the building by an exterior wall opening or from a source outside the building by a 2-hour fire-rated air transfer system.

Δ **(B)** For generators supplying Level 1 EPSS, discharge air shall be directed outside the building by an exterior wall opening or to an exterior opening by a 2-hour fire-rated air transfer system.

Δ **(C)** Fire dampers, shutters, or other self-closing devices shall not be permitted in ventilation openings or ductwork for supply or return/discharge air to generator equipment for Level 1 EPSS.

6.7.1.3.4.3 Ventilation air supply shall be from outdoors or from a source outside the building by an exterior wall opening or from a source outside the building by a 2-hour fire-rated air transfer system. [**110:**7.7.3]

Δ **6.7.1.3.4.4** Ventilation air shall be provided to supply and discharge cooling air for radiator cooling of the generator when running at rated load.

Δ **(A)** Ventilation air supply and discharge for a radiator-cooled generator shall have a maximum static restriction of 125 Pa (0.5 in. of water column) in the discharge duct at the radiator outlet.

(B) Radiator air discharge shall be ducted outdoors or to an exterior opening by a 2-hour rated air transfer system. [**110:**7.7.4.2]

Δ **6.7.1.3.4.5** Motor-operated dampers, when used, shall be spring operated to open and motor closed. Fire dampers, shutters, or other self-closing devices shall not be permitted in ventilation openings or ductwork for supply or return/discharge air to generator equipment for Level 1 systems.

Δ **6.7.1.3.4.6** The ambient air temperature in the generator equipment room or outdoor housing containing Level 1 rotating equipment shall stabilize at not less than 4.5°C (40°F) when the equipment is not operating.

6.7.1.3.5* Energy Converters. Internal combustion engine energy converters and associated cranking batteries shall be in accordance with the requirements of NFPA 110.

6.7.1.3.6 Compressed Air Starting Devices. Other types of stored energy starting systems (except pyrotechnic) shall be permitted to be used where recommended by the manufacturer of the prime mover and subject to approval of the authority having jurisdiction, under the following conditions:

(1) Where two complete periods of cranking cycles are completed without replacement of the stored energy
(2) Where a means for automatic restoration from the emergency source of the stored energy is provided
(3) Where the stored energy system has the cranking capacity specified in 5.6.4.2.1 of NFPA 110
(4) Where the stored energy system has a "black start" capability in addition to normal discharge capability
[**110:**5.6.4.1.2]

6.7.1.3.7 Fuel Supply. The fuel supply for the generator set shall comply with Sections 5.5 and 7.9 of NFPA 110.

6.7.1.3.8 Requirements for Safety Devices.

6.7.1.3.8.1 Internal Combustion Engines. Internal combustion engines serving generator sets shall be equipped with the following:

(1) Sensor device plus visual warning device to indicate a water-jacket temperature below that required in 6.7.1.3.3

(2) Sensor devices plus visual prealarm warning device to indicate the following:

   (a) High engine temperature (above manufacturer's recommended safe operating temperature range)

   (b) Low lubricating oil pressure (below manufacturer's recommended safe operating range)

   (c) Low water coolant level

(3) Automatic engine shutdown device plus visual device to indicate that a shutdown took place due to the following:

   (a) Overcrank (failed to start)

   (b) Overspeed

   (c) Low lubricating oil pressure

   (d) Excessive engine temperature

(4) Common audible alarm device to warn that one or more of the prealarm or alarm conditions exist

6.7.1.3.8.2 Safety Indications and Shutdowns. Safety indications and shutdowns shall be in accordance with Table 6.7.1.3.8.2.

6.7.1.3.8.3 Individual visual signals plus a common audible signal to warn of an engine-generator alarm condition shall indicate the following:

(1) Low lubricating oil pressure

(2) Low water temperature (below that required in 6.7.1.3.3)

(3) Excessive water temperature

(4) Low fuel when the main fuel storage tank contains less than a 4-hour operating supply

(5) Overcrank (failed to start)

(6) Overspeed

6.7.1.4 Health Care Microgrid. A health care microgrid in accordance with Section 6.10 shall be permitted to serve as the EPS for all or part of an essential electrical system.

6.7.2* Distribution.

6.7.2.1 General Requirements.

6.7.2.1.1* Coordination.

6.7.2.1.1.1 Overcurrent protective devices serving the essential electrical system shall be coordinated for the period of time that a fault's duration extends beyond 0.1 second.

6.7.2.1.1.2 Coordination shall not be required as follows:

(1) Between transformer primary and secondary overcurrent protective devices, where only one overcurrent protective device or set of overcurrent protective devices exists on the transformer secondary

(2) Between overcurrent protective devices of the same size (ampere rating) in series

N **6.7.2.1.2 Ground-Fault Protection of Equipment, Essential Electrical System.**

N **6.7.2.1.2.1** Ground-fault protection of equipment with automatic disconnecting means shall not be required on alternate power supply sources, between alternate power supply

△ **Table 6.7.1.3.8.2 Safety Indications and Shutdowns**

Indicator Function (at Battery Voltage)	Level 1		
	CV	S	RA
(a) Overcrank	X	X	X
(b) Low water temperature	X	—	X
(c) High engine temperature prealarm	X	—	X
(d) High engine temperature	X	X	X
(e) Low lube oil pressure prealarm	X	—	X
(f) Low lube oil pressure	X	X	X
(g) Overspeed	X	X	X
(h) Low fuel main tank	X	—	X
(i) Low coolant level	X	O	X
(j) EPS supplying load	X	—	—
(k) Control switch not in automatic position	X	—	X
(l) High battery voltage	X	—	—
(m) Low cranking voltage	X	—	X
(n) Low voltage in battery	X	—	—
(o) Battery charger ac failure	X	—	—
(p) Lamp test	X	—	—
(q) Contacts for local and remote common alarm	X	—	X
(r) Audible alarm-silencing switch	—	—	X
(s) Low starting air pressure	X	—	—
(t) Low starting hydraulic pressure	X	—	—
(u) Air shutdown damper when used	X	X	X
(v) Remote emergency stop	—	X	—

CV: Control panel–mounted visual. S: Shutdown of EPS indication. RA: Remote audible. X: Required. O: Optional.

Notes:

(1) Item (p) is to be provided, but a separate remote audible signal is not required when the regular work site in 5.6.6 of NFPA 110 is staffed 24 hours a day.

(2) Item (b) is not required for combustion turbines.

(3) Item (r) or (s) is required only where used as a starting method.

(4) Item (j): EPS ac ammeter is permitted for this function.

(5) All required CV functions are to be visually annunciated by a remote, common visual indicator.

(6) All required functions indicated in the RA column are to be annunciated by a remote, common audible alarm as required in 5.6.5.2(4) of NFPA 110.

(7) Item (i) requires a low gas pressure alarm on gaseous systems.

(8) Item (b) must be set at 11°C (20°F) below the regulated temperature determined by the EPS manufacturer, as required in 5.3.1 of NFPA 110.

sources and any essential electrical system transfer switch, or on the load side of any essential electrical system transfer switch.

N **6.7.2.1.2.2** Ground-fault indication without automatic disconnection shall be provided at any on-site power source.

6.7.2.1.3 Automatic Transfer Switch Features.

6.7.2.1.3.1 Source Monitoring.

△ **(A)*** Undervoltage-sensing devices shall be provided to monitor all ungrounded lines of the primary power source as follows:

(1) When the voltage on any phase falls below the minimum operating voltage of any load to be served, the transfer

switch shall automatically initiate engine start and the process of transfer to the other power source.

(2)* When the voltage on all phases of the primary source returns to within specified limits for a designated period of time, the process of transfer back to the primary power source shall be initiated.

Δ **(B)** Both voltage-sensing and frequency-sensing equipment shall be provided to monitor one ungrounded line of the power sources.

Δ **(C)** Transfer to a power source shall be inhibited until the voltage and frequency are within a specified range to handle loads to be served.

(D) Sensing equipment shall not be required in the transfer switch, provided it is included with the engine control panel. [**110:**6.2.2.3.1]

Δ **(E)** Frequency-sensing equipment shall not be required for monitoring the off-site power source.

Δ **6.7.2.1.3.2 Interlocking.** Mechanical interlocking or an approved alternate method shall prevent the inadvertent interconnection of any two separate power sources.

6.7.2.1.3.3* Manual Operation. Instruction and equipment shall be provided for safe manual nonelectric transfer in the event the transfer switch malfunctions. [**110:**6.2.4]

Δ **6.7.2.1.3.4* Time Delay on Starting of Power Sources.**

N **(A)** A time-delay device shall be provided to delay starting of the on-site power source.

N **(B)** The time-delay device shall prevent nuisance starting of the power source and possible subsequent load transfer in the event of harmless momentary power dips and interruptions of the primary power source.

6.7.2.1.3.5 Time Delay at Engine Control Panel. Time delays shall be permitted to be located at the engine control panel in lieu of in the transfer switches. [**110:**6.2.6]

Δ **6.7.2.1.3.6 Time Delay on Transfer.** An adjustable time-delay device shall be provided to delay transfer and sequence load transfer to the power source to avoid excessive voltage drop when the transfer switch is installed for Level 1 use.

Δ **(A) Time Delay Commencement.** The time delay shall commence when proper voltage and frequency are achieved.

(B) Time Delay at Engine Control Panel. Time delays shall be permitted to be located at the engine control panel in lieu of in the transfer switches. [**110:**6.2.7.2]

Δ **6.7.2.1.3.7* Time Delay on Retransfer to Primary Power Source.** An adjustable time-delay device with automatic bypass shall be provided to delay retransfer from one power source to the other power source, and allow the power source to stabilize before retransfer of the load.

Δ **6.7.2.1.3.8 Time Delay Bypass If a Power Source Fails.** The time delay shall be automatically bypassed if a power source fails.

Δ **(A)** The transfer switch shall be permitted to be programmed for a manually initiated retransfer to the on-site power source to provide for a planned momentary interruption of the load.

Δ **(B)** If used, the arrangement in 6.7.2.1.3.8(A) shall be provided with a bypass feature to allow automatic retransfer in the event that the on-site power source fails and the other power source is available.

Δ **6.7.2.1.3.9 Time Delay on Engine Shutdown.** A minimum time delay of 5 minutes shall be provided for unloaded running of a generator prior to shutdown to allow for engine cooldown.

(A) The minimum 5-minute delay shall not be required on small (15 kW or less) air-cooled prime movers. [**110:**6.2.10.1]

Δ **(B)** A time-delay device shall not be required if it is included with the engine control panel or if a utility feeder is used as a power source.

Δ **6.7.2.1.3.10 Test Switch.** A test means shall be provided on each automatic transfer switch (ATS) that simulates failure of one power source and then transfers the load to another power source(s).

6.7.2.1.3.11* Indication of Transfer Switch Position. Two pilot lights with identification nameplates or other approved position indicators shall be provided to indicate the transfer switch position. [**110:**6.2.13]

Δ **6.7.2.1.3.12 Motor Load Transfer.** Provisions shall be included to reduce currents resulting from motor load transfer if such currents could damage power source equipment or cause nuisance tripping of power source overcurrent protective devices.

Δ **6.7.2.1.3.13* Isolation of Neutral Conductors.** Provisions shall be included for ensuring continuity, transfer, and isolation of the power source neutral conductors wherever they are separately grounded to achieve ground-fault sensing.

6.7.2.1.3.14 Retransfer. If a power source or set of power sources fails during a test, provisions shall be made to immediately retransfer to the other power source or set of power sources.

6.7.2.1.3.15 Switch Rating. The rating of the transfer switches shall be adequate for switching all classes of loads to be served and for withstanding the effects of available fault currents without contact welding.

Δ **6.7.2.1.3.16* Automatic Transfer Switch.**

N **(A)** Transfer of all loads shall be accomplished using an automatic transfer switch(es).

N **(B)** Each automatic transfer switch of 600 V or less shall be listed for the purpose and marked for emergency use.

6.7.2.1.3.17* Nonautomatic Transfer Switch Features. Switching devices shall be mechanically held and shall be operated by direct manual or electrical remote manual control. [**110:**6.2.16]

Δ **(A) Interlocking.** Reliable mechanical interlocking or an approved alternate method shall prevent the inadvertent interconnection of the [primary] power source and the EPS. [**110:**6.2.16.1]

Δ **(B) Indication of Transfer Switch Position.** Two pilot lights with identification nameplates or other approved position indicators shall be provided to indicate the switch position. [**110:**6.2.16.2]

6.7.2.1.4 Nonautomatic Transfer Device Classification. Nonautomatic transfer devices of 600 V or less shall be listed for the purpose and approved.

6.7.2.1.5 Nonautomatic Transfer Device Features.

6.7.2.1.5.1 General. Switching devices shall be mechanically held and shall be operated by direct manual or electrical remote manual control. [**110**:6.2.16]

Δ **6.7.2.1.5.2 Interlocking.** Reliable mechanical interlocking or an approved alternate method shall prevent the inadvertent interconnection of two power sources.

6.7.2.1.5.3 Indication of Switch Position. Two pilot lights with identification nameplates, or other approved position indicators, shall be provided to indicate the switch position. [**110**:6.2.16.2]

6.7.2.1.6 Bypass and Isolating Transfer Switches. Bypass-isolation switches shall be permitted for bypassing and isolating the transfer switch and installed in accordance with 6.4.2, 6.4.3, and 6.4.4 of NFPA 110. [**110**:6.4.1]

6.7.2.1.6.1 Bypass-Isolation Switch Rating. The bypass-isolation switch shall have a continuous current rating and a current rating compatible with that of the associated transfer switch. [**110**:6.4.2]

6.7.2.1.6.2 Bypass-Isolation Switch Classification. Each bypass-isolation switch shall be listed for emergency electrical service as a completely factory-assembled and factory-tested apparatus. [**110**:6.4.3]

6.7.2.1.6.3* Operation. With the transfer switch isolated or disconnected, the bypass-isolation switch shall be designed so it can function as an independent nonautomatic transfer switch and allow the load to be connected to either power source. [**110**:6.4.4]

6.7.2.1.6.4 Reconnection of Transfer Switch. Reconnection of the transfer switch shall be possible without a load interruption greater than the maximum time, in seconds, specified by the type of system. [**110**:6.4.5]

6.7.2.2 Branches.

6.7.2.2.1 The division between the branches shall occur at transfer switches where more than one transfer switch is required.

6.7.2.2.2 Each branch shall be arranged for connection, within the time limits specified in this chapter, to another power source following a loss of a power source or set of sources.

6.7.2.2.3 The number of transfer switches to be used shall be based upon reliability, design, and load considerations.

6.7.2.2.3.1 Each branch of the essential electrical system shall have one or more transfer switches.

6.7.2.2.3.2 One transfer switch shall be permitted to serve one or more branches in a facility with a continuous load on the switch of 150 kVA (120 kW) or less.

Δ **6.7.2.2.3.3**

N **(A)** Where a single transfer switch is used as permitted in 6.7.2.2.3.2, the following requirements shall apply:

(1) The single transfer switch shall include a bypass-isolation switch to facilitate maintenance of the transfer switch without jeopardizing continuity of power to the connected load.
(2) Division into separate branches shall not be required.

N **(B)** A bypass-isolation switch in accordance with 6.7.2.2.3.3(A) shall not be required where any of the following conditions exist:

(1) All processes that rely on the essential electrical system are capable of being disabled during maintenance or repair activities.
(2) The building or structure is unoccupied and fire protection systems are fully functional and do not require an alternate power source.
(3) Other temporary means are permitted to be substituted for the essential electrical system.

6.7.2.2.4 Feeders from On-Site Power Source.

6.7.2.2.4.1 A single feeder supplied by the on-site power source shall be permitted to supply the essential electrical system to the point at which the life safety, critical, and equipment branches are separated.

6.7.2.2.4.2 Installation of the transfer equipment shall be permitted at locations other than that of the on-site power source.

6.7.2.2.5 Receptacles. The requirements for receptacles shall comply with 6.7.2.2.5(A) and 6.7.2.2.5(B).

(A) Branch-circuit overcurrent devices shall be readily accessible to authorized personnel.

(B)* The electrical receptacles or the cover plates for the electrical receptacles supplied from the life safety and critical branches shall have a distinctive color or marking so as to be readily identifiable.

6.7.2.2.6 Switches. Switches of all types shall be permitted in the lighting circuits connected to the essential electrical system in accordance with NFPA *101*.

6.7.2.2.7 Secondary circuits of transformer-powered communication or signaling systems shall not be required to be enclosed in raceways unless otherwise specified by Chapters 7 or 8 of *NFPA 70*.

6.7.3 Performance Criteria and Testing.

Δ **6.7.3.1 Transfer Switches.** All ac-powered support and accessory equipment necessary for the operation of the on-site power source shall be supplied from the load side of the automatic transfer switch(es), or the output terminals of the on-site power source, ahead of the main overcurrent protection to ensure continuity of operation and performance.

6.7.3.2 The essential electrical system shall be served by the normal power source, except when the normal power source is interrupted or drops below a predetermined voltage level. Settings of the sensors shall be determined by careful study of the voltage requirements of the load.

Δ **6.7.3.3** Failure of the normal source shall automatically start the other power source after a short delay, as described in 6.7.2.1.3.4.

N **6.7.3.3.1** When the other power source has attained a voltage and frequency that satisfies the minimum operating requirements of the essential electrical system, the load shall be connected automatically to the that source.

N 6.7.3.4 Generator Control Wiring. Control conductors installed between the transfer switch and the emergency generator(s) shall be kept entirely independent of all other wiring.

N 6.7.3.4.1 The integrity of the generator remote start circuit shall be monitored for broken, disconnected, or short-circuited wires.

N 6.7.3.4.2 Loss of integrity shall start the generator(s).

Δ 6.7.3.5 Upon connection of a power source, the loads comprising the life safety and critical branches shall be automatically re-energized.

N 6.7.3.5.1 The load comprising the equipment branch shall be connected either automatically after a time delay, as described in 6.7.2.1.3.6, or nonautomatically and in a sequential manner that will not overload the other power source.

Δ 6.7.3.6 When the first power source is restored, and after a time delay as described in 6.7.2.1.3.7, the automatic transfer switches shall disconnect the other power source and connect the loads to the first power source.

N 6.7.3.6.1 The other power source shall continue to run unloaded for a preset time delay, as described in 6.7.2.1.3.9.

6.7.3.7 If a power source fails and the other power source has been restored, retransfer to the other power source shall be immediate, bypassing the retransfer delay timer.

Δ 6.7.3.8 Nonautomatic transfer switching devices shall be restored as soon as possible or at the discretion of the operator.

6.7.4 Administration.

6.7.4.1 Maintenance and Testing of Essential Electrical System.

6.7.4.1.1 Maintenance and Testing of On-Site Power Source, Transfer Switches, and Associated Equipment.

6.7.4.1.1.1 Maintenance of On-Site Power Source. The on-site power source and associated equipment, including all appurtenance parts, shall be maintained such that it is capable of supplying service within the shortest time practicable and within the 10-second interval specified in 6.7.1.2.5 and 6.7.5.3.1.

Δ 6.7.4.1.1.2

N (A) The 10-second criterion shall not apply during the monthly testing of an essential electrical system.

N (B) If the 10-second criterion is not met during the monthly test, a process shall be provided to annually confirm the capability of the life safety and critical branches to comply with 6.7.5.3.1.

Δ 6.7.4.1.1.3 Maintenance shall be performed in accordance with Section 6.9.

6.7.4.1.1.4 Maintenance of the electrical equipment for the life safety branch, critical branch, and equipment branch shall be maintained in accordance with the manufacturer's instructions and preventative maintenance programs.

6.7.4.1.1.5 Inspection and Testing. Criteria, conditions, and personnel requirements shall be in accordance with 6.7.4.1.1.5(A) through 6.7.4.1.1.5(C).

(A)* Test Criteria. Testing criteria shall be as follows:

(1) Generator sets shall be tested 12 times a year, with testing intervals of not less than 20 days nor more than 40 days.
(2) Generator sets serving essential electrical systems shall be tested in accordance with Chapter 8 of NFPA 110.

(B) Test Conditions. The scheduled test under load conditions shall include a complete simulated cold start and appropriate automatic and manual transfer of all essential electrical system loads.

(C) Test Personnel. The scheduled tests shall be conducted by qualified personnel to keep the machines ready to function and, in addition, serve to detect causes of malfunction and to train personnel in operating procedures.

N 6.7.4.1.1.6 When a transfer switch is bypassed to facilitate maintenance, one of the following conditions shall apply:

(1) The bypass switch automatically transfers the load between power sources upon loss of the connected power source.
(2) The bypass switch remains actively supervised by a qualified person who can manually initiate a transfer of the load between power sources.

N 6.7.4.1.1.7 Where bypass isolation switches are used, inadvertent parallel operation shall be avoided.

6.7.4.1.2 Maintenance and Testing of Circuitry.

6.7.4.1.2.1 Insulation Resistance. The resistance readings of main feeder insulation shall be taken prior to acceptance and whenever damage is suspected.

6.7.4.1.2.2 Maintenance of Batteries. Batteries for on-site generators shall be maintained in accordance with NFPA 110.

6.7.4.2 Record Keeping. A written record of inspection, performance, exercising period, and repairs shall be regularly maintained and available for inspection by the authority having jurisdiction.

6.7.5* Type 1 Essential Electrical System Requirements.

6.7.5.1* Branches.

6.7.5.1.1 The essential electrical system shall be divided into the following three branches:

(1) Life safety
(2) Critical
(3) Equipment

6.7.5.1.2 Life Safety Branch.

6.7.5.1.2.1 The life safety branch shall be limited to circuits essential to life safety.

6.7.5.1.2.2 The life safety branch shall supply power as follows:

(1) Illumination of means of egress in accordance with NFPA *101*
(2) Exit signs and exit directional signs in accordance with NFPA *101*
(3)* Communications systems, where used for issuing instruction during emergency conditions
(4) Generator set location as follows:

   (a) Task illumination
   (b) Battery charger for emergency battery-powered lighting unit(s)

(c) Select receptacles at the generator set location and essential electrical system transfer switch locations

(5) Elevator cab lighting, control, communications, and signal systems

(6) Electrically powered doors used for building egress

(7) Fire alarms and auxiliary functions of fire alarm combination systems complying with *NFPA 72*

6.7.5.1.2.3 Alarm and alerting systems (other than fire alarm systems) shall be connected to the life safety branch or critical branch.

6.7.5.1.2.4 Loads dedicated to a specific generator, including the fuel transfer pump(s), ventilation fans, electrically operated louvers, controls, cooling system, and other generator accessories essential for generator operation, shall be connected to the life safety branch or the output terminals of the generator with overcurrent protective devices.

6.7.5.1.2.5 No functions other than those in 6.7.5.1.2.2, 6.7.5.1.2.3, and 6.7.5.1.2.4 shall be connected to the life safety branch, except as specifically permitted in 6.7.5.1.2.

N **6.7.5.1.2.6 Branch Circuits for Life Safety Lighting.** Branch circuits supplying life safety lighting shall be served from a source in compliance with 6.7.1 when the normal supply for lighting is interrupted or where single circuits supply luminaires containing secondary batteries.

N **6.7.5.1.2.7 Life Safety Lighting Circuit Switches.** Life safety lighting circuit switches shall meet the following requirements:

(1) The switch(es) for the life safety lighting circuits shall be arranged so that only authorized persons have control of the life safety lighting switch(es) unless one of the following conditions are met:

(a) Where two or more single-throw switches are connected in parallel to control a single circuit, at least one of these switches is accessible only to authorized persons.

(b) Additional switches are included that act only to put life safety lights into operation, but not to disconnect them.

(2) Switches connected in series or 3- and 4-way switches shall not be used.

(3) All manual switches for controlling life safety lighting shall meet the following requirements:

(a) The manual switches shall be in locations convenient to authorized persons responsible for their actuation unless there are multiple switches provided.

(b) One of the switches shall be permitted to be located so that it can only energize, but not de-energize, the circuit.

N **6.7.5.1.2.8 Life Safety Lighting Dimmer and Relay Systems.** A dimmer or relay system containing more than one dimmer or relay and listed for emergency use shall be permitted to be used as a control device for energizing life safety lighting circuits.

N **(A)** Upon failure of normal power, the dimmer or relay system shall be permitted to selectively energize only those branch circuits necessary to provide the minimum required illumination using a control bypass function.

N **(B)** Where the dimmer or relay system is supplied by an upstream transfer switch, normal power sensing for this function shall be permitted to be from a normal-only power source upstream of the transfer switch.

N **6.7.5.1.2.9 Directly Controlled Life Safety Luminaires.** Where life safety illumination is provided by a directly controlled life safety luminaire(s) that responds to an external control input, or loss thereof, to bypass normal control upon loss of normal power, the luminaire(s) and external bypass control(s) shall be individually listed for emergency use.

N **6.7.5.1.2.10 Life Safety Lighting Automatic Load Control Relay.**

N **(A)** If a life safety lighting load is automatically energized upon loss of the normal supply, a listed automatic load control relay shall be permitted to energize the load.

N **(B)** The load control relay shall not be used as transfer equipment.

6.7.5.1.3* Critical Branch.

6.7.5.1.3.1 The critical branch shall be permitted to be subdivided into two or more branches.

6.7.5.1.3.2 The critical branch shall supply power for task illumination, fixed equipment, select receptacles, and select power circuits serving the following spaces and functions related to patient care:

(1) Category 1 spaces where deep sedation or general anesthesia is administered, task illumination, select receptacles, and fixed equipment

(2) Task illumination and select receptacles in the following:

(a) Patient care spaces, including infant nurseries, selected acute nursing areas, psychiatric bed areas (omit receptacles), and ward treatment rooms

(b) Medication preparation spaces

(c) Pharmacy dispensing spaces

(d) Nurses' stations — unless adequately lighted by corridor luminaires

(3) Additional specialized patient care task illumination and receptacles, where needed

(4) Nurse call systems

(5) Blood, bone, and tissue banks

(6)* Telecommunications entrance facility, telecommunications equipment rooms, and telecommunication rooms and equipment in these rooms.

(7) Task illumination, select receptacles, and select power circuits for the following areas:

(a) Category 1 or 2 spaces with at least one duplex receptacle per patient bed location, and task illumination as required by the governing body of the health care facility

(b) Angiographic labs

(c) Cardiac catheterization labs

(d) Coronary care units

(e) Hemodialysis rooms or areas

(f) Emergency room treatment areas (select)

(g) Human physiology labs

(h) Intensive care units

(i) Postoperative recovery rooms (select)

(8) Clinical IT-network equipment

(9) Wireless phone and paging equipment for clinical staff communications

(10) Additional task illumination, receptacles, and select power circuits needed for effective facility operation,

including single-phase fractional horsepower motors, which are permitted to be connected to the critical branch

6.7.5.1.4 Equipment Branch.

6.7.5.1.4.1 General. The equipment branch shall be connected to equipment described in 6.7.5.1.4.3 through 6.7.5.1.4.4.

6.7.5.1.4.2 Connection to On-Site Power Source.

Δ **(A)** The equipment branch shall be installed and connected to the on-site power source such that equipment described in 6.7.5.1.4.3 is automatically restored to operation at appropriate time-lag intervals following the energizing of the life safety and critical branches.

(B) The arrangement of the connection to the on-site power source shall also provide for the subsequent connection of equipment described in 6.7.5.1.4.4.

6.7.5.1.4.3* Equipment for Delayed-Automatic Connection.

(A) The following equipment shall be permitted to be arranged for delayed-automatic connection to the on-site power source:

(1) Central suction systems serving medical and surgical functions, including controls, with such suction systems permitted to be placed on the critical branch
(2) Sump pumps and other equipment required to operate for the safety of major apparatus, including associated control systems and alarms
(3) Compressed air systems serving medical and surgical functions, including controls, with such air systems permitted to be placed on the critical branch
(4) Smoke control and stair pressurization systems
(5) Kitchen hood supply or exhaust systems, or both, if required to operate during a fire in or under the hood
(6) Supply, return, and exhaust ventilating systems for the following:
 (a) Airborne infectious/isolation rooms
 (b) Protective environment rooms
 (c) Exhaust fans for laboratory fume hoods
 (d) Nuclear medicine areas where radioactive material is used
 (e) Ethylene oxide evacuation
 (f) Anesthetic evacuation

(B) Where delayed-automatic connection is not appropriate, the ventilation systems specified in 6.7.5.1.4.3(A)(6) shall be permitted to be placed on the critical branch.

Δ **6.7.5.1.4.4* Equipment for Delayed-Automatic or Manual Connection.** The following equipment shall be permitted to be arranged for either delayed-automatic or manual connection to the on-site power source *(also see A.6.7.5.1.4.3)*:

(1) Heating equipment used to provide heating for operating, delivery, labor, recovery, intensive care, and coronary care spaces; nurseries; infection/isolation rooms; emergency treatment spaces; and general patient rooms and pressure maintenance (i.e., jockey or make-up) pumps for water-based fire protection systems
(2)* Heating of general patient rooms during disruption of the normal source shall not be required under any of the following conditions:
 (a) Outside design temperature is higher than –6.7°C (+20°F)

(b) Outside design temperature is lower than –6.7°C (+20°F), where a selected room(s) is provided for the needs of all confined patients [then only such room(s) need be heated]
(3) Elevator(s) selected to provide service to patient, surgical, obstetrical, and ground floors during interruption of normal power
(4) Supply, return, and exhaust ventilating systems for surgical and obstetrical delivery suites; intensive care and coronary care spaces; nurseries; and emergency treatment spaces
(5) Hyperbaric facilities
(6) Hypobaric facilities
(7) Autoclaving equipment, which is permitted to be arranged for either automatic or manual connection to the alternate source
(8) Controls for equipment listed in 6.7.5.1.3
(9)* Other selected equipment

6.7.5.1.5 Generator load-shed circuits designed for the purpose of load reduction or for load priority systems shall not shed life safety branch loads, critical branch loads serving Category 1 spaces, medical air compressors, medical–surgical vacuum pumps, fire pumps, the pressure maintenance (i.e., jockey) pump(s) for water-based fire protection systems, generator fuel pumps, or other generator accessories.

6.7.5.2 Wiring Requirements.

6.7.5.2.1* Separation from Other Circuits. The life safety branch and critical branch shall be kept independent of all other wiring and equipment.

6.7.5.2.2 Mechanical Protection of the Life Safety and Critical Branches. The wiring of the life safety and critical branches shall be mechanically protected by raceways, as defined in *NFPA 70*.

6.7.5.2.3 Flexible power cords of appliances or other utilization equipment connected to the life safety and critical branches shall not be required to be enclosed in raceways.

6.7.5.3 Performance Criteria and Testing.

Δ **6.7.5.3.1 Source.** The life safety and critical branches shall be installed and connected to the on-site power source specified in 6.7.1.1.2 so that all functions specified herein for the life safety and critical branches are automatically restored to operation within 10 seconds after interruption of power.

6.7.6* Type 2 Essential Electrical System Requirements.

6.7.6.1 Sources. The requirements for sources for Type 2 essential electrical systems shall conform to those listed in 6.7.1.

6.7.6.2 Distribution.

6.7.6.2.1* Branches.

6.7.6.2.1.1 The number of transfer switches to be used shall be based upon reliability, design, and load considerations.

6.7.6.2.1.2 The essential electrical system shall be divided into the following two branches:

(1) Life safety branch
(2) Equipment branch

6.7.6.2.1.3 Each branch of the essential electrical system shall have one or more transfer switches.

6.7.6.2.1.4 One transfer switch shall be permitted to serve one or more branches in a facility with a continuous load on the switch of 150 kVA (120 kW) or less.

6.7.6.2.1.5 Life Safety Branch.

(A) Required to be Connected. The life safety branch shall supply power to the following:

(1) Illumination of means of egress in accordance with NFPA *101*
(2) Exit signs and exit directional signs in accordance with NFPA *101*
(3) Alarm and alerting systems, including the following:

   (a) Fire alarms
   (b) Alarms required for systems used for the piping of nonflammable medical gases as specified in Chapter 5

(4)* Communications systems, where used for issuing instructions during emergency conditions
(5) Task illumination and select receptacles at the generator set location
(6) Elevator cab lighting, control, communications, and signal systems

Δ **(B) Prohibited to be Connected.** No functions other than those listed in 6.7.6.2.1.5(A)(1) through 6.7.6.2.1.5(A)(6) shall be connected to the life safety branch.

N **(C) Branch Circuits for Life Safety Lighting.** Branch circuits that supply life safety lighting shall be served from a source in accordance with 6.7.1 when the normal supply for lighting is interrupted or where single circuits supply luminaries containing secondary batteries.

N **(D) Life Safety Lighting Circuit Switches.** Life safety lighting circuit switches shall meet the following requirements:

(1) The switch(es) for the life safety lighting circuits shall be arranged so that only authorized persons have control of the life safety lighting switch(es) unless one of the following conditions are met:

   (a) Where two or more single-throw switches are connected in parallel to control a single circuit, at least one of these switches is accessible only to authorized persons.
   (b) Additional switches are included that act only to put life safety lights into operation, but not to disconnect them.

(2) Switches connected in series or 3- and 4-way switches shall not be used.
(3) All manual switches for controlling life safety lighting shall meet the following requirements:

   (a) The manual switches shall be in locations convenient to authorized persons responsible for their actuation unless there are multiple switches provided.
   (b) One of the switches shall be permitted to be located so that it can only energize, but not de-energize, the circuit.

N **(E) Life Safety Lighting Dimmer and Relay Systems.** A dimmer or relay system containing more than one dimmer or relay and listed for emergency use shall be permitted to be used as a control device for energizing life safety lighting circuits. Upon failure of normal power, the dimmer or relay system shall be permitted to selectively energize only those

branch circuits necessary to provide minimum required illumination using a control bypass function. Where the dimmer or relay system is supplied by an upstream transfer switch, normal power sensing for this function shall be permitted to be from a normal-only power source upstream of the transfer switch.

N **(F) Life Safety Lighting Automatic Load Control Relay.** If a life safety lighting load is automatically energized upon loss of the normal supply, a listed automatic load control relay shall be permitted to energize the load. The load control relay shall not be used as transfer equipment.

6.7.6.2.1.6 Equipment Branch.

(A) Equipment Automatically Restored to Operation. The equipment branch shall be installed and connected to the on-site power source such that equipment listed in 6.7.6.2.1.6(C) is automatically restored to operation at appropriate time-lag intervals following the restoration of the life safety branch to operation.

Δ **(B) Connection of Additional Equipment.** The equipment branch arrangement shall provide for the additional connection of equipment listed in 6.7.6.2.1.6(D).

(C) AC Equipment for Nondelayed-Automatic Connection. Generator accessories including, but not limited to, the transfer fuel pump, electrically operated louvers, and other generator accessories essential for generator operation shall be arranged for automatic connection to the on-site power source.

(D) Delayed-Automatic Connections to Equipment Branch. The following equipment shall be permitted to be connected to the equipment branch and shall be arranged for delayed-automatic connection to the on-site power source:

(1) Task illumination and select receptacles in the following:

   (a) Patient care spaces
   (b) Medication preparation spaces
   (c) Pharmacy dispensing spaces
   (d) Nurses' stations — unless adequately lighted by corridor luminaires

(2) Supply, return, and exhaust ventilating systems for airborne infectious isolation rooms
(3) Sump pumps and other equipment required to operate for the safety of major apparatus and associated control systems and alarms
(4) Smoke control and stair pressurization systems
(5) Kitchen hood supply or exhaust systems, or both, if required to operate during a fire in or under the hood
(6) Nurse call systems
(7) HVAC systems serving the EF, TER, and TR

Δ **(E)* Delayed-Automatic or Manual Connections to Equipment Branch.** The following equipment shall be permitted to be connected to the equipment branch and shall be arranged for either delayed-automatic or manual connection to the alternate power source:

(1) *Heating Equipment to Provide Heating for General Patient Rooms.* Heating of general patient rooms during disruption of the normal source shall not be required under any of the following conditions:

   (a)* The outside design temperature is higher than −6.7°C (+20°F).
   (b) The outside design temperature is lower than −6.7°C (+20°F) and, where a selected room(s) is

provided for the needs of all confined patients, then only such room(s) need be heated.

    (c)   The facility is served by a dual source of normal power. *(See A.6.7.1.1 for more information.)*

(2)* *Elevator Service.* In instances where interruptions of power would result in elevators stopping between floors, throw-over facilities shall be provided to allow the temporary operation of any elevator for the release of passengers.

(3)   *Optional Connections to the Equipment Branch.* Additional illumination, receptacles, and equipment shall be permitted to be connected only to the equipment branch.

(4)   *Multiple Systems.* Where one switch serves multiple systems as permitted in 6.7.6.2, transfer for all loads shall be nondelayed automatic.

6.7.6.3 Wiring Requirements.

6.7.6.3.1* Separation from Other Circuits. The life safety and equipment branches shall be kept entirely independent of all other wiring and equipment.

6.7.6.3.2* Receptacles. The electrical receptacles or the cover plates for the electrical receptacles supplied from the life safety and equipment branches shall have a distinctive color or marking so as to be readily identifiable.

6.7.6.4 Performance Criteria and Testing.

Δ **6.7.6.4.1 Source.** The life safety and equipment branches shall be installed and connected to the on-site power source specified in 6.7.1.1.2 so that all functions specified herein for the life safety and equipment branches are automatically restored to operation within 10 seconds after interruption of power.

6.8 Site Acceptance Testing.

6.8.1* Site acceptance testing shall be performed on the electrical system and all electrical components serving Category 1 and Category 2 spaces.

6.8.1.1 Acceptance testing is required after initial installation or major renovation prior to the system being placed into service.

6.8.2* Site acceptance testing procedures shall be in accordance with industry-recognized standards and practices for equipment testing and system commissioning.

6.8.3 Site Acceptance Testing Records.

6.8.3.1 A record of all site acceptance testing procedures required in 6.8.1 and testing results shall be maintained.

6.8.3.2 Site acceptance testing records shall be retained for 5 years.

6.8.3.3 Record Medium.

6.8.3.3.1 The records shall be on a medium that will survive the retention period.

6.8.3.3.2 Paper or electronic media shall be permitted.

6.8.3.4 Record Reporting and Archiving.

6.8.3.4.1 The record shall be available for examination and, if required, reported to the authority having jurisdiction.

6.8.3.4.2 Archiving of records by any means shall be permitted if hard copies of the records can be provided promptly when requested.

Δ **6.9 Electrical Maintenance Program (EMP).**

6.9.1 EMP Program.

Δ **6.9.1.1*** All electrical components which are part of an electrical system serving a Category 1 and Category 2 space shall be part of an electrical maintenance program (EMP).

6.9.1.2 The EMP shall include the following elements:

(1)   Listing of all equipment and systems included as part of the program

(2)   Schedule of inspection, testing, and servicing (maintenance) of equipment

(3)   Survey and analysis of electrical equipment and systems to determine maintenance requirements and priorities

(4)   Scheduled routine inspections and tests

(5)   Review of inspection and test reports so that proper corrective measures can be prescribed

(6)   Performance of necessary work

(7)   Complete records

6.9.2 EMP Records.

6.9.2.1 A record of all testing and maintenance described in 6.9.4 shall be maintained.

6.9.2.2 EMP inspection, testing, and maintenance records shall be retained for 5 years.

6.9.2.3 EMP Record Medium.

6.9.2.3.1 The records shall be on a medium that will survive the retention period.

6.9.2.3.2 Paper or electronic media shall be permitted.

6.9.2.4 EMP Record Reporting and Archiving.

6.9.2.4.1 The record shall be available for examination and, if required, reported to the authority having jurisdiction.

6.9.2.4.2 Archiving of records by any means shall be permitted if hard copies of the records can be provided promptly when requested.

6.9.3 Corrective Measures.

6.9.3.1* Analysis of Inspection, Testing, and Maintenance Reports. Analysis of inspection, testing, and maintenance reports shall be followed by the implementation of appropriate corrective measures.

6.9.3.2 All corrective measures shall be documented in accordance with the requirements of 6.9.2.

6.9.4 EMP Intervals.

6.9.4.1* EMP intervals shall be in accordance with Table 6.9.4.1.

6.9.4.2* Alternative Equipment Maintenance (AEM) Program.

6.9.4.2.1 EMP intervals shall be permitted to be developed as part of an alternative equipment maintenance (AEM) program.

6.9.4.2.2 The AEM shall include the following elements:

(1)*   The AEM program shall be based on accepted standards of practice for electrical equipment maintenance.

(2)   The AEM program requirements (including EMP schedules) shall be clearly documented and available for inspection by the authority having jurisdiction.

Δ **Table 6.9.4.1 Electrical Maintenance Program (EMP) Intervals**

Item	Inspection Period	Testing Period	Maintenance Period
Medium-voltage switchgear	Every 3 months	Every 3 years	Every 3 years
Power distribution transformers (≥ 750 kVA)	Monthly	Every 3 years	Every 3 years
Generator (alternate source)	*(See Chapter 8 of NFPA 110.)*	*(See Chapter 8 of NFPA 110.)*	*(See Chapter 8 of NFPA 110.)*
Generator paralleling switchgear	Monthly	Annually	Every 3 years
Low-voltage switchgear/switchboards	Every 3 years	Every 3 years	Every 3 years
Overcurrent Protective Devices			
Fuses (≥ 400 A)	Every 3 years	Every 3 years	Every 3 years
Low-voltage power circuit breakers (≥ 400 A)	Every 3 years	Every 3 years	Every 3 years
Low-voltage molded-case circuit breakers (≥ 400 A)	Every 3 years	Every 3 years	Every 3 years
Medium-voltage circuit breakers	Every 3 years	Every 3 years	Every 3 years
Relays (including polyphase ground-fault equipment protection)	Every 3 years	Every 3 years	Every 3 years
Transfer equipment	Monthly	Every 3 years	Every 3 years
Bus duct	Every 3 years	Every 3 years	Every 3 years
Uninterruptible power supplies (≥ 100 kW)	Every 3 months	Every 6 months	Every 6 months
Isolated power panels	*(See 6.3.3.3.3.)*	*(See 6.3.3.3.3.)*	*(See 6.3.3.3.3.)*
Motor control equipment	Annually	Every 3 years	Every 3 years
Branch-circuit panelboards	Annually	Every 3 years	N/A
Wiring devices	*(See 6.3.3.2.)*	*(See 6.3.3.2.)*	*(See 6.3.3.2.)*
Battery-powered lighting units	*(See 6.3.2.6.8.)*	*(See 6.3.2.6.8.)*	*(See 6.3.2.6.8.)*

N/A: not applicable.

(3) The AEM program shall be developed and administered by qualified personnel, regardless of whether they are health care facility employees or contractors.

(4)* The AEM program shall consider the typical health and safety risks associated with the equipment's use, including "critical equipment" for which there exists a risk of serious injury or death to a patient or staff person if the equipment fails.

6.10 Health Care Microgrids.

6.10.1 General Requirements.

6.10.1.1 Applicability. (Reserved)

6.10.1.2* Purpose. The purpose of Section 6.10 shall be to describe requirements for multiple-source health care microgrid systems, ac or dc, utilized as all or a portion of EPSSs for health care facilities.

6.10.1.3* Campuses. Health care microgrids shall be permitted to serve individual buildings or campuses consisting of several buildings.

6.10.1.4 Non–Health Care Buildings. Health care microgrids shall be permitted to serve buildings that fall into multiple use categories as described in Chapter 4.

6.10.2 Sources.

6.10.2.1 All sources shall meet the installation and maintenance requirements of the applicable NFPA code.

Δ **6.10.2.2** Any combination of generation, storage, or transformation assets shall be permitted to serve as the on-site power source for all or a portion of health care microgrids.

N **6.10.2.2.1** The combination of sources shall provide performance equivalent to that of the requirements of 6.7.1.2.1.

6.10.3 Reliability.

6.10.3.1 Health care microgrid systems shall be designed with sufficient reliability to provide effective facility operation consistent with the facility's emergency operations plan.

6.10.3.2* Health care microgrid system components shall not be compromised by failure of the normal source.

6.10.4 Interconnection to an Electrical Utility. Health care microgrids that are interconnected to an external electrical utility shall comply with regulations relevant to the serving utility.

6.10.5 Distribution System. (Reserved)

6.10.6* Control System. Health care microgrid control systems shall comply with the requirements of this subsection.

6.10.6.1* Network Segregation.

6.10.6.1.1 Health care microgrid control system networks shall be segregated from other networks.

6.10.6.1.2 Intelligence and memory of health care microgrid control systems shall not be dependent on off-site resources.

6.10.6.2 Source Monitoring. (Reserved)

6.10.6.3 Design. The design of health care microgrid control systems shall include a sequence of operations for manual controlling of sources in the event of system failure.

6.10.6.4 Controller Backup Power. Health care microgrid controllers shall have a dedicated battery backup having a minimum 90-minute capacity.

6.10.6.5 Annunciation.

6.10.6.5.1 Health care microgrid control systems shall be capable of providing readouts that indicates which sources are operating.

6.10.6.5.2 The amount of power provided to the health care microgrid by each source shall be visible at all times.

6.10.6.6 Security. (Reserved)

6.10.7 Commissioning. Health care microgrid systems shall be commissioned in accordance with their sequence of operations.

6.10.7.1 Verification of Means and Methods. Health care microgrid system installers or commissioning agents shall prepare a written commissioning plan that provides a description of the means and methods necessary to document and verify that the system and its associated controls and safety systems are in proper working condition.

6.10.7.2 Commissioning Plan. Commissioning plans shall include the following:

(1) An overview of the commissioning process developed specifically for the health care microgrid and its controller to be installed and a narrative description of the activities to be conducted

(2)* Roles and responsibilities for all those involved in the planning, design, construction, installation, and operation of the health care microgrid

(3) Means and methods whereby the commissioning plan will be made available during the implementation of the health care microgrid project

(4) Plans and specifications necessary to understand the installation and operation of the health care microgrid and all associated components, operational controls, and safety systems

(5) A detailed description of each activity to be conducted during the commissioning process, who will perform each activity, and at what point in time each activity is to be conducted

(6) Procedures to be used in documenting the proper operation of the health care microgrid and all associated components, operational controls, and safety systems

(7) Guidelines and format for a commissioning checklist, relevant operational testing forms, and necessary commissioning

(8) Means and methods whereby facility operation and maintenance staff will be trained on the system

(9) Identification of personnel qualified to service, maintain, and respond to incidents involving the system

6.10.7.3 Commissioning Report. A commissioning report documenting the commissioning process and the results shall be provided.

6.10.7.3.1 The commissioning report shall be prepared by the health care microgrid system commissioning agent and summarize the commissioning process, the operation of the system, the associated operational controls, and the safety systems.

6.10.7.3.2 The commissioning report shall include the final commissioning plan and the results of the commissioning process, as well as a copy of the plans and specifications associated with the as-built health care microgrid system design and installation.

6.10.7.3.3 The commissioning report shall include any issues identified during commissioning and the measures taken to resolve them.

6.10.8 Inspection, Testing, and Maintenance.

6.10.8.1 The health care microgrid system shall be inspected, tested, and maintained by qualified personnel.

6.10.8.2 All health care microgrid components shall be inspected and maintained in accordance with manufacturers' instructions or annually, whichever occurs first.

6.10.8.3 Health care microgrid system components shall be tested in accordance with the manufacturers' requirements.

6.10.8.4 Health care microgrid systems shall be recommissioned for operation when the system configuration changes or every five years, whichever occurs first.

6.11 Classification of Emergency Power Supply Systems (EPSSs).

△ **6.11.1 General.** The EPSS shall provide a source of electrical power of required capacity, reliability, and quality to loads for a length of time as specified in Table 6.11.1(a) and within a specified time following loss or failure of power as specified in Table 6.11.1(b).

Table 6.11.1(a) Classification of EPSSs

Class	Minimum Time
Class 0.083	0.083 hr (5 min)
Class 0.25	0.25 hr (15 min)
Class 2	2 hr
Class 6	6 hr
Class 48	48 hr
Class X	Other time, in hours, as required by the application, code, or user

[**110:**Table 4.1(a)]

Table 6.11.1(b)   Types of EPSSs

Designation	Power Restoration
Type U	Basically uninterruptible (UPS systems)
Type 10	10 sec
Type 60	60 sec
Type 120	120 sec
Type M	Manual stationary or nonautomatic — no time limit

[**110**:Table 4.1(b)]

6.11.2 Class. The class defines the minimum time, in hours, for which the EPSS is designed to operate at its rated load without being refueled or recharged. *[See Table 6.11.1(a).]* [**110**:4.2]

6.11.3 Type. The type defines the maximum time, in seconds, that the EPSS will permit the load terminals of the transfer switch to be without acceptable electrical power. Table 6.11.1(b) provides the types defined by this standard. [**110**:4.3]

6.11.4 Level. This standard recognizes two levels of equipment installation, performance, and maintenance. [**110**:4.4]

6.11.4.1 Level 1 systems shall be installed where failure of the equipment to perform could result in loss of human life or serious injuries. [**110**:4.4.1]

6.11.4.2 Level 2 systems shall be installed where failure of the EPSS to perform is less critical to human life and safety. [**110**:4.4.2]

6.11.4.3 All equipment shall be permanently installed. [**110**:4.4.3]

Δ **6.11.4.4** Level 1 and Level 2 systems shall ensure that all loads served by the EPSS are supplied by an on-site power source that meets all the following criteria:

(1) It is of a quality within the operating limits of the load.
(2) It operates for a duration specified for the class as defined in Table 6.11.1(a).
(3) It operates within the time specified for the type as defined in Table 6.11.1(b).

Chapter 7   Information Technology and Communications Systems

7.1* Applicability. This chapter shall apply to new health care facilities as specified in Section 1.3.

7.2 Reserved.

7.3 Category 1 Systems.

7.3.1 Information Technology and Communications Systems Infrastructure.

7.3.1.1 Premises Distribution System (Fiber and Copper).

7.3.1.1.1 Cables and installation shall be in compliance with *NFPA 70* and TIA/EIA 568-B, *Commercial Building Telecommunications Cabling Standard.*

7.3.1.1.2 Distribution system cable labeling, record keeping, and alphanumeric schemes shall be in accordance with

TIA/EIA 606-B, *Administration Standard for Commercial Telecommunications Infrastructure.*

7.3.1.2* Telecommunications Systems' Spaces and Pathways.

7.3.1.2.1 Entrance Facility (EF).

7.3.1.2.1.1 General. The EF location shall be permitted to be combined with the telecommunications equipment room (TER).

7.3.1.2.1.2 Not less than two physically separated service entrance pathways into this location shall be required.

7.3.1.2.1.3 Remote Primary Data Center. In a facility where the primary data center is located remotely, two EFs and redundant telecommunications service entrances shall be provided.

7.3.1.2.1.4 Location Requirements and Restrictions.

(A) The EF shall be permitted to be located with the TER.

(B) Where the EF is combined with the TER, the space and electrical power and cabling shall be added to the TER to accommodate the telecommunications service provider's space and access requirements.

(C)* The EF shall be dedicated to low-voltage communication systems.

(D) Electrical equipment or fixtures (e.g., transformers, panelboards, conduit, wiring) that are not directly related to the support of the EF shall not be installed in or pass through the EF.

(E) Mechanical equipment and fixtures (e.g., water or drainage piping of any kind, ductwork, pneumatic tubing) that are not directly related to the support of the EF shall not be installed in, pass through, or enter the EF.

(F) The EF shall be located in an area not subject to flooding.

(G) The EF shall be as close as practicable to the building communications service entrance point.

7.3.1.2.1.5 Working Space. (Reserved)

7.3.1.2.1.6 Security. Access to the EF shall be determined based on a security vulnerability assessment.

7.3.1.2.1.7 Power Requirements.

(A) Circuits serving the EF shall be dedicated to serving the EF.

(B) Circuits serving equipment in the EF shall be connected to the critical branch of the essential electrical system.

(C) A minimum of one duplex receptacle served from normal power shall be provided on one wall of the EF for service and maintenance.

7.3.1.2.1.8 Environmental Requirements.

(A) Temperature and humidity in the EF shall be controlled in accordance with the manufacturer's equipment requirements.

(B)* HVAC systems serving the EF shall be connected to the equipment branch of the essential electrical system.

(C)* A positive-pressure differential with respect to surrounding areas shall be provided.

(D) Sprinklers shall be provided with wire cages or shall be recessed to prevent accidental operation.

7.3.1.2.1.9 Other Requirements. (Reserved)

7.3.1.2.2 Telecommunications Equipment Room (TER). Each facility shall have at least one TER space that meets the minimum requirements of this chapter.

7.3.1.2.2.1 General.

(A) The TER houses the main networking equipment and shall be permitted to also house application servers and data storage devices that serve the health care facility.

(B) Central equipment for other communications systems shall be permitted to be housed in the TER.

7.3.1.2.2.2* The EF shall be permitted to be combined with the TER space.

7.3.1.2.2.3 Reserved.

7.3.1.2.2.4 Location Requirements and Restrictions.

(A) Electrical equipment or fixtures (e.g., transformers, panelboards, conduit, wiring) that are not directly related to the support of the TER shall not be installed in, pass through, or enter the TER.

(B) Any mechanical equipment or fixtures (e.g., water or drainage piping of any kind, ductwork, pneumatic tubing) not directly related to the support of the TER shall not be installed in, pass through, or enter the TER.

(C) The TER shall be located in a nonsterile area of the facility.

(D) In geographic areas prone to hurricanes or tornadoes, the TER shall be located away from exterior curtain walls to prevent wind and water damage.

(E) The TER shall be located or designed to avoid vibration from mechanical equipment or other sources.

7.3.1.2.2.5 Working Space. Working space about communications cabinets, racks, or other equipment shall be in accordance with 110.26(A) of *NFPA 70*.

7.3.1.2.2.6 Security. Access to the TER shall be determined based on a security vulnerability assessment.

7.3.1.2.2.7 Power Requirements.

(A) Circuits serving the TER and the equipment within the TER shall be dedicated to serving the TER.

(B) Circuits serving other communications equipment in the TER shall be connected to the essential electrical system.

(C) A minimum of one duplex outlet shall be provided on each wall and shall be connected to normal power for service and maintenance.

7.3.1.2.2.8 Environmental Requirements.

(A) Temperature and humidity in the TER shall be controlled in accordance with the manufacturer's equipment requirements.

(B) HVAC systems serving the TER shall be connected to the equipment branch of the essential electrical system.

(C) A positive-pressure differential with respect to surrounding areas shall be provided.

7.3.1.2.2.9 Other Requirements. (Reserved)

7.3.1.2.3 Telecommunications Room (TR).

7.3.1.2.3.1 General. A TR houses telecommunications equipment, cable terminations, and cross-connect cabling.

7.3.1.2.3.2 Sufficient TRs shall be provided so that the horizontal cable to any data or communications outlet in the building can be reached without exceeding 90 m (295 ft) maximum cable length as tested electrically from the termination point in the TR to the outlet.

7.3.1.2.3.3 Reserved.

7.3.1.2.3.4 Location Requirements and Restrictions.

(A) Switchboards, panelboards, transformers, and similar electrical equipment that are not directly related to the support of the TR shall not be installed in the TR.

(B) Any mechanical equipment or fixtures (e.g., water or drainage piping of any kind, ductwork, pneumatic tubing) not directly related to the support of the TR shall not be installed in, pass through, or enter the TR.

(C) In geographic areas prone to hurricanes or tornadoes, TRs shall be located away from exterior curtain walls to prevent wind and water damage.

(D) A minimum of one TR shall be on each floor of the facility.

(E) A TR shall only serve the floor where it is located and shall be located so as to not exceed the maximum cable length in 7.3.1.2.3.2.

7.3.1.2.3.5 Working Space. Working space about communications cabinets, racks, or other equipment shall be in accordance with 110.26(A) of *NFPA 70*.

7.3.1.2.3.6 Security. Access to TRs shall be determined based on a security vulnerability assessment.

7.3.1.2.3.7 Power Requirements.

(A) Circuits serving the TR and the equipment within the TR shall be dedicated to serving the TR.

(B) Circuits serving the TR shall be connected to the critical branch of the essential electrical system.

(C) A minimum of one duplex receptacle shall be provided in each TR and shall be connected to normal power for service and maintenance.

7.3.1.2.3.8 Environmental Requirements.

(A) Temperature and humidity in the TR shall be controlled in accordance with the manufacturer's equipment requirements.

(B) Sprinklers shall be provided with wire cages or shall be recessed to prevent accidental discharge.

7.3.1.2.3.9 Other Requirements. Suspended ceilings shall not be required in the EF, TER, and TR.

7.3.1.2.4 Cabling Pathways and Raceway Requirements.

7.3.1.2.4.1 Backbone Distribution. Redundant pathways shall be provided between the EF and TER.

7.3.1.2.4.2 Conduits shall be provided for cabling in inaccessible ceiling spaces.

7.3.1.2.5 Outside Plant (OSP) Infrastructure.

7.3.1.2.5.1 General. OSP infrastructure shall consist of the conduits, vaults, and other pathways and cabling used to connect buildings on a campus and to provide services from off-campus service providers.

7.3.1.2.5.2 Pathways.

(A) Dual telecommunications service entrance pathways shall be provided to the EF.

(B) Service entrance pathways shall be a minimum of 6.1 m (20 ft) apart.

(C) Underground conduits for technology systems shall be a minimum of 0.61 m (2 ft) from underground steam and water piping if crossing perpendicularly, and a minimum of 1.83 m (6 ft) if parallel.

(D) Underground conduits for technology systems shall be a minimum of 0.61 m (2 ft) below grade.

7.3.1.3 Antennas. (Reserved)

7.3.2 Voice, Data, Communications, and Cable Television Systems.

7.3.2.1 Voice/Telecommunications. (Reserved)

7.3.2.2 Local Area Networks (LANs). (Reserved)

7.3.2.3 Wireless Local Area Network (LAN) Systems and Public WiFi Hot Spots. (Reserved)

7.3.2.4 Wireless Voice Systems and In-Building Cellular Networks. (Reserved)

7.3.2.5 UHF, VHF, 800 MHz, and 900 MHz Radio Communication Systems. (Reserved)

7.3.2.6 Cable Television. (Reserved)

7.3.3 Other Communications Systems.

7.3.3.1 Nurse Call Systems.

7.3.3.1.1* General. The nurse call systems shall communicate patient and staff calls for assistance and information in health care facilities.

7.3.3.1.1.1 The nurse call systems shall be the audiovisual type or tone visual type and listed for the purpose.

Δ **7.3.3.1.1.2** The recognized standard for a listed nurse call system shall be UL 1069, *Hospital Signaling and Nurse Call Equipment.*

7.3.3.1.1.3* The nurse call system shall provide event notifications for one or more of the following: medical device alarms, staff emergency calls, code calls, and staff or patient requests for help or assistance.

7.3.3.1.1.4 Primary notification of nurse call events shall be provided by a listed nurse call system in accordance with 7.3.3.1.8.

7.3.3.1.1.5* Supplemental features shall be permitted to include call notification to alphanumeric pagers and other wireless devices carried by health care facility staff.

7.3.3.1.2 Patient Area Call Stations. The locations of call stations and calling devices shall be in accordance with the requirements set forth by federal, state, and local codes.

7.3.3.1.2.1* Each patient bed location shall be provided with a call station.

7.3.3.1.2.2* A single call station that provides two-way voice communications shall not serve more than two adjacent beds with calling devices.

7.3.3.1.2.3* Call stations at patient bed locations shall be permitted to provide supplemental signaling of medical device alarms.

7.3.3.1.2.4 When provided, supplemental signaling of a medical device alarm shall be in accordance with 7.3.3.1.8.

7.3.3.1.2.5 Bath stations shall be provided at each inpatient toilet, bath, shower, or sitz bath and shall be accessible to a patient lying on the floor.

7.3.3.1.2.6 A pull cord shall be permitted to enable access by a patient lying on the floor.

7.3.3.1.3 Staff Emergency Call. The locations of staff emergency call stations shall be in accordance with the requirements set forth by federal, state, and local codes.

7.3.3.1.3.1* A staff emergency call shall be turned off only at the station, room, or space from where it originates.

7.3.3.1.4* Code Call. The nurse call system shall include provisions to summon assistance from medical emergency resuscitation teams in locations set forth by federal, state, and local codes.

7.3.3.1.4.1* A code call shall be turned off only at the station, room, or space from where it originates.

7.3.3.1.5 Call stations located in areas where patients are under constant visual surveillance, such as pre-op, recovery, and emergency units shall be permitted to be limited to the staff emergency call and the code call, and two-way communication with the patient bed location shall not be required.

7.3.3.1.6 Nurse call system provisions shall be provided for geriatric, Alzheimer's, and other dementia units where:

(1) All call stations shall have tamper-resistant fasteners.
(2) Provisions shall be made for the removal or covering of call buttons and outlets.
(3) Call cords or pull strings in excess of 152 mm (6 in.) shall not be permitted.

7.3.3.1.7 Nurse call system provisions shall not be required in psychiatric units, except for psychiatric seclusion ante/exam rooms where staff emergency call stations shall be provided:

(1) Call stations shall have tamper-resistant fasteners.
(2) Provisions shall be made for the removal or covering of call buttons and outlets.
(3) Call cords or pull strings shall not be permitted.
(4) Control to limit unauthorized use shall be permitted.

7.3.3.1.8 Notification Signals. The nurse call system shall annunciate each call visibly and audibly to all areas to where calls need to be directed and as required by state and local codes.

7.3.3.1.8.1 Notification signals for a code call and staff emergency call shall be individually identifiable and distinct from all other nurse call signals.

7.3.3.1.8.2 Activation of a call station including patient station, bath station, staff emergency station, and code call station shall activate the following notification signals:

(1) Visual signal in the corridor at the patient room door or care space
(2) Visual signals at corridor intersections where individual patient room door or care space signals are not directly visible from the associated nursing station
(3) Visible and audible signals at the nurse master station and associated duty stations
(4) Visible signals at the calling station from which the call originates
(5) A visual or aural signal indication at each audio calling station to indicate voice circuit operation

7.3.3.2 Patient Tracking. (Reserved)

7.3.3.3 Equipment and Asset Tracking. (Reserved)

7.3.3.4 Staff and Visitor Tracking. (Reserved)

7.3.3.5 Wireless Phone and Paging Integration.

7.3.3.5.1 Wireless phone and paging systems that are used for enhanced clinical staff communications and that can be integrated with the nurse call system or with a shared interoperable clinical IT network shall provide listed electrical safety and FCC certifications that are appropriate for the intended use.

7.3.3.5.2* Wireless phone and paging systems that are used for enhanced clinical staff communications and notification of nurse call events or interoperable clinical alarm events shall be managed and controlled as described in 7.3.3.7.1.

7.3.3.6 Patient and Equipment Monitoring Systems. (Reserved)

7.3.3.7 Clinical Information Systems.

7.3.3.7.1* The clinical IT network shall be managed and controlled in accordance with the following:

(1) The overall responsibility for risk management of the clinical IT network shall be that of the responsible organization.
(2) The responsible organization shall establish, maintain, and be accountable for the clinical IT network risk management file.
(3) The health care facility's governing body shall be accountable for all policies, resources, and risk management processes.
(4) The health care facility's governing body shall appoint a clinical IT network risk manager.
(5) The clinical IT network risk manager shall be responsible for all duties.
(6) Manufacturers for each device placed on the clinical IT network shall provide all required documentation.
(7) The health care facility's governing body shall be accountable for document control and procedures.

Δ **7.3.3.7.2*** It shall be permitted for the nurse call system to utilize the interoperable clinical IT network provided that the nurse call system is listed to UL 1069, *Hospital Signaling and*

Nurse Call Equipment, and identified for use in a shared network environment.

7.3.3.7.3* The clinical IT network shall provide at least two independent pathways where the operational capability of each pathway to each device shall be verified through end-to-end communication.

7.3.3.7.3.1 Where one single addressable device is served (e.g., an end-point terminal device with a single connection to the clinical IT network, which is not part of the network infrastructure transporting clinical information between end points), only one pathway shall be required.

7.3.3.7.4 Conditions that affect the operation of the normal and redundant clinical IT network pathways shall be annunciated as a trouble signal when minimal operational requirements cannot be met.

7.3.3.7.5* Requirements for utilizing the independent redundant network paths and monitoring the operational integrity of the clinical IT network shall be established in the clinical IT network risk management plan maintained by the health care facility's governing body.

7.3.3.7.6 An event management process for the clinical IT network shall be documented by the health care facility's governing body and include at least the following:

(1) Switchover from one pathway to the other when deemed necessary
(2) Record all negative events and remediation actions
(3) Report of events, actions, and findings by the clinical IT network risk manager
(4) Evaluate events, reassess risks, and propose appropriate changes through change-release management processes and, track all corrective and preventive actions

7.3.3.8 Pharmacy. (Reserved)

7.3.3.9 Material Management Information Systems. (Reserved)

7.3.3.10 Electronic Medical Records and Dictation Systems. (Reserved)

7.3.3.11 Medical Imaging Systems. (Reserved)

7.3.3.12 Archiving Systems. (Reserved)

7.3.4 Security Systems.

7.3.4.1 Internet Protocol (IP) Security Cameras Systems. (Reserved)

7.3.4.2 Digital Video Recording. (Reserved)

7.3.4.3 Intrusion Detection Systems. (Reserved)

7.3.4.4 Sitewide Monitoring. (Reserved)

7.3.4.5 Access Control Systems. (Reserved)

7.3.4.6 ID Badging Systems Integrated with Point of Sales Systems. (Reserved)

7.3.4.7 Threat Protection Systems. (Reserved)

7.3.4.8 Parking Access Systems. (Reserved)

7.4 Category 2 Systems.

7.4.1 Information Technology and Communications Systems Infrastructure.

7.4.1.1 Requirements for information technology and communications systems infrastructure shall be in accordance with 7.3.1, except as specified in 7.4.1.1.1.

7.4.1.1.1 Redundant pathways and cabling for the backbone distribution system shall not be required.

7.4.2 Voice, Data, Communications, and Cable Television Systems.

7.4.2.1 Voice/Telecommunications. (Reserved)

7.4.2.2 Local Area Networks (LANs). (Reserved)

7.4.2.3 Wireless Local Area Network (LAN) Systems and Public WiFi Hot Spots. (Reserved)

7.4.2.4 Wireless Voice Systems and In-Building Cellular Networks. (Reserved)

7.4.2.5 Cable Television. (Reserved)

7.4.3 Other Communications Systems.

7.4.3.1 Nurse Call Systems.

7.4.3.1.1 General. The nurse call system shall be in accordance with the requirements in 7.3.3.1.

7.4.3.1.2 Provisions for medical device alarms and code calls shall not be required. *(See 7.3.3.1.1.3.)*

7.4.3.2 Patient Tracking. (Reserved)

7.4.3.3 Equipment and Asset Tracking. (Reserved)

7.4.3.4 Staff and Visitor Tracking. (Reserved)

7.4.3.5 Wireless Phone and Paging Integration. Wireless phone and paging integration systems shall be in accordance with 7.3.3.5.

7.4.3.6 Patient and Equipment Monitoring Systems. (Reserved)

7.4.3.7 Clinical Information Systems. Clinical information systems shall be in accordance with 7.3.3.7.

7.4.3.8 Electronic Medical Records and Dictation Systems. (Reserved)

7.4.3.9 Medical Imaging Systems. (Reserved)

7.4.3.10 Archiving Systems. (Reserved)

7.4.4 Security Systems.

7.4.4.1 Internet Protocol (IP) Security Cameras Systems. (Reserved)

7.4.4.2 Digital Video Recording. (Reserved)

7.4.4.3 Intrusion Detection Systems. (Reserved)

7.4.4.4 Sitewide Monitoring. (Reserved)

7.4.4.5 Access Control Systems. (Reserved)

7.4.4.6 ID Badging Systems Integrated with Point of Sales Systems. (Reserved)

7.4.4.7 Threat Protection Systems. (Reserved)

7.4.4.8 Parking Access Systems. (Reserved)

7.5 Category 3 Systems.

7.5.1 Information Technology and Communications Systems Infrastructure.

7.5.1.1 Requirements for information technology and communications systems infrastructure shall be in accordance with 7.3.1, with exceptions as noted in 7.5.1.1.1 through 7.5.1.1.4.

7.5.1.1.1 Dual service entrance pathways into the EF are not required.

7.5.1.1.2 Power circuits serving equipment in the EF, the TER, and TRs shall not be required to be connected to the essential electrical system.

7.5.1.1.3 HVAC systems serving the EF, the ER, and TRs shall not be required to be connected to the essential electrical system.

7.5.1.1.4 Redundant pathways and cabling for the backbone distribution system shall not be required.

7.5.2 Voice, Data, Communications, and Cable Television Systems.

7.5.2.1 Voice/Telecommunications. (Reserved)

7.5.2.2 Local Area Networks (LANs). (Reserved)

7.5.2.3 Cable Television. (Reserved)

7.5.3 Other Communications Systems.

7.5.3.1 Nurse Call Systems. (Reserved)

7.5.3.2 Electronic Medical Records and Dictation Systems. (Reserved)

7.5.3.3 Medical Imaging Systems. (Reserved)

7.5.3.4 Archiving Systems. (Reserved)

7.5.4 Security Systems.

7.5.4.1 Internet Protocol (IP) Security Cameras Systems. (Reserved)

7.5.4.2 Digital Video Recording. (Reserved)

7.5.4.3 Intrusion Detection Systems. (Reserved)

7.5.4.4 Access Control Systems. (Reserved)

Chapter 8   Plumbing

8.1 Applicability.

8.1.1 This chapter shall apply to construction of new health care facilities, except as noted in 8.1.2 and 8.1.3.

8.1.2 This chapter shall also apply to the altered, renovated, or modernized portions of existing systems or individual components.

8.1.3 An existing system that is not in strict compliance with the provisions of this code shall be permitted to be continued in use, unless the authority having jurisdiction has determined that such use constitutes a distinct hazard to life.

8.2 System Category Criteria. The health care facility's governing body that has the responsibility for the building system components as identified in this chapter shall designate, in accordance with the function of each space, building system categories in accordance with Sections 4.1 and 4.2.

8.2.1* The category of risk applied to each plumbing system serving a space shall be independent of the category of risk applied to other systems serving that same space.

8.3 General Requirements.

8.3.1 Potable Water. Potable water systems shall comply with applicable plumbing codes and the applicable volume of FGI guidelines.

8.3.2 Nonpotable Water. Nonpotable water systems shall comply with applicable plumbing codes and the applicable volume of FGI guidelines.

8.3.3 Water Heating. Maximum hot water temperatures shall comply with applicable plumbing codes and the applicable volume of FGI guidelines.

8.3.4 Water Conditioning. Water shall be treated or heated to control pathogens in the water.

8.3.5 Nonmedical Compressed Air.

8.3.5.1 Nonmedical air compressors shall be listed or approved.

8.3.5.2 Nonmedical compressed air shall not be used for powering medical instruments or for human respiration.

8.3.5.3 Nonmedical compressed air shall meet the quality and pressure requirements of the equipment connected to the system.

8.3.6 Special Use Water Systems. When special use water systems are required, the applicable volume of FGI guidelines or the applicable ANSI-reviewed standard shall be followed.

8.3.7 Grease Interceptors.

8.3.7.1 Sizing for grease interceptors shall be permitted in accordance with local plumbing codes or an engineered calculation factoring meals served per day.

8.3.8 Fixtures. Plumbing fixtures shall be in accordance with the applicable volume of FGI guidelines.

8.3.9 Black Waste Water. Black waste water shall be discharged to a sanitary sewer or private on-site waste treatment system as permitted by applicable plumbing codes.

8.3.10 Gray Waste Water.

8.3.10.1 Gray waste water shall be permitted to be stored on-site and used for nonpotable water systems as permitted by applicable plumbing codes.

8.3.10.2 Gray waste water shall not be used for any system that aerosolizes the water in a breathing zone or has direct contact with humans.

8.3.10.3 Excess gray waste water shall be discharged to a sanitary sewer or private on-site waste treatment system as permitted by applicable plumbing codes.

8.3.11 Clear Waste Water.

8.3.11.1 Clear waste water shall be permitted to be stored on-site and used for nonpotable water systems as permitted by applicable plumbing codes.

8.3.11.2 Clear waste water that has been treated to potable water standards shall be permitted to be used as nonpotable water.

8.3.11.3 Clear waste water that has not been treated to potable water standards shall not be used for any system that aerosolizes the water in a breathing zone or has direct contact with humans.

8.3.11.4 Excess clear waste water shall be discharged to a storm sewer, held in detention ponds, or recharged into the water table as permitted by applicable plumbing codes.

8.3.12 Drainage Systems. Drainage systems shall comply with applicable plumbing codes and the applicable volume of FGI guidelines.

8.4 Category 1. (Reserved)

8.5 Category 2. (Reserved)

8.6 Category 3. (Reserved)

Shaded text = Revisions.   **Δ** = Text deletions and figure/table revisions.   • = Section deletions.   *N* = New material.

2024 Edition

Chapter 9 Heating, Ventilation, and Air Conditioning (HVAC)

9.1 Applicability.

9.1.1 This chapter shall apply to construction of new health care facilities, except as noted in 9.1.2 and 9.1.3.

9.1.2 This chapter shall also apply to the altered, renovated, or modernized portions of existing systems or individual components.

9.1.3 An existing system that is not in strict compliance with the provisions of this code shall be permitted to be continued in use, unless the authority having jurisdiction has determined that such use constitutes a distinct hazard to life.

9.2 System Category Criteria. The health care facility's governing body that has the responsibility for the building system components as identified in this chapter shall designate, in accordance with the function of each space, building system categories in accordance with Sections 4.1 and 4.2.

9.2.1* The category of risk applied to each HVAC system serving a space shall be independent of the category of risk applied to other systems serving that same space.

9.3 General.

9.3.1 Heating, Cooling, Ventilating, and Process Systems.

9.3.1.1 Heating, cooling, ventilating, and process systems serving spaces or providing health care functions covered by this code or listed within ASHRAE 170, *Ventilation of Health Care Facilities*, shall be provided in accordance with ASHRAE 170.

9.3.1.2 Laboratories shall comply with NFPA 45.

9.3.1.3* Anesthetizing Locations. Anesthetizing locations shall not be required to have a smoke purge system.

9.3.2 Energy Conservation. Heating, cooling, and ventilating systems serving spaces or providing health care functions covered by this code shall comply with ASHRAE 90.1, *Energy Standard for Buildings Except Low-Rise Residential Buildings*, or another locally adopted energy code.

9.3.3 Commissioning.

9.3.3.1 Heating, cooling, ventilating, and process systems serving spaces or providing health care functions covered by this code shall be commissioned in accordance with ASHRAE 90.1, *Energy Standard for Buildings Except Low-Rise Residential Buildings*.

9.3.3.2* Commissioning shall follow any publicly reviewed document acceptable to the authority having jurisdiction.

9.3.4 Piping. Heating, cooling, ventilating, and process systems serving spaces or providing health care functions covered by this code shall utilize piping systems complying with applicable mechanical codes.

9.3.5 Ductwork. Heating, cooling, ventilating, and process systems serving spaces or providing health care functions covered by this code shall utilize ductwork systems complying with NFPA 90A or applicable mechanical codes.

9.3.6 Medical Gas Storage or Transfilling.

9.3.6.1 All gases, other than medical gases, shall be provided with ventilation per NFPA 55.

9.3.6.2 Outdoor storage/installations for medical gases and cryogenic fluids shall be provided with ventilation per NFPA 55.

9.3.6.3* Medical gases and cryogenic fluids that are in use per Chapter 11 shall not require special ventilation.

9.3.6.4 Transfilling area shall be provided with ventilation in accordance with NFPA 55.

9.3.6.5 Indoor storage or manifold areas and storage or manifold buildings for medical gases and cryogenic fluids shall be provided with natural ventilation or mechanical exhaust ventilation in accordance with 9.3.6.5.1 through 9.3.6.8.

9.3.6.5.1* For the purposes of this section the volume of fluid (gas and liquid) to be used in determining the ventilation requirements shall be the volume of the stored fluid when expanded to standard temperature and pressure (STP) of either the largest single vessel in the enclosed space or of the entire volume of the connected vessels that are on a common manifold in the enclosed space, whichever is larger.

9.3.6.5.2 Natural Ventilation.

Δ **9.3.6.5.2.1*** Natural ventilation shall consist of two nonclosable louvered openings, each having an aggregate free opening area of at least 155 cm^2 (24 in.^{2}) for each 28.3 m^3 (1000 ft^3) of the gas designed to be stored in the space and in no case less than 465 cm^2 (72 in.^{2}).

9.3.6.5.2.2 One opening shall be located within 30 cm (1 ft) of the floor, and one shall be located within 30 cm (1 ft) of the ceiling.

9.3.6.5.2.3 The openings shall be located to ensure cross ventilation.

9.3.6.5.2.4 Natural ventilation openings shall be directly to the outside atmosphere without ductwork.

9.3.6.5.2.5 Mechanical ventilation shall be provided if natural ventilation requirements cannot be met.

9.3.6.5.3 Mechanical Ventilation.

9.3.6.5.3.1 Mechanical exhaust to maintain a negative pressure in the space shall be provided continuously, unless an alternative design is approved by the authority having jurisdiction.

9.3.6.5.3.2 Mechanical exhaust shall be at a rate of 1 L/sec of airflow for each 300 L (1 cfm per 5 ft^3 of fluid) designed to be stored in the space and not less than 24 L/sec (50 cfm) nor more than 235 L/sec (500 cfm).

9.3.6.5.3.3 Mechanical exhaust inlets shall be unobstructed and shall draw air from within 300 mm (1 ft) of the floor and adjacent to the cylinder or containers.

9.3.6.5.3.4 Mechanical exhaust air fans shall be supplied with electrical power from the essential electrical system. Where an essential electrical system is not provided, a risk assessment shall be conducted to determine if continuous ventilation shall be provided by alternate means.

9.3.6.5.3.5 Dedicated exhaust systems shall not be required, provided that the system does not connect to spaces that contain combustible or flammable materials.

9.3.6.5.3.6 The exhaust duct material shall be noncombustible.

Δ **9.3.6.5.3.7** A means of make-up air shall be provided according to one of the following:

(1) Air shall be permitted to be transferred through noncombustible ductwork from spaces, inside or outside the building, that do not contain combustible or flammable materials.
(2) Air shall be permitted to be transferred from a corridor under the door up to the greater of 24 L/sec (50 cfm) or 15 percent of the room exhaust in accordance with NFPA 90A.
(3) Supply air shall be permitted from any building ventilation system that does not contain flammable or combustible vapors.

9.3.6.6 Discharge from the natural and mechanical ventilation systems shall be sited by a minimum separation distance in accordance with NFPA 55.

9.3.6.7 A storage room shall maintain a temperature not greater than 52°C (125°F).

9.3.6.8 A transfer or manifold room shall maintain a temperature not greater than 52°C (125°F) and not less than −7°C (20°F).

9.3.7 Waste Gas.

Δ **9.3.7.1*** Removal of excess anesthetic gases from the anesthesia circuit shall be accomplished by an active system, or by a semi-active or passive scavenging ventilation system.

9.3.7.1.1 Semi-Active Systems. A dedicated exhaust system with an exhaust fan shall be provided to interconnect all of the anesthesia gas circuits to provide sufficient airflow and negative pressure in the gas disposal tubing so that cross contamination does not occur in the other circuits connected to the system.

9.3.7.1.2 Passive Systems.

9.3.7.1.2.1 A dedicated exhaust system with an exhaust fan shall be provided to exhaust snorkels at all of the anesthesia gas circuits to provide sufficient airflow to capture the gases, vapors, and particles expelled from the gas disposal tubing.

9.3.7.1.2.2 The snorkel shall include a minimum 25.4 mm (1 in.) diameter tubing connected to the exhaust system.

9.3.7.2 All the exhausted air shall be vented to the external atmosphere.

9.3.7.3 The excess anesthetic gases shall be deposited into the exhaust stream either at the exhaust grille or further downstream in the exhaust duct.

9.3.8* Medical Plume (Surgical Smoke) Evacuation and Filtration.

9.3.8.1* All medical plumes (i.e., surgical smoke) generated by the use of energy devices (e.g., electrosurgical units, lasers) during medical and surgical procedures shall be captured as close as possible to the point of generation (i.e., point where the energy device contacts the tissue) by one or a combination of the following methods:

(1)* Dedicated local exhaust ventilation system that discharges in accordance with 9.3.8.2
(2) Connection to return or exhaust duct after air cleaning through ULPA and gas phase filtration (e.g., activated carbon)
(3) Point of use surgical smoke evacuator with ULPA and gas phase filtration (e.g., activated carbon) for air cleaning and return to the space
(4) Medical-surgical vacuum system with an in-line filter with ULPA and gas phase filtration (e.g., activated carbon) for small amounts of plume in accordance with 5.1.3.7.4

9.3.8.2 The exhaust discharge for a dedicated exhaust system in accordance with 9.3.8.1(1) shall be located as follows:

(1) Outdoors
(2) At least 7.5 m (25 ft) from any doors, windows, air intakes, or other openings in buildings or places of public assembly
(3) At an elevation different from air intakes
(4) Where prevailing winds, adjacent buildings, topography, or other influences will not divert the exhaust into occupied areas or prevent dispersion of the exhaust

N **9.3.8.3*** Plume evacuation exhausts shall be permitted to be shared with waste gas as described in 9.3.7.

9.3.9 Emergency Power System Room. Heating, cooling, and ventilating of the emergency power system shall be in accordance with 6.7.1.3.4.

9.3.10 Ventilation During Construction. Ventilation during construction shall comply with the applicable volume of FGI guidelines.

9.4 Category 1. (Reserved)

9.5 Category 2. (Reserved)

9.6 Category 3. (Reserved)

Chapter 10   Electrical Equipment

10.1* Applicability.

10.1.1 This chapter shall apply to the performance, maintenance, and testing of electrical equipment in new and existing health care facilities.

10.1.2 Experimental or research apparatus built to order or under development shall be used under qualified supervision and shall have a degree of safety that is equivalent to that described herein or that has been deemed acceptable by the facility.

10.1.3* Reserved.

10.2 Performance Criteria for Patient Care–Related Electrical Appliances and Equipment.

10.2.1 Permanently Connected — Fixed Equipment. Patient-connected electric appliances shall be grounded to the equipment grounding bus in the distribution panel by an insulated grounding conductor run with the power conductors.

10.2.2 Cord- and Plug-Connected — Portable Equipment.

10.2.2.1 Grounding of Appliances.

10.2.2.1.1 All cord-connected electrically powered appliances that are not double insulated and are used in the patient care vicinity shall be provided with a three-wire power cord and a three-pin grounding-type plug.

10.2.2.1.2 Double-insulated appliances shall be permitted to have two conductor cords and shall be rated as Class II devices.

10.2.2.2 Attachment Plugs. Attachment plugs listed for the purpose shall be used on all cord-connected appliances.

10.2.2.3 Construction and Use. The attachment plug shall be a two-pole, three-wire grounding type.

10.2.2.3.1 Appliances supplied by other than 120-V single-phase systems shall use the grounding-type plug (cap) appropriate for the particular power system.

10.2.2.3.2 The grounding prong of the plug shall be the first to be connected to, and the last to be disconnected from, the receptacle.

10.2.2.3.3 If screw terminals are used, the stranded conductor shall be twisted to prevent stray strands, but the bundle shall not be tinned after twisting.

10.2.2.3.4 If the conductor is not twisted, it shall be attached by an approved terminal lug.

10.2.2.3.5 The power cord conductors shall be arranged so that the conductors are not under tension in the plug.

10.2.2.3.6 The grounding conductor shall be the last one to disconnect when a failure of the plug's strain relief allows the energized conductors to be disrupted.

10.2.2.3.7 Strain Relief. Strain relief shall be provided.

10.2.2.3.7.1 The strain relief shall not cause thinning of the conductor insulation.

10.2.2.3.7.2 The strain relief of replaceable plugs shall be capable of being disassembled.

10.2.2.3.7.3 Plugs shall be permitted to be integrally molded onto the cord jacket if the design is listed for the purpose.

10.2.2.3.8 Testing. The wiring of each cord assembly shall be tested for continuity and polarity at the time of manufacture, when assembled into an appliance, and when repaired.

10.2.3 Power Cords.

10.2.3.1 Material and Gauge.

10.2.3.1.1 The flexible cord, including the grounding conductor, shall be of a type suitable for the particular application; shall be listed for use at a voltage equal to or greater than the rated power line voltage of the appliance; and shall have an ampacity, as given in Table 400.5(A) of *NFPA 70*, equal to or greater than the current rating of the device.

10.2.3.1.2 "Hard Service" (SO, ST, or STO), "Junior Hard Service" (SJO, SJT, or SJTO), or equivalent listed flexible cord shall be used, except where an appliance with a cord of another designation has been listed for the purpose.

10.2.3.2 Grounding Conductor.

10.2.3.2.1 Each electric appliance shall be provided with a grounding conductor in its power cord.

10.2.3.2.2 The grounding conductor shall be not smaller than 18 AWG.

10.2.3.2.3 The grounding conductor of cords longer than 4.6 m (15 ft) shall be not smaller than 16 AWG.

10.2.3.2.4* A grounding conductor in the power cord shall not be required for double-insulated appliances, but a functional ground conductor (functional earth conductor) shall be permitted.

10.2.3.3 Detachable Power Cords.

10.2.3.3.1 A detachable power cord shall be permitted if an accidental disconnection would not present an unacceptable hazard or if a mechanism that reliably prevents inadvertent disconnection is used.

10.2.3.3.2 Detachable power cords shall be designed so that the grounding conductor is the first to be connected and the last to be disconnected.

10.2.3.3.3 The cord set to the appliance shall be listed for the purpose.

10.2.3.4 Connection to Circuit and Color Codes.

10.2.3.4.1 Power cords, regardless of whether intended for use on grounded or isolated power systems, shall be connected in accordance with the conventions of a grounded system.

10.2.3.4.2 The circuit conductors in the cord shall be connected to the plug and the wiring in the appliance so that any of the following devices, when used in the primary circuit, are connected to the ungrounded conductor:

(1) Center contact of an Edison base lampholder
(2) Solitary fuseholder
(3) Single-pole, overcurrent protective device
(4) Any other single-pole, current-interrupting device

10.2.3.4.3 A second fuseholder or other overcurrent protective device provided in the appliance shall be permitted to be placed in the grounded side of the line.

10.2.3.5 Cord Strain Relief.

10.2.3.5.1 Cord strain relief shall be provided at the attachment of the power cord to the appliance so that mechanical stress, either pull, twist, or bend, is not transmitted to internal connections.

10.2.3.5.2 A strain relief molded onto the cord shall be bonded to the jacket and shall be of compatible material.

10.2.3.6* Relocatable Power Taps (RPTs). Relocatable power taps (RPTs) shall be permitted to be used to supply power to plug-connected components of a movable equipment assembly that is pole-, rack-, table-, pedestal-, or cart-mounted, provided that all of the following conditions are met:

(1)* The RPT is securely attached.
(2)* The sum of the ampacity of all appliances connected to the outlets does not exceed 75 percent of the ampacity of the flexible cord supplying the RPT.
(3) The ampacity of the flexible cord is in accordance with *NFPA 70*.
(4) The RPT attachment plug must not be connected to another RPT or extension cord.
(5) The electrical and mechanical integrity of the assembly and its securement method are regularly verified and documented.

10.2.4 Adapters and Extension Cords.

10.2.4.1 Three-prong to two-prong adapters shall not be permitted.

10.2.4.2 Adapters and extension cords meeting the requirements of 10.2.4.2.1 through 10.2.4.2.3 shall be permitted.

10.2.4.2.1 All adapters shall be listed for the purpose.

10.2.4.2.2 Attachment plugs and fittings shall be listed for the purpose.

10.2.4.2.3 The cabling shall comply with 10.2.3.

10.2.4.3 Overhead power receptacles shall be permitted to be supplied by a flexible cord with strain relief (ceiling drop) that is connected at a ceiling-mounted junction box in either of the following ways:

(1) Permanently
(2)* Utilizing a locking-type attachment plug cap and receptacle combination, or other method of retention

10.3 Testing Requirements — Patient Care–Related Electrical Appliances and Equipment.

10.3.1* Physical Integrity. The physical integrity of the power cord assembly composed of the power cord, attachment plug, and cord-strain relief shall be confirmed by visual inspection.

10.3.2* Resistance.

10.3.2.1 For appliances that are used in the patient care vicinity, the resistance between the appliance chassis, or any exposed conductive surface of the appliance, and the ground pin of the attachment plug shall be less than 0.50 ohm under the following conditions:

(1) The cord shall be flexed at its connection to the attachment plug or connector.
(2) The cord shall be flexed at its connection to the strain relief on the chassis.

10.3.2.2 The requirement of 10.3.2.1 shall not apply to accessible metal parts that achieve separation from main parts by insulation or metallic screening or that are unlikely to become energized (e.g., escutcheons or nameplates, small screws).

10.3.3* Leakage Current Tests.

10.3.3.1 General.

10.3.3.1.1 The requirements in 10.3.3.2 through 10.3.3.4 shall apply to all tests.

10.3.3.1.2 Tests shall be performed with the power switch ON and OFF.

10.3.3.2 Resistance Test. The resistance tests of 10.3.2 shall be conducted before undertaking any leakage current measurements.

10.3.3.3* Techniques of Measurement. The test shall not be made on the load side of an isolated power system or separable isolation transformer.

10.3.3.4 Leakage and Touch Current Limits. The leakage and touch current limits in 10.3.4.2 and 10.3.5.4 shall be followed.

10.3.4 Leakage Current — Fixed Equipment.

10.3.4.1 Permanently wired appliances in the patient care vicinity shall be tested prior to installation while the equipment is temporarily insulated from ground.

10.3.4.2 The leakage current flowing through the ground conductor of the power supply connection to ground of permanently wired appliances installed in Category 1 or Category 2 spaces shall not exceed 10.0 mA (ac or dc) with all grounds lifted.

10.3.5 Touch Current — Portable Equipment.

10.3.5.1 Single Power Cord Supplying Power. If multiple devices are connected together and one power cord supplies power, the touch current shall be measured as an assembly.

10.3.5.2 Multiple Power Cords Supplying Power. When multiple devices are connected together and more than one power cord supplies power, the devices shall be separated into groups according to their power supply cord, and the touch current shall be measured independently for each group as an assembly.

10.3.5.3 Touch Leakage Test Procedure. Measurements shall be made using the circuit, such as the one illustrated in Figure 10.3.5.3, with the appliance ground broken in two modes of appliance operation as follows:

(1) Power plug connected normally with the appliance on
(2) Power plug connected normally with the appliance off (if equipped with an on/off switch)

10.3.5.3.1 If the appliance has fixed redundant grounding (e.g., permanently fastened to the grounding system), the touch leakage current test shall be conducted with the redundant grounding intact.

10.3.5.4* Touch Current — Portable Equipment. The touch current for cord connected equipment shall not exceed 500 μA with normal polarity and the ground wire disconnected (if a ground wire is provided).

FIGURE 10.3.5.3   Example Test Circuit for Measuring Touch Leakage Current.

10.3.6* Lead Leakage Current Tests and Limits — Portable Equipment.

10.3.6.1 The leakage current between all patient leads connected together and ground shall be tested with the power plug connected normally and the device powered on.

10.3.6.2 The leakage current between all patient leads connected together and ground shall be measured with the ground switch open and with the ground switch closed.

10.3.6.3 An acceptable test configuration shall be as illustrated in Figure 10.3.6.3.

10.3.6.4 The leakage current shall not exceed 100 μA for ground wire closed and 500 μA ac for ground wire open.

10.4 Nonpatient Electrical Appliances and Equipment.

10.4.1 Permanently Connected — Fixed. (Reserved)

10.4.2 Cord- and Plug-Connected — Portable Equipment in Patient Care Vicinity.

10.4.2.1 Nonpatient care–related electrical equipment, including facility- or patient-owned appliances that are used in the patient care vicinity and will, in normal use, contact patients, shall be visually inspected by the patient's care staff or other personnel.

10.4.2.2 Any equipment that appears not to be in proper working order or in a worn condition shall be removed from service or reported to the appropriate maintenance staff.

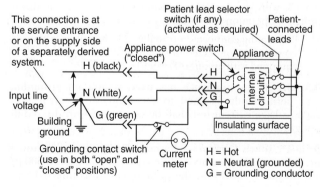

FIGURE 10.3.6.3   Test Circuit for Measuring Leakage Current Between Patient Leads and Ground — Nonisolated.

10.4.2.3 Household or office appliances not commonly equipped with grounding conductors in their power cords shall be permitted, provided that they are not located within the patient care vicinity. Double-insulated appliances shall be permitted in the patient care vicinity.

10.5 Administration.

10.5.1 Responsibilities of the Health Care Facility's Governing Body. (Reserved)

10.5.2 Policies.

10.5.2.1 Testing Intervals.

10.5.2.1.1 The facility shall establish policies and protocols to identify what patient care–related electrical equipment requires periodic inspection and, where applicable, the type of test and intervals of testing.

10.5.2.1.2 All patient care–related electrical equipment used in the patient care vicinity shall be tested in accordance with 10.3.5.3 or 10.3.6 before being put into service for the first time and after any repair or modification that might have compromised electrical safety.

10.5.2.2* Protection of Patients with Direct Electrical Pathways to the Heart. Only equipment that is specifically designed for the purpose [i.e., provided with suitable isolated patient leads or connections (cardiac floating, also known as CF, according to ANSI/AAMI ES60601-1, *Medical electrical equipment — Part 1: General requirements for basic safety and essential performance*)] shall be connected directly to electrically conductive pathways to a patient's heart.

10.5.2.3 Adapters and Extension Cords.

10.5.2.3.1 Adapters and extension cords meeting the requirements of 10.2.4 shall be permitted to be used.

10.5.2.3.2 Three- to two-prong adapters shall not be permitted.

10.5.2.3.3 The wiring shall be tested for all of the following:

(1) Physical integrity
(2) Polarity
(3) Continuity of grounding at the time of assembly and periodically thereafter

10.5.2.4 Devices Likely to Be Used During Defibrillation. Devices that are critical to patient safety and that are likely to be attached to the patient when a defibrillator is used (such as ECG monitors) shall be marked as "defibrillation proof," as defined in ANSI/AAMI ES60601-1, *Medical electrical equipment — Part 1: General requirements for basic safety and essential performance.*

10.5.2.5* System Demonstration. Any system consisting of several electric appliances shall be demonstrated to comply with this code as a complete system.

10.5.2.6 Appliances Not Provided by the Facility. Policies shall be established for the control of appliances not supplied by the facility.

10.5.3 Servicing and Maintenance of Equipment.

10.5.3.1 The manufacturer of the appliance shall furnish documents containing at least a technical description, instructions for use, and a means of contacting the manufacturer.

10.5.3.2 The documents specified in 10.5.3.1 shall include the following, where applicable:

(1) Illustrations that show the location of controls
(2) Explanation of the function of each control
(3) Illustrations of proper connection to the patient or other equipment, or both
(4) Step-by-step procedures for testing and proper use of the appliance
(5) Safety considerations in use and servicing of the appliance
(6) Precautions to be taken if the appliance is used on a patient simultaneously with other electric appliances
(7) Schematics, wiring diagrams, mechanical layouts, parts lists, and other pertinent data for the appliance
(8) Instructions for cleaning, disinfection, or sterilization
(9) Utility supply requirements (electrical, gas, ventilation, heating, cooling, and so forth)
(10) Explanation of figures, symbols, and abbreviations on the appliance
(11) Technical performance specifications
(12) Instructions for unpacking, inspection, installation, adjustment, and alignment
(13) Preventive and corrective maintenance, inspection, and repair procedures

10.5.4 Administration of Oxygen Therapy.

10.5.4.1 Electrical Equipment in Oxygen-Enriched Atmospheres. Appliances, or a part(s) of an appliance or a system (e.g., pillow speaker, remote control, pulse oximeter probe), to be used in the site of intentional expulsion shall comply with one of the following:

(1) They shall be listed for use in oxygen-enriched atmospheres.
(2) They shall be sealed so as to prevent an oxygen-enriched atmosphere from reaching electrical components, with sealing material of the type that will still seal even after repeated exposure to water, oxygen, mechanical vibration, and heating from the external circuitry.
(3) They shall be ventilated so as to limit the oxygen concentration surrounding electrical components to below 23.5 percent by volume.
(4) They shall have both of the following characteristics:

(a) No hot surfaces over 300°C (573°F), except for small (less than 2 W) hermetically sealed heating elements, such as light bulbs
(b) No exposed switching or sparking points of electrical energy that fall to the right of the curve for the appropriate type of circuit illustrated in Figure 10.5.4.1(a) through Figure 10.5.4.1(f), with the dc (or peak ac) open-circuit voltage and short-circuit current required to be used

10.5.4.2 When only the remote control or signal leads of a device are to be used in the site of intentional expulsion, only the control or signal leads shall be required to comply with 10.5.4.1.

10.5.4.3 Subparagraphs 10.5.4.1 and 10.5.4.2 shall not apply to small (less than 2 W), hermetically sealed heating elements such as light bulbs.

10.5.4.4 Electrical equipment sold with the intent to be used in oxygen-enriched atmospheres shall be listed for use in oxygen-enriched atmospheres.

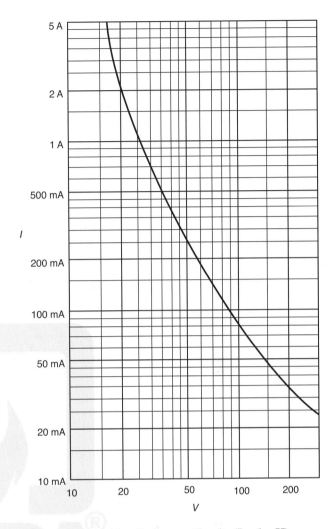

FIGURE 10.5.4.1(a) Resistance Circuits (L < 1 mH): Minimum Igniting Currents, Applicable to All Circuits Containing Cadmium, Zinc, or Magnesium.

10.5.4.5* Electrical equipment used within oxygen delivery equipment shall be listed for use in oxygen-enriched atmospheres in accordance with ANSI/AAMI ES60601-1, *Medical electrical equipment — Part 1: General requirements for basic safety and essential performance.*

10.5.4.6* High-energy-delivering probes (such as defibrillator paddles) or other electrical devices that do not comply with 10.5.4.1 and 10.5.4.2, that are deemed essential to the care of an individual patient, and that must be used within an administration site or within oxygen-delivery equipment shall be permitted.

10.5.5 Laboratory.

10.5.5.1* The laboratory shall establish policies and protocols for the type of test and intervals of testing for appliances.

FIGURE 10.5.4.1(b)   Resistance Circuits (L < 1 mH): Minimum Igniting Currents, Applicable to Circuits Where Cadmium, Zinc, or Magnesium Can Be Excluded.

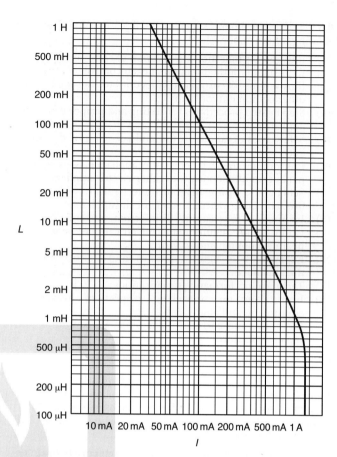

FIGURE 10.5.4.1(c)   Inductance Circuits (L > 1 mH): Minimum Igniting Currents at 24 V, Applicable to All Circuits Containing Cadmium, Zinc, or Magnesium.

10.5.6 Record Keeping — Patient Care Appliances.

10.5.6.1 Instruction Manuals.

10.5.6.1.1 Instruction and maintenance manuals shall be accessible to the group responsible for the maintenance of the appliance.

10.5.6.1.2 Instruction and user maintenance manuals shall be accessible to the user.

10.5.6.1.3 Any safety labels and condensed operating instructions on an appliance shall be maintained in legible condition.

10.5.6.2* Documentation.

10.5.6.2.1 A record shall be maintained of the tests required by this chapter and associated repairs or modifications.

10.5.6.2.2 At a minimum, the record shall contain all of the following:

(1) Date
(2) Unique identification of the equipment tested

(3) Indication of which items have met or have failed to meet the performance requirements of Section 10.2

10.5.6.3 Records Retention. The records shall be maintained and kept for a period of time in accordance with a health care facility's record retention policy.

10.5.7 Use. (Reserved)

10.5.8 Qualification and Training of Personnel.

10.5.8.1* Personnel concerned for the application or maintenance of electric appliances shall be trained on the risks associated with their use.

10.5.8.1.1 The health care facilities shall provide programs of continuing education for its personnel.

10.5.8.1.2 Continuing education programs shall include periodic review of manufacturers' safety guidelines and usage requirements for electrosurgical units and similar appliances.

10.5.8.2 Personnel involved in the use of energy-delivering devices including, but not limited to, electrosurgical, surgical laser, and fiber-optic devices shall receive periodic training in fire prevention and suppression.

10.5.8.3* Equipment shall be serviced by qualified personnel only.

FIGURE 10.5.4.1(d)   Inductance Circuits (L > 1 mH): Minimum Igniting Currents for Various Voltages, Applicable to All Circuits Containing Cadmium, Zinc, or Magnesium.

FIGURE 10.5.4.1(e)   Inductance Circuits (L > 1 mH): Minimum Igniting Currents at 24 V, Applicable Only to Circuits Where Cadmium, Zinc, or Magnesium Can Be Excluded.

FIGURE 10.5.4.1(f) **Capacitance Circuits Minimum Ignition Voltages. (The curves correspond to values of current-limiting resistance as indicated. The curve marked *Sn* is applicable only where cadmium, zinc, or magnesium can be excluded.)**

Chapter 11   Gas Equipment

11.1 Applicability.

11.1.1 This chapter shall apply to the performance, maintenance, and testing of gas equipment in new and existing health care facilities.

11.1.2* This chapter shall apply to the use, at normal atmospheric pressure, of all of the following:

(1) Nonflammable medical gases
(2) Vapors and aerosols
(3) Equipment required for the administration of 11.1.2(1) and 11.1.2(2)

11.1.3 When used in this chapter, the term *oxygen* shall be intended to mean oxygen USP as well as mixtures of oxygen and air.

11.1.4* This chapter shall not apply to special atmospheres, such as those encountered in hyperbaric chambers.

11.1.5* Reserved.

11.2 Portable Cylinder and Container Source.

11.2.1 Cylinder valve outlet connections shall conform to the mandatory requirements of CGA V-1, *Standard for Compressed*

Gas Cylinder Valve Outlet and Inlet Connections (ANSI B57.1) (includes Pin-Index Safety System for medical gases).

11.2.2 When low-pressure threaded connections are employed, they shall be in accordance with the mandatory requirements of CGA V-5, *Diameter Index Safety System (Noninterchangeable Low Pressure Connections for Medical Gas Applications)*, for noninterchangeable, low-pressure connections for medical gases, air, and suction.

11.2.3 Low-pressure quick coupler connections shall be noninterchangeable between gas services.

11.2.4 Pressure-reducing regulators and gauges intended for use in high-pressure service shall be listed for such service.

11.2.5 Pressure-reducing regulators shall be used on high-pressure cylinders to reduce the cylinder pressure to operating pressures.

11.2.6 Approved pressure-reducing regulators or other gas-flow control devices shall be used to reduce the cylinder pressure of every cylinder used for medical purposes. All such devices shall have connections so designed that they attach only to cylinders of gas for which they are designated.

11.2.7* Equipment that could allow the intermixing of different gases, either through defects in the mechanism or through error in manipulation in any portion of the high-pressure side of any system in which these gases might flow, shall not be used for joining cylinders containing compressed gases.

11.2.8 Cylinder valve outlet connections for oxygen shall be Connection No. 540 or Connection No. 870 as described in the mandatory requirements of CGA V-1, *Standard for Compressed Gas Cylinder Valve Outlet and Inlet Connections* (ANSI B57.1).

11.2.9 Cylinder valve outlet connections for nitrous oxide shall be Connection No. 326 or Connection No. 910 as described in the mandatory requirements of CGA V-1, *Standard for Compressed Gas Cylinder Valve Outlet and Inlet Connections* (ANSI B57.1).

11.3 Cylinder and Container Storage Requirements.

11.3.1 For the purpose of this section, the health care facility's governing body shall define criteria for determining full cylinders and containers.

11.3.2 Full cylinders and containers shall be stored in accordance with Section 11.3.

11.3.3 Full cylinders and containers shall be segregated from all others.

11.3.4 Full and empty cylinders shall be prevented from reaching temperatures in excess of 52°C (125°F).

11.3.5* Design and Construction.

11.3.5.1 Storage for nonflammable gases equal to or greater than 85 m³ (3000 ft³) at STP shall comply with 11.3.5.2 unless such installations are approved existing installations, which shall be permitted to be continued in service.

11.3.5.2 Locations for the storage of nonflammable gases shall meet the following requirements:

(1) They shall be constructed with access to move cylinders and containers in and out of the location on hand trucks complying with 11.4.3.1.1.

(2) They shall be provided with lockable doors or gates or otherwise able to be secured.

(3) If outdoors, they shall be provided with an enclosure constructed of noncombustible materials.

(4) If indoors, they shall have interior finishes of noncombustible or limited-combustible materials.

(5)* If indoors, the room shall be separated from the rest of the building by walls and floors having a 1-hour fire resistance rating with doors and other opening protectives having a ¾-hour fire protection rating.

(6)* They shall comply with *NFPA 70* for unclassified (nonhazardous) locations.

(7)* Fuel-fired equipment shall not be located in the room.

(8) If they require heat, the maximum allowable temperature of the in-room heating element shall be 130°C (266°F).

(9) They shall be provided with racks, chains, or other fastenings to secure all cylinders from falling, whether full or empty.

(10) They shall be supplied with electrical power compliant with the requirements for essential electrical systems as described in Chapter 6.

(11) They shall have racks, shelves, and supports, where provided, constructed of noncombustible materials or limited-combustible materials.

(12)* They shall protect electrical devices from physical damage.

(13)* They shall allow access by delivery vehicles and management of cylinders.

(14) If indoors, ventilation for medical gas storage rooms shall comply with 9.3.6.

11.3.6* Storage for nonflammable gases greater than 8.5 m³ (300 ft³), but less than 85 m³ (3000 ft³), at STP shall comply with the requirements in 11.3.6.1 through 11.3.6.8.

11.3.6.1 Storage locations shall be outdoors in an enclosure or within an enclosed interior space of noncombustible or limited-combustible construction, with doors (or gates outdoors) that can be secured against unauthorized entry.

11.3.6.2 Oxidizing gases such as oxygen and nitrous oxide shall not be stored with any flammable gas, liquid, or vapor.

11.3.6.3 Oxidizing gases such as oxygen and nitrous oxide shall be separated from combustibles or flammable materials by any of the following:

(1) Minimum distance of 6.1 m (20 ft)

(2) Minimum distance of 1.5 m (5 ft) if the entire storage location is protected by an automatic sprinkler system designed in accordance with NFPA 13

(3) A gas cabinet in accordance with NFPA 55

11.3.6.4 Full and empty cylinders shall be prevented from reaching temperatures in excess of 52°C (125°F).

11.3.6.5 Cylinder or container restraints shall comply with 11.6.2.3.

11.3.6.6 Smoking, open flames, electric heating elements, and other sources of ignition shall be prohibited within storage locations and within 6.1 m (20 ft) of outside storage locations.

11.3.6.7 Cylinder valve protection caps shall comply with 11.6.2.2(4).

11.3.6.8 Ventilation for indoor medical gas storage rooms shall comply with 9.3.6.

11.3.7 Storage for nonflammable gases with a total volume equal to or less than 8.5 m³ (300 ft³) shall comply with the requirements in 11.3.7.1 and 11.3.7.2.

11.3.7.1 Individual cylinder storage associated with a smoke compartment in accordance with NFPA *101* shall not be required to be stored in enclosures.

11.3.7.2 Precautions in handling cylinders specified in 11.3.7.1 shall be in accordance with 11.6.2.

11.3.8* Storage for nonflammable gases less than 85 m³ (3000 ft³) at STP shall be permitted to be stored in a gas cabinet constructed in accordance with NFPA 55, provided that the following also applies:

(1) Storage is limited to cylinders.

(2) There are no flammables or combustibles in the cabinet.

(3) The temperature limitations of 5.1.3.2.11 are met.

(4) The cylinders are secured.

(5) When storing nitrous oxide, the cabinets are lockable.

11.3.9 When small-size (A, B, D, or E) cylinders are in use, they shall be attached to a cylinder stand or to medical equipment designed to receive and hold compressed gas cylinders.

11.3.10 Individual small-size (A, B, D, or E) cylinders available for immediate use in patient care spaces shall not be considered to be in storage.

11.3.11 Cylinders shall not be chained to portable or movable apparatus such as beds and oxygen tents.

11.3.12 Signs.

11.3.12.1 Storage locations meeting the requirements of 11.3.5 or 11.3.6 shall have precautionary signage, readable from a distance of 1.5 m (5 ft), displayed on each door or gate of the storage room or enclosure.

11.3.12.2 Signs for inert gases shall include the following wording as a minimum:

CAUTION

NO Smoking or Open Flame

Positive-Pressure Gases

Room May Have Insufficient Oxygen

Open Door and Allow Room to Ventilate Before Entering

11.3.12.2.1 Existing signage that is not in strict compliance with the provisions of this code shall be permitted to be continued in use as long as the authority having jurisdiction has determined that such use does not constitute a distinct hazard to life.

11.3.12.3 In health care facilities where smoking is permitted, signs shall include the following wording as a minimum:

CAUTION

NO SMOKING OR OPEN FLAME

OXIDIZING GAS(ES) STORED WITHIN

11.3.12.3.1 Existing signage that is not in strict compliance with the provisions of this code shall be permitted to be continued in use as long as the authority having jurisdiction has determined that such use does not constitute a distinct hazard to life.

11.3.12.4 In health care facilities where smoking is prohibited, signs shall include the following wording as a minimum:

CAUTION

NO OPEN FLAME

OXIDIZING GAS(ES) STORED WITHIN

11.3.12.4.1 Existing signage that is not in strict compliance with the provisions of this code shall be permitted to be continued in use as long as the authority having jurisdiction has determined that such use does not constitute a distinct hazard to life.

11.3.12.5 Replacement of existing signage that includes "No Smoking" for health care facilities that prohibit smoking shall not be required.

11.4 Performance Criteria and Testing.

11.4.1 Portable Patient Care Gas Equipment.

11.4.1.1* Each yoke on anesthetic apparatus constructed to allow attachment of a small cylinder equipped with a flush-type valve shall have two pins installed as specified in the mandatory requirements of CGA V-1, *Standard for Compressed Gas Cylinder Valve Outlet and Inlet Connections* (ANSI B57.1).

11.4.1.2 Testing.

11.4.1.2.1 Interventions requiring testing shall include, but not be limited to, the following:

(1) Alteration of pipeline hose or pipeline fittings
(2) Alteration of internal piping
(3) Adjustment of selector switches or flush valves
(4) Replacement or repair of flowmeters or bobbins

11.4.1.2.2 After any adjustment or repair involving use of tools, or any modification of the gas piping supply connections or the pneumatic power supply connections for the anesthesia ventilator, or other pneumatically powered device, if one is present, and before use on patients, the gas anesthesia apparatus shall be tested at the final common path to the patient to determine that oxygen, and only oxygen, is delivered from the oxygen flowmeters and the oxygen flush valve, if any.

11.4.1.2.3 Before the gas anesthesia apparatus is returned to service, each fitting and connection shall be checked to verify its proper indexing to the respective gas service involved.

11.4.1.2.4 Before the gas anesthesia apparatus is returned to service, an oxygen analyzer, or a similar device, shall be used to verify the oxygen concentration.

11.4.1.3* Yoke-type connections between anesthesia apparatus and flush-type cylinder valves (commonly used with anesthetic gas cylinders) shall be of the Connection No. 860 type in accordance with the mandatory requirements of CGA V-1, *Standard for Compressed Gas Cylinder Valve Outlet and Inlet Connections* (ANSI B57.1).

11.4.2 Apparatus for Administering Respiratory Therapy.

11.4.2.1 Oxygen-delivery equipment intended to rest on the floor shall be equipped with a base designed to render the entire assembly stable during storage, transport, and use.

11.4.2.2 Oxygen enclosures of rigid materials shall be fabricated of noncombustible materials.

11.4.2.3 Equipment supplied from cylinders or containers shall be designed and constructed for service at full cylinder or container pressure or constructed for use with, or equipped with, pressure reducing regulators.

11.4.2.4 Humidification or reservoir jars containing liquid to be dispersed into a gas stream shall be made of transparent or translucent material, shall be impervious to contained solutions and medications, and shall allow observation of the liquid level and consistency.

11.4.2.5 Humidifiers and nebulizers shall be equipped with provisions for overpressure relief or alarm if the flow becomes obstructed.

11.4.2.6 Humidifiers and nebulizers shall be incapable of tipping or shall be mounted so that any tipping or alteration from the vertical shall not interfere with function or accuracy.

11.4.3 Nonpatient Gas Equipment.

11.4.3.1 Carts and Hand Trucks.

11.4.3.1.1 Construction. Carts and hand trucks for cylinders and containers shall be constructed for the intended purpose, be self-supporting, and be provided with appropriate chains or stays to retain cylinders or containers.

11.4.3.2 Medical Devices. Medical devices not for patient care that require medical gases or medical support gases shall meet the following:

(1) Be listed for the intended purpose by the US Food and Drug Administration
(2) Be under the direction of a licensed medical professional
(3) Not be permanently attached to the piped distribution system (*see 5.1.3.5.2*)
(4) Undergo a risk assessment conducted by the health care facility's governing body to determine the character of the processes and operations conducted in the facility and whether medical gases or medical support gases are acceptable for use by the medical device

11.5 Administration.

11.5.1 Policies.

11.5.1.1 Elimination of Sources of Ignition.

11.5.1.1.1 Smoking materials (e.g., matches, cigarettes, lighters, lighter fluid, tobacco in any form) shall be removed from patients receiving respiratory therapy.

11.5.1.1.2* When a nasal cannula and its associated supply tubing are delivering oxygen outside of a patient care space, no sources of open flame shall be permitted in the site of intentional expulsion.

11.5.1.1.3* When any other oxygen delivery equipment not specified in 11.5.1.1.2 is in use, no sources of open flame shall be permitted in the area of administration.

11.5.1.1.4* Solid fuel-burning appliances shall not be permitted in the area of administration.

11.5.1.1.5* Sparking toys shall not be permitted in any patient care space.

11.5.1.1.6 Nonmedical appliances that have hot surfaces or sparking mechanisms shall not be permitted within oxygen-delivery equipment or within the site of intentional expulsion.

11.5.1.2 Misuse of Flammable Substances.

11.5.1.2.1 Flammable or combustible aerosols or vapors, such as alcohol, shall not be used in oxygen-enriched atmospheres.

11.5.1.2.2 Oil, grease, or other flammable substances shall not be used on/in oxygen equipment.

11.5.1.2.3 Flammable and combustible liquids shall not be permitted within the site of intentional expulsion.

11.5.1.3 Servicing and Maintenance of Equipment.

11.5.1.3.1 Defective equipment shall be immediately removed from service.

11.5.1.3.2 Areas designated for the servicing of oxygen equipment shall be clean and free of oil, grease, or other flammable substances.

11.5.1.3.3* A scheduled preventive maintenance program shall be followed.

11.5.2 Gases in Cylinders and Liquefied Gases in Containers.

11.5.2.1 Qualification and Training of Personnel.

11.5.2.1.1* Personnel concerned with the application and maintenance of medical gases and others who handle medical gases and the cylinders that contain the medical gases shall be trained on the risks associated with their handling and use.

11.5.2.1.2 Health care facilities shall provide programs of continuing education for their personnel.

11.5.2.1.3 Continuing education programs shall include periodic review of safety guidelines and usage requirements for medical gases and their cylinders.

11.5.2.1.4 Equipment shall be serviced only by personnel trained in the maintenance and operation of the equipment.

11.5.2.1.5 If a cryogenic fluid central supply system is present, the supplier shall provide annual training on its operation.

11.5.2.2 Transfilling Cylinders.

11.5.2.2.1 Mixing of compressed gases in cylinders shall be prohibited.

11.5.2.2.2* Transfilling of gaseous oxygen from one cylinder to another shall be in accordance with the mandatory requirements in the mandatory requirements of CGA P-2.5, *Standard for Transfilling of High Pressure Gaseous Oxygen Used for Respiration*.

11.5.2.2.3 Transfilling of any gases from one cylinder to another in the patient care vicinity shall be prohibited.

11.5.2.3 Transfilling Liquid Oxygen. Transfilling of liquid oxygen shall comply with 11.5.2.3.1 or 11.5.2.3.2, as applicable.

11.5.2.3.1 Transfilling to liquid oxygen base reservoir containers or to liquid oxygen portable containers over 344.74 kPa (50 psi) shall include the following:

(1) A designated area is separated by a fire barrier of 1-hour fire-resistive construction from any portion of a facility where patients are housed, examined, or treated.
(2) The area is mechanically ventilated, is sprinklered, and has ceramic or concrete flooring.
(3) The area is posted with signs indicating that transfilling is occurring and that smoking in the immediate area is not permitted.

(4) The individual transfilling the container(s) has been properly trained in the transfilling procedures.

11.5.2.3.2* Where transfilling to liquid oxygen portable containers at 344.74 kPa (50 psi) and under, the following conditions shall be met:

(1) The area is well ventilated and has noncombustible flooring.
(2) The area is posted with signs indicating that smoking in the area is not permitted.
(3) The individual transfilling the liquid oxygen portable container has been properly trained in the transfilling procedure.
(4) The mandatory requirements of CGA P-2.6, *Standard for Transfilling of Liquid Oxygen Used for Respiration*, are met.

11.5.2.4* Filling Cylinders from Oxygen Concentrators. Filling cylinders from oxygen concentrators, including in the patient care vicinity, shall be in accordance with the manufacturer's instructions, not to exceed the limits in 11.5.2.4.1 through 11.5.2.4.4.

11.5.2.4.1 The cylinder contents shall not exceed 700 L (25 ft^3).

11.5.2.4.2 The flow shall not exceed 5 L/min (0.2 ft^3/min).

11.5.2.4.3 The pressure shall not exceed the DOT rating of the cylinder or 20,700 kPa (3000 psi), whichever is less.

11.5.2.4.4 The cylinders shall be in accordance with DOT requirements or those of the applicable regulatory agency.

11.5.2.5 Ambulatory Patients. Areas where ambulatory patients on oxygen therapy are permitted access shall be flame- and smoke-free areas.

11.5.3 Use (Including Information and Warning Signs).

11.5.3.1 Labeling.

11.5.3.1.1 Equipment listed for use in oxygen-enriched atmospheres shall be so labeled.

11.5.3.1.2 Oxygen-metering equipment and pressure reducing regulators shall be conspicuously labeled as follows:

OXYGEN — USE NO OIL

11.5.3.1.3 Flowmeters, pressure reducing regulators, and oxygen-dispensing apparatus shall be clearly and permanently labeled, designating the gas or mixture of gases for which they are intended.

11.5.3.1.4 Apparatus whose calibration or function is dependent on gas density shall be labeled as to the proper supply gas gauge pressure (kPa/psi) for which it is intended.

11.5.3.1.5 Oxygen-metering equipment, pressure reducing regulators, humidifiers, and nebulizers shall be labeled with the name of the manufacturer or supplier.

11.5.3.1.6 Cylinders and containers shall be labeled in accordance with the mandatory requirements of CGA C-7, *Guide to Classification and Labeling of Compressed Gases*. Color coding shall not be utilized as a primary method of determining cylinder or container content.

11.5.3.1.7 All labeling shall be durable and withstand cleansing or disinfection.

11.5.3.2* Signs.

11.5.3.2.1 In health care facilities where smoking is not prohibited, precautionary signs readable from a distance of 1.5 m (5 ft) shall be conspicuously displayed wherever supplemental oxygen is in use and in aisles and walkways leading to such an area.

11.5.3.2.2 The signs shall be attached to adjacent doorways or to building walls or be supported by other appropriate means.

11.5.3.2.3 In health care facilities where smoking is prohibited and signs are prominently (strategically) placed at all major entrances, secondary signs with no smoking language shall not be required.

11.5.3.2.4 The nonsmoking policies shall be strictly enforced.

11.5.3.3 Transportation, Storage, and Use of Equipment.

11.5.3.3.1 Flow-control valves on administering equipment shall be closed prior to connection and when not in use.

11.5.3.3.2 Apparatus shall not be stored or transported with liquid agents in reservoirs.

11.5.3.3.3 Care shall be taken in attaching connections from gas services to equipment and from equipment to patients.

11.5.3.3.4 Fixed or adjustable orifice mechanisms, metering valves, pressure reducing regulators, and gauges shall not be connected directly to high pressure cylinders, unless specifically listed for such use and provided with appropriate safety devices.

11.5.3.3.5 Equipment shall only be serviced by qualified personnel.

11.6 Operation and Management of Cylinders.

11.6.1 Administration. Administrative authorities of health care organizations shall provide policies and procedures for safe practices.

11.6.1.1 Purchase specifications shall include the following:

(1) Specifications for cylinders
(2) Marking of cylinders, regulators, and valves
(3) Proper connections on the cylinders supplied to the facility

11.6.1.2 Training procedures shall include the following:

(1) Maintenance programs in accordance with the manufacturer's recommendations for the piped gas system
(2) Use and transport of equipment and the proper handling of cylinders, containers, hand trucks, supports, and valve protection caps
(3) Verification of gas content and mechanical connection specificity of each cylinder or container prior to placing it into service

11.6.1.3 Policies for enforcement shall include the following:

(1) Regulations for the storage and handling of cylinders and containers of oxygen and nitrous oxide
(2) Prompt evaluation of all signal warnings and all necessary measures taken to re-establish the proper functions of the medical gas and vacuum systems
(3) Organizational capability and resources to cope with a complete loss of any medical gas or vacuum system

(4) Successful completion of all tests required in 5.1.12.4 prior to the use of any medical gas or vacuum piping system for patient care
(5) Locations intended for the delivery vehicle delivering cryogenic liquid to cryogenic fluid central supply systems to remain open and not be used for any other purpose (e.g., vehicle parking, storage of trash containers)

11.6.2 Special Precautions for Handling Oxygen Cylinders and Manifolds. Handling of oxygen cylinders and manifolds shall be based on the mandatory requirements of CGA G-4, *Oxygen.*

11.6.2.1 Oxygen cylinders, containers, and associated equipment shall be protected from contact with oil or grease by means of the following specific precautions:

(1) Oil, grease, or readily flammable materials shall not be permitted to come in contact with oxygen cylinders, valves, pressure reducing regulators, gauges, or fittings.
(2) Pressure reducing regulators, fittings, or gauges shall not be lubricated with oil or any other flammable substance.
(3) Oxygen cylinders or apparatus shall not be handled with oily or greasy hands, gloves, or rags.

11.6.2.2 Equipment associated with oxygen shall be protected from contamination by means of the following specific precautions:

(1) Particles of dust and dirt shall be cleared from cylinder valve openings by slightly opening and closing the valve before applying any fitting to the cylinder valve.
(2) The high-pressure valve on the oxygen cylinder shall be opened slowly before bringing the apparatus to the patient or the patient to the apparatus.
(3) An oxygen cylinder shall not be draped with any materials such as hospital gowns, masks, or caps.
(4) Cylinder-valve protection caps, where provided, shall be kept in place and be hand-tightened, except when cylinders are in use or connected for use.
(5) Valves shall be closed on all empty cylinders in storage.

11.6.2.3 Cylinders shall be protected from damage by means of the following specific procedures:

(1) Oxygen cylinders shall be protected from abnormal mechanical shock, which is liable to damage the cylinder, valve, or safety device.
(2) Oxygen cylinders shall not be stored near elevators or gangways or in locations where heavy moving objects will strike them or fall on them.
(3) Cylinders shall be protected from tampering by unauthorized individuals.
(4) Cylinders or cylinder valves shall not be repaired, painted, or altered.
(5) Safety relief devices in valves or cylinders shall not be tampered with.
(6) Valve outlets clogged with ice shall be thawed with warm — not boiling — water.
(7) A torch flame shall not be permitted, under any circumstances, to come in contact with a cylinder, cylinder valve, or safety device.
(8) Sparks and flame shall be kept away from cylinders.
(9) Even if they are considered to be empty, cylinders shall not be used as rollers, supports, or for any purpose other than that for which the supplier intended them.
(10) Large cylinders (exceeding size E) and containers larger than 45 kg (100 lb) weight shall be transported on a proper hand truck or cart complying with 11.4.3.1.

Shaded text = Revisions. Δ = Text deletions and figure/table revisions. • = Section deletions. *N* = New material.

(11) Freestanding cylinders shall be properly chained or supported in a proper cylinder stand or cart.

(12) Cylinders shall not be supported by radiators, steam pipes, or heat ducts.

11.6.2.4 Cylinders and their contents shall be handled with care, which shall include the following specific procedures:

(1) Oxygen fittings, valves, pressure reducing regulators, or gauges shall not be used for any service other than that of oxygen.

(2) Gases of any type shall not be mixed in an oxygen cylinder or any other cylinder.

(3) Oxygen shall always be dispensed from a cylinder through a pressure reducing regulator.

(4) The cylinder valve shall be opened slowly, with the face of the indicator on the pressure reducing regulator pointed away from all persons.

(5) Oxygen shall be referred to by its proper name, *oxygen*, not air, and liquid oxygen shall be referred to by its proper name, not liquid air.

(6) Oxygen shall not be used as a substitute for compressed air.

(7) The markings stamped on cylinders shall not be tampered with, because it is against federal statutes to change these markings.

(8) Markings used for the identification of contents of cylinders shall not be defaced or removed, including decals, tags, and stenciled marks, except those labels/tags used for indicating cylinder status (e.g., full, in use, empty).

(9) The owner of the cylinder shall be notified if any condition has occurred that might allow any foreign substance to enter a cylinder or valve, giving details and the cylinder number.

(10) Neither cylinders nor containers shall be placed in the proximity of radiators, steam pipes, heat ducts, or other sources of heat.

(11) Very cold cylinders or containers shall be handled with care to avoid injury.

11.6.2.5 Oxygen equipment that is defective shall not be used until one of the following tasks has been performed:

(1) It has been repaired by competent in-house personnel.

(2) It has been repaired by the manufacturer or his or her authorized agent.

(3) It has been replaced.

11.6.2.6 Pressure reducing regulators that are in need of repair or cylinders having valves that do not operate properly shall not be used.

11.6.3 Special Precautions for Making Cylinder and Container Connections.

11.6.3.1 Cylinder valves shall be opened and connected in accordance with the following procedure:

(1) Make certain that apparatus and cylinder valve connections and cylinder wrenches are free of foreign materials.

(2) Turn the cylinder valve outlet away from personnel following these safety procedures:

(a) Stand to the side — not in front and not in back.

(b) Before connecting the apparatus to the cylinder valve, momentarily open the cylinder valve to eliminate dust.

(3) Make connection of the apparatus to the cylinder valve, and tighten the connection nut securely with a wrench.

(4) Release the low-pressure adjustment screw of the pressure-reducing regulator completely.

(5) Slowly open cylinder valve to the full-open position.

(6) Slowly turn in the low-pressure adjustment screw on the pressure reducing regulator until the proper operating pressure is obtained.

(7) Open the valve to the utilization apparatus.

11.6.3.2 Connections for containers shall be made in accordance with the container manufacturer's operating instructions.

11.6.4 Special Precautions for the Care of Safety Mechanisms.

11.6.4.1 Personnel using cylinders and containers and other equipment covered in this chapter shall be familiar with the mandatory requirements of CGA Pin-Index Safety System and the CGA Diameter-Index Safety System, which are both designed to prevent utilization of the wrong gas.

11.6.4.2 Safety relief mechanisms, noninterchangeable connectors, and other safety features shall not be removed, altered, or replaced.

11.6.5 Special Precautions — Storage of Cylinders and Containers.

11.6.5.1 Storage shall be planned so that cylinders can be used in the order in which they are received from the supplier.

11.6.5.2 If empty and full cylinders are stored within the same enclosure, empty cylinders shall be segregated from full cylinders.

11.6.5.2.1 When the facility employs cylinders with integral pressure gauge, it shall establish the threshold pressure at which a cylinder is considered empty.

11.6.5.3 Empty cylinders shall be marked to avoid confusion and delay if a full cylinder is needed in a rapid manner.

11.6.5.4 Cylinders stored in exterior locations shall be as follows:

(1) Secured against falling or tipping

(2) Stored in a well-drained location and protected from prolonged contact with soil

(3) Prevented from reaching temperatures lower than the recommendations of the medical gas supplier

(4) Screened against continuous exposure to direct rays of the sun where the ambient temperature exceeds 52°C (125°F)

11.6.5.5* Storage of nitrous oxide cylinders shall be secured against unauthorized access.

11.7 Liquid Oxygen Equipment.

11.7.1 General. The storage and use of liquid oxygen in liquid oxygen base reservoir containers and liquid oxygen portable containers shall comply with the following, or storage and use shall be in accordance with the adopted fire prevention code.

11.7.2 Information and Instructions. The liquid oxygen seller shall provide the user with documentation that includes, but is not limited to, the following:

(1) Manufacturer's instructions, including labeling for storage and use of the containers

(2) Requirements for storage and use of containers away from ignition sources, exits, electrical hazards, and high-temperature devices

(3) Methods for container restraint to prevent falling

(4) Requirements for container handling

(5) Safeguards for refilling of containers

11.7.3 Container Storage, Use, and Operation.

11.7.3.1* Containers shall be stored, used, and operated in accordance with the manufacturer's instructions and labeling.

11.7.3.2 Containers shall not be placed in the following areas:

(1) Where they can be tipped over by the movement of a door

(2) Where they interfere with foot traffic

(3) Where they are subject to damage from falling objects

(4) Where exposed to open flames and high-temperature devices

11.7.3.3* Liquid oxygen base reservoir containers shall be secured by one of the following methods while in storage or use to prevent tipping over caused by contact, vibration, or seismic activity:

(1) Securing to a fixed object with one or more restraints

(2) Securing within a framework, stand, or assembly designed to resist container movement

(3) Restraining by placing the container against two points of contact

11.7.3.4 Liquid oxygen base reservoir containers shall be transported by a cart or hand truck designed for such use, unless a container is equipped with a roller base.

11.7.3.5* Liquid Oxygen Portable Containers.

11.7.3.5.1 Liquid oxygen portable containers shall be kept in an upright position.

11.7.3.5.2 Liquid oxygen portable containers shall not be carried under clothing or other covering.

11.7.3.5.3 Liquid oxygen portable containers shall be kept away from ignition sources, electrical hazards, and high temperature devices during filling and use.

11.7.3.6 The transfilling of containers shall be in accordance with the manufacturer's instructions and the requirements of 11.7.3.6.1 through 11.7.3.6.2.

11.7.3.6.1 Liquid oxygen containers shall be filled outdoors or in compliance with 11.5.2.3.1.

11.7.3.6.1.1* A drip pan compatible with liquid oxygen shall be provided under the liquid oxygen base reservoir container's filling and vent connections used during the filling process, unless the filling is performed on a noncombustible surface such as concrete.

11.7.3.6.2 Liquid oxygen portable containers shall be permitted to be filled indoors when the liquid oxygen base reservoir container is designed for filling such containers and the written instructions provided by the container manufacturer are followed.

11.7.4 Maximum Quantity.

11.7.4.1 The maximum total quantity of liquid oxygen permitted in storage and in use in a patient bed location or patient care vicinity shall be 120 L (31.6 gal), provided that the patient bed location or patient care vicinity, or both, are separated from the remainder of the facility by fire barriers and horizontal assemblies having a minimum fire resistance rating of 1 hour in accordance with the adopted building code.

11.7.4.2 One liquid oxygen portable container [limited to 1.5 L (0.396 gal) capacity] per patient is permitted to be stored or used in a patient bed location or patient care vicinity without having to meet the fire separation requirements of 11.7.4.1.

Chapter 12 Emergency Management

12.1* Applicability. This chapter shall apply to new and existing health care facilities.

12.1.1* This chapter shall provide those with the responsibility for emergency management in health care facilities with the criteria to assess, mitigate, prepare for, respond to, and recover from emergencies of any origin.

Δ **12.1.2*** This chapter shall be the source for emergency management in health care facilities.

12.1.3 This chapter shall aid in developing, maintaining, and evaluating effective emergency management programs in new and existing facilities.

12.2 Responsibilities.

12.2.1* Authority Having Jurisdiction.

12.2.1.1 The authority having jurisdiction shall be cognizant of the requirements of a health care facility with respect to its uniqueness for continued operation of the facility in an emergency.

12.2.1.2 The authority having jurisdiction shall ensure health care facility emergency management programs meet the requirements of this chapter.

12.2.2 Senior Management.

12.2.2.1 The senior management shall actively participate in and support emergency management planning.

12.2.2.2 Senior management shall provide the required resources to develop and support the emergency management program.

12.2.2.3 At least one representative of senior management shall provide a documented review of after-action reports and the annual evaluation of the emergency operations plan (EOP).

12.2.2.4 Senior management shall direct the prioritization of opportunities for improvement identified during exercises, events, and incidents.

12.2.2.5 Senior management shall appoint a program coordinator.

12.2.3* Emergency Management Committee. The emergency management committee shall include representatives of senior management and clinical and support services.

12.2.3.1* The membership of the emergency management committee shall include a chairperson, the emergency program coordinator, and leadership representatives of those departments, services, and areas that have a significant role in the facility's emergency management activities.

12.2.3.2 The emergency management committee shall have the responsibility for the emergency management program within the facility.

12.2.3.3* The emergency management committee shall model the emergency operations plan on an incident command system (ICS) in coordination with federal, state, and local emergency response agencies, as applicable.

12.3 Emergency Management Categories. The application of requirements in this chapter shall be based on the emergency management category of the health care facility as defined in Table 12.3.

12.4 General.

12.4.1* Health care facilities shall develop an emergency management program with a documented emergency operations plan based on the category of the health care facility as defined in Table 12.3.

12.4.1.1* The emergency management program shall include elements as required to manage an emergency during all four phases: mitigation, preparedness, response, and recovery.

12.4.1.2 The emergency management program shall comply with applicable regulations, directives, policies, and industry standards of practice.

12.4.2* When developing its emergency management program, the facility shall communicate its needs and vulnerabilities to community emergency response agencies and identify the capabilities of its community in supporting their mission.

12.4.3 The health care facility, in combination with local authorities, federal authorities, or both, shall establish the required emergency management category as defined in Table 12.3.

12.5 Emergency Management Category 1 and Emergency Management Category 2 Requirements.

12.5.1 All emergency management Category 1 and emergency management Category 2 health care facilities shall be required to develop and maintain an emergency management program that addresses all program elements as prescribed in 12.5.2 and 12.5.3.

12.5.2 The elements and complexity of the subsequent code sections in this chapter shall apply, as appropriate to the hazard vulnerability analysis (HVA), the community's expectations, and the leadership's defined mission of the health care facility.

Table 12.3 Emergency Management Categories

Emergency Management Category	Definition
1	Those inpatient facilities that remain operable to provide advanced life support services to injured responders and disaster victims, or those inpatient facilities that serve as a receiving facility for evacuating health care facilities. These facilities manage the existing inpatient load as well as plan for the influx of additional patients as a result of an emergency.
2	Those inpatient or outpatient facilities that augment the critical mission. These facilities manage the existing inpatient or outpatient loads but do not plan to receive additional patients as a result of an emergency or do not plan to remain operable should essential utilities or services be lost.

12.5.3 Program Elements.

12.5.3.1 Hazard Vulnerability Analysis (HVA).

12.5.3.1.1 A hazard vulnerability analysis (HVA) shall be conducted to identify and prioritize hazards that pose a threat to the facility and can affect the demand for its services.

Δ **12.5.3.1.2*** The hazards to be considered shall include, but not be limited to, the following:

(1) Natural (geological, meteorological, and biological)
(2) Human-caused (accidental and intentional)
(3) Technological

12.5.3.1.3 The analysis shall include the potential impact of the hazards on conditions including, but not limited to, the following:

(1)* Continuity of operations
(2) Care for new and existing patients/residents/clients
(3) Health, safety, and security of persons in the affected area
(4) Support of staff
(5) Property, facilities, and infrastructure
(6) Environmental impact
(7) Economic and financial conditions
(8) Regulatory and contractual obligations
(9) Reputation of, or confidence in, the facility

12.5.3.1.4 The facility shall prioritize the hazards and threats identified in the HVA with input from the community.

12.5.3.2 Mitigation.

12.5.3.2.1 The facility shall develop and implement a strategy to eliminate hazards or mitigate the effects of hazards that cannot be eliminated.

12.5.3.2.2 A mitigation strategy shall be developed for priority hazards defined by the HVA.

12.5.3.2.3 The mitigation strategy shall consider, but not be limited to, the following:

(1) Use of applicable building construction standards
(2) Hazard avoidance through appropriate land-use practices
(3) Relocation, retrofitting, or removal of structures at risk
(4) Removal or elimination of the hazard
(5) Reduction or limitation of the amount or size of the hazard
(6) Segregation of the hazard from that which is to be protected
(7)* Modification of the basic characteristics of the hazard
(8) Control of the rate of release of the hazard
(9) Provision of protective systems or equipment for both cyber or physical risks
(10) Establishment of hazard warning and communications procedures
(11) Redundancy or duplication of essential personnel, critical systems, equipment, information, operations, or materials

12.5.3.3 Preparedness.

12.5.3.3.1 The facility shall prepare for any emergency as determined by the HVA by organizing and mobilizing essential resources.

12.5.3.3.2 The facility shall maintain a current, documented inventory of the assets and resources it has on-site that would be needed during an emergency, such as medical, surgical, and pharmaceutical resources; water; fuel; staffing; food; and linen.

12.5.3.3.3 The facility shall identify the resource capability shortfalls from 96 hours of sustainability and determine if mitigation activities are necessary and feasible.

12.5.3.3.4 The facility shall establish a protocol for monitoring the quantity of assets and resources as they are utilized.

12.5.3.3.5 The facility shall write an emergency operations plan (EOP) that describes a command structure and the following critical functions within the facility during an emergency:

(1) Communications
(2) Resources and assets
(3) Safety and security
(4) Clinical support activities
(5) Essential utilities
(6) Exterior connections
(7) Staff roles

12.5.3.3.6 Critical Function Strategies. During the development of the EOP, the facility shall consider the strategies required in 12.5.3.3.6.1 through 12.5.3.3.6.8 in order to manage critical functions during an emergency within the facility.

Δ **12.5.3.3.6.1 Communications.** The facility shall plan for the following during an emergency:

(1) Initial notification and ongoing communication of information and instructions to staff
(2) Initial notification and ongoing communication with external authorities
(3) Communication with the following:

　(a) Patients and their families (i.e., responsible parties)
　(b) Responsible parties when patients are relocated to alternative care sites
　(c) Community and the media
　(d) Suppliers of essential materials, services, and equipment
　(e) Alternative care sites

(4) Definition of when and how to communicate patient information to third parties
(5)* Establishment of backup communications systems
(6) Cooperative planning with other local or regional health care facilities, including the following:

　(a) Exchange of information relating to command operations, including contact information
　(b) Staffing, resources, and assets that could be shared
　(c) A process and system to identify and track patients and fatalities related to the planned event or incident

12.5.3.3.6.2 Resources and Assets. The facility shall plan for the following during an emergency:

(1) Acquiring medical, pharmaceutical, and nonmedical supplies
(2) Replacing medical supplies and equipment that will be used throughout response and recovery
(3) Replacing pharmaceutical supplies that will be consumed throughout response and recovery
(4) Replacing nonmedical supplies that will be depleted throughout response and recovery

(5) Managing staff support activities, such as housing, transportation, incident stress debriefing, sanitation, hydration, nutrition, comfort, morale, and mental health
(6) Managing staff family support needs, such as child care, elder care, pet care, and communication to home
(7) Providing staff, equipment, and transportation vehicles needed for evacuation

12.5.3.3.6.3* Safety and Security. The facility shall plan for the following during an emergency:

(1) Internal security and safety operations
(2) Roles of agencies such as police, sheriff, and national guard
(3) Managing hazardous materials and waste
(4) Radioactive, biological, and chemical isolation and decontamination
(5) Patients susceptible to wandering
(6) Controlling entrance into the health care facility during emergencies
(7) Conducting a risk assessment with applicable authorities if it becomes necessary to control egress from the health care facility
(8) Controlling people movement within the health care facility
(9) Controlling traffic access to the facility

12.5.3.3.6.4 Clinical Support Activities. The facility shall plan for the following during an emergency:

(1) Clinical activities that could need modification or discontinuation during an emergency, such as patient scheduling, triage, assessment, treatment, admission, transfer, discharge, and evacuation
(2) Clinical services for special needs populations in the community, such as pediatric, geriatric, disabled, and chronically ill patients, and those with addictions (Emergency Management Category 1 only)
(3) Process to shelter patients in place
(4) Patient cleanliness and sanitation
(5) Behavioral needs of patients
(6) Mortuary services
(7) Evacuation both horizontally and, when required by circumstances, vertically, when the environment cannot support care, treatment, and services
(8) Transportation of patients, and their medications and equipment, and staff to an alternative care site(s) when the environment cannot support care, treatment, and services
(9) Transportation of pertinent patient information, including essential clinical and medication-related information, to an alternative care site(s) when the environment cannot support care, treatment, and services
(10) Documentation and tracking of patient location and patient clinical information

12.5.3.3.6.5* Essential Utilities and Systems. The facility shall plan for continuity of operations during the loss or interruption of the following utilities and systems during an emergency, as applicable:

(1) Electricity
(2) Potable water
(3) Nonpotable water
(4) Wastewater
(5) HVAC
(6) Fire protection
(7) Fuel for building operations

(8) Fuel for essential transportation
(9) Medical gas and vacuum
(10) Information technology

12.5.3.3.6.6 Exterior Connections. For essential utility systems in Emergency Management Category 1 facilities only, and based on the facility's HVA, consideration shall be given to the installation of exterior building connectors to allow for the attachment of portable emergency utility modules.

12.5.3.3.6.7 Staff Roles.

(A) Staff roles shall be defined for the areas of communications, resources and assets, safety and security, essential utilities, and clinical activities.

(B) Staff shall receive training for their assigned roles in the EOP.

(C) The facility shall communicate to licensed independent health care providers their roles in the EOP.

(D) The facility shall ensure that staff, volunteers, and other personnel are credentialed by the facility for their assignment and wear visible identification demonstrating such credentialing while on-site at the facility.

(E) The facility shall include in its plan the alerting, managing, and tracking of all staff in an emergency.

(F) The facility shall include in its plan a process for integrating the use of volunteers, including those of the federal government, in their emergency response.

12.5.3.3.6.8 The facility shall include the following in its EOP:

(1)* Standard command structure that is consistent with its community
(2) Reporting structure consistent with the command structure
(3) Activation and deactivation of the response and recovery phases, including the authority and process
(4) Facility capabilities and appropriate response efforts when the facility cannot be supported from the outside for extended periods in the six critical areas with an acceptable response, including examples such as the following:

  (a) Resource conservation
  (b) Service curtailment
  (c) Partial or total evacuation consistent with the staff's designated role in community response plan

(5) Alternative treatment sites to meet the needs of the patients

12.5.3.3.7 Staff Education.

12.5.3.3.7.1 Each facility shall implement an educational program in emergency management that includes training, drills, and exercises.

12.5.3.3.7.2 The educational program shall include an overview of the components of the emergency management program and concepts of the incident command system (ICS).

12.5.3.3.7.3 Individuals who are expected to perform as incident commanders or to be assigned to specific positions within the command structure shall be trained in and familiar with the ICS and the particular levels at which they are expected to perform.

12.5.3.3.7.4 Education concerning the staff's specific duties and responsibilities shall be conducted.

12.5.3.3.7.5 General overview education of the emergency management program and the ICS shall be conducted at the time of hire.

12.5.3.3.7.6 Department- and staff-specific education shall be conducted upon appointment to department/staff assignments or positions and annually thereafter.

12.5.3.3.8* **Testing Emergency Plans and Operations.**

Δ **12.5.3.3.8.1** The facility shall test its EOP at least twice annually through functional or full-scale exercises, events, or incidents.

12.5.3.3.8.2 Exercises shall be based on the HVA priorities and be as realistic as feasible.

Δ **12.5.3.3.8.3** For Emergency Management Category 1 only, an influx of volunteer or simulated patients shall be tested annually through a functional or full-scale exercise, event, or incident. *(See Table 12.3.)*

12.5.3.3.8.4 Annual table top, functional, or full-scale exercises shall include the following:

(1) Community integration
(2) Assessment of sustainability

12.5.3.3.8.5 For Emergency Management Category 1 only, if so required by the community designation to receive infectious patients, the facility shall conduct at least one exercise a year that includes a surge of infectious patients. *(See Table 12.3.)*

12.5.3.3.8.6 The identified exercises shall be conducted independently or in combination.

12.5.3.3.9 **Scope of Exercises.**

12.5.3.3.9.1 Exercises shall be monitored by at least one designated evaluator who has knowledge of the facility's plan and who is not involved in the exercise.

12.5.3.3.9.2 Exercises shall monitor the critical functions.

12.5.3.3.9.3 The facility shall conduct a debriefing session not more than 72 hours after the conclusion of the exercise, event, or incident.

12.5.3.3.9.4* The debriefing shall include key representatives from all of the following:

(1) Incident management team
(2) Clinical leadership
(3) Administrative leadership
(4) Physician(s)
(5) Nursing
(6) Support staff

12.5.3.3.9.5 Exercises, events, and incidents shall be critiqued to identify areas for improvement.

12.5.3.3.9.6 The critiques required by 12.5.3.3.9.5 shall identify deficiencies and opportunities for improvement based upon monitoring activities and observations during the exercise.

12.5.3.3.9.7 Opportunities for improvement identified in critiques shall be incorporated in the facility's improvement plan.

12.5.3.3.9.8* Improvements made to the emergency management program shall be evaluated in subsequent exercises.

12.5.3.4 **Response.**

12.5.3.4.1* The facility shall declare itself in an emergency mode based on current conditions that leadership considers extraordinary.

12.5.3.4.2 Once an emergency mode has been declared, the facility shall activate its EOP.

12.5.3.4.3 The decision to activate the EOP shall be made by the incident commander designated within the plan, in accordance with the facility's activation criteria.

12.5.3.4.4 The decision to deactivate the EOP shall be made by the incident commander in the health care organization in coordination with the applicable external command authority.

12.5.3.4.5* The organization shall make provisions for emergency credentialing of volunteer clinical staff.

12.5.3.4.5.1 At a minimum, a peer evaluation of skill shall be conducted to validate proficiency for volunteer clinical staff.

12.5.3.4.5.2 Prior to beginning work, the identity of other volunteers offering to assist during response activities shall be verified.

12.5.3.4.5.3 Personnel designated or involved in the EOP of the health care facility shall be supplied with a means of identification, which shall be worn at all times in a visible location.

12.5.3.4.5.4 Identification issued to volunteers shall distinguish volunteers from staff members.

12.5.3.4.6 The command staff shall actively monitor conditions present in the environment and remain in communication with community emergency response agencies during an emergency response.

12.5.3.4.7 When conditions approach untenable, the command staff, in combination with community emergency response agencies, shall determine when to activate the facility evacuation plan.

12.5.3.4.8 Evacuation to the alternative care site shall follow the planning conducted during the preparedness phase.

12.5.3.4.9* **Crisis Standards of Care.** Crisis standards of care shall be developed through a communitywide approach, as approved by the authority having jurisdiction.

12.5.3.4.9.1 The decision to implement crisis standards of care shall be coordinated with the community leadership.

12.5.3.4.9.2 Upon implementation of crisis standards of care in a community, the following shall be considered:

(1) The triage process
(2) The allocation of medical services across the population

12.5.3.4.9.3 Standards of care shall be returned to normal at the earliest feasible time.

12.5.3.4.10 **Medical Surge Capacity and Capability.** The requirements of 12.5.3.4.10.1 and 12.5.3.4.10.2 shall apply only to those facilities designated as Emergency Management Category 1 as defined by the HVA.

12.5.3.4.10.1* The facility shall plan for medical surge capacity and capability.

12.5.3.4.10.2 The triage process shall be implemented as follows:

(1) The arriving victim shall be assessed into the following cohorts:

    (a) Risk to others, as follows:

        i. Mentally unstable
        ii. Contaminated
        iii. Infectious

    (b) Risk to self, as follows:

        i. Emotionally impaired
        ii. Suicidal

    (c) Risk of death or permanent injury, as follows:

        i. Walking wounded
        ii. Severely injured but stable
        iii. Suffering from life-threatening injury
        iv. Beyond care

(2) Patients shall be admitted for treatment depending on facility capacity, the facility's specialty, and clinical need.

(3) Creation of ancillary clinical space shall have adequate utility support for the following:

    (a) HVAC
    (b) Sanitation
    (c) Lighting
    (d) Proximity to operating room (OR)

12.5.3.4.11 Health care facilities shall have a designated media spokesperson to facilitate news releases during the response process.

12.5.3.4.12 An area shall be designated for media representatives to assemble where they will not interfere with the operations of the health care facility.

12.5.3.5* Recovery.

12.5.3.5.1 Plans shall reflect measures needed to restore operational capability to predisaster levels.

12.5.3.5.2 Fiscal aspects shall be considered with respect to restoration costs and possible cash flow losses associated with the disruption.

12.5.3.5.3 Facility leadership shall accept and accommodate federal, state, and local assistance that will be beneficial for recovery of operations.

12.5.3.5.4 No party to recovery shall take action to unfairly limit lawful competition once recovery operations are completed.

12.5.3.5.5 Recovery shall not be deemed complete until infection control decontamination efforts are validated.

12.5.3.6 Administration.

Δ **12.5.3.6.1** The facility shall modify, as necessary, its HVA, EOP, supply chain (including the current emergency supplies inventory), and other components of the emergency management program as a result of exercises, events, incidents, and annual review.

12.5.3.6.2 The facility shall maintain written records of drills, exercises, and training as required by this chapter for a period of 3 years.

Chapter 13　Security Management

13.1* Applicability. This chapter shall apply to new and existing health care facilities.

13.2* Security Management Plan.

13.2.1 A health care facility shall have a security management plan.

13.2.2* The scope, objectives, performance, and effectiveness of the security plan shall be tested at a frequency shown to be necessary by review of the security vulnerability assessment (SVA) in accordance with Section 13.3.

13.3 Security Vulnerability Assessment (SVA).

13.3.1* At least annually, the health care facility shall conduct a security vulnerability assessment (SVA).

13.3.2 The facility shall modify, as necessary, its SVA as a result of exercises, national or local events, and annual review.

13.3.3 The SVA shall evaluate the potential security risks posed by the physical and operational environment of the health care facility to all individuals in the facility.

13.3.4 The facility shall implement procedures and controls in accordance with the risks identified by the SVA.

13.4 Responsible Person.

13.4.1 A person(s) shall be appointed by the leadership of the health care facility to be responsible for all security management activities.

13.4.2 The duties of the person assigned as required by 13.4.1 shall include, but not be limited to, the following, as identified in the SVA:

(1) Provide identification for patients, staff, and other people entering the facility
(2) Control access in and out of security-sensitive areas
(3) Define and implement procedures as follows:

   (a) Security incident
   (b) Hostage situation
   (c)* Bomb (explosive device or threat)
   (d) Criminal threat
   (e) Labor action
   (f) Disorderly conduct
   (g) Workplace violence
   (h) Restraining order
   (i) Prevention of, and response to, infant or pediatric abduction
   (j) Situations involving VIPs or the media
   (k) Maintenance of access to emergency areas
   (l) Civil disturbance
   (m) Forensic patients
   (n) Patient elopement
   (o) National Terrorism Advisory System (NTAS) or equivalent
   (p) Suspicious material or package
   (q) Suspicious powder or substance
   (r) Use of force policy
   (s) Security staffing augmentation
   (t) Active shooter
(4) Provide security at alternate care sites or vacated facilities
(5) Control vehicular traffic on the facility property

(6) Protect the facility assets, including property and equipment
(7) Provide policy for interaction with law enforcement agencies
(8) Comply with applicable laws, regulations, and standards regarding security management operations
(9) Educate and train the facility security force to address the following:

   (a) Customer service
   (b) Use of physical restraints
   (c) Use of force
   (d) Response criteria
   (e) Fire watch procedures
   (f) Lockdown procedures
   (g) Emergency notification procedures
   (h) Emergency communications procedures

13.5 Security-Sensitive Areas.

13.5.1 All security-sensitive areas, as identified by the SVA, shall be protected as appropriate.

13.5.2 Emergency department security shall include appropriate protection, including the following:

(1)* Control and limitation of access by the general public
(2) Private duress alarm at the nurses' station and reception for summoning immediate assistance
(3) Access-control of treatment area
(4) Lockdown procedure to secure the area when conditions threaten the viability of the department
(5) Bullet-resisting glazing material, as deemed necessary by review of the SVA

13.5.3 Pediatric and infant care areas shall have a security plan for the prevention of, and response to, pediatric and infant abduction that shall include appropriate protections, such as the following:

(1) Control and limitation of access by the general public
(2) Screening by nursing prior to allowing persons access to infant care areas
(3) Matching protocol with staff clearance to pair infants with parents
(4) System to monitor and track the location of pediatric and infant patients
(5)* Facility alert system and lockdown procedures
(6) Use of electronic monitoring, tracking, and access control equipment
(7) Use of an automated and standardized facility-wide alerting system to announce pediatric or infant abduction
(8) Remote exit locking or alarming
(9) Staff observation of all persons and inspection of all packages leaving the premises
(10) Prohibition on birth announcements by staff
(11) Detection of the presence of a nonidentified individual constitutes a security breach
(12) Movement of infants restricted to basinets only — no hand carries
(13) Health care staff wear unique identification or uniforms
(14) Secure storage of scrubs and uniforms, both clean and dirty
(15) Education in pediatric and infant abduction as follows:

   (a) Health care staff are familiar with infant abduction scenarios
   (b) Parents know not to leave a child or an infant unattended or in the care of an unidentified person

     (c) Parents know that they have the right to refuse to release their child to any individual without validation of official hospital identification

(16) Visiting family and friends not permitted to enter any nursery area with an infant or a newborn from the outside

(17) Infant abduction drills conducted periodically, based on SVA, to test effectiveness of chosen measures

(18) Video surveillance equipment, where it does not violate HIPAA or other patient rights

13.5.4* Medication storage and work areas shall be secured against admittance of unauthorized personnel through the use of the following:

(1) Access control
(2) Unique identification for the area
(3) Secure storage and controlled dispensing of drugs

13.5.5 Clinical and research laboratories shall be secured against admittance of unauthorized personnel through appropriate protections, such as the following:

(1) Access control
(2) Unique identification for the area
(3) Secure storage and controlled dispensing of regulated chemical, biological, and radiological materials
(4) Video surveillance

13.5.6 Dementia or behavioral health units shall be secured against the admittance or release of unauthorized personnel through appropriate protections, such as the following:

(1) Access control
(2) Unique identification for the area
(3)* Procedure to prevent entry of contraband prior to a person being admitted into the unit or department
(4) Elopement precautions
(5) Maintenance of color photos with the medical information of current patients to aid in identification

13.5.7 Forensic patient treatment areas shall provide appropriate protections, such as the following:

(1)* Law enforcement attending the patient at all times
(2) Treatment performed in an area separate from other patients
(3) Restraints applied or removed only under forensic staff control

13.5.8 Communications, data infrastructure, and medical records storage areas shall be secured against the admittance of unauthorized personnel or unauthorized release of confidential information through the use of appropriate protections, such as the following:

(1) Access control
(2) Unique identification for the area
(3) Surveillance equipment
(4) Data encryption and password protection

13.6 Access and Egress Security Measures.

13.6.1 Public visitation controls shall be enforced.

13.6.2 After-hours entrance by the public shall be restricted to designated areas, such as entrance lobbies and emergency departments.

13.6.3 Health care facility security controls and procedures shall comply with life safety requirements for egress.

13.6.3.1* Security plans for health care occupancies shall address access and egress control during periods of quarantine and other events in conjunction with emergency agencies.

13.7* Media Control.

13.7.1 The security management plan shall include procedures to accommodate media representatives.

13.7.1.1* A person shall be designated to serve as media contact and representative for the organization in regard to media interactions.

13.7.2* An area shall be designated for assembly of media representatives.

13.7.3 A security or facility staff member shall remain with the media representative(s) at all times.

13.7.4 Media representatives shall be escorted when granted access to the health care facility outside of the area designated in 13.7.2.

13.8* Crowd Control.

13.8.1 The security management plan shall include processes and procedures for controlling access to the health care facility.

13.8.2 The security management plan shall provide procedures for crowd control for management of those demanding access to a health care facility.

13.8.3 The procedures for crowd control shall provide for the coordination and collaboration of security and law enforcement.

13.9 Access Control Equipment.

13.9.1 Exterior entrances shall be provided with locking devices.

13.9.2 Locking devices shall comply with applicable federal, state, and local requirements.

13.9.3 Locking devices shall be properly installed and be in good working order.

13.9.4* The facility shall operate a key control program.

13.10* Employment Practices. Employers shall ensure a high level of integrity in the workplace by using the following practices:

(1) Background checks of employees with access to critical assets
(2) Background checks of outside contractors' employees
(3) Drug testing program for employees

13.11* Security Operations.

13.11.1* Post orders shall be written for security personnel.

13.11.2 Security personnel training shall include, but not be limited to, the following:

(1) Customer service
(2) Emergency procedures
(3) Patrol methods
(4) De-escalation training
(5) Use of physical restraints
(6) Use of force

13.12 Program Evaluation.

13.12.1* Periodic drills shall be conducted at various times and locations.

13.12.2 The drills shall be critiqued for plan effectiveness and to identify opportunities for improvement.

13.12.3 Identified opportunities for improvement shall be incorporated into the security plan.

13.12.4 The security plan shall be evaluated at least annually.

13.12.5 The evaluation of the security management plan shall include a review of laws, regulations, and standards applicable to the security program.

Chapter 14   Hyperbaric Facilities

14.1* Scope. The scope of this chapter shall be as specified in 1.1.12.

14.1.1 Applicability.

14.1.1.1 This chapter shall apply to new facilities.

Δ **14.1.1.2** The following sections of this chapter shall apply to both new and existing facilities:

(1)   14.2.4.1.1 (excluding subsections)
(2)   14.2.4.1.1.1
(3)   14.2.4.1.2
(4)   14.2.4.1.3 (excluding subsections)
(5)   14.2.4.1.3.3
(6)   14.2.4.4 (and subsections)
(7)   14.2.5.4
(8)   14.2.6.1.4
(9)   14.2.6.1.5
(10) 14.2.6.1.7
(11) 14.3.4.3.5 (and subsections)
(12) 14.2.8.1
(13) 14.2.8.2 (and subsections)
(14) 14.2.9.3.1 through 14.2.9.3.4
(15) 14.2.9.3.8 (and subsection)
(16) 14.2.9.3.14.4
(17) 14.2.9.3.15.5
(18) 14.2.9.3.16 (and subsections)
(19) 14.2.9.4.1.3
(20) 14.2.9.6 (and subsections)
(21) 14.2.10.3 through 14.2.10.6.3 (and subsections)
(22) 14.2.11.2.5
(23) 14.3.1 (and subsections)
(24) 14.3.2.1.1 through 14.3.2.1.5
(25) 14.3.2.4 through 14.3.2.6 (and subsection)
(26) 14.3.3 and 14.3.4 (and subsections)

14.1.1.3 This chapter shall also apply to the altered, renovated, or modernized portion of an existing system or individual component.

14.1.1.4 Existing construction or equipment shall be permitted to be continued in use when such use does not constitute a distinct hazard to life.

14.1.2 Classification of Chambers.

14.1.2.1 General. Chambers shall be classified according to occupancy in order to establish appropriate minimum essentials in construction and operation.

14.1.2.2 Occupancy. Hyperbaric chambers shall be classified according to the following criteria:

(1)   Class A — Human, multiple occupancy
(2)   Class B — Human, single occupancy
(3)   Class C — Animal, no human occupancy

14.1.3 Category.

14.1.3.1 Category 1 Hyperbaric Care.

14.1.3.1.1 Where interruption or failure of medical gas supply is likely to cause major injury or death of patients, staff, or visitors, the medical gas system shall be Category 1 for use in this chapter.

14.1.3.1.2 Where interruption or failure of electrical service is likely to cause major injury or death of patients, staff, or visitors, the electrical service shall be Category 1 for use in this chapter.

14.1.3.2 Category 2 Hyperbaric Care.

14.1.3.2.1 Where interruption or failure of medical gas supply is likely to cause minor injury of patients, staff, or visitors, the medical gas system shall be considered Category 2 for use in this chapter.

14.1.3.2.2 Where interruption or failure of electrical service is likely to cause minor injury of patients, staff, or visitors, the electrical service shall be Category 2 for use in this chapter.

14.1.3.3 Category 3 Hyperbaric Care.

14.1.3.3.1 Where interruption or failure of medical gas supply is not likely to cause injury to patients, staff, or visitors, the medical gas system shall be considered Category 3 for use in this chapter.

14.1.3.3.2 Where interruption or failure of electrical service is not likely to cause injury to patients, staff, or visitors, the electrical service shall be Category 3 for use in this chapter.

14.1.3.4 Category 4 Hyperbaric Care. (Reserved)

14.1.4 Applicable Code. Hyperbaric facilities that are conducting any form of treatment and are not located in a designated health care facility, including residential occupancies, shall comply with the requirements of the applicable code.

14.2 Construction and Equipment.

14.2.1 Housing for Hyperbaric Facilities.

14.2.1.1 For Class A chambers located inside a building, the chamber(s) and all ancillary service equipment shall be protected by 2-hour fire-resistant-rated construction.

14.2.1.1.1* Freestanding, dedicated buildings containing only a Class A chamber(s) and ancillary service equipment shall not be required to be protected by 2-hour fire-resistant-rated construction.

14.2.1.1.2 Class B and C chambers located inside a building shall not be required to be protected by 2-hour fire-resistant-rated construction.

14.2.1.1.3 Trailer or vehicle-mounted facilities shall be permitted without a 2-hour fire-resistant-rated perimeter.

14.2.1.1.4 When trailer or vehicle-mounted facilities are located contiguous to a health care facility or another structure, a

2-hour fire-resistant-rated barrier shall be placed between the facility and the contiguous structure.

14.2.1.1.5 Where building exterior walls form part of the facility boundary, that portion of the facility boundary shall not require 2-hour fire-resistant-rated construction.

14.2.1.1.6* If there are connecting doors through such common walls of contiguity, they shall be at least B-label, 1½-hour fire doors.

14.2.1.1.7 When used for hyperbaric procedures, the room or rooms housing the Class A or Class B chambers shall be for the exclusive use of the hyperbaric operation.

14.2.1.1.8 Service equipment (e.g., compressors) shall be permitted to be located in multi-use spaces meeting the requirements of 14.2.1.1.

14.2.1.1.9 The supporting foundation for any chamber shall be designed to support the chamber.

14.2.1.1.9.1 If on-site hydrostatic testing will be performed, the chamber supporting foundation shall be designed to support an additional water weight.

14.2.1.2* The room housing a Class A or Class B chamber and any ancillary equipment rooms shall be provided protection by one of the following systems:

(1)* A hydraulically calculated automatic wet pipe sprinkler system meeting the requirements of NFPA 13
(2) An automatic water mist fire protection system installed in accordance with NFPA 750
(3)* A clean agent fire protection system in accordance with NFPA 2001

14.2.1.2.1 Class A or Class B chambers not contiguous to a health care facility and located in a mobile vehicle-mounted facility shall not be required to be protected as specified in 14.2.1.2.

14.2.1.2.2 The room housing a Class A, Class B, or Class C chamber shall contain a minimum of one 2-A:10B:C portable fire extinguisher.

14.2.1.3 Hyperbaric Piping Requirements.

14.2.1.3.1* Except where otherwise required by this chapter, piping systems dedicated to the hyperbaric chamber shall meet the requirements of ASME PVHO-1, *Safety Standard for Pressure Vessels for Human Occupancy*, for hyperbaric facility piping systems.

14.2.1.3.2 Shutoff valves accessible to facility personnel shall be provided for piping specified in 14.2.1.3.1 at the point of entry to the room housing the chamber(s).

14.2.1.3.3* Gas supplies from cylinders and portable containers shall include particulate filters to protect downstream components in the piping system.

14.2.1.4 Hyperbaric Medical Oxygen System Requirements.

14.2.1.4.1 Where medical oxygen systems are installed for hyperbaric use, the hyperbaric area(s) or facility shall be treated as a separate zone.

14.2.1.4.2 The requirements of Chapter 5 shall apply to the medical oxygen system for hyperbaric use, from the source of supply to the first in-line valve located downstream of the zone valve(s).

Δ **14.2.1.4.3** The requirements of ASME PVHO-1, *Safety Standard for Pressure Vessels for Human Occupancy*, shall apply to the medical oxygen system for hyperbaric use, starting immediately downstream of the first in-line valve located after the zone valve(s).

14.2.1.4.4 Hyperbaric oxygen systems for Category 1, Category 2, and Category 3 hyperbaric care connected directly to a hospital's oxygen system shall comply with Section 5.1, as applicable, except as noted in 14.2.1.4.4.1.

14.2.1.4.4.1 Central Supply Systems. Oxygen systems shall comply with 5.1.3.5, as applicable, except as follows:

(1) An emergency oxygen supply connection (EOSC) shall not be required for the hyperbaric oxygen system.
(2) An in-building emergency reserve (IBER) shall not be required for the hyperbaric oxygen system.

14.2.1.4.5 Hyperbaric stand-alone oxygen systems for Category 1 and Category 2 hyperbaric care shall comply with Section 5.1, as applicable, except as noted in 14.2.1.4.5.1.

14.2.1.4.5.1 Central Supply Systems. Oxygen systems shall comply with 5.1.3.5, as applicable, except as follows:

(1) An EOSC shall not be required for the hyperbaric oxygen system.
(2) An IBER shall not be required for the hyperbaric oxygen system.

14.2.1.4.6 Warning Systems.

14.2.1.4.6.1 Oxygen systems shall comply with 5.1.9, as applicable, except that warning systems shall be permitted to be a single master/area alarm panel.

14.2.1.4.6.2 The alarm panel shall be located in the room housing the chamber(s) to allow for easy audio and visual monitoring by the chamber operator.

14.2.1.4.7 Hyperbaric stand-alone oxygen systems for Category 3 hyperbaric care shall comply with Section 5.2, as applicable, except as noted in 14.2.1.4.7.1.

14.2.1.4.7.1 Central Supply Systems. Oxygen systems shall comply with 5.1.3.5, as applicable, except as follows:

(1) If the operating oxygen supply consists of high-pressure cylinders designed with a primary and secondary source, no reserve supply shall be required.
(2) If the operating oxygen supply consists of liquid containers designed with a primary and secondary source, a reserve with a minimum supply of 15 minutes shall be required.
(3) If the operating oxygen supply consists of a bulk primary, a reserve with a minimum supply of 15 minutes shall be required.
(4) An EOSC shall not be required for the hyperbaric oxygen system.
(5) An IBER shall not be required for the hyperbaric oxygen system.

14.2.1.5 Hyperbaric Medical Air System Requirements.

14.2.1.5.1 Where medical air systems are installed for hyperbaric use, the hyperbaric area(s) or facility shall be treated as a separate zone.

14.2.1.5.2 Chapter 5 requirements shall apply to the medical air system for hyperbaric use, from the source of supply to the first in-line valve located downstream of the zone valve(s).

Δ **14.2.1.5.3** ASME PVHO-1, *Safety Standard for Pressure Vessels for Human Occupancy*, requirements shall apply to the medical air system for hyperbaric use, starting immediately downstream of the first in-line valve located after the zone valve(s).

14.2.1.5.4 Where a medical air system is installed for hyperbaric treatments, it shall comply with the requirements for the appropriate level as determined in 14.2.1.5.4.1 through 14.2.1.5.4.7.

14.2.1.5.4.1 Hyperbaric medical air systems for Category 1, Category 2, and Category 3 hyperbaric care connected directly to a hospital's medical air system shall comply with Section 5.2, as applicable.

14.2.1.5.4.2 Reserved.

14.2.1.5.4.3 Hyperbaric stand-alone medical air systems for Category 1 and Category 2 hyperbaric care shall comply with Section 5.2, as applicable.

14.2.1.5.4.4 Reserved.

14.2.1.5.4.5 Medical air systems for Category 1 and Category 2 hyperbaric care shall comply with Section 5.2, as applicable, except that warning systems shall be permitted to be a single master/area alarm panel.

14.2.1.5.4.6 Hyperbaric stand-alone medical systems for Category 3 hyperbaric care shall comply with Section 5.2, as applicable, except as noted in 14.2.1.5.4.7.

14.2.1.5.4.7 Medical air systems shall comply with Section 5.2 as applicable, except as follows:

(1) Area and master alarms shall not be required for Category 3 hyperbaric care.
(2) A gas cylinder header per Section 5.2 with sufficient cylinder connections to provide for at least an average day's supply with the appropriate number of connections being determined after consideration of delivery schedule, proximity of the facility to alternate supplies, and the facility's emergency plan shall be permitted.
(3) A medical air cylinder directly connected to a Class B or Class C chamber and used to provide air to that chamber shall be permitted to be in the same room as the chamber.
(4) Where a cylinder is used as described in 14.2.1.5.4.7(3), the cylinder shall be considered to be "in use" and shall not be counted when determining the total volume of medical gas outside a storage area in Section 11.3.

14.2.1.6 Storage and Handling of Medical Gases. Storage and handling of medical gases shall meet the applicable requirements of Chapter 5 and Chapter 11.

14.2.2 Fabrication of the Hyperbaric Chamber.

14.2.2.1* Chambers for human occupancy and their supporting systems shall be designed and fabricated to meet the requirements of ASME PVHO-1, *Safety Standard for Pressure Vessels for Human Occupancy*, by personnel qualified to fabricate vessels under such codes.

N **14.2.2.1.1*** The primary pressure relief device on a chamber shall be capable of preventing any increase in pressure above the design pressure.

N **14.2.2.1.2*** A means to provide secondary pressure relief capable of preventing pressure exceeding 200 percent of the design pressure shall be provided.

14.2.2.1.3 Piping systems for hyperbaric facilities shall be required to meet only the requirements of this chapter and Section 4, "Piping Systems," of ASME PVHO-1, *Safety Standard for Pressure Vessels for Human Occupancy*.

Δ **14.2.2.1.4** Piping installed in concealed locations in the building that houses the hyperbaric facility, such as inside building walls or above false ceilings, shall use only those joining procedures permitted by Chapter 5.

14.2.2.2 The chamber shall be stamped in accordance with ASME PVHO-1, *Safety Standard for Pressure Vessels for Human Occupancy*.

14.2.2.3 Class C chambers shall be designed, fabricated, and stamped to meet Division 1 or Division 2 code requirements of Section VIII of the ASME *Boiler and Pressure Vessel Code*.

14.2.2.4* The viewports for Class C chambers shall be designed, fabricated, and marked to meet Section 2 of ASME PVHO-1, *Safety Standard for Pressure Vessels for Human Occupancy*.

14.2.2.5 The floor of a Class A chamber shall be designed to support equipment and personnel necessary for the operation of the chamber according to its expected purpose.

14.2.2.5.1 The floor of Class A chambers shall be noncombustible.

14.2.2.5.2 If a bilge is installed, access to the bilge shall be provided for cleaning purposes.

14.2.2.5.3 If the interior floor of a Class A chamber consists of removable floor (deck) plates, the plates shall be mechanically secured and electrically bonded to the chamber to ensure a positive electrical ground and to prevent movement of the plate, which could cause injury to personnel.

14.2.2.6 The interior surface of Class A chambers shall be unfinished or treated with a paint/coating in accordance with 14.2.2.6.1.

Δ **14.2.2.6.1*** Interior paint/coating shall meet the performance criteria of NFPA *101*, Class A interior finish, when tested in accordance with ASTM E84, *Standard Test Method for Surface Burning Characteristics of Building Materials*, or UL 723, *Test for Surface Burning Characteristics of Building Materials*.

14.2.2.6.2* One additional application of paint shall be permitted, provided total paint thickness does not exceed $\frac{1}{28}$ in. (0.9 mm).

14.2.2.6.3 If the interior of a Class A chamber is treated (painted), the cure procedure and minimum duration for each layer of paint/coating to off-gas shall be in accordance with the manufacturer's application instructions.

14.2.2.6.4* If sound-deadening materials are employed within a hyperbaric chamber, they shall be limited-combustible materials.

14.2.2.7* Viewing ports, access ports for piping and wiring or monitoring, and related leads shall be installed during initial fabrication of the chamber.

14.2.2.7.1 Access ports in Class A chambers, access ports for monitoring, and other electrical circuits shall be housed in enclosures that are weatherproof, both inside and outside the chamber, for protection in the event of sprinkler activation.

Δ 14.2.2.7.2 Viewports and penetrator plates shall be designed and fabricated according to ASME PVHO-1, *Safety Standard for Pressure Vessels for Human Occupancy*.

14.2.3 Illumination.

14.2.3.1 Sources of illumination mounted outside the pressure chamber and arranged to shine through chamber ports or through chamber penetrators designed for fiber-optic or similar lighting shall meet the following requirements:

(1) Lighting fixtures used in conjunction with viewports shall be designed so that temperature ratings for the viewport material given in ASME PVHO-1, *Safety Standard for Pressure Vessels for Human Occupancy*, are not exceeded.
(2) Gasket material shall be of a type that allows the movement of thermal expansion and shall be selected for the temperatures, pressures, and composition of gases involved.
(3) Gaskets or O-rings shall be confined to grooves or enclosures, which will prevent their being blown out or squeezed from the enclosures or compression flanges.

14.2.3.2 Emergency lighting for the interior of the chamber shall be provided.

14.2.4 Chamber Ventilation.

14.2.4.1 Ventilation of Class A Chambers.

14.2.4.1.1 The minimum ventilation rate for a Class A chamber shall be 0.085 m³/min (3 ft³/min) of air per chamber occupant who is not using a breathing-mask overboard dump system that exhausts exhaled gases.

14.2.4.1.1.1 The minimum threshold rate shall be 0.085 m³/min (3 ft³/min).

14.2.4.1.1.2 Provision shall be made for ventilation during nonpressurization of Class A chambers as well as during pressurization.

14.2.4.1.2* Ventilation shall not be required when saturation operations are conducted in the chamber, provided that carbon dioxide removal and odor control are accomplished and that the monitoring requirements of 14.2.10.4.3 and 14.2.10.5 are met.

Δ 14.2.4.1.3* Individual breathing apparatus for use by each occupant shall be available inside a Class A chamber in the event that the chamber atmosphere is fouled by combustion or otherwise.

14.2.4.1.3.1 The breathing mixture supplied to breathing apparatus shall be independent of the chamber atmosphere.

14.2.4.1.3.2 The breathing gas supply shall be designed for simultaneous use of all breathing apparatus.

14.2.4.1.3.3 Breathing apparatus shall function at all pressures that can be encountered in the chamber.

Δ 14.2.4.1.3.4 Provisions shall be made to simultaneously switch all breathing apparatus to an air supply independent of the chamber atmosphere in the event of a fire within the chamber.

14.2.4.2 Sources of Air for Chamber Atmospheres.

14.2.4.2.1* Sources of air for chamber atmospheres shall be such that toxic or flammable gases are not introduced.

14.2.4.2.2 Compressor intakes shall be located away from air contaminated by exhaust from activities of vehicles, internal combustion engines, stationary engines, or building exhaust outlets.

14.2.4.2.3 Air supply for chamber atmosphere shall be monitored as required in 14.2.10.6.

14.2.4.2.4 The use of conventional oil-lubricated compressors shall be permitted, provided that they are fitted with air treatment packages designed to meet the requirements of 14.2.10.6.

14.2.4.2.5 Air compressor installations shall consist of two or more individual compressors with capacities such that required system flow rates can be maintained on a continuous basis with any single compressor out of operation, unless 14.2.9.2.6 is satisfied.

14.2.4.2.5.1 Each compressor shall be supplied from separate electrical branch circuits.

14.2.4.2.6 Air compressor installations that supply medical air to piped gas systems as well as to hyperbaric facilities shall meet the requirements of 5.1.3.6.3 and this chapter.

14.2.4.2.7 Air compressor installations that are used exclusively for hyperbaric facilities shall meet the requirements of this chapter only.

14.2.4.3 Temperature and Humidity Control.

14.2.4.3.1 Warming or cooling of the atmosphere within a Class A chamber shall be permitted by circulating the ambient air within the chamber over or past coils through which a constant flow of warm or cool water or water/glycol mixture is circulated.

14.2.4.3.2 Dehumidification shall be permitted through the use of cold coils.

14.2.4.3.3 Humidification by the use of an air-powered water nebulizer shall be permitted.

14.2.4.3.4 Noncombustible packing and nonflammable lubricant shall be employed on the fan shaft.

14.2.4.4 Ventilation of Class B Chambers.

14.2.4.4.1* The minimum ventilation rate for a Class B chamber shall be 0.0283 m³/min (1 ft³/min).

14.2.4.4.2 Class B chambers not designed for 100 percent oxygen environment shall comply with the monitoring requirements of 14.2.10.4.

14.2.4.4.3 For Class B chambers equipped with a breathing apparatus, the breathing apparatus shall function at all pressures that can be encountered in the chamber.

14.2.5 Emergency Depressurization.

14.2.5.1 Class A chambers shall be capable of depressurizing from 3 ATA (304.0 kPa absolute) to ambient pressure in not more than 6 minutes.

14.2.5.2 Class B chambers shall be capable of depressurizing from 3 ATA (304.0 kPa absolute) to ambient pressure in not more than 2 minutes.

14.2.5.3 Class C chambers shall be capable of rapid depressurization.

14.2.5.4* A risk assessment shall be performed to determine if means for respiratory and eye protection from combustion products allowing unrestricted mobility is required to be available outside all classes of hyperbaric chambers for use by personnel in the event the air in the vicinity of the chamber is fouled by smoke or other combustion products.

14.2.6 Fire Protection in Class A Chambers.

14.2.6.1 General.

14.2.6.1.1 Fire suppression consisting of a primary fire suppression system and a secondary fire suppression system shall be installed in all Class A chambers.

Δ **14.2.6.1.2** Design of fire suppression systems shall be such that failure of components in either the primary or secondary fire suppression system will not render the other system inoperative.

14.2.6.1.3 System design shall be such that activation of the primary fire suppression system automatically causes the following:

(1) An alarm signal shall be transmitted to the facility's central fire alarm system, if present.
(2) Visual and audible indication of activation shall occur at the chamber operator's console.
(3) All ungrounded electrical leads for power and lighting circuits contained inside the chamber shall be disconnected.
(4) Emergency lighting (*see 14.2.3.2*) and communication, where used, shall be activated.

14.2.6.1.3.1 Intrinsically safe circuits, including sound-powered communications, shall be permitted to remain connected when either the primary or secondary fire suppression system is activated.

14.2.6.1.4 A means of communication shall be provided at the chamber operator's control console for notifying the fire department.

14.2.6.1.5* Fire blankets and portable carbon dioxide extinguishers shall not be installed in or carried into the chamber.

14.2.6.1.6 Booster pumps, control circuitry, and other electrical equipment involved in fire suppression system operation shall be powered from a critical branch of the essential electrical system as specified in 14.2.9.2.1.2.

14.2.6.1.7* At least one sign prohibiting the introduction of flammable liquids, gases, and other articles not permitted by this chapter into the chamber shall be posted in the room housing the chamber(s).

14.2.6.1.8 Fire suppression systems shall be permitted to be supplied from the local potable water service.

N **14.2.6.1.9*** Design and performance of primary fire suppression systems shall comply with either 14.2.6.2 or 14.2.6.4.

N **14.2.6.1.10*** Design and performance of secondary fire suppression systems shall comply with either 14.2.6.3 or 14.2.6.5.

14.2.6.2 Deluge System. Where fixed water deluge extinguishing systems serve as primary fire suppression systems in accordance with 14.2.6.1.9, they shall be installed in all chamber compartments that are designed for manned operations.

14.2.6.2.1 In chambers that consist of more than one chamber compartment (lock), the design of the deluge system shall meet the requirements of 14.2.6.2 when the chamber compartments are at different depths (pressures).

14.2.6.2.2 The deluge system in different compartments (locks) shall operate independently or simultaneously.

14.2.6.2.3* Manual activation and deactivation deluge controls shall be located at the operator's console and in each chamber compartment (lock) containing a deluge system.

14.2.6.2.3.1 Controls shall be designed to prevent unintended activation.

14.2.6.2.4 Water shall be delivered from the fixed discharge nozzles as specified in 14.2.6.2.6 within 3 seconds of activation of any affiliated deluge control.

14.2.6.2.5* Average spray density at floor level shall be not less than 81.5 L/min/m² (2 gpm/ft²), with no floor area larger than 1 m² (10.76 ft²) receiving less than 40.75 L/min/m² (1 gpm/ft²).

14.2.6.2.6 Water shall be available in the deluge system to maintain the flow specified in 14.2.6.2.5 simultaneously in each chamber compartment (lock) containing the deluge system for at least 1 minute.

14.2.6.2.6.1 The limit on maximum extinguishment duration shall be governed by the chamber capacity (bilge capacity also, if so equipped) or its drainage system, or both.

Δ **14.2.6.2.7** The deluge system shall have stored pressure to operate for at least 1 minute without electrical power.

14.2.6.2.8 All dedicated storage vessels used to provide the deluge system with water shall be fitted with a suitable water level indicator, with the level displayed at the chamber console.

14.2.6.2.9 Deluge systems using pressurized water vessels shall be designed to prevent the driving gas supply from pressurizing the hyperbaric chamber if all the water is driven out of the water vessel.

N **14.2.6.2.10*** Water storage vessels capable of producing or containing corrosion or other products capable of blocking outlet nozzles shall be equipped with a strainer complying with 14.2.6.2.10.1 through 14.2.6.2.10.3.

N **14.2.6.2.10.1** The strainer shall be located where water exits the vessel into the fire suppression system piping.

N **14.2.6.2.10.2** The strainer shall be capable of opening for inspection and cleaning of the filter device during periodic system maintenance inspections.

N **14.2.6.2.10.3** The strainer mesh or pore size shall be selected to protect deluge nozzles and any inline flow control equipment from blockage or damage and to ensure the filter does not clog between fire suppression system testing intervals specified in 14.3.4.3.5.

14.2.6.3 Handline System. Where handline extinguishing systems serve as secondary fire suppression systems in accordance with 14.2.6.1.10, they shall be installed in all chamber compartments (locks) designed for manned operations.

14.2.6.3.1 At least two handlines shall be strategically located in treatment compartments (locks).

14.2.6.3.2 At least one handline shall be located in each personnel transfer compartment (lock).

14.2.6.3.3 If any chamber compartment (lock) is equipped with a bilge access panel, at least one handline shall reach the bilge area.

14.2.6.3.4 Handlines shall have a 12.7 mm (0.5 in.) minimum internal diameter and shall have a rated operating pressure greater than the highest supply pressure of the supply system.

14.2.6.3.5 Each handline shall be activated by a manual, quick-opening, quarter-turn valve located within the compartment (lock).

14.2.6.3.5.1 A hand-operated spring-return to close valves at the discharge end of handlines shall be permitted.

14.2.6.3.6 Handlines shall be equipped with override valves that are accessible to personnel outside the chamber.

14.2.6.3.7 The water supply for the handline system shall be designed to ensure a 345 kPa (50 psi) minimum water pressure above the maximum chamber pressure.

14.2.6.3.7.1 The system shall be capable of supplying a minimum of 18.9 L/min (5 gpm) simultaneously to each of any two of the handlines at the maximum chamber pressure for a period of not less than 4 minutes.

N **14.2.6.3.8** System design shall be such that activation of the handline system automatically causes the following to occur:

(1) Visual and audible indication of activation shall occur at the chamber operator's console.
(2) All ungrounded electrical leads for power and lighting circuits contained inside the chamber shall be disconnected.
(3) Emergency lighting *(see 14.2.3.2)* and communication, where used, shall be activated.

N **14.2.6.4 Alternative Primary Fire Suppression System.** Where alternative fire suppression systems serve as primary fire suppression systems in accordance with 14.2.6.1.9, they shall be installed in all chamber compartments designed for manned operations.

N **14.2.6.4.1*** The fire suppression system shall be designed to suppress a fire in all areas of the compartment where an occupant could be sitting or lying.

N **14.2.6.4.1.1*** Fire suppression shall be demonstrated by lowering the temperature at the head of the occupant to 50°C (122°F) or lower within 20 seconds of activation.

N **14.2.6.4.1.2** Testing shall be conducted at the maximum operating pressure of the chamber and at surface (i.e., normal) pressure.

N **14.2.6.4.2** The system shall have sufficient capacity to operate for at least 1 minute after activation.

N **14.2.6.4.3** The fire suppression media shall be safe for human exposure.

N **14.2.6.5 Alternative Secondary Fire Suppression System.** Where alternative fire suppression systems serve as secondary fire suppression systems in accordance with 14.2.6.1.10, portable, handheld fire extinguishers shall be available in all chamber compartments designed for manned operations.

N **14.2.6.5.1** At least two portable fire extinguishers shall be strategically located in treatment compartments.

N **14.2.6.5.2** At least one portable fire extinguisher shall be located in each personnel transfer compartment.

N **14.2.6.5.3** Portable fire extinguishers shall be designed to function at the maximum operating pressure of the chamber.

N **14.2.6.5.4** The fire extinguishing media shall be safe for human exposure.

14.2.6.6 Automatic Detection System. Automatic fire detection systems shall not be required.

14.2.6.6.1 Surveillance fire detectors responsive to the radiation from flame shall be employed.

14.2.6.6.1.1 The type and arrangement of detectors shall be such as to respond within 1 second of flame origination.

14.2.6.6.2* The number of detectors employed and their location shall be selected to cover the chamber interior.

14.2.6.6.3 The system shall be powered from the critical branch of the essential electrical system or shall have automatic battery backup.

14.2.6.6.4 If used to automatically activate the deluge system, the requirements for manual activation/deactivation in 14.2.6.2.3 and deluge system response time in 14.2.6.2.4 shall still apply.

14.2.6.6.5 The system shall include self-monitoring functions for fault detection and fault alarms and indications.

14.2.6.6.6 Automatic fire detection equipment, when used, shall meet the applicable requirements in 14.2.9.3.

14.2.7 Pneumatic Controls for Class A Chambers. Class A chambers that utilize pneumatically operated controls that are related to fire suppression system operation, breathing gases, or rapid exhaust valves shall be equipped with a means to operate such controls or intended function in the event that the pneumatic supply fails.

14.2.8 Fire Protection in Class B and Class C Chambers. Class B and Class C chambers shall not be required to comply with 14.2.6.

14.2.8.1* At least one sign prohibiting the introduction of flammable liquids, gases, and other articles not permitted by this chapter into the chamber shall be posted in the room housing the chamber(s).

14.2.8.2 A means for communication shall be provided within the room housing the chamber(s) for notifying the fire department.

14.2.8.2.1 If the building housing the hyperbaric facility has a central fire alarm system, the communication shall be a pull-station connected to the system.

14.2.8.2.2 Trailer or vehicle-mounted facilities not contiguous to a health care facility shall conform to one of the following:

(1) They shall comply with 14.2.8.2.
(2) They shall have a means for immediately contacting the local fire department.

14.2.9 Electrical Systems.

14.2.9.1 General.

14.2.9.1.1 The requirements of *NFPA 70* or local electrical codes shall apply to electrical wiring and equipment in hyperbaric facilities within the scope of this chapter, except as such rules are modified in 14.2.9.

14.2.9.1.2 All hyperbaric chamber service equipment, switchboards, panels, or control consoles shall be located outside of, and in the vicinity of, the chamber.

14.2.9.1.3 Console or module spaces containing both oxygen piping and electrical equipment shall be either one of the following:

(1) Mechanically or naturally ventilated
(2) Continuously monitored for excessive oxygen concentrations whenever the electrical equipment is energized

14.2.9.1.4 For the fixed electrical installation, none of the following shall be permitted inside the chamber:

(1) Circuit breakers
(2) Line fuses
(3) Motor controllers
(4) Relays
(5) Transformers
(6) Ballasts
(7) Lighting panels
(8) Power panels

14.2.9.1.5 All electrical equipment connected to, or used in conjunction with, hyperbaric patients shall comply with the requirements of Chapter 10 and with the applicable subparagraphs of 14.2.9.3.

14.2.9.1.6 In the event of activation of the room sprinkler system, electrical equipment shall be protected from sprinkler water but shall not be required to remain functional if manual means to control and decompress the chamber are provided.

14.2.9.2 Electrical Service.

14.2.9.2.1* All hyperbaric facilities equipped with any of the following electrically driven feature shall be provided with some means of backup electric power:

(1)* Chamber room emergency lighting, installed per Section 7.9 of NFPA *101*.
(2)* Chamber emergency lighting, whether internally or externally mounted
(3)* Chamber intercommunications
(4)* Alarm systems, including flame detectors
(5)* Chamber fire suppression system equipment and controls
(6)* Electrical controls used for chamber pressurization and ventilation control

14.2.9.2.1.1 Electrical control and alarm system design shall be such that hazardous conditions (e.g., loss of chamber pressure control, deluge activation, spurious alarms) do not occur during power interruption or during power restoration.

14.2.9.2.1.2 Booster pumps in the chamber fire suppression system shall be on separate branch circuits serving no other loads.

14.2.9.2.2 Article 700 of *NFPA 70* shall apply to hyperbaric systems located in facilities other than health care facilities.

14.2.9.2.3 Hyperbaric electrical service for Category 1 or 2 hyperbaric care shall be supplied from two independent sources of electric power.

14.2.9.2.3.1 For hyperbaric facilities using a prime-mover–driven generator set, they shall be designated as the life safety and critical branches and shall meet the requirements of Chapter 6 for hyperbaric systems based in health care facilities.

14.2.9.2.3.2 Electrical equipment associated with life-support functions of hyperbaric facilities shall be connected to the critical branch of the essential electrical system, which requires that such equipment shall have electrical power restored within 10 seconds of interruption of normal power.

14.2.9.2.4 Electric motor–driven compressors and auxiliary electrical equipment normally located outside the chamber and used for chamber atmospheric control shall be connected to the equipment system *(see Chapter 6)* or the life safety and critical branches *(see Article 700 of NFPA 70)* as applicable.

14.2.9.2.5 Electric motor–driven compressors and auxiliary electrical equipment shall be arranged for delayed-automatic or manual connection to the alternate power source so as to prevent excessive current draw on the system during restarting.

14.2.9.2.6 Where reserve air tanks or a nonelectric compressor(s) is provided to maintain ventilation airflow within the chamber and supply air for chamber pressurization, the compressor(s) and auxiliary equipment shall not be required to have an alternate power source.

14.2.9.3* Wiring and Equipment Inside Class A Chambers. The general rules of 14.2.9.3.1 through 14.2.9.3.16.5 shall be satisfied in the use of electrical devices and equipment. These requirements are intended to protect against the elevated fire risks known to exist in a pressurized air environment and shall not be construed as classifying the chamber interior as a Class I (as defined in Article 500 of *NFPA 70*) hazardous location.

14.2.9.3.1 Equipment or equipment components installed in, or used in, the chamber shall not present an explosion or implosion hazard under the conditions of hyperbaric use.

14.2.9.3.2 All equipment shall be rated, or tested and documented, for intended hyperbaric conditions prior to use.

Δ **14.2.9.3.3** Only electrical equipment necessary for safe operation of the chamber, required patient care, and patient entertainment provided by the facility shall be permitted in the chamber.

N **14.2.9.3.3.1** Fixed patient entertainment equipment shall be permitted where installed by the manufacturer.

N **14.2.9.3.3.2*** Portable patient entertainment equipment shall be permitted where approved by the manufacturer or hyperbaric safety coordinator.

Δ **14.2.9.3.4** Only portable equipment necessary for logistical, operational, and patient-care support shall be permitted in the chamber.

14.2.9.3.5 Wires and Cables. Wires and cables used inside the chamber shall be resistant to the spread of fire by complying with 14.2.9.3.5.1 or shall be contained within equipment described in 14.2.9.3.5.2.

Δ **14.2.9.3.5.1** Wires and cables shall comply with the spread of fire requirements of "UL Flame Exposure, Vertical Tray Flame Test" in UL 1685, *Vertical-Tray Fire-Propagation and Smoke-Release Test for Electrical and Optical-Fiber Cables*, or shall exhibit damage (char length) not to exceed 1.5 m (4 ft 11 in.) when performing the CSA "Vertical Flame Test — Cables in Cable Trays," as described in CSA C22.2 No. 0.3, *Test Methods for Electrical Wires and Cables*.

14.2.9.3.5.2 Wires and cables that form an integral part of electrical equipment approved or listed specifically for use inside hyperbaric chambers, including patient leads, shall not be required to comply with the requirements of 14.2.9.3.5.1.

14.2.9.3.6 Wiring Methods.

14.2.9.3.6.1 Fixed wiring shall be installed in conduit using the following components and be watertight after installation:

(1) Threaded metal joints
(2) Fittings
(3) Boxes
(4) Enclosures

14.2.9.3.6.2 A continuous ground shall be maintained between all conductive surfaces enclosing electrical circuits and the chamber hull using approved grounding means unless prohibited by 14.2.9.3.6.3.

N **14.2.9.3.6.3** Grounding to the chamber hull shall be prohibited where electrical circuits require an independent ground.

Δ **14.2.9.3.6.4** All threaded conduit shall be threaded with an NPT standard conduit cutting die that provides a 0.75 in. taper per 1 ft or the equivalent tapered metric thread in accordance with ISO 724, *ISO general-purpose metric screw threads — Basic dimensions*.

14.2.9.3.6.5 All threaded conduit shall be made wrench-tight to prevent sparking when fault current flows through the conduit system.

14.2.9.3.6.6 Wiring classified as intrinsically safe for any group location and installed in accordance with Article 504 of *NFPA 70* shall be permitted.

14.2.9.3.6.7 Threaded, liquidtight flexible metal conduit installed in accordance with Article 350 of *NFPA 70* shall be permitted when protected from damage by physical barriers such as equipment panels.

14.2.9.3.7 Drainage. Means of draining fixed conduit and fixed equipment enclosures shall be provided at points where fluids can collect.

14.2.9.3.8 Flexible Electrical Cords. Flexible cords used to connect portable utilization equipment to the fixed electrical supply circuit shall meet all the following requirements:

(1) They shall be of a type approved for extra-hard use in accordance with Table 400.4 of *NFPA 70*.
(2) Electrically conductive casings of all portable equipment for use inside the chamber shall be grounded.
(3) They shall meet the requirements of 501.140 of *NFPA 70*.

14.2.9.3.8.1 The normal cord supplied with the portable utilization equipment shall be permitted when the portable device is rated at less than 2 A and the cord is positioned out of traffic and protected from physical abuse.

14.2.9.3.9* Receptacles Installed Inside the Chamber.

14.2.9.3.9.1 Receptacles shall be waterproof.

14.2.9.3.9.2 Receptacles shall be of the type providing for connection to the grounding conductor of the flexible cord.

14.2.9.3.9.3 Receptacles shall be capable of conducting ungrounded power between each isolated external power circuit meeting the requirements of 14.2.9.4.2 and the device inside the chamber.

14.2.9.3.9.4 The design of the receptacle shall be such that sparks cannot be discharged into the chamber environment when the plug is inserted or withdrawn under electrical load.

14.2.9.3.9.5 One of the following shall be satisfied to protect against inadvertent withdrawal of the plug under electrical load:

(1) The receptacle–plug combination shall be of a locking type.
(2) The receptacle shall carry a label warning against unplugging under load, and the power cord shall not present a trip hazard for personnel moving in the chamber.

14.2.9.3.10 Switches. Switches in the fixed wiring installation shall be waterproof.

14.2.9.3.10.1* Switch make and break contacts shall be housed in the electrical enclosure so that no sparks from arcing contacts can reach the chamber environment.

14.2.9.3.11* Temperature. No electrical equipment installed or used in the chamber shall have an operating surface temperature in excess of 85°C (185°F).

14.2.9.3.12 Exposed Live Electrical Parts. No exposed live electrical parts shall be permitted, except as specified in 14.2.9.3.12.1 and 14.2.9.3.12.2.

14.2.9.3.12.1 Exposed live electrical parts that are intrinsically safe shall be permitted.

14.2.9.3.12.2 Exposed live electrical parts that constitute patient monitoring leads, which are part of electromedical equipment, shall be permitted, provided that they meet the requirements of 14.2.9.3.16.

Δ **14.2.9.3.13* Motors.** Motors located in the chamber that are not a component of medical equipment shall meet one of the following requirements:

(1) They shall comply with 501.125(A)(1) of *NFPA 70*.
(2) They shall be totally enclosed in accordance with 501.125(A)(2) or 501.125(A)(3) of *NFPA 70*.
(3) They shall comply with all of the following:

    (a) The motor shall be of the brushless, dc type with no flammable lubricants.
    (b) Any internal control circuitry attached to the motor shall be potted in an oxygen-compatible compound to prevent exposure to the chamber atmosphere.
    (c) No powered switches shall be permitted inside the chamber.

14.2.9.3.14* Lighting.

14.2.9.3.14.1 Lighting installed or used inside the chamber shall be of a type that is not damaged by exposure to 1½ times the maximum allowable working pressure (MAWP).

14.2.9.3.14.2 Permanently installed fixtures shall meet the following requirements:

(1) They shall be rated and approved for Class I (Division 1 or 2) classified areas.
(2) They shall have lens guards installed.
(3) They shall be located away from areas where they would experience physical damage from the normal movement of people and equipment.

14.2.9.3.14.3 Ballasts and other energy storage components that are part of the lighting circuit shall be installed outside the chamber in accordance with 14.2.9.1.4.

14.2.9.3.14.4 Portable fixtures intended for spot illumination shall be shatterproof or protected from physical damage.

14.2.9.3.15 Low-Voltage, Low-Power Equipment. The requirements of 14.2.9.3.15.1 through 14.2.9.3.15.5 shall apply to sensors and signaling, alarm, communications, and remote-control equipment installed or used in the chamber for operation of the chamber.

14.2.9.3.15.1* Equipment shall be isolated from main power by one of the following means:

(1) Design of the power supply circuit
(2) Opto-isolation
(3) Other electronic isolation means

14.2.9.3.15.2 Circuits such as headset cables, sensor leads, and so forth, not enclosed as required in 14.2.9.3.6, shall meet one of the following requirements:

(1) They shall be part of approved intrinsically safe equipment.
(2) They shall be limited by circuit design to not more than 28 V and 0.5 A under normal or circuit-fault conditions.

14.2.9.3.15.3 Chamber speakers shall be of a design in which the electrical circuitry and wiring is completely enclosed.

14.2.9.3.15.4 The electrical rating of chamber speakers shall not exceed 28 V rms and 25 W.

14.2.9.3.15.5 Battery-operated, portable intercom headset units shall meet the requirements of 14.2.9.3.16.4 for battery-operated devices.

14.2.9.3.16 Portable Patient Care–Related Electrical Appliances.

14.2.9.3.16.1 The appliance shall be designed, constructed, inspected, and maintained in accordance with Chapter 10.

14.2.9.3.16.2 The electrical and mechanical integrity of the appliance shall be verified and documented through an ongoing maintenance program as required in Chapter 10.

14.2.9.3.16.3 Appliances that utilize oxygen shall not allow oxygen accumulation in the electrical portions of the equipment under normal and abnormal conditions.

14.2.9.3.16.4 Battery-Operated Devices. Battery-operated devices shall meet the following requirements:

(1) Batteries shall be fully enclosed and secured within the equipment enclosure.
(2) Batteries shall not be damaged by the maximum chamber pressure to which they are exposed.
(3) Batteries shall be of a sealed type that does not off-gas during normal use.
(4) Batteries or battery-operated equipment shall not undergo charging while located in the chamber.
(5) Batteries shall not be changed on in-chamber equipment while the chamber is in use.
(6) The equipment electrical rating shall not exceed 12 V and 48 W.

14.2.9.3.16.5 Cord-Connected Devices. Cord-connected devices shall meet the following requirements:

(1) All portable, cord-connected equipment shall have an on/off power switch.
(2) The equipment electrical rating shall not exceed 120 V and 2 A, unless the electrical portions of the equipment are inert-gas purged.
(3) The plug of cord-connected devices shall not be used to interrupt power to the device.

14.2.9.3.17* Gas Purging. Gas purging of AC and DC equipment used inside the chamber shall be permitted using inert gas or air.

14.2.9.4 Grounding and Ground-Fault Protection.

14.2.9.4.1 All chamber hulls shall be grounded to an electrical ground or grounding system that meets the requirements of Part III of Article 250 of *NFPA 70*.

14.2.9.4.1.1 Grounding conductors shall be secured as required by Part III of Article 250 of *NFPA 70*.

14.2.9.4.1.2 The material, size, and installation of the grounding conductor shall meet the requirements of Part VI of Article 250 of *NFPA 70* for equipment grounding conductors.

Δ **14.2.9.4.1.3** The resistance between the grounded chamber and electrical supply system ground shall not exceed 1 ohm.

14.2.9.4.2 All ac electrical power circuits located within the chamber shall be supplied from an ungrounded electrical system.

14.2.9.4.2.1 The circuits specified in 14.2.9.4.2 shall meet the requirements of 517.160(A) and 517.160(B) of *NFPA 70*.

14.2.9.4.2.2 Branch circuits shall not exceed 125 V or 15 A.

14.2.9.4.3 Wiring located both inside and outside the chamber, that serves line level circuits and equipment located inside the chamber, shall meet the grounding and bonding requirements of 501.30 of *NFPA 70*.

14.2.9.5 Wiring Outside the Chamber. Those electrical components that must remain functional for the safe termination of chamber operations following activation of the room sprinkler system shall be enclosed in waterproof housing.

14.2.9.5.1 All associated conduits shall meet the following requirements:

(1) They shall be waterproof.
(2) They shall meet the requirements of *NFPA 70*.
(3) They shall be equipped with approved drains.

14.2.9.5.2* All other electrical devices outside the chamber shall meet the requirements of *NFPA 70*.

14.2.9.6 Additional Wiring and Equipment Requirements Inside Class B and Class C Chambers. The requirements in 14.2.9.6 shall apply to Class C chambers pressurized with oxygen and to Class B chambers whether they are pressurized with oxygen or with air.

14.2.9.6.1 Electrical equipment inside chambers shall be restricted to communications functions and patient physiological monitoring leads.

14.2.9.6.1.1* Each circuit shall be designed to limit the electrical energy to wire leads into the chamber under normal or fault conditions to not more than 28 V and 4.0 W. This requirement shall not exclude more stringent requirements imposed by other codes governing electromedical apparatus.

14.2.9.6.1.2 Communications wires shall be protected from physical damage and from coming into contact with flammable materials in the chamber by barriers or conduit.

14.2.9.6.1.3 Patient monitoring leads shall be part of approved electromedical apparatus meeting the requirements in 14.2.9.3.16.

14.2.9.6.2 Lighting inside the chamber shall be supplied from external sources.

14.2.9.6.3 No materials shall be permitted in a chamber whose temperature exceeds 50°C (122°F), nor shall any electrical circuit inside a chamber operate at a temperature exceeding 50°C (122°F).

N **14.2.9.6.4** Equipment not specified by 14.2.9.6 shall be permitted in the chamber, with the approval of the hyperbaric medical director and the hyperbaric safety coordinator, if any of the following conditions exists:

(1) The equipment is intrinsically safe.
(2) The equipment is compliant with Class 1 requirements specified in Article 500 of *NFPA 70*.
(3) The equipment meets all of the following conditions:

    (a) The batteries and circuitry are sealed or isolated from the chamber environment.
    (b) The equipment has a maximum voltage of 3 volts and a power requirement of 4 W.
    (c) The equipment contains no volatile lubricants or hydrocarbons.

14.2.10 Communications and Monitoring.

14.2.10.1 General.

14.2.10.1.1 Electrical monitoring equipment used inside the chamber shall comply with the applicable requirements of 14.2.9.

14.2.10.1.2 Detectors, sensors, transducers, and communications equipment located inside the chamber shall meet the requirements of 14.2.9.3.15 for Class A chambers and 14.2.9.6 for Class B chambers.

14.2.10.1.3 Wiring methods in the chamber shall meet the applicable requirements in 14.2.9.3.

14.2.10.1.4 The following equipment shall be installed outside the chamber or shall meet the requirements of 14.2.9.3.15:

(1) Control equipment

(2) Power amplifiers
(3) Output transformers
(4) Monitors associated with communications and monitoring equipment

14.2.10.2* Intercommunications.

14.2.10.2.1* An intercommunications system shall connect all personnel compartments (locks) and the chamber operator's control console.

14.2.10.2.2* Closed-circuit television monitoring of the chamber interior shall be employed for chamber operators who do not have direct visual contact with the chamber interior from their normal operating location.

14.2.10.2.3 Oxygen mask microphones shall be intrinsically safe at the maximum proposed pressure and 95 ± 5 percent oxygen.

14.2.10.3 Combustible Gas Detection.

14.2.10.3.1 The chamber atmosphere shall be continuously monitored for combustible gas concentrations whenever any volatile agents are used in the chamber.

14.2.10.3.1.1 The monitor shall be set to provide audible and visual alarms at 10 percent lower explosive limit (LEL) for the particular gas used.

14.2.10.4 Oxygen Monitoring.

N **14.2.10.4.1** Where required, oxygen monitors shall be equipped with audible and visual alarms.

N **14.2.10.4.2** Where required, oxygen monitors shall have a sample response time of no more than 30 seconds at all treatment levels.

14.2.10.4.3 Oxygen levels shall be continuously monitored in any chamber in which nitrogen is added to the chamber or to reduce the volumetric concentration of oxygen in the atmosphere.

14.2.10.4.4* Oxygen levels shall be continuously monitored in Class A chambers when breathing mixtures containing greater than 21 percent oxygen by volume are being breathed by patients or attendants, when any flammable agents are present in the chamber, or when both conditions exist.

14.2.10.4.4.1 Audible and visual alarms shall indicate volumetric oxygen concentrations greater than 23.5 percent range for Class A chambers.

14.2.10.4.4.2* At least one sample port shall be equipped with a removable extension to allow for spot-checking of any location within the chamber.

14.2.10.5 Carbon Dioxide Monitoring. The chamber atmosphere shall be monitored for carbon dioxide levels during saturation operations whenever ventilation is not used.

14.2.10.6* Chamber Gas Supply Monitoring.

14.2.10.6.1* As a minimum, the air supplied from compressors to all classes of chambers shall meet the requirements for CGA Grade E with the added requirement that condensed hydrocarbons and particulates shall be less than 0.1 mg/m^3.

14.2.10.6.2 When air cylinders are used to provide breathing air in chambers, the breathing air shall be medical air USP.

14.2.10.6.3 When cylinders are used to provide oxygen in chambers, the gas shall be oxygen USP.

14.2.11 Other Equipment and Fixtures.

14.2.11.1 All furniture permanently installed in the hyperbaric chamber shall be grounded.

14.2.11.2* Exhaust from all classes of chambers shall be piped outside of the building.

14.2.11.2.1 Each Class B and Class C chamber shall have an independent exhaust line.

14.2.11.2.2 The point of exhaust shall not create a hazard.

14.2.11.2.3 The point of exhaust shall not allow reentry of gases into the building.

14.2.11.2.4 The point of exhaust shall be protected by the provision of a minimum of 0.3 cm (0.12 in.) mesh screen and situated to prevent the intrusion of rain, snow, or airborne debris.

14.2.11.2.5* The point of exhaust shall be identified as an oxygen exhaust by a sign prohibiting smoking or open flame and the sign shall include a pictograph indicating "no smoking" and "no open flame — flame" in accordance with NFPA 170.

14.3 Administration and Maintenance.

14.3.1 General.

14.3.1.1 Purpose. Section 14.3 contains requirements for administration and maintenance that shall be followed as an adjunct to physical precautions specified in Section 14.2.

14.3.1.2* Recognition of Hazards. The nature and recognition of hyperbaric hazards are outlined in Annex B of this document and shall be reviewed by the hyperbaric safety coordinator.

14.3.1.3 Responsibility.

14.3.1.3.1* Personnel responsible for the hyperbaric facility, and those responsible for licensing, accrediting, or approving institutions or other facilities in which hyperbaric installations are employed, shall establish and enforce programs to fulfill the provisions of this chapter.

14.3.1.3.2* For each hyperbaric facility, a hyperbaric safety coordinator shall be designated as responsible for all hyperbaric equipment and the operational safety requirements of this chapter.

14.3.1.3.2.1 The hyperbaric safety coordinator shall develop operation and maintenance procedures for the hyperbaric facility with facility management personnel and the hyperbaric physician(s).

14.3.1.3.2.2 The hyperbaric safety coordinator shall make recommendations for departmental safety policies and procedures.

14.3.1.3.2.3 The hyperbaric safety coordinator shall have the authority to restrict or remove any potentially hazardous supply or equipment items from the chamber.

14.3.1.3.3* By virtue of its responsibility for the professional conduct of members of the medical staff of the health care facility, the organized medical staff shall adopt and enforce

regulations with respect to the use of hyperbaric facilities located in health care facilities.

14.3.1.3.3.1 The hyperbaric safety coordinator shall participate in the enforcement of the regulations required by 14.3.1.3.3.

14.3.1.3.4* The hyperbaric safety coordinator shall ensure that electrical, monitoring, life-support, fire protection, and ventilating arrangements in the hyperbaric chamber are inspected and tested as part of the routine maintenance program of the facility.

14.3.1.4 Rules and Regulations.

14.3.1.4.1* General. The administrative, technical, and professional staffs shall jointly develop policies for management of the hyperbaric facility.

N **14.3.1.4.1.1** The hyperbaric safety coordinator shall participate in the development of the policies required by 14.3.1.4.1.

14.3.1.4.1.2 Upon adoption, the management policies shall be available in the facility.

14.3.1.4.2 The physician in charge of hyperbaric medicine and the hyperbaric safety coordinator shall jointly develop the minimum staff qualifications, experience, and complement based on the following:

(1) Number and type of hyperbaric chambers in use
(2) Maximum treatment capacity
(3) Type of hyperbaric therapy normally provided

14.3.1.4.3 All personnel, including those involved in maintenance and repair of the hyperbaric facility, shall be trained on the purpose, application, operation, and limitations of emergency equipment.

14.3.1.4.4 When an inspection, test, or maintenance procedure of the fire suppression system results in the system being placed out of service, a protocol shall be followed that notifies appropriate personnel and agencies of the planned or emergency impairment.

14.3.1.4.5 A sign indicating the fire suppression system is out of service shall be conspicuously placed on the operating console until the fire suppression system is restored to service.

14.3.1.4.6* During chamber operations with an occupant(s) in a chamber, the operator shall be physically present and shall maintain visual or audible contact with the control panel or the chamber occupant(s).

14.3.1.5 Emergency Procedures.

14.3.1.5.1 Emergency procedures specific to the hyperbaric facility shall be established.

14.3.1.5.2* All personnel shall be trained in emergency procedures.

14.3.1.5.3 Personnel shall be trained to control the chamber and decompress occupants when all powered equipment has been rendered inoperative.

14.3.1.5.4* Emergency procedures and fire training drills shall be conducted at least annually and documented by the hyperbaric safety coordinator.

14.3.1.5.4.1 The time required to evacuate all persons from a hyperbaric area with a full complement of chamber occupants all at treatment pressure shall be measured annually.

14.3.1.5.4.2 The occupants for the timed evacuation drill shall be permitted to be simulated.

14.3.1.6 General.

14.3.1.6.1 Potential Ignition Sources.

14.3.1.6.1.1* The following shall be prohibited from inside the chamber and the immediate vicinity outside the chamber:

(1) Smoking
(2) Open flames
(3) Hot objects

14.3.1.6.1.2 The following shall be prohibited from inside the chamber:

(1) Personal warming devices (e.g., therapeutic chemical heating pads, hand warmers, pocket warmers)
(2) Personal electrically powered devices (e.g., laptops, electronic tablets, cell phones, pagers)
(3) Sparking toys
(4) Personal entertainment devices

14.3.1.6.1.3* Prior to each hyperbaric treatment, a pretreatment safety check to identify and remove prohibited items shall be performed and documented by a qualified person.

14.3.1.6.2 Flammable Gases and Liquids.

14.3.1.6.2.1 Flammable agents, including devices such as laboratory burners employing bottled or natural gas and cigarette lighters, shall be prohibited inside the chamber and from the proximity of the compressor intake.

14.3.1.6.2.2 For Class A chambers, flammable agents used for patient care, such as alcohol swabs, parenteral alcohol-based pharmaceuticals, and topical creams, shall be permitted in the chamber if the following conditions are met:

(1) Such use is approved by the hyperbaric safety coordinator or other authority having jurisdiction.
(2)* The quantities of such agents are limited so that they are incapable of releasing sufficient flammable vapor into the chamber atmosphere to exceed the LEL for the material.
(3) A safety factor is included to account for the localized concentrations, stratification, and the absence of ventilation.
(4) The oxygen monitoring requirement of 14.2.10.4.4 is observed.

14.3.1.6.2.3 Flammable liquids, gases, or vapors shall not be permitted inside any Class B chamber.

14.3.1.6.3* Personnel.

14.3.1.6.3.1 Antistatic procedures, as directed by the hyperbaric safety coordinator, shall be employed whenever atmospheres containing more than 23.5 percent oxygen by volume are used.

14.3.1.6.3.2 In Class A and Class B chambers with atmospheres containing more than 23.5 percent oxygen by volume, electrical grounding of the patient shall be ensured by the provision of a high-impedance conductive pathway in contact with the patient's skin.

14.3.1.6.3.3 Shoes having ferrous nails that make contact with the floor shall not be permitted to be worn in Class A chambers.

14.3.1.6.4* Textiles.

14.3.1.6.4.1 Except where permitted in 14.3.1.6.4.3, silk, wool, or synthetic textile materials, or any combination thereof, shall be prohibited in Class A or Class B chambers.

14.3.1.6.4.2* Garments permitted inside of chambers shall be as follows:

(1) Garments fabricated of 100 percent cotton or a blend of cotton and polyester fabric shall be permitted in Class A chambers.
(2) Garments fabricated of 100 percent cotton, or a blend of cotton and polyester fabric containing no more than 50 percent polyester, shall be permitted in Class B chambers.

Δ **14.3.1.6.4.3*** The hyperbaric physician in charge, with the concurrence of the hyperbaric safety coordinator, shall be permitted to use materials that are prohibited or not specifically permitted by this chapter.

14.3.1.6.4.4* Approval by the hyperbaric physician in charge and the hyperbaric safety coordinator to use prohibited items shall be stated in writing for all prohibited items employed.

14.3.1.6.4.5 Upholstered Furniture.

(A) Upholstered furniture (fixed or portable) shall be resistant to smoldering (or cigarette) ignition in accordance with one of the following:

(1) The components of the upholstered furniture shall meet the requirements for Class 1 when tested in accordance with NFPA 260.
(2) Mocked-up composites of the upholstered furniture shall have a char length not exceeding 38 mm (1½ in.) when tested in accordance with NFPA 261.

(B) Upholstered furniture shall have limited rates of heat release when tested in accordance with ASTM E1537, *Standard Test Method for Fire Testing of Upholstered Furniture*, or with California Technical Bulletin 133, *Flammability Test Procedure for Seating Furniture for Use in Public Occupancies*, as follows:

(1) The peak rate of heat release for the single upholstered furniture item shall not exceed 80 kW.
(2) The total heat released by the single upholstered furniture item during the first 10 minutes of the test shall not exceed 25 MJ.

14.3.1.6.4.6 Mattresses.

(A) Mattress components shall have a char length not exceeding 2 in. (51 mm) when tested in accordance with 16 CFR 1632, "Standard for the Flammability of Mattresses and Mattress Pads (FF 4-72)," or NFPA 260.

(B) Mattresses shall have limited rates of heat release when tested in accordance with ASTM E1590, *Standard Test Method for Fire Testing of Mattresses*, or California Technical Bulletin 129, *Flammability Test Procedure for Mattresses for Use in Public Buildings*, as follows:

(1) The peak rate of heat release for the mattress shall not exceed 100 kW.

(2) The total heat released by the mattress during the first 10 minutes of the test shall not exceed 25 MJ.

14.3.1.6.4.7 Fill materials contained within upholstered furniture and mattresses shall comply with the open flame test in Section A-1 of the 2000 edition of California Technical Bulletin 117, *Requirements, Test Procedure and Apparatus for Testing the Flame Retardance of Resilient Filling Materials Used in Upholstered Furniture.*

14.3.1.6.4.8 For materials with fire-retardant coatings, the material shall be maintained in accordance with the manufacturer's instructions to retain the fire-retardant properties.

14.3.1.6.4.9 Exposed foamed plastic materials shall be prohibited.

14.3.1.6.5 The use of flammable hair sprays, hair oils, and skin oils shall be prohibited for all chamber occupants/patients as well as personnel.

14.3.1.6.5.1 Whenever possible, patients shall be stripped of all clothing, particularly if it is contaminated by dirt, grease, or solvents, and then reclothed. *(See A.14.3.1.6.4.)*

14.3.1.6.5.2 All cosmetics, lotions, and oils shall be removed from the patient's body and hair.

14.3.1.6.6 All other fabrics used in the chamber, such as sheets, pillow cases, and blankets, shall conform to 14.3.1.6.4.1 and 14.3.1.6.4.2.

14.3.1.6.7 Drapes used within the chamber shall meet the flame propagation performance criteria contained in Test 1 or Test 2, as appropriate, of NFPA 701.

14.3.1.6.8 Clothing worn by patients in Class A or Class B chambers and personnel in Class A chambers shall, prior to each treatment, conform to the following:

(1) They shall be issued by the hyperbaric facility or specifically approved by the hyperbaric safety coordinator for hyperbaric use.
(2) They shall be uncontaminated.
(3) They shall be devoid of prohibited articles prior to chamber pressurization.

14.3.1.6.9* Paper brought into the chamber shall be stored in a closed metal container.

14.3.2 Equipment.

14.3.2.1 All equipment used in the hyperbaric chamber shall comply with Section 14.2, including the following:

(1) All electrical and mechanical equipment necessary for the operation and maintenance of the hyperbaric facility
(2) Any medical devices and instruments used in the facility

14.3.2.1.1 Use of unapproved equipment shall be prohibited.

14.3.2.1.2 The following devices shall not be operated in the hyperbaric chamber unless approved for such use by the hyperbaric safety coordinator and medical director of hyperbaric medicine:

(1) Portable x-ray devices
(2) Electrocautery equipment
(3) High-energy devices

14.3.2.1.3 Photographic equipment employing the following shall not remain in the chamber when the chamber is pressurized:

(1) Photoflash
(2) Flood lamps

14.3.2.1.4 The use of Class 1 or Class 2 lasers as defined by ANSI Z136.3, *American National Standard for Safe Use of Lasers in Health Care,* shall be permitted.

14.3.2.1.5 Equipment known to be, or suspected of being, defective shall not be introduced into any hyperbaric chamber or used in conjunction with the operation of such chamber until repaired, tested, and accepted by qualified personnel and approved by the hyperbaric safety coordinator. *(See 14.3.1.3.2.)*

14.3.2.2* The following shall be all-metal to the extent possible:

(1) Oxygen containers
(2) Valves
(3) Fittings
(4) Interconnecting equipment

14.3.2.3 The following shall be compatible with oxygen under service conditions:

(1) Valve seats
(2) Gaskets
(3) Hose
(4) Lubricants

14.3.2.4 Equipment used inside the chamber requiring lubrication shall be lubricated with oxygen-compatible material.

14.3.2.4.1 Factory-sealed antifriction bearings shall be permitted to be used with standard hydrocarbon lubricants in Class A chambers that do not employ atmospheres of increased oxygen concentration.

14.3.2.5* Equipment made of the following shall be prohibited from the chamber interior:

(1) Cerium
(2) Magnesium
(3) Magnesium alloys

14.3.2.6* In the event that radiation equipment is introduced into a hyperbaric chamber, hydrocarbon detectors shall be installed.

14.3.2.6.1 In the event that flammable gases are detected in excess of 1000 ppm, radiation equipment shall not be operated until the chamber atmosphere is cleared.

14.3.3 Handling of Gases.

14.3.3.1 The institution's administrative personnel shall develop policies for safe handling of gases in the hyperbaric facility. *(See 14.3.1.6.2.)*

14.3.3.2 Oxygen and other gases shall not be introduced into the chamber in the liquid state.

14.3.3.3 Flammable gases shall not be used or stored in the chamber or in the hyperbaric facility.

14.3.3.4* Pressurized containers of gas shall be permitted to be introduced into the hyperbaric chamber, provided that the container and its contents are approved for such use by the hyperbaric safety coordinator.

14.3.4 Inspection, Testing, and Maintenance.

14.3.4.1 General.

14.3.4.1.1 The hyperbaric safety coordinator shall ensure that all valves, regulators, meters, and similar equipment used in the hyperbaric chamber are compensated for use under hyperbaric conditions and tested as part of the routine maintenance program of the facility.

14.3.4.1.1.1 Pressure relief valves shall be tested and calibrated as part of the routine maintenance program of the facility.

N **14.3.4.1.1.2** Where employed, a rupture disc shall be inspected periodically and replaced at intervals specified by the chamber manufacturer.

14.3.4.1.2 The hyperbaric safety coordinator shall ensure that all gas outlets are labeled or stenciled in accordance with CGA C-7, *Guide to Classification and Labeling of Compressed Gases.*

14.3.4.1.3 The requirements set forth in Section 5.1 and NFPA 55 concerning the storage, location, and special precautions required for medical gases shall be followed.

14.3.4.1.4 Storage areas for hazardous materials shall not be located in the room housing the hyperbaric chamber. *(See 14.2.1.)*

14.3.4.1.4.1 Flammable gases, except as provided in 14.3.1.6.2.2(1), shall not be used or stored in the hyperbaric room.

14.3.4.1.5 All replacement parts and components shall conform to original design specification.

14.3.4.1.6* Air from compressors shall be sampled at least every 6 months and after major repair or modification of the compressor(s).

14.3.4.2 Maintenance Logs.

14.3.4.2.1 Installation, repairs, and modifications of equipment related to a chamber shall be evaluated by engineering personnel, tested under pressure, and approved by the hyperbaric safety coordinator.

14.3.4.2.1.1 Logs of all tests shall be maintained.

14.3.4.2.2 Operating equipment logs shall be maintained by engineering personnel.

14.3.4.2.2.1 Operating equipment logs shall be signed before chamber operation by the person in charge. *(See A.14.3.1.3.2.)*

14.3.4.2.3 Operating equipment logs shall not be taken inside the chamber.

14.3.4.3 Fire Protection Equipment for Class A Hyperbaric Chambers.

14.3.4.3.1 Electrical switches, valves, and electrical monitoring equipment associated with fire protection shall be visually inspected before each chamber pressurization.

14.3.4.3.1.1 Where provided, water level indicators shall be visually inspected before each chamber pressurization.

14.3.4.3.1.2 Where provided, air pressure gauges shall be visually inspected before each chamber pressurization.

14.3.4.3.2 Fire detection equipment, if installed, shall be tested each week.

14.3.4.3.2.1 Testing shall include activation of trouble circuits and signals.

14.3.4.3.3 Full testing, including discharge of extinguishing media, shall be conducted annually.

14.3.4.3.4 Inspection, testing, and maintenance of the water storage tanks for Class A chambers shall be in accordance with applicable sections of Chapter 9 of NFPA 25.

14.3.4.3.5* Fire extinguishing systems shall be functionally tested at least semiannually as follows:

(1) For deluge systems, in accordance with the requirements of 14.2.6.2.4 and 14.2.6.2.6
(2) For handline systems, in accordance with the requirements of 14.2.6.3.7.1

14.3.4.3.5.1 Following the test, all valves shall be placed in their baseline position.

14.3.4.3.5.2 If a bypass system is used, it shall not remain in the test mode after completion of the test.

14.3.4.3.5.3 During initial construction, or whenever changes are made to the installed deluge system that will affect the spray pattern, testing of spray coverage to demonstrate conformance to the requirements of 14.2.6.2.5 shall be performed at surface pressure and at maximum operating pressure.

△ **14.3.4.3.5.4** A detailed record of the test results shall be maintained and a copy sent to the hyperbaric safety coordinator.

14.3.4.3.5.5 Inspection, testing, and maintenance of hyperbaric fire suppression systems shall be performed by a qualified person.

14.3.4.4 Electrical Safeguards.

14.3.4.4.1 All electrical circuits shall be tested in accordance with the routine maintenance program of the facility.

14.3.4.4.1.1 Electrical circuit tests shall include the following:

(1) Ground-fault check to verify that no conductors are grounded to the chamber
(2) Test of normal functioning *(see 14.2.9.2.3.2)*

14.3.4.4.1.2 In the event of fire, all nonessential electrical equipment within the chamber shall be de-energized before extinguishing the fire.

(A) Smoldering, burning electrical equipment shall be de-energized before extinguishing a localized fire involving only the equipment. *(See 14.2.6.)*

14.3.4.5 Furniture and Grounding.

14.3.4.5.1 Conductive devices on furniture and equipment shall be inspected to ensure that they are free of wax, lint, or other extraneous material that could insulate them and defeat the conductive properties.

14.3.4.5.2* Casters or furniture leg tips shall not be capable of impact sparking.

14.3.4.5.3 Casters shall not be lubricated with oils or other flammable materials.

14.3.4.5.4 Lubricants shall be oxygen compatible.

Shaded text = Revisions. △ = Text deletions and figure/table revisions. • = Section deletions. *N* = New material.

2024 Edition

14.3.4.5.5 Wheelchairs and gurneys with bearings lubricated and sealed by the manufacturer shall be permitted in Class A chambers where conditions prescribed in 14.2.10.4 are met.

14.3.4.6* Electrostatic Safeguards.

14.3.4.6.1 Conductive accessories shall meet conductivity and antistatic requirements.

14.3.4.6.2* Patient ground shall be verified in Class B chambers prior to each chamber operation.

14.3.4.6.3* Patient ground shall be verified in Class A chambers prior to chamber operation whenever atmospheres containing more than 23.5 percent oxygen by volume are used.

14.3.4.6.4 Chamber ground shall be verified to be in accordance with 14.2.9.4.1.3 for Class A and Class B chambers as part of the preventive maintenance program of the facility.

14.3.4.6.5* Materials containing rubber shall be inspected as part of the routine maintenance program of the facility, especially at points of kinking.

14.3.4.7* Housekeeping. A housekeeping program shall be implemented, whether or not the facility is in regular use.

14.3.4.7.1 The persons assigned to the task of housekeeping shall be trained in the following:

(1) Potential damage to the equipment from cleaning procedures
(2) Potential personal injury
(3) Specific cleaning procedures
(4) Equipment not to be cleaned

Chapter 15   Dental Gas and Vacuum Systems

15.1 Applicability. This chapter shall apply to dental health care facilities that qualify to install dental gas and vacuum piping systems.

N **15.1.1** Category 1 dental piped gas and piped vacuum system requirements shall be applied in facilities where general anesthesia and deep sedation is performed, as defined in 3.3.70.1 and 3.3.70.2.

15.1.2 Category 2 dental piped gas and piped vacuum system requirements shall be applied in facilities where only moderate and minimal sedation is performed, as defined in 3.3.70.3 and 3.3.70.4.

15.1.3 Category 3 dental piped gas and piped vacuum system requirements shall be applied in facilities where minimal or no sedation is performed, as defined in 3.3.70.4.

15.1.4 A single facility shall be permitted to include dental gas and vacuum systems for more than one category of dental piped gas and vacuum systems.

15.1.5 An existing system that is not in strict compliance with the requirements of this code shall be permitted to continue in use unless the authority having jurisdiction has determined that such use constitutes a distinct hazard to life.

N **15.1.6** This chapter shall apply to new health care facilities as specified by Section 1.3 unless otherwise specified by 15.1.7, 15.1.8, or 15.1.9.

15.1.7 The requirements for Category 1 dental gas and vacuum systems for the operation, management, and mainte-

nance of gas and vacuum piping systems shall apply to both new and existing facilities within the scope of this chapter and in accordance with 5.1.1.5.

Δ **15.1.8** The following sections of this chapter shall apply to the operation, management, and maintenance of Category 2 dental gas and vacuum systems in both new and existing facilities:

(1) 15.1.5
(2) Section 15.2
(3) 15.4.2.4.3
(4) 15.4.2.4.6
(5) 15.4.2.4.12
(6) 15.4.2.5.14
(7) 15.4.2.6.4
(8) 15.4.2.9

15.1.9 The following sections of this chapter shall apply to the operation, management, and maintenance of Category 3 dental gas and vacuum systems in both new and existing facilities:

(1) 15.1.5
(2) Section 15.2
(3) 15.5.8

15.1.10 Where the term *responsible facility authority* is used, that entity shall follow the requirements of 5.1.14.1.

15.2 Nature of Hazards of Gas and Vacuum Systems. Potential fire and explosion hazards associated with positive-pressure dental gas systems and vacuum systems shall be considered in the design, installation, testing, operation, and maintenance of these systems.

15.3 Category 1 Dental Gas and Vacuum Systems.

15.3.1 General. Facilities that perform deep sedation and general anesthesia associated with dental treatment shall meet the requirements for Category 1 dental gas and vacuum systems.

15.3.2 Category 1 Medical Gas Systems (Dental).

15.3.2.1 Medical Gas and Vacuum Sources.

15.3.2.1.1 Central Supply System Identification and Labeling. Category 1 systems shall comply with 5.1.3.1.

15.3.2.1.2 Central Supply Operations. Category 1 systems shall comply with 5.1.3.2.

15.3.2.1.3 Central Supply System Locations. Category 1 systems shall comply with 5.1.3.3.

15.3.2.1.4 Central Supply Systems. Category 1 systems shall comply with 5.1.3.5.

15.3.2.1.5 Medical Air Supply Systems. Category 1 systems shall comply with 5.1.3.6, except as follows:

(1) Medical air compressors, dryers, aftercoolers, filters, and regulators shall be permitted to be simplex.
(2) The facility staff shall develop an emergency plan to deal with the loss of medical air.

15.3.2.1.6 Oxygen Supply Systems Using Concentrators. Oxygen supply systems using concentrators shall be permitted to consist of two sources, one of which being a cylinder header with sufficient cylinder connections for an average day's supply.

15.3.2.1.7 Dental–Surgical Vacuum Systems. Category 1 systems shall comply with 5.1.3.7, except as follows:

(1) Dental–surgical vacuum systems shall be permitted to be simplex.
(2) The facility staff shall develop an emergency plan to deal with the loss of dental–surgical vacuum.

15.3.2.1.8 WAGD Systems. Category 1 systems shall comply with 5.1.3.8, except as follows:

(1) Medical WAGD pumps shall be permitted to be simplex.
(2) The facility staff shall develop an emergency plan to deal with the loss of WAGD.

15.3.2.2 Valves. Category 1 systems shall comply with 5.1.4.

15.3.2.3 Station Outlets and Inlets. Category 1 systems shall comply with 5.1.5.

15.3.2.4 Manufactured Assemblies. Category 1 systems shall comply with 5.1.6.

15.3.2.5 Surface-Mounted Medical Gas Rails. Category 1 systems shall comply with 5.1.7.

15.3.2.6 Pressure and Vacuum Indicators. Category 1 systems shall comply with 5.1.8.

15.3.2.7 Warning Systems. Warning systems associated with Category 1 systems shall provide the master, area, and local alarm functions of a Category 1 system as required in 5.1.9, except as follows:

(1) Warning systems shall be permitted to be a single alarm panel.
(2) The alarm panel shall be located in an area of continuous surveillance while the facility is in operation.
(3) Pressure and vacuum switches/sensors shall be mounted at the source equipment with a pressure indicator at the master alarm panel.

15.3.2.8 Medical Gas Distribution. Category 1 systems shall comply with 5.1.10.

15.3.2.9 Labeling and Identification. Category 1 systems shall comply with 5.1.11.

15.3.2.10 Performance Criteria and Testing (Medical Gas, Medical–Surgical Vacuum, and WAGD). Category 1 systems shall comply with 5.1.12.

15.3.2.11 Support Gases. Category 1 systems shall comply with 5.1.13, except as follows:

(1) Nitrogen source equipment shall be permitted to be installed in enclosures for Category 3 medical gases or in a mechanical room.
(2) Nitrogen source equipment shall include the following:
    (a) One or more cylinders of nitrogen NF, sufficient for at least one average day's supply
    (b) A manifold, if primary and secondary cylinders are provided
    (c) A line pressure regulating valve
    (d) A check valve downstream from the pressure regulating valve
    (e) A pressure relief valve set at 50 percent above the normal line pressure and located downstream from the check valve
    (f) A pressure relief valve discharge piped to the outdoors at a point that will not create a probable

hazard and that is turned down to prevent the entry of rain or snow

15.3.2.12 Medical Gas and Vacuum Operation and Management. Category 1 systems shall comply with 5.1.14.

15.3.3 Category 1 Dental Air and Vacuum Piping Systems.

15.3.3.1 General.

15.3.3.1.1 Dental vacuum systems shall include dental vacuum and nitrous oxide scavenging.

15.3.3.2 Equipment Locations for Dental Air and Vacuum Systems.

15.3.3.2.1 General. Any of the following systems shall be permitted to be located together in the same room:

(1) Medical air compressor supply sources
(2) Dental air compressor sources and reserve headers
(3) Dental–surgical vacuum sources
(4) Dental vacuum sources
(5) WAGD sources
(6) Any other compressor, vacuum pump, or electrically powered machinery

15.3.3.2.2 Cylinders and Containers. Cylinders and containers for gases shall be handled in accordance with Chapter 11.

15.3.3.2.3 Ventilation. The following source locations for motor-driven equipment shall be adequately ventilated to prevent accumulation of heat:

(1) Medical air sources
(2) Instrument air sources
(3) Dental compressed air sources
(4) Dental–surgical vacuum sources
(5) Dental vacuum sources
(6) WAGD sources

15.3.3.3 Dental Gas and Vacuum Source Equipment.

Δ **15.3.3.3.1** The capacity of source equipment shall be based on the design requirements for the facility, including the number of gas outlets, vacuum inlets, and other connections, and their individual capacities.

15.3.3.3.2 The system design requirements shall be included in the data used for testing and verifying the operation of the gas and vacuum piping systems.

15.3.3.4* Dental Air.

15.3.3.4.1 General.

15.3.3.4.1.1 Dental air use shall comply with the following requirements:

(1) Dental air shall be used for driving dental tools.
(2) Dental air shall be permitted to be used to supply air-driven equipment.
(3) Dental compressed air shall not be permitted to be used for respiration.

Δ **15.3.3.4.1.2** Dental air outlets shall not be interchangeable with any other gas outlets.

15.3.3.4.2 Dental Air Compressor Units.

15.3.3.4.2.1 Dental air compressor units shall include dental air compressors, vibration isolation, air receivers, coalescent air filters, adsorption dryers, exhaust silencer/filters, moisture indicators, and service access manifolds, electrical disconnects, motor wiring, and controls.

15.3.3.4.2.2 Air compressors shall be scroll dental, reciprocating dental, or the oil-free dental types.

N **15.3.3.4.2.3** Dental air sources for compressors located inside the building shall meet the following requirements:

(1) Be located in a space where no chemical-based materials are stored or used

(2) Be located in a space that is not used for patient treatment or dental procedures

(3) Be taken from a room or space in which there is no open or semi-open discharge from a dental vacuum or dental scavenging system

(4) Drawn from a remote location, such as the building return air system, when the compressor is located in a room with an open or semi-open discharge from a dental vacuum or dental scavenging system

15.3.3.5* Dental Vacuum.

15.3.3.5.1 General.

15.3.3.5.1.1 Dental vacuum shall be used for oral evacuation and nitrous oxide scavenging.

15.3.3.5.1.2 Dental vacuum inlets shall not be interchangeable with any other vacuum inlets, including dental–surgical vacuum.

15.3.3.5.2 Dental Vacuum Units.

15.3.3.5.2.1 Dental vacuum units shall include dental vacuum pumps, vibration isolation, separation tanks, vacuum inlet, vacuum exhaust, condensate drain, motor wiring, and controls.

15.3.3.5.2.2 Dental vacuum pumps shall be dental dry vacuum or dental liquid (wet) ring pumps. Pumps shall be oil-free or oil-lubricated, and suitable for nitrous oxide scavenging.

N **15.3.3.5.2.3** Dental vacuum exhaust shall comply with one of the following requirements:

(1) Be exhausted to the outdoors in accordance with the manufacturer's recommendations

(2) Be filtered and diffused locally with a ULPA filter element capable of retaining 99.99 percent of particulates

(3) Discharge outdoors if used for nitrous oxide scavenging

N **15.3.3.5.2.4** Dental vacuum system piping shall comply with all of the following:

(1) Horizontal piping in dental vacuum systems shall be sloped a minimum of 7 mm per 3.05 m (¼ in. per 10 ft) toward the vacuum source equipment.

(2) Horizontal piping shall include no sags or low points that would permit fluid or debris to accumulate in the piping.

(3) Voids in the vacuum piping shall be avoided to prevent buildup and obstructions.

(4) Accessible cleanouts shall be permitted to be installed in the vertical downflow pipe to clear obstructions, where necessary.

(5) Dental vacuum cleanouts shall not to be installed on horizontal piping.

(6) Dental vacuum inlets shall be capable of 283 L/min (10 SCFM) or greater flow capacity.

15.3.3.6 Nitrous Oxide Scavenging.

15.3.3.6.1 General.

15.3.3.6.1.1 The use of scavenging shall be limited to portions of dental facilities where moderate or minimal sedation is administered. WAGD shall be provided where the dental treatment involves general anesthesia or deep sedation.

15.3.3.6.1.2 Active nitrous oxide scavenging shall include the use of a nasal mask on the patient. The nasal mask shall be connected to a scavenging inlet in the dental vacuum system through a flow-limiting adapter.

15.3.3.6.1.3 Nitrous oxide scavenging inlets shall not be interchangeable with any other vacuum inlets, including medical–surgical vacuum, dental vacuum, and WAGD.

15.3.3.6.2 Connection to Dental Vacuum. Scavenging connections to the dental vacuum system shall be a direct high-volume evacuation (HVE) connection to a high-volume vacuum port with a capacity of 45 L/min (1.6 cfm).

15.3.3.7 Piping for Dental Air and Vacuum Systems.

15.3.3.7.1 General.

15.3.3.7.1.1 Piping for dental compressed air systems shall comply with 15.3.3.7.2.

15.3.3.7.1.2 Piping for dental vacuum systems and scavenging systems shall comply with 15.3.3.7.3.

15.3.3.7.2 Piping for Dental Air Systems.

15.3.3.7.2.1 General. Pipe, fittings, and joints in piping for dental compressed air systems shall be in accordance with 15.3.3.7.2.2 through 15.3.3.7.2.5.

15.3.3.7.2.2 Pipe. Piping materials for dental air systems shall comply with one of the following:

(1) ASTM B88, *Standard Specification for Seamless Copper Water Tube,* Type L or K

(2) ASTM B819, *Standard Specification for Seamless Copper Tube for Medical Gas Systems,* Type L or K

(3) ASTM B280, *Standard Specification for Seamless Copper Tube for Air Conditioning and Refrigeration Field Service,* ACR tube (O.D. size)

(4) ASTM B103/B103M, *Standard Specification for Phosphor Bronze Plate, Sheet, Strip, and Rolled Bar,* listed corrugated medical tubing (CMT) fabricated from copper alloy No. 51000 strip, as follows:

    (a) Having a design margin of 3.5

    (b) Externally coated with a nonmetallic sheath marked with the manufacturer's marking

    (c) Listing includes testing to demonstrate that CMT systems can be consistently gas-purged with results equivalent to comparable medical gas copper tubing

15.3.3.7.2.3 Copper Tube. Copper tube shall be hard temper or annealed (soft temper).

15.3.3.7.2.4 Fittings. Fittings for dental air piping systems shall be permitted to be any of the following acceptable joining methods:

(1) Brazed or soldered fittings complying with ASME B16.22, *Wrought Copper and Copper Alloy Solder-Joint Pressure Fittings*

(2) Brazed fittings complying with ANSI/ASME B16.50, *Wrought Copper and Copper Alloy Braze-Joint Pressure Fittings*

(3) Brazed fittings complying with ASME B16.22, with socket depths equal to or greater than braze-joint pressure fittings complying with ANSI/ASME B16.50

(4) Flared fittings complying with ASME B16.26, *Cast Copper Alloy Fittings for Flared Copper Tubes*

(5) Compression fittings (¾ in. maximum size)

(6) Axially swaged fittings complying with 5.1.10.7

15.3.3.7.2.5 Joints. Joints for piping under 15.3.3.7.2 shall comply with the following:

(1) Joints shall be brazed, soldered, threaded, flared, or the compression type.

(2) Where joints are brazed, they shall comply with the requirements of 15.4.6.

(3) Soldered joints shall be made in accordance with ASTM B828, *Standard Practice for Making Capillary Joints by Soldering of Copper and Copper Alloy Tube and Fittings*, using a "lead-free" solder filler metal containing not more than 0.2 percent lead by volume that complies with ASTM B32, *Standard Specification for Solder Metal*.

15.3.3.7.3 Piping for Dental Vacuum Systems and Scavenging Systems.

15.3.3.7.3.1 General. Piping for dental vacuum systems and scavenging systems shall be copper, PVC plastic, or CPVC plastic.

15.3.3.7.3.2 Copper Piping. Copper piping under 15.3.3.7.3 shall be in accordance with 15.3.3.7.3.2(A) through 15.3.3.7.3.2(C).

(A) Copper Tube. Copper tubing shall be hard temper or annealed (soft temper) and comply with the following:

(1) ASTM B88, *Standard Specification for Seamless Copper Water Tube*, Type L or K

(2) ASTM B819, *Standard Specification for Seamless Copper Tube for Medical Gas Systems*, Type L or K

(3) ASTM B280, *Standard Specification for Seamless Copper Tube for Air Conditioning and Refrigeration Field Service*, ACR tube (O.D. size)

(B) Copper Fittings. Copper fittings shall comply with the following:

(1) Brazed or soldered fittings conforming to ASME B16.22, *Wrought Copper and Copper Alloy Solder-Joint Pressure Fittings*

(2) Brazed fittings conforming to ANSI/ASME B16.50, *Wrought Copper and Copper Alloy Braze-Joint Pressure Fittings*

(3) Brazed fittings conforming to ASME B16.22 with socket depths equal to or greater than braze-joint pressure fittings conforming to ANSI/ASME B16.50

(4) Flared fittings conforming to ASME B16.26, *Cast Copper Alloy Fittings for Flared Copper Tubes*

(5) Compression fittings (¾ in. maximum size)

(C) Joints for Copper Piping. Joints in copper tubing shall comply with the following:

(1) Joints shall be brazed, soldered, threaded, flared, or the compression type.

(2) Where joints are brazed, they shall comply with the requirements of 15.4.6.

(3) Soldered joints shall be made in accordance with ASTM B828, *Standard Practice for Making Capillary Joints by Soldering of Copper and Copper Alloy Tube and Fittings*, using a "lead-free" solder filler metal containing not more than 0.2 percent lead by volume that complies with ASTM B32, *Standard Specification for Solder Metal*.

15.3.3.7.3.3 PVC Plastic Piping. PVC plastic piping under 15.3.3.7.3 shall comply with the following:

(1) PVC plastic pipe shall be Schedule 40 or Schedule 80, conforming to ASTM D1785, *Standard Specification for Poly(Vinyl Chloride) (PVC) Plastic Pipe, Schedules 40, 80, and 120.*

(2) PVC plastic fittings shall be Schedule 40 or Schedule 80 to match the pipe, conforming to ASTM D2466, *Standard Specification for Poly(Vinyl Chloride) (PVC) Plastic Pipe Fittings, Schedule 40*, or ASTM D2467, *Standard Specification for Poly(Vinyl Chloride) (PVC) Plastic Pipe Fittings, Schedule 80.*

(3) Joints in PVC plastic piping shall be solvent-cemented in accordance with ASTM D2672, *Standard Specification for Joints for IPS PVC Pipe Using Solvent Cement.*

15.3.3.7.3.4 CPVC Plastic Piping. CPVC plastic piping under 15.3.3.7.3 shall comply with the following:

(1) CPVC IPS plastic pipe shall be Schedule 40 or Schedule 80, conforming to ASTM F441/F441M, *Standard Specification for Chlorinated Poly(Vinyl Chloride) (CPVC) Plastic Pipe, Schedules 40 and 80.*

(2) CPVC IPS plastic fittings shall be Schedule 40 or Schedule 80 to match the pipe, conforming to ASTM F438, *Standard Specification for Socket-Type Chlorinated Poly (Vinyl Chloride) (CPVC) Plastic Pipe Fittings, Schedule 40*, or ASTM F439, *Standard Specification for Chlorinated Poly(Vinyl Chloride) (CPVC) Plastic Pipe Fittings, Schedule 80.*

(3) CPVC CTS plastic pipe and fittings ½ in. through 2 in. nominal size shall be SDR 11, conforming to ASTM D2846/D2846M, *Standard Specification for Chlorinated Poly(Vinyl Chloride) (CPVC) Plastic Hot- and Cold-Water Distribution Systems.*

(4) Solvent cement for joints in CPVC plastic piping shall comply with ASTM F493, *Standard Specification for Solvent Cements for Chlorinated Poly(Vinyl Chloride)(CPVC) Plastic Pipe and Fittings.*

N **15.3.3.7.3.5 Piping Within Floor Slabs Prohibited.** Dental gas and vacuum piping shall not be installed within floor slabs.

N **15.3.3.8 Dental Air and Vacuum Systems Testing.**

N **15.3.3.8.1 General.**

N **15.3.3.8.1.1** Inspection and testing shall be performed on all new piped dental gas and vacuum systems, additions, renovations, temporary installations, or repaired systems to ensure, by a documented procedure, that the following have been completed:

(1) All applicable requirements of this code have been followed.

(2) System integrity has been achieved or maintained.

(3) Piping systems are ready for testing and verification.

(4) Piping systems are performing in accordance with their design requirements.

N **15.3.3.8.1.2** The inspection and testing reports shall be submitted directly to the party that contracted for the testing, who then submits the reports through channels to the responsible facility authority and any others that are required.

N **15.3.3.8.1.3** Reports shall contain detailed listings of all findings and results.

N **15.3.3.8.1.4** The responsible facility authority shall review the inspection and testing records prior to the use of any systems to ensure that all findings and results of the inspection and testing have been successfully completed before use.

N **15.3.3.8.1.5** All documentation pertaining to inspections and testing shall be maintained on-site within the facility.

N **15.3.3.8.2 Category 1 Dental Air and Vacuum Systems.**

N **15.3.3.8.2.1** All Category 1 dental air and vacuum piping systems indicated in 15.3.3 shall be initially tested in accordance with 15.3.3.8.3.

N **15.3.3.8.2.2** Dental air, vacuum, and scavenging systems shall be final tested in accordance with 15.3.3.8.3.5 and 15.3.3.8.3.6.

N **15.3.3.8.3 Initial Testing of Piping Systems.**

N **15.3.3.8.3.1 General.**

N **(A)** Where plastic vacuum and plastic scavenging piping systems are installed, they shall be visually inspected for cross-connections to oxygen and nitrous oxide systems before applying positive test pressures to the copper piping systems.

N **(B)** During the process of initial testing, the identification and labeling of the dental gas and vacuum piping shall be checked.

N **15.3.3.8.3.2 Initial Cross-Connection Test for Plastic Vacuum and Plastic Scavenging Piping Systems.**

N **(A)** Plastic piping shall be tested before copper piping.

N **(B)** Tests shall be conducted to determine that no cross-connections exist between any plastic vacuum piping systems or plastic scavenging piping systems and any copper piping systems.

N **(C)** The vacuum or scavenging source shutoff valves for the vacuum or scavenging piping systems shall remain closed during the tests, unless they are being used for the cross-connection test vacuum source.

N **(D)** The cross-connection test vacuum shall be a minimum of 300 mm (12 in.) HgV.

N **(E)** The source of test vacuum shall be connected only to the vacuum or scavenging piping system being tested.

N **(F)** All individual gas system outlets and vacuum or scavenging system inlets shall be checked to determine that the test vacuum is only present in the vacuum or scavenging piping system being tested.

N **(G)** The cross-connection tests shall be repeated for each installed vacuum and scavenging system with plastic piping.

N **(H)** Any cross-connections shall be removed and the associated piping repaired and leak tested.

N **(I)** The proper labeling and identification of system outlets/inlets shall be confirmed during the initial tests.

N **15.3.3.8.3.3 Initial Pressure Test.**

N **(A)** Each section of the piping in dental air systems and copper vacuum systems shall be pressure tested. Plastic vacuum and plastic scavenging piping shall not be pressure tested.

N **(B)** Initial pressure tests shall be conducted as follows:

(1) After installation of station outlet/inlet rough-in assemblies

(2) Prior to the installation of components of the distribution piping system that would be damaged by the test pressure (e.g., pressure/vacuum alarm devices, pressure/vacuum indicators, line pressure relief valves)

N **(C)** The source shutoff valve shall remain closed during the pressure tests.

N **(D)** The test pressure for dental air piping and copper vacuum piping shall be 1.5 times the system operating pressure but not less than a gauge pressure of 1035 kPa (150 psi).

N **(E)** The test pressure shall be maintained until each joint has been examined for leakage by means of a leak detectant that is safe for use with oxygen and does not contain ammonia.

N **(F)** Any leaks shall be located, repaired (if permitted) or replaced (if required) by the installer, and retested.

N **15.3.3.8.3.4 Initial Piping Purge Test.**

N **(A)** The outlets in each dental air piping system shall be purged to remove any particulate matter from the distribution piping.

N **(B)** Using appropriate adapters, each outlet shall be purged with an intermittent high-volume flow of test gas until the purge produces no discoloration in a clean white cloth.

N **(C)** The purging shall be started at the closest outlet to the piping shutoff valve and continue to the furthest outlet from the shutoff valve.

N **15.3.3.8.3.5 Standing Pressure Test for Dental Air and Copper Vacuum Piping.**

N **(A)** After successful completion of the initial pressure tests in 15.4.8.1, the dental air systems and copper vacuum systems shall be subject to a standing pressure test.

N **(B)** Tests shall be conducted after the final installation of station outlet valve bodies, faceplates, and other distribution system components (e.g., pressure alarm devices, pressure indicators, line pressure relief valves, manufactured assemblies, hoses).

N **(C)** The source valve shall be closed during this test.

N **(D)** The piping systems shall be subjected to 24-hour standing pressure tests using oil-free, dry nitrogen NF.

N **(E)** Test pressures shall be 20 percent above the normal system operating line pressure.

N **(F)** At the conclusion of the tests, there shall be no change in the test pressure except that attributed to specific changes in ambient temperature.

N **(G)** Any leaks shall be located, repaired (if permitted) or replaced (if required) by the installer, and retested. The piping shall be repurged if necessary.

N **15.3.3.8.3.6 Standing Vacuum Test for Plastic Vacuum Piping.**

N **(A)** After successful completion of the initial pressure tests in 15.4.8.1, vacuum distribution piping, including scavenging, shall be subjected to a standing vacuum test.

N **(B)** Tests shall be conducted after installation and connection of all components of the vacuum system.

N **(C)** The piping systems shall be subjected to a 24-hour standing vacuum test.

N **(D)** Test pressure shall be between 300 mm (12 in.) HgV and full vacuum.

N **(E)** During the test, the source of test vacuum shall be disconnected from the piping system.

N **(F)** At the conclusion of the test, there shall be no change in the vacuum pressure other than that attributed to changes of ambient temperature.

N **(G)** Any leaks shall be located, repaired (if permitted) or replaced (if required) by the installer, and retested.

N **15.3.3.8.4 Operation and Management.**

N **15.3.3.8.4.1 System Shutdowns.**

N **(A)** Gas and vacuum piping systems shall be shut down at the end of each workday.

N **(B)** Emergency shutoff valves or remote actuators shall not be used for daily shutdown of the systems.

N **(C)** Cylinder gas valves shall be used for daily shutdowns.

N **15.3.3.8.4.2 Prohibited Interconnections.** Two or more piping systems for different gases or different vacuums shall not be interconnected for testing or any other reason.

N **15.3.3.8.4.3 Manufacturer's Instructions.**

N **(A)** Piping system components shall be installed, adjusted, operated, and maintained in accordance with the manufacturer's instructions.

N **(B)** Copies of the manufacturer's instructions shall be provided to and maintained at the facility.

N **15.3.3.8.4.4 Maintenance.**

N **(A)** Gas and vacuum system equipment shall be maintained by a qualified person.

N **(B)** Every facility shall establish a procedure for manually turning off the gas supply at the cylinder valves of Category 2 dental gas and vacuum systems at the end of each day.

N **15.3.3.8.5 Periodic Testing.** Station outlets for oxygen and nitrous oxide shall be tested for flow and pressure on an approved schedule.

15.4 Category 2 Dental Gas and Vacuum Systems.

15.4.1 General.

15.4.1.1 Category 2 dental gas and vacuum system shall be limited to facilities that, at most, provide moderate and minimal sedation.

15.4.1.2 The medical gases shall be limited to oxygen and nitrous oxide.

15.4.1.3 Dental air shall be provided from a dental air source system.

15.4.1.4 The vacuum systems shall be dental vacuum and nitrous oxide scavenging.

15.4.1.5 All connections within Category 2 medical gas (oxygen and nitrous oxide) shall be gas-specific to prevent cross-connections with other piping systems, including vacuum, water, and dental air.

15.4.1.6 Station outlets and piped outlets for Category 2 medical gas and dental air having nonstandard operating pressures shall comply with the following additional requirements:

(1) They shall be gas specific.
(2) They shall be pressure specific where a single gas is piped at more than one operating pressure.
(3) They shall be a D.I.S.S connection if operated at a gauge pressure in excess of 550 kPa (80 psi).
(4) They shall be designed to prevent the removal of the adapter until the pressure has been relieved, if operated at a gauge pressure between 1380 kPa and 2070 kPa (200 psi and 300 psi).

15.4.1.7 Requirements for Category 2 dental gas and vacuum systems relating to the operation, management, and maintenance of oxygen and nitrous oxide piping systems shall apply both new and existing facilities as specified in 15.1.8.

15.4.2 Medical Gas Systems (Oxygen and Nitrous Oxide).

15.4.2.1 Installer Qualifications (Oxygen and Nitrous Oxide).

15.4.2.1.1 Installers of medical gas systems shall be certified in accordance with ASSE/IAPMO/ANSI 6010, *Professional Qualifications Standard for Medical Gas Systems Installers*, regardless of the capacity of the source equipment.

15.4.2.1.2 Installers of medical gas systems shall not use their certification to oversee installation by noncertified personnel.

15.4.2.1.3 Brazing of medical gas piping systems shall be performed by individuals who are qualified in accordance with 15.4.6.1.

15.4.2.1.4 Prior to any installation work involving brazing, the installer of the medical gas piping systems shall provide documentation required by 15.4.6.1 for the qualifications of the brazing procedures and individual brazers.

15.4.2.2 Central Supply System Identification and Labeling (Oxygen and Nitrous Oxide).

Δ **15.4.2.2.1** Cylinders, containers, and tanks shall be designed, fabricated, tested, and marked (i.e., stamped) in accordance with Department of Transportation (DOT) regulations, Transport Canada's (TC) *Transportation of Dangerous Goods Regulations*, or the ASME *Boiler and Pressure Vessel Code*. [**55:**7.1.5.1]

15.4.2.2.2 Cylinder contents shall be identified by attached labels or stencils naming the contents in accordance with the mandatory requirements of CGA C-7, *Guide to Classification and Labeling of Compressed Gases*.

15.4.2.2.3 Liquid containers shall have additional product identification visible from all directions with a minimum of 51 mm (2 in.) high letters, such as a 360-degree wraparound tape for medical liquid containers.

15.4.2.2.4 Cryogenic liquid containers shall be provided with gas-specific outlet connections in accordance with the mandatory requirements of CGA V-5, *Standard for Diameter Index Safety System (Noninterchangeable Low Pressure Connections for Medical Gas Applications)*, or CGA V-1, *Standard for Compressed Gas Cylinder Valve Outlet and Inlet Connections*.

15.4.2.2.5 Cylinder and cryogenic liquid container outlet connections shall be affixed in such a manner as to be integral to the valve(s), unremovable with ordinary tools, or so designed as to render the attachment point unusable when removed.

15.4.2.2.6 The contents of cylinders and cryogenic liquid containers shall be verified prior to use.

15.4.2.2.7 Labels shall not be defaced, altered, or removed, and connecting fittings shall not be modified.

15.4.2.2.8 Locations containing positive-pressure gases other than oxygen and medical air shall have their door(s) labeled as follows:

Positive-Pressure Gases
NO Smoking or Open Flame
Room May Have Insufficient Oxygen
Open Door and Allow Room to Ventilate Before Entering

15.4.2.2.9 Locations containing central supply systems or cylinders containing only oxygen or medical air shall have their door(s) labeled as follows:

Medical Gases
NO Smoking or Open Flame

15.4.2.3 Central Supply System Operations (Oxygen and Nitrous Oxide).

15.4.2.3.1 The use of adapters or conversion fittings to adapt one gas-specific fitting to another shall be prohibited.

15.4.2.3.2 Cylinders and containers shall be handled in strict accordance with 11.6.2.

15.4.2.3.3 Only gas cylinders, reusable shipping containers, and their accessories shall be permitted to be stored in rooms containing central supply systems or gas cylinders.

15.4.2.3.4 No flammable materials, cylinders containing flammable gases, or containers containing flammable liquids shall be stored in rooms with gas cylinders.

15.4.2.3.5 If cylinders are wrapped when received, the wrappers shall be removed prior to storage.

15.4.2.3.6 Cylinders without correct markings or whose markings and gas-specific fittings do not match shall not be used.

15.4.2.3.7 Cryogenic liquid storage units intended to supply gas to the facility shall not be used to transfill other liquid storage vessels.

15.4.2.3.8 Care shall be exercised when handling cylinders that have been exposed to freezing temperatures or containers that contain cryogenic liquids to prevent injury to the skin.

15.4.2.3.9 Cylinders containing compressed gases and containers for volatile liquids shall be kept away from radiators, steam piping, and like sources of heat.

15.4.2.3.10 Where cylinder valve protection caps are supplied, they shall be secured tightly in place unless the cylinder is connected for use.

15.4.2.3.11 Containers shall not be stored in a tightly closed space.

15.4.2.3.12 Cylinders in use and in storage shall be prevented from reaching temperatures in excess of 52°C (125°F).

Δ 15.4.2.3.13 Central supply systems for nitrous oxide and carbon dioxide using cylinders or portable containers shall be prevented from reaching temperatures lower than the recommendations of the central supply system's manufacturer but never be lower than −7°C (20°F) or greater than 52°C (125°F).

15.4.2.4 Locations of Medical Gas Source Equipment (Oxygen and Nitrous Oxide).

Δ 15.4.2.4.1 Gas storage locations in facilities with Category 2 medical gas systems with a total of all gases in cylinders or containers, except nitrogen, connected and in storage at one time that does not exceed 85 m³ (3000 ft³) at standard temperature and pressure (STP), or 142 m³ (5000 ft³) STP if oxygen is stored in a DOT specification 4 L (cryogenic liquid) container shall comply with 15.4.2.4.3 through 15.4.2.4.15.

15.4.2.4.2* Gas storage locations in facilities with Category 2 medical gas systems with a total of all gases in cylinders or containers exceeding quantities listed in 15.4.2.4.1 shall comply with 5.1.3.3.

15.4.2.4.3 Enclosures shall serve no purpose other than to contain the medical gas source equipment (oxygen and nitrous oxide), except that nitrogen source equipment and compressed air cylinders shall be permitted in the enclosure.

N 15.4.2.4.4 Natural or mechanical ventilation for oxygen and nitrous oxide manifold locations shall be in accordance with 9.3.6.5.

15.4.2.4.5 Storage of full or empty gas cylinders, or both, shall be permitted in the same enclosure.

15.4.2.4.6 Air compressors, vacuum pumps, and other equipment shall not be located in enclosures for medical gas cylinders (oxygen and nitrous oxide source equipment).

15.4.2.4.7* If enclosures are outdoors or remote from the treatment facilities that they serve, they shall be kept locked.

15.4.2.4.8 Cylinders in use and in storage shall be prevented from reaching temperatures in excess of 52°C (125°F). Nitrous oxide cylinders shall be prevented from reaching temperatures lower than −7°C (20°F).

15.4.2.4.9 Indoor enclosures shall not communicate directly with medical gas (oxygen and nitrous oxide) use points or storage locations for flammable materials or gases.

15.4.2.4.10 Outdoor enclosures that are adjacent to a building wall shall be located such that the distance to any window or door of the adjacent building is greater than 3.05 m (10 ft).

15.4.2.4.11 Enclosures for medical gas (oxygen and nitrous oxide) source equipment shall be provided with doors or gates.

15.4.2.4.12 Cylinders in service or in storage shall be individually secured and located to prevent falling or being knocked over.

N 15.4.2.4.13 Locations containing positive-pressure gases or cylinders containing oxygen, nitrous oxide, or both shall be separated from the rest of the building by walls and floors having a 1-hour fire resistance rating with doors and other opening projective having a ¾-hour fire protection rating.

N 15.4.2.4.14 Locations containing positive-pressure gases or cylinders containing positive-pressure gases shall be ventilated in accordance with 9.3.6.5.

N **15.4.2.4.15** Locations containing positive-pressure gases or cylinders containing positive-pressure gases shall be provided with an automatic sprinkler system in accordance with NFPA 13.

15.4.2.5 Medical Gas Source Equipment (Oxygen and Nitrous Oxide).

15.4.2.5.1 Mechanical means shall be provided to ensure that the medical gas source equipment is connected to the correct medical gas distribution piping system.

15.4.2.5.2 Cylinder valve outlets for oxygen and nitrous oxide shall comply with CGA V-1, *Standard for Compressed Gas Cylinder Valve Outlet and Inlet Connections.*

15.4.2.5.3 Threaded connections to manifolds shall comply with CGA V-5, *Standard for Diameter Index Safety System (Noninterchangeable Low Pressure Connections for Medical Gas Applications).*

15.4.2.5.4 A check valve shall be provided downstream of each pressure regulator.

15.4.2.5.5 A pressure relief valve set at 50 percent above the normal line pressure shall be located downstream of the check valve in 15.4.2.5.4.

15.4.2.5.6 Pressure relief valves shall be brass, bronze, or stainless steel and designed for oxygen service.

15.4.2.5.7 Hose and flexible connectors shall have a gauge pressure rating not less than 6895 kPa (1000 psi).

Δ **15.4.2.5.8** Materials used in central supply systems shall meet the following requirements:

(1) In those portions of systems intended to handle oxygen at gauge pressures greater than 3000 kPa (435 psi), interconnecting hose shall contain no polymeric materials.
(2) In those portions of systems intended to handle oxygen or nitrous oxide material, construction shall be compatible with oxygen under the temperatures and pressures to which the components can be exposed.
(3) If potentially exposed to cryogenic temperatures, materials shall be designed for low temperature service.
(4) If intended for outdoor installation, materials shall be installed in accordance with the manufacturer's requirements.

15.4.2.5.9 Nonmetallic hoses and flexible connectors shall not exceed 1.52 m (5 ft) in length nor be concealed or penetrate walls, floors, ceilings, or partitions.

15.4.2.5.9.1 Source equipment shall not be connected to the piping system through flexible connectors.

15.4.2.5.10 Medical gas source equipment that serves one or two treatment facilities shall include two banks of one or more cylinders of oxygen and (if used) two banks of one or more cylinders of nitrous oxygen, each bank containing at least one average day's supply.

15.4.2.5.11 The two banks of each medical gas source shall be manifolded so that either bank can supply its distribution piping system.

15.4.2.5.12 Where the source equipment is remote from a single treatment facility and an in-use bank is unable to supply the system, the manifold shall automatically switch to the secondary bank.

15.4.2.5.13 Where the source equipment serves multiple treatment facilities and an in-use bank is unable to supply the system, the manifold shall automatically switch to the secondary bank.

15.4.2.5.14 Where the source equipment is not remote and is accessible from a single treatment facility served and an in-use bank is unable to supply the system, the manifold shall be manually or automatically switched to the secondary bank.

15.4.2.6 Emergency Shutoff Valves (Oxygen and Nitrous Oxide).

15.4.2.6.1* All Category 2 medical gas systems shall have an emergency shutoff valve accessible from all use-point locations in an emergency.

Δ **15.4.2.6.2** Where a central medical gas supply system supplies two treatment facilities, each facility shall be provided with an emergency shutoff valve located in that treatment facility accessible from all use-point locations in an emergency.

15.4.2.6.3 Each emergency shutoff valve shall be labeled to indicate the gas it controls and shut off only the gas to the treatment facility that it serves.

15.4.2.6.4 A remotely activated shutoff valve at a gas supply manifold shall not be used for emergency shutoff.

Δ **15.4.2.6.4.1** For clinical purposes, a remote valve actuator shall not fail-close in the event of loss of electric power.

Δ **15.4.2.6.4.2** Where remote actuators are the type that fail-open, cylinder shutoff valves shall be closed whenever the system is not in-use.

N **15.4.2.6.4.3** Emergency shutoff valves shall be located to meet the following requirements:

(1) Be readily operable from a standing position
(2) Be installed where visible and accessible at all times
(3) Be installed where they will not be hidden from plain view, such as not behind normally open or normally closed doors
(4) Be installed in the egress pathway near the exit from the treatment area that will be used in an emergency
(5) Be installed in rooms, areas, or closets that are not capable of being closed or locked

15.4.2.7 Station Outlets and Risers (Oxygen and Nitrous Oxide).

15.4.2.7.1 Each gas outlet shall be gas specific.

15.4.2.7.2 Gas outlets shall consist of a primary and a secondary valve or assembly.

15.4.2.7.3 Each gas outlet shall be legibly identified.

15.4.2.7.4 Threaded outlets shall be noninterchangeable connections complying with the mandatory requirements of CGA V-5, *Standard for Diameter Index Safety System (Noninterchangeable Low Pressure Connections for Medical Gas Applications).*

15.4.2.7.5 Factory-installed copper inlet tubes on station outlets extending no further than 205 mm (8 in.) from the body of the terminal shall be not less than DN8 (NPS ¼) (⅜ in. O.D.) size, with 8 mm (0.3 in.) minimum inside diameter.

15.4.2.8 Manufactured Assemblies (Oxygen and Nitrous Oxide). Category 2 systems shall comply with 5.1.6.

15.4.2.9 Pressure and Vacuum Indicators (Oxygen and Nitrous Oxide). Category 2 systems shall comply with 5.1.8.

Δ **15.4.2.10 Warning Systems (Oxygen and Nitrous Oxide).** Category 2 warning systems shall comply with 5.2.9, except as follows:

(1) Warning systems shall be permitted to be a single alarm panel.
(2) The alarm panel shall be located in an area of continuous surveillance while the facility is in operation.
(3) Pressure and vacuum switches/sensors shall be mounted at the source equipment with a pressure indicator at the master alarm panel.
(4) Warning systems for medical gas systems shall provide the following alarms:

  (a) Oxygen main line pressure low
  (b) Oxygen main line pressure high
  (c) Oxygen changeover to secondary bank or about to changeover (if automatic)
  (d) Nitrous oxide main line pressure low
  (e) Nitrous oxide main line pressure high
  (f) Nitrous oxide changeover to secondary bank or about to changeover (if automatic)

(5) Audible and noncancelable alarm visual signals shall indicate if the pressure in the main line increases or decreases 20 percent from the normal operating pressure.
(6) Visual indications shall remain until the situation that caused the alarm is resolved.
(7) Pressure switches/sensors shall be installed downstream of any emergency shutoff valves and any other shutoff valves in the system and cause an alarm for the medical gas if the pressure decreases or increases 20 percent from the normal operating pressure.
(8) A cancelable audible indication of each alarm condition that produces a sound at the alarm panel shall reinitiate the audible signal if another alarm condition occurs while the audible signal is silenced.

15.4.2.11 Labeling and Identification. Category 2 systems shall comply with 5.1.11.

15.4.3 Category 2 Dental Air and Vacuum Piping Systems.

15.4.3.1 General. Dental vacuum systems shall include dental vacuum and nitrous oxide scavenging.

15.4.3.2 Equipment Locations for Dental Air and Vacuum Systems.

15.4.3.2.1 General. Any of the following systems shall be permitted to be located together in the same room:

(1) Dental air compressor sources and reserve headers
(2) Dental–surgical vacuum sources
(3) Dental vacuum sources
(4) Any other compressor, vacuum pump, or electrically powered machinery

15.4.3.2.2 Cylinders and Containers. Cylinders and containers for gases shall be handled in accordance with Chapter 11.

15.4.3.2.3 Ventilation for Motor-Driven Equipment. The following source locations shall be adequately ventilated to prevent accumulation of heat:

(1) Medical air sources
(2) Instrument air sources
(3) Dental compressed air sources

(4) Dental–surgical vacuum sources
(5) Dental vacuum sources
(6) WAGD sources

15.4.3.3 Dental Gas and Vacuum Source Equipment.

15.4.3.3.1 General.

15.4.3.3.1.1 The capacity of source equipment shall be based on the design requirements for the facility, including the number of gas outlets, vacuum inlets, and other connections, and their individual capacities.

15.4.3.3.1.2 The system design requirements shall be included in the data used for testing and verifying the operation of the gas and vacuum piping systems.

15.4.3.3.2 Dental Air.

15.4.3.3.2.1 General.

(A) Dental air use shall comply with the following requirements:

(1) Dental air shall be used for driving dental tools.
(2) Dental air shall be permitted to be used to supply air-driven equipment.
(3) Dental compressed air shall not be permitted to be used for respiration.

(B) Dental air outlets shall not be interchangeable with any other gas outlets, including oxygen, nitrous oxide, medical air, instrument air, and nitrogen.

15.4.3.3.2.2 Dental Air Compressor Units.

(A) Dental air compressor units shall include dental air compressors, vibration isolation, air receivers, coalescent air filters, adsorption dryers, exhaust silencer/filters, moisture indicators, service access manifolds, electrical disconnects, motor wiring, and controls.

(B) Air compressors shall be scroll dental, reciprocating dental, or the oil-free dental types.

N **(C)** Dental air sources for compressors located inside the building shall meet the following requirements:

(1) Be located in a space where no chemical-based materials are stored or used
(2) Be located in a space that is not used for patient treatment or dental procedures
(3) Be taken from a room or space in which there is no open or semi-open discharge from a dental vacuum or dental scavenging system
(4) Be drawn from a remote location, such as the building return air system, when the compressor is located in a room with an open or semi-open discharge from a dental vacuum or dental scavenging system

15.4.3.3.3 Dental Vacuum.

15.4.3.3.3.1 General.

(A) Dental vacuum shall be used for oral evacuation and nitrous oxide scavenging.

(B) Dental vacuum inlets shall not be interchangeable with any other vacuum inlets, including dental–surgical vacuum.

15.4.3.3.3.2 Dental Vacuum Units.

(A) Dental vacuum units shall include dental vacuum pumps, vibration isolation, separation tanks, vacuum inlet, vacuum exhaust, condensate drain, motor wiring, and controls.

(B) Dental vacuum pumps shall comply with both of the following:

(1) Pumps shall be dental dry vacuum or dental liquid (wet) ring pumps.
(2) Pumps shall be oil-free or oil-lubricated and suitable for nitrous oxide scavenging.

N **(C)** Dental vacuum exhaust shall comply with one of the following requirements:

(1) It shall be exhausted to the outdoors in accordance with the manufacturer's recommendations.
(2) It shall be filtered and diffused locally with a ULPA filter element capable of retaining 99.99 percent of particulates.
(3) If used for nitrous oxide scavenging, it shall discharge outdoors.

N **(D)** Dental vacuum system piping shall comply with all of the following:

(1) Horizontal piping in dental vacuum systems shall be sloped a minimum of 7 mm per 3.05 m (¼ in. per 10 ft) toward the vacuum source equipment.
(2) Horizontal piping shall include no sags or low points that would permit fluid or debris to accumulate in the piping.
(3) Voids in the vacuum piping shall be avoided to prevent buildup and obstructions.
(4) Accessible cleanouts shall be permitted to be installed in the vertical downflow pipe to clear obstructions, where necessary.
(5) Dental vacuum cleanouts shall not to be installed on horizontal piping.
(6) Dental vacuum inlets shall be capable of 283 L/min (10 SCFM) or greater flow capacity.

15.4.3.3.4 Nitrous Oxide Scavenging.

15.4.3.3.4.1 General.

△ **(A)** The use of scavenging shall be limited to portions of dental facilities where moderate or minimal sedation is administered.

(B) Active nitrous oxide scavenging shall include the use of a nasal mask on the patient that is connected to a scavenging inlet in the dental vacuum system through a flow-limiting adapter.

(C) Nitrous oxide scavenging inlets shall not be interchangeable with any other vacuum inlets, including medical–surgical vacuum, dental vacuum, and WAGD.

15.4.3.3.4.2 Connection to Dental Vacuum. Scavenging connections to the dental vacuum system shall be a direct HVE connection to a high-volume vacuum port with a capacity of 45 L/min (1.6 cfm).

15.4.3.4 Category 2 Warning Systems (Oxygen and Nitrous Oxide).

15.4.3.4.1 General.

15.4.3.4.1.1 The warning systems in Category 2 dental gas and vacuum systems shall comply with applicable requirements of 5.2.9 and 15.4.3.4.2 through 15.4.3.4.4.

15.4.3.4.1.2 The master, area, and local alarm functions shall be permitted to be provided by a single alarm panel, as indicated in 5.2.9.

15.4.3.4.2 Master Alarm Panels.

15.4.3.4.2.1 A master alarm panel shall be located in the facility at a point of continuous surveillance when the facility is in operation.

15.4.3.4.2.2 The master alarm panel shall indicate the following:

(1) Oxygen supply pressure ±20 percent from normal
(2) Nitrous oxide supply pressure ±20 percent from normal
(3) Changeover of oxygen supply source
(4) Changeover of nitrous oxide supply source

15.4.3.4.3 Area Alarm Panels.

15.4.3.4.3.1 An area alarm panel shall be centrally located where two or more treatment areas are supplied from the same zoned dental gas and vacuum piping.

15.4.3.4.3.2 Area alarm panels shall indicate the following:

(1) Oxygen supply pressure ±20 percent from normal
(2) Nitrous oxide supply pressure ±20 percent from normal

15.4.3.4.4 Local Alarms.

15.4.3.4.4.1 Local alarms shall be located in source equipment control panels or separate control panels in the equipment rooms for source equipment.

15.4.4 Piping for Category 2 Medical Gas, Dental Air, and Vacuum Systems.

15.4.4.1 General.

15.4.4.1.1 Piping for the following systems shall comply with 15.4.4.2:

(1) Oxygen
(2) Nitrous oxide

15.4.4.1.2 Piping for dental air systems shall comply with 15.4.4.3.

15.4.4.1.3 Piping for dental vacuum systems and scavenging systems shall comply with 15.4.4.4.

15.4.4.2 Piping for Oxygen and Nitrous Oxide Systems.

△ **15.4.4.2.1 Cleaning for Oxygen Service.**

N **15.4.4.2.1.1** For oxygen and nitrous oxide, the pipe, fittings, valves, gas/vacuum outlets/inlets, and other piping components shall be cleaned for oxygen by the manufacturer prior to installation in accordance with CGA G-4.1, *Cleaning Equipment for Oxygen Service.*

N **15.4.4.2.1.2** Fittings shall be permitted to be cleaned by a supplier or agency other than the manufacturer.

15.4.4.2.2 Pipe. Piping materials for oxygen and nitrous oxide shall be one of the following:

(1) Hard-drawn seamless copper in accordance with ASTM B819, *Standard Specification for Seamless Copper Tube for Medical Gas Systems,* medical gas tube, Type L or Type K
(2) Listed corrugated medical tubing (CMT) fabricated from copper alloy No. 51000 strip, meeting ASTM B103/B103M, *Standard Specification for Phosphor Bronze Plate, Sheet, Strip, and Rolled Bar,* as follows:

  (a) Having a design margin of 3.5
  (b) Externally coated with a nonmetallic sheath marked with the manufacturer's marking
  (c) Listing includes testing to demonstrate that CMT systems can be consistently gas-purged with results equivalent to comparable medical gas copper tubing

N **15.4.4.2.2.1** CMT shall have a flame spread index of 25 or less and a smoke developed index of 50 or less as determined by ASTM E84, *Standard Test Method for Surface Burning Characteristics of Building Materials.*

N **15.4.4.2.2.2** CMT shall be identified by the manufacturer as suitable for oxygen service at a minimum of every 0.92 m (3 ft).

15.4.4.2.3 Fittings.

15.4.4.2.3.1 Fittings shall be brazed, memory metal, or axially swaged.

15.4.4.2.3.2 Brazed fittings shall be the wrought copper capillary type complying with the following:

(1) ASME B16.22, *Wrought Copper and Copper Alloy Solder-Joint Pressure Fittings*
(2) ANSI/ASME B16.50, *Wrought Copper and Copper Alloy Braze-Joint Pressure Fittings*
(3) ASME B16.22 with socket depths equal to or greater than brazed joint pressure fittings in accordance with ANSI/ASME B16.50

15.4.4.2.3.3 Cast copper alloy fittings shall not be used with field-brazed joints.

Δ **15.4.4.2.3.4** Memory metal fittings shall be rated for not less than 538°C (1000°F) and 2070 kPa (300 psi) and be installed by qualified technicians in accordance with the manufacturer's instructions.

Δ **15.4.4.2.3.5** Axially swaged couplings shall include metal-to-metal seats, shall be rated for not less than 538°C (1000°F) and 2070 kPa (300 psi), and provide permanent, nonseparable joints. Fittings shall be installed by qualified technicians in accordance with the manufacturer's instructions.

15.4.4.2.4 Joints.

15.4.4.2.4.1 Brazed. Brazing of copper joints shall be in accordance with 15.4.6.

15.4.4.2.4.2 Threaded. Threaded joints shall be limited to connections to pressure indicators, alarm devices, and source equipment and shall comply with the following:

(1) Threads shall be tapered complying with ASME B1.20.1, *Pipe Threads, General Purpose, Inch.*

(2) Threads shall be made up with polytetrafluoroethylene (PTFE) tape or other thread sealant recommended for oxygen service, with the sealant applied to the male threads only.

15.4.4.2.4.3 Prohibited Joints. The following joints shall be prohibited under 15.4.4.2.4:

(1) Flared and compression connections, including connections to station outlets, alarm devices, and other components
(2) Push-lock connections
(3) Straight-threaded connections, including unions
(4) Pipe crimping tools used to permanently stop the flow of medical gas and vacuum piping

15.4.4.3 Piping for Dental Air Systems.

15.4.4.3.1 General. Pipe, fittings, and joints in piping for dental compressed air systems shall be in accordance with 15.4.4.3.2 through 15.4.4.3.4.

Δ **15.4.4.3.2 Pipe.** Piping materials for dental air systems shall comply with one of the following:

(1) ASTM B88, *Standard Specification for Seamless Copper Water Tube,* Type L or K
(2) ASTM B819, *Standard Specification for Seamless Copper Tube for Medical Gas Systems,* Type L or K
(3) ASTM B280, *Standard Specification for Seamless Copper Tube for Air Conditioning and Refrigeration Field Service,* ACR tube (O.D. size)
(4) ASTM B103/B103M, *Standard Specification for Phosphor Bronze Plate, Sheet, Strip, and Rolled Bar,* listed corrugated medical tubing (CMT) fabricated from copper alloy No. 51000 strip, as follows:

  (a) Having a design margin of 3.5
  (b) Externally coated with a nonmetallic sheath marked with the manufacturer's marking
  (c) Listing includes testing to demonstrate that CMT systems can be consistently gas purged with results equivalent to comparable medical gas copper tubing

15.4.4.3.2.1 Copper tube shall be hard temper or annealed (soft temper).

15.4.4.3.3 Fittings. Fittings for dental air piping systems shall be permitted to be any of the following acceptable joining methods:

(1) Brazed or soldered fittings complying with ASME B16.22, *Wrought Copper and Copper Alloy Solder-Joint Pressure Fittings*
(2) Brazed fittings complying with ANSI/ASME B16.50, *Wrought Copper and Copper Alloy Braze-Joint Pressure Fittings*
(3) Brazed fittings complying with ASME B16.22, with socket depths equal to or greater than braze-joint pressure fittings complying with ANSI/ASME B16.50
(4) Flared fittings complying with ASME B16.26, *Cast Copper Alloy Fittings for Flared Copper Tubes*
(5) Compression fittings (¾ in. maximum size)
(6) Axially swaged fittings complying with 15.4.4.2.3.5

15.4.4.3.4 Joints. Joints for piping under 15.4.4.3 shall comply with 15.4.4.3.4.1 through 15.4.4.3.4.3.

15.4.4.3.4.1 Joints shall be brazed, soldered, threaded, flared, or the compression type.

15.4.4.3.4.2 Where joints are brazed, they shall comply with the requirements of 15.4.6.

15.4.4.3.4.3 Soldered joints shall be made in accordance with ASTM B828, *Standard Practice for Making Capillary Joints by Soldering of Copper and Copper Alloy Tube and Fittings*, using a "lead-free" solder filler metal containing not more than 0.2 percent lead by volume that complies with ASTM B32, *Standard Specification for Solder Metal*.

15.4.4.4 Piping for Dental Vacuum Systems and Scavenging Systems.

15.4.4.4.1 General. Piping for dental vacuum systems and scavenging systems shall be copper, PVC plastic, or CPVC plastic.

15.4.4.4.2 Copper Piping. Copper piping under 15.4.4.4 shall be in accordance with 15.4.4.4.2.1 through 15.4.4.4.2.3.

15.4.4.4.2.1 Copper Tube. Copper tubing shall be hard temper or annealed (soft temper) and shall comply with the following:

(1) ASTM B88, *Standard Specification for Seamless Copper Water Tube*, Type L or K
(2) ASTM B819, *Standard Specification for Seamless Copper Tube for Medical Gas Systems*, Type L or K
(3) ASTM B280, *Standard Specification for Seamless Copper Tube for Air Conditioning and Refrigeration Field Service*, ACR tube (O.D. size)

15.4.4.4.2.2 Copper Fittings. Copper fittings shall comply with the following:

(1) Brazed or soldered fittings conforming to ASME B16.22, *Wrought Copper and Copper Alloy Solder-Joint Pressure Fittings*
(2) Brazed fittings conforming to ANSI/ASME B16.50, *Wrought Copper and Copper Alloy Braze-Joint Pressure Fittings*
(3) Brazed fittings conforming to ASME B16.22 with socket depths equal to or greater than braze-joint pressure fittings conforming to ANSI/ASME B16.50
(4) Flared fittings conforming to ASME B16.26, *Cast Copper Alloy Fittings for Flared Copper Tubes*
(5) Compression fittings (¾ in. maximum size)

15.4.4.4.2.3 Joints for Copper Piping. Joints in copper tubing shall be in accordance with the following:

(1) Joints shall be brazed, soldered, threaded, flared, or the compression type.
(2) Where joints are brazed, they shall comply with the requirements of 15.4.6.
(3) Soldered joints shall be made in accordance with ASTM B828, *Standard Practice for Making Capillary Joints by Soldering of Copper and Copper Alloy Tube and Fittings*, using a "lead-free" solder filler metal containing not more than 0.2 percent lead by volume that complies with ASTM B32, *Standard Specification for Solder Metal*.

15.4.4.4.3 PVC Plastic Piping. PVC plastic piping under 15.4.4.4 shall be in accordance with the following:

(1) PVC plastic pipe shall be Schedule 40 or Schedule 80, conforming to ASTM D1785, *Standard Specification for Poly(Vinyl Chloride) (PVC) Plastic Pipe, Schedules 40, 80, and 120.*
(2) PVC plastic fittings shall be Schedule 40 or Schedule 80 to match the pipe, conforming to ASTM D2466, *Standard Specification for Poly(Vinyl Chloride) (PVC) Plastic Pipe Fittings, Schedule 40*, or ASTM D2467, *Standard Specification for Poly(Vinyl Chloride) (PVC) Plastic Pipe Fittings, Schedule 80.*
(3) Joints in PVC plastic piping shall be solvent-cemented in accordance with ASTM D2672, *Standard Specification for Joints for IPS PVC Pipe Using Solvent Cement.*

15.4.4.4.4 CPVC Plastic Piping. CPVC plastic piping under 15.4.4.4 shall be in accordance with the following:

(1) CPVC IPS plastic pipe shall be Schedule 40 or Schedule 80, conforming to ASTM F441/F441M, *Standard Specification for Chlorinated Poly(Vinyl Chloride) (CPVC) Plastic Pipe, Schedules 40 and 80.*
(2) CPVC IPS plastic fittings shall be Schedule 40 or Schedule 80 to match the pipe, conforming to ASTM F438, *Standard Specification for Socket-Type Chlorinated Poly(Vinyl Chloride) (CPVC) Plastic Pipe Fittings, Schedule 40*, or ASTM F439, *Standard Specification for Chlorinated Poly(Vinyl Chloride) (CPVC) Plastic Pipe Fittings, Schedule 80.*
(3) CPVC CTS plastic pipe and fittings ½ in. through 2 in. size shall be SDR 11, conforming to ASTM D2846/D2846M, *Standard Specification for Chlorinated Poly(Vinyl Chloride) (CPVC) Plastic Hot- and Cold-Water Distribution Systems.*
(4) Solvent cement for joints in CPVC plastic piping shall comply with ASTM F493, *Standard Specification for Solvent Cements for Chlorinated Poly(Vinyl Chloride) (CPVC) Plastic Pipe and Fittings.*

15.4.4.5 Piping for Nitrogen. Nitrogen piping in dental facilities shall comply with 15.4.4.2, including cleaning for oxygen service.

15.4.5 Installation of Medical Gas, Dental Air, and Vacuum Piping.

15.4.5.1 General.

15.4.5.1.1 Gas and vacuum piping systems shall be as listed in Section 15.4.

15.4.5.1.2 Piping materials shall be as listed in 15.4.4.

15.4.5.2 Pipe Sizing. Piping systems shall be designed and sized to deliver the required flow rates at the utilization pressures.

15.4.5.3 Minimum Pipe Sizes. The minimum size of the following piping shall be as follows:

(1) Category 2 oxygen piping shall be not less than DN10 (NPS ⅜ in.) (½ in. O.D.) size.
(2) Category 2 nitrous oxide piping shall be not less than DN8 (NPS ¼ in.) (⅜ in. O.D.) size.
(3) Category 2 oxygen piping shall be at least 1 size larger than piping for nitrous oxide.

15.4.5.4 Location of Piping. Piping shall not be located where subject to contact with oil.

15.4.5.5 Protection of Piping.

15.4.5.5.1 Piping shall be protected against freezing, corrosion, and physical damage.

15.4.5.5.2 Piping exposed in corridors and other locations where subject to physical damage from the movement of equipment shall be protected.

15.4.5.6 Pipe Support.

15.4.5.6.1 Piping shall be supported from the building structure.

15.4.5.6.2 Hangers and supports shall comply with and be installed in accordance with MSS SP-58, *Pipe Hangers and Supports — Materials, Design, Manufacture, Selection, Application, and Installation.*

15.4.5.6.3 Hangers and supports shall be sized for the tube or pipe being supported.

15.4.5.6.4 In potentially damp locations, copper tube hangers and supports that are in contact with the tube shall be plastic-coated or otherwise electrically insulated from the tube.

15.4.5.6.5 The maximum support spacing for copper tube shall be in accordance with Table 15.4.5.6.5.

15.4.5.6.6 The maximum support spacing for plastic pipe shall be in accordance with Table 15.4.5.6.6.

15.4.5.7 Underground Piping Outside of Buildings.

15.4.5.7.1 Buried piping outside of buildings shall be installed below the local level of frost penetration.

15.4.5.7.2 The installation procedure for underground piping shall prevent physical damage to the piping while being backfilled.

Table 15.4.5.6.5 Maximum Copper Tube Support Spacing

Pipe Size	Hanger Spacing	
	mm	ft
DN8 (NPS ¼) (⅜ in. O.D.)	1520	5
DN10 (NPS ⅜) (½ in. O.D.)	1830	6
DN15 (NPS ½) (⅝ in. O.D.)	1830	6
DN20 (NPS ¾) (⅞ in. O.D.)	2130	7
DN25 (NPS 1) (1⅛ in. O.D.)	2440	8
DN32 (NPS 1¼) (1⅜ in. O.D.)	2740	9
DN40 (NPS 1½) (1⅝ in. O.D.) and larger	3050	10
Vertical risers, all sizes, every floor, but not to exceed	4570	15

Table 15.4.5.6.6 Maximum Plastic Pipe Support Spacing

Pipe Size	Hanger Spacing	
	mm	ft
DN15 (NPS ½) (⅝ in. O.D.)	1220	4
DN20 (NPS ¾) (⅞ in. O.D.)	1220	4
DN25 (NPS 1) (1⅛ in. O.D.)	1320	4.33
DN32 (NPS 1¼) (1⅜ in. O.D.)	1320	4.33
DN40 (NPS 1½) (1⅝ in. O.D.)	1420	4.66
DN50 (NPS 2) (2⅜ in. O.D.)	1420	4.66
DN65 (NPS 2½) (2⅞ in. O.D.) and larger	1520	5
Vertical risers, all sizes, every floor, but not to exceed	3040	10

15.4.5.7.3 If the underground piping is protected by a conduit, cover, or other enclosure, the following requirements shall be met:

(1) Access during construction shall be provided at the joints for visual inspection and leak testing.
(2) The conduit, cover, or enclosure shall be self-draining and not retain groundwater in prolonged contact with copper tubing.

15.4.5.7.4 Buried piping that is subject to surface loads shall be buried at a depth that will protect the piping, its enclosure, or both, from excessive stresses.

15.4.5.7.5 The minimum backfill cover above the top of the piping or its enclosure shall be 900 mm (36 in.), except that the minimum cover shall be permitted to be reduced to 450 mm (18 in.) where there is no potential for damage from surface loads or surface conditions.

15.4.5.7.6 Trenches shall be excavated so that the piping or its enclosure has firm, substantially continuous bearing on the bottom of the trench.

15.4.5.7.7 Backfill shall be clean, free from material that can damage the pipe, and compacted.

15.4.5.7.8 A continuous warning tape or marker shall be placed immediately above the piping or its enclosure to clearly identify the pipeline by specific name.

15.4.5.7.9 A continuous warning means shall also be placed above the pipeline at approximately one-half the depth of burial.

15.4.5.7.10 Where buried piping is extended into a building through a wall sleeve, the outdoor end of the sleeve shall be sealed watertight to prevent the entrance of groundwater into the building.

15.4.5.8 Underground Piping Within Buildings.

15.4.5.8.1 The installation procedure for underground piping shall prevent physical damage to the piping while being backfilled.

15.4.5.8.2 If the underground piping is protected by a conduit, cover, or other enclosure, access shall be provided at the joints during construction for visual inspection and leak testing.

15.4.5.8.3 The piping shall be backfilled with clean sand or gravel.

15.4.5.9 Piping Within Floor Slabs Prohibited. Dental gas and vacuum piping shall not be installed within floor slabs.

15.4.5.10 Hose and Flexible Connectors.

15.4.5.10.1 Hose and flexible connectors, both metallic and nonmetallic, shall be no longer than necessary nor penetrate or be concealed in walls, floors, ceilings, or partitions.

15.4.5.10.2 Hose and flexible connectors, metallic or nonmetallic, shall have a minimum burst gauge pressure of 6895 kPa (1000 psi).

15.4.5.10.3 Medical gas hose and flexible connectors shall be oxygen compatible.

15.4.5.10.4 Hose and flexible connectors shall be clearly identified as to the gas content.

Shaded text = Revisions.   Δ = Text deletions and figure/table revisions.   • = Section deletions.   *N* = New material.

15.4.5.10.5 Hose and flexible connectors for dental medical gases shall be gas-specific and not be permitted to conduct any other gas, gas mixture, or liquid.

15.4.6 Brazing Copper Tubing.

15.4.6.1 Qualification of Brazing Procedures and Brazers.

15.4.6.1.1 Brazing procedures and brazer performance for the installation of dental piping shall be in accordance with either Section IX, "Welding and Brazing Qualifications," of the ASME *Boiler and Pressure Vessel Code*, or AWS B2.2/B2.2M, *Specification for Brazing Procedure and Performance Qualification*, both as modified by 15.4.6.

15.4.6.1.2 Brazers shall be qualified by visual examination of the test coupons followed by sectioning.

15.4.6.1.3 The brazing procedure specification shall address cleaning, joint clearance, overlap, internal purge gas, purge gas flow rate, and filler metal.

15.4.6.1.4 The brazing procedure qualification record and the record of brazer performance qualification shall document the filler metal used, cleaning, joint clearance, overlap, internal purge gas and flow rate during brazing of the coupon, and the absence of internal oxidation in the completed coupon.

15.4.6.1.5 Brazing procedures qualified by a technically competent group or agency shall be permitted under the following conditions:

(1) The brazing procedure specification and the procedure qualification record meet the requirements of this code.
(2) The employer obtains a copy of both the brazing procedure specification and the supporting qualification record from the group or agency and signs and dates these records, thereby accepting responsibility for the qualifications that were performed by the group or agency.
(3) The employer qualifies at least one brazer following each brazing procedure specification used.

15.4.6.1.6 An employer shall be permitted to accept brazer qualification records of a previous employer under the following conditions:

(1) The brazer has been qualified following the same procedure that the new employer uses or an equivalent procedure.
(2) The new employer obtains a copy of the record of brazer performance qualification tests from the previous employer and signs and dates these records, thereby accepting responsibility for the qualifications performed by the previous employer.

15.4.6.1.7 Performance qualifications of brazers shall remain in effect indefinitely, unless the brazer does not braze with the qualified procedure for a period exceeding 6 months or there is a specific reason to question the ability of the brazer.

15.4.6.2 Brazed Joints.

15.4.6.2.1 Brazed tube joints shall be of the socket type.

15.4.6.2.2 Brazed joints shall be made using a brazing alloy that exhibits a melting temperature in excess of 538°C (1000°F) to retain the integrity of the piping system in the event of fire exposure.

15.4.6.2.3 Filler metals shall bond with and be metallurgically compatible with the base metal being joined.

15.4.6.2.4 Filler metals shall comply with ANSI/AWS A5.8M/A5.8, *Specification for Filler Metals for Brazing and Braze Welding*.

15.4.6.2.5 Copper-to-copper joints shall be brazed using a copper-phosphorus or copper-phosphorus-silver brazing filler metal (i.e., BCuP series) without flux.

15.4.6.2.6 Joints to be brazed in place shall be accessible for necessary preparation, assembly, heating, filler application, cooling, cleaning, and inspection.

15.4.6.3 Cutting Tube Ends.

15.4.6.3.1 Tube ends shall be cut square using a sharp tubing cutter to avoid deforming the tube.

15.4.6.3.2 The cutting wheels on tubing cutters shall be free from grease, oil, or other lubricants not recommended for oxygen service.

15.4.6.3.3 The cut ends of the tube shall be rolled smooth or deburred with a sharp, clean deburring tool, taking care to prevent chips from entering the tube.

15.4.6.4 Cleaning Joints for Brazing.

15.4.6.4.1 The interior surfaces of tubes, fittings, and other components that are cleaned for oxygen service shall be stored and handled to avoid contamination prior to assembly and brazing.

15.4.6.4.2 The exterior surfaces of tube ends shall be cleaned prior to brazing to remove any oxides and surface dirt and to roughen the surfaces to prepare them for brazing.

15.4.6.4.3 Nonabrasive pads shall be used to clean the exterior surfaces of tube ends.

15.4.6.4.4 The use of steel wool, sand cloth, or wire brushes shall be prohibited.

15.4.6.4.5 The cleaning process shall not result in grooving the surfaces to be joined.

15.4.6.4.6 After being abraded, the surfaces shall be wiped using a clean, lint-free white cloth.

15.4.6.4.7 Tubes, fittings, valves, and other components shall be visually examined internally before being joined to verify that they have not become contaminated for oxygen service and that they are free of obstructions or debris.

15.4.6.4.8 Material that has become contaminated internally and is not clean for oxygen service shall not be installed.

15.4.6.4.9 Joints shall be brazed within 8 hours after being cleaned for brazing.

15.4.6.5 Brazing Dissimilar Metals.

15.4.6.5.1 Flux shall only be used when brazing dissimilar metals, such as copper and bronze or brass, using a silver brazing filler metal (i.e., BAg series).

15.4.6.5.2 Cast metals shall not be field brazed.

15.4.6.5.3 Surfaces shall be cleaned for brazing in accordance with 15.4.6.4.

15.4.6.5.4 Flux shall be applied sparingly to minimize contamination of the inside of the tube with flux.

15.4.6.5.5 The flux shall be applied and worked over the cleaned surfaces to be brazed using a stiff bristle brush to ensure complete coverage and wetting of the surfaces with flux.

15.4.6.5.6 Where possible, short sections of copper tube shall be brazed onto the noncopper component, and the interior of the subassembly shall be cleaned of flux prior to installation in the piping system.

15.4.6.5.7 On joints DN20 (NPS ¾) (⅞ in. O.D.) size and smaller, flux-coated brazing rods shall be permitted to be used in lieu of applying flux to the surfaces to be joined.

15.4.6.6 Nitrogen Purge.

15.4.6.6.1 While being brazed, joints shall be continuously purged with oil-free, dry nitrogen NF to prevent the formation of copper oxide on the inside surface of the joint.

15.4.6.6.2 The source of the nitrogen purge gas shall be monitored, and the installer shall be audibly alerted when the content is low.

15.4.6.6.3 The nitrogen purge gas flow rate shall not be high enough to produce a positive pressure in the piping system.

15.4.6.6.4 The nitrogen purge gas flow shall be controlled by the use of both a pressure regulator and a flowmeter or a combination thereof.

15.4.6.6.5 Pressure regulators alone shall not be used to control nitrogen purge gas flow rates.

15.4.6.6.6 During and after installation, openings in the piping system shall be kept capped or plugged to maintain a nitrogen atmosphere within the piping and to prevent debris or other contaminants from entering the system.

15.4.6.6.7 While a joint is being brazed, a discharge opening shall be provided on the opposite side of the joint from where the nitrogen purge gas is being introduced.

15.4.6.6.8 The flow of nitrogen purge gas shall be maintained until the joint is cool to the touch.

15.4.6.6.9 After the joint has cooled, the purge discharge opening shall be plugged or capped to prevent contamination of the inside of the tube and maintain the nitrogen atmosphere within the piping system.

15.4.6.7 Assembling and Heating Brazed Joints.

15.4.6.7.1 Tube ends shall be inserted either fully into the depth of the fitting socket or to a mechanically limited depth that is not less than the minimum cup depth (i.e., overlap) specified in ANSI/ASME B16.50, *Wrought Copper and Copper Alloy Braze-Joint Pressure Fittings.*

15.4.6.7.2 Where flux is permitted, joints shall be heated slowly until the flux has liquefied.

15.4.6.7.3 After flux has liquefied, or where flux is not permitted to be used, the joint shall be heated quickly to the brazing temperature, taking care not to overheat the joint.

15.4.6.7.4 Techniques for heating joints, applying the brazing filler metal, and making the horizontal, vertical, and large-diameter joints shall be as described in sections on applying heat and brazing horizontal and vertical joints in Chapter VIII, "Brazed Joints," in the CDA *Copper Tube Handbook.*

15.4.6.8 Inspection of Brazed Joints.

15.4.6.8.1 After brazing, the outside of all joints shall be cleaned by washing with water and a wire brush to remove any residue and allow clear visual inspection of the joint.

15.4.6.8.2 Where flux has been used, the wash water shall be hot.

15.4.6.8.3 Each joint shall be visually inspected after cleaning the outside surfaces.

15.4.6.8.4 Joints exhibiting the following conditions shall not be permitted:

(1) Flux or flux residue (where flux or flux-coated BAg rods are used with dissimilar metals)
(2) Base metal melting or erosion
(3) Unmelted filler metal
(4) Failure of the filler metal to be clearly visible all the way around the joint at the interface between the socket and the tube
(5) Cracks in the tube or component
(6) Cracks in the filler metal
(7) Failure of the joint to hold the test pressure under the installer-performed initial pressure test *(see 15.4.7.4.4)* and standing pressure test *(see 15.4.7.4.6)*

15.4.6.8.5 Joints that are identified as defective under conditions specified in 15.4.6.8.4(2) or 15.4.6.8.4(5) shall be replaced.

15.4.6.8.6 Joints that are found to be defective under conditions specified in 15.4.6.8.4(1), 15.4.6.8.4(3), 15.4.6.8.4(4), 15.4.6.8.4(6), or 15.4.6.8.4(7) shall be permitted to be repaired, except that no joint shall be reheated more than once before being replaced.

15.4.7 Performance Criteria and Testing (Oxygen and Nitrous Oxide).

15.4.7.1 Testing and Verification.

15.4.7.1.1 General.

15.4.7.1.1.1 Inspection and testing shall be performed on all new piped oxygen and nitrous oxide systems, additions, renovations, temporary installations, or repaired systems to ensure, by a documented procedure, that the following have been completed:

(1) All applicable requirements of this code have been followed.
(2) System integrity has been achieved or maintained.
(3) Piping systems are ready for testing and verification.
(4) Piping systems are performing in accordance with their design requirements.

15.4.7.1.1.2 The inspection and testing reports shall be submitted directly to the party that contracted for the testing, who then submits the reports through channels to the responsible facility authority and any others that are required.

15.4.7.1.1.3 Reports shall contain detailed listings of all findings and results.

15.4.7.1.1.4 The responsible facility authority shall review the inspection and testing records prior to the use of any systems to ensure that all findings and results of the inspection and testing have been successfully completed before use.

15.4.7.1.1.5 All documentation pertaining to inspections and testing shall be maintained on-site within the facility.

15.4.7.2 Required Testing and Verification.

15.4.7.2.1 Category 2 Medical Gas Systems (Oxygen and Nitrous Oxide). All Category 2 oxygen and nitrous oxide piping systems indicated in 15.4.2 shall be initially tested in accordance with 15.4.7.4.

15.4.7.2.2 The oxygen and nitrous oxide piping systems shall be verified in accordance with 15.4.7.5.

15.4.7.3 Qualification of System Testers and Verifiers (Oxygen and Nitrous Oxide).

15.4.7.3.1 Individuals who perform the initial and final tests of the oxygen and nitrous oxide piping systems shall be certified to ASSE 6010, *Professional Qualifications Standard for Medical Gas Systems Installers*, or verifiers who comply with 15.4.7.3.2.

15.4.7.3.2 Individuals who verify the oxygen and nitrous oxide piping systems shall be certified to ASSE 6030, *Professional Qualifications Standard for Medical Gas Systems Verifiers*.

15.4.7.4 Initial Testing of Piping Systems (Oxygen and Nitrous Oxide).

15.4.7.4.1 General.

15.4.7.4.1.1 The initial tests required by 15.4.7.4 shall be performed prior to either the final tests or the verification tests listed in 15.4.7.5.

15.4.7.4.1.2 The test gas for gas piping systems shall be oil-free, dry nitrogen NF.

15.4.7.4.1.3 Where manufactured assemblies are to be installed, the initial tests required by 15.4.7.4 shall be performed as follows:

(1) After completion of the distribution piping but before the standing pressure test
(2) Prior to installation of manufactured assemblies supplied through flexible hose or flexible tubing
(3) For all station outlets/inlets on installed manufactured assemblies supplied through copper tubing

15.4.7.4.1.4 Where plastic vacuum and plastic scavenging piping systems are installed, they shall be visually inspected for cross-connections to positive-pressure systems before applying positive test pressures to the copper piping systems.

15.4.7.4.1.5 Where brazed joints in copper tubing are found to be defective, they shall be repaired if permitted by 15.4.6.8.6 or replaced if required by 15.4.6.8.5, and retested. The piping shall be repurged if necessary.

15.4.7.4.1.6 During the process of initial testing, the identification and labeling of the medical gas and vacuum piping shall be checked.

15.4.7.4.2 Initial Piping Blowdown (Oxygen and Nitrous Oxide). Piping in dental air and vacuum distribution systems shall be blown clear by means of oil-free, dry nitrogen NF after installation of the distribution piping but before installation of station outlet/inlet rough-in assemblies and other system components (e.g., pressure/vacuum alarm devices, pressure/

vacuum indicators, pressure relief valves, manifolds, and source equipment).

15.4.7.4.3 Initial Cross-Connection Test for Copper Piping Systems.

15.4.7.4.3.1 Copper piping shall not be tested before any plastic piping.

15.4.7.4.3.2 It shall be determined that no cross-connections exist between the various medical gas and vacuum piping systems.

15.4.7.4.3.3 All piping systems shall be reduced to atmospheric pressure.

15.4.7.4.3.4 Sources of test gas shall be disconnected from all piping systems except for the one system being tested.

15.4.7.4.3.5 The system under test shall be charged with oil-free, dry nitrogen NF to a gauge pressure of 345 kPa (50 psi).

15.4.7.4.3.6 After the installation of the individual faceplates with appropriate adapters matching outlet/inlet labels, each individual outlet/inlet in each installed medical gas and vacuum piping system shall be checked to determine that the test gas is dispensed only from the piping system tested.

15.4.7.4.3.7 The initial cross-connection test in 15.4.7.4.3 shall be repeated for each installed medical gas and vacuum piping system with copper piping.

15.4.7.4.3.8 Any cross-connections shall be removed and the associated piping repaired and leak tested.

15.4.7.4.3.9 The proper labeling and identification of system outlets/inlets shall be confirmed during these tests.

15.4.7.4.4 Initial Pressure Test.

15.4.7.4.4.1 Each section of the piping in positive-pressure gas systems and copper vacuum systems shall be pressure tested. Plastic vacuum and plastic scavenging piping shall not be pressure tested.

15.4.7.4.4.2 Initial pressure tests shall be conducted as follows:

(1) After blowdown of the distribution piping
(2) After installation of station outlet/inlet rough-in assemblies
(3) Prior to the installation of components of the distribution piping system that would be damaged by the test pressure (e.g., pressure/vacuum alarm devices, pressure/vacuum indicators, and line pressure relief valves)

15.4.7.4.4.3 The source shutoff valve shall remain closed during the pressure tests.

15.4.7.4.4.4 The test pressure for oxygen and nitrous oxide piping shall be 1.5 times the system operating pressure but not less than a gauge pressure of 1035 kPa (150 psi).

15.4.7.4.4.5* The test pressure shall be maintained until each joint has been examined for leakage by means of a leak detectant that is safe for use with oxygen and does not contain ammonia.

15.4.7.4.4.6 Any leaks shall be located, repaired (if permitted), or replaced (if required) by the installer, and retested.

15.4.7.4.5 Initial Piping Purge Test.

15.4.7.4.5.1 The outlets in each oxygen and nitrous oxide piping system shall be purged to remove any particulate matter from the distribution piping.

15.4.7.4.5.2 Using appropriate adapters, each outlet shall be purged with an intermittent high-volume flow of test gas until the purge produces no discoloration in a clean white cloth.

15.4.7.4.5.3 The purging shall be started at the closest outlet to the piping shutoff valve and continue to the furthest outlet from the shutoff valve.

15.4.7.4.6 Standing Pressure Test for Oxygen and Nitrous Oxide Piping.

15.4.7.4.6.1 After successful completion of the initial pressure tests in 15.4.7.4.4, the gas distribution piping shall be subject to a standing pressure test.

15.4.7.4.6.2 Tests shall be conducted after the final installation of station outlet valve bodies, faceplates, and other distribution system components (e.g., pressure alarm devices, pressure indicators, line pressure relief valves, manufactured assemblies, and hoses).

15.4.7.4.6.3 The source valve shall be closed during this test.

15.4.7.4.6.4 The piping systems shall be subjected to 24-hour standing pressure tests using oil-free, dry nitrogen NF.

15.4.7.4.6.5 Test pressures shall be 20 percent above the normal system operating line pressure.

15.4.7.4.6.6 At the conclusion of the tests, there shall be no change in the test pressure except that attributed to specific changes in ambient temperature.

15.4.7.4.6.7 Any leaks shall be located, repaired (if permitted), or replaced (if required) by the installer, and retested. The piping shall be repurged if necessary.

15.4.7.4.6.8 The 24-hour standing pressure tests shall be witnessed by the authority having jurisdiction or its designee. A form indicating that these tests have been performed and witnessed shall be provided to the verifier at the start of the verification tests in 15.4.7.5.

15.4.7.5 Verification of Piping Systems (Oxygen and Nitrous Oxide).

15.4.7.5.1 General.

15.4.7.5.1.1 The oxygen and nitrous oxide piping systems requiring initial testing and verification shall be as indicated in 15.4.7.2 for the different dental facilities.

15.4.7.5.1.2 Required verification of oxygen and nitrous oxide piping systems shall be performed only after all initial tests required in 15.4.7.4 have been completed.

15.4.7.5.1.3 The test gas shall be oil-free, dry nitrogen NF or the system gas or vacuum where permitted.

15.4.7.5.1.4 Verification shall be conducted by a party technically competent and experienced in the field of medical gas and vacuum piping system testing and certified for ASSE 6030, *Professional Qualifications Standard for Medical Gas Systems Verifiers.*

15.4.7.5.1.5 Verification shall be performed by a party other than the installing contractor.

15.4.7.5.1.6 All required verification tests shall be performed after installation of any manufactured assemblies supplied through tubing or flexible hose.

15.4.7.5.1.7 Where there are multiple possible connection points for terminals, each possible position shall be tested independently.

15.4.7.5.1.8 Where brazed joints in copper tubing are found to be defective, they shall be repaired if permitted by 15.4.6.8.6 or replaced if required by 15.4.6.8.5, and retested. The piping shall be repurged if necessary.

15.4.7.5.1.9 During the process of verification, the presence and proper labeling of source equipment, station outlets/inlets, zone valve boxes, shutoff valves, and alarms shall be checked.

15.4.7.5.2 Verifier Standing Pressure Test. Oxygen and nitrous oxide piping systems requiring verification shall be subjected to a 10-minute standing pressure test at operating line pressure using the following procedure:

(1) After the system is filled with nitrogen or the source gas, the source valve shall be closed.
(2) The piping system shall show no decrease in pressure after not less than 10 minutes.
(3) Any leaks shall be located, repaired (if permitted), or replaced (if required) by the installer, and retested.

15.4.7.5.3 Verifier Cross-Connection Test. The piping systems shall be tested for cross-connections between the systems using the following procedure:

(1) All medical gas and vacuum piping systems shall be reduced to atmospheric pressure.
(2) All sources of test gas for all of the gas and vacuum systems, with the exception of the one system to be checked, shall be disconnected.
(3) The system being checked shall be pressurized to a gauge pressure of 345 kPa (50 psi).
(4) With adapters matching outlet labels, each individual station outlet/inlet of all medical gas and vacuum systems installed shall be checked to determine that test gas is dispensed only from the outlets/inlets of the piping system being tested.
(5) The source of test gas shall be disconnected, and the system that was tested reduced to atmospheric pressure.
(6) Each additional piping system shall be tested until all gas and vacuum piping systems requiring verification are free of cross-connections.
(7) Any cross-connections shall be removed and the associated piping repaired and tested for leaks.

15.4.7.5.4 Verifier Piping Purge Test.

15.4.7.5.4.1 To remove any traces of particulate matter deposited in the oxygen and nitrous oxide piping during construction, a heavy, intermittent purging of the piping shall be done.

15.4.7.5.4.2 The appropriate adapter shall be obtained and high purge rates of at least 225 Nl/min (8 SCFM) shall be put on each outlet.

15.4.7.5.4.3 After each purge is started, it shall be rapidly interrupted several times until the purge produces no discoloration in a white cloth loosely held over the adapter during the purge.

15.4.7.5.4.4 To avoid possible damage to the outlet and its components, this test shall not be conducted using any implement other than the proper adapter.

15.4.7.5.4.5 No pronounced or objectionable odor shall be discernible from any positive-pressure outlet.

15.4.7.5.5 Verifier Piping Particulate Test.

15.4.7.5.5.1 For each oxygen and nitrous oxide system, the cleanliness of the piping system shall be verified.

15.4.7.5.5.2 The test shall be performed with the use of oil-free, dry nitrogen NF.

15.4.7.5.5.3 A minimum of 1000 L (35 ft^3) of gas shall be filtered through a clean, white 0.45 micron filter at a minimum flow rate of 100 Nl/min (3.5 SCFM).

15.4.7.5.5.4 Twenty five percent of the zones shall be tested at the outlet most remote from the source.

15.4.7.5.5.5 The filter shall accrue no more than 0.001 g (1 mg) of matter from any outlet tested.

15.4.7.5.5.6 If any outlet fails this test, the most remote outlet in every zone shall be tested.

15.4.7.5.6 Verifier Piping Purity Test.

15.4.7.5.6.1 For each oxygen and nitrous oxide system, the purity of the piping system shall be verified in accordance with 15.4.7.5.6.

15.4.7.5.6.2 These tests shall be performed with oil-free, dry nitrogen NF or the system gas.

15.4.7.5.6.3 The outlet most remote from the source shall be tested for total nonmethane hydrocarbons and compared to the test of the source gas.

15.4.7.5.6.4 If the system gas is used as the source gas, it shall be tested at the source equipment.

15.4.7.5.6.5 The difference between the two tests shall in no case exceed 5 ppm of total nonmethane hydrocarbons.

15.4.7.5.6.6 The difference between the two tests shall in no case exceed 5 ppm of halogenated hydrocarbons.

15.4.7.5.6.7 The moisture concentration of the outlet test shall not exceed 500 ppm or an equivalent pressure dew point of $-12°C$ ($10°F$) at a gauge pressure of 345 kPa (50 psi).

15.4.7.5.7 Verifier Final Tie-in Test.

15.4.7.5.7.1 Prior to the connection of any work or any extension or addition to an existing piping system, the verification tests in 15.4.7.5 shall be successfully performed on the new work.

15.4.7.5.7.2 Each joint in the final connection between the new work and the existing system shall be leak-tested with the gas of system designation at the normal operating pressure by means of a leak detectant that is safe for use with oxygen and does not contain ammonia.

15.4.7.5.7.3 For oxygen and nitrous oxide, immediately after the final brazed connection is made and leak-tested, an outlet in the new piping and an outlet in the existing piping that are immediately downstream from the point or area of intrusion shall be purged in accordance with the applicable requirements of 15.4.7.5.4.

15.4.7.5.7.4 Before the new work is used for patient care, oxygen and nitrous oxide shall be tested for operational pressure and gas concentration in accordance with 15.4.7.5.8 and 15.4.7.5.9.

15.4.7.5.7.5 Permanent records of these tests shall be maintained.

15.4.7.5.8 Verifier Operational Pressure Test.

15.4.7.5.8.1 Operational pressure tests shall be performed at each station outlet or terminal where the user makes connections and disconnections.

15.4.7.5.8.2 Tests shall be performed with the gas of system designation.

15.4.7.5.8.3 All medical gas outlets with a gauge pressure of 345 kPa (50 psi), including oxygen and nitrous oxide, shall deliver 50 SLPM (1.8 SCFM) with a pressure drop of not more than 35 kPa (5 psi) and static pressure of 345 kPa to 380 kPa (50 psi to 55 psi).

15.4.7.5.9 Verifier Gas Concentration Test. After purging each system with the gas of system designation, the following shall be performed:

(1) Each pressure gas source and outlet shall be analyzed for concentration of gas, by volume.
(2) Analysis shall be conducted with instruments designed to measure the specific gas dispensed.
(3) Allowable concentrations shall be as follows:

    (a) Oxygen ≥99 percent
    (b) Nitrous oxide ≥99 percent
    (c) Other gases ±1 percent unless otherwise specified

15.4.8 Performance Criteria and Testing (Dental Air and Vacuum).

15.4.8.1 Dental Air and Vacuum Systems Testing.

15.4.8.1.1 General.

15.4.8.1.1.1 Inspection and testing shall be performed on all new piped dental gas and vacuum systems, additions, renovations, temporary installations, or repaired systems to ensure, by a documented procedure, that the following have been completed:

(1) All applicable requirements of this code have been followed.
(2) System integrity has been achieved or maintained.
(3) Piping systems are ready for testing and verification.
(4) Piping systems are performing in accordance with their design requirements.

15.4.8.1.1.2 The inspection and testing reports shall be submitted directly to the party that contracted for the testing, who then submits the reports through channels to the responsible facility authority and any others that are required.

15.4.8.1.1.3 Reports shall contain detailed listings of all findings and results.

15.4.8.1.1.4 The responsible facility authority shall review the inspection and testing records prior to the use of any systems to ensure that all findings and results of the inspection and testing have been successfully completed before use.

15.4.8.1.1.5 All documentation pertaining to inspections and testing shall be maintained on-site within the facility.

15.4.8.1.2 Category 2 Dental Air and Vacuum Systems.

15.4.8.1.2.1 All Category 2 dental air and vacuum piping systems indicated in 15.4.3 shall be initially tested in accordance with 15.4.8.1.

15.4.8.1.2.2 Dental air, vacuum, and scavenging systems shall be final tested in accordance with 15.4.8.1.7 and 15.4.8.1.8.

15.4.8.1.3 Initial Testing of Piping Systems.

△ **15.4.8.1.3.1** Where plastic vacuum and plastic scavenging piping systems are installed, they shall be visually inspected for cross-connections to oxygen and nitrous oxide systems before applying positive test pressures to the copper piping systems.

15.4.8.1.3.2 During the process of initial testing, the identification and labeling of the dental gas and vacuum piping shall be checked.

15.4.8.1.4 Initial Cross-Connection Test for Plastic Vacuum and Plastic Scavenging Piping Systems.

15.4.8.1.4.1 Plastic piping shall be tested before copper piping.

15.4.8.1.4.2 Tests shall be conducted to determine that no cross-connections exist between any plastic vacuum piping systems or plastic scavenging piping systems and any copper piping systems.

15.4.8.1.4.3 The vacuum or scavenging source shutoff valves for the vacuum or scavenging piping systems shall remain closed during the tests, unless they are being used for the cross-connection test vacuum source.

15.4.8.1.4.4 The cross-connection test vacuum shall be a minimum of 300 mm (12 in.) HgV.

15.4.8.1.4.5 The source of test vacuum shall be connected only to the vacuum or scavenging piping system being tested.

15.4.8.1.4.6 All individual gas system outlets and vacuum or scavenging system inlets shall be checked to determine that the test vacuum is only present in the vacuum or scavenging piping system being tested.

15.4.8.1.4.7 The cross-connection tests shall be repeated for each installed vacuum and scavenging system with plastic piping.

15.4.8.1.4.8 Any cross-connections shall be removed and the associated piping repaired and leak tested.

15.4.8.1.4.9 The proper labeling and identification of system outlets/inlets shall be confirmed during the initial tests.

15.4.8.1.5 Initial Pressure Test.

15.4.8.1.5.1 Each section of the piping in dental air systems and copper vacuum systems shall be pressure tested. Plastic vacuum and plastic scavenging piping shall not be pressure tested.

△ **15.4.8.1.5.2** Initial pressure tests shall be conducted as follows:

(1) After installation of station outlet/inlet rough-in assemblies
(2) Prior to the installation of components of the distribution piping system that would be damaged by the test pressure (e.g., pressure/vacuum alarm devices, pressure/vacuum indicators, line pressure relief valves)

15.4.8.1.5.3 The source shutoff valve shall remain closed during the pressure tests.

15.4.8.1.5.4 The test pressure for dental air piping and copper vacuum piping shall be 1.5 times the system operating pressure but not less than a gauge pressure of 1035 kPa (150 psi).

15.4.8.1.5.5 The test pressure shall be maintained until each joint has been examined for leakage by means of a leak detectant that is safe for use with oxygen and does not contain ammonia.

△ **15.4.8.1.5.6** Any leaks shall be located, repaired (if permitted) or replaced (if required) by the installer, and retested.

15.4.8.1.6 Initial Piping Purge Test.

15.4.8.1.6.1 The outlets in each dental air piping system shall be purged to remove any particulate matter from the distribution piping.

15.4.8.1.6.2 Using appropriate adapters, each outlet shall be purged with an intermittent high-volume flow of test gas until the purge produces no discoloration in a clean white cloth.

15.4.8.1.6.3 The purging shall be started at the closest outlet to the piping shutoff valve and continue to the furthest outlet from the shutoff valve.

15.4.8.1.7 Standing Pressure Test for Dental Air and Copper Vacuum Piping.

15.4.8.1.7.1 After successful completion of the initial pressure tests in 15.4.8.1, the dental air systems and copper vacuum systems shall be subject to a standing pressure test.

△ **15.4.8.1.7.2** Tests shall be conducted after the final installation of station outlet valve bodies, faceplates, and other distribution system components (e.g., pressure alarm devices, pressure indicators, line pressure relief valves, manufactured assemblies, hoses).

15.4.8.1.7.3 The source valve shall be closed during this test.

15.4.8.1.7.4 The piping systems shall be subjected to 24-hour standing pressure tests using oil-free, dry nitrogen NF.

15.4.8.1.7.5 Test pressures shall be 20 percent above the normal system operating line pressure.

15.4.8.1.7.6 At the conclusion of the tests, there shall be no change in the test pressure, except that attributed to specific changes in ambient temperature.

△ **15.4.8.1.7.7** Any leaks shall be located, repaired (if permitted) or replaced (if required) by the installer, and retested. The piping shall be repurged if necessary.

15.4.8.1.8 Standing Vacuum Test for Plastic Vacuum Piping.

15.4.8.1.8.1 After successful completion of the initial pressure tests in 15.4.8.1, vacuum distribution piping, including scavenging, shall be subjected to a standing vacuum test.

15.4.8.1.8.2 Tests shall be conducted after installation and connection of all components of the vacuum system.

15.4.8.1.8.3 The piping systems shall be subjected to a 24-hour standing vacuum test.

15.4.8.1.8.4 Test pressure shall be between 300 mm (12 in.) HgV and full vacuum.

15.4.8.1.8.5 During the test, the source of test vacuum shall be disconnected from the piping system.

15.4.8.1.8.6 At the conclusion of the test, there shall be no change in the vacuum pressure other than that attributed to changes of ambient temperature.

15.4.8.1.8.7 Any leaks shall be located, repaired (if permitted), or replaced (if required) by the installer, and retested.

15.4.9 Operation and Management.

15.4.9.1 System Shutdowns.

15.4.9.1.1 Gas and vacuum piping systems shall be shut down at the end of each workday.

Δ **15.4.9.1.2** Emergency shutoff valves or remote actuators shall not be used for daily shutdown of the systems.

N **15.4.9.1.3** Cylinder gas valves shall be used for daily shutdowns.

15.4.9.2 Prohibited Interconnections. Two or more piping systems for different gases or different vacuums shall not be interconnected for testing or any other reason.

15.4.9.3 Manufacturer's Instructions.

15.4.9.3.1 Piping system components shall be installed, adjusted, operated, and maintained in accordance with the manufacturer's instructions.

15.4.9.3.2 Copies of the manufacturer's instructions shall be provided to the facility and maintained at the facility.

15.4.9.4 Maintenance.

15.4.9.4.1 Gas and vacuum system equipment shall be maintained by a qualified person.

15.4.9.4.2 Every facility shall establish a procedure for manually turning off the gas supply at the cylinder valves of Category 2 dental gas and vacuum systems at the end of each day.

15.4.9.5 Periodic Testing. Station outlets for oxygen and nitrous oxide shall be tested for flow and pressure on an approved schedule.

15.5 Category 3 Dental Gas and Vacuum Systems.

15.5.1 General.

15.5.1.1 Category 3 dental gas and vacuum systems shall be limited to facilities that perform minimal or no sedation.

15.5.1.2 There shall be no medical gases.

15.5.1.3 Dental air shall be provided from a dental air source system.

15.5.1.4 The vacuum system shall be dental vacuum.

15.5.2 Category 3 Dental Air and Vacuum Piping Systems. Dental vacuum systems shall include dental vacuum and nitrous oxide scavenging.

15.5.3 Equipment Locations for Dental Air and Vacuum Systems.

15.5.3.1 General. Any of the following systems shall be permitted to be located together in the same room:

(1) Dental air compressor sources and reserve headers

(2) Dental vacuum sources
(3) Any other compressor, vacuum pump, or electrically powered machinery

15.5.3.2 Cylinders and Containers. Cylinders and containers for gases shall be handled in accordance with Chapter 11.

15.5.3.3 Ventilation for Motor-Driven Equipment. The following source locations shall be adequately ventilated to prevent accumulation of heat:

(1) Dental compressed air sources
(2) Dental vacuum sources

15.5.4 Dental Gas and Vacuum Source Equipment.

15.5.4.1 General.

15.5.4.1.1 The capacity of source equipment shall be based on the design requirements for the facility, including the number of gas outlets, vacuum inlets, and other connections, and their individual capacities.

15.5.4.1.2 The system design requirements shall be included in the data used for testing and verifying the operation of the gas and vacuum piping systems.

15.5.4.2 Dental Air.

15.5.4.2.1 General.

15.5.4.2.1.1 Dental air use shall comply with the following:

(1) Be used for driving dental tools
(2) Be permitted to be used to supply air-driven equipment
(3) Be prohibited from being used for respiration

15.5.4.2.1.2 Dental air outlets shall not be interchangeable with any other gas outlets, including oxygen, nitrous oxide, medical air, instrument air, and nitrogen.

15.5.4.2.2 Dental Air Compressor Units.

15.5.4.2.2.1 Dental air compressor units shall include dental air compressors, vibration isolation, air receivers, coalescent air filters, adsorption dryers, exhaust silencer/filters, moisture indicators, and service access manifolds, electrical disconnects, motor wiring, and controls.

15.5.4.2.2.2 Air compressors shall be scroll dental, reciprocating dental, or the oil-free dental types.

N **15.5.4.2.2.3** Dental air sources for compressors located inside the building shall meet the following requirements:

(1) Sources shall be located in a space where no chemical-based materials are stored or used.
(2) Sources shall be located in a space that is not used for patient treatment or dental procedures.
(3) Sources shall not be taken from a room or space in which there is an open or semi-open discharge from a dental vacuum or dental scavenging system.
(4) When the compressor is located in a room with an open or semi-open discharge from a dental vacuum or dental scavenging system, the air shall be drawn from a remote location such as the building return air system.

15.5.4.3 Dental Vacuum.

15.5.4.3.1 General.

15.5.4.3.1.1 Dental vacuum shall be used for oral evacuation and nitrous oxide scavenging.

15.5.4.3.1.2 Dental vacuum inlets shall not be interchangeable with any other vacuum inlets, including dental–surgical vacuum.

15.5.4.3.2 Dental Vacuum Units.

15.5.4.3.2.1 Dental vacuum units shall include dental vacuum pumps, vibration isolation, separation tanks, vacuum inlet, vacuum exhaust, condensate drain, motor wiring, and controls.

15.5.4.3.2.2 Dental vacuum pumps shall be dental dry vacuum or dental liquid (wet) ring pumps. Pumps shall be oil-free or oil-lubricated and suitable for nitrous oxide scavenging.

N 15.5.4.3.2.3 Dental vacuum exhaust shall comply with one of the following:

(1) Dental vacuum shall be exhausted to the outdoors in accordance with the manufacturer's recommendations.
(2) Dental vacuum exhaust shall be filtered and diffused locally with a ULPA filter element capable of retaining 99.99 percent of particulates.
(3) Dental vacuum exhaust shall discharge outdoors if used for nitrous oxide scavenging.

N 15.5.4.3.2.4 Dental vacuum system piping shall comply with all of the following:

(1) Horizontal piping in dental vacuum systems shall be sloped a minimum of 7 mm per 3.05 m (¼ in. per 10 ft) toward the vacuum source equipment.
(2) Horizontal piping shall include no sags or low points that would permit fluid or debris to accumulate in the piping.
(3) Voids in the vacuum piping shall be avoided to prevent buildup and obstructions.
(4) Accessible cleanouts shall be permitted to be installed in the vertical downflow pipe to clear obstructions, where necessary.
(5) Dental vacuum cleanouts shall not to be installed on horizontal piping.
(6) Dental vacuum inlets shall be capable of 283 L/min (10 SCFM) or greater flow capacity.

15.5.5 Piping for Category 3 Dental Gas and Vacuum Systems.

15.5.5.1 General.

15.5.5.1.1 Piping for dental air systems shall comply with 15.5.5.2.

15.5.5.1.2 Piping for dental vacuum systems and scavenging systems shall comply with 15.5.5.3.

15.5.5.2 Piping for Dental Air Systems.

15.5.5.2.1 General. Pipe, fittings, and joints in piping for dental compressed air systems shall be in accordance with 15.5.5.2.2 through 15.5.5.2.4.

15.5.5.2.2 Pipe. Piping materials for dental air systems shall comply with one of the following:

(1) ASTM B88, *Standard Specification for Seamless Copper Water Tube*, Type L or K
(2) ASTM B819, *Standard Specification for Seamless Copper Tube for Medical Gas Systems*, Type L or K
(3) ASTM B280, *Standard Specification for Seamless Copper Tube for Air Conditioning and Refrigeration Field Service*, ACR tube (O.D. size)
(4) ASTM B103/B103M, *Standard Specification for Phosphor Bronze Plate, Sheet, Strip, and Rolled Bar*, listed corrugated

medical tubing (CMT) fabricated from copper alloy No. 51000 strip, as follows:

(a) Having a design margin of 3.5
(b) Externally coated with a nonmetallic sheath marked with the manufacturer's marking
(c) Listing includes testing to demonstrate that CMT systems can be consistently gas purged with results equivalent to comparable medical gas copper tubing

15.5.5.2.2.1 Copper tube shall be hard temper or annealed (soft temper).

15.5.5.2.3 Fittings. Fittings for dental air piping systems shall be permitted to be any of the following acceptable joining methods:

(1) Brazed or soldered fittings complying with ASME B16.22, *Wrought Copper and Copper Alloy Solder-Joint Pressure Fittings*
(2) Brazed fittings complying with ANSI/ASME B16.50, *Wrought Copper and Copper Alloy Braze-Joint Pressure Fittings*
(3) Brazed fittings complying with ASME B16.22, with socket depths equal to or greater than braze-joint pressure fittings complying with ANSI/ASME B16.50
(4) Flared fittings complying with ASME B16.26, *Cast Copper Alloy Fittings for Flared Copper Tubes*
(5) Compression fittings (¾ in. maximum size)
(6) Axially swaged fittings complying with 5.1.10.7

15.5.5.2.4 Joints. Joints for piping under 15.5.5.2 shall comply with the following:

(1) Joints shall be brazed, soldered, threaded, flared, or the compression type.
(2) Where joints are brazed, they shall comply with the requirements of 15.4.6.
(3) Soldered joints shall be made in accordance with ASTM B828, *Standard Practice for Making Capillary Joints by Soldering of Copper and Copper Alloy Tube and Fittings*, using a "lead-free" solder filler metal containing not more than 0.2 percent lead by volume that complies with ASTM B32, *Standard Specification for Solder Metal*.

15.5.5.3 Piping for Dental Vacuum Systems and Scavenging Systems.

15.5.5.3.1 General. Piping for dental vacuum systems and scavenging systems shall be copper, PVC plastic, or CPVC plastic.

15.5.5.3.2 Copper Piping. Copper piping under 15.5.5.3 shall be in accordance with 15.5.5.3.2.1 through 15.5.5.3.2.3.

15.5.5.3.2.1 Copper Tube. Copper tubing shall be hard temper or annealed (soft temper) and comply with the following:

(1) ASTM B819, *Standard Specification for Seamless Copper Tube for Medical Gas Systems*, Type L or K
(2) ASTM B88, *Standard Specification for Seamless Copper Water Tube*, Type L or K
(3) ASTM B280, *Standard Specification for Seamless Copper Tube for Air Conditioning and Refrigeration Field Service*, ACR tube (O.D. size)

15.5.5.3.2.2 Copper Fittings. Copper fittings shall comply with the following:

(1) Brazed or soldered fittings conforming to ASME B16.22, *Wrought Copper and Copper Alloy Solder-Joint Pressure Fittings*

(2) Brazed fittings conforming to ANSI/ASME B16.50, *Wrought Copper and Copper Alloy Braze-Joint Pressure Fittings*

(3) Brazed fittings conforming to ASME B16.22 with socket depths equal to or greater than braze-joint pressure fittings conforming to ANSI/ASME B16.50

(4) Flared fittings conforming to ASME B16.26, *Cast Copper Alloy Fittings for Flared Copper Tubes*

(5) Compression fittings (¾ in. maximum size)

15.5.5.3.2.3 Joints for Copper Piping. Joints in copper tubing shall be in accordance with the following:

(1) Joints shall be brazed, soldered, threaded, flared, or the compression type.

(2) Where joints are brazed, they shall comply with the requirements of 15.4.6.

(3) Soldered joints shall be made in accordance with ASTM B828, *Standard Practice for Making Capillary Joints by Soldering of Copper and Copper Alloy Tube and Fittings*, using a "lead-free" solder filler metal containing not more than 0.2 percent lead by volume that complies with ASTM B32, *Standard Specification for Solder Metal*.

15.5.5.3.3 PVC Plastic Piping. PVC plastic piping for dental vacuum systems and scavenging systems shall be in accordance with the following:

(1) PVC plastic pipe shall be Schedule 40 or Schedule 80 and comply with ASTM D1785, *Standard Specification for Poly(Vinyl Chloride) (PVC) Plastic Pipe, Schedules 40, 80, and 120*.

(2) PVC plastic fittings shall be Schedule 40 or Schedule 80 to match the pipe and comply with ASTM D2466, *Standard Specification for Poly(Vinyl Chloride) (PVC) Plastic Pipe Fittings, Schedule 40*; ASTM D2467, *Standard Specification for Poly(Vinyl Chloride) (PVC) Plastic Pipe Fittings, Schedule 80*; or ASTM D2665, *Standard Specification for Poly(Vinyl Chloride) (PVC) Plastic Drain, Waste, and Vent Pipe and Fittings*.

(3) Joints in PVC plastic piping shall be solvent-cemented in accordance with ASTM D2672, *Standard Specification for Joints for IPS PVC Pipe Using Solvent Cement*.

15.5.5.3.4 CPVC Plastic Piping. CPVC plastic piping under 15.5.5.3 shall be in accordance with the following:

(1) CPVC IPS plastic pipe shall be Schedule 40 or Schedule 80, conforming to ASTM F441/F441M, *Standard Specification for Chlorinated Poly(Vinyl Chloride) (CPVC) Plastic Pipe, Schedules 40 and 80*.

(2) CPVC IPS plastic fittings shall be Schedule 40 or Schedule 80 to match the pipe, conforming to ASTM F438, *Standard Specification for Socket-Type Chlorinated Poly(Vinyl Chloride) (CPVC) Plastic Pipe Fittings, Schedule 40*, or ASTM F439, *Standard Specification for Chlorinated Poly(Vinyl Chloride) (CPVC) Plastic Pipe Fittings, Schedule 80*.

(3) CPVC CTS plastic pipe and fittings ½ in. through 2 in. size shall be SDR 11, conforming to ASTM D2846/D2846M, *Standard Specification for Chlorinated Poly(Vinyl Chloride) (CPVC) Plastic Hot- and Cold-Water Distribution Systems*.

(4) Solvent cement for joints in CPVC plastic piping shall comply with ASTM F493, *Standard Specification for Solvent Cements for Chlorinated Poly(Vinyl Chloride) (CPVC) Plastic Pipe and Fittings*.

15.5.6 Installation of Dental Air and Vacuum Piping.

15.5.6.1 General.

15.5.6.1.1 Dental air and vacuum piping systems shall be as listed in 15.5.2.

15.5.6.1.2 Piping materials shall be as listed in 15.5.5.

15.5.6.2 Pipe Sizing. Piping systems shall be designed and sized to deliver the required flow rates at the utilization pressures.

15.5.6.3 Protection of Piping.

15.5.6.3.1 Piping shall be protected against freezing, corrosion, and physical damage.

15.5.6.3.2 Piping exposed in corridors and other locations where subject to physical damage from the movement of equipment shall be protected.

15.5.6.4 Pipe Support.

15.5.6.4.1 Piping shall be supported from the building structure.

15.5.6.4.2 Hangers and supports shall comply with and be installed in accordance with MSS SP-58, *Pipe Hangers and Supports — Materials, Design, Manufacture, Selection, Application, and Installation*.

15.5.6.4.3 Hangers and supports shall be sized for the tube or pipe being supported.

15.5.6.4.4 The maximum support spacing for copper tube shall be in accordance with Table 15.5.6.4.4.

Table 15.5.6.4.4 Maximum Copper Tube Support Spacing

Pipe Size	Hanger Spacing	
	mm	ft
DN8 (NPS ¼) (⅜ in. O.D.)	1520	5
DN10 (NPS ⅜) (½ in. O.D.)	1830	6
DN15 (NPS ½) (⅝ in. O.D.)	1830	6
DN20 (NPS ¾) (⅞ in. O.D.)	2130	7
DN25 (NPS 1) (1⅛ in. O.D.)	2440	8
DN32 (NPS 1¼) (1⅜ in. O.D.)	2740	9
DN40 (NPS 1½) (1⅝ in. O.D.) and larger	3050	10
Vertical risers, all sizes, every floor, but not to exceed	4570	15

15.5.6.4.5 The maximum support spacing for plastic pipe shall be in accordance with Table 15.5.6.4.5.

15.5.6.5 Underground Piping Outside of Buildings.

15.5.6.5.1 Buried piping outside of buildings shall be installed below the local level of frost penetration.

15.5.6.5.2 The installation procedure for underground piping shall prevent physical damage to the piping while being backfilled.

Table 15.5.6.4.5 Maximum Plastic Pipe Support Spacing

Pipe Size	Hanger Spacing	
	mm	ft
DN15 (NPS ½) (⅝ in. O.D.)	1220	4
DN20 (NPS ¾) (⅞ in. O.D.)	1220	4
DN25 (NPS 1) (1⅛ in. O.D.)	1320	4.33
DN32 (NPS 1¼) (1⅜ in. O.D.)	1320	4.33
DN40 (NPS 1½) (1⅝ in. O.D.)	1420	4.66
DN50 (NPS 2) (2⅜ in. O.D.)	1420	4.66
DN65 (NPS 2½) (2⅞ in. O.D.) and larger	1520	5
Vertical risers, all sizes, every floor, but not to exceed	3040	10

15.5.6.5.3 If the underground piping is protected by a conduit, cover, or other enclosure, the following requirements shall be met:

(1) Access during construction shall be provided at the joints for visual inspection and leak testing.
(2) The conduit, cover, or enclosure shall be self-draining and not retain groundwater in prolonged contact with copper tubing.

15.5.6.5.4 Buried piping that is subject to surface loads shall be buried at a depth that will protect the piping, its enclosure, or both, from excessive stresses.

15.5.6.5.5 The minimum backfill cover above the top of the piping or its enclosure shall be 900 mm (36 in.), except that the minimum cover shall be permitted to be reduced to 450 mm (18 in.) where there is no potential for damage from surface loads or surface conditions.

15.5.6.5.6 Trenches shall be excavated so that the piping or its enclosure has firm, substantially continuous bearing on the bottom of the trench.

15.5.6.5.7 Backfill shall be clean, free from material that can damage the pipe, and compacted.

15.5.6.5.8 A continuous warning tape or marker shall be placed immediately above the piping or its enclosure to clearly identify the pipeline by specific name.

15.5.6.5.9 A continuous warning means shall also be placed above the pipeline at approximately one-half the depth of burial.

15.5.6.5.10 Where buried piping is extended into a building through a wall sleeve, the outdoor end of the sleeve shall be sealed watertight to prevent the entrance of groundwater into the building.

15.5.6.6 Underground Piping Within Buildings.

15.5.6.6.1 The installation procedure for underground piping shall prevent physical damage to the piping while being backfilled.

15.5.6.6.2 The piping shall be backfilled with clean sand or gravel.

15.5.6.7 Piping Within Floor Slabs Prohibited. Dental gas and vacuum piping shall not be installed within floor slabs.

15.5.7 Performance Criteria and Testing (Dental Air and Vacuum).

15.5.7.1 Dental Air and Vacuum Systems Testing.

15.5.7.1.1 General.

15.5.7.1.1.1 Inspection and testing shall be performed on all new piped dental gas and vacuum systems, additions, renovations, temporary installations, or repaired systems to ensure, by a documented procedure, that the following have been completed:

(1) All applicable requirements of this code have been followed.
(2) System integrity has been achieved or maintained.
(3) Piping systems are ready for testing and verification.
(4) Piping systems are performing in accordance with their design requirements.

15.5.7.1.1.2 The inspection and testing reports shall be submitted directly to the party that contracted for the testing, who then submits the reports through channels to the responsible facility authority and any others that are required.

15.5.7.1.1.3 Reports shall contain detailed listings of all findings and results.

15.5.7.1.1.4 The responsible facility authority shall review the inspection and testing records prior to the use of any systems to ensure that all findings and results of the inspection and testing have been successfully completed before use.

15.5.7.1.1.5 All documentation pertaining to inspections and testing shall be maintained on-site within the facility.

15.5.7.1.2 Required Testing.

Δ **15.5.7.1.2.1** All Category 3 dental gas and vacuum piping systems indicated in 15.5.2 shall be initially tested in accordance with 15.5.7.1.3.

15.5.7.1.2.2 Dental air, vacuum, and scavenging systems shall be final tested in accordance with 15.5.7.1.3.4 and 15.5.7.1.3.5.

15.5.7.1.3 Initial Testing of Piping Systems.

15.5.7.1.3.1 General.

(A) Where plastic vacuum and plastic scavenging piping systems are installed, they shall be visually inspected for cross-connections to oxygen and nitrous oxide systems before applying positive test pressures to the copper piping systems.

(B) During the process of initial testing, the identification and labeling of the dental gas and vacuum piping shall be checked.

15.5.7.1.3.2 Initial Pressure Test.

(A) Each section of the piping in dental air systems and copper vacuum systems shall be pressure tested. Plastic vacuum and plastic scavenging piping shall not be pressure tested.

Δ **(B)** Initial pressure tests shall be conducted as follows:

(1) After installation of station outlet/inlet rough-in assemblies
(2) Prior to the installation of components of the distribution piping system that would be damaged by the test pressure (e.g., pressure/vacuum alarm devices, pressure/vacuum indicators, line pressure relief valves)

(C) The source shutoff valve shall remain closed during the pressure tests.

(D) The test pressure for dental air piping and copper vacuum piping shall be 1.5 times the system operating pressure but not less than a gauge pressure of 1035 kPa (150 psi).

(E) The test pressure shall be maintained until each joint has been examined for leakage by means of a leak detectant that is safe for use with oxygen and does not contain ammonia.

Δ **(F)** Any leaks shall be located, repaired (if permitted) or replaced (if required) by the installer, and retested.

15.5.7.1.3.3 Initial Piping Purge Test.

(A) The outlets in each dental air piping system shall be purged to remove any particulate matter from the distribution piping.

(B) Using appropriate adapters, each outlet shall be purged with an intermittent high-volume flow of test gas until the purge produces no discoloration in a clean white cloth.

(C) The purging shall be started at the closest outlet to the piping shutoff valve and continue to the furthest outlet from the shutoff valve.

15.5.7.1.3.4 Standing Pressure Test for Dental Air and Copper Vacuum Piping.

(A) After successful completion of the initial pressure tests in 15.5.7.1.3.2, the dental air systems and copper vacuum systems shall be subject to a standing pressure test.

(B) Tests shall be conducted after the final installation of station outlet valve bodies, faceplates, and other distribution system components (e.g., pressure alarm devices, pressure indicators, line pressure relief valves, manufactured assemblies, and hoses).

(C) The source valve shall be closed during this test.

(D) The piping systems shall be subjected to 24-hour standing pressure tests using oil-free, dry nitrogen NF.

(E) Test pressures shall be 20 percent above the normal system operating line pressure.

(F) At the conclusion of the tests, there shall be no change in the test pressure except that attributed to specific changes in ambient temperature.

Δ **(G)** Any leaks shall be located, repaired (if permitted) or replaced (if required) by the installer, and retested. The piping shall be repurged if necessary.

15.5.7.1.3.5 Standing Vacuum Test for Plastic Vacuum Piping.

(A) After successful completion of the initial pressure tests in 15.5.7.1.3.2, vacuum distribution piping, including scavenging, shall be subjected to a standing vacuum test.

(B) Tests shall be conducted after installation and connection of all components of the vacuum system.

(C) The piping systems shall be subjected to a 24-hour standing vacuum test.

(D) Test pressure shall be between 300 mm (12 in.) HgV and full vacuum.

(E) During the test, the source of test vacuum shall be disconnected from the piping system.

(F) At the conclusion of the test, there shall be no change in the vacuum pressure other than that attributed to changes of ambient temperature.

Δ **(G)** Any leaks shall be located, repaired (if permitted) or replaced (if required) by the installer, and retested.

15.5.8 Operation and Management.

15.5.8.1 System Shutdowns. Gas and vacuum piping systems shall be shut down at the end of each workday.

15.5.8.2 Manufacturer's Instructions.

15.5.8.2.1 Piping system components shall be installed, adjusted, operated, and maintained in accordance with the manufacturer's instructions.

15.5.8.2.2 Copies of the manufacturer's instructions shall be provided to the facility and maintained at the facility.

15.5.8.3 Maintenance. Dental air and vacuum system equipment shall be maintained by a qualified representative of the equipment manufacturer.

Chapter 16 Features of Fire Protection

16.1 Applicability.

16.1.1 This chapter shall apply to all new and existing health care facilities.

Δ **16.1.2** Continued use of an existing system that is noncompliant with the requirements of this code shall be permitted unless the authority having jurisdiction has determined that such use poses a distinct hazard to life.

16.2 Construction and Compartmentation. Buildings or structures housing a health care facility shall meet the minimum construction and compartmentation requirements of the applicable code.

16.3 Special Hazard Protection for Flammable Liquids and Gases.

16.3.1 Where required by the provisions of Chapters 11 through 43 of NFPA *101*, occupancies with storage, use, and handling of hazardous materials shall comply with the following codes unless otherwise modified by other provisions of this *Code:* NFPA 30, NFPA 54, NFPA 55, NFPA 58, NFPA 400, and NFPA 495. [*101*:8.7.3.1]

16.3.2* No storage, use, or handling of hazardous materials shall be permitted in any location where such storage, use, or handling would jeopardize egress from the structure, unless otherwise permitted by a document listed in 16.3.1. [*101*:8.7.3.2]

16.4 Laboratories. Laboratories that use chemicals shall comply with NFPA 45 unless otherwise modified by other provisions of this code. [*101*:8.7.4.1]

16.5 Utilities.

16.5.1 General. Utilities shall comply with the requirements of 16.5.1.1 through 16.5.1.3.

16.5.1.1 Gas. Equipment using gas and related gas piping shall be in accordance with NFPA 54 or NFPA 58 unless such installations are approved existing installations, which shall be permitted to be continued in service. [*101*:9.1.1]

Δ **16.5.1.2 Electrical Systems.** Electrical wiring and equipment shall be in accordance with Chapter 6.

16.5.1.3 Stored Electrical Energy Systems. Stored electrical energy systems shall be installed, tested, and maintained in accordance with NFPA 111. [*101*:9.1.4]

16.5.2 Heating, Ventilating, and Air-Conditioning. [*101*:9.2]

16.5.2.1* Heating, Ventilating, and Air Conditioning. Air-conditioning, heating, ventilating ductwork, and related equipment shall be in accordance with NFPA 90A, unless such installations are approved existing installations, which shall be permitted to be continued in service.

Δ **16.5.2.2 Ventilating or Heat-Producing Equipment.** Ventilating or heat-producing equipment shall be in accordance with NFPA 31, NFPA 54, *NFPA 70*, NFPA 91, or *NFPA 211*, as applicable, unless such installations are approved existing installations, which shall be permitted to be continued in service. [*101*:9.2.2]

16.5.2.3 Commercial Cooking Operations. Commercial cooking operations shall be protected in accordance with NFPA 96 unless such installations are approved existing installations, which shall be permitted to be continued in service. [*101*:9.2.3]

16.5.2.4 Ventilating Systems in Laboratories Using Chemicals. Ventilating systems in laboratories using chemicals shall be in accordance with NFPA 45. [*101*:9.2.4]

16.5.3 Elevators, Escalators, and Conveyors. [*101*:9.4]

16.5.3.1 Code Compliance. [*101*:9.4.2]

16.5.3.1.1 Except as modified herein, new elevators, escalators, dumbwaiters, and moving walks shall be in accordance with the requirements of ASME A17.1/CSA B44, *Safety Code for Elevators and Escalators.* [*101*:9.4.2.1]

16.5.3.1.2 Except as modified herein, existing elevators, escalators, dumbwaiters, and moving walks shall be in accordance with the requirements of ASME A17.3, *Safety Code for Existing Elevators and Escalators.* [*101*:9.4.2.2]

16.5.3.2 Firefighters' Emergency Operations. [*101*:9.4.3]

16.5.3.2.1 All new elevators shall conform to the firefighters' emergency operations requirements of ASME A17.1/CSA B44, *Safety Code for Elevators and Escalators.* [*101*:9.4.3.1]

16.5.3.2.2 All existing elevators having a travel distance of 25 ft (7620 mm) or more above or below the level that best serves the needs of emergency personnel for firefighting or rescue purposes shall conform to the firefighters' emergency operations requirements of ASME A17.3, *Safety Code for Existing Elevators and Escalators.* [*101*:9.4.3.2]

16.5.3.3* Elevator Machine Rooms. Elevator machine rooms that contain solid-state equipment for elevators, other than existing elevators, having a travel distance exceeding 50 ft (15 m) above the level of exit discharge, or exceeding 30 ft (9.1 m) below the level of exit discharge, shall be provided with a natural or mechanical means to maintain temperature during firefighters' emergency operations for elevator operation *(see 9.4.3 of NFPA 101).* The operating temperature shall be established by the elevator equipment manufacturer's specifications. When standby power is connected to the elevator, the means to control the temperature in the machine room shall be connected to standby power, if applicable. [*101*:9.4.5]

Δ **16.5.3.4 Elevator Testing.**

N **16.5.3.4.1** Elevators shall be subject to periodic inspections and tests as specified in ASME A17.1/CSA B44, *Safety Code for Elevators and Escalators.* [*101*:9.4.6.1]

N **16.5.3.4.2** All elevators equipped with firefighters' emergency operations in accordance with 9.4.3 of NFPA *101* shall be subject to a monthly operation with a written record of the findings made and kept on the premises as required by ASME A17.1/CSA B44, *Safety Code for Elevators and Escalators.* [*101*:9.4.6.2]

16.6 Waste Chutes, Incinerators, and Linen Chutes. Waste chutes, linen chutes, and incinerators shall be installed and maintained in accordance with NFPA 82 unless such installations are approved existing installations, which shall be permitted to be continued in service.

16.6.1 Any waste chute or linen chute, including pneumatic waste and linen systems, shall be provided with automatic extinguishing protection in accordance with Section 9.7 of NFPA *101.* [*101*:19.5.4.3]

16.7 Fire Detection, Alarm, and Communications Systems. [*101*:9.6]

16.7.1* General. [*101*:9.6.1]

16.7.1.1 Buildings or structures housing a health care facility shall meet the fire detection, alarm, and communications systems requirements of the applicable code.

16.7.1.2 A fire alarm system required for life safety shall be installed, tested, and maintained in accordance with the applicable requirements of *NFPA 70* and *NFPA 72*.

16.7.1.3 An approved existing installation shall be permitted to be continued in use, provided it is tested and maintained in accordance with the requirements of *NFPA 72*.

16.7.1.4 For the purposes of this code, a complete fire alarm system shall provide functions for initiation, notification, and control, and shall perform as follows:

(1) The initiation function provides the input signal to the system.
(2) The notification function advises that human action is required in response to a particular condition.
(3) The control function provides outputs to control building equipment to enhance protection of life.

16.7.2 Signal Initiation.

16.7.2.1 Buildings or structures housing a health care facility shall meet the minimum signaling and alarm initiation requirements of the applicable code.

16.7.2.2 Manual fire alarm boxes shall be used only for fire-protective signaling purposes.

16.7.2.2.1 Combination fire alarm and guard's tour stations shall be acceptable.

16.7.2.3 A manual fire alarm box shall be provided in the natural exit access path near each required exit from an area, unless modified by another section of this code.

16.7.2.4* Additional manual fire alarm boxes shall be located so that, on any given floor in any part of the building, no horizontal distance on that floor exceeding 60 m (200 ft) shall need to be traversed to reach a manual fire alarm box. [*101*:9.6.2.5]

16.7.2.5 For fire alarm systems using automatic fire detection or waterflow detection devices, not less than one manual fire alarm box shall be provided to initiate a fire alarm signal.

16.7.2.5.1 The manual fire alarm box shall be located where required by the authority having jurisdiction.

16.7.2.6 Manual fire alarm boxes shall be accessible, unobstructed, and visible. [*101*:9.6.2.7]

16.7.2.7 Where a sprinkler system provides automatic detection and alarm system initiation, it shall be provided with an approved alarm initiation device that operates when the flow of water is equal to or greater than that from a single automatic sprinkler.

16.7.3 Smoke Alarms.

16.7.3.1 Where required by the applicable code, single-station and multiple-station smoke alarms shall be in accordance with *NFPA 72*.

16.7.3.2 System smoke detectors in accordance with *NFPA 72* and arranged to function in the same manner as single-station or multiple-station smoke alarms shall be permitted in lieu of smoke alarms. [*101*:9.6.2.10.8]

16.7.3.3 The alarms shall sound only within an individual dwelling unit, suite of rooms, or similar area and shall not actuate the building fire alarm system, unless otherwise permitted by the authority having jurisdiction. Remote annunciation shall be permitted.

16.7.4 Occupant Notification. [*101*:9.6.3]

16.7.4.1 Where required by the applicable code, occupant notification shall be provided to alert occupants of a fire or other emergency.

16.7.4.2 Occupant notification shall be in accordance with 16.7.4.3 unless otherwise provided in 16.7.4.2.1 and 16.7.4.2.2. [*101*:9.6.3.2]

16.7.4.2.1* Elevator lobby, hoistway, and associated machine room smoke detectors used solely for elevator recall, and heat detectors used solely for elevator power shutdown, shall not be required to activate the building evacuation alarm if the power supply and installation wiring to such detectors are monitored by the building fire alarm system, and if the activation of such detectors initiates a supervisory signal at a constantly attended location. [*101*:9.6.3.2.1]

16.7.4.2.2* Smoke detectors used solely for closing dampers or HVAC system shutdown shall not be required to activate the building evacuation alarm, provided that the power supply and installation wiring to the detectors are monitored by the building fire alarm system, and the activation of the detectors initiates a supervisory signal at a constantly attended location. [*101*:9.6.3.2.2]

16.7.4.3 Defend in Place. For new and existing facilities, where the response to a fire is to defend in place within a safe place in the building, occupant notification shall be in accordance with the facility fire plan.

16.7.4.3.1* Where buildings are required to be subdivided into smoke compartments, fire alarm notification zones shall coincide with one or more smoke compartment boundaries or shall be in accordance with the facility fire plan.

16.7.4.3.2* The private operating mode, as defined in *NFPA 72*, shall be permitted to be used for the placement of notification appliances within the health care and ambulatory health care occupancies of the building.

16.7.4.3.3* The notification signal shall readily identify the smoke zone or the floor area, floor, and building in need of staff response.

16.7.4.3.4 The notification signal shall be heard in all locations in accordance with the facility fire plan.

16.7.4.3.5* In patient care spaces where alarm notification adversely affects patient care, as determined by a risk assessment, alarm notification appliances shall not be required as long as an alternative means of alarm notification is provided.

16.7.4.3.6 Visible signals shall not be required inside surgical operating rooms, patient sleeping rooms, or psychiatric care areas where their operation would interfere with patient treatment.

16.7.4.3.7 Visible signals shall not be required inside exam rooms, special procedure rooms, dressing rooms, and nonpublic toilet rooms where staff is required to respond to those areas in accordance with the facility fire plan.

16.8* Heliports.

16.8.1 New heliports shall be designed and constructed in accordance with the requirements of NFPA 418.

16.8.2 Heliports shall be maintained in accordance with NFPA 418.

16.9 Automatic Sprinklers and Other Extinguishing Equipment.

16.9.1 Automatic Sprinklers.

16.9.1.1 Buildings or structures housing a health care facility shall meet the automatic sprinkler system requirements of the applicable code.

16.9.1.2 Where provided, automatic sprinkler systems shall be installed in accordance with NFPA 13.

16.9.1.3* Defend in Place. For new and existing facilities, where the response to a fire is to defend in place within a safe place in the building and not to automatically evacuate the building, sprinkler system zones shall coincide with smoke compartment boundaries or shall be in accordance with the facility fire plan.

16.9.1.4* Closets. Sprinklers shall not be required in clothes closets of patient sleeping rooms in hospitals where the area of the closet does not exceed 6 ft^2 (0.55 m^2) provided the distance from the sprinkler in the patient sleeping room to the back wall of the closet does not exceed the maximum distance permitted by NFPA 13. [*101*:18.3.5.10]

16.10 Manual Extinguishing Equipment.

16.10.1* Portable fire extinguishers shall be selected, installed, inspected, and maintained in accordance with NFPA 10.

16.10.1.1 Fire extinguishers shall be provided in MRI rooms and associated spaces.

16.10.1.1.1* Fire extinguishers and associated hardware rated as MR conditional or MR safe shall be provided in MRI rooms and associated spaces.

16.10.1.2 Class K fire extinguishers shall be provided for hazards where there is a potential for fires involving combustible cooking media (vegetable or animal oils and fats). [*10*:6.6.1]

16.10.1.3* Class K fire extinguishers shall not be required where residential cooking equipment is used for food warming or limited cooking, or where an occupancy prohibits deep fat frying.

16.10.1.4* Clean agent– or water mist–type fire extinguishers shall be provided in operating rooms.

16.10.1.5 Clean agent–type fire extinguishers shall be provided in telecommunication entrance facilities and telecommunication equipment rooms.

16.10.2 Where provided, standpipe and hose systems shall be in accordance with NFPA 14.

16.10.2.1 Where standpipe and hose systems are installed in combination with automatic sprinkler systems, installation shall be in accordance with the appropriate provisions established by NFPA 13 and NFPA 14.

16.10.2.2* Hose or hose outlets shall be permitted to be removed from existing standpipe and hose systems that are not required by the applicable code.

16.11* Compact Storage.
Compact storage shall be protected by sprinklers in accordance with NFPA 13.

16.12 Compact Mobile Storage.

16.12.1 Rooms with compact mobile storage units greater than 50 ft^2 (4.65 m^2) shall be protected as a hazardous area in accordance with the applicable code.

16.12.2 Smoke detection shall be installed above compact mobile storage units greater than 50 ft^2 (4.65 m^2) in accordance with *NFPA 72*.

16.12.3* Compact mobile storage units greater than 50 ft^2 (465 m^2) shall be protected by automatic sprinklers in accordance with NFPA 13.

16.13 Maintenance and Testing.

16.13.1 All water-based fire protection systems shall be inspected, tested, and maintained in accordance with NFPA 25.

16.13.2 All non-water-based fire protection systems shall be inspected, tested, and maintained in accordance with the applicable NFPA standards.

16.14 Fire Loss Prevention in Operating Rooms.

16.14.1 Hazard Assessment.

16.14.1.1 An evaluation shall be made of hazards that could be encountered during surgical procedures.

16.14.1.2 The evaluation shall include hazards associated with the properties of electricity, hazards associated with the operation of surgical equipment, and hazards associated with the nature of the environment.

16.14.1.3 Periodic reviews of surgical operations and procedures shall be conducted with special attention given to any change in materials, operations, or personnel.

16.14.2 Fire Prevention Procedures. Fire prevention procedures shall be established.

16.14.3 Germicides and Antiseptics.

16.14.3.1 Medicaments and alcohol-based hand sanitizers, including those dispersed as aerosols, shall be permitted to be used in anesthetizing locations.

16.14.3.2* Flammable liquid germicides or antiseptics used in anesthetizing locations, whenever the use of electrosurgery, cautery, or a laser is contemplated, shall be packaged to ensure controlled delivery to the patient in unit dose applicators, swabs, and other similar applicators.

16.14.3.3 Whenever the application of flammable liquid germicides or antiseptics is employed in surgeries where the use of electrosurgery, cautery, or a laser is contemplated, time shall be allowed to elapse between application of the germicide or antiseptic and the following:

(1) Application of drapes, to allow complete evaporation and dissipation of any flammable vehicle remaining
(2) Use of electrosurgery, cautery, or a laser, to ensure the solution is completely dry and to allow thorough evaporation and dissipation of any flammable vehicle remaining

16.14.3.4 Prior to draping or use of electrosurgery, cautery, or a laser, any flammable liquid–soaked materials shall be removed from the patient care vicinity.

16.14.3.5 Pooling of flammable liquid germicides or antiseptics shall be avoided; if pooling occurs, excess solution shall be wicked, and the germicide or antiseptic shall be allowed to completely dry.

16.14.3.6 A preoperative "time out" period shall be conducted prior to the initiation of any surgical procedure using flammable liquid germicide or antiseptic solutions to verify the following:

(1) Application site of solution is dry prior to draping and use of electrosurgery, cautery, or a laser.
(2) Pooling of solution has not occurred or has been corrected.
(3) Any solution-soaked materials have been removed from the patient care vicinity.

16.14.3.7 Whenever flammable aerosols or antiseptics are employed, sufficient time shall be allowed to elapse between deposition and application of drapes to allow complete evaporation and dissipation of any flammable vehicle remaining.

16.14.3.8 Health care organizations shall establish policies and procedures outlining safety precautions related to the use of flammable liquid or aerosol germicides or antiseptics used in anesthetizing locations, as required in 16.14.3.9, whenever the use of electrosurgery, cautery, or a laser is contemplated.

16.14.3.9 Emergency Procedures.

16.14.3.9.1 Procedures for operating room/surgical suite emergencies shall be developed.

16.14.3.9.2 Procedures shall include alarm actuation, evacuation, and equipment shutdown procedures and provisions for control of emergencies that could occur in the operating room, including specific detailed plans for control operations by an emergency control group within the organization or a public fire department.

16.14.3.9.3 Emergency procedures shall be established for controlling chemical spills.

16.14.3.9.4 Emergency procedures shall be established for extinguishing drapery, clothing, or equipment fires.

16.14.3.10 Orientation and Training.

16.14.3.10.1 New operating room/surgical suite personnel, including physicians and surgeons, shall be taught general safety practices for the area and specific safety practices for the equipment and procedures they will use.

16.14.3.10.2 Continuing safety education and supervision shall be provided, incidents shall be reviewed monthly, and procedures shall be reviewed annually.

16.14.3.10.3 Fire exit drills shall be conducted annually or more frequently as determined by the applicable code.

Annex A   Explanatory Material

Annex A is not a part of the requirements of this NFPA document but is included for informational purposes only. This annex contains explanatory material, numbered to correspond with the applicable text paragraphs.

A.1.1.10 Because no single model of an emergency management plan is feasible for every health care facility, this chapter is intended to provide criteria for the preparation and implementation of an individual plan. The principles involved are universally applicable; the implementation needs to be tailored to the specific facility.

A.1.1.12 Hyperbaric chambers are found in a variety of settings, including but not limited to hospitals, doctor's offices, private clinics, and business occupancies. Not all hyperbaric facilities are designed or equipped the same. Hyperbaric treatment and facilities are used for a variety of emergent and nonemergent conditions, and the acuity of patients ranges from stable to critical. These variations lead to differences in hyperbaric equipment, ancillary support equipment, and facility location. This chapter is intended to provide minimum safeguards for hyperbaric patients and personnel regardless of the location of the facility.

A.1.3.1.3 This subsection clarifies that if a provision of this code becomes applicable due to the installation or use of a system, equipment, or assembly regulated herein, the facility does not automatically become subject to the code in its entirety.

A.1.5 Although it is common practice for medical appliances to use metric units on their dials, gauges, and controls, many components of systems within the scope of this document are manufactured and used in the United States and employ nonmetric dimensions. Since these dimensions (such as nominal pipe sizes) are not established by the National Fire Protection Association, the Technical Correlating Committee on Health Care Facilities cannot independently change them. Accordingly, this document uses dimensions that are presently in common use by the building trades in the United States. Trade units vary from SI to US customary units, depending on the equipment devices or material.

A.2.1 The documents referenced in this chapter or portions of such documents are referenced within this code and are considered part of the requirements of this document.

Documents referenced in this chapter or portions of such documents are only applicable to the extent called for within other chapters of this code.

Where the requirements of a referenced code or standard differ from the requirements of this code, the requirements of this code govern.

Δ **A.3.2.1 Approved.** The National Fire Protection Association does not approve, inspect, or certify any installations, procedures, equipment, or materials nor does it approve or evaluate testing laboratories. In determining the acceptability of installations or procedures, equipment, or materials, the "authority having jurisdiction" may base acceptance on compliance with NFPA or other appropriate standards. In the absence of such standards, said authority may require evidence of proper installation, procedure, or use. The "authority having jurisdiction" may also refer to the listings or labeling practices of an organization that is concerned with product evaluations and is thus in a position to determine compliance with appropriate standards for the current production of listed items.

A.3.2.2 Authority Having Jurisdiction (AHJ). The phrase "authority having jurisdiction," or its acronym AHJ, is used in NFPA standards in a broad manner because jurisdictions and approval agencies vary, as do their responsibilities. Where public safety is primary, the authority having jurisdiction may be a federal, state, local, or other regional department or individual such as a fire chief; fire marshal; chief of a fire prevention bureau, labor department, or health department; building official; electrical inspector; or others having statutory authority. For insurance purposes, an insurance inspection department, rating bureau, or other insurance company representative may be the authority having jurisdiction. In many circumstances, the property owner or his or her designated agent assumes the role of the authority having jurisdiction; at government installations, the commanding officer or departmental official may be the authority having jurisdiction.

A.3.2.3 Code. The decision to designate a standard as a "code" is based on such factors as the size and scope of the NFPA standard, its intended use and form of adoption, and whether it contains substantial enforcement and administrative provisions.

A.3.2.6 Listed. The means for identifying listed equipment may vary for each organization concerned with product evaluation; some organizations do not recognize equipment as listed unless it is also labeled. The authority having jurisdiction should utilize the system employed by the listing organization to identify a listed product.

A.3.3.10 Applicator. In the given sense, an applicator is not an electrode, because it does not use a conductive connection to the patient in order to function. A radio frequency "horn" of a diathermy machine is a typical applicator. (MED)

A.3.3.12 Atmosphere. As employed in this code, the term *atmosphere* can refer to the environment within or outside of a hyperbaric facility. When used as a measure of pressure, atmosphere is expressed as a fraction of standard air pressure [101.4 kPa (14.7 psi)]. *(See the first column of Table D.1 in NFPA 99B.)* (HYP)

A.3.3.12.2 Atmosphere of Increased Burning Rate. The degree of fire hazard of an oxygen-enriched atmosphere varies with the concentration of oxygen and diluent gas and the total pressure. The definition contained in the current edition of NFPA 53 and in editions of NFPA 56D prior to 1982 did not necessarily reflect the increased fire hazard of hyperbaric and hypobaric atmospheres.

The definition of *atmosphere of increased burning rate* used in Chapter 14 and in NFPA 99B defines an oxygen-enriched atmosphere with an increased fire hazard as it relates to the increased burning rate of material in the atmosphere. It is based on a 1.2 cm/sec (0.47 in./sec) burning rate (at 23.5 percent oxygen at 1 atmosphere absolute) as described in Figure A.3.3.12.2.

This rate can be determined as follows:

[A.3.3.12.2]

$$\frac{23.45}{\sqrt{TP_{atmos}}}$$

where:
TP_{atmos} = total pressure in atmospheres

(HYP)

A.3.3.20.3 Bulk Oxygen System. The oxygen containers can be stationary or movable, and the oxygen can be stored as gas or liquid. The bulk oxygen system terminates at the point where oxygen at service pressure first enters the supply line. (PIP)

A.3.3.21 Central Supply System. Central supply systems comprise the equipment necessary to produce, condition, control, and monitor the gases or vacuum. They include all equipment from the atmospheric intake on air compressors, exhaust on vacuum pumps, and cylinders or containers for pressurized gases through to the source valve *(see 5.1.4.2).* Examples of central supply systems include air compressor sources, vacuum pump sources, cylinder and container headers and manifolds, liquid bulk gas systems proportioning systems and combinations thereof. (PIP)

A.3.3.23 Clinical IT Network. A clinical IT network comprises the servers, switches, routers, and voice and data communications equipment that are employed to transport patient patient-critical clinical data, information, and staff communications over a shared interoperable IT network infrastructure. (ELS)

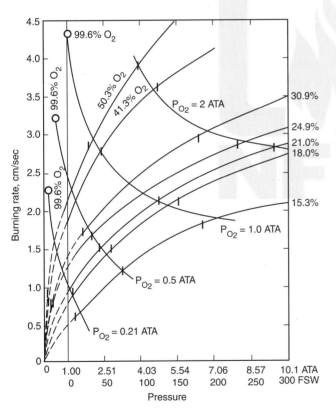

ATA = Atmospheres absolute
FSW = Feet of sea water

FIGURE A.3.3.12.2 Burning Rates of Filter Paper Strips at an Angle of 45 Degrees in N_2–O_2 Mixtures. (Adapted from Figure 4 of "Technical Memorandum UCRI-721, Chamber Fire Safety.")

A.3.3.25 Combustible Liquid. See NFPA 30 for further information on flash point test procedures. (FUN)

A.3.3.26 Combustion. Combustion is not limited to a chemical reaction always involving oxygen. Certain metals, such as calcium and aluminum, will burn in nitrogen; nitrous oxide will support the combustion of phosphorus and carbon; and so on. However, this document deals with the more common process of fuels burning in air. (HYP)

A.3.3.28 Compressed Medical Gases (CMG). CMG classifications are defined in 201(g)(1) of the Federal Food, Drug, and Cosmetic Act, 21 USC 321(g)(1). This includes gases recognized in the current *United States Pharmacopeia and National Formulary (USP-NF)* or supplements and gases intended for direct use or as a component of gases in the diagnosis, cure, mitigation, treatment, or prevention of diseases in man or in animals that achieves its intended purpose through chemical rather than physical means. [**55, 2023**] (PIP)

A.3.3.36 Defend in Place. The concept of the term *defend in place* includes, but is not limited to, elements related to moving building occupants from an area of immediate danger to a safe location in the building and containment of the emergency or dangerous condition. (FUN)

A.3.3.43 Direct Electrical Pathway to the Heart. Electrodes, such as those used for pacing the heart, and catheters filled with conductive fluids, are examples of direct electrical pathways to the heart. (MED)

A.3.3.44 Disaster. A disaster can be either an event that causes, or threatens to cause, physical damage and injury to facility personnel or patients within the facility, or an event that requires expansion of facilities to receive and care for a large number of casualties resulting from a disaster that produces no damage or injury to the health care facility and staff, or a combination thereof.

Such a situation creates the need for emergency expansion of facilities, as well as operation of this expanded facility in an unfamiliar environment. Under this definition, the recognition of a disaster situation will vary greatly from one facility to another and from time to time in any given facility. Such recognition and concomitant activation of the Health Care Emergency Preparedness Plan is dependent on mutual aid agreements, facility type, geographic location, bed capacity, bed occupancy at a given time, staff size, staff experience with disaster situations, and other factors. For example, the routine workload of the emergency department of a large metropolitan general hospital would constitute a disaster, requiring activation of the Health Care Emergency Preparedness Plan, were this same workload to be suddenly applied to a small community hospital.

Disasters have a variety of causes, all of which should be considered for effective emergency preparedness planning. Among the most common are natural disasters such as earthquakes, hurricanes, tornadoes, and floods; mass food poisoning; industrial accidents involving explosion or environmental release of toxic chemicals; transportation accidents involving crashes of trains, planes, or automobiles with resulting mass casualties; civil disturbances; building fires; extensive or prolonged utility failure; collapse of buildings or other occupied structures; and toxic smogs in urban areas. Arson attempts and bomb threats have been made on health care facilities and should, therefore, be considered. Potential admission to the facility of high-profile persons should be addressed. Although a high-profile admission does not involve mass casualties or the potential for mass casualties, the degree of disruption of normal routine will be sufficient to qualify it as a disasterlike situation.

Disaster plans should reflect a facility's location from potential internal and external disasters. As an example, areas subject to frequent wildland fires should invoke countermeasures for smoke management and air quality maintenance. (HES)

A.3.3.46 Double-Insulated Appliances. Double-insulated appliances can be identified by a symbol consisting of a square within a square or wording such as "double-insulated" marked on the appliance. Appliance packaging and documents can also provide identification. Although double-insulated appliances do not require a third wire or pin, some double-insulated appliances have a third conductor or pin solely for purposes of electromagnetic compatibility (EMC). (MED)

N A.3.3.48 Electrical Maintenance Program (EMP). Electrical maintenance relies on knowing the electrical systems and equipment being maintained and on knowing the operating experience, loss exposures, potential for injury, and maintenance resources. [**70B,** 2023] (ELS)

A.3.3.54 Essential Electrical System. The essential electrical system can be comprised of three branches: life safety branch, critical branch, and equipment branch. (ELS)

A.3.3.58 Facility Fire Plan. This plan can be either a standalone plan or be a part of the emergency operations plan. (FUN)

A.3.3.61 FGI Guidelines. When the phrase "the applicable volume of FGI Guidelines" is used within this code, it is meant to allow users to select the FGI Guidelines that are applicable to their facility. (FUN)

A.3.3.62 Flammable. Flammables can be solids, liquids, or gases exhibiting these qualities. Many substances that are nonflammable in air become flammable if the oxygen content of the gaseous medium is increased above 0.235 ATA. (FUN)

A.3.3.65 Flash Point. Note that the flash point temperature is heavily dependent on the test used to determine it. (FUN)

A.3.3.67 Flowmeter. A pressure compensated flowmeter should be used to indicate an accurate flow of gas whether the gas is discharged into ambient pressure or into a system at nonambient pressure. (MED)

A.3.3.68 Frequency. Formerly, the unit of frequency was cycles per second, a terminology no longer preferred. The waveform can consist of components having many different frequencies, in which case it is called a complex or nonsinusoidal waveform. (MED)

A.3.3.69 Fume Hood. Laboratory fume hoods prevent toxic, flammable, or noxious vapors from entering the laboratory; present a physical barrier from chemical reactions; and serve to contain accidental spills.

This definition does not include canopy hoods or recirculation laminar-flow biological-safety cabinets that are not designed for use with flammable materials. (ELS)

A.3.3.70 General Anesthesia and Levels of Sedation/Analgesia. It should be noted that these are not static conditions. Minimal sedation can easily become moderate sedation, and moderate sedation can progress to deep sedation or general anesthesia.

Δ A.3.3.71 Ground-Fault Circuit Interrupter (GFCI). See UL 943, *Standard for Ground-Fault Circuit Interrupters,* for further information. Class A ground-fault circuit interrupters trip when the ground-fault current is 6 mA or higher and do not trip when the ground-fault current is less than 4 mA. [**70,** 2023] (ELS)

A.3.3.73 Grounding System. It coordinates with, but can be locally more extensive than, the grounding system described in Article 250 of *NFPA 70.* (ELS)

A.3.3.75 Health Care Facilities. Health care facilities include, but are not limited to, hospitals, nursing homes, limited care facilities, clinics, medical and dental offices, and ambulatory health care centers, whether permanent or movable. This definition applies to normal, regular operations and does not pertain to facilities during declared local or national disasters. A health care facility is not a type of occupancy classification as defined by NFPA *101.* Therefore, the term *health care facility* should not be confused with the term *health care occupancy.* All health care occupancies (and ambulatory health care occupancies) are considered health care facilities; however, not all health care facilities are considered health care occupancies, as health care facilities also include ambulatory health care occupancies and business occupancies. (FUN)

A.3.3.76 Health Care Facility's Governing Body. This definition excludes political governmental agencies, such as authorities having jurisdiction, that exercise local, regional, or national legal jurisdiction over the design, construction, inspection, and operation of a particular health care facility. (FUN)

A.3.3.77 Health Care Microgrid. The health care microgrid can connect and disconnect from the utility to enable it to operate in both grid-connected or island mode. (ELS)

A.3.3.79 Home Care. For the purposes of this definition, *home care* should not include commercially operated facilities housing of four or more occupants not related by blood or marriage receiving personal care or medical services.

Facilities, regardless of occupancy classification, that provide or facilitate the provision of personal care or medical services to four or more persons should not be classified as home care and should be subject to the applicable provisions of this standard. An example would be a residential board and care occupancy or an apartment building with an oxygen storage room. (FUN)

A.3.3.83 Hyperbaric Operations. Such procedures include but are not limited to (a) therapy inside a hyperbaric chamber, (b) changing clothes, (c) vital signs assessments, (d) noninvasive transcutaneous oxygen monitoring, (e) clinical and medical assessments, and (f) minor dressing changes. Debridement or other surgical procedures, application of casting material, application of skin substitutes, and application of bioengineered grafts are not recommended in the chamber room. (HYP)

A.3.3.88 Impedance. The circuit element can consist of any combination of resistance, capacitance, or inductance. (MED)

A.3.3.91 Instrument Air. Instrument air is intended for the powering of medical devices unrelated to human respiration (e.g., to remove excess moisture from instruments before further processing, or to operate medical–surgical tools, air-driven booms, pendants, or similar applications). (PIP)

A.3.3.93 Intrinsically Safe. "Abnormal conditions" can include accidental damage to any part of the equipment or wiring, damage to insulation or other failure of electrical components, application of overvoltage, adjustment and maintenance operations, and other similar conditions. (HYP)

A.3.3.96 Isolated Power System (IPS). See *NFPA 70.* (ELS)

A.3.3.98 Laboratory. These laboratories are not intended to include isolated frozen section laboratories; areas in which oxygen is administered; blood donor rooms in which flammable, combustible, or otherwise hazardous materials normally used in laboratory procedures are not present; and clinical service areas not using hazardous materials. (FUN)

A.3.3.101 Limited-Combustible (Material). Material subject to increase in combustibility or flame spread index beyond the limits herein established through the effects of age, moisture, or other atmospheric condition is considered combustible.

See NFPA 259 and NFPA 220. (FUN)

A.3.3.103 Liquid. When not otherwise identified, the term *liquid* includes both flammable and combustible liquids. *(See also B.11.1.1.)* (FUN)

A.3.3.104 Local Signal. Examples would include a gauge, a flag, a light, or some other possible manifestation that allows a maintenance person to stand at the equipment and know what conditions are present (e.g., which header of cylinders is in service). The elements to be displayed are typically those that will also be monitored at the master alarm, but the local signal is visible at the equipment rather than remotely. (PIP)

A.3.3.107 Manufactured Assembly. Examples are headwalls, columns, ceiling columns, ceiling-hung pendants, movable track systems, and so on. (PIP)

A.3.3.110 Medical Air. Air supplied from on-site compressors and associated air treatment systems (as opposed to medical air USP supplied in cylinders) that complies with the specified limits is considered medical air. Hydrocarbon carryover from the compressor into the pipeline distribution system could be detrimental to the safety of the end user and to the integrity of the piping system. Mixing of air and oxygen is a common clinical practice, and the hazards of fire are increased if the air is thus contaminated. Compliance with these limits is thus considered important to fire and patient safety. The quality of local ambient air should be determined prior to its selection for compressors and air treatment equipment. (PIP)

A.3.3.114 Medical Office. Examples include a dental office/clinic, a medical office/clinic, an immediate care facility, and a podiatry office. (FUN)

A.3.3.130 Nonflammable Medical Gas System. See Chapter 5. (PIP)

A.3.3.134 Oxidizing Gas. Oxygen and nitrous oxide are examples of oxidizing gases. There are many others, including halogens. (HYP)

A.3.3.135 Oxygen. Oxygen's outstanding property is its ability to sustain life and to support combustion. Although oxygen is nonflammable, materials that burn in air will burn much more vigorously and create higher temperatures in oxygen or in oxygen-enriched atmospheres. (MED)

A.3.3.135.2 Liquid Oxygen. If spilled, the liquid can cause frostbite on contact with skin. (MED)

A.3.3.137 Oxygen Delivery Equipment. If an enclosure such as a mask, hood, incubator, canopy, or tent is used to contain the oxygen-enriched atmosphere, that enclosure is considered to be oxygen-delivery equipment. (MED)

A.3.3.138 Oxygen Hood. For additional information, see A.3.3.12.2 and Figure A.3.3.12.2. (HYP)

A.3.3.140 Oxygen Toxicity (Hyperbaric). Under the pressures and times of exposure normally encountered in hyperbaric treatments, toxicity is a direct function of concentration and time of exposure. (HYP)

A.3.3.145 Patient Care Space. Business offices, corridors, lounges, day rooms, dining rooms, or similar areas typically are not classified as patient care spaces. (FUN)

A.3.3.148 Patient Lead. A patient lead can be a surface contact (e.g., an ECG electrode), an invasive connection (e.g., implanted wire or catheter), or an incidental long-term connection (e.g., conductive tubing).

It is not intended to include adventitious or casual contacts, such as a push button, bed surface, lamp, hand-held appliance, and so forth.

(Also see 3.3.95, Isolated Patient Lead.) (MED)

A.3.3.156.5 Operating Pressure. The operating pressure for patient medical gases is typically 345 kPA to 380 kPa (50 psig to 55 psig). The operating pressure for medical support gases is typically 345 kPa to 1275 kPA (160 psig to 185 psig). (PIP)

A.3.3.156.6 Partial Pressure. The pressure contributed by other gases in the mixture is ignored. For example, oxygen is one of the constituents of air; the partial pressure of oxygen in standard air, at a standard air pressure of 14.7 psia, is 3.06 psia or 0.208 ATA or 158 mm Hg. (HYP)

A.3.3.157 Pressure-Reducing Regulator. In hospitals, the term *regulator* is frequently used to describe a regulator that incorporates a flow-measuring device. (MED)

A.3.3.159 Producer. Examples of these producers include vacuum pumps, fans, blowers, and venturis. (PIP)

A.3.3.161 psig. Under standard conditions, 0 psig is equivalent to 14.7 psia. (HYP)

N **A.3.3.164 Receptacle.** A duplex receptacle is an example of a multiple receptacle that has two receptacles on the same yoke or strap. [**70,** 2023] (ELS)

A.3.3.167 Remote. A gas storage supply system can be remote from the single treatment facility, but all use points must be contiguous within the facility. (PIP)

A.3.3.176 Single Treatment Facility. The definition of single treatment facility was established to take into consideration principally single-level installations or those of a practice that could be two-level, but are reached by open stairs within the confines of the single treatment facility. *(See Figure A.3.3.176.)* (PIP)

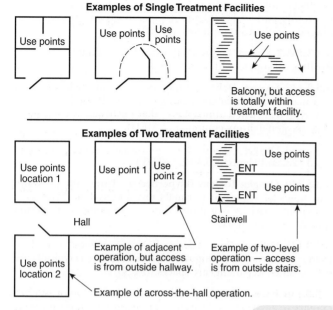

FIGURE A.3.3.176   Examples of Treatment Facilities.

A.3.3.177 Site of Intentional Expulsion. This definition addresses the site of intended expulsion. Actual expulsion can occur at other sites remote from the intended site due to disconnections, leaks, or rupture of gas conduits and connections. Vigilance on the part of the patient care team is essential to ensure system integrity.

For example, for a patient receiving oxygen via a nasal cannula or face mask, the site of expulsion normally surrounds the mask or cannula; for a patient receiving oxygen while enclosed in a canopy or incubator, the site of intentional expulsion normally surrounds the openings to the canopy or incubator; for a patient receiving oxygen while on a ventilator, the site of intentional expulsion normally surrounds the venting port on the ventilator. (MED)

A.3.3.184 Surface-Mounted Medical Gas Rail Systems. It is the intent that surface-mounted medical gas rail systems would be permitted in individual patient rooms but would not be permitted to go directly through room walls to adjacent patient rooms. However, it is the intent to permit surface-mounted medical gas rails to be used in a given Category 1 space where there can be a partition separating certain patient care functions, essentially leaving the system within the given Category 1 space. As an example, two adjacent patient rooms outside of a Category 1 space care unit would not be permitted to have a surface-mounted medical gas rail interconnect between the two rooms through the wall. However, in a nursery where there might be one or two segregated areas for isolation, a medical gas rail system supplying more than one isolation room, but within the nursery area, would be permitted to be interconnected with the nursery system. (PIP)

A.3.3.189.1 Endotracheal Tube. An endotracheal tube can be equipped with an inflatable cuff. (MED)

A.3.3.195 Wet Procedure Locations. Routine housekeeping procedures and incidental spillage of liquids do not define a wet procedure location. (FUN)

A.4.1 Four levels of systems categories are defined in this code, based on the risks to patients and caregivers in the facilities. The categories are as follows:

(1) Category 1: Systems are expected to work or be available at all times to support patient needs.
(2) Category 2: Systems are expected to provide a high level of reliability; however, limited short durations of equipment downtime can be tolerated without significant impact on patient care. Category 2 systems support patient needs but are not critical for life support.
(3) Category 3: Normal building system reliabilities are expected. Such systems support patient needs, but failure of such equipment would not immediately affect patient care. Such equipment is not critical for life support.
(4) Category 4: Such systems have no impact on patient care and would not be noticeable to patients in the event of failure.

The category definitions apply to equipment operations and are not intended to consider intervention by caregivers or others. Potential examples of areas/systems and their categories of risk follow. A risk assessment should be conducted to evaluate the risk to the patients, staff, and visitors.

(1) Ambulatory surgical center, two patients with full OR services, Category 1
(2) Reconstructive surgeon's office with general anesthesia, Category 1
(3) Procedural sedation site for outpatient services, Category 2
(4) Cooling Towers in Houston, TX, Category 2
(5) Cooling Towers in Seattle, WA, Category 3
(6) Dental office, no general anesthesia, Category 3
(7) Typical doctor's office/exam room, Category 4
(8) Lawn sprinkler system, Category 4

A.4.1.1 Major injury can include the following:

(1) Any amputation
(2) Loss of the sight of an eye (whether temporary or permanent)
(3) Chemical or hot metal burn to the eye or any penetrating injury to the eye
(4) Any injury that results in electric shock and electric burns leading to unconsciousness and that requires resuscitation or admittance to a hospital for 24 hours or more
(5) Any other injury leading to hypothermia, heat induced illness, or unconsciousness requiring resuscitation or admittance to a hospital for 24 hours or more
(6) Loss of consciousness caused by asphyxia or lack of oxygen or exposure to a biological agent or harmful substance
(7) Absorption of any substance by inhalation, skin, or ingestion causing loss of consciousness or acute illness requiring medical treatment
(8) Acute illness requiring medical treatment where there is reason to believe the exposure was to biological agents, its toxins, or infected materials

A.4.1.2 A minor injury means *not serious* or *involving risk of life.*

A.4.1.5 In some situations, it might be desirable to design to a higher risk category. For example, it might only be required to design a system to a Category 4 but it is permissible to design to a Category 1, Category 2, or Category 3. The converse is not allowed. For example, a required Category 1 system must be designed to a Category 1 and cannot be designed to a Category 2, Category 3, or Category 4.

A.4.2 Risk assessment should follow procedures such as those outlined in ISO/IEC 31010, *Risk Management — Risk Assessment Techniques*; NFPA 551; SEMI S10-0307E, *Safety Guideline for Risk Assessment and Risk Evaluation Process*; SFPE's *Engineering Guide to Fire Risk Assessment*; or other formal process. The results of the assessment procedure should be documented and records retained. Figure A.4.2 is a sample risk assessment model that can be used to evaluate the categories.

A.4.2.2 Classification of risk categories requires a collaborative effort between the health care facility's governing body and the authority having jurisdiction.

A.4.4.1 The provisions of 4.4.1 do not require inherently noncombustible materials to be tested in order to be classified as noncombustible materials.

A.4.4.2 Material subject to increase in combustibility or flame spread index beyond the limits herein established through the effects of age, moisture, or other atmospheric condition is considered combustible. *(See NFPA 259 and NFPA 220.)* [**5000**:A.7.1.4.2]

Δ **A.5.1.1** Section 5.1 covers Category 1 piped gas and vacuum systems; Section 5.2 covers Category 2 piped gas and vacuum systems; and Section 5.3 covers Category 3 piped gas and vacuum systems.

The health care facility's governing body should designate a category in accordance with Chapter 4 for each patient care space in the facility. This process should include areas being used for medical support (e.g., decontamination or sterilization, lab work, post mortem) that are not strictly patient care spaces themselves (i.e., there are no patients there) but share utilities such as medical gases or medical support gases with such spaces. Because it is not realistic to create separate supply systems for each category, it is desirable that one supply system be used for spaces of all categories to supply medical gases, medical support gases, and vacuums to terminals.

The principle is set out at the start of the requirements for each category in Chapter 5 *(see 5.1.1, 5.2.1, and 5.3.1)* that a higher category source and piping system is permitted to supply terminals in any lower Category space; a Category 1 system can supply terminals in Category 2 and Category 3 spaces, but a Category 2 system cannot supply terminals in a Category 1 space.

N **A.5.1.1.1** Category 1 piped gas or piped vacuum system requirements should be applied where any of the following criteria is met:

(1) General anesthesia, as defined in 3.3.70.1, or deep sedation, as defined in 3.3.70.2, is performed.
(2) The loss of the piped gas or piped vacuum systems is likely to cause major injury or death of patients, staff, or visitors.

A.5.1.1.2 These requirements do not restrict the distribution of other inert gases through piping systems.

A.5.1.1.3 The intent is that an existing system built in accordance with an earlier edition of this code is permitted to be continued in use as long as no element is disturbed. For this purpose, "disturbed" includes replacing or changing of elements (except simple like-for-like exchange as part of a

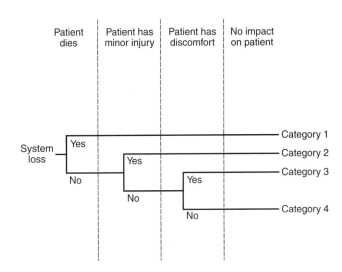

FIGURE A.4.2   Sample Risk Assessment.

repair or normal maintenance), portions added to or removed from the system in a manner that requires system shutdown, and opening of any part of the system to the atmosphere.

When any element(s) of the system is disturbed, the following should occur:

(1) The specific element(s) that was disturbed should be brought into compliance with the most recent edition of this code.
(2) An evaluation should be conducted and documented for any portions of the system affected by the change.
(3) Through risk analysis, the responsible facility authority should document any elements where a distinct hazard to life is apparent or is created by the changes. These elements should then be brought into compliance with the currently adopted edition of this code. All other portions can remain undisturbed.
(4) After completion of any corrections and updates resulting from the risk analysis, and appropriate testing if required under 5.1.12, the entire system can then be considered an "existing system" for the purposes of this code.
(5) The decisions and results of the risk analysis and final testing, if required, should be made part of the permanent records of the facility for future reference.

A.5.1.3 See Figure A.5.1.3. Category 1 source drawings in this annex are representational, demonstrating a possible arrangement of components required by the text. The diagrams are not intended to imply method, materials of construction, or more than one of many possible and equally compliant arrangements. Alternative arrangements are permitted if they meet the intent of the text. Listed paragraphs might not be the only paragraphs that apply.

A.5.1.3.1.1 Regulations of the US Department of Transportation (formerly US Interstate Commerce Commission) outline specifications for transportation of explosives and dangerous articles (49 CFR 171–190). In Canada, the regulations of the Canadian Transport Commission, Union Station, Ottawa, Ontario, apply.

FIGURE A.5.1.3   Legend for Typical Category 1 Source Drawings.

A.5.1.3.1.2 CGA documents contain both mandatory and nonmandatory language. Enforceable language uses the word "shall"; nonmandatory language uses the word "should." This section indicates that this code is making reference only to the mandatory requirements in the CGA document.

A.5.1.3.2.5 Wrappers (or overpacks) are intended to provide an outer package for transport, such as a cardboard box, and typically present a significant combustible fire load. Cylinders should not be stored in health care facilities in overpacks when the overpack is made of a combustible material with a significant fire load. Valve shrink wraps used to seal valve connections, and outer netting applied to cylinders that does not cover more than 50 percent of the cylinder surface and is only intended to protect the cylinder paint coatings and side wall labels from damage, are not considered wrappers.

A.5.1.3.3 The bulk supply system should be installed on a site that has been prepared to meet the requirements of NFPA 55 or CGA G-8.1, *Standard for Nitrous Oxide Systems at Customer Sites.* A storage unit(s), reserve, pressure regulation, and a signal

actuating switch(es) are components of the supply system. Shutoff valves, piping from the site, and electric wiring from a signal switch(es) to the master signal panels are components of the piping system.

The bulk supply system is normally installed on the site by the owner of this equipment. The owner or the organization responsible for the operation and maintenance of the bulk supply system is responsible for ensuring that all components of the supply system — main supply, reserve supply, supply system signal-actuating switch(es), and delivery pressure regulation equipment — function properly before the system is put in service.

In the locating of central supply systems, consideration should be given to ensuring the resilience of the facility under reasonably anticipated adverse conditions. Examples have included the following:

(1) Flooding of systems located in basements from extraordinary weather, water main breaks, and sprinkler head failures

(2) Seismic events that rendered the supply system inoperative

(3) Degradation of the quality of air at the intake due to a nearby fire and chemical release

(4) Electrical problems, including failure of motor control centers and failure of switchgear to properly connect

Many of these risks can be ameliorated by care when siting the central supply systems and their utility connections.

A.5.1.3.3.1.1(4) Examples include the concentrator unit, the oxygen reservoir, and regulating devices.

A.5.1.3.3.1.2(5) Examples include the concentrator unit, the oxygen reservoir, and regulating devices.

A.5.1.3.3.1.3(6) This includes individual components on the air side of concentrators.

N A.5.1.3.3.1.6 See 5.1.3.3.2.5 for maximum allowable quantities in health care facilities.

A.5.1.3.3.1.10 Examples of inert gases include but are not limited to helium and nitrogen.

A.5.1.3.3.2 Electric wiring and equipment are not required to be explosionproof.

Δ A.5.1.3.3.2.2(6) The fire resistance rating for walls and floors is determined in accordance with ASTM E119, *Standard Test Methods for Fire Tests of Building Construction and Materials*, or UL 263, *Fire Tests of Building Construction and Materials*. The fire protection rating for doors is determined in accordance with NFPA 252.

A.5.1.3.3.2.2(7) Electrical devices should be physically protected, such as by use of a protective barrier around the electrical devices, or by location of the electrical device such that it will avoid causing physical damage to the cylinders or containers. For example, the device could be located at or above 1.5 m (5 ft) above finished floor or other location that will not allow the possibility of the cylinders or containers to come into contact with the electrical device as required by this section.

A.5.1.3.3.2.2(8) Examples of indirect heating include steam, hot water, and electric heating.

A.5.1.3.3.2.2(11) Chapter 6 specifies medical gas equipment that should be powered by the essential electrical systems. Electrical equipment that is not essential for the operation of the supply system can be powered by nonessential power (e.g., telemetry, site lighting).

A.5.1.3.3.2.2(14) Considerations for this access include proximity to loading docks, access to elevators, and passage of cylinders through public areas.

N A.5.1.3.3.2.5 Table 5.1.3.3.2.5 specifies the MAQs permitted within health care facilities. In accordance with Section 2.1(2), this table supersedes the MAQs and related tables in NFPA 55 for health care facilities.

N A.5.1.3.3.2.7 The documented risk assessment by the health care facility's governing body should consider clinical needs, emergency needs for proper patient care, hazards associated with storing larger quantities of gases, and any mitigation requirements for patient, personnel, and visitor safety. The risk assessment should be done for each location independently because these conditions might change due to factors including, but not limited to, the floor on which the gas is being stored and how many smoke compartments are provided in the area.

A.5.1.3.3.4.2 Exhaust fan motors, fan-coil motors, or similar small motors used for ventilation purposes are not intended to be prohibited from the storage enclosure.

A.5.1.3.5 See Figure A.5.1.3.5. A four-valve bypass arrangement is illustrated. Three-way valves are permitted in lieu of the four valves shown.

A.5.1.3.5.4 Components include, but are not limited to, containers, valves, valve seats, lubricants, fittings, gaskets, and interconnecting equipment, including hose. Easily ignitable materials should be avoided.

Compatibility involves both combustibility and ease of ignition. Materials that burn in air will burn violently in pure oxygen at normal pressure and explosively in pressurized oxygen. Also, many materials that do not burn in air will do so in pure oxygen, particularly under pressure. Metals for containers and piping have to be carefully selected, depending on service conditions. The various steels are acceptable for many applications, but some service conditions can call for other materials (usually copper or its alloys) because of their greater resistance to ignition and lower rate of combustion.

Similarly, materials that can be ignited in air have lower ignition energies in oxygen. Many such materials can be ignited by friction at a valve seat or stem packing or by adiabatic compression produced when oxygen at high pressure is rapidly introduced into a system initially at low pressure.

FIGURE A.5.1.3.5   Typical Arrangement for Line Controls at Pressure Sources.

A.5.1.3.5.5.1 The intent of 5.1.3.5.5.1 is to ensure that the pressure at the station outlet is steady and maintained safely within the limits of Table 5.1.11. Traditionally, line pressure regulators were required here as the only allowed control-of-pressure devices. Other methods of control are becoming possible (e.g., variable speed controlled on pressure). The present wording is intended to achieve the performance requirement *(see Table 5.1.11)* and to allow not only traditional pressure regulators but other control methods as well.

A.5.1.3.5.9 See Figure A.5.1.3.5.9(a) and Figure A.5.1.3.5.9(b). Connection to the gas outlet connection is illustrated. If the liquid outlet connection were used, an external vaporizer could be required.

A.5.1.3.5.9(1) The appropriate number of cylinders should be determined after consideration of delivery schedules, proximity of the facility to alternate supplies, and the emergency plan.

A.5.1.3.5.10 See Figure A.5.1.3.5.10.

A.5.1.3.5.11 See Figure A.5.1.3.5.11.

A.5.1.3.5.12 See Figure A.5.1.3.5.12.

If the relief valve on the emergency oxygen supply connection is moved downstream from the check valve in the emergency oxygen line, it should be connected to the system with a demand check fitting.

The emergency oxygen supply connection (EOSC) can be used as a part of the emergency operation plan (EOP) for an unplanned loss of oxygen supply. However, a risk assessment should be conducted by the facility to determine the contingency plan for vital life support and Category 1 space. There might need to be interim measures for dealing with the loss of oxygen (e.g., high-pressure oxygen cylinders available for back feeding Category 1 space).

A.5.1.3.5.12.2(8) Monitoring temporary supply in use is essential to patient safety. The facility's emergency operations plan (EOP) should address how the facility will monitor the temporary supply while in use. The length of time the EOSC will be in use, the availability of staff to monitor temporary supply, and the type of temporary supply should all be considered when determining the means to accomplish this item.

N **A.5.1.3.5.14** The preferred location for the auxiliary connection should consider how it will be used in event of need, including space for or access to the temporary source, access to electrical power, and alarm connections.

Similar auxiliary connections (tee, valve, and plug or cap), as illustrated in Figure A.5.1.3.5.14, might also be useful in other locations that the responsible facility authority determines appropriate for operating or supplementing their systems during maintenance, construction, or emergencies (e.g., at zone valves in high-dependency areas). They are generally superior to "backfeeding" through outlets or gauge ports, which might be the only other option.

A.5.1.3.6 Air supplied from on-site compressor and associated air treatment systems (as opposed to medical air USP supplied in cylinders) that complies with the specified limits is considered medical air. Hydrocarbon carryover from the compressor into the pipeline distribution system could be detrimental to the safety of the end user and to the integrity of the piping system. Mixing of air and oxygen is a common clinical practice, and the hazards of fire are increased if the air is contaminated.

FIGURE A.5.1.3.5.9(a) **Header for Gas in Cylinders.**

Compliance with these limits is thus considered important to fire and patient safety. The quality of local ambient air should be determined prior to its selection for compressors and air treatment equipment. See Figure A.5.1.3.6.

A.5.1.3.6.1 Supply systems for medical air using compressors draw air of the best available quality from a source of clean local ambient air; add no contaminants in the form of particulate matter, odor, or other gases; and dry, filter, regulate, and supply that air only via the medical air piping distribution system for use exclusively in the application of human respiration.

The utilization of an air treatment system is the joint responsibility of the system designer, the hospital clinical and engineering staffs, and the authority having jurisdiction. Different types of compressors have characteristics that affect the selection of the type of air treatment system. Some air treatment systems impose an additional load upon the compressors that has to be accounted for in the sizing of the system (usable capacity). The compressor duty cycle has to be chosen in accordance with the manufacturer's recommendation.

The type of air compressor and air condition at the intake will govern the type of filter provided for the air compressor supply system. All filters should be examined quarterly for the presence of liquids or excessive particulates and replaced according to the manufacturer's instructions.

FIGURE A.5.1.3.5.9(b)   Header for Cryogenic Gas in Containers.

One procedure for reaching a decision on the quality of the medical air is the following:

(1) Test at the intake and at the sample connection valve.
(2) If the two purities agree within the limits of accuracy of the test, the compressor system can be accepted.
(3) If the air is found to exceed the values for medical compressed air as defined in 5.1.3.6.1, the facility can elect to install purification apparatus for the contaminants in question.

A.5.1.3.6.2 It is the intent that the medical air piping distribution system support only the intended need for breathable air for such items as intermittent positive-pressure breathing (IPPB) and long-term respiratory assistance needs, anesthesia machines, and so forth. The system is not intended to be used to provide engineering, maintenance, and equipment needs for general hospital support use. It is the intent that the life safety nature of the medical air be protected by a system dedicated solely for its specific use.

As a compressed air supply source, a medical air compressor should not be used to supply air for other purposes, because such use could increase service interruptions, reduce service life, and introduce additional opportunities for contamination.

A.5.1.3.6.3 See Figure A.5.1.3.6.

A.5.1.3.6.3.4(A) Examples of 5.1.3.6.3.4(A)(1) are liquid ring and permanently sealed bearing compressors.

An example of 5.1.3.6.3.4(A)(2) is an extended head reciprocating compressor with an atmospheric vent between the compression chamber and the crankcase.

An example of 5.1.3.6.3.4(A)(3) is a rotating element compressor with the compression chamber being nonlubricated and separated from the lubricated gears by at least one shaft seal with an atmospheric vent on both sides. The vent on the lubricated side is provided with a gravity drain to atmosphere.

N **A.5.1.3.6.3.7(5)** The sample port allows for purging the offline air dryer prior to switching from one dryer to the other, which is a common and regularly performed maintenance task. This requirement allows maintenance personnel to purge and test the dew point prior to placing the air dryer online. This purging and testing can reduce false alarms and ensures that the proper air quality is introduced into the pipeline during this maintenance task.

A.5.1.3.6.3.9(D) A typical example of valving the receiver is shown in Figure A.5.1.3.6.3.9(D).

A.5.1.3.6.3.9(F) The two configurations are equally acceptable. The components can be arranged in either of the arrangements shown in Figure A.5.1.3.6.3.9(F).

A.5.1.3.6.3.10 The intent of 5.1.3.6.3.10 is to ensure that the pressure at the station outlet is steady and maintained safely within the limits of Table 5.1.11. Traditionally, line pressure regulators were required here as the only allowed control-of-pressure devices. Other methods of control are becoming possible (e.g., variable speed controlled on pressure). The present wording is intended to achieve the performance requirement *(see Table 5.1.11)* and to allow not only traditional pressure regulators but other control methods as well.

A.5.1.3.6.3.14(A)(1) The proportioning system might require approval from regulatory bodies that have medical device authority, such as the FDA in the United States.

A.5.1.3.6.3.14(A)(9) The proportioning system should be monitored for conditions that can affect air quality during use or in the event of failure, based on the type of proportioning system design used in the system, including monitoring for the following systems and conditions:

(1) Where proportioning systems used are configured with a primary proportioning system and a reserve medical air manifold per 5.1.3.5.10
(2) Where proportioning systems used are configured with a primary proportioning system and a reserve proportioning system
(3) Where proportioning systems used are configured with a primary proportioning system and a reserve medical air compressor per 5.1.3.5.3
(4) Alarm at a predetermined set point, before the reserve supply begins to supply the system, indicating reserve supply in use
(5) Alarm at a predetermined set point, before the reserve supply contents fall to one average day's supply, indicating reserve low

Water-in-receiver alarms are not required for a proportioning system.

The engineering controls should include, as a minimum, the following:

(1) Engineering controls should be in place when the sources of oxygen USP or nitrogen NF, or both, are the same sources as those supplying the oxygen USP or nitrogen

FIGURE A.5.1.3.5.10   Manifold for Gas Cylinders.

NF pipelines, or both, for other uses within the health care facility, and the following should apply:

(a)   In cases where a new supply system is installed, or in cases where one or more bulk supplies are used to supply the mixer, bulk systems and vaporizers should be sized for total peak demand flow, including peak demand flow to the mixer and any other areas of utilization.

(b)   Operating limits should be established, at a minimum, for the oxygen and nitrogen source pressures, both high and low, and for the medical air oxygen concentration, both high and low, based upon USP specifications. A process upset can be defined as an excursion in the process windows established for oxygen and nitrogen source pressures or medical air oxygen concentration, or both. A means to detect excursion from these process limits and power failure should be provided.

(c)   At least one dedicated valve or other control should be installed in the proportioning system and/or the line(s) between the oxygen and/or nitrogen supply system(s) and proportioning system. The purpose of the dedicated control(s) is to prevent the cross contamination of the oxygen and nitrogen lines due to product backflow as follows:

    i.   The control(s) should be separate from the valve(s) or other device(s) used to control oxygen flow and nitrogen flow in normal operation.

    ii.   The control(s) should not cycle in normal operation.

    iii.   If installed in the line(s) between the oxygen or nitrogen supply system(s), or both, and proportioning system, upon activation of the control(s), an alarm should be sent to the facility. The control(s) cannot exist exclusively via the use of check valves.

(d)   In the event of a process upset, the dedicated control(s) should either positively isolate the supply of oxygen or nitrogen, or both, from the mixer, or the dedicated control(s) should reduce the mixer pressure to less than half of the minimum final line pressure values, each, for the oxygen and nitrogen lines. In the event of a process upset, the control(s) should operate. Manual reset should be required to restart the proportioning system.

FIGURE A.5.1.3.5.11   Typical Source of Supply for Cryogenic Gas in Containers.

FIGURE A.5.1.3.5.12   Emergency Oxygen Supply Connection.

A.5.1.3.6.3.14(C)(9) The proportioning system should be monitored for conditions that can affect air quality during use or in the event of failure, based on the type of proportioning system design used in the system, including the following situations:

(1) Where proportioning systems that are configured with a primary proportioning system and a reserve medical air manifold per 5.1.3.5.10 are used

(2) Where proportioning systems that are configured with a primary proportioning system and a reserve proportioning system are used

(3) Where proportioning systems that are configured with a primary proportioning system and a reserve medical air compressor per 5.1.3.5.10 are used

(4) When proportioning systems are configured to alarm at a predetermined set point before the reserve supply begins to supply the system, indicating reserve supply in use

(5) When proportioning systems are configured to alarm at a predetermined set point before the reserve supply contents fall to one average day's supply, indicating reserve low

Water-in-receiver alarms are not required for proportioning systems.

A.5.1.3.7 See Figure A.5.1.3.7.

A.5.1.3.8 A functioning WAGD system allows the facility to comply with occupational safety requirements by preventing the accumulation of waste anesthetic gases in the work environment.

WAGD using an HVAC (heating, ventilation, and air-conditioning) system are not within the scope of Chapter 5.

Flammable and nonflammable gases are known to be incompatible with some seals and piping used in medical–surgical vacuum systems. If WAGD is to be included as part of the medical–surgical vacuum system, it should be recognized that this activity might cause deterioration of the vacuum system. The station inlet performance tests outlined in 5.1.12.4.10 are extremely important in maintaining the integrity of the medical–surgical vacuum system, and they should be made at more frequent intervals if WAGD is included in the vacuum system.

A.5.1.3.8.1 Interfaces are provided with overpressure, underpressure, overflow, and underflow compensation to ensure the breathing circuit is isolated from the WAGD system.

A.5.1.3.9 See Figure A.5.1.3.9(a), Figure A.5.1.3.9(b), and Figure A.5.1.3.9(c).

A.5.1.3.9.1 See Figure A.5.1.3.9.1.

A.5.1.3.9.2(2) Oxygen concentrators have inherent risks because they might not be able to instantaneously begin producing oxygen of the necessary concentration and quantity from a "cold start." For these reasons, cylinder header(s) are often preferable as one or more of the three sources. The cylinders will supply the system while the concentrator pressurizes and purges itself to the desired concentration of oxygen. Cylinders are also independent of electricity and can provide a supply of oxygen in the event of power interruption.

A.5.1.3.9.2(5) The method used elsewhere in this document to provide these characteristics will be found in the final line regulator requirements under 5.1.3.5.5. This method would be suitable for oxygen supply systems using concentrator(s) as well. However, the pressure differential between the output of the concentrator and the system line pressure is often very small, making the use of regulators problematic. In this case, alternate control arrangements (e.g., pressure control through variable speed drives) might be more effective.

△ **A.5.1.3.10** Figure A.5.1.3.10(a) illustrates distances between bulk oxygen systems and exposures for cryogenic fluid central

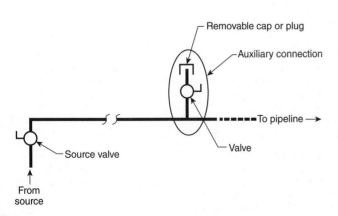

N **FIGURE A.5.1.3.5.14   Typical Configuration of an Auxiliary Connection.**

FIGURE A.5.1.3.6   Elements of a Typical Duplex Medical Air Compressor Source System (Category 1 Gas Systems).

supply oxygen systems. Figure A.5.1.3.10(b) illustrates typical sources of supply for cryogenic gas in bulk.

A.5.1.3.10.1.1 The cryogenic fluid central supply system should be installed on a site that has been prepared to meet the requirements of NFPA 55. A storage unit(s), reserve, pressure regulation, and signal actuating switch(es) are components of the supply system. Shutoff valves, piping from the site, and electric wiring from a signal switch(es) to the master signal panels are components of the piping system. [**55:**A.17.1.1]

The cryogenic fluid central supply system is normally installed on the site by the owner of the equipment. The owner

or the organization responsible for the operation and maintenance of the bulk supply system is responsible for ensuring that all components of the supply system — main supply, reserve supply, supply system signal-actuating switch(es), and delivery pressure regulation equipment — function properly before the system is put in service. [**55:**A.17.1.1]

A.5.1.3.10.8.3 For example, 2400 psi (16,550 kPa) rated cylinders are not connected to the same manifold as 2015 psi (13,890 kPa) rated cylinders unless all cylinders, including the 2400 psi (16,550 kPa) cylinders, are filled no greater than 2015 psi (13,890 kPa). [**55:**A.17.8.3]

FIGURE A.5.1.3.6.3.9(D) Receiver Valving Arrangement.

A.5.1.3.10.11.4(A) A typical alternate material is stainless steel. [**55:**A.17.11.4.1]

A.5.1.3.10.12 The local signal arose from the simple need of a maintenance person to know what is going on with any given piece of source equipment. Note that it is not an alarm in the sense of a local or master alarm. It is simply an indicator, which might be a gauge, a flag, a light, or some other possible manifestation that allows a maintenance person to stand at the equipment and know what conditions are present (e.g., which header of cylinders is in service). The elements to be displayed are typically those that will also be monitored at the master alarm, but the local signal is visible at the equipment rather than remotely. [**55:**A.17.12]

A.5.1.4 See Figure A.5.1.4.

Area alarms are required in critical care locations (e.g., intensive care units, coronary care units, angiography laboratories, cardiac catheterization laboratories, post-anesthesia recovery rooms, and emergency rooms) and anesthetizing locations (e.g., operating rooms and delivery rooms). Refer to definitions for these areas.

A.5.1.4.3 The presence of a main line shutoff valve is optional where the source valve can equally or more effectively perform the same function. An example is a case where the source is within the building or just on the outside of the building and,

FIGURE A.5.1.3.6.3.9(F) Alternate Valving Sequences for Line Controls in Medical Air.

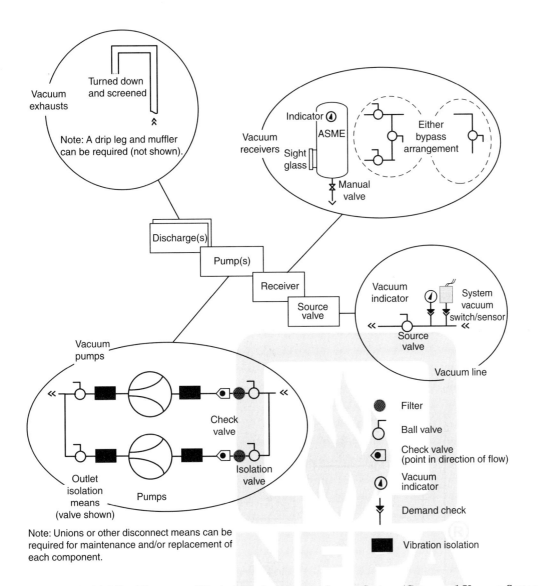

FIGURE A.5.1.3.7   Elements of Typical Duplex Vacuum Source System (Category 1 Vacuum Systems).

therefore, there would be no great distance separating the two valves. A source that was physically separate from the building would require both valves to ensure the intervening piping could be controlled.

A.5.1.4.6.1(2) A "standing position" is meant to refer to an average-height individual standing with their feet on the floor in front of the zone valve.

A.5.1.4.6.1(3) Wheeled equipment, such as what is permitted to be located in a corridor in accordance with 18.2.3.4 and 19.2.3.4 of NFPA *101*, does not render zone valves inaccessible if located in front of the zone valve. Those sections permit wheeled equipment and emergency equipment in use, medical emergency equipment not in use, and patient lift and transport equipment. The zone valve needs to remain visible.

N **A.5.1.4.6.2** Category 1 spaces include, but are not limited to, ICUs, NICUs, ERs, and PACUs. Zone valves installed in these Category 1 spaces might control multiple rooms within the area or zone. For example, an ICU zone valve for oxygen might control ICU Rooms 1–10.

Category 1 spaces that also administer general anesthesia, deep sedation, or moderate sedation to patients include, but are not limited to, ORs, DRs, and trauma rooms. Zone valves are required to be installed outside of each room in these Category 1 spaces. For example, an OR zone valve for oxygen might control OR 1 only, and not multiple OR rooms.

A.5.1.5 Station outlets and inlets should be located at an appropriate height above the floor to prevent physical damage to equipment attached to the outlet. The minimum number of station outlets and inlets for each system that is installed should be provided per the applicable volume of FGI guidelines or other federal, state, or local codes.

A.5.1.6 Manufactured assembly examples include headwalls, columns, ceiling columns, ceiling-hung pendants, movable track systems, and so forth. See Figure A.5.1.6.

Note: Drawing is illustrative, alternative arrangements might be acceptable.

FIGURE A.5.1.3.9(a)   Elements of an Oxygen Concentrator Central Supply Source.

Note: In this example, Source A will act as the primary source, and B will act as the reserve.

Δ FIGURE A.5.1.3.9(b)   Elements of an Oxygen Concentrator Central Supply Source with Two Sources.

A.5.1.7 It is the intent that surface-mounted medical gas rail systems would be permitted in individual patient rooms but would not be permitted to go directly through room walls to adjacent patient rooms. However, it is the intent to permit surface-mounted medical gas rails to be used in a given Category 1 space where there can be a partition separating certain patient care functions, essentially leaving the system within the given Category 1 space. As an example, two adjacent patient rooms outside of a Category 1 space care unit would not be permitted to have a surface-mounted medical gas rail interconnect between the two rooms through the wall. However, in a nursery where there might be one or two segregated areas for

isolation, a medical gas rail system supplying more than one isolation room, but within the nursery area, would be permitted to be interconnected with the nursery system.

A.5.1.8.1.3 This gauge would therefore be suitable for any operating pressure of 690 kPa to 1380 kPa (100 psig to 200 psig).

A.5.1.9.4 See Table A.5.1.9.4.

A.5.1.9.4(2) Examples of Category 1 space include post-anesthesia recovery, intensive care units, and emergency departments.

FIGURE A.5.1.3.9(c)   One Example of an Oxygen Concentrator Central Supply Source in Practice.

Note: Alternative arrangement might be acceptable

FIGURE A.5.1.3.9.1   Elements of an Oxygen Concentrator Supply Source.

A.5.1.9.4.1 Area alarm panels should be placed in a location that will most closely fulfill the following criteria (recognizing that no existing location might fulfill all criteria):

(1) Near or within the location where the staff will most often be present (e.g., a staff base, a nurses' station)

(2) Where the audible alert will best carry throughout the unit being surveilled

(3) Where the panel is visible from the largest number of rooms, beds, or stations within the zone

(4) Where visualization of the panel will not be blocked (e.g., by cabinet doors, carts, room doors, curtains, supplies)

(5) At a height above the floor at which the panel can be comfortably viewed and at which the mute button can be conveniently accessed

A.5.1.9.4.4 See Figure A.5.1.4.

A.5.1.9.4.4(1) This signal is intended to provide immediate warning for loss of, or increase in, system pressure for each individual vital life support and Category 1 space.

A.5.1.9.4.4(2) This signal is intended to provide immediate warning for loss of, or increase in, system pressure for all anesthetizing locations supplied from a single branch line — not for each individual operating or delivery room.

A.5.1.9.5 Activation of any of the warning signals should immediately be reported to the department of the facility responsible for the medical gas piping system involved. If the medical gas is supplied from a bulk supply system, the owner or the organization responsible for the operation and maintenance of that system, usually the supplier, should also be notified. As much detail as possible should be provided. See Table A.5.1.9.5.

A.5.1.10.1.4 Operation of piped medical gas systems at gauge pressures in excess of 1275 kPa (185 psi) involves certain restrictions because of the limitations in materials.

A.5.1.10.1.4(2) The listing should include a specific system geometry representative of medical gas systems.

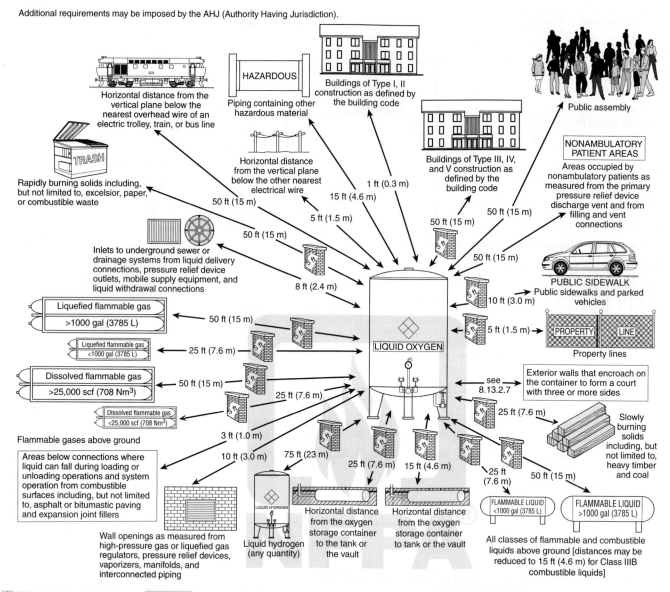

△ **FIGURE A.5.1.3.10(a)** **Distances Between Bulk Oxygen Systems and Exposures. [55:Figure A.9.3.2]**

A.5.1.10.2.3.2 Such dual labeling should include the source, piping, valves, and alarms.

A.5.1.10.3.1 A distinction is made between deep-socket solder-joint fittings (ASME B16.22, *Wrought Copper and Copper Alloy Solder-Joint Pressure Fittings*) and those having shallow sockets for brazing (ANSI/ASME B16.50, *Wrought Copper and Copper Alloy Braze-Joint Pressure Fittings*). The use of shallow-socket brazing fittings improves the quality of the brazement without decreasing its strength, particularly in larger sizes, which are difficult to heat. See Table A.5.1.10.3.1 for socket depths conforming to ANSI/ASME B16.50. The installer can use ANSI/ASME B16.50 fittings (if available) or have the sockets on ASME B16.22 fittings cut down to ANSI/ASME B16.50 depths. Where shallow-socket fittings are used for the medical gas piping, care should be taken to avoid their use in other piping systems where joints could be soldered instead of brazed.

A.5.1.10.4.5 The intent is to provide an oxygen-free atmosphere within the tubing and to prevent the formation of copper oxide scale during brazing. This is accomplished by filling the piping with a low-volume flow of low-pressure inert gas.

A.5.1.10.4.5.12 This is to ensure a quality joint and to prevent the formation of copper oxide on the inside and outside surfaces of the joint.

A.5.1.10.5.1.5 Gas mixtures are commonly used in GTAW autogenous fusion welding. The identification of a gas mixture as "75He 25Ar" is a common industry term to define a commercially available grade from gas suppliers. If test welding results lead to questions about the mixture percentage or gas quality, another bottle should be substituted and test welds performed.

A.5.1.10.8(3) It is intended that the "recommended for oxygen service" apply to both polytetrafluoroethylene tape as well as the "other thread sealant."

FIGURE A.5.1.3.10(b) **Typical Source of Supply for Cryogenic Gas in Bulk.**

N A.5.1.10.9.2 Examples of fittings with internal seals include, but are not limited to, dielectric fittings and zero clearance fittings for facilitating the connection of source equipment.

A.5.1.10.11.4.4 CMT is coated with a nonmetallic jacket with an O.D. equal to a larger copper tube size than CMT. The CMT manufacturer's installation instructions should identify acceptable solutions.

A.5.1.11 It is recommended that the facility's normal operating pressure of nitrous oxide be initially set and continually maintained at least 34.5 kPag (5 psig) below the normal operating pressures of the oxygen and medical air.

Piping systems that are connected through blending devices are in effect cross-connected through the device. In the rare event of a failure of the safeties inside the equipment, the possibility of having the gases flow across the device exists. When the device is an anesthesia machine, and one of the gases is nitrous oxide, a pressure in the nitrous oxide pipeline greater than the pressure in the medical air or oxygen system opens the possibility of nitrous oxide flowing into the other pipelines. A patient could then receive a lethal quantity of nitrous oxide from a labeled and indexed medical air or oxygen outlet. Adjusting the pressure as recommended can reduce the likelihood of the causative equipment failure and

Note: Single service valves are shown, but multiple zones can branch off a single service valve.

FIGURE A.5.1.4 **Arrangement of Pipeline Components.**

Notes:

1. Drawing is representational, demonstrating a possible arrangement of components required by the text. The diagram is not intended to imply a method, materials of construction, or more than one of many possible and equally compliant arrangements. Alternative arrangements are permitted if they meet the intent of the text.

2. Area alarms are required in critical care locations (examples might include intensive care units, coronary care units, angiography laboratories, cardiac catheterization laboratories, post-anesthesia recovery rooms, and emergency rooms) and anesthetizing locations (examples might include operating rooms and delivery rooms). Refer to definitions for these areas.

3. Locations for switches/sensors are not affected by the presence of service or in-line valves.

also reduce the severity of the problem in the event it does occur.

A.5.1.11.2.3 It is not intended that all valves on a medical–surgical vacuum system be labeled as both medical–surgical vacuum and WAGD. Rather, any valve when closed or opened that would affect the medical–surgical vacuum and WAGD should be labeled to indicate that it controls both of those systems. Valves that would cause no change in the WAGD system should be labeled to indicate medical–surgical vacuum only.

A.5.1.11.2.8 It is not intended that every room be listed on the label, but an area that is easily identifiable by staff needs to be indicated. This can be accomplished with text or by graphical means such as a map or color coding. The label should be

permanently affixed outside and near valve box. The label should not be affixed to a removable cover.

A.5.1.11.4.2 It is not intended that every room be listed on the label, but an area that is easily identifiable by staff needs to be indicated. This can be accomplished with text or by graphical means such as a map or color coding.

A.5.1.12 All testing should be completed before putting a new piping system, or an addition to an existing system, into service. Test procedures and the results of all tests should be made part of the permanent records of the facility of which the piping system forms a part. They should show the room and area designations, dates of the tests, and name(s) of the person(s) conducting the tests.

FIGURE A.5.1.6   Terminals in Manufactured Assemblies.

Δ **Table A.5.1.9.4 Requirements for Category 1 Area Alarms**

Alarm Condition	Requirement Location
High line pressure (for each gas piped to the area)	5.1.9.4 5.1.9.4.1 5.1.9.4.2 5.1.9.4.4
Low line pressure (for each gas piped to the area)	5.1.9.4 5.1.9.4.1 5.1.9.4.2 5.1.9.4.4
Low medical–surgical vacuum (if piped to the area)	5.1.9.4 5.1.9.4.1 5.1.9.4.3 5.1.9.4.4
Low WAGD vacuum (if piped to the area)	5.1.9.4 5.1.9.4.1 5.1.9.4.3 5.1.9.4.4

N **A.5.1.12.1.3** Distribution piping and new gas source examples include, but are not limited to, cryogenic fluid central supply systems, manifolds, compressors, dryers, and alarms.

N **A.5.1.12.1.11** Due to the nature of the initial pressure testing requirements, it is unsafe to have a new piping system connected to an existing piping system with only a shutoff valve between them. The initial test pressure of 1034 kPa (150 psig) is much higher than many of the standard operating pressures of positive pressure systems. Back-feeding into the existing systems from the new system has occurred during testing due to the differential pressures and has caused valves to leak by the valve seals.

N **A.5.1.12.2.2** Examples of system components addressed by 5.1.12.2.2 include, but are not limited to, pressure/vacuum alarm devices, pressure/vacuum indicators, pressure relief valves, manifolds, source equipment, manufactured assemblies, and manufactured rough-in assemblies.

N **A.5.1.12.2.3.2(3)** Examples of components of the distribution piping system that would be damaged by the test pressure required by 5.1.12.2.3.2 include, but are not limited to, pressure/vacuum alarm devices, pressure/vacuum indicators, line pressure relief valves, and station outlet/inlet primary valves or assemblies.

A.5.1.12.2.3.5 Ammonia is known to cause stress cracking in copper and its alloys.

A.5.1.12.2.6.1 Examples of distribution system components include, but are not limited to, pressure alarm devices, pressure indicators, line pressure relief valves, manufactures assemblies, and hose.

Δ **A.5.1.12.2.6.5** The effect of temperature changes on the pressure of a confined gas is based on the Ideal Gas Law. The final absolute pressure (P2a) equals the initial absolute pressure (P1a) times the final absolute temperature (T2a), divided by the initial absolute temperature (T1a). The relationship is the same for nitrogen, nitrous oxide, oxygen, and compressed air.

Absolute pressure is the gauge pressure reading plus the absolute atmospheric pressure. See Table A.5.1.12.2.6.5(b) for the absolute atmospheric pressures for elevations at and above sea level.

Absolute temperature K (°R) is the temperature gauge reading °C (°F) plus the absolute zero temperature 273°C (460°F).

Examples of pressure test data at sea level in SI and IP units follow.

The initial test pressure is 415 kPag (60 psig) at 27°C (80°F). A temperature decrease to 18°C (65°F) will cause the test pressure to drop to 400 kPag (57.9 psig).

$P1a = 415 + 101 = 516$ kPa	$P1a = 60 + 14.7 = 74.7$ psia
$T1a = 27 + 273 = 300$K	$T1a = 80 + 460 = 540°R$
$T2a = 18 + 273 = 291$K	$T2a = 65 + 460 = 525°R$
$P2a = 516 \times 291/300 = 501$ kPa	$P2a = 74.7 \times 525/540 = 72.6$ psia
$P2g = 501 - 101 = 400$ kPag	$P2g = 72.6 - 14.7 = 57.9$ psig

A.5.1.12.2.7.5 The effect of temperature changes on the vacuum of a confined gas is based on the Ideal Gas Law. The final absolute vacuum (V2a) equals the initial absolute vacuum (V1a) times the final absolute temperature (T2a), divided by the initial absolute temperature (T1a).

Δ **Table A.5.1.9.5 Requirements for Category 1 Local Alarms**

	Medical Air Compressors						
Alarm Condition	Oil-less (Sealed Bearing) 5.1.3.6.3.4(A)(1)	Oil-Free (Separated) 5.1.3.6.3.4(A)(2)	Liquid Ring (Water-Sealed) 5.1.3.6.3.4(A)(1)	Instrument Air Compressors	Medical–Surgical Vacuum Pumps	WAGD Producers	Oxygen Concentrators
Low medical air reserve Capacity	5.1.3.6.3.12(F) 5.1.9.5.3(1)	5.1.3.6.3.12(F) 5.1.9.5.3(1)	5.1.3.6.3.12(F) 5.1.9.5.3(1)				
Low medical vacuum reserve capacity					5.1.3.7.8 5.1.9.5.3(4)		
Low WAGD reserve capacity						5.1.3.8.3.2 5.1.9.5.3(5)	
Low instrument air reserve capacity				5.1.13.3.7.11(A) 5.1.9.5.3(7)			
Carbon monoxide high	5.1.3.6.3.13(2) 5.1.9.5.3(2)	5.1.3.6.3.13(2) 5.1.9.5.3(2)	5.1.3.6.3.13(2) 5.1.9.5.3(2)				
High discharge air temperature	5.1.3.6.3.12(D) 5.1.9.5.3(10)	5.1.3.6.3.12(E)(1) 5.1.9.5.3(10)					
High water in receiver	5.1.3.6.3.12(B) 5.1.9.5.3(8)	5.1.3.6.3.12(B) 5.1.9.5.3(8)	5.1.3.6.3.12(B) 5.1.9.5.3(8)				
High water in separator			5.1.3.6.3.12(C) 5.1.9.5.3(9)				
Medical air dew point high	5.1.3.6.3.13(1) 5.1.9.5.3(3)	5.1.3.6.3.13(1) 5.1.9.5.3(3)	5.1.3.6.3.13(1) 5.1.9.5.3(3)				
Instrument air dew point high				5.1.9.5.3(6) 5.1.13.3.7.11(A)(2)			
Oxygen concentrator low concentration							5.1.3.9.1.13(1) 5.1.3.9.3(10)(c) 5.1.3.9.5.1(3)
Oxygen concentrator high concentration							5.1.3.9.1.13(1) 5.1.3.9.5.1(3)
Oxygen reserve in use							5.1.3.9.5.3(2) 5.1.9.5.3(13)(a)
Oxygen reserve supply less than 1 day (low contents)							5.1.3.9.5.3(3) 5.1.9.5.3(13)(b)
Oxygen main line low concentration							5.1.3.9.5.2(3) 5.1.9.5.3(13)(e)
Oxygen main line high concentration							5.1.3.9.5.2(3) 5.1.9.5.3(13)(f)
Oxygen change of source							5.1.9.5.3(13)(c) 5.1.3.9.5.4(1)(a)
Oxygen concentrator internal pressure low							5.1.3.9.5.4(2) 5.1.9.5.3(13)(d)

Absolute vacuum is the absolute zero pressure 101 kPa (30 inHg) less the vacuum reading below atmospheric. See Table A.5.1.12.2.6.5(b) for the absolute atmospheric pressures for elevations at and above sea level.

Absolute temperature K (°R) is the temperature gauge reading °C (°F) plus the absolute zero temperature 273°C (460°F).

Examples of vacuum test data at sea level in SI and IP units follow.

The initial test vacuum is 54 kPa or 16 inHg at 18°C (65°F). A temperature increase to 27°C (80°F) will cause the test vacuum to decrease to 52.5 kPa (15.6 inHg).

For SI units:

$V1g = 54$ kPa, $T1g = 18°C$, $T2g = 27°C$

$V1a = 101 - 54 = +47$ kPaV

$T1a = 18 + 273 = 291K$

$T2a = 27 + 273 = 300K$

$V2a = 47 \times 300/291 = +48.5$ kPaV

$V2g = 101 - 48.5 = 52.5$ kPa

For IP units:

$V1g = 16$ inHg, $T1g = 65°F$, $T2g = 80°F$

$V1a = 30 - 16 = +14$ inHgV

$T1a = 65 + 460 = 525°R$

$T2a = 80 + 460 = 540°R$

$V2a = 14 \times 540/525 = +14.4$ inHgV

$V2g = 30 - 14.4 = 15.6$ inHg

Table A.5.1.10.3.1 Socket Depths for ANSI/ASME B16.50 Brazing Fittings

Tube Size (in.)	Socket Depth (in.)
¼ (⅜ O.D.)	0.17
⅜ (½ O.D.)	0.2
½ (⅝ O.D.)	0.22
¾ (⅞ O.D.)	0.25
1 (1⅛ O.D.)	0.28
1¼ (1⅜ O.D.)	0.31
1½ (1⅝ O.D.)	0.34
2 (2⅛ O.D.)	0.40
2½ (2⅝ O.D.)	0.47
3 (3⅛ O.D.)	0.53
4 (4⅛ O.D.)	0.64
5 (5⅛ O.D.)	0.73
6 (6⅛ O.D.)	0.83

Δ **Table A.5.1.12.2.6.5(b) Pressure Corrections for Elevation**

Elevation (ft)	Absolute Atmospheric Pressure			
	kPa	psia	mmHg	inHg
0	101.33	14.70	760.0	29.92
500	99.49	14.43	746.3	29.38
1000	97.63	14.16	733.0	28.86
1500	95.91	13.91	719.6	28.33
2000	94.19	13.66	706.6	27.82
2500	92.46	13.41	693.9	27.32
3000	90.81	13.17	681.2	26.82
3500	89.15	12.93	668.8	26.33
4000	87.49	12.69	656.3	25.84
4500	85.91	12.46	644.4	25.37
5000	84.33	12.23	632.5	24.90

A.5.1.12.4.2 This is the final pressure test of the completely installed system and is intended to locate any leaks that would be more likely to occur at lower pressure (e.g., leaks in station outlet valve seals).

A.5.1.12.4.6.4 Odor is checked by sniffing a moderate flow of gas from the outlet being tested. Specific measure of odor in gas is impractical. Gas might have a slight odor but the presence of a pronounced odor should render the piping unsatisfactory.

A.5.1.12.4.8 The detector used for total hydrocarbons is calibrated with a gas that has a known quantity of methane. When a sample is run with this calibrated detector, the result will be total hydrocarbons as methane. Since methane is the one hydrocarbon that does not interact with the body and is present in all air and most oxygen, the actual amount of methane in the sample is subtracted from the total hydrocarbon result to give total non-methane hydrocarbons.

A.5.1.12.4.10.6 A sleep lab is an example of a location where gas flow and concentration are frequently modified.

A.5.1.12.4.11(3) The committee recognizes that current clinical practice is to use analyzers that might not be able to analyze oxygen to current USP requirements of 99 percent and that these analyzers frequently have an error of up to 3 percent.

A.5.1.13.1 Medical support gas systems are subject to the same hazards as are present in any piped medical gas system, with the additional hazard of operating at higher pressures.

Δ **A.5.1.13.1.2** Examples of medical support gas uses include, but are not limited to, removing excess moisture from instruments before further processing and operating gas-driven booms, boom brakes, pendants, or similar applications. Air of other grades and from sources other than instrument air can be appropriate for general utility use, as well. See Chapter 8 for general utility systems requirements.

A.5.1.13.3.7 See Figure A.5.1.13.3.7.

A.5.1.13.3.7.7 Drawing intake air from outside in compliance with 5.1.3.6.3.11 is recommended.

A.5.1.14 All cylinders containing compressed gases, such as anesthetic gases, oxygen, or other gases used for medicinal purposes, whether these gases are flammable or not, should comply with the specifications and be maintained in accordance with regulations of the US Department of Transportation.

Cylinder and container temperatures greater than 52°C (125°F) can result in excessive pressure increase. Pressure relief devices are sensitive to temperature and pressure. When relief devices actuate, contents are discharged.

A.5.1.14.2.1 The process can be a subset of a currently utilized system, such as a preconstruction risk assessment.

A.5.1.14.2.2(4) A procedure for the shutdown and restoration of medical gases during installation or maintenance of these systems can be found in Annex J, "Recommended Guidelines for Conducting Planned Medical Gas Systems Shutdowns and Temporary Backfeed," of ASSE/IAPMO/ANSI 6000, *Professional Qualifications Standard for Medical Gas Systems Personnel.*

A.5.1.14.3.1 Piping systems for the distribution of flammable gases (e.g., hydrogen, acetylene, natural gas) are outside the scope of this chapter.

A.5.1.14.3.3 Vacuum systems from station inlets to the exhaust discharge should be considered contaminated unless proven otherwise. Methods exist to disinfect the system or portions thereof.

Clogging of regulators, for example, with lint, debris, or dried body fluids, reduces vacuum system performance.

A.5.1.14.3.4 Other examples of prohibited use of medical–surgical vacuum would be scope cleaning, decontamination, and laser plume.

A.5.1.14.3.5 When spaces are converted, the inlets and outlets should be addressed in one of the following ways:

(1) Inlets and outlets removed and tubing capped
(2) Inlets and outlets plugged and provided with a blank-off plate
(3) Inlets and outlets remain accessible for maintenance and testing
(4) Other means deemed appropriate by the AHJ

Proper decommissioning of systems should include identifying them as not in service. The associated zone valve box and alarm panels should be kept up-to-date with the changes made to rooms no longer served.

△ FIGURE A.5.1.13.3.7   Elements of Typical Instrument Air Source.

Note: Unions or other disconnect means can be required for maintenance and/or replacement of each component.

N **A.5.1.14.3.6** Ensuring access to and protection of outdoor central supply systems, both day-to-day and in case of adverse events (e.g., snow, ice, flooding), is essential to effective operation of the systems. Examples of elements the emergency operations plan should consider include designating and enforcing restrictions on parking, ensuring access to the fill connection for the tanker truck, spill control, maintenance of the pathway for cylinder and container carts, and preventing accumulations of detritus in the enclosure.

Examples of elements that might be considered when planning for adverse events include snow and ice accumulation and flooding of the pathways to the central supply systems.

A.5.1.14.4.1 The facility should retain a written or an electronic copy of all findings and any corrections performed.

A.5.1.14.4.2.2 In addition to the minimum inspection and testing in 5.1.14, facilities should consider annually inspecting equipment and procedures and correcting any deficiencies.

A.5.1.14.4.3 The following should be considered in a routine testing, maintenance, and inspection program:

(1) Medical air source, as follows:

    (a) Room temperature
    (b) Shaft seal condition
    (c) Filter condition
    (d) Presence of hydrocarbons
    (e) Room ventilation
    (f) Water quality, if so equipped
    (g) Intake location
    (h) Carbon monoxide monitor calibration
    (i) Air purity
    (j) Dew point

(2) Medical vacuum source — exhaust location
(3) WAGD source — exhaust location
(4) Instrument air source — filter condition
(5) Manifold sources (including systems complying with 5.1.3.5.9, 5.1.3.5.10, 5.1.3.5.11, and 5.1.3.10), as follows:

    (a) Ventilation
    (b) Enclosure labeling

(6) Cryogenic fluid central supply system source inspected in accordance with NFPA 55
(7) Final line regulation for all positive pressure systems — delivery pressure
(8) Valves — labeling
(9) Alarms and warning systems — lamp and audio operation
(10) Alarms and warning systems, as follows:

    (a) Master alarm signal operation
    (b) Area alarm signal operation
    (c) Local alarm signal operation

(11) Station outlets/inlets, as follows:

    (a) Flow
    (b) Labeling
    (c) Latching/delatching
    (d) Leaks

(12) Medical gas quality, as follows:

    (a) Purity — percent concentration
    (b) Permanent particulates and contaminants
    (c) Odor and moisture

A.5.1.14.7.11 Accessibility of valves and the visibility and audibility of alarms are inherent to the functions for which they are installed. The hazard involved in placing any equipment in front of a valve that blocks the line of sight is obvious.

Access to alarms involves both seeing and hearing the alarms. Any obstruction of sight lines (e.g., with a computer monitor, signs, boxes, carts) or impairment of the alarm's audio (e.g., by taping over or plugging the speaker or sounder) can delay or prevent response.

During routine safety checks, a facility should include visual checks of the visibility, access, and condition of all zone valves and alarms.

A.5.1.14.7.11(2)(a) The intended operator's position is where the person who will operate the valve can see and reach the valve to open or close it. This can involve opening access doors, standing on a ladder, or other actions that would put the operator into the correct position.

A.5.2.1 Section 5.1 covers Category 1 piped gas and vacuum systems; Section 5.2 covers Category 2 piped gas and vacuum systems; and Section 5.3 covers Category 3 piped gas and vacuum systems.

The health care facility's governing body should designate a category in accordance with Chapter 4 for each patient care space in the facility. This process should include areas being used for medical support (e.g., decontamination or sterilization, lab work, post mortem) that are not strictly patient care spaces themselves (i.e., there are no patients there) but share utilities such as medical gases or medical support gases with such spaces. Because it is not realistic to create separate supply systems for each category, it is desirable that one supply system be used for spaces of all categories to supply medical gases, medical support gases, and vacuums to terminals.

The principle is set out at the start of the requirements for each category in Chapter 5 (*see 5.1.1, 5.2.1, and 5.3.1*) that a higher category source and piping system is permitted to supply terminals in any lower Category space; a Category 1 system can supply terminals in Category 2 and Category 3 spaces, but a Category 2 system cannot supply terminals in a Category 1 space.

N **A.5.2.1.1** Category 2 piped gas or piped vacuum system requirements should be applied when all of the following criteria are met:

(1) Only moderate sedation (*as defined in 3.3.70.3*), minimal sedation (*as defined in 3.3.70.4*), or no sedation is performed. Deep sedation and general anesthesia are not permitted.
(2) The loss of the piped gas or piped vacuum systems is likely to cause minor injury to patients, staff, or visitors.
(3) The facility piped gas or piped vacuum systems are intended for Category 2 patient care spacesin accordance with 3.3.146.2.

A.5.2.14 Medical gas and vacuum systems should be surveyed at least annually for the items that follow and deficient items corrected.

Survey of medical air and instrument air sources should include, but not be limited to, the following:

(1) Dew point monitor (operation and calibration)
(2) Carbon monoxide monitor (medical air only) (operation and calibration)
(3) Aftercoolers (condition, operation of drains)

(4) Operating pressures (cut-in, cut-out, and control pressures)
(5) All local alarms (verify presence of required alarms, perform electrical test, test lag alarm)
(6) Receiver elements (auto drain, manual drain, sight glass, pressure gauge)
(7) Filters (condition)
(8) Pressure regulators (condition, output pressure)
(9) Source valve (labeling)
(10) Intake (location and condition)
(11) Housekeeping around compressors

Survey of the medical vacuum and the WAGD source(s) should include, but not be limited to, the following:

(1) Operating vacuum (cut-in, cut-out, and control pressures)
(2) All local alarms (verify presence of required alarms, perform electrical test, test lag alarm)
(3) Receiver elements (manual drain, sight glass, vacuum gauge)
(4) Source valve (labeling)
(5) Exhaust (location and condition)
(6) Housekeeping around pump

Survey of the medical gas manifold source(s) should include, but not be limited to, the following:

(1) Number of cylinders (damaged connectors)
(2) Cylinder leads (condition)
(3) Cascade (switching from one header to another)
(4) All local alarms (verify presence of required alarms, perform electrical test, test all alarms)
(5) Source valve (labeling)
(6) Relief valves (discharge location and condition)
(7) Leaks
(8) Security (door or gate locks and signage)
(9) Ventilation (general operation, housekeeping)
(10) Housekeeping around manifolds

Survey of medical gas area alarms should include, but not be limited to, the following:

(1) Locations (visible to staff)
(2) Signals (audible and visual, use test function)
(3) Activation at low pressure
(4) Activation at high pressure
(5) Housekeeping around alarm

Survey of medical gas master alarms should include, but not be limited to, the following:

(1) Locations (visible to appropriate staff)
(2) Signals (audible and visual, use test function)
(3) Activation at low pressure
(4) Activation at high pressure
(5) Housekeeping around alarm

Survey of zone valves should include, but not be limited to, the following:

(1) Locations (relationship to terminals controlled)
(2) Leaks
(3) Labeling
(4) Housekeeping around alarm

Survey of medical gas outlet/inlets should include, but not be limited to, the following:

(1) Flow and function
(2) Latching/delatching

(3) Leaks
(4) General condition (noninterchangeable indexing)

The facility should retain a written or an electronic copy of all findings and any corrections performed.

A.5.3.1 The health care facility's governing body should designate a category in accordance with Chapter 4 for each patient care space in the facility. This process should include areas being used for medical support (e.g., decontamination or sterilization, lab work, post mortem) that are not strictly patient care spaces themselves (i.e., there are no patients there) but share utilities such as medical gases or medical support gases with such spaces. Because it is not realistic to create separate supply systems for each category, it is desirable that one supply system be used for spaces of all categories to supply medical gases, medical support gases, and vacuums to terminals.

The principle is set out at the start of the requirements for each category in Chapter 5 *(see 5.1.1, 5.2.1, and 5.3.1)* that a higher category source and piping system is permitted to supply terminals in any lower Category space; a Category 1 system can supply terminals in Category 2 and Category 3 spaces, but a Category 3 system cannot supply terminals in Category 1 or Category 2 spaces.

N **A.5.3.1.1** Category 3 piped gas or piped vacuum system requirements should be applied when all of the following criteria are met:

(1) Only minimal sedation, as defined in 3.3.70.4, or no sedation is performed. Deep sedation, moderate sedation, and general anesthesia are not permitted.
(2) The loss of the piped gas or piped vacuum systems is not likely to cause injury to patients, staff, or visitors but can cause discomfort.
(3) The facility piped gas or piped vacuum systems are intended for Category 3 patient care spaces in accordance with 3.3.146.3.

A.5.3.3.5.10(3) Medical gases include, but are not limited to, oxygen, nitrous oxide, nitrogen, medical air, carbon dioxide, and helium.

N **A.5.4.1** Cryogenic liquids might be drawn from containers for use in liquid form for the preservation of items including, but not limited to, specimens, embryos, and material samples.

Specific hazards are present whenever cryogenic liquefied gases are manipulated or used, including, but not limited to, the following:

(1) Hazards due to exposure to very low temperatures (e.g., frost burns, frostbite)
(2) Hazards due to rapid vaporization (i.e., expansion of volume) of the liquid into gas (e.g., explosion)
(3) Hazards due to depletion of the supply of liquid or pipeline interruption of liquid through equipment failure, operator error, vapor lock, or other phenomena inherent to the use of liquefied gases, which can result in the loss of cryogenically preserved materials
(4) Hazards due to vaporization of the liquid and the management of the resulting gas (e.g., liquid nitrogen discharge into room air with the consequence of depleting the room oxygen)
(5) Icing and condensate formation around the piping
(6) Hazards natural to the gas itself (e.g., oxygen as an oxidizer)
(7) Hazards due to the handling and storage of containers

N **A.5.4.5.2** The need to ventilate the discharged gas to ensure a safe atmosphere shall be considered.

N **A.5.4.6.2** Automated ventilation systems that operate with a room monitor are acceptable. Ventilation should consider the potential for liquid boiloff and resultant venting.

N **A.5.4.6.5(1)** Systems that allow limited liquid withdrawal from the secondary header to reduce boiloff are acceptable.

N **A.5.4.6.9.1.3** Special purpose devices include, but are not limited to, phase separator valves and diverter valves.

N **A.5.4.6.10(4)** Criteria for the testing of liquid cryogen withdrawal piping will vary with the technology, design, site conditions, and installation techniques employed. The test criteria to be employed should be established during the design of the system.

Δ **A.6.1** Although complete compliance with this chapter is desirable, variations in existing health care facilities should be considered acceptable in instances where wiring arrangements are in accordance with prior editions of this document or afford an equivalent degree of performance and reliability. Such variations could occur, particularly with certain wiring in separate or common raceways, with certain functions connected to one or another system or branch, or with certain provisions for automatically or manually delayed restoration of power.

A.6.2.1 Electrical systems can be subject to the occurrence of electrical fires. Grounding systems, overcurrent protective devices, and other subjects discussed in this code could be intended for fire prevention as well as other purposes. This aspect of electrical systems is the primary focus of other NFPA standards and will not be emphasized herein.

A.6.3.2.1 Assignment of degree of reliability of electrical systems in health care facilities depends on the careful evaluation of the variables at each particular installation. For further information, see ANSI/IEEE 493, *Recommended Practice for the Design of Reliable Industrial and Commercial Power Systems.*

Δ **A.6.3.2.2.1** It is best, if possible, to employ only one type of receptacle (i.e., standard three-prong type) for as many receptacles being served by the same line voltage to avoid the inability to connect life-support equipment in emergencies. The straight-blade, three-prong receptacle is now permitted in all locations in a hospital. Previously, special receptacles were specified in operating room locations and caused compatibility problems.

Hospital grade requirements are in addition to the basic construction and performance requirements for general-purpose receptacles. These requirements enhance the safety of patients who might be more susceptible to stray currents, evaluate the integrity of the receptacle's grounding path where subjected to the conditions encountered in health care facilities, and apply to receptacles that are non-locking-type, 125-volt, 15- or 20-ampere grounding receptacles of NEMA configurations 5-15R, 5-20R, 5-20RA, 6-15R, 6-20R, and 6-20RA. For the evaluation requirements of hospital-grade receptacles, see UL 498, *Attachment Plugs and Receptacles.* For receptacle configuration dimensions, see ANSI/NEMA WD 6, *Wiring Devices — Dimensional Specifications.*

A.6.3.2.2.5 Care should be taken in specifying a system containing isolated ground receptacles, because the grounding impedance is controlled only by the grounding wires and does not benefit from any conduit or building structure in parallel with it.

A.6.3.2.2.7 A clinical laboratory is a space where diagnostic tests are performed as part of patient care.

A.6.3.2.3.1 Moisture can reduce the contact resistance of the body, and electrical insulation is more subject to failure.

A.6.3.2.3.4 In conducting a risk assessment, the health care governing body should consult with all relevant parties, including, but not limited to, clinicians, biomedical engineering staff, and facility safety engineering staff.

A.6.3.2.3.8 The health care health care facility's governing body and designer of record should evaluate the type of protection to be provided against electrical shock to patients and caregivers in wet procedure locations. The application considerations should include but not be limited to the reliability of power to critical equipment and systems.

A.6.3.2.4 The requirement that branch circuits be fed from not more than one distribution panel was introduced for several reasons. A general principle is to minimize possible potential differences between the grounding pins of receptacles in one area by bringing the grounding conductors to a common point. A specific reason is to simplify maintenance by making it easier to find the source for the receptacles in a room. This is particularly a problem in hospitals where emergency conditions might require rapid restoration of power.

A.6.3.2.5.1.5 The requirement for grounding interconnection between the normal and essential power systems follows the principle of minimizing possible potential differences between the grounding pins of receptacles in one area by bringing the grounding conductors to a common point.

A.6.3.2.5.3 Special grounding methods could be required in patient vicinities immediately adjacent to rooms containing high-power or high-frequency equipment that causes electrical interference with monitors or other electromedical devices. In extreme cases, electromagnetic induction can cause the voltage limits of 6.3.3.1 to be exceeded.

Electromagnetic interference problems can be due to a variety of causes, some simple, others complex. Such problems are best solved one at a time. In some locations, grounding of stretchers, examining tables, or bed frames will be helpful. Where necessary, a patient equipment grounding point should be installed. This can usually be accomplished even after completion of construction by installing a receptacle faceplate fitted with grounding posts. Special grounding wires should not be used unless they are found to be essential for a particular location, because they can interfere with patient care procedures or present trip hazards.

A.6.3.2.9 Patient protection is provided primarily by an adequate grounding system. The ungrounded secondary of the isolation transformer reduces the cross-sectional area of grounding conductors necessary to protect the patient against voltage resulting from fault current by reducing the maximum current in case of a single probable fault in the grounding system. The line isolation monitor is used to provide warning when a single fault occurs. Excessive current in the grounding conductors will not result in a hazard to the patient unless a second fault occurs. If the current in the grounding system does not exceed 10 mA, even under fault conditions, the voltage across 3 m (9.84 ft) of No. 12 AWG wire will not exceed

0.2 mV, and the voltage across 3 m (9.84 ft) of No. 18 AWG grounding conductor in a flexible cord will not exceed 0.8 mV. Allowing 0.1 mV across each connector, the voltage between two pieces of patient-connected equipment will not exceed 2 mV.

The reference grounding point is intended to ensure that all electrically conductive surfaces of the building structure, which could receive heavy fault currents from ordinary (grounded) circuits, are grounded in a manner to bypass these heavy currents from the operating room.

A.6.3.2.9.2.1 It is desirable to limit the size of the isolation transformer to 10 kVA or less and to use conductor insulation with low leakage to meet the impedance requirements. Keeping branch circuits short and using insulation with a dielectric constant less than 3.5 and insulation resistance constant greater than 6100 megohmmeters at 16°C (20,000 megohm-ft at 60°F) reduces leakage from line to ground.

To correct milliammeter reading to line impedance, use the following equation:

$$[A.6.3.2.9.2.1]$$

$$\text{Line impedance (in ohms)} = \frac{V \cdot 1000}{I}$$

where:
V = isolated power system voltage
I = milliammeter reading made during impedance test

A.6.3.2.9.3.1 Protection for the patient is provided primarily by a grounding system. The ungrounded secondary of the isolation transformer reduces the maximum current in the grounding system in case of a single fault between either isolated power conductor and ground. The line isolation monitor provides warning when a single fault occurs, or when excessively low impedance to ground develops, which might expose the patient to an unsafe condition if an additional fault occurs. Excessive current in the grounding conductors will not result from a first fault. A hazard exists if a second fault occurs before the first fault is cleared.

A.6.3.2.9.3.3 It is desirable to reduce this monitor hazard current, provided that this reduction results in an increased "not alarm" threshold value for the fault hazard current.

A.6.3.2.9.3.4 It is desirable to locate the ammeter such that it is conspicuously visible to persons in the anesthetizing location.

The line isolation monitor can be a composite unit, with a sensing section cabled to a separate display panel section on which the alarm and test functions are located, if the two sections are within the same electric enclosure.

A.6.3.3.1.1 In a conventional grounded power distribution system, one of the line conductors is deliberately grounded, usually at some distribution panel or the service entrance. This grounded conductor is identified as the neutral conductor. The other line conductor(s) is the high side of the line. The loads to be served by this distribution system are fed by the high and neutral conductors.

In addition to the high and neutral conductors, a grounding conductor is provided. One end is connected to the neutral at the point where the neutral is grounded, and the other end leads out to the connected loads. For purposes here, the load connection point will be considered to be a convenience receptacle, with the grounding conductor terminating at the grounding terminal of that receptacle.

This grounding conductor can be a separate wire running from the receptacle back to the remote grounding connection (where it joins the neutral conductor). If that separate conductor does not make any intermediate ground contacts between the receptacle and the remote ground, then the impedance of the connection between the receptacle and the remote ground is primarily the resistance of the grounding conductor itself and is, therefore, predictable.

If, however, the receptacle is also interconnected with the remote ground point by metallic conduit or other metallic building structures, the impedance of the circuit between the receptacle and remote ground is not easily predictable; nor is it easy to measure accurately, although one can be sure that the impedance will be less than that of the grounding wire itself because of the additional parallel paths.

Fortunately, as will become apparent in the paragraphs that follow, the absolute value of the apparent impedance between the grounding contact of an outlet and the remote ground point need not be known or measured with great accuracy.

Ideally, and under no-fault conditions, the grounding system described earlier is supposed to be carrying no current at all. If this were true, then no voltage differences would be found between exposed conductive surfaces of any electrical appliances that were grounded to the grounding contacts of the receptacles that powered them. Similarly, there would be no voltage differences between these appliances and any other exposed metal surface that was also interconnected with the grounding system, provided that no currents were flowing in that interconnection.

Ideal conditions, however, do not prevail, and even when there are no "faults" within an appliance, residual "leakage" current does flow in the grounding conductor of each of the appliances, producing a voltage difference between the chassis of that appliance and the grounding contact of the receptacle that feeds it. Furthermore, this current can produce voltage differences among other appliances plugged into various receptacles on the system.

If, however, a breakdown of insulation between the high side of the line and the chassis of an appliance occurs, the leakage condition becomes a fault condition, the magnitude of which is limited by the nature of the breakdown, or, in the case of a dead short circuit in the appliance, the magnitude of the fault current is limited only by the residual resistance of the appliance power cord conductors and that of the power distribution system. In the event of such a short circuit, the impedance of the grounding circuit, as measured between the grounding contact of the receptacle that feeds the defective appliance and the remote ground point where the neutral and grounding conductors are joined, should be so small that a large enough fault current will flow to ensure a rapid breaking of the circuit by the overcurrent protective device that serves that receptacle.

For a 20-A branch circuit, a fault current of 40 A or more would be required to ensure a rapid opening of the branch-circuit overcurrent protective device. This corresponds to a circuit impedance of 3 ohms or less, of which the grounding system should contribute 1 ohm or less.

During the time this large fault current flows in the grounding system, the chassis of the defective appliance is raised many volts above other grounded surfaces in the same vicinity. The hazard represented by this condition is minimized by the fact that it exists for only a short time, and, unless a patient simultaneously contacts both the defective appliance and some other grounded surface during this short time interval, there is no hazard. Furthermore, the magnitude of an applied voltage required to produce a serious shock hazard increases as its duration decreases, so the rapidity with which the circuit is interrupted helps reduce shock hazard even if such a patient contact occurs.

If, however, the defect in the appliance is not such as to cause an immediate circuit interruption, then the effect of this intermediate level of fault current on the voltages appearing on various exposed conductive surfaces in the patient care vicinity should be considered.

Because all of this fault current flows in the grounding conductor of the defective appliance's power cord, the first effect is to raise the potential of this appliance above that of the receptacle that feeds it by an amount proportional to the power cord grounding conductor resistance. This resistance is required to be less than 0.15 ohm, so fault currents of 20 A or less, which will not trip the branch-circuit overcurrent protective device, will raise the potential of the defective appliance above the grounding contact of its supply receptacle by only 3 V or less. This value is not hazardous for casual contacts.

The fault current that enters the grounding system at the grounding contact of any receptacle in the patient care vicinity could affect the potential at the grounding contacts of all the other receptacles, and, more importantly, it could produce significant voltage differences between them and other grounded surfaces, such as exposed piping and building structures.

If one grounded point is picked as a reference (a plumbing fixture in or near the patient care vicinity, for example), and the voltage difference is then measured between that reference and the grounding contact of a receptacle, produced by driving some known current into that contact, a direct measure of the effectiveness of the grounding system within the patient care vicinity is obtained. The "figure of merit" can be stated as so many volts per ampere of fault current. The ratio volts per ampere is, of course, impedance; but because the exact path taken by the fault current is not known, and because the way in which the reference point is interconnected with the grounding system is not known, it cannot be stated that this value is the impedance between the receptacle and some specific point, such as the joining of the neutral and grounding conductors. However, it can be stated that this measured value of "effective impedance" is indicative of the effectiveness with which the grounding system minimizes voltage differences between supposedly grounded objects in the patient care vicinity that are produced by ground faults in appliances used in that vicinity. This impedance, which characterizes the ability of the grounding system to maintain nearly equipotential conditions within the patient care vicinity, is of prime importance in assessing shock hazard; but this impedance is not necessarily the same as the impedance between receptacle and remote ground point, which controls the magnitude of the short-circuit current involved in tripping the branch-circuit overcurrent protective device.

Fault currents on the grounding system can also come from neutral-to-ground faults, which allow some current to flow in the neutral and some in the ground. This type of fault is often the cause of interference on EEG and ECG equipment. It is often not recognized easily because, except for 60 Hz interference, the equipment works perfectly properly. It is most easily found by causing a substantial change in the line-to-line load and noting changes in the ground-to-reference voltage.

A.6.3.3.1.1.4 The grounding system (reference ground and conduit) is to be tested as an integral system. Lifting of grounds from receptacles and fixed equipment is not required or recommended for the performance of this test.

A.6.3.3.1.3 Effective grounding to safely handle both fault and leakage currents requires following the requirements of both Chapter 6 and Article 250 of *NFPA 70*; having good workmanship; and using some techniques that are not found in these documents.

The performance of the grounding system is made effective through the existence of the green grounding wire, the metal raceway, and all of the other building metal. Measurements have shown that it is the metal raceway and building steel that provide most of the effective grounding path of less than 10 milliohms at the receptacle, including plug-to-receptacle impedance. The green grounding wire becomes a backup, not a primary grounding path performer.

Good practice calls for each receptacle to have a good jumper grounding connection to the metal raceway at the receptacle location in addition to having the green grounding wire connecting these points to the grounding bus in the distribution panel. Good workmanship includes seeing that these grounding connections are tight at each receptacle and that all metal raceway joints are secure and tight.

The voltage difference measurements listed in 6.3.3.1.3 in connection with power distribution grounding systems should ideally be made with an oscilloscope or spectrum analyzer in order to observe and measure components of leakage current and voltage differences at all frequencies.

For routine testing, such instruments could be inconvenient. An alternative is to use a metering system that weighs the contribution to the meter reading of the various components of the signal being measured in accordance with their probable physiological effect.

A meter specifically designed for this purpose would have an impedance of approximately 1000 ohms, and a frequency characteristic that was flat to 1 kHz, dropped at the rate of 20 decibels per decade to 100 kHz, and then remaining flat to 1 MHz or higher. This frequency response characteristic could be achieved by proper design of the internal circuits of the amplifier that probably precedes the indicating instrument or by appropriate choice of a feedback network around the amplifier. These details are, of course, left to the instrument designer.

If a meter specifically designed for these measurements is not available, a general-purpose laboratory millivoltmeter can be adapted for the purpose by adding a frequency response–shaping network ahead of the meter. One such suggested network is shown in Figure A.6.3.3.1.3(a).

The circuit shown Figure A.6.3.3.1.3(a) in is especially applicable to measurements of leakage current, where the current being measured is derived from a circuit whose source impedance is high compared to 1000 ohms. Under these conditions, the voltage developed across the millivoltmeter will be proportional to the impedance of the network. The network impedance will be 1000 ohms at low frequencies and 10 ohms at high frequencies, and the transition between these two values will occur in the frequency range between 1 kHz and 100 kHz.

The basic low-frequency sensitivity will be 1 mV of meter reading for each 1 mA of leakage current.

The millivoltmeter's own input impedance needs to be very large compared to 1000 ohms (100 kilohms), and the meter should have a flat frequency response to well beyond 100 kHz. (If the meter impedance is lower than 100 kilohms, then the 1000 ohm resistor can be raised to a higher value, such that the impedance of that resistor in parallel with the meter will still be 1000 ohms.)

The circuit in Figure A.6.3.3.1.3(a) can be used for the voltage difference measurements required in Section 6.5, but, because the source impedance will be very low compared to 1000 ohms, the frequency response of the measurement system will remain flat. If any high-frequency components produced, for example, by pickup from nearby radio frequency transmitters appear on the circuit being measured, then they will not be attenuated, and the meter reading will be higher than it should be.

For meter readings below any prescribed limits, this possible error is of no consequence. For borderline cases, it could be significant. To avoid this uncertainty when making voltage-difference measurements, a slightly more elaborate version of a frequency response–shaping network is given in Figure A.6.3.3.1.3(b).

Here the source being measured is separated from the frequency response–shaping network by the combination of the 900 ohm and 100 ohm resistors. The frequency response characteristic is now independent of the circuit being tested.

The millivoltmeter should have an input impedance of 150 kilohms and a frequency response that is flat to well beyond 100 kHz.

This independence is achieved, however, at a loss in signal delivered to the millivoltmeter. The basic low-frequency sensitivity of this metering circuit is 1 mV of meter reading for 10 A of leakage current or, on a voltage basis, 1 mV of meter reading for 10 mV at the input terminals of the network.

For either of the suggested networks, the resistors and capacitors should be mounted in a metal container close to the millivoltmeter to avoid stray pickup by the leads going to the meter.

A.6.3.3.1.4 It is not the intent that each receptacle be tested. It is intended that compliance be demonstrated through random

FIGURE A.6.3.3.1.3(a)   Circuit Used to Measure Leakage Current with High Source Impedance.

i_{lkg} = Leakage current being measured

FIGURE A.6.3.3.1.3(b)   Circuit Used to Measure Leakage Current with Low Source Impedance.

testing. The 10 percent random testing should include a mixture of both normal and emergency receptacles.

A.6.3.4.1.1 Although several approaches to documentation exist in hospitals, the minimum acceptable documentation should identify what was tested, when it was tested, and whether it performed successfully. Adopting a system of exception reporting can be the most efficient form of record keeping for routine rechecks of equipment or systems, thereby minimizing technicians' time in recording the value of each measurement taken. For example, once a test protocol is established, which simply means testing the equipment or system consistent with Chapter 6, the only item (value) that needs to be recorded is the failure or the deviation from the requirements of the chapter that was detected when a corrective action (repair) was undertaken. This approach can serve to eliminate, for example, the need to keep individual room sheets to record measured results on each receptacle or to record measurement values of all types of leakage current tests.

A.6.7 Requirements found in 6.7.1 through 6.7.4 are general requirements for both Type 1 and Type 2 EES.

Δ **A.6.7.1.1** *Connection to Dual Source of Off-Site Power.* For the greatest assurance of electrical service continuity, an off-site source should consist of two separate full-capacity services, each independent of the other. Such services should be selected and installed with full recognition of local hazards of interruption, such as icing and flooding. Where more than one full-capacity service is installed, they should be connected such that one will pick up the load automatically upon loss of the other, and should be so arranged that the load of the essential electrical system will be transferred to the on-site power source only when both off-site services are de-energized, unless this arrangement is impractical and waived by the authority having jurisdiction. Such services should be interlocked to prevent paralleling of utility services on either primary or secondary voltage levels. Note that in any installation where it is possible to parallel utility supply circuits (e.g., to prevent interruption of service when switching from one utility source to another), it is imperative to consult the power companies affected as to problems of synchronization. Facilities whose off-site power is supplied by two or more separate central station–fed services (dual sources) experience greater reliability than those with only a single feed.

Installation of Generator Sets. For additional material on diesel engines, see National Research Council Publication 1132, *Diesel Engines for Use with Generators to Supply Emergency and Short-Term Electric Power.*

A.6.7.1.2.1 A Class X system is intended to give the facility the flexibility to provide the appropriate duration before refueling operations are needed. The hospital should determine the appropriate run time for the EES and size the fuel tanks accordingly. Careful consideration should be given to the potential types of outages anticipated and the availability of fuel. It should be noted that in some situations it might be permissible to size the fuel system to accommodate less than 48 hours of fuel. If life safety systems are included on the EES, other codes and standards might have minimum durations of required operation.

A.6.7.1.2.2.2 Some sources, such as photovoltaic cells, operate intermittently. The systems should be able to operate with sources out of service and still be able to provide this redundancy.

A.6.7.1.2.2.3 The intent of 6.7.1.2.2.3 is as follows:

(1) Contiguous or same-site nonhospital buildings can be served by the generating equipment. However, such loads should not compromise the integrity of the system serving the hospital. Thus, any such contiguous or same-site nonhospital buildings can be served by the generating equipment only if the transfer means operates in accordance with 6.7.1.2.2.3.
(2) Within a hospital building, 6.7.5.1.3.2(10) permits "additional" loads on the critical branch and 6.7.5.1.4.4(9) permits "other equipment" on the equipment system in order to provide limited flexibility to a facility to add one or two loads not otherwise listed in 6.7.5.1.3.2(1) through 6.7.5.1.3.2(10), 6.7.5.1.4.3, or 6.7.5.1.4.4(1) through 6.7.5.1.4.4(9) to a critical branch panel or an equipment system panel. This is permitted to prevent the need for an additional panel to serve a small number of selected circuits in a particular area. These sections are not intended to permit large blocks of loads not listed in these sections to be on the critical branch or equipment system. The intent of the division of the essential system loads into systems and branches is to ensure maximum reliability of service to loads considered essential. Every additional load placed onto a system somewhat increases the probability of a failure on the system that threatens the integrity of service to the balance of loads served by the system. Therefore, while "additional" loads and "other equipment" are permitted to be placed onto the critical branch and equipment system in very limited situations, where a facility wants to put large blocks of loads not listed in 6.7.5.1.3.2(1) through 6.7.5.1.3.2(10), 6.7.5.1.4.3, or 6.7.5.1.4.4(1) through 6.7.5.1.4.4(9) onto the generating equipment, the facility is permitted to do so, but only by designating these large blocks of loads as "optional loads" and by complying with 6.7.1.2.2.3.

A.6.7.1.2.4 Paragraph 12.5.3.3.5 includes the requirements and components for an emergency operations plan. For additional loads to be considered, see 6.7.1.2.2.1.

A.6.7.1.2.7.2(B) As a supplement to hard-wired alarm annunciations, it is permissible to have Level 1 and Level 2 EPS and ATS functions monitored off-site. Monitoring stations can include pagers, cell phones, and Internet-connected devices.

A.6.7.1.2.7.2(H) An example of a centralized computer system is a building automation system.

A.6.7.1.3.4 During operation, EPS and related equipment reject considerable heat that needs to be removed by proper ventilation or air-cooling. In some cases, outdoor installations rely on natural air circulation, but enclosed installations need properly sized, properly positioned ventilation facilities, to prevent recirculation of cooling air. The optimum position of air-supply louvers and radiator air discharge is on opposite walls, both to the outdoors. [110:A.7.7.1]

A.6.7.1.3.4.2 See 110.3(b) of *NFPA 70* for more information on the manufacturer's installation instructions.

A.6.7.1.3.5 Refer to the following sections in NFPA 110 for specific requirements:

(1) Section 5.3 for requirements on energy converters — temperature maintenance
(2) Section 5.4 for requirements on energy converters — capacity
(3) Section 5.5 for requirements on energy converters — fuel supply
(4) Subsections 5.6.1 through 5.6.4.7 for requirements on rotating equipment

A.6.7.2 It should be emphasized that the type of system selected and its area and type of coverage should be appropriate to the medical procedures being performed in the facility. For example, a battery-operated emergency light that switches "on" when normal power is interrupted and an alternate power source for suction equipment, along with the immediate availability of some portable handheld lighting, would be advisable where oral and maxillofacial surgery (e.g., extraction of impacted teeth) is performed. On the other hand, in dental offices where simple extraction, restorative, prosthetic, or hygienic procedures are performed, remote corridor lighting for purposes of egress only would be sufficient. Emergency power for equipment would not be necessary. As with oral surgery locations, a surgical clinic requiring use of life-support or emergency devices, such as suction machines, ventilators, cauterizers, or defibrillators, would require both emergency light and power.

Distribution system arrangements should be designed to minimize interruptions to the electrical systems due to internal failures by the use of adequately rated equipment.

The following factors should be considered in the design of the distribution system:

(1) Abnormal voltages, such as single phasing of three-phase utilization equipment; switching or lightning surges, or both; and voltage reductions
(2) Capability of achieving the fastest possible restoration of any given circuit(s) after clearing a fault
(3) Effects of future changes, such as increased loading or supply capacity, or both
(4) Stability and power capability of the prime mover during and after abnormal conditions
(5) Sequence reconnection of loads to avoid large current inrushes that trip overcurrent devices or overload the generator(s)
(6) Bypass arrangements to allow testing and maintenance of system components that could not otherwise be maintained without disruption of important hospital functions
(7) Effects of any harmonic currents on neutral conductors and equipment

Careful consideration should be given to the location of the spaces housing the components of the essential electrical system (EES) to minimize interruptions caused by natural forces common to the area (e.g., storms, floods, or earthquakes; or hazards created by adjoining structures or activities).

Consideration should also be given to the possible interruption of normal electrical services resulting from similar causes as well as possible disruption of normal electrical service due to internal wiring and equipment failures. Consideration should be given to the physical separation of the main feeders of the EES from the normal wiring of the facility to prevent possible simultaneous destruction as a result of a local catastrophe.

In selecting electrical distribution arrangements and components for the EES, high priority should be given to achieving maximum continuity of the electrical supply to the load. Higher consideration should be given to achieving maximum reliability of the alternate power source and its feeders rather than protection of such equipment, provided that the protection is not required to prevent a greater threat to human life, such as fire, explosion, and electrocution, than would be caused by the lack of an essential electrical supply.

A.6.7.2.1.1 It is important that the various overcurrent devices be coordinated, as far as practicable, to isolate faulted circuits and to protect against cascading operation on short-circuit faults. In many systems, however, full coordination could compromise safety and system reliability. Primary consideration also should be given to prevent overloading of equipment by limiting the possibilities of large current inrushes due to instantaneous re-establishment of connections to heavy loads. The terms coordination and coordinated as used in 6.7.2.1.1 do not cover the full range of overcurrent conditions.

A.6.7.2.1.3.1(A) Where special loads require more rapid detection of power loss, underfrequency monitoring also might be provided. Upon frequency decay below the lower limit necessary for proper operation of the loads, the transfer switch should automatically initiate transfer to the alternate source. *(See A.6.2.15 of NFPA 110.)* [**110:**A.6.2.2.1]

A.6.7.2.1.3.1(A)(2) See 6.2.5 and 6.2.7 of NFPA 110. [**110:**A.6.2.2.1(2)]

A.6.7.2.1.3.3 Authorized personnel should be available and familiar with manual operation of the transfer switch and should be capable of determining the adequacy of the alternate power source prior to manual transfer. [**110:**A.6.2.4]

A.6.7.2.1.3.4 For most applications, a nominal delay of 1 second is adequate. The time delay should be short enough so that the generator can start and be on the line within the time specified for the type classification. [**110:**A.6.2.5]

A.6.7.2.1.3.7 It is recommended that the timer for delay on retransfer to the primary source be set for 30 minutes. The 30-minute recommendation is to establish a "normalized" engine temperature, when it is beneficial for the engine. *NFPA 70* establishes a minimum time requirement of 15 minutes. [**110:**A.6.2.8]

A.6.7.2.1.3.11 For maintenance purposes, consideration should be given to a transfer switch counter. [**110:**A.6.2.13]

Δ **A.6.7.2.1.3.13** Automatic transfer switches (ATS) can be provided with accessory controls that provide a signal to operate remote motor controls that disconnect motors prior to transfer and to reconnect them after transfer when the residual voltage has been substantially reduced. Another method is to provide in-phase monitors within the ATS in order to prevent retransfer to the primary source until both sources are nearly synchronized. A third method is to use a programmed neutral position transfer switch. [**110:**A.6.2.15]

N **A.6.7.2.1.3.16** See 700.5 of *NFPA 70.*

A.6.7.2.1.3.17 Standards for nonautomatic transfer switches are similar to those for automatic transfer switches, as defined in 3.3.14.1 and 3.3.14.3 of NFPA 110, with the omission of automatic controls. [**110:**A.6.2.16]

A.6.7.2.1.6.3 Consideration should be given to the effect that load interruption could have on the load during maintenance and service of the transfer switch.

A.6.7.2.2.5(B) If color is used to identify these receptacles, the same color should be used throughout the facility.

A.6.7.4.1.1.5(A) When events, such as the issuance of storm warnings, indicate that power outages might be likely, good practice recommends the warming up of generator sets by a regular exercise period. Operation of generator sets for short intervals should be avoided, particularly with compression ignition engines, since it is harmful to the engines.

Records of changes to the essential electrical system should be maintained so that the actual demand likely to be produced by the connected load will be within the available capacity.

A.6.7.5 General requirements from 6.7.1 through 6.7.4 are also applicable to Type 1 EES.

A.6.7.5.1 Type 1 essential electrical systems are comprised of three separate branches capable of supplying a limited amount of lighting and power service that is considered essential for life safety and effective facility operation during the time the normal electrical service is interrupted for any reason. These three separate branches are the life safety, critical, and equipment branches.

A.6.7.5.1.2.2(3) Departmental installations such as digital dialing systems used for intradepartmental communications could have impaired use during a failure of electrical service to the area. In the event of such failure, those systems that have lighted selector buttons in the base of the telephone instrument or in the desk units known as "director sets" will be out of service to the extent that the lights will not function and that the buzzer used to indicate incoming calls will be silenced. The lack of electrical energy will not prevent the use of telephones for outgoing calls, but incoming calls will not be signaled, nor will intercommunicating calls be signaled. This communication failure should be taken into consideration in planning essential electrical systems.

A.6.7.5.1.3 It is recommended that facility authorities give consideration to providing and properly maintaining automatic battery-powered lighting units or systems to provide minimal task illumination in operating rooms, delivery rooms, and certain special-procedure radiology rooms, where the loss of lighting due to failure of the essential electrical system could cause severe and immediate danger to a patient undergoing surgery or an invasive radiographic procedure.

A.6.7.5.1.3.2(6) Departmental installations such as digital dialing systems used for intradepartmental communications could have impaired use during a failure of electrical service to the area. In the event of such failure, those systems that have lighted selector buttons in the base of the telephone instrument or in the desk units known as "director sets" will be out of service to the extent that the lights will not function and that the buzzer used to indicate incoming calls will be silenced. The lack of electrical energy will not prevent the use of telephones for outgoing calls, but incoming calls will not be signaled, nor will intercommunicating calls be signaled. This communication failure should be taken into consideration in planning essential electrical systems.

A.6.7.5.1.4.3 The equipment in 6.7.5.1.4.3(A)(1) through 6.7.5.1.4.3(A)(3) can be arranged for sequential delayed-automatic connection to the on-site power source to prevent overloading it where engineering studies indicate that it is necessary.

A.6.7.5.1.4.4 For elevator cab lighting control and signal system requirements, see 6.7.5.1.2.2(5).

In instances where interruption of normal power would result in other elevators stopping between floors, throw-over facilities should be provided to allow the temporary operation of any elevator for the release of patients or other persons who are confined between floors.

A.6.7.5.1.4.4(2) The outside design temperature is based on the 97½ percent design value, as shown in Chapter 24 of the *ASHRAE Handbook — Fundamentals.*

A.6.7.5.1.4.4(9) Consideration should be given to selected equipment in kitchens, laundries, and radiology rooms and to selected central refrigeration.

It is desirable that, where heavy interruption currents can be anticipated, the transfer load be reduced by the use of multiple transfer devices. Elevator feeders, for instance, might be less hazardous to electrical continuity if they are fed through an individual transfer device.

A.6.7.5.2.1 See *NFPA 70* for installation requirements.

A.6.7.6 General requirements from 6.7.1 through 6.7.4 are also applicable to Type 2 EES.

A.6.7.6.2.1 Type 2 essential electrical systems are comprised of two separate branches capable of supplying a limited amount of lighting and power service that is considered essential for the protection of life and safety and effective operation of the institution during the time normal electrical service is interrupted for any reason. These two separate branches are the life safety and equipment branches.

The number of transfer switches to be used should be based upon reliability, design, and load considerations. Each branch of the essential electrical system should have one or more transfer switches. One transfer switch should be permitted to serve one or more branches in a facility with a maximum demand on the essential electrical system of 150 kVA (120 kW).

A.6.7.6.2.1.5(A)(4) Departmental installations such as digital dialing systems used for intradepartmental communications could have impaired use during a failure of electrical service to the area. In the event of such failure, those systems that have lighted selector buttons in the base of the telephone instrument or in the desk units known as "director sets" will be out of service to the extent that the lights will not function and that the buzzer used to indicate incoming calls will be silenced. The lack of electrical energy will not prevent the use of telephones for outgoing calls, but incoming calls will not be signaled, nor will intercommunicating calls be signaled. This communication failure should be taken into consideration in planning essential electrical systems.

A.6.7.6.2.1.6(E) Other selected equipment can be served by the equipment branch. Note that consideration should be

given to selected equipment in kitchens and laundries and to selected central refrigeration.

It is desirable that, where heavy interruption currents can be anticipated, the transfer load be reduced by the use of multiple transfer devices. Elevator feeders, for instance, might be less hazardous to electrical continuity if they are fed through an individual transfer device.

A.6.7.6.2.1.6(E)(1)(a) The outside design temperature is based on the 97½ percent design value, as shown in Chapter 24 of the *ASHRAE Handbook — Fundamentals.*

A.6.7.6.2.1.6(E)(2) For elevator cab lighting, control, and signal system requirements, see 6.7.6.2.1.5(A)(6).

A.6.7.6.3.1 See *NFPA 70* for installation requirements.

A.6.7.6.3.2 If color is used to identify these receptacles, the same color should be used throughout the facility.

△ A.6.8.1 The intent of these tests is to assure that all electrical equipment is operational within industry-recognized standards and the manufacturer's tolerances and that equipment is installed and functioning in the system in the manner intended. The tests and inspections should determine suitability for initial and continued reliable operation and provide a baseline for the ongoing electrical maintenance program (EMP).

A.6.8.2 The intent of this requirement is that the components of the electrical system feeding Category 1 and Category 2 spaces are tested to ensure that the complete system operates in the manner anticipated and continues operating reliably. This requires testing of the individual electrical components of the system, as well as the development of functional performance tests to confirm proper operation of the system as a whole. Examples of industry-recognized standards for the development of site acceptance test procedures include ANSI/NETA ATS, *Standard for Acceptance Testing Specifications for Electrical Power Equipment and Systems*, and Chapter 31 of NFPA 70B.

△ A.6.9.1.1 The purpose of any electrical maintenance program (EMP) is to establish the condition of equipment, determine what work should be done, and verify the equipment will continue to function until the next scheduled servicing occurs. Inspection and testing are best done in conjunction with routine maintenance. In this way, many minor items that require no special tools, training, or equipment can be corrected as they are found. The inspection and testing program is probably the most important function of a maintenance department because it establishes what should be done to keep the system in service performing the function for which it is required.

A.6.9.3.1 Appropriate corrective measures can include, but are not limited to, repair, replacement, and adjustment. Follow-through with necessary repairs, replacement, and adjustment is the end purpose of an effective EMP.

A.6.9.4.1 See Table A.6.9.4.1 for sources with recommended maintenance activities.

A.6.9.4.2 Health care facilities that choose to establish alternate equipment maintenance (AEM) activities and/or schedules must develop, implement, and maintain a documented AEM program to minimize risk to patients and others in the facility associated with the use of electrical utility equipment. Generally, multiple factors must be considered because differ-

Table A.6.9.4.1 Recommended Maintenance Activities

Item	References
Medium-voltage switchgear	See Sections 11.10 and 15.5 of NFPA 70B.
Power distribution transformers (≥ 750 kVA)	See 11.11.2, 11.11.8, 21.2.2.2, and 21.3.5 of NFPA 70B.
Generator (alternate source)	See 6.7.4.1 of this code.
Generator paralleling switchgear	See 8.3.5 of NFPA 110.
Overcurrent Protective Devices	
Fuses (≥ 400 A)	See 18.1.2 and 18.2.3 of NFPA 70B.
Low-voltage power circuit breakers (≥ 400 A)	See Sections 11.10 and 15.4 of NFPA 70B.
Low-voltage molded-case circuit breakers (≥ 400 A)	See Sections 17.7 through 17.11 and 11.10.5 of NFPA 70B.
Medium-voltage circuit breakers	See Sections 15.4 through 15.8 of NFPA 70B.
Relays (including polyphase ground-fault equipment protection)	See Section 11.12, 13.3.5, and 15.9.7.3 of NFPA 70B.
Transfer equipment	See 8.3.4 of NFPA 110.
Uninterruptible power supplies (≥ 100 kW)	See NFPA 111.
Isolated power panels	See 6.3.3.3.3 of this code.
Motor control equipment	See NEMA ICS 2.3, *Instructions for the Handling, Installation, Operation and Maintenance of Motor Control Centers Rated Not More than 600 V.*
Branch-circuit panelboards	See ANSI/NEMA PB 1.1, *General Instructions for Proper Installation, Operation and Maintenance of Panelboards Rated 600 V or Less.*
Wiring devices	See 6.3.3.2 of this code.
Battery-powered lighting units	See 6.3.2.6.8 of this code.

ent types of equipment present different combinations of severity of potential harm and likelihood of failure.

A.6.9.4.2.2(1) Standard examples for physical plant equipment maintenance can be found in the American Society for Healthcare Engineering (ASHE) document, *Maintenance Management for Health Care Facilities*, and in NFPA 70B.

A.6.9.4.2.2(4) An example of "critical equipment" is electrical utility equipment.

A.6.10.1.2 Health care facilities are increasingly implementing various on-site generation using a wide variation in technologies. These designs optimize the use of different sources both on and off site and provide numerous advantages, including resilience, efficiency, lowered operating costs, and reduced environmental impact. Health care microgrids with sophisticated controls and bundles of sources and storage assets can provide better outcomes than the conventional design that envisions a "normal" and an "emergency" source.

A.6.10.1.3 Areas served by health care microgrids should be identified.

A.6.10.3.2 A method for determining reliability for a health care microgrid can be found in IEEE's 3006 standard series *(see listed IEEE references in D.2.8)* and in NFPA 70B.

A.6.10.6 The health care microgrid controller is a decision-making software and/or hardware. The scheduling of health care microgrid distributed energy resources (DER) in grid-connected and island modes is performed by the controller based on economic and reliability considerations. The controller determines the health care microgrid's interaction with the utility grid, the decision to switch between grid-connected and island modes, frequency regulation and voltage control, and optimal operation of local resources. It also provides any decisions on load curtailment and shifting.

A.6.10.6.1 Health care microgrid systems monitored remotely should include safeguards to mitigate malicious control of or damage to the health care microgrid.

A.6.10.7.2(2) This should include all those involved in the planning, design, construction, installation, and operation of each source and control within the health care microgrid.

A.7.1 Additional information on these systems can be found in IEEE 602, *Recommended Practice for Electric Systems in Health Care Facilities*, and the applicable volume of FGI guidelines.

A.7.3.1.2 Additional information can be found in ANSI/TIA 569-D, *Telecommunications Pathways and Spaces.*

A.7.3.1.2.1.4(C) Such systems can include security, nurse call, cable television, patient education, voice, data, head end equipment for clinical systems, and similar low voltage systems.

A.7.3.1.2.1.8(B) Supplying the circuits serving equipment in the telecommunications entrance facility through an uninterrupted power system (UPS) provides a desirable level of redundancy.

A.7.3.1.2.1.8(C) Consideration should be given to the reliability of power supply to the HVAC equipment because of its important function within the telecommunications entrance facility.

A.7.3.1.2.2.2 In combined spaces, care should be taken to provide separation of, and adequate service access for, service provider equipment.

A.7.3.3.1.1 Depending on the size and scope of the Category 1 space, an audiovisual type system or tone visual type system may be used for the nurse call system. While both system types provide audible tones and illuminated light sources to annunciate call events, the audiovisual system provides voice communication capabilities to enable staff to speak with patients or other staff at locations remote from the patient's room. Depending on the requirements for the different care areas, combinations of audiovisual and tone visual nurse call system equipment can be used.

A.7.3.3.1.1.3 The fundamental operation of a listed nurse call system provides alerts and notifications of call system events. In addition to the call notifications activated by call stations, a nurse call system should also provide alert notifications for system self-monitoring events to annunciate trouble conditions that can occur within the system itself.

△ **A.7.3.3.1.1.5** A nurse call system can be integrated with a wireless communication system for the purposes of providing supplemental call notifications to staff-carried wireless devices. Such notifications are considered supplemental unless the wireless communication system is listed to UL 1069, *Hospital Signaling and Nurse Call Equipment.* Supplemental communication systems should be provided with appropriate NRTL safety certifications and listings that are consistent with the intended use as a stand-alone wireless communication system.

The requirements in ANSI/IEC/ISO 80001-1-1, *Application of Risk Management for IT Networks Incorporating Medical Devices — Part 1-1: Risk Management of Medical IT Networks,* and ANSI/IEC/ISO 80001-2-5, *Application of Risk Management for IT Networks Incorporating Medical Devices — Part 2-5: Application Guidance — Guidance for Distributed Alarm Systems,* should be followed whenever a nurse call system is integrated with a supplemental communication system.

A.7.3.3.1.2.1 Patient care spaces and nursing unit support areas can contain many types of call stations with varying combinations of call initiation functions (e.g., code call, staff emergency, medical device alarm, help, assistance). A single call station can be equipped and configured to activate a single call type or a number of different call types, and can have bidirectional voice communication capability.

A.7.3.3.1.2.2 Patient stations provide a means for patients to summon assistance from the nursing staff. Calling devices such as listed wired or wireless pillow speakers, pendant controls call cords, and patient- or staff-worn personal pendants are permitted to initiate patient or staff calls. A call station that serves two beds is permitted when beds are located adjacent to each other.

A.7.3.3.1.2.3 Primary signaling of a medical device alarm is a requirement of the medical device itself, per the governing regulatory standard, and is beyond the scope of this code.

A.7.3.3.1.3.1 When two or more call stations are located in the same area and all are visible from any call location, the alarm should be capable of being canceled at any of these locations. This method of call cancelation can be applied to all call station types.

A.7.3.3.1.4 A code call can also be referred to as an emergency resuscitation alarm.

A.7.3.3.1.4.1 When two or more call stations are located in the same area and all are visible from any call location, the alarm should be capable of being canceled at any of these locations. This method of call cancelation can be applied to all call station types.

△ **A.7.3.3.5.2** Currently, no standard exists for the certification of a wireless communication system having the specific intended use as a clinical alarm communication and notification system. While desirable for enhancing clinical communications and optimizing clinical workflow, these types of communication systems have inherent reliability limitations. For example, there is no notification at a wireless pager when it is out of range for receiving messages and there is no alert at the central station that the communication device is unreachable or return confirmation that a message has been delivered or received.

A document with information on how to manage and control risk is ANSI/AAMI/IEC 80001-1, *Application of Risk Management for IT Networks Incorporating Medical Devices — Part 1: Roles, Responsibilities and Activities.*

There might be manufacturers of FDA-cleared medical equipment that can have wireless communication capabilities and that might be FDA cleared for a specific intended use. Such medical equipment would typically be certified to one or more ANSI/AAMI ES60601 standards (e.g., 60601-1, *Medical electrical equipment — Part 1: General requirements for basic safety and essential performance;* 60601-2, *Medical electrical equipment — Part 2: Collateral standard: Electromagnetic disturbances — Requirements and tests;* 60601-8, *Medical electrical equipment — Part 8: Collateral standard: Alarm systems — General requirements, tests and guidance for alarm systems in medical electrical equipment and medical electrical systems;* and so forth).

The responsible organization can also contract with a provider of communication equipment to integrate a wireless communication system with nurse call system or with the clinical IT network for the purposes of enhanced clinical staff communications. However, such an integration would not be listed to any governing standard.

Therefore, where a wireless communication system is integrated with the clinical IT network and used as a clinical alarm notification or enhanced communication system, it is necessary for the responsible organization to follow and enact the risk management requirements established in ANSI/AAMI/IEC 80001-1, *Application of Risk Management for IT Networks Incorporating Medical Devices — Part 1: Roles, Responsibilities and Activities.*

Further in this context, the end-to-end system integration and its management need to also conform to the guidelines established in ANSI/IEC/ISO 80001-2-5, *Application of Risk Management for IT Networks Incorporating Medical Devices — Part 2-5: Application Guidance — Guidance for Distributed Alarm Systems.*

A.7.3.3.7.1 As the clinical environment becomes more and more automated, integrated, and evolved, there is a need to ensure that the servers and networking equipment that transport interoperable clinical data and communications over a clinical IT network are properly instituted and sufficiently managed. ANSI/AAMI/IEC 80001-1, *Application of Risk Management for IT Networks Incorporating Medical Devices — Part 1: Roles, Responsibilities and Activities,* is the governing standard by which the clinical IT network needs to be managed.

△ **A.7.3.3.7.2** While all nurse call systems need to be listed to UL 1069, *Hospital Signaling and Nurse Call Equipment,* not all nurse call systems can be identified for use on a shared clinical IT network. Only those nurse call systems that are listed for use on a shared network are permitted to use the clinical IT network infrastructure.

A.7.3.3.7.3 To ensure an effective, reliable, and resilient clinical IT network, two independent physical pathways providing network communications need to be provided. Both paths need to be at operational readiness at all times. Operational readiness can be ensured by continuous self-monitoring of each path. All equipment items comprising each clinical IT network path need to be verified for availability by means of communication. End-point terminal equipment items (e.g., computers, monitors, discrete medical devices, discrete devices comprising the nurse call system, and so forth), which are connected to but are not part of the clinical IT network, only require one physical connection to the clinical IT network.

A.7.3.3.7.5 Examples for operational monitoring of the clinical IT network includes, but is not limited to, the following:

(1) Environmental changes, including risks associated with data and system security vulnerabilities
(2) Operational/performance feedback from both automated measurement and user feedback (e.g., speed problems, high error rates, equipment failure, malicious software attacks, and so forth)

A.8.2.1 There are no interdependencies for each type of system (e.g., medical gas, electrical, potable water, nonpotable water, nonmedical compressed air, heating). A risk assessment of each system should be conducted to evaluate the risk to the patient, staff, and visitors.

A.9.2.1 There are no interdependencies for each type of system (e.g., medical gas, electrical, potable water, nonpotable water, nonmedical compressed air, plumbing). A risk assessment of each system should be conducted to evaluate the risk to the patient, staff, and visitors. It is possible when applying this section to identify multiple categories of systems serving a single patient. For example, see A.4.1.

A.9.3.1.3 Previous editions had required smoke purge systems in these locations. The elimination of flammable anesthetics and limited use of combustible material in modern ORs makes this requirement obsolete.

A.9.3.3.2 ASHRAE Guideline 0, *The Commissioning Process*, ASHRAE Guideline 1.1, *HVAC&R Technical Requirements for the Commissioning Process*, and ASHRAE Standard 202, *Commissioning Process for Buildings and Systems*, while not mandatory, can provide guidance for this requirement.

A.9.3.6.3 Paragraph 9.3.6.3 only covers fluids that are stored in enclosed spaces.

A.9.3.6.5.1 See Table A.11.3.5.

N **A.9.3.6.5.2.1** The opening calculation is based on the volume of gas released if the vessel is open to atmospheric temperature and pressure. A typical release rate is 28.3 m^3 (1000 ft^3) of gas from 32.88 L (8.69 gal) of liquid.

N **A.9.3.7.1** An example of an active system is a waste anesthetic gas disposal (WAGD) as described in Chapter 5.

N **A.9.3.8** More details or specific information can be found in ISO 16571, *Systems for evacuation of plume generated by medical devices*; NIOSH 96-128, "Control of Smoke From Laser/Electric Surgical Procedures"; and CSA Z305.13, *Plume Scavenging in Surgical, Diagnostic, Therapeutic, and Aesthetic Settings*.

A.9.3.8.1 Inlets can be of any design suitable for the plume capture device in use, provided the design does not permit interconnection to any medical vacuum, WAGD, or housekeeping vacuum systems.

Flow control for the inlets should be as appropriate for the plume capture device in use.

A warning system, such as one that uses a building automation system, that monitors the operation of the source equipment should be provided.

A.9.3.8.1(1) A dedicated medical plume evacuation system can serve multiple locations. The discharge of a dedicated system can be filtered or unfiltered.

N **A.9.3.8.3** Where used for plume evacuation exhaust, a semi-active waste gas exhaust system in accordance with 9.3.7.1.1 should be sized for the sum of the flow from all producers.

A.10.1 An appliance that yields erroneous data or functions poorly is potentially harmful. Quality and assurance of full appliance performance is not covered, except as it relates to direct electrical or fire injury to patients or personnel.

The material in this annex, as it relates to electrical safety, interprets some of the basic criteria by presenting different methodologies and alternative procedures to achieve the level of safety defined by the criteria.

A.10.1.3 Risk categorization is not appropriate for this chapter. Much of the chapter deals with electrical safety issues. Any line-powered device that does not meet these requirements poses the risk of electric shock to patients or personnel, regardless of where it is used or the clinical application of the device. Shock and fire risk is not dependent on the required reliability of the device or the extent to which patient diagnosis and treatment depends on the device. Even categorization regarding direct cardiac connection or patient contact are not relevant as death or injury can occur in any case.

A.10.2.3.2.4 ANSI/AAMI ES60601-1, *Medical electrical equipment — Part 1: General requirements for basic safety and essential performance*, defines the terms *protective earth conductor* and *functional earth conductor*. A protective earth conductor is relied upon for safety and provides one means of protection from electric shock. A functional earth conductor has no safety function and does not provide a means of protection against electric shock. A double-insulated medical product is permitted (but not required) to have a functional earth conductor that is referred to as a *functional ground conductor*.

A.10.2.3.6 Consideration should be given to certification of relocatable power taps in accordance with UL 1363A, *Outline of Investigation for Special Purpose Relocatable Power Taps*, which addresses the requirements currently in this code and additional safety requirements, such as use of hospital-grade receptacle outlets and plugs, integrity of the enclosures, and testing for grounding and leakage current.

A.10.2.3.6(1) Tape, adhesive, and hook-and-loop fasteners are not considered to be secure means of attachment. A clamp or bracket that has been hand or tool tightened is considered securely attached.

A.10.2.3.6(2) A means of meeting the requirement is through summation of nameplate ampacity of connected equipment and proactive administrative actions (e.g., education, signs). A circuit protective device (e.g., circuit breaker, surge protector, supplementary protector), alone, is not considered sufficient.

A.10.2.4.3(2) The disconnection means is permitted only to facilitate replacement; as such, ceiling drop cords cannot be disconnected for alternative usage. See Chapter 6 for criteria of receptacles.

A.10.3.1 Visual inspections do not have to be formal or documented by any particular staff member. All staff are expected to be observant of the condition of the equipment they use, including power cord assemblies.

A.10.3.2 There are several methods for measuring ground-wire resistance accurately. Three examples are described as follows and shown in Figure A.10.3.2(a) through Figure A.10.3.2(c):

(1) *Two-Wire Resistance Technique.* A known current is fed through the unknown resistance. A high-input-impedance voltmeter measures the voltage drop across the resistance, *R*, and *R* is calculated as voltage divided by impedance, *V*/*I*. This technique measures the lead resistance in series with the unknown resistance. When the unknown resistance is a ground wire (less than 0.15 ohm), the lead resistance is appreciable. This is accounted for by shorting the lead wires together and "zeroing" the voltmeter. The actual resistance, in effect, subtracts out the lead wire resistance. In order for this technique to be reasonably accurate for measuring ground wires, an active high-impedance millivoltmeter has to be used.

(2) *Four-Wire Resistance Technique.* This technique is very similar to the two-wire resistance technique. The difference is that the known current is fed to the resistance to be measured through a pair of leads separate from the pair of leads to the voltmeter. The voltmeter is measuring the true voltage across the resistance to be measured, regardless of the resistance of the measuring leads. This method eliminates the need for zeroing out the measuring lead resistance.

(3) *AC Current Method.* This technique utilizes a step-down transformer of known voltage output to feed current through the ground wire and measure the current that flows. The impedance of the ground wire is then calculated by Ohm's law.

Note that the internal impedance of the measuring circuit has to be established with the test leads shorted. This value needs to be subtracted from the test measurement.

A.10.3.3 For complex leakage current waveforms, a single reading from an appropriate metering system can represent the physiologically effective value of the composite waveform, provided that the contribution of each component to the total reading is weighted in accordance with 10.3.3.

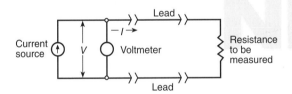

FIGURE A.10.3.2(a)   Two-Wire Resistance Technique.

FIGURE A.10.3.2(b)   Four-Wire Resistance Technique.

FIGURE A.10.3.2(c)   AC Current Method.

This weighting can be achieved by a frequency response–shaping network that precedes a flat-response meter, or by a meter whose own frequency response characteristic matches that of 10.3.3.

If the required performance is obtained by a meter with integral response-shaping properties, then that meter should have a constant input resistance of 1000 ohms. (A high-input-impedance meter can be used by shunting a 1000 ohm resistor across the meter's input terminals.)

If, however, the required frequency response is obtained by a network that precedes an otherwise flat-response meter, then the input impedance of the network should be 1000 ohms ± 10 percent, over the frequency range from 0 to 1 MHz, and the frequency response of the network–meter combination should be substantially independent of the impedance of the signal source.

For maximum chassis leakage current permitted (i.e., 300 µA) below 1 kHz, this network will yield the limiting current of 10 mA above 30 kHz.

A suggested input network is shown in Figure A.10.3.3.

A.10.3.3.3 This test is not valid when performed on the load side of an isolation transformer or an isolated power system, because the values obtained will be falsely low.

A.10.3.5.4 Where existing equipment exceeds 500 µA, methods to reduce leakage current, such as the addition of small isolation transformers to that equipment, or methods that provide equivalent safety by adding redundant equipment ground, are permissible.

A.10.3.6 Although the touch current value is 500 µA, the patient lead leakage current limit for nonisolated input has been intentionally limited to 100 µA. This decision is in recognition of the need for a greater level of electrical safety for those portions of devices that make direct electrical patient connection.

A.10.5.2.2 The reference to ANSI/AAMI ES60601-1, *Medical electrical equipment — Part 1: General requirements for basic safety and essential performance,* is the US version and includes deviations for use in the United States. Other countries often use the IEC version or other versions with deviations.

A.10.5.2.5 Systems should comply with the appropriate medical device or system standards such as ANSI/AAMI ES60601-1, *Medical electrical equipment — Part 1: General requirements for basic safety and essential performance.* Consideration should also be given to the guidance provided as part of the documentation supplied with the individual medical equipment.

A.10.5.4.5 The use of electrical equipment in spaces where there is a high oxygen content is a matter of concern because

FIGURE A.10.3.3   Leakage Current Measurements (1.0 Millivoltmeter Reading Corresponds to Input Current of 1.0 Microampere).

of the fire hazard. It is particularly a problem where the oxygen is "pure," that is, 80 percent to 90 percent, because materials that are not very flammable in ordinary air become extremely flammable in pure oxygen.

In medical practice, particularly in surgery, patients are often given supplemental oxygen via respirator, anesthesia machines, and so forth. Such supplemental oxygen can range from room air to 100 percent oxygen. Clearly, different levels of protection are needed.

This code addresses the problem by defining the following three elements of the situation:

(1) *Type of Air.* An oxygen-enriched atmosphere (OEA) is air that ranges from slightly enriched (23.5 percent, rather than 21 percent) to total oxygen (100 percent).
(2) *Type of Apparatus.* Oxygen delivery equipment (ODE) is a device that delivers an OEA to a patient.
(3) *Type of Space.* A site of intentional expulsion (SIE) is a small-volume space where oxygen that has been delivered to the patient is discharged to the ambient air.

When an OEA is within ODE, it is much more likely to have a high concentration of oxygen. Paragraph 10.5.4 therefore advises manufacturers, and A.10.5.4.5 advises users, of precautions to take to reduce the fire hazard. Paragraph 10.5.4 lists four ways of attacking the problem. Note that an OEA can be created not only in a ventilator or oxygen tubing, but also in an oxygen tent or incubator. Special precautions should be taken.

At the other extreme of hazard is a space in the open air, the site of intentional expulsion (SIE). This space is defined as located within 30.5 cm (12 in.) of the exhaust port, because, in most instances, dilution to ambient levels occurs within a few inches of the port; 30.5 cm (12 in.) provides an adequate safety factor. Paragraph 10.5.4.1 provides guidance to minimize this hazard by requiring that only those parts of the apparatus that are intended to be within the SIE are to be of concern. Even these components, such as nurse call buttons, leads, and so forth, do not necessarily need to be listed for use in OEA, because they usually conform to provisions of 10.5.4.1(4); that is, they do not have hot surfaces, and they meet the requirements of Figure 10.5.4.1(a) through Figure 10.5.4.1(f).

The intent of A.10.5.4.5 is to advise users to specify appliances that meet higher requirements where the hazard is higher but not to overspecify where the hazard is minimal. Thus, as they are ordinarily used, nurse call buttons, pillow speakers, and so forth, do not need to be listed for use in oxygen-enriched atmospheres.

Note, however, that these requirements apply only to the intended use. The user should exercise vigilance to guard against an unintended use or an accidental failure, which can vastly increase the hazard.

A.10.5.4.6 Where possible, combustible materials such as hair, fabric, and paper should be removed from the vicinity where the energy is delivered. Water-soluble surgical jelly has been shown to dramatically reduce the combustibility of such materials.

A.10.5.5.1 Most laboratory fires involve biomedical or other electronic equipment failures. The most common ignition factors are short circuits or ground faults. Electrical wire or cable insulation is the material most likely to first ignite in a clinical laboratory fire. (*See Hoeltge, G.A., Miller, A., Klein, B.R., Hamlin, W.B., "Accidental Fires in Clinical Laboratories."*)

A.10.5.6.2 Although several approaches to documentation exist in hospitals, the minimum acceptable documentation should identify what was tested, when it was tested, and whether it performed successfully. Adopting a system of exception reporting can be the most efficient form of record keeping for routine rechecks of equipment or systems, thereby minimizing technicians' time in recording the value of each measurement taken. For example, once a test protocol is established, which simply means testing the equipment or system consistent with Chapter 10, the only item (value) that needs to be recorded is the failure or the deviation from the requirements of the chapter that was detected when a corrective action (repair) was undertaken. This approach can serve to eliminate, for example, the need to keep individual room sheets to record measured results on each receptacle or to record measurement values of all types of leakage current tests.

A.10.5.8.1 "Personnel" includes physicians, nurses, nursing assistants, engineers, and technicians.

A.10.5.8.3 Qualification for equipment servicing does not always include manufacturer training, as required knowledge and skills can be obtained by other means.

A.11.1.2 Respiratory therapy is an allied health specialty employed with medical direction in the treatment, management, control, diagnostic evaluation, and care of patients with deficiencies and abnormalities of the cardiopulmonary system. (Courtesy of the American Association for Respiratory Therapy, 1720 Regal Row, Dallas, TX 75235.)

Respiratory therapy includes the therapeutic use of the following: medical gases and administration apparatus, environmental control systems, humidification, aerosols, medications, ventilatory support, bronchopulmonary drainage, pulmonary rehabilitation, cardiopulmonary resuscitation, and airway management. (Courtesy of the American Association for Respiratory Therapy, 1720 Regal Row, Dallas, TX 75235.)

There is a continual need for human diligence in the establishment and maintenance of safe practices for respiratory therapy. It is essential for personnel having responsibility for respiratory therapy to establish and enforce appropriate programs to fulfill the provisions of this chapter.

It is the responsibility of the administrative and professional staff of a hospital, or safety director, if one is appointed, to adopt and enforce appropriate regulations for a hospital. In other health care facilities, responsibility could be assigned to a safety director, or other responsible person, who is, in turn, responsible to the administration.

In institutions having a respiratory therapy service, it is recommended that this service be directly responsible for the administration of Chapter 11. Hazards can be mitigated only when there is continual recognition and understanding.

A.11.1.4 See Chapter 14.

A.11.1.5 Risk categorization is not appropriate for this chapter. Much of the chapter deals with gas equipment safety issues. Any storage or use of gas equipment in a health care facility presents risks that the requirements of this chapter reduce. Any gas-related device that does not meet these requirements poses the same risk to patients or personnel, regardless of where it is used or its clinical application.

A.11.2.7 It is particularly important that the intermixing of oxidizing and flammable gases under pressure be scrupulously avoided. Such mixing can result in a violent explosion.

A.11.3.5 Electric wiring and equipment are not required to be explosionproof. See Table A.11.3.5.

A.11.3.5.2(5) The fire resistance rating for walls and floors is determined in accordance with ASTM E119, *Standard Test Methods for Fire Tests of Building Construction and Materials*, or UL 263, *Fire Tests of Building Construction and Materials*. The fire protection rating for doors is determined in accordance with NFPA 252.

A.11.3.5.2(6) Electrical devices should be physically protected, such as by use of a protective barrier around the electrical devices, or by location of the electrical device such that it will avoid causing physical damage to the cylinders or containers. For example, the device could be located at or above 1.5 m (5 ft) above finished floor or other location that will not allow the possibility of the cylinders or containers to come into contact with the electrical device as required by this section.

A.11.3.5.2(7) Examples of indirect heating include steam, hot water, and electric heating.

Table A.11.3.5 Typical Medical Gas Cylinders' Volume and Weight of Available Contents [All Volumes at 21.1°C (70°F) and 101.325 kPa (14.696 psi)]

Cylinder Style and Dimensions	Nominal Volume [L (in.³)]	Contents	Air	Carbon Dioxide	Helium	Nitrogen	Nitrous Oxide	Oxygen	Mixtures of Oxygen — Helium	CO₂
B 8.89 × 33 cm (3½ in. O.D. × 13 in.)	1.43 (87)	kPa (psig)		5778 (838)				13,100 (1900)		
		L (ft³)		370 (13)				200 (7)		
		kg (lb-oz)		0.68 (1–8)				—		
D 10.8 × 43 cm (4¼ in. O.D. × 17 in.)	2.88 (176)	kPa (psig)	13,100 (1900)	5778 (838)	11,032 (1600)	13,100 (1900)	5137 (745)	13,100 (1900)	*	*
		L (ft³)	375 (13)	940 (33)	300 (11)	370 (13)	940 (33)	400 (14)	300 (11)	400 (14)
		kg (lb-oz)	—	1.73 (3–13)	—	—	1.73 (3–13)	—	*	*
E 10.8 × 66 cm (4¼ in. O.D. × 26 in.)	4.80 (293)	kPa (psig)	13100 (1900)	5778 / 5778 (838)	11,032 (1600)	13,100 (1900)	5137 (745)	13,100 (1900)	*	*
		L (ft³)	625 (22)	1590 (56)	500 (18)	610 (22)	1590 (56)	660 (23)	500 (18)	660 (23)
		kg (lb-oz)	—	2.92 (6–7)	—	—	2.92 (6–7)	—	*	*
M 17.8 × 109 cm (7 in. O.D. × 43 in.)	21.9 (1337)	kPa (psig)	13,100 (1900)	5778 (838)	11,032 (1600)	15,169 (2200)	5137 (745)	15,169 (2200)	*	*
		L (ft³)	2850 (101)	7570 (267)	2260 (80)	3200 (113)	7570 (267)	3450 (122)	2260 (80)	3000 (106)
		kg (lb-oz)	—	13.9 (30–10)	—	—	13.9 (30–10)	—	*	*
G 21.6 × 130 cm (8½ in. O.D. × 51 in.)	38.8 (2370)	kPa (psig)	13,100 (1900)	5778 (838)	11,032 (1600)	15,169 (2200)	5137 (745)	15,169 (2200)	*	*
		L (ft³)	5050 (178)	12,300 (434)	4000 (141)	5000 (176)	13,800 (487)	6000 (211)	4000 (141)	5330 (188)
		kg (lb-oz)	—	22.7 (50–0)	—	—	25.4 (56–0)	—	*	*
H or K 23.5 × 130 cm (9¼ in. O.D. × 51 in.)	43.6 (2660)	kPa (psig)	15,169 (2200)	5778 (838)	15,169 (2200)	15,169 (2200)	5137 (745)	15,169† (2200†)	*	*
		L (ft³)	6550 (231)	15,840 (559)	6000 (212)	6400 (226)	15,800 (558)	6900 (244)	6000 (212)	15,840 (559)
		kg (lb-oz)	—	29.1 (64)	—	—	29.1 (64)	—	*	*

Notes:

These are computed contents based on nominal cylinder volumes and rounded to no greater variance than ±1 percent.

*The pressure and weight of mixed gases will vary according to the composition of the mixture.

†275 ft³/7800 L cylinders at 2490 psig are available on request.

Source: Compressed Gas Association, Inc.

Shaded text = Revisions. Δ = Text deletions and figure/table revisions. • = Section deletions. *N* = New material.

2024 Edition

A.11.3.5.2(12) Electrical devices should be physically protected, such as by use of a protective barrier around the electrical devices, or by location of the electrical device such that it will avoid causing physical damage to the cylinders or containers. For example, the device could be located at or above 1.5 m (5 ft) above finished floor or other location that will not allow the possibility of the cylinders or containers to come into contact with the electrical device as required by this section.

A.11.3.5.2(13) Considerations for this access include proximity to loading docks, access to elevators, and passage of cylinders through public areas.

A.11.3.6 When determining the volume of storage, do not consider cylinders and containers that are in use. Only the volume of stored gas that is in excess of 8.5 m³ (300 ft³) is required to be located in an enclosure, since 11.3.7 already permits up to 8.5 m³ (300 ft³) without any special storage requirements.

A.11.3.8 Limited quantities of combustibles applicable to the cylinders, such as cylinder labels, gauges, posted safety signs, and similar, are permitted.

A.11.4.1.1 The Pin-Index Safety System consists of a combination of two pins projecting from the yoke assembly of the apparatus and so positioned as to fit into matching holes drilled into the cylinder valves. It is intended to protect against the possibility of error in attaching the flush-type valves, with which gas cylinders and other sources of gas supply are equipped, to gas apparatus having yoke connections.

Δ **A.11.4.1.3** Fabrication specifications are contained in CGA V-1, *Standard for Compressed Gas Cylinder Valve Outlet and Inlet Connections* (ANSI B57.1). Connection No. 860, shown in that document, illustrates the system. Connection No. 870 (Oxygen, Medical), Connection No. 880 (Oxygen–Carbon Dioxide Mixture), Connection No. 890 (Oxygen–Helium Mixture), Connection No. 900 (Ethylene), Connection No. 910 (Nitrous Oxide), Connection No. 920 (Cyclopropane), Connection No. 930 (Helium), and Connection No. 940 (Carbon Dioxide) are for specific medical gases and gas mixtures and utilize the basic dimensions of Connection 860.

A.11.5.1.1.2 Outside of a patient care room, 11.5.1.1.2 prohibits sources of open flames within the site of intentional expulsion [1 ft (0.3 m)] of a nasal cannula. No sources of open flame are permitted within the area of administration [15 ft (4.3 m)] for other types of oxygen delivery equipment or in patient care spaces *(see 11.5.1.1.3)*.

The amount of oxygen delivered by a nasal cannula is limited. One ft (0.3 m) is sufficient separation from an oxygen-enriched atmosphere produced by a nasal cannula, which is oxygen delivery equipment used outside of patient care spaces. In the open air, dilution goes to ambient levels (not oxygen-enriched atmosphere) within a few inches of the cannula openings, but 12 in. (300 mm) provides an adequate safety factor. Other oxygen delivery equipment, such as masks, are not included since masks would not typically be associated with mobile patients in health care facilities and can deliver greater quantities of oxygen than nasal cannula.

The household-style nursing homes that include kitchens intended for residents' use and enclosed gas fireplaces present a source of flame ignition to which residents will be exposed. Residents utilizing a nasal cannula would potentially not be allowed to participate in the cooking because it would place the cooking flame within the site of intentional expulsion. However, they would be allowed in the kitchen area to assist in preparing the food and to socialize with other residents and staff in the kitchen similar to what happens in the kitchens of residential environments.

The primary concern is that flame-producing equipment exists in many places in a nursing home and that it would be impractical to maintain a resident with a nasal cannula a minimum of 15 ft (4.3 m) (Area of Administration) away from the flame-producing equipment. Typical flame-producing equipment found in a nursing home includes the following:

(1) Candles in chapels
(2) Open kitchens using gas cooking equipment
(3) Fireplaces
(4) Fuel-fired heating equipment
(5) Private family dining rooms using fuel-fired equipment
(6) Canned cooking fuel (e.g., used under chafing dishes)

A.11.5.1.1.3 Patients and hospital personnel in the area of administration should be advised of respiratory therapy hazards and regulations.

Visitors should be cautioned of these hazards through the prominent posting of signs. *(See 11.3.12.)*

A.11.5.1.1.4 Solid fuel-burning appliances include wood-burning fireplaces, wood stoves, and similar appliances. These pose a greater risk in locations where oxygen is being provided than gas-fueled appliances, in part due to their ability to emit embers into the environment.

A.11.5.1.1.5 Such toys have been associated with fire incidents in health care facilities.

A suggested text for precautionary signs for oxygen tent canopies and oxygen hoods used in pediatric nursing units is the following:

CAUTION: OXYGEN IN USE

ONLY TOYS APPROVED BY

NURSES MAY BE GIVEN TO CHILD

A.11.5.1.3.3 Service manuals, instructions, and procedures provided by the manufacturer should be considered in the development of a program for maintenance of equipment. The experience accumulated by the facility and others (evidence-based maintenance) should be used to adjust manufacturer's recommendations whenever and wherever appropriate, even if they indicate no maintenance program is required.

A.11.5.2.1.1 "Personnel" typically includes physicians, nurses, nursing assistants, respiratory therapists, engineers, technicians, and others.

A.11.5.2.2.2 CGA P-2.5, *Standard for Transfilling of High Pressure Gaseous Oxygen Used for Respiration*, contains both mandatory and nonmandatory language. Enforceable language uses the term shall; nonmandatory language uses the term should. This section indicates that this code is making reference only to the mandatory requirements in that document.

A.11.5.2.3.2 CGA P-2.6, *Standard for Transfilling of Liquid Oxygen Used for Respiration*, describes the recommended precautions and safety procedures when transfilling liquid oxygen used for respiration. Mishandling of oxygen presents potential hazards to both trained and untrained persons. Organizations engaged in the transfilling of liquid oxygen should ensure that personnel are familiar with the hazards of cryogenic liquid oxygen and that they comply with applicable regulations and safety practices.

A.11.5.2.4 Oxygen concentrator filling systems are FDA approved and have been in use for many years with excellent safety records. The inherent risks associated with typical transfilling do not apply to oxygen concentrator filling compressors.

Limitations were placed on these systems in order to prevent the risks associated with larger, higher flow, or higher pressure systems being introduced into the patient environment. The cylinder size was limited to cylinders normally used for patient ambulation. The filling rate was limited to prevent excessive heating of the cylinder contents. The filling pressure was limited based on the existing industry practice.

A.11.5.3.2 Precautionary signs should be at least 21 cm × 28 cm (8 in. × 11 in.).

Any material that can burn in air will burn more rapidly in the presence of oxygen.

Special signs and additional precautionary measures should be employed whenever foreign languages present a communication problem. *(See Figure A.11.5.3.2.)*

No electrical equipment is permitted within an oxygen enclosure or within 1.5 m (5 ft) of the enclosure.

A.11.6.5.5 For further guidance, refer to CGA P-50, *Standard for Site Security.*

A.11.7.3.1 The seller has a responsibility to provide written instructions to the user in accordance with 11.7.2. In fulfilling this responsibility, the seller should explain to the user the use of the equipment being delivered and precautions that are to be taken. The seller's written instructions are intended to make the user aware of the hazards of the material and to provide recommendations that will address the location, restraint, movement, and refill of portable containers when these containers are to be refilled by the user. However, the user has the responsibility to receive, read, and understand the written material regarding storage and use of liquid oxygen and the containers and equipment that are furnished by the seller. In addition to specific information or instructions provided by the seller or equipment manufacturer regarding the storage or use of the equipment and of the liquid oxygen or the containers used, the user remains responsible to see that the containers are used or maintained in accordance with the seller's instructions to ensure that they are as follows:

(1) Located and maintained in accordance with the requirements of 11.7.3.2

FIGURE A.11.5.3.2   Suggested Minimum Text for Precautionary Signs.

(2) Restrained in accordance with the requirements of 11.7.3.3
(3) Handled or transported in accordance with the requirements of 11.7.3.4
(4) Refilled in accordance with the requirements of 11.7.3.6 and the manufacturer's instructions when liquid oxygen portable containers are to be refilled by the user

CGA P-2.7, *Guideline for the Safe Storage, Handling, and Use of Small Portable Liquid Oxygen Systems in Health Care Facilities,* describes the recommended precautions and safety procedures to be followed when liquid oxygen systems are used within health care facilities. Mishandling of oxygen presents potential hazards to both trained and untrained persons. Therefore, it is important that personnel who assume responsibility for oxygen equipment and its use be familiar with the hazards of oxygen, the operational characteristic of the equipment, and the precautions to be observed while using it.

A.11.7.3.3 Two points of contact can be provided by using elements of a room or furnishings in the room, such as the walls of a corner of a room, or a wall and a furnishing or object, such as a table or a desk.

A.11.7.3.5 CGA P-2.7, *Guideline for the Safe Storage, Handling, and Use of Small Portable Liquid Oxygen Systems in Health Care Facilities,* describes the recommended precautions and safety procedures to be followed when liquid oxygen systems are used within health care facilities, such as a 1.5 m (5 ft) separation from electrical appliances during filling and use.

Mishandling of oxygen presents potential hazards to both trained and untrained persons. It is therefore important that personnel who assume responsibility for oxygen equipment and its use be familiar with the hazards of oxygen, the operational characteristic of the equipment, and the precautions to be observed while using it.

A.11.7.3.6.1.1 Drip pans or similar containment devices are used in order to protect against liquid oxygen spillage coming into contact with combustible surfaces, including asphalt, which would elevate the potential for ignition.

A.12.1 Such facilities include, but are not limited to, hospitals, convalescent or nursing homes, and emergency receiving stations. A government authority could formally designate such facilities as disaster treatment centers. Such facilities would not normally include doctors' or dentists' offices, medical laboratories, or school nurseries, unless such facilities are used for treatment of disaster victims. National bioterrorism preparedness efforts call for the use of schools and other large public facilities to provide facilities for mass immunization.

Δ **A.12.1.1** Wherever the term *hospital* is used in Chapter 12, the term should also apply to other types of health care facilities. Applicable facilities include, but are not limited to, hospitals, convalescent or nursing homes, and emergency receiving stations. A government authority could formally designate such facilities as disaster treatment centers. Such facilities would not normally include doctors' or dentists' offices, medical laboratories, or school nurseries, unless such facilities are used for treatment of disaster victims. National bioterrorism preparedness efforts call for the use of schools and other large public facilities to provide for mass immunization. An emergency management program (formerly known as a disaster plan or internal/external plan) encompasses activities across four phases: mitigation, preparedness, response, and recovery. Mitigation activities are those designed to reduce or eliminate the impact of hazards. Preparedness activities include those that build organizational and individual capabilities to deal with disasters. Response activities include all necessary actions to stop ongoing negative effects of a disaster. Recovery activities are those that restore the organization, its employees, and the community back to normal.

NFPA 1660 includes an internationally accepted framework for an emergency program. Chapter 12 of NFPA 99 recognizes this overall structure and provides additional information useful to health care organizations.

N **A.12.1.2** Chapter 12 is based on the foundations of NFPA 1660.

A.12.2.1 In time of disaster, all persons are subject to certain constraints or authorities not present during normal circumstances. The emergency operations plans written by a health care facility should be reviewed and coordinated with such authorities so as to prevent confusion. Such authorities include, but are not limited to, civil authorities (such as a fire department, a police department, a public health department, or emergency medical service councils), Centers for Disease Control, Federal Bureau of Investigation, and emergency management or military authorities. See Annex D for publications explaining how the out-of-hospital response is organized to multiple and mass casualty incidents. Further, an authority having jurisdiction can impose upon the senior management of the facility the responsibility for participating in a community emergency management program.

A.12.2.3 It is strongly recommended that executive and medical leadership representatives play a key role in the emergency management committee and planning process. The following list is not intended to be all-inclusive, and additional representatives might be needed based on the level of care provided or the structure of the organization:

(1) Bioterrorism coordination
(2) Communications/data management
(3) Finance
(4) Human resources
(5) Legal/risk management
(6) Public relations
(7) Purchasing/materials management
(8) Quality management
(9) Training and education

A.12.2.3.1 An individual member can represent multiple disciplines, as appropriate, to the facility. Those departments, services, and areas that have a significant role in the facility's emergency management activities can include, but are not limited to, the following key areas:

(1) Senior management
(2) Medical staff
(3) Nursing
(4) Infection prevention
(5) Emergency department
(6) Facility engineering
(7) Safety/industrial hygiene
(8) Security
(9) Information technology
(10) Materials management
(11) Marketing/public relations
(12) Food services
(13) Environmental services
(14) Other key areas within the organization

A.12.2.3.3 Federal, state, and local governments are required to use an incident command system (ICS) based on the National Incident Management System (NIMS). Although private sector hospitals are not required to be NIMS compliant, many are choosing to comply, not only to integrate with other emergency responders but also to remain eligible to receive certain federal grant monies. HICS, the Hospital Incident Command System, was specifically designed to be NIMS compliant, and, therefore, many hospitals use this model, either as developed or with some customization. HICS can be customized and adapted to other types of health care facilities.

HICS is led by an incident commander and assisted by command staff consisting of the public information officer, safety officer, and liaison officer, and those medical/technical specialists who are appropriate to the event. Section chiefs are responsible for each of the following sections:

(1) Operations Section: Conducts the tactical operations to carry out the incident action plan using defined objectives and directing all necessary resources
(2) Planning Section: Collects and evaluates information for decision support, maintains resource status information, prepares the Incident Action Plan, and maintains documentation
(3) Logistics Section: Provides support, resources, and other services to meet the operational objectives
(4) Finance/Administration: Monitors costs related to the incident and provides accounting services, time recording, and cost analyses

Each section is composed of subordinate positions that are divided into branches or units.

Features of HICS include the following:

(1) Clear chain of command
(2) Manageable span of control
(3) Common terminology
(4) Adaptability to unified command

HICS tools include the following:

(1) Job action sheets detailing position responsibilities
(2) Forms to document the event

HICS was intended to be used not only for emergencies but also for planned events. Complete HICS documentation is free and available for download at www.emsa.ca.gov.

A.12.4.1 Consideration should be given to all sites affiliated with the organization. Each component of the health care organization should either have their own emergency management program and plan or be part of the overall organization's emergency management program and plan.

A.12.4.1.1 Organizations that are part of an integrated health care system can choose to develop an emergency operations plan (EOP) using a system approach, rather than individual facility EOPs.

A.12.4.2 The Assistant Secretary of Preparedness and Response (ASPR) defines the term *health care coalition (HCC)* in *2017-2022 Health Care Preparedness and Response Capabilities* as "A group of individual health care and response organizations [e.g., hospitals, emergency medical services (EMS), emergency management organizations, public health agencies] in a defined geographic location. HCCs play a critical role in developing health care delivery system preparedness and response capabilities. HCCs serve as multiagency coordinating groups that support and integrate with [Emergency Support Function-8] ESF-8 [health and medical services] activities in the context of incident command system (ICS) responsibilities."

Health care facilities should participate in health care coalitions to improve community emergency planning, resource sharing, and other collaborative efforts. Participation in other types of collaborative groups can also be beneficial.

A.12.5.3.1.2 By basing the planning of health care emergency management on realistic conceptual events, the program reflects those issues or events that are predictable for the environment in which the organization operates. Thus, such conceptual planning should focus on issues, such as severe weather typical in the locale, situations that can occur due to close proximity of industrial, government, or transportation complexes, or earthquake possibilities due to local seismic activity. Planning should also incorporate knowledge available in the emergency management research about how individuals, small groups, organizations, communities, and societies behave during emergencies.

A.12.5.3.1.3(1) Continuity of operations can include, but is not limited to, maintaining staffing levels, resources and assets, ability to obtain support from the outside environment, and leadership sustainability. At a minimum, plans should include the following:

(1) Leadership succession
(2) Delegation of legal authority
(3) Restoration of critical systems

A.12.5.3.2.3(7) This should include additional information on the development, maintenance, and evaluation of hazardous materials first receivers decontamination programs.

A.12.5.3.3.6.1(5) Emergency internal and external communications systems should be established to facilitate communication with security forces and other authorities having jurisdiction, as well as internal patient care and service units in the event normal communications methods are rendered inoperative. The basic form of communication in a disaster is the telephone system. As part of the contingency plan to maintain communication, a plan for restoring telephone systems or using alternate systems is necessary. Typically, the first line of internal defense for a system outage is strategically placed power-failure telephones that are designed to continue to function in the event of system failure (e.g., dedicated lines, fax lines). Plans for external outages and load control should include the use of pay phones, where available, that have first priority status in external system restoration. Facilities should preplan restoration activities and prioritization with their telephone service providers. A review with the state and other communications agencies (Government Emergency Telecommunications Service, Wireless Priority Service, Health and Homeland Alert Network) should be conducted.

Contingency plans should also contain strategies for the use of radio frequency communications to supplement landline usage. The plan should include a means to distribute and use two-way radio communication throughout the facility. A plan for the incorporation and use of amateur radio operators should also be considered.

It should be recognized that single-channel radio communication is less desirable than telephone system restoration due to the limited number of messages that can be managed. Cellular telephones, although useful in some disaster situations, should not be considered a contingency that has high reliability due to their vulnerability to the load control schemes of telephone companies. Text messaging has been proven to be more reliable than cellular phone calls. Social media can be an important tool for emergency communication, but it must be managed so that responses to inquiries can be provided. Portable email devices, satellite telephones, and audio- and videoconferencing services are useful tools to link key staff and organizations.

A.12.5.3.3.6.3 Prior to a disaster, facilities should formally coordinate their security needs with local law enforcement agencies. The health care institution will find it necessary to share its emergency operations plans with local law enforcement agencies or, better still, involve them in the process of planning for security support during disasters. The information should at least include availability of parking for staff, patients, and visitors, and normal vehicular, emergency vehicular, and pedestrian traffic flow patterns in and around the facility. The extent of the security and traffic control problems for any given health care facility will depend upon its geographical location, physical arrangement, availability of visitor parking areas, number of entrances, and so forth.

Crowd Control. Visitors can be expected to increase in number with the severity of the disaster. They should not be allowed to disrupt the functioning of the facility disaster plan. Ideally, a visitor reception center should be established away from the main facility itself, particularly in the case of major disasters. Volunteer personnel such as community emergency response teams (CERT), Red Cross, Explorer Scouts, or other helpers can be utilized as liaisons between the visitors and the health care facility itself.

Vehicular Traffic Control. Arrangement for vehicular traffic control into and on the facility premises should be made in the disaster planning period. It will be necessary to direct ambulances and other emergency vehicles carrying casualties to triage areas or the emergency room entrance, and to direct incoming and outgoing vehicles carrying people, supplies, and equipment. Charts showing traffic flow and indicating entrances to be used, evacuation routes to be followed, and so forth, should be prepared and included in the emergency operations plan. Parking arrangements should not be overlooked.

Internal Security and Traffic Control. Internal security and traffic control are best conducted by facility-trained personnel (i.e., regular health care facility security forces) with reinforcements as necessary. Potential additional assistance from the local law enforcement agencies should be coordinated in the disaster planning phase. Upon activation of the emergency operations plan, security guards should be stationed at all unlocked entrances and exits to the extent possible. Entrance to the facility should be restricted to personnel bearing staff identification cards and to casualties. In the case of major access corridors between key areas of the facility, pedestrian traffic should be restricted to one side of the corridor, keeping the other side of the corridor free for movement of casualties. Traffic flow charts for internal traffic should also be prepared in the planning phase, as is the case with external traffic control.

A.12.5.3.3.6.5 Consideration should be given to preemptively installing parallel components such that maintenance can be performed on operating equipment. This will necessitate the installation of additional valves, circuits, or controls to isolate those parts to be removed and replaced, such as air or fuel filters. This work should not violate any other code, standard, or safety device. The desired outcome is system resiliency despite part failure.

When planning for emergency utility systems, consideration should be given for maintaining temperature and humidity levels appropriate for patients and supply storage. This could be done by providing HVAC on emergency power, by relocation of patients and supplies to an appropriately heated or cooled area of the facility, or evacuation.

Δ **A.12.5.3.3.6.8(1)** The command structure should also follow the National Incident Management System (NIMS) as provided in NFPA 1660.

A.12.5.3.3.8 Experiences show the importance of drills to rehearse the implementation of all elements of a specific response, including the entity's role in the community, space management, staff management, and patient management activities. To document an exercise, the following aspects are typically incorporated. A general overview of the scenario, documented activation of the emergency operations plan, reports from an identified evaluator(s), evaluation of all involved participants (departments) and any observer(s), a written critique following the drill, and any identified follow-up training or improvement action(s) to correct or manage any deficiencies.

N **A.12.5.3.3.9.4** Other participants can include observers and subject matter experts.

A.12.5.3.3.9.8 When improvements require substantive resources that cannot be accomplished by the next planned exercise, interim improvements should be put in place until final resolution.

A.12.5.3.4.1 In emergency situations that occur without warning and impact the facility, staff at the scene of the problem are expected to follow established protocols to protect life, notify others, and conserve property. Senior management can establish a hospital command center (HCC) or participate in unified command with other responding agencies at a designated emergency operations center (EOC). In emergency situations with warning or whose impacts require extended periods to resolve, designated leadership reports to the HCC. Not all incidents require an HCC.

The HCC provides centralized locations for information collection, display, coordination, documentation, and dissemination.

A.12.5.3.4.5 Note that care should be taken to ensure that identification cards are recalled whenever personnel terminate association with the health care facility. Members of the news media should be asked to wear some means of identification, such as a press card, on their outside garments so that they are readily identifiable by security guards controlling access to the facility or certain areas therein. Clergy also will frequently accompany casualties or arrive later for visitations and require some means of identification. Water storage systems should be inventoried and protected to the greatest extent possible.

A.12.5.3.4.9 For additional information, see the 2012 Institute of Medicine (IOM) Report, *Crisis Standards of Care: A Systems Framework for Catastrophic Disaster Response*.

A.12.5.3.4.10.1 Based on the facility's hazard vulnerability analysis (HVA), consideration should include, but not be limited to, preparation to do the following:

(1) Provide services to injured responders and disaster victims
(2) Receive large numbers of victims from a mass casualty incident (trauma or medical)
(3) Be a receiving facility for a health care facility evacuation
(4) Handle uncontrolled increased census (e.g., due to a flu outbreak)

A.12.5.3.5 Recovery measures could involve a simple repositioning of staff, equipment, supplies, and information services; or recovery could demand extensive cleanup and repair. It can, under certain circumstances, be a means to identify opportunities for structural and nonstructural mitigation efforts. Filing of loss claims might require special approaches. Health care facilities should have access to cash or negotiable instruments to procure immediately needed supplies.

A.13.1 This chapter is the source for security management in health care facilities and is based on the foundations of NFPA 730.

A.13.2 A health care facility security plan can be formulated from security-sensitive areas that need the highest level of protection outward to the perimeter of the health care facility campus in concentric rings. Viewed from the outside, security is thus open and welcoming to patients and visitors. As an individual proceeds into the interior, public spaces might have minimal surveillance, but those sensitive areas that cannot be entered are layered with protections and countermeasures.

A.13.2.2 The security plan should be reviewed annually or more frequently if new challenges present themselves.

A.13.3.1 For general information regarding the SVA and premises security, see NFPA 730.

A.13.4.2(3)(c) The emergency potential inherent in the telephoned bomb threat warrants inclusion of this contingency in the health care emergency operations plan. Experience has shown that facility personnel have to accompany police or military bomb demolition personnel in searching for the suspected bomb, because speed is of the essence, and only individuals familiar with a given area can rapidly spot unfamiliar or suspicious objects or conditions in the area. This is particularly true in health care facilities. The facility switchboard operator should have a checklist, to be kept available at all times, in order to obtain as much information as possible from the caller concerning the location of the supposed bomb, time of detonation, and other essential data, which should be considered in deciding whether or not to evacuate all or part of the facility.

A.13.5.2(1) A visible presence is normally accomplished by the placement of a security officer at the ambulance entrance. This serves the dual purpose of monitoring the security cameras throughout the emergency department as well as the activity at the ambulance entrance.

A.13.5.3(5) The facility-wide alerting system should be activated for all reports of pediatric or infant abduction. The use of a standardized "code alert" system can facilitate the announcement; for example, "code pink" for an infant abduction or "code purple" for a pediatric abduction.

A.13.5.4 Video surveillance and motion detection can be used as additional protection for these areas. Some controlled drugs should be stored in safes.

A.13.5.6(3) Reasons for a contraband check procedure would be to control items such as tobacco, drugs, or tools that could cause harm to the patient or staff.

A.13.5.7(1) Law enforcement personnel should have orientation on the emergency procedures and layout of the facility. There should be good communication between law enforcement and health care facility security staff.

A.13.6.3.1 There can be times where full or partial facility access or egress is not desirable. Planning for these events should be conducted in coordination with local emergency agencies, such as police, fire, and public health agencies.

A.13.7 Patients that generate media interest should be subject to special security procedures. VIP or media representatives present the need for a unique set of security requirements. Protection of VIPs is normally accomplished by restricting the use of names on charts and rooms and by assigning a dedicated security watch.

Admission of a high-profile person to a health care facility creates two sets of problems that might require partial activation of the health care emergency management plan. These problems are security and the reception of news media.

Provision of security forces in this situation might be provided by a governmental agency or private security forces. However, activation of facility security forces might be required to prevent hordes of curious onlookers from entering facility work areas and interfering with routine facility functioning. Routine visiting privileges and routine visiting hours might need to be suspended in parts of the facility.

A.13.7.1.1 The marketing department of the hospital might be best suited to assist security personnel with media control.

A.13.7.2 Ideally, news media personnel should be provided with a media briefing area or a media staging area, or both, with access to telephone communication and, if possible, an expediter who, though not permitted to act as a spokesperson for news releases, could provide other assistance to such personnel. News media personnel should not be allowed into the health care facility without proper identification. Media representatives should be requested to wear some means of identification for security purposes. Members of the news media should be asked to wear some means of identification, such as a press card, on their outside garments so that they are readily identifiable by security guards controlling access to the facility or certain areas therein.

A.13.8 Crowd control of persons demanding access to care will create additional demands on security. Because of the intense public interest in disaster casualties, news media representatives should be given as much consideration as the situation will allow. To alert off-duty health care staff and to reassure the public, use of broadcast media should be planned.

Where feasible, photo identification or other means to ensure positive identification should be used. Visitor and crowd control create the problem of distinguishing staff from visitors. Such identification should be issued to all facility personnel, including volunteer personnel who might be utilized in disaster functions. Note that care should be taken to ensure that identification cards are recalled whenever personnel terminate asso-

ciation with the health care facility. Clergy also will frequently accompany casualties or arrive later for visitations and require some means of identification.

A.13.9.4 Key cards are preferable to traditional keys because they can be immediately deactivated if lost or not returned by a terminated employee.

Facility keys should not be identified in any manner such that a person finding a lost key could trace it back to the facility. A policy should be established to restrict duplication of keys without written permission. All keys should be marked "DO NOT DUPLICATE" to deter the unauthorized copying of keys.

There should be a log of keys issued to employees and vendors maintained at the facility. A responsible individual should be in charge of issuing keys and maintaining complete, up-to-date records of the disposition of keys, including copies. The records should show the issuance and return of keys, including the name of the person to whom the key was issued, as well as the date and time. Records of key issuance should be secured and kept separate from keys.

Keys should be restricted to those who need them, and extra copies of keys should be kept locked in a secure cabinet with access control.

Procedures should be established for collecting keys from terminated employees, employees on vacation, and vacated tenants. Lost keys should be reported immediately and procedures established for the rekeying or replacement of the affected locks.

A master key system should be designed so that the grandmaster key is the only key that will open every restricted area of the facility. A master key system is used to limit the number of keys carried by personnel requiring access to multiple areas of the building. It is important that such a system not be designed so that the loss of a single key could provide an unauthorized individual unrestricted access to all areas of the building. The sophistication of the master key system should depend upon an assessment of employees' or tenants' needs and the criticality, risk, and sensitivity of restricted areas.

The number of grandmaster keys should be limited to the least number necessary for operation of the health care facility. Master key distribution should be limited to the personnel requiring access to multiple restricted areas. A log should be maintained showing who is in possession of master keys.

A.13.10 Background checks should include criminal record checks, employment histories, and references. This function is typically managed by the human resources department.

A.13.11 The number of guards needed at any given time will depend on the size of the facility, the hours of operation, and the current risk factors. Many states have laws that require background checks and specific training for security personnel, especially armed personnel. It is essential that facilities using security personnel train them in the legal and practical applications of their employment. Training must reflect changes in regulations and the enactment of new laws.

A.13.11.1 Post orders should contain a list of the duties of the security officer and instructions to cover all foreseeable events the security officer can encounter. Post orders should list the name of the facility, the date issued, the effective date, and the purpose. Duties of security personnel should be listed, including job classification, uniforms, carrying of firearms, reporting times, watch tours, hours of coverage, and other duties to be assigned. Instructions should be lawful and protect the safety of the security officer and those they encounter. Reviews of post orders should be conducted regularly with facility management and security officers. Post orders should be updated regularly and at least annually. A procedure should be established to inform security officers of changes in post orders.

A.13.12.1 The effectiveness of the security plan is tested by performing drills. Drills should be conducted on all work schedules, so that all personnel are familiar with the plan. Practicing the plan helps personnel react as needed during a security incident.

A.14.1 Chapter 14 does not apply to respiratory therapy employing oxygen-enriched atmospheres at ambient pressures. *(See Chapter 11.)*

A.14.2.1.1.1 For guidance on minimum construction requirements, depending on occupancy classification, see NFPA *101*.

A.14.2.1.1.6 Characteristics of building construction housing hyperbaric chambers and ancillary facilities are no less important to safety from fire hazards than are the characteristics of the hyperbaric chambers themselves. It is conceivable that a fire emergency occurring immediately outside a chamber, given sufficient fuel, could seriously endanger the life or lives of those inside the chamber. Since the service facilities, such as compressors, cooling equipment, reserve air supply, oxygen, and so forth, will, in all probability, be within the same building, these facilities will also need protection while in themselves supplying life-maintaining service to those inside.

A.14.2.1.2 In addition to the functions of building protection, the chamber room sprinkler system should be designed to ensure a degree of protection to chamber operators who likely will not be able to immediately evacuate the premises in the event of a fire.

A.14.2.1.2(1) Where the area to be covered is small (six sprinklers or less), 9.7.1.2 of NFPA *101* permits fire sprinkler systems required to be installed in accordance with NFPA 13 to be supplied from the local domestic water system, provided that the local domestic water system has sufficient pressure and flow capacity.

A.14.2.1.2(3) When selecting a clean agent fire protection system, careful consideration should be given to the selection of agent based on permissible exposure levels.

A.14.2.1.3.1 Hyperbaric chamber systems often require piping materials, pressure ratings, and joining techniques that are not permitted by Chapter 5 of this code.

N **A.14.2.1.3.3** This requirement is meant to protect regulators and other components from particles in the piping system. Many pressure regulators incorporate a particulate filter meeting this requirement. If filtration is added, the particulate filter should be in accordance with CGA E-7, *Standard for Medical Gas Pressure Regulators, Flowmeters, and Orifice Flow Selectors.*

A.14.2.2.1 Other chapters in this code contain many requirements that could appear to relate to hyperbaric facilities but could be inappropriate. The requirements of other chapters in this code should be applied to hyperbaric facilities only where specifically invoked by this chapter.

N **A.14.2.2.1.1** The primary pressure relief device is intended to overcome the pressurization supply system. Hyperbaric chamber volume and maximum flow of the pressurization supply system determine the sizing of the primary relief device.

N **A.14.2.2.1.2** In the event of fire inside the hyperbaric chamber, a rapid rise in pressure might overwhelm the capability of the primary pressure relief device. The means of secondary pressure relief is intended to prevent catastrophic failure of the hyperbaric chamber in this scenario.

A.14.2.2.4 A definition for the term *viewport* can be found in ASME PVHO-1, *Safety Standard for Pressure Vessels for Human Occupancy.*

A.14.2.2.6.1 In past editions of this code, "high quality epoxy" was specified as interior finish in these chambers, without a specific fire performance. Although not the only option, this type of material offers suitable physical properties. The interior finish of a Class A chamber should be smooth, impermeable, durable, provide corrosion resistance, and be compatible with infection control procedures.

A.14.2.2.6.2 One common hazard of paint fires in ships is related to welding or burning operations on one side of a metal bulkhead that heats the metal to a point where the paint on the opposite side ignites. Most paints are not flammable when installed as thin layers over a substantial heat sink, such as the thick steel walls of a hyperbaric chamber, unless the walls are heated first. The same paints, when ground into a powder or installed over a very thin metal substrate, can burn readily. The paint selected for use in the interior walls of a hyperbaric chamber should be selected both for suitability to the requirements of the application and for its combustibility properties. The hazard of a fire increases as the amount of heat sink is reduced. Therefore, combustion is easier to achieve when paint is applied over thin materials and when there are multiple layers of paint. On thin section materials that are easily heated, care should be exercised in selecting the flammability characteristics of the paint and the amount of paint applied.

A.14.2.2.6.4 Many commercial sound-deadening materials that might be nonflammable are porous and will absorb water from activation of the fire-suppression system and retain odor. Metallic panels that contain a large quantity of small holes or are made of wire mesh and are installed about 2.5 cm (1 in.) away from the chamber wall can be used to form an acoustic baffle. These panels should be made from corrosive-resistant materials, such as stainless steel or aluminum, and are permitted to be painted in accordance with 14.2.2.6.3.

A.14.2.2.7 Prudent design considerations suggest that at least 50 percent excess pass-through capacity be provided, for future use, given the difficulty of adding pass-throughs to the chamber after it is constructed and tested.

A.14.2.4.1.2 Experience and practice can dictate the need for a threshold ventilation rate in excess of the minimum specified for sanitary reasons. It is recommended that consideration be given, if necessary, to the use of odor filters in the chamber circulation system as a means of keeping sanitary ventilation rate requirements to a minimum.

N **A.14.2.4.1.3** The intent of this requirement is to allow options for chamber occupants. A risk assessment should be conducted to determine the breathing apparatus appropriate to the environment and identify the potential hazards.

A.14.2.4.2.1 If intakes are located where it could be possible for maintenance to be conducted in the immediate vicinity, a warning sign should be posted.

A.14.2.4.4.1 Ventilation is permitted to be provided by closed- or open-circuit systems.

A.14.2.5.4 The risk assessment should be documented. When performing a risk assessment, consider using available internal resources (e.g., safety officer, risk management, public safety). Risk assessments should include, but not be limited to, the following factors:

(1) The time required to evacuate to a safe area (as required by 14.3.1.5.4.1)
(2) Building and room architecture (e.g., egress versus defend-in-place architecture)
(3) Accessible means of egress
(4) Room layout, number, and configuration of the chambers
(5) Possible need for slow decompression or decompression stops
(6) Response time of internal and external emergency responders

A.14.2.6.1.5 Experience has shown that fire blankets, portable carbon dioxide extinguishers, and other methodology intended to "snuff out" fires by excluding air are not effective in controlling fires in oxygen-enriched atmospheres. Valuable time can be lost in attempting to use such devices.

N **A.14.2.6.1.7** The required signage should be visible to the patients preparing to go into the hyperbaric chamber. The intent of this requirement is to remind patients of prohibited items before they enter. Best practice is to use signage in multiple zones of control. Locating signage in the chamber waiting area, visible to patients and their family members or caregivers, should be considered. Placing one or more posters in the patient changing area should also be considered. Additionally, if the chamber has a separate entry compartment, placing a sign near the entry compartment should be considered.

N **A.14.2.6.1.9** The intent of 14.2.6.2 is to prescribe specific design features and performance requirements for a water deluge fire suppression system. The intent of 14.2.6.4 is to allow alternative design features and alternative suppression media if the fire suppression system is demonstrated to be effective.

N **A.14.2.6.1.10** The intent of 14.2.6.5 is to allow portable fire extinguishers and alternative extinguishing media.

A.14.2.6.2.3 More than one control station could be required in a compartment (lock), depending on its size.

A.14.2.6.2.5 Experience has shown that, when water is discharged through conventional sprinkler heads into a hyperbaric atmosphere, the spray angle is reduced because of increased resistance to water droplet movement in the denser atmosphere. This is so, even though the water pressure differential is maintained above chamber pressure. Therefore, it is necessary to compensate by increasing the number of sprinkler heads. It is recommended that spray coverage tests be conducted at maximum chamber pressure.

Some chamber configurations, such as small-diameter horizontal cylinders, could have a very tiny floor, or even no floor at all. For horizontal cylinder chambers and spherical chambers, the term *floor level* should be taken to mean the level at ¼ diameter below the chamber centerline or actual floor level, whichever yields the larger floor area.

N **A.14.2.6.2.10** Carbon steel water storage vessels are likely to produce rust. Stainless steel and epoxy-lined vessels, and vessels with polymer-based bladders, might not need strainers. However, a strainer might be prudent in areas with hard water.

N **A.14.2.6.4.1** Fire suppression performance requires a hot test on a simulated burning occupant in a fire under hyperbaric conditions. At commencement of testing, the chamber environmental oxygen level should be at least 23.5 percent. The test is typically performed using a clothed manikin surrounded by materials specifically permitted in this code, including clothing, mattresses, pillows, cushions, and blankets.

N **A.14.2.6.4.1.1** The system should preferably be able to extinguish the fire within 40 seconds of activation. The system should prevent the subsequent rise of temperature elsewhere in the chamber.

A.14.2.6.6.2 Additional detectors are recommended to avoid "blind" areas if the chamber contains compartmentation.

N **A.14.2.8.1** The required signage should be visible to the patients preparing to go into the hyperbaric chamber. The intent of this requirement is to remind patients of prohibited items before they enter. Best practice is to use signage in multiple zones of control. Locating signage in the chamber waiting area, visible to patients and their family members or caregivers, should be considered. Placing one or more posters in the patient changing area should also be considered.

A.14.2.9.2.1 A backup generator or backup power system for the hyperbaric facility might not be necessary, but certain electrically driven features of hyperbaric facilities should have some type of backup. This could be addressed with a single backup power system or with multiple, smaller power sources. The source for such backup power and emergency lighting can be battery supplied.

A.14.2.9.2.1(1) Chamber room emergency lighting should be provided and does not require a unique type of emergency lighting because it is a hyperbaric facility.

A.14.2.9.2.1(2) Chamber emergency lighting requirements vary. For chambers with a large acrylic window, found in most Class B chambers, the room emergency lighting is sufficient to meet this requirement. For chambers made primarily of steel, with a small window(s), lighting dedicated to the chamber interior might be necessary. In this case, at least on light should be provided with backup power.

A.14.2.9.2.1(3) Chamber intercommunication power requirements vary. The duration of backup power for communications depends on the type of hyperbaric treatments performed but should not have to exceed the duration of a hyperbaric treatment conducted in the facility.

A.14.2.9.2.1(4) Class A chambers might employ flame detectors. If employed, these detectors should have backup power. Flame detectors are typically not employed in Class B chambers.

A.14.2.9.2.1(5) Class A chambers are required to have a fire suppression system. All electrical controls related to activation and performance of the fire suppression system should have backup power. Fire suppression systems are not typically employed in Class B chambers.

A.14.2.9.2.1(6) Some Class A and Class B chambers employ electrical controls as part of the pressurization and ventilation system of the chamber. These controls should have backup power.

A.14.2.9.3 This subsection contains requirements for the safe use of electrical equipment in the hyperbaric, oxygen-enriched environment of the Class A chamber.

N A.14.2.9.3.3.2 Portable patient entertainment equipment does not include personal entertainment devices prohibited by 14.3.1.6.1.2.

A.14.2.9.3.9 It should be recognized that interruption of any powered circuit, even of very low voltage, could produce a spark sufficient to ignite a flammable agent.

A.14.2.9.3.10.1 It is recommended that all control switching functions inside the chamber be accomplished using intrinsically safe circuits that control power and control circuits located outside of the chamber.

A.14.2.9.3.11 It is the intention of 14.2.9.3.11 that equipment used in the chamber be incapable of igniting, by heating, any material or fabric that could come into contact with the surface of the equipment.

A.14.2.9.3.13 It is recommended that electric motors not be located inside the chamber. This recommendation is not intended to apply to a motor that is within a piece of portable medical equipment.

A.14.2.9.3.14 It is strongly recommended that high-intensity local task lighting be accomplished using through-hull fiber-optic lights. Many high-intensity lights will not meet the temperature requirements specified in 14.2.9.3.11.

A.14.2.9.3.15.1 The requirement for isolation from main supply in 14.2.9.3.15.1 is not the same as the requirement in 14.2.9.4.2 that circuits supplying power to portable utilization equipment inside the chamber be isolated, monitored, and alarmed.

It is recommended that intrinsically safe sensors and controls be used whenever possible.

A.14.2.9.3.16 These requirements are only the minimum requirements for electrical safety. There are many other safety concerns that should be addressed on a case-by-case basis. Meeting the requirements of 14.2.9.3.16 does not indicate that proper device performance will occur in the hyperbaric environment and that the device will be safe for use with patients.

A.14.2.9.3.17 The intent of this section is to mitigate the risks of fire when an electrical device is placed inside the chamber and put under pressure.

The requirements of this section are not intended for things such as approved wristwatches and similar approved small battery-powered devices. See B.14.5 for additional information on inert gas or air purging.

A.14.2.9.5.2 It is necessary that these circuits be protected from exposure to water from the room sprinkler system protecting the chamber housing in the event of a fire in the vicinity of the chamber while it is in operation.

A.14.2.9.6.1.1 Limiting current using a suitable current sensing device (e.g., a rapid acting fuse or circuit breaker, located

outside the chamber) would provide appropriate protection and prevent circuits from exceeding the 4.0 W power limit.

A.14.2.10.2 Intercommunications equipment is mandatory for safe operation of a hyperbaric facility.

A.14.2.10.2.1 It is recommended that multiple-compartment (lock) Class A chambers be equipped with multiple channel systems and that, in addition, a sound-powered telephone or surveillance microphone be furnished.

A.14.2.10.2.2 It is recommended that information about the status of an anesthetized or otherwise monitored patient be transmitted to the inside chamber attendants via the intercommunications system. As an alternative, the monitor indicators can be placed adjacent to a chamber viewport (or viewports) for direct observation by inside personnel.

A.14.2.10.4.4 Oxygen levels in Class A chambers should be sampled from at least two sample ports at disparate locations in the chamber, and the chamber should be equipped with an oxygen monitor for each sample port.

Chamber atmospheres are typically not homogenous. Oxygen can accumulate in pools or pockets around patients with levels that are dangerously high. A single oxygen sample port inside the chamber might not be sufficient to detect increased oxygen levels in another area of the chamber. In this case, a serious increase of oxygen, well above the allowed level of 23.5 percent, can go undetected. Providing at least two sample ports allows for better assessment of the oxygen levels inside the chamber. The size of the vessel should be factored into determining how many ports are necessary.

A dedicated oxygen analyzer on each line prevents false readings from two or more sample lines feeding into one oxygen sensor.

For example, one sample line might come from an area of 21 percent, and the other line might come from an area of 50 percent or more. When both lines come together, they will mix and give a false low oxygen reading. Having a dedicated oxygen monitor for each sample line will avoid this unsafe situation.

A.14.2.10.4.4.2 The ability to spot check for oxygen leaks and oxygen pooling is essential for the safe management of oxygen levels. If the minimum 30-second response time is not compromised, the extension or "snooping wand" can remain connected for easy use.

A.14.2.10.6 The purity of the various gas supplies should be ensured. A purity statement for any cryogenic or high-pressure cylinder gas should be supplied by the vendor. Gas cylinder purity statements should be cross-referenced, where possible, with the delivered gas.

For additional verification, some facilities have installed sampling ports for monitoring oxygen and other gases.

A.14.2.10.6.1 CGA Grade E permits quantities of hydrocarbons and water in air. In piping systems where air and oxygen might be used interchangeably, hydrocarbon buildup can occur and increase the risk of fire when oxygen is used. There is also a concern about pneumatic components being fouled and functionally impaired by hydrocarbons or water from compressed air. Ideally, there should be no condensed hydrocarbons in an oxygen system and no liquid water in pneumatic control systems.

A.14.2.11.2 Exhaust piping extending from the building can create a lightning risk. Lightning protection should be considered.

A.14.2.11.2.5 The facility should consider bilingual signage that is appropriate to the location. The hyperbaric safety coordinator should be aware of any work performed on the roof near exhaust vent.

See Figure A.14.2.11.2.5 for examples of the pictographs required by NFPA 170.

A.14.3.1.2 The hazards involved in the use of hyperbaric facilities can be mitigated successfully only when all of the areas of hazard are fully recognized by all personnel and when the physical protection provided is complete and is augmented by attention to detail by all personnel of administration and maintenance having any responsibility for the functioning of the hyperbaric facility. Since Section 14.3 is expected to be used as a text by those responsible for the mitigation of hazards of hyperbaric facilities, the requirements set forth are frequently accompanied by explanatory text.

N **A.14.3.1.3.1** It is incumbent upon the personnel responsible for the hyperbaric facility to insist that rules and regulations with respect to practices and conduct in hyperbaric facilities — including qualifications and training of hyperbaric personnel — be adopted by the medical or administrative staff of the institution, and that regulations for inspection and maintenance are in use by the administrative, maintenance, and ancillary (and, in hospitals, nursing and other professional) personnel.

Personnel responsible for the hyperbaric facility should adopt or correlate regulations and standard operating procedures to ensure that both the physical qualities and the operating maintenance methods pertaining to hyperbaric facilities meet the safety standards in accordance with Chapter 14. The controls adopted should cover the conduct of personnel in and around hyperbaric facilities and the apparel and footwear allowed. They should also cover periodic inspection of static-dissipating materials and of all electrical equipment, including the testing of ground contact indicators.

Δ **A.14.3.1.3.2** The complexity of hyperbaric chambers necessitates that at least one person be designated as hyperbaric safety coordinator. Regardless of the terminology used for this designee, the intent is for someone to manage the operational responsibilities of this chapter. This requirement can be met by creating a hyperbaric safety coordinator job description for the designee or by merely assigning the additional responsibilities to someone with another job description. In either case, a hyperbaric safety coordinator designation document should be created and signed by a person responsible for the hyperbaric facility.

Because of variations in the management structure of hyperbaric facilities, this designation could be made by a variety of people including the hyperbaric medical director, the hyperbaric department manager/director, hospital administration, or a management company responsible for the hyperbaric facility. It is not the intent of this requirement for the designation to be made by an authority having jurisdiction (e.g., fire marshal, health department inspector).

The hyperbaric safety coordinator does not have to be present during all chamber operations but should be accessible to the hyperbaric physicians and staff and, where unavailable, have a process in place to manage safety decisions based on the responsibilities referenced below. The designee should have firsthand knowledge of the hyperbaric equipment, personnel, training, operating procedures, and maintenance procedures in their facility. Due to a conflict of responsibility, the designee should not be the hyperbaric medical director.

Safety, operational, and maintenance criteria of other organizations have been published (e.g., in Undersea & Hyperbaric Medical Society Safety Committee documents and Compressed Gas Association pamphlets) and should be reviewed by the hyperbaric safety coordinator. The hyperbaric safety coordinator should also serve on the health care facility safety committee.

Hyperbaric safety coordinator responsibilities can be found in the following paragraphs:

(1) 14.2.9.6.4
(2) 14.3.1.2

No Open Flame — Flame			
	Circular field Red circle and slash Black image White background	The identification of areas in which open flame is prohibited	The identification of areas, such as combustible storage areas, gas stations, and hazardous areas

No Smoking			
	Circular field Red circle and slash Black image White background	The identification of areas in which smoking is prohibited	The identification of areas, such as those for flammable liquid storage, where smoking could lead to fire or explosion

FIGURE A.14.2.11.2.5   Fire Safety Symbols from NFPA 170.

(3) 14.3.1.3.2, including 14.3.1.3.2.1 through 14.3.1.3.2.3
(4) 14.3.1.3.3.1
(5) 14.3.1.3.4
(6) 14.3.1.4.1.1
(7) 14.3.1.4.2
(8) 14.3.1.5.4
(9) 14.3.1.6.2.2
(10) 14.3.1.6.3.1
(11) 14.3.1.6.4.3
(12) 14.3.1.6.4.4
(13) 14.3.2.1.2
(14) 14.3.2.1.5
(15) 14.3.3.4
(16) 14.3.4.1.1 and 14.3.4.1.2
(17) 14.3.4.2.1
(18) 14.3.4.3.5.4

A.14.3.1.3.3 It is recommended that training of hyperbaric chamber personnel be closely monitored, following the guidelines and publications of the Undersea & Hyperbaric Medical Society, the Baromedical Nurses Association, and the National Board of Diving and Hyperbaric Medical Technology.

A.14.3.1.3.4 In the case of a hyperbaric facility located in a hospital, hospital licensing and other approval bodies, in meeting their responsibilities to the public, should include in their inspections not only compliance with requirements for physical installations in hyperbaric facilities, but also compliance with the requirements set forth in Section 14.3.

A.14.3.1.4.1 It is recommended that all personnel, including trainees and those involved in the operation and maintenance of hyperbaric facilities, and including professional personnel and (in the case of hospitals) others involved in the direct care of patients undergoing hyperbaric therapy, be familiar with Chapter 14. Personnel concerned should maintain proficiency in the matters of life and fire safety by periodic review of Chapter 14, as well as any other pertinent material.

Positive measures are necessary to acquaint all personnel with the rules and regulations established and to ensure enforcement. Training and discipline are necessary.

A.14.3.1.4.6 The complexity of hyperbaric chambers is such that one person should be designated chamber operator, such as a person in a position of responsible authority. Before starting a hyperbaric operation, this person should record, in an appropriate log, the purpose of the operation or test, the duties of all personnel involved, and a statement that he or she is satisfied with the condition of all equipment. Exceptions should be itemized in the statement.

A.14.3.1.5.2 All full- and part-time personnel should receive training in emergency management appropriate to their job descriptions.

A.14.3.1.5.4 A calm reaction (without panic) to an emergency situation can be expected only if the recommendations are familiar to and rehearsed by all concerned.

A suggested outline for emergency action in the case of fire is contained in B.14.2.

A.14.3.1.6.1.1 Oxygen-filled chambers dump oxygen into the room each time the door is opened at the end of a treatment. Oxygen could also be dumped into the room by the chamber pressure relief device. Air-filled chambers could leak oxygen into the room from the breathing gas piping. This oxygen enrichment lowers the ignition temperature of combustible materials. Therefore, extra caution should be used in the area around the chamber as well as inside the chamber.

A.14.3.1.6.1.3 Precautions should be in place for monitoring items used to prepare a patient or staff member for entry into the hyperbaric chamber to prevent the entry of prohibited items into the hyperbaric chamber.

In addition to monitoring prohibited items, the following items should be verified:

(1) Patient identity
(2) Pretreatment orders
(3) Appropriate safety measures
(4) Appropriate staffing
(5) Appropriate textiles
(6) Patient grounding

A.14.3.1.6.2.2(2) Allowable quantities complying with 14.3.1.6.2.2(2) can be determined from the chamber volume, flammable agent vapor density, and lower explosive limit (LEL). Experience has shown that increased pressure has little effect on LEL for a given flammable gas and oxygen concentration. A safety factor of 10 is recommended. Flammable liquids should be confined to nonbreakable, nonspill containers.

Sample Determination. An example of limiting quantity of flammable agent substance:

Isopropyl alcohol (2-propanol)

LEL = 2%/vol. (irrespective of chamber pressure)

Vapor density = 2.1 relative to air

Liquid density = 786 g/L (49.1 lb/ft^3)

Air density = 0.075 lb/ft^3 (1.2 kg/m^3) at STP

The limiting case occurs at the lowest ambient pressure, that is, 1 atmosphere:

$$\text{Alcohol vapor density at LEL} \begin{aligned} &= 0.02 \times 2.1 \times 0.075 \\ &= 0.00315 \text{ lb/ft}^3 \ (0.05 \text{ kg/m}^3) \\ &= 1.43 \text{ g/ft}^3 \ (0.05 \text{ kg/m}^3) \end{aligned}$$

For a relatively small 500 ft^3 (14.2 m^3) chamber, this implies:

1.43 × 500 = 715 g (1.58 lb) alcohol vapor at LEL

Using a safety factor of 10 to account for uneven vapor concentrations gives 71.5 g = 91 mL (3 oz) alcohol.

One could conclude that even 90 mL (3 oz) of alcohol is more than would be needed for almost any medical procedure. The preceding calculation also does not account for the mitigating effect of ventilation.

Many "inert" halogenated compounds have been found to act explosively in the presence of metals, even under normal atmospheric conditions, despite the fact that the halogen compound itself does not ignite in oxygen or, in the case of solids such as polytetrafluoroethylene, is self-extinguishing. Apparently these materials are strong oxidizers, whether gases, liquids (solvents, greases), or solids (electrical insulation, fabric, or coatings). Some halogenated hydrocarbons that will not burn in the presence of low-pressure oxygen will ignite and continue to burn in high-pressure oxygen. Customarily, Class A chambers maintain internal oxygen concentration that does not exceed 23.5 percent.

Parts of Chapter 14 deal with the elements required to be incorporated into the structure of the chamber to reduce the possibility of electrostatic spark discharges, which are a possible cause of ignition in hyperbaric atmospheres. The elimination of static charges is dependent on the vigilance of administrative activities in materials, purchase, maintenance supervision, and periodic inspection and testing. It cannot be emphasized too strongly that an incomplete chain of precautions generally will increase the electrostatic hazard. For example, conductive flooring can contribute to the hazard unless all personnel wear conductive shoes, all objects in the room are electrically continuous with the floor, and humidity is maintained.

The limitations in 14.3.1.6.2.2 on the use in the chamber of alcohol and other agents that emit flammable vapors should be strictly observed, and such restrictions should be prominently posted.

A.14.3.1.6.3 The number of occupants of the chamber should be kept to the minimum number necessary to carry out the procedure.

A.14.3.1.6.4 It is recommended that all chamber personnel should wear garments of the overall or jumpsuit type that completely cover all skin areas to the extent possible and that are as tight-fitting as possible. It can be impractical to clothe some patients (depending upon their disease or the site of any surgery) in such garments. Hospital gowns can be employed in such a case.

A.14.3.1.6.4.2 Selection of textiles for the hyperbaric chamber should be based on a variety of factors, including comfort, lint production, ignition temperature, static-producing properties, and fuel load of the material. The amount of polyester in a cotton/polyester blend will likely have an effect on all of these factors.

Historically, all synthetic fabrics were prohibited from the chamber. Previous editions of this code allowed an "antistatic blend of cotton and polyester" because of one specific fabric — a blend of cotton and polyester with steel fibers to make it conductive. This blended fabric was intended for surgical scrubs, but its conductive properties made it a good choice for hyperbaric garments. The polyester in the fabric was acceptable because the conductive properties of the fabric actually afforded some protection from static production that cotton fabric did not. This particular fabric is no longer made. Selection of textiles has always been about balancing various safety concerns; primarily fire-resistance and static production. For further guidance on selecting appropriate textiles, see A.14.3.1.6.4.3.

Δ **A.14.3.1.6.4.3** The intent of this requirement is to allow for exceptions, where appropriate. The risk assessment process below is a tool to guide the decision. Although the process was designed for textiles and wound dressings, it could be used to assess any material. In addition to exceptions, this risk assessment should be used to develop a "use" list (i.e., locally approved items) and a "do not use" list (i.e., locally prohibited items). Documentation should include the "use" and "do not use" lists as well as a worksheet for each item identifying the reference material used and rationale for continuing or not continuing at each decision step in the process.

The textiles definitions and risk assessment process for hyperbaric wound dressings are as follows:

Combustion. A chemical process of oxidation that occurs at a rate fast enough to produce heat in the form of either a glow or flame.

Flammable. A combustible (solid, liquid, or gas) that is capable of easily being ignited and rapidly consumed by fire.

Flash Point. The minimum temperature at which a liquid or a solid emits vapor sufficient to form an ignitible mixture with oxygen under specified environmental conditions.

Ignition Temperature. The minimum temperature required to initiate or cause self-sustaining combustion under specified environmental conditions.

Lower Explosive Limit (LEL) or Lower Flammable Limit (LFL). The minimum concentration of fuel vapor (percent by volume) over which combustion will occur on contact with an ignition source.

General Risk Assessment Information. This risk assessment process was designed to evaluate wound dressing products for use in a hyperbaric chamber. However, the same decision process can be applied to the evaluation of textiles for hyperbaric use. Wound dressings are commonly used inside hyperbaric chambers and play an important role in infection control and patient outcome. Important safety concerns include production of heat, production of static electricity, production of flammable vapor, ignition temperature, and total fuel load. Many wound dressings employ fabrics and other materials that are gas permeable. It is a common misconception that a gauze bandage will isolate an undesirable product from the chamber environment. Gauze is gas permeable and will allow oxygen from the chamber to interact with the product and allow vapors from the product to interact with the chamber environment. Also, gas permeable materials exposed to hyperbaric oxygen will hold additional oxygen for some time after the exposure. These materials should be kept away from open flames for at least 20 minutes after the hyperbaric treatment.

Risk Assessment Process (see Figure A.14.3.1.6.4.3).

(1) Is there a more suitable alternative to this dressing? The issue of need must first be addressed. There might be a substitute dressing that has already been deemed acceptable for the hyperbaric environment. The wound dressing orders can be changed to the more desirable substitute if there is no negative impact on patient outcome. It might be viable to remove the dressing before the hyperbaric treatment, leave it off during the treatment, and replace it after the treatment. Before making this decision, it is important to remember that some dressings should not be disturbed (e.g., in the case of a new skin graft); some dressings are designed to stay in place for several days; some dressings are very expensive; and it can be detrimental for the wound to remain undressed during the treatment. If there is a suitable alternative to using this dressing, the rest of the decision process can be eliminated.

(2) Does this dressing produce heat in the chamber? Dressings are made from a large variety of materials. The concern is that materials in a dressing can rapidly oxidize and produce heat (i.e., cause an exothermic reaction) when exposed to additional oxygen. For example, air-activated heat patches (commonly used for pain relief)

have been tested in hyperbaric environments. The average operating temperature increased from 48.1°C (119°F) in normobaric air to 121.8°C (251°F) in hyperbaric oxygen. In this circumstance, the patient's skin would be burned, and the heat could ignite combustible material in the chamber. Information on oxygen compatibility can be found in a product material safety data sheet (MSDS).

(3) Does this dressing produce too much static electricity? All common textiles will contribute to static production. Wool and synthetic materials generally contribute more to static production than cotton. Although static charge is constantly accumulating, it will dissipate into the environment when humidity is present. At less than 30 percent relative humidity, static charge can accumulate faster than it can dissipate. At greater than 60 percent relative humidity, static charge is all but eliminated. Use of conductive surfaces and electrical grounding will allow static charge to dissipate. Paragraph 14.2.9.4.1 requires all hyperbaric chambers to be grounded. Paragraph 14.2.11.1 requires any furniture installed inside a chamber to be grounded. Paragraph 14.3.1.6.3.2 requires all occupants of the chamber to be grounded when the oxygen percentage in the chamber is above 23.5 percent. The continuity of electrical grounds should be verified periodically.

(4) Does this dressing have a low ignition temperature/flash point? ASTM G72/G72M, *Standard Test Method for Autogenous Ignition Temperature of Liquids and Solids in a High-Pressure Oxygen-Enriched Environment*, can be used to determine the autogenous ignition temperatures of products entering a hyperbaric chamber. In 2016, ASTM G72/G72M added a new test for oxygen-enriched environments of less than 300 psi (2068 kPa) of pressure. In all hyperbaric environments, the partial pressure of oxygen is higher than at normal atmospheric conditions. Increasing the partial pressure of oxygen can change the classification of a material from nonflammable to flammable. Many materials are flammable in a 100 percent oxygen environment. Any material used in a hyperbaric chamber should have an ignition temperature higher than the temperature to which it could be exposed. Paragraph 14.2.9.3.11 limits electrical equipment inside a Class A (i.e., multi-place) chamber to a maximum operating surface temperature of 85°C (185°F). Paragraph 14.2.9.6.3 limits electrical circuits inside a Class B (i.e., monoplace) chamber to a maximum operating temperature of 50°C (122°F). As the oxygen percentage increases, it takes less energy to ignite materials. This leads to more conservative decisions in a 100 percent oxygen environment. A greater margin of safety is achieved when there is a greater difference between the temperature limit of the equipment inside a Class A or Class B chamber and the ignition temperature of the material in question. A material will release vapor into the chamber environment as it approaches its flash point temperature. Once sufficient vapor is present in the chamber (i.e., LEL), it takes very little energy for ignition to occur. Paragraph 14.3.1.6.2.2 sets limits on flammable agents inside Class A (i.e., multi-place) chambers. Paragraph 14.3.1.6.2.3 specifically prohibits flammable liquids, gases, and vapors inside Class B (i.e., monoplace) chambers. Information on ignition temperature and flash point in air can be found in a product MSDS.

(5) Is the total fuel load too high? If a fire does occur, the energy produced is a function of the partial pressure of oxygen and the total fuel load. In a hyperbaric environment, the partial pressure of oxygen is higher and contributes to greater energy production. Any dressing product placed inside of a hyperbaric chamber is a combustible material and adds to the fuel load. Therefore, total fuel load inside the chamber should be minimized to only what is necessary.

(6) Is there an adverse effect when this product is used inside the hyperbaric chamber? It has been reported that the antibacterial agent mafenide acetate, in combination with hyperbaric oxygen, has a poorer clinical result than either one by itself. There can be other drug interactions with hyperbaric oxygen that are undesirable. The mechanical effects of pressure change can cause a dressing material to rupture. If the material is capable of venting/equalizing during pressure change, this should not occur.

(7) The hyperbaric facility should maintain a "use" list and a "do not use" list of items that have been evaluated for hyperbaric use. In addition to this list, it is important to keep documentation on file explaining the risk assessment for each item. This will prevent future duplication of effort. It also serves as evidence that due diligence was used.

N A.14.3.1.6.4.4 Documentation of the exception(s) should include the rationale, any limits, and at least one additional measure to mitigate the hazard(s). The following is an example of such written documentation: "Available chamber-approved clothing is too small for Patient X. To protect patient dignity, we will allow Patient X to wear their own clothing in the chamber for the duration of their course of treatment. The clothing must be made of material allowed by NFPA 99. The clothing will be inspected daily for contraband and cleanliness."

See also A.14.3.1.3.2.

A.14.3.1.6.9 The use of paper should be kept to an absolute minimum in hyperbaric chambers.

A.14.3.2.2 Users should be aware that many items, if ignited in pressurized oxygen-enriched atmospheres, are not self-extinguishing. Iron alloys, aluminum, and stainless steel are, to various degrees, in this category, as well as human skin, muscle, and fat, and plastic tubing such as polyvinyl chloride. Testing for oxygen compatibility is very complicated. Very little data exists, and many standards still have to be determined. Suppliers do not normally have facilities for testing their products in controlled atmospheres, especially high-pressure oxygen. Both static conditions and impact conditions are applicable. Self-ignition temperatures normally are unknown in special atmospheres.

A.14.3.2.5 See A.14.3.2.2.

A.14.3.2.6 Radiation equipment, whether infrared or roentgen ray, can make hyperbaric chambers even more hazardous.

A.14.3.3.4 Quantities of oxygen stored in the chamber should be kept to a minimum.

A.14.3.4.1.6 The frequency of such monitoring should depend on the location of the air intake relative to potential sources of contamination.

A.14.3.4.3.5 The primary focus for the semiannual test of a water-based extinguishing system is to ensure water flow

FIGURE A.14.3.1.6.4.3 Risk Assessment Process.

through the system (i.e., inspector's test). Other vitally important benefits are the activation of water flow devices, alarm appliances, and notification and annunciator systems.

A.14.3.4.5.2 Ferrous metals can cause such sparking, as can magnesium or magnesium alloys, if contact is made with rusted steel.

A.14.3.4.6 The elimination of static charges is dependent on the vigilance of administrative supervision of materials purchased, maintenance, and periodic inspection and testing.

A.14.3.4.6.2 Verification of patient grounding should include actual testing of ground, not just a visual verification. Ideally,

the verification will include connecting the patient to the ground pathway and measuring no more than 100,000,000 ohms with a meter. This value comes from NFPA 77.

A.14.3.4.6.3 See A.14.3.4.6.2.

A.14.3.4.6.5 Materials containing rubber deteriorate rapidly in oxygen-enriched atmospheres.

A.14.3.4.7 It is absolutely essential that all areas of, and components associated with, the hyperbaric chamber be kept meticulously free of grease, lint, dirt, and dust.

A.15.3.3.4 Dental air systems are used primarily to drive gas-powered power devices. See Figure A.15.3.3.4 for an illustration of this type of system. Similar applications are found in podiatry and plastic surgery. Examples of these are air used to drive turbine-powered drills and air used to dry teeth and gums. Some dental hand pieces have an internal self-contained air return system, while other hand pieces discharge air into the atmosphere. Some discharge a mixture of air and water. Nitrogen is often piped as an alternative or reserve supply to the compressor system.

Dental compressed air is not used for life-support purposes, such as respirators, intermittent positive-pressure breathing (IPPB) machines, analgesia, anesthesia, and so forth. Air discharged into the oral cavity is incidental and not a primary source of air to sustain life.

A dental compressed air system should not be used to provide power for an air-powered evacuation system without specific attention paid to the discharge of the evacuated gases and liquids. An open discharge of evacuated gases into the general environment of an operatory could compromise the quality of breathing air in the treatment facility. Air discharge should be vented to the outside of the building through a dedicated vent.

An air-powered evacuation system might require significant quantities of air to operate.

Manufacturer's recommendations should be followed regarding proper sizing of the air compressor. Inadequate sizing can result in overheating, premature compressor failures, and inadequate operating pressures and flows.

A.15.3.3.5 A dental vacuum system is not intended for medical–surgical vacuum applications. A wet piping system is designed to accommodate liquid, air–gas, and solids through the service inlet. A dry piping system is designed to accommodate air–gas only through the service inlet, with liquids and solids being trapped before entering the system. *[See Figure A.15.3.3.5(a) through Figure A.15.3.3.5(d).]*

A.15.4.2.4.2 Requirements for the location of these enclosures, including, but not limited to, design and construction, ventilation, and cylinder storage, are located in 5.1.3.3. For additional information on ventilation, see 9.3.6. For additional information on cylinder storage, see Chapter 11.

A.15.4.2.4.7 When the storage/supply enclosure is remote from the single treatment facility, it should be locked for security reasons (i.e., to prevent tampering). Access should only be allowed for authorized staff or fire departments. When the enclosure is within the single treatment facility, it is left to the discretion of facility management as to whether a greater benefit is achieved by immediate access or by higher security. An

Notes:
1. Dotted lines indicate optional items.
2. Either the nitrogen/compressed air manifold system or the air compressor system can be primary, and the other can be optional.

M	Moisture indicator	◇	Drain plug
F	Filter(s)	U.C.	Utility center
↕	Check valve	S	Service outlet
⬒	Automatic drain	✕	Shutoff valve

FIGURE A.15.3.3.4   Dental Air Supply System.

enclosure with direct access from a public hallway should be locked. See Figure A.15.2.2.4.7 for examples of enclosures with doors that open to access corridors.

A.15.4.2.6.1 See Figure A.15.2.2.6.1 for an illustration of single treatment locations.

A.15.4.7.4.4.5 Ammonia is known to cause stress cracking in copper and its alloys.

A.16.3.2 NFPA 58 permits the use of portable butane-fueled appliances in restaurants and in attended commercial food catering operations where fueled by a maximum of two 0.28 kg (10 oz) LP-Gas capacity, nonrefillable butane containers with a water capacity not in excess of 0.4 kg (1.08 lb) per container. Containers are required to be directly connected to the appliance, and manifolding of containers is not permitted. Storage of cylinders is limited to 24 containers, with an additional 24 permitted where protected by a 2-hour fire resistance–rated

barrier. *(See 4.1.3 and Annex C of NFPA 101 for referenced documents on hazardous materials.)* [*101*:A.8.7.3.2]

A.16.5.2.1 This section is different from 9.2.1 of NFPA *101* because NFPA 90B, referenced in NFPA *101*, is not applicable to health care facilities.

A.16.5.3.3 Continued operation of solid-state elevator equipment is contingent on maintaining the ambient temperature in the range specified by the elevator manufacturer. If the machine room ventilation/air-conditioning is connected to the general building system, and that system is shut down during a fire, the fire department might lose the use of elevators due to excessive heat in the elevator machine room. [*101*:A.9.4.5]

A.16.7.1 The provisions of Section 16.7 cover the basic functions of a complete fire alarm system, including fire detection, alarm, and communications. These systems are primarily intended to provide the indication and warning of abnormal conditions, the summoning of appropriate aid, and the control of occupancy facilities to enhance protection of life.

Some of the provisions of Section 16.7 originated with *NFPA 72.* For purposes of this Code, some provisions of Section 16.7 are more stringent than those of *NFPA 72,* which should be consulted for additional details. [*101*:A.9.6.1]

A.16.7.2.4 It is not the intent of 16.7.2.4 to require manual fire alarm boxes to be attached to movable partitions or to equipment, nor is it the intent to require the installation of permanent structures for mounting purposes only. [*101*:A.9.6.2.5]

A.16.7.4.2.1 Elevator lobbies have been considered areas subject to unwanted alarms due to factors such as low ceilings and smoking. In the past several years, new features have become available to reduce this problem. These features are, however, not necessarily included in any specific installation. [*101*:A.9.6.3.2.1]

A.16.7.4.2.2 The concept addressed is that detectors used for releasing service, such as door or damper closing and fan shutdown, are not required to sound the building alarm. [*101*:A.9.6.3.2.2]

A.16.7.4.3.1 It is not the intent of this paragraph to require fire alarm system zones to coincide with smoke compartment boundaries, provided that the facility fire plan addresses the differences between fire alarm system zones and building smoke compartments.

A.16.7.4.3.2 In the private operating mode, audible and visible signaling is required only to those persons directly concerned with the implementation and direction of emergency action. Provided that those persons receive alarm notification, audible and visible signaling is not required to patients or other building occupants who are not responsible for the implementation and direction of emergency action.

N A.16.7.4.3.3 The requirement in 16.7.4.3.3 does not mandate the use of voice communication systems in all health care facilities, only that the signal readily identifies the zone, area, floor, and building that requires attention by staff. This could be accomplished with voice communication systems or a non-voice audio and/or visual system. Examples of non-voice systems include a remote annunciator panel at each nurse station or a coded system.

△ FIGURE A.15.3.3.5(a)   Typical Wet or Dry Piping System with Single Vacuum Pump Source.

△ FIGURE A.15.3.3.5(b)   Typical Wet or Dry Piping System with Duplex Vacuum Source with Air/Liquid Separator.

△ FIGURE A.15.3.3.5(c)   Typical Wet or Dry Piping System with Single Vacuum Source.

△ **FIGURE A.15.3.3.5(d)**   Typical Wet or Dry Piping System with Duplex Vacuum Source with Waste Holding Tank.

FIGURE A.15.4.2.4.7   Examples of Storage/Supply Enclosures.

FIGURE A.15.4.2.6.1   Examples of Single Treatment Locations.

A.16.7.4.3.5 Paragraph 16.7.4.3.5 allows the omission of either or both audible and visual notification appliances in any patient care space, regardless of the risk category, where a risk assessment determines the alarm notification can adversely affect patient care. The risk assessment should carefully review the additional duties, responsibilities, and associated training expected for the staff at the facility to learn and respond accordingly. Examples of such areas can include, but are not limited to, intensive care units, coronary care units, angiography laboratories, cardiac catheterization laboratories, nurseries, delivery rooms, operating rooms, post-anesthesia recovery rooms, emergency departments, and similar areas.

A.16.8 Health care facilities utilizing heliports should ensure that they are registered with the US Federal Aviation Administration's (FAA's) Airport Master Record program to ensure that their heliport and the airspace servicing it is registered. Once registered, the health care facility should ensure that their airport identifier and related information in the FAA's Airport Master Record is always up-to-date. If outside of the FAA's jurisdiction, facilities should comply with the applicable aviation authority.

A.16.9.1.3 It is not the intent of this paragraph to require sprinkler system zones to coincide with smoke compartment boundaries, provided that the facility fire plan addresses the differences between sprinkler systems zones and building smoke compartments.

Δ **A.16.9.1.4** This exception is limited to hospitals, as nursing homes and many limited care facilities might have more combustibles within the closets. The limited amount of clothing found in the small clothes closets in hospital patient rooms is typically far less than the amount of combustibles in casework cabinets that do not require sprinkler protection, such as nurse servers. In many hospitals, especially new hospitals, it is difficult to make a distinction between clothes closets and cabinet work. The exception is far more restrictive than similar exceptions for hotels and apartment buildings. NFPA 13 already permits the omission of sprinklers in wardrobes . It is not the intent of 16.9.1.4 to affect the wardrobe provisions of NFPA 13. It is the intent that the sprinkler protection in the room covers the closet as if there were no door on the closet . [*101*:A.18.3.5.10]

A.16.10.1 The selection of portable fire extinguishers for health care facilities is a vital step in preparing the facility to effectively deal with a fire in its incipient stage. There are special extinguisher requirements such as nonferrous fire extinguisher components of fire extinguishers in an MRI room or area, and Class K extinguishers in kitchens. There is a need to consider extinguishing agents for various areas of a facility that are nontoxic, noncorrosive, and/or nonconductive. Chapters 5 and 6 and their Annex A notes of NFPA 10 need very careful review. Annex C, "Fire Extinguisher Selection" and Annex D, "Operation and Use" of NFPA 10 provide additional valuable guidance.

A.16.10.1.1.1 MR safe or MR conditional fire extinguishers should meet the requirements of ASTM F2503, *Standard Practice for Marking Medical Devices and Other Items for Safety in the Magnetic Resonance Environment*, and ASTM F2213, *Standard Test Method for Measurement of Magnetically Induced Torque on Medical Devices in the Magnetic Resonance Environment*.

Extinguishers that are appropriate for MRI rooms and associated spaces (i.e., safe zones) are typically labeled with information regarding their safe use in an MRI environment. See Figure A.16.10.1.1.1 for an example of such a label.

A.16.10.1.3 This provision is intended to permit appliances used for reheating, limited cooking, and food preparation, such as microwave ovens, hot plates, electric skillets, toasters, and nourishment centers to be exempt from the requirements for commercial cooking equipment and hazardous area protection. Limited quantities of butter, cooking spray, or oil can be used. [*101*:A.18.3.2.5.2]

A.16.10.1.4 Dry chemical fire extinguishers should not be provided in operating rooms. While a clean agent or water mist extinguisher is required by this code for operating rooms, a carbon dioxide fire extinguisher shares the electrically nonconductive properties of clean agent and water mist fire extinguishers and, on that basis, could be used in lieu of a clean agent extinguisher. However, it should be noted that carbon dioxide fire extinguishers do not have Class A ratings. A clean agent extinguisher for use in an operating room should have a Class A rating of some form.

A.16.10.2.2 Hose and hose outlets can be required by a building code or by the authority having jurisdiction.

A.16.11 Compact storage is characterized by shelving units that are manually or electrically moved on fixed tracks to provide access aisles. Such systems are also known as mobile shelving, track files, compaction files, or movable files.

A floor loading calculation should be performed.

A.16.12.3 NFPA 13 contains protection criteria for limited configurations of compact mobile storage units and materials stored. Storage arrangements not specifically addressed in NFPA 13 are outside the scope of the standard (i.e., protection for plastic commodities in compact mobile storage units does not simply follow high piled storage protection criteria for shelves or racks). Where compact mobile storage configurations outside the scope of NFPA 13 are to be utilized, they must be addressed on a case-by-case basis, with consideration given to the fact that no known sprinkler protection criteria is currently available. The storage of paper administrative and medical records with limited plastic labels or folders is typically a Class III commodity with less than 5 percent plastics. The storage of most office supplies, engineering parts, food products, garments, and other general supplies is typically a Class IV commodity with 5 percent to 25 percent plastics. The storage of x-rays, medicines, and plastic-based medical supplies is typically a Group A plastics commodity with greater than 25 percent plastics.

A.16.14.3.2 Some tinctures and solutions of disinfecting agents provide significant clinical benefits in reducing the risk of surgical infections. However, they can be flammable and can be used improperly during surgical procedures. Tipping containers, accidental spillage, and the pouring of excessive amounts of such flammable agents on patients expose them to injury in the event of accidental ignition of the flammable solvent. To control this risk, flammable germicides or antiseptics that are used when electrosurgery, cautery, or a laser is contemplated should be packaged to ensure controlled delivery to the patient (e.g., unit dose applicator, swab) in small volumes appropriate for single application.

	MR CONDITIONAL
/MR\	THIS EXTINGUISHER HAS BEEN TESTED TO OPERATE PROPERLY AND POSE NO SAFETY HAZARD IN AN MRI ENVIRONMENT ASSOCIATED WITH MR SYSTEMS OPERATING AT 11.7 TESLA OR LESS.

FIGURE A.16.10.1.1.1   Example of a Label on an Extinguisher for an MRI Environment.

Annex B   Additional Explanatory Notes

This annex is not a part of the requirements of this NFPA document but is included for informational purposes only.

B.1 Reserved.

B.2 Reserved.

B.3 Reserved.

B.4 Reserved.

B.5 Additional Information on Chapter 5. Numbers in brackets refer to paragraphs in Chapter 5.

B.5.1 General. This section sets out a minimum recommended guide for testing. Testing requirements are listed in 5.1.12 and summarized in Table B.5.1. Tests specified in 5.1.12 should be carried out by an experienced person or persons designated by the administration of the health care facility. Such a person(s) should certify the results of tests to the administra-

tion. The designated person(s) should be experienced in medical gas testing and verification of piping systems with cross-connection testing. A member of the health care facility should be present to verify the testing.

B.5.2 Retesting and Maintenance of Nonflammable Medical Piped Gas Systems (Category 1 Systems).

B.5.2.1 [5.1.3.5.9] These systems should be checked daily to ensure that proper pressure is maintained and that the change-over signal has not malfunctioned. Periodic retesting of the routine changeover signal is not necessary, as it will normally be activated on a regular basis.

B.5.2.2 [5.1.3.5.10] These systems should be checked daily to ensure that proper pressure is maintained and that the change-over signal has not malfunctioned. Periodic retesting of the routine changeover signal is not required. Annual retesting of the operation of the reserve and activation of the reserve-in-use signal should be performed.

Δ **Table B.5.1 Performance Criteria and Testing — Level 1 (Gases, Medical–Surgical Vacuum, and WAGD)**

Responsibility	Test Reference	Test (as Applicable)	Purpose of Test
Installer	5.1.12.2.1	General	
Installer	5.1.12.2.2	Initial blow down	Distribution piping is blown down to remove particulates
Installer	5.1.12.2.3	Initial pressure test	Distribution piping is free from pressure loss
Installer	5.1.12.2.4	Cross-connection test	Distribution piping is free from cross-connections
Installer	5.1.12.2.5	Piping purge test	Distribution piping is purged to remove particulates
Installer	5.1.12.2.6	Standing pressure test for positive pressure medical gas piping	Distribution piping is free from excessive pressure loss
Installer	5.1.12.2.7	Standing vacuum test for vacuum system	Distribution piping is free from excessive vacuum loss
System verification	5.1.12.4.1	General	
System verification	5.1.12.4.2	Standing pressure test	Distribution piping is free from leaks
System verification	5.1.12.4.3	Cross-connection test	Distribution piping is free from cross-connections
	5.1.12.4.3.1	Individual pressurization	
	5.1.12.4.3.2	Pressure differential	
System verification	5.1.12.4.4	Valve test	Shutoff valves are functioning and labeled properly
System verification	5.1.12.4.5	Alarm test	Alarms are functioning and labeled properly
	5.1.12.4.5.1	General	
	5.1.12.4.5.2	Master alarm	
	5.1.12.4.5.3	Area alarm	
System verification	5.1.12.4.6	Piping purge test	Distribution piping is purged to remove particulates
System verification	5.1.12.4.7	Piping particulate test	Distribution piping is free from particulates
System verification	5.1.12.4.8	Piping purity test	Distribution piping is free from excessive water vapor, total hydrocarbons, and halogenated hydrocarbons
System verification	5.1.12.4.9	Final tie-in test	The new and existing distribution system is free from leaks at the point of connection, and no additional contamination was added to the existing system
System verification	5.1.12.4.10	Operational pressure test	Distribution piping is free from excessive pressure/vacuum loss
System verification	5.1.12.4.11	Medical gas concentration test	Proper concentration of system gas is present at each outlet
System verification	5.1.12.4.12	Medical air purity test (compressor system)	Proper quality of medical air is present
System verification	5.1.12.4.13	Labeling	Distribution piping, outlets/inlets, shutoff valves, alarms, and source equipment are labeled correctly
System verification	5.1.12.4.14	Source equipment verification	Source equipment properly functions
	5.1.12.4.14.1	General	
	5.1.12.4.14.2	Gas supply sources	
	5.1.12.4.14.3	Medical air compressor systems	
	5.1.12.4.14.6	Medical–surgical vacuum systems	

     Shaded text = Revisions.   **Δ** = Text deletions and figure/table revisions.   • = Section deletions.   **N** = New material.

B.5.2.3 [5.1.3.5.10] If the system has an actuating switch and signal to monitor the contents of the reserve, it should be retested annually.

B.5.2.4 [5.1.3.5.11] Maintenance and periodic testing of the bulk system is the responsibility of the owner or the organization responsible for the operation and maintenance of that system.

The staff of the facility should check the supply system daily to ensure that medical gas is ordered when the content's gauge drops to the reorder level designated by the supplier. Piping system pressure gauges and other gauges designated by the supplier should be checked regularly, and gradual variation, either increases or decreases, from the normal range should be reported to the supplier. These variations might indicate the need for corrective action.

Periodic testing of the master signal panel system, other than the routine changeover signal, should be performed. Assistance should be requested from the supplier or detailed instruction if readjustment of bulk supply controls is necessary to complete these tests.

B.5.2.5 [5.1.8.2.3] The main line pressure gauge should be checked daily to ensure the continued presence of the desired pressure. Variation, either increases or decreases, should be investigated and corrected.

B.5.2.6 [5.1.3.6.3.14] Quarterly rechecking of the location of the air intake should be made to ensure that it continues to be a satisfactory source for medical compressed air.

B.5.2.7 [5.1.3.6.3.14] Proper functioning of the pressure gauge and high water level sensor should be checked at least annually. The receiver drain should be checked daily to determine if an excessive quantity of condensed water has accumulated in the receiver.

B.5.2.8 [5.1.3.6] An important item required for operation of any medical compressed air supply system is a comprehensive preventive maintenance program. Worn parts on reciprocating compressors can cause high discharge temperatures, resulting in an increase of contaminants in the discharge gas. Adsorber beds, if not changed at specified time intervals, can become saturated and lose their effectiveness. It is important that all components of the system be maintained in accordance with the manufacturers' recommendations. It is important that any instrumentation, including analytical equipment, be calibrated routinely and maintained in operating order. Proper functioning of the dew point sensor should be checked at least annually.

B.5.2.9 [5.1.9] When test buttons are provided with signal panels, activation of the audible and visual signals should be performed on a regular basis (monthly).

B.5.2.10 [5.1.9.2.4] Changeover Warning Signals. As these are routine signals that are activated and deactivated at frequent intervals, there is no need for retesting unless they fail. If the reserve-in-use signal is activated because both units of the operating supply are depleted without the prior activation of the changeover signal, it should be repaired and retested.

B.5.2.11 [5.1.9.2.4] Reserve-In-Use Warning Signal. All components of this warning signal system should be retested annually. Audible and visual signals should be tested periodically during the year (monthly).

B.5.2.12 [5.1.9.2.4] Reserve Supply Low (Down to an Average One-Day Supply) High Pressure Cylinder or Liquid Reserve. All components of these signal warning systems should be retested annually. If test buttons are provided, audible and visual signals should be periodically tested throughout the year (monthly).

B.5.2.13 [5.1.9.2.4] The medical compressed air system alarms in 5.1.3.6.3.12 should be checked at least annually.

B.5.2.14 [5.1.8.2.2(1)] This pressure gauge should be checked on a daily basis to ensure proper piping system pressure. A change, increase or decrease, if noted, could be evidence that maintenance is required on the line pressure regulator and could thus avoid a problem.

B.5.2.15 [5.1.9] Annual retesting of all components of warning systems, if it can be done without changing piping system line pressure, should be performed.

B.5.2.16 [5.1.9] If test buttons are provided, the retesting of audible and visual alarm indicators should be performed monthly.

B.5.2.17 [5.1.4] Shutoff valves should be periodically checked for external leakage by means of a test solution or other equally effective means of leak detection that is safe for use with oxygen.

B.5.2.18 [5.1.5] Station outlets should be periodically checked for leakage and flow. Manufacturer instructions should be followed in making this examination.

B.5.3 Oxygen Service–Related Documents. The following publications can be used for technical reference:

(1) ASTM G63, *Standard Guide for Evaluating Nonmetallic Materials for Oxygen Service*
(2) ASTM G88, *Standard Guide for Designing Systems for Oxygen Service*
(3) ASTM G93/G93M, *Standard Guide for Cleanliness Levels and Cleaning Methods for Materials and Equipment Used in Oxygen-Enriched Environments*
(4) ASTM G94, *Standard Guide for Evaluating Metals for Oxygen Service*

B.6 Additional Information on Chapter 6.

B.6.1 Typical Hospital Wiring Arrangement. See Figure B.6.1. Separate transfer switches for each branch, as shown, are required only if dictated by load considerations. Smaller facilities can be served by a single transfer switch.

B.6.2 Maintenance Guide for an Essential Electrical System. This generalized maintenance guide is provided to assist administrative, supervisory, and operating personnel in establishing and evaluating maintenance programs for emergency electric generating systems. See Figure B.6.2.

Δ **FIGURE B.6.1   Typical Hospital Wiring Arrangement.**

Δ **B.6.3 Suggested Format for Listing Functions to Be Served by the Essential Electrical System in a Hospital.** It might be advantageous in listing the specific functions for a given construction project or building review to list them, at the outset, by geographical location within the project in order to ensure comprehensive coverage *(see Figure B.6.3)*. Every room or space should be reviewed for possible inclusion of the following:

(1) Lighting (partial or all)
(2) Receptacles (some or all)
(3) Permanently wired electrical apparatus

The format suggested herein is offered as a convenient tool, not only for identifying all functions to be served and their respective time intervals for being re-energized by the on-site source, but also for documenting other functions that were considered, discussed, and excluded as nonessential. The last column in Figure B.6.3 is considered worthy of attention. It might be that the hospital engineer or the reviewing authority will wish to keep on file a final copy of the list, which would be the basis for the electrical engineer's detailed engineering design.

Although this suggested format is intended for use by a hospital, it might, with suitable changes, be useful for other health care facilities.

B.7 Reserved.

B.8 Reserved.

B.9 Reserved.

B.10 Reserved.

B.11 Additional Information on Chapter 11.

B.11.1 Medical Safeguards — Respiratory Therapy.

B.11.1.1 General.

B.11.1.1.1 Personnel setting up, operating, and maintaining respiratory therapy equipment, including suction apparatus, should familiarize themselves with the problems of the use of each individual unit.

B.11.1.1.2 Personnel must be aware of the exact location of equipment in storage to facilitate emergency use.

B.11.1.1.3 Suction tubing employed in a hazardous location is to be electrically conductive.

B.11.2 Glossary of Respiratory Therapy Terminology.

B.11.2.1 Arrhythmia. Irregularity of heartbeats.

B.11.2.2 Asphyxia. Suffocation from lack of oxygen and an accumulation of carbon dioxide.

B.11.2.3 Aspiration. Removal of accumulated mucus by suction.

B.11.2.4 Bronchi. The two primary divisions of the trachea.

B.11.2.5 CPAP. Continuous positive airway pressure.

B.11.2.6 CPR. Cardiopulmonary resuscitation.

B.11.2.7 Croup Tent. Equipment utilized to provide environmental control inside a canopy in relation to oxygen concentration, temperature, humidity, and filtered gas.

MAINTENANCE GUIDE

Monthly

(1) Testing of generator sets and transfer switches under load and operating temperature conditions at least every 30 days. A 30-minute exercise period is an absolute minimum, or the engine manufacturer's recommendations should be followed.

(2) Permanently record all available instrument readings during the monthly test.

(3) During the monthly test, check the following system or systems applicable to your installation:

Natural Gas or Liquid Petroleum Gas System:
- ❏ Operation of solenoids and regulators
- ❏ Condition of all hoses and pipes
- ❏ Fuel quantity

Gasoline Fuel System:
- ❏ Main tank fuel level
- ❏ Operation of system

Diesel Fuel System:
- ❏ Main tank fuel level
- ❏ Day tank fuel level
- ❏ Operation of fuel supply pump and controls

Turbine Prime Movers:
- ❏ Follow manufacturer's recommended maintenance procedure

Engine Cooling System:
- ❏ Coolant level
- ❏ Rust inhibitor in coolant
- ❏ Antifreeze in coolant (if applicable)
- ❏ Adequate cooling water to heat exchangers
- ❏ Adequate fresh air to engine and radiators
- ❏ Condition of fan and alternator belts
- ❏ Squeeze and check condition of hose and connections
- ❏ Functioning of coolant heater (if installed)

Engine Lubricating System:
- ❏ Lubricating oil level
- ❏ Crankcase breather not restricted
- ❏ Appearance of lubricating oil
- ❏ Correct lubricating oil available to replenish or change
- ❏ Operation of lubricating oil heater (if installed)
- ❏ Oil pressure correct

Engine Electrical Starting System:
- ❏ Battery terminals clean and tight
- ❏ Add distilled water to maintain proper electrolyte level
- ❏ Battery charging rate
- ❏ Battery trickle charging circuit operating properly
- ❏ Spare batteries charged (if provided)

Engine Compressed Air Starting System:
- ❏ Air compressor operating properly
- ❏ Air compressor lubricating oil level
- ❏ Spare compressed air tanks full
- ❏ Main compressed air tanks full
- ❏ Drain water from compressed air tanks

Engine Exhaust System:
- ❏ Condensate trap drained
- ❏ No exhaust leaks
- ❏ Exhaust not restricted
- ❏ All connections tight

Transfer Switch:
- ❏ Inside clean and free of foreign matter
- ❏ No unusual sounds
- ❏ Terminals and connectors normal color
- ❏ Condition of all wiring insulation
- ❏ All covers tight
- ❏ Doors securely closed

General:
- ❏ Any unusual condition of vibration, deterioration, leakage, or high surface temperatures or noise
- ❏ Maintenance manuals, service log, basic service tools, jumpers, and supplies readily available
- ❏ Check and record the time intervals of the various increments of the automatic start-up and shutdown sequences
- ❏ Overall cleanliness of room
- ❏ No unnecessary items in room

(4) After the monthly test: Take prompt action to correct all improper conditions indicated during test. Check that the standby system is set for automatic start and load transfer.

Quarterly

(1) Generator Sets:

Engine Electrical Starting System:
- ❏ Check battery electrolyte specific gravity
- ❏ Check battery cap vents

Engine Lubricating System:
- ❏ Check lubricating oil (or have analyzed if part of an engineered lube oil program)

(2) Fuel System:
- ❏ Drain water from fuel filters (if applicable)
- ❏ Drain water from day tank (if applicable)
- ❏ Check fuel gauges and drain water from main fuel tanks
- ❏ Inspect all main fuel tank vents

© 2023 National Fire Protection Association   (NFPA 99, 1 of 2)

Δ **FIGURE B.6.2   Maintenance Guide for Essential Electrical System.**

MAINTENANCE GUIDE (Continued)

Semiannually

Generator Sets:

  Engine Lubricating System:
- ❏ Change oil filter (if sufficient hours)
- ❏ Clean crankcase breather

  Fuel System:
- ❏ General inspection of all components
- ❏ Change fuel filter
- ❏ Change or clean air filter

  Governor:
- ❏ Check all linkages and ball joints
- ❏ Check oil level (if applicable)
- ❏ Observe for unusual oil leakage

  Generator:
- ❏ Check brush length and pressure
- ❏ Check appearance of slip rings and clean if necessary
- ❏ Blow out with clean, dry compressed air

  Engine Safety Controls:
- ❏ Check operation of all engine-operating alarms and safety shutdown devices (generator not under load during this check)

Annually

(1) Generator Sets:

  Fuel System:

  Diesel:
- ❏ Analyze fuel for condition (replace if required)

  Gasoline:
- ❏ Replace fuel

  Natural Gas or Liquefied Petroleum Gas:
- ❏ Examine all supply tanks, fittings, and lines

  Lubricating Systems:
- ❏ Change oil
- ❏ Change oil filter
- ❏ Replace carburetor air filter

  Cooling System:
- ❏ Check condition and rod-out heat exchangers if necessary
- ❏ Change coolant on closed systems
- ❏ Clean exterior of all radiators
- ❏ Check all engine water pumps and circulating pumps
- ❏ Examine all duct work for looseness
- ❏ Clean and check motor-operated louvers

  Exhaust System:
- ❏ Check condition of mufflers, exhaust lines, supports, and connections

  Ignition System:
- ❏ Spark ignition engines
- ❏ Replace points and plugs
- ❏ Check ignition timing
- ❏ Check condition of all ignition leads

  Generator:
- ❏ Clean generator windings
- ❏ Check generator bearings
- ❏ Measure and record resistance readings of generator windings using insulation tester (megger)

  Engine Control:
- ❏ General cleaning
- ❏ Check appearance of all components
- ❏ Check meters

(2) Transfer Switch:
- ❏ Inspect transfer switch and make repairs or replacements if indicated

(3) On Main Switchgear and Generator Switchgear:
- ❏ Operate every circuit breaker manually
- ❏ Visually check bus bars, bracing, and feeder connections for cleanliness and signs of overheating

Every 3 Years

(1) System Controls:
- ❏ Reevaluate the settings of the voltage-sensing and time delay relays.

(2) Main Switchgear and Generator Switchgear:
- ❏ Determine whether changes to the electrical supply system have been made that require a revision of the main circuit breaker, fuse, or current-limiting bus duct coordination.
- ❏ Calibrate and load test main circuit breakers. Spot-check bus bar bolts and supports for tightness. Obtain and record insulation tester readings on bus bars and circuit breakers. Obtain and record insulation tester readings on internal distribution feeders.

Periodically

(1) Prime Mover Overhaul:
- ❏ Each prime mover should have a periodic overhaul in compliance with the manufacturer's recommendation or as conditions warrant.

(2) Connected Load:
- ❏ Update the record of demand and connected load and check for potential overload.

© 2023 National Fire Protection Association   (NFPA 99, 2 of 2)

Δ **FIGURE B.6.2** *Continued*

Essential Electrical Systems

Hospital _____ Date _____

Room No.	Room Name	Function Served*	Emergency system		Equipment system		Nonessential
			Life Safety Branch	Critical Branch	Delayed Auto.†	Delayed Manual	

* Indicate precise lighting, receptacles, and/or equipment. Use a separate line for each function.

† Indicate time interval.

FIGURE B.6.3   Essential Electrical Systems.

B.11.2.8 Cyanosis. A bluish discoloration of skin and mucus membranes due to excessive concentration of reduced hemoglobin in the blood.

B.11.2.9 Defibrillate. Use of electrical shock to synchronize heart activity.

B.11.2.10 Diffusion. Transfer of gases across the alveolar capillary membrane.

B.11.2.11 EKG, ECG. Electrocardiogram.

B.11.2.12 Hemoglobin. The chemical compound in red blood cells that carries oxygen.

B.11.2.13 Hypoxia. An abnormally decreased supply or concentration of oxygen.

B.11.2.14 IMV. Intermittent mandatory ventilation.

B.11.2.15 IPPB. Intermittent positive-pressure breathing.

B.11.2.16 PEEP. Positive end expiratory pressure.

B.11.2.17 Respiration. The exchange by diffusion of gases between the alveoli, the blood, and the tissue.

B.11.2.18 Retrolental Fibroplasia. A disease entity of the premature infant causing blindness.

B.11.2.19 Thorax. The chest; the upper part of the trunk between the neck and the abdomen.

B.11.2.20 Trachea. The windpipe leading from the larynx to the bronchi.

B.11.2.21 Ultrasonic Nebulizer. A device that produces sound waves that are utilized to break up water into aerosol particles.

B.11.2.22 Ventilation. Movement of air into and out of the lungs.

B.11.2.23 Ventilator. Machine used to support or assist nonbreathing or inadequately breathing patient.

B.11.3 Suggested Fire Response — Respiratory Therapy. The suggested procedure in the event of fire involving respiratory therapy apparatus is given in B.11.3.1 through B.11.3.6.

B.11.3.1 General. Fires in oxygen-enriched atmospheres spread rapidly, generate intense heat, and produce large volumes of heated and potentially toxic gases. Because of the immediate threat to patients and personnel, as well as the damage to equipment and possible spread to the structure of the building, it is important that all personnel be aware of the steps necessary to save life, to preserve limb, and, within reason, to extinguish or contain the fire.

B.11.3.2 Steps to Take in Event of Fire.

B.11.3.2.1 The following steps are recommended in the event of a fire, in the approximate order of importance:

(1) Remove the patient or patients immediately exposed from the site of the fire if their hair and clothing are not burning; if they are burning, extinguish the flames. *(See B.11.3.4 and B.11.3.5.)*

(2) Sound the fire alarm by whatever mode the hospital fire plan provides.

(3) Close off the supply of oxygen to the therapy apparatus involved if this step can be accomplished without injury to personnel. *(See B.11.3.3.)*

(4) Carry out any other steps specified in the fire plan of the hospital including, but not limited to, the following examples:

    (a) Remove patients threatened by the fire.

    (b) Close the doors leading to the site of the fire.

    (c) Attempt to extinguish or contain the fire *(see B.11.3.4)*.

    (d) Direct firefighters to the site of the fire.

    (e) Take whatever steps necessary to protect or evacuate patients in adjacent areas.

B.11.3.3 Closing Off of Oxygen Supply.

B.11.3.3.1 In the event of a fire involving respiratory therapy equipment connected to an oxygen station outlet, the zone valve supplying that station is to be closed.

B.11.3.3.1.1 All personnel are cautioned to be aware of the hazard of the step specified in B.11.3.3.1 to other patients receiving oxygen supplied through the same zone valve. Steps should be taken to minimize such hazards, realizing that closing the valve is of foremost importance.

B.11.3.3.2 In the case of oxygen therapy apparatus supplied by a cylinder or container of oxygen, it is desirable to close the valve of the cylinder or container, provided that such closure can be accomplished without injury to personnel.

Note that metallic components of regulators and valves can become exceedingly hot if exposed to flame. Personnel are cautioned not to use their bare hands to effect closure.

B.11.3.4 Extinguishment or Containment of Fire.

B.11.3.4.1 Fire originating in or involving respiratory therapy apparatus generally involves combustibles such as rubber, plastic, linen, blankets, and the like. Water or water-based extinguishing agents are most effective in such fires.

B.11.3.4.1.1 Precautions should be observed if electrical equipment is adjacent to, or involved in, the fire because of the danger of electrocution of personnel if streams of water contact live 115-V circuits.

B.11.3.4.1.2 Before attempting to fight the fire with water or a water-based extinguishing agent, electrical apparatus should be disconnected from the supply outlet, or the supply circuit should be de-energized at the circuit panel.

B.11.3.4.1.3 If de-energization at the circuit panel cannot be accomplished, water should not be employed. *(See B.11.3.4.2.)*

B.11.3.4.2 Fires involving or adjacent to electrical equipment with live circuits can be fought with extinguishers suitable for Class C fires in accordance with NFPA 10.

Note that chemical extinguishers are not effective against fires in oxygen-enriched atmospheres unless the source of oxygen is shut off. See B.11.3.3 for closing off the oxygen supply.

B.11.3.5 Protection of Patients and Personnel.

B.11.3.5.1 Because of the intense heat generated, serious and even fatal burns of the skin or of the lungs from inhaling heated gases are possible sequelae to a fire in an oxygen-enriched atmosphere. Thus, it is essential that patients be removed from the site of the fire whenever practical.

Note that, where a nonambulatory patient is connected to a burning piece of therapy equipment, it might be more practical, as the initial step, to remove the equipment or extinguish the fire, or both, than to remove the patient.

B.11.3.5.2 The large quantities of noxious gases produced constitute a threat to life from asphyxia, beyond the thermal burn problem.

B.11.3.5.2.1 Personnel are cautioned not to remain in the fire area after patients are evacuated if quantities of gaseous combustion products are present.

B.11.3.6 Indoctrination of Personnel. It is highly desirable that personnel involved in the care of patients, including nurses, aides, ward secretaries, and physicians, irrespective of whether or not they are involved in respiratory therapy practices, be thoroughly indoctrinated in all aspects of fire safety, including the following:

(1) Location of zone valves of nonflammable medical gas systems where employed, and the station outlets controlled by each valve

(2) Location of electrical service boxes and the areas served thereby

(3) Location of fire extinguishers, indications for their use, and techniques for their application

(4) Recommended methods of evacuating patients and routes by which such evacuation is accomplished most expeditiously, with reference made to the facility's fire plan

(5) Steps involved in carrying out the fire plan of the hospital

(6) Location of fire alarm boxes, or knowledge of other methods, for summoning the local fire department

B.11.4 Typical Gas Cylinders. See Table A.11.3.5.

B.12 Additional Information on Chapter 12.

B.12.1 Emergency Management Program Development. The program development process illustrated in Figure B.12.1 is an example of a tool that can be used to develop an emergency management program; other tools or processes are acceptable as long as the tasks of identification, planning, education, evaluation, and improvement are addressed.

B.12.1.1 Program Development Steps and Activities.

B.12.1.1.1 Review the Hazard Vulnerability Analysis (HVA) and Determine Priorities for Developing Standard Operating Procedures (SOPs). Using the input submitted by operating unit managers, the Emergency Management Committee (EMC) must prioritize threats/events and develop a list of SOPs that must be developed to address those hazards. Figure B.12.1.1.1 displays a sample standard operating procedure format.

B.12.1.1.2 Implement Mitigation and Preparedness Strategies. Using the SOPs developed for prioritized threats/events, develop and implement actions that will eliminate or reduce the impact of adverse events to the facility and build capabilities to manage them. The committee should review the SOPs to identify resources needed for mitigation and preparedness, develop cost estimates or resources required, and submit the resource request to the director for funding. The committee is responsible for tracking mitigation and preparedness planning activities until completed.

B.12.1.1.3 Report Results of Mitigation and Preparedness Activities to the Emergency Management Committee. Operating unit managers and the emergency program coordinator should regularly report results of mitigation and preparedness activities to the committee. Reports should include mitigation activities taken that effectively reduced or eliminated adverse impacts to the facility; mitigation activities that did not reduce or eliminate adverse impacts to the facility operation; and recommendations for mitigation and preparedness activities, budget, and timelines.

Δ **B.12.1.1.4 Develop, Publish, and Distribute the Emergency Operations Plan (EOP).** There are numerous resources that provide guidance on the development of emergency operations plans, or EOPs. The EOP is designed to address all hazards, and it accomplishes this through its organization by functions, not departments, hazards, or individuals. Flexibility is a key feature of this type of format, as only the functions needed to address the problems are activated, not the entire plan. This type of EOP format (a basic plan and functional annexes) is used by communities, states, and the Federal Response Framework. *(See Annex D.)*

Hard copies of the EOP need not be widely distributed. Staff members need access to incident-specific plans, but not the entire document. Several copies of the full EOP should be available in the Hospital Command Center, in the administrative offices, and with the chair of the Emergency Management Committee. Posting the EOP on the hospital intranet with links

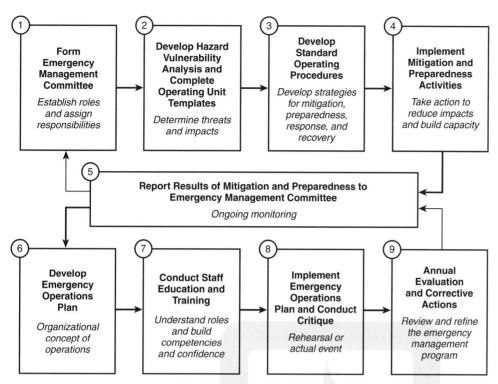

FIGURE B.12.1   Emergency Management Program Development Process.

to enhance movement through the plan can also be very effective; however, a few hard copies should still be available in the event of computer failure.

B.12.1.1.5 Train Staff on the EOP. See 12.5.3.5.

B.12.1.1.6 Delegate the Emergency Management Committee (EMC), Identify Department Roles, and Assign Responsibilities. The EMC is a multidisciplinary committee established to coordinate and oversee the emergency management program and should have a close relationship with the Safety Committee or Environment of Care Committee, or both.

The functions of the EMC include defining the role of the organization in the communitywide emergency management program; conducting/reviewing a hazard vulnerability analysis (HVA), which addresses all hazards that threaten the facility; developing/reviewing standard operating procedures (SOPs) that address hazards identified in the HVA; developing/reviewing the emergency operations plan and coordinating it with other health care organizations in the communitywide emergency management program; assigning roles and responsibilities of operating unit managers and key operators/managers; overseeing the development and maintenance of the EMP; ensuring that all employees have received appropriate training; conducting an annual evaluation of the effectiveness of the program; and ensuring a telephone roster of key personnel responsible for critical operations is kept current.

B.12.1.1.7 Test and Evaluate the EOP in Response to a Drill or Actual Event. See 12.5.3.3.7.

B.12.2 Personnel Notification and Recall. Medical staff, key personnel, and other personnel needed will be notified and recalled as required. In order to relieve switchboard congestion, it is desirable to utilize a pyramidal system to recall individuals who are off duty or otherwise out of the facility. Under the pyramidal system, an individual who has been notified will notify two other individuals, who, in turn, will each notify two other individuals, and so on. A current copy of the notification and recall roster, with current home and on-call telephone numbers, will be maintained at the hospital switchboard at all times. In case the pyramidal system is to be utilized, each individual involved in the system has to maintain a current copy of the roster at all times, in order that each knows who they are to notify and the telephone numbers concerned. It is essential that key personnel rosters be kept current.

B.12.3 Special Considerations and Protocols.

B.12.3.1 Fire and Explosion. In the event that the health care facility does not need to be completely evacuated immediately, the actions staff should take when they are alerted to a fire are detailed in Sections 18.7, 19.7, 20.7, and 21.7 of NFPA *101.*

B.12.3.2 During the past decade, the health care industry has been struck by numerous natural disasters. A study of these disasters has provided a series of "lessons learned." Examples follow.

_____

(Name of Facility)

Standard Operating Procedure #: _____　_____

(Date)

SUBJECT: _____

(Insert Hazard, Threat, or Event Name)

1. Description of hazard, threat, or event: _____

_____

_____

2. Impact on mission-critical systems: _____

_____

_____

3. Operating units and key personnel with responsibility: _____

_____

_____

4. Mitigation and preparedness activities

   a. Hazard reduction strategies and resource issues: _____

   _____

   b. Preparedness strategies and resource issues: _____

   _____

5. Response and recovery activities

   a. Hazard control strategies and resource issues: _____

   _____

   b. Hazard monitoring strategies: _____

   _____

   c. Recovery strategies and resource issues: _____

6. Notification procedures

   a. Internal: _____

   b. External: _____

7. Specialized staff training: _____

_____

_____

8. References and further assistance: _____

_____

_____

9. Review date: _____

_____　　_____

(Name)　　　　　　　　　　　　　　　　　　　　　　(Position/Title)

© 2023 National Fire Protection Association　　　　　　　　　　　　　　　　NFPA 99

△ **FIGURE B.12.1.1.1　Sample Standard Operating Procedure Format.**

B.12.3.2.1 Alert. Alerting is often provided through the local Office of Emergency Management and the National Oceanic and Atmospheric Administration. Based on the facility's geographical location, these alerts often come in the form of a "watch," which indicates the strong possibility of a natural disaster, or a "warning," which indicates the immediate threat of a disaster. A hazard vulnerability analysis (HVA) of the area would result in actions that should be taken at different stages of the alert. Such actions could indicate monitoring reports by a liaison with the Office of Emergency Management; the Internal Incident Command of a facility would assess existing staffing and supply issues and make decisions to activate staff call-back plans and augment critical supplies. Some facilities have also indicated they have found it useful to complete a prestorm patient census reduction to discharge, where possible, or to move preselected high-acuity patients, such as neonatal intensive care patients, bariatric patients, or patients with severe respiratory complications, or a combination thereof. Also, during this prestorm patient relocation, selected patients could be moved to what are considered to be safer areas within the facility.

Some natural disasters provide absolutely no warning, such as an earthquake. During such a situation, staff would have to assume immediate operations plan procedures.

B.12.3.2.2 Isolation Survival for up to 96 Hours. Recent disasters have shown it could be 96 hours (in some cases, longer) before outside help is able to reach the facility. Those facilities with sufficient resources in-house for critical areas fared the best during disasters. Facilities that had corporate structures or associations with out-of-area organizations also received help in a timely manner.

B.12.3.2.3 Wind. When wind knocked down communications antennas, the result was severe difficulties in facility communication with staff, other health care facilities, and so forth. One solution was construction of antennas with hinges so they could be laid down during a prestorm warning. In other cases, the history of high winds or the HVA, or both, showed that certain windows should be boarded and certain doors should be braced and sandbagged.

B.12.3.2.4 Flooding. Flooding into a facility's lower levels where utilities are often housed results in a disruption of these services. In a recovery effort, the following procedures were helpful:

(1) Keep the electrical service turned off until the electrical device completely dries.
(2) Secure environmental waste containers and portable medical gas containers.

One contractor dealing with the hospitals of the Gulf states stated that, based on its experience with floods, it would never again use "fail return" elevators to a basement level. Many times elevators returned to the basement level upon loss of power, resulting in the wires that are located in the cab flooring being soaked, rendering the elevator useless.

B.12.3.2.5 Power Loss. Power is lost typically as a result of high winds and flooding. Generators and transfer switches have been lost due to their location below the high water mark. Another problem surfacing with generators is that they often were not powerful enough to provide HVAC services to the facility. In some of the Gulf states, this alone forced evacuation of the hospital or long-term care facility. Another problem encountered was fuel, designed for another type of generator

(such as military), contaminating the unit. When ordering backup generators, it is important to know the size needed and the method to be used to connect the generator to the facility.

Services, in priority, which should be up and running for the facility to be operational, are as follows:

(1) Clinical care:
  (a) Life-support systems
  (b) Life safety (exits and fire alarm and fire suppression)
  (c) Lab services
  (d) Pharmaceutical services
  (e) Diagnostic services
(2) Infrastructure:
  (a) Heating, ventilation, and air-conditioning
  (b) Water supply and removal systems
  (c) Information technology
  (d) Food and liquids
  (e) Elevators

B.12.3.2.6 Loss of Communications. Loss of communications is one of the major problems during a disaster. There have been many suggested solutions, including satellite phones and websites to communicate to staff and responsible parties. A successful solution has been communications conducted through Amateur Radio Emergency Services (ARES). Health care facilities have also reported that it was important to have either a liaison to, or a liaison position within, the community emergency operations center.

B.12.3.2.7 Loss of Water. Loss of water can result in problems with sewer service, air-conditioning, generator and refrigeration cooling systems, sterilization, dialysis services, liquid consumption, laundry, dishwashing, staff and patient hygiene, and fire suppression. It is recommended that hospitals perform risk assessments in these areas and prepare themselves for 96 hours of isolation, without outside water delivery. If this is not possible, evacuation might have to be considered.

B.12.3.2.8 Staff Issues. The following staff issues were found to be important to address:

(1) Transportation, including knowledge of which roads are open and actually transporting staff to the facility. The health care organization should work with the state and local agencies to identify qualified volunteer groups or other organizations that could provide transportation services to staff.
(2) Addressing the safety of families of staff.
(3) Provision of food, liquids, and lodging for staff and family members.

B.12.3.2.9 Civil Disturbance. Civil disturbance resulted mostly from members of the disaster-struck community seeking drugs, food, and shelter. During such disturbances, facilities initiate lockdown procedures and request local police assistance to protect the facility. It was noted that police departments were often overburdened during disasters that involved civil disturbance, and facilities had to rely on private security or the National Guard, or both.

B.12.3.2.10 Influx of Patients. Even though the facility is trying to keep its patients alive and safe, it must be recognized that some outside patients might come to the facility due to serious injuries that occur during the disaster or other medical needs. Others might have power at home or home health care providers to assist them with special needs and may not need to go to the health care facility. Community members might come to the facility simply to seek shelter or medications in the event their normal pharmacy is shut down. Some patients might come from an evacuating facility.

Recognizing these situations, facilities might be able to redirect the special needs population to a special needs shelter if the community has set up such provisions. It was found helpful to establish an outside (under cover) preemergency/triage room to relieve stress from the critical care emergency room within the hospital.

B.12.3.2.11 Evacuation. Often evacuation was accomplished in two phases. Phase I was a prestorm evacuation. It was found that, if this was going to be undertaken, it had to begin early enough to avoid traffic congestion to get patients to their ultimate destination in an acceptable length of time; otherwise, Phase II, or full hospital evacuation, could not take place until the disaster had subsided and transportation was once again available to move patients. Additional problems occurred with tracking patients and moving their medical records. Medical records that were on the Electronic Health Records System were at times unattainable if they could not be accessed from a remote site. Hard copy records, in some cases, were lost during transport.

B.12.3.3 Evacuation. Evacuation can be partial or total. It might involve moving from one story to another, from one lateral section or wing to another, or moving out of the structure. Even partial evacuations can involve all categories of patients. Where patients are those who would not routinely be moved, extraordinary measures might be required to support life. It is also necessary to ensure movement of supplies in conjunction with any evacuation. Decisions to evacuate might be made as a result of internal problems or under the menace of engulfing external threats. In all cases, the following considerations should govern:

(1) Move to predesignated areas, whether in the facility, nearby, or in remote zones. Evacuation directives will normally indicate destinations. Note that it is recommended to predesign a mutual aid evacuation plan with other health care facilities in the community. *(See Annex D, US Government Publication 3152, Hospitals and Community Emergency Response — What You Need to Know, on the subject of health care community mutual aid and evacuation planning.)* Receiving facilities can also be designated based on the scope of the event, activation of state or federal resources, or by local emergency medical services (EMS), based on availability.
(2) Ensure movement of equipment, supplies, and medical records to accompany or meet patients and staff in the new location.
(3) Execute predetermined staffing plans. Some staff will accompany patients; others will rendezvous in the new location. Maintenance of shifts is more complex than normal, especially when some hard-to-move patients stay behind in the threatened location, and when staff might be separated from their own relocated families.
(4) Protect patients and staff (during and after movement) against the threatening environment.
(5) When planning, consider transportation arrangements and patient tracking.

B.12.3.3.1 The Emergency Management Committee oversees the HVA process to ensure that all major threats to the facility are accounted for and assessed. Input to the HVA by operating unit managers is very important. Once a list of priority hazards, threats, and events has been compiled, managers should complete an operating unit template for their particular service or department. Some threats to individual operating units are so severe that they might interrupt the continuity of critical operations in the facility. The operating unit template is a unit level contingency plan, useful in staff education, drills, and actual events. Figure B.12.3.3.1(a) illustrates a sample HVA format. Figure B.12.3.3.1(b) shows a sample operating unit template.

B.12.3.4 Activation of Emergency Utility Resources. Loss of utility resources can occur at any time due to a natural disaster, an internal system failure, or even a supply shortage. Redundancy in system design and support is fundamental to avoiding loss of utilities. Critical points of failure in systems and supply chains should be identified, and their malfunction, disruption, or loss mitigated.

The key to a successful response to a loss of utilities is planning. Assessment of the organization's utility systems is an excellent starting point and should consist of identifying essential utility systems, such as electricity, water/sewer, piped medical gas and vacuum systems, HVAC systems, and vertical and horizontal transports. Once the systems are identified, they should be broken down to the component level and evaluated for importance. This allows the organization to establish priorities and the capabilities of the systems and their components.

Organizations should evaluate their self-sufficiency for at least 96 hours. This evaluation will assist in establishing gaps in the utility systems. For example, if a facility loses electricity and has backup generators, the organization must establish how long it can operate on those generators. By looking at different components of the generator system, the organization might determine that only enough fuel for 24 hours is maintained. If the same generator is cooled by water and the water supply is disrupted, that is an additional limitation. This concept should be applied to all systems and key components of each utility.

By establishing the limitations of the utility systems and components, an organization can identify the need to mitigate with alternative means, such as extra equipment, generators, bottled medical gas, bottled water, or formal documented agreements and understandings with other organizations. Contingency plans should be established and tested for effectiveness on a regular basis. It is essential that an organization understands its limitations and uses this information to determine if it can sustain itself for 96 hours or if it is appropriate to stop or limit services.

B.12.3.5 Civil Disturbance. Large-scale civil disturbances have shown that health care facilities and their personnel are not immune to the direct effects of human violence during such disturbances. Hospitals in large urban areas have to make special provisions in their disaster plans to ensure the physical safety of their employees in transit from the hospital exit to and from a secure means of transportation to their homes. In extreme cases, it might be necessary to house employees within the health care facility itself during such civil disturbances. Another aspect of civil disturbances not to be overlooked in facility security planning is the possibility that a given health care facility might have to admit and treat large numbers of prisoners during such emergencies; however, security guards for such patients will normally be provided by the local police department.

Type of Event	Severity Classification — Low, Moderate, High				Rank
	Probability	Human Impact	Property Impact	Operational Impact	
	Likelihood this will occur within 1 year	Possibility of death or injury	Physical losses and damage	Interruption of services	Score of 2 or higher in any category requires an SOP
Score	0 = N/A 1 = Low 2 = Moderate 3 = High	0 = N/A 1 = Low 2 = Moderate 3 = High	0 = N/A 1 = Low 2 = Moderate 3 = High	0 = N/A 1 = Low 2 = Moderate 3 = High	SOP required — yes or no?
(Hazard Type)					

NFPA 99

Δ **FIGURE B.12.3.3.1(a)   Sample Hazard Vulnerability Analysis (HVA) Format.**

Operating Unit: _____   Operating Unit Manager: _____

Mission-Critical System	Potential Problems	Contact for Assistance in Preparing	Mitigation Actions	If this mission-critical system is interrupted, then:	
				Assess situation for:	Action required:
(Lighting)					
(Electrical Power)					
(Steam Distribution)					
(HVAC)					
(Room or Hood Exhaust)					
(Water Delivery)					
(Waste Stream)					
(Communications)					

© 2023 National Fire Protection Association   NFPA 99

Δ **FIGURE B.12.3.3.1(b)   Sample Operating Unit Template.**

Shaded text = Revisions.   Δ = Text deletions and figure/table revisions.   • = Section deletions.   *N* = New material.

B.12.3.6 Hazardous Materials. There are at least three major sources of concern with regard to nonradioactive hazardous materials unrelated to the intentional use of chemical agents to harm people *(see B.12.3.8)*. The first is the possibility of a large spill or venting of hazardous materials near the facility; this is especially likely near major rail or truck shipping routes, near pipelines, or near heavy manufacturing plants. Second, every facility contains within its boundaries varying amounts of such materials, especially in the laboratory and custodial areas. A spill of a highly volatile chemical can quickly contaminate an entire structure by way of the air ducts. Finally, contaminated patients can pose a risk to staff, though on a more localized basis. Usually, removal of their clothing will reduce the risk materially. In any case, staff has to be prepared to seek advice on unknown hazards. This type of advice is not usually available from poison centers, but rather from a central referral, such as CHEMTREC, and its toll-free emergency information service number (800-424-9300).

See Annex D for publications concerning hazardous materials regulations and reports on various types of chemical protective equipment.

B.12.3.7 Volcanic Eruptions. Although most of the direct effects of a volcanic eruption are covered in other protocols for disasters (e.g., fire, explosion), it is necessary to make special provisions for functioning in areas of heavy to moderate ash fall. This hazard can exist hundreds of miles downwind from the eruption.

Volcanic ash is actually finely pulverized rock blown out of the volcano. Outside the area of direct damage, the ash varies from a fine powder to a coarse sand. General housekeeping measures can exclude much ash. It should be noted, however, that people move about freely during and after ash fall.

Ash fall presents the following four problems for health care facilities:

(1) People require cleanup (brushing, vacuuming) before entering the building.
(2) Electromechanical and automotive equipment and air-filtering systems require special care because of the highly abrasive and fine-penetration nature of the ash.
(3) Increased flow of patients with respiratory complaints can be expected.
(4) Eye protection is required for people who have to be out in the dust. (No contact lenses should be worn; goggles are suggested.) Dust masks are available that are approved by the National Institute for Occupational Safety and Health (NIOSH) and are marked TC-21 plus other digits.

B.12.3.8 Weapons of Mass Destruction. Weapons of mass destruction, or WMD, are defined as any weapon or device that is intended to cause, or has the capability to cause, death or serious bodily injury to a significant number of people through the release, dissemination, or impact of toxic or poisonous chemicals or their precursors; a disease organism; or radiation or radioactivity. Many federal departments and agencies are involved in supporting WMD preparedness and response activities at the state and local level. The Department of Health and Human Services manages two cooperative grant programs administered by the Centers for Disease Control and Prevention (CDC) and the Assistant Secretary for Preparedness and Response (ASPR). These programs are aimed at enhancing the readiness of the public health and hospital system.

The Department of Justice maintains a help line (1-800-368-6498) offering technical assistance in nonemergency cases and provides information on the following subjects: detection equipment; personal protective equipment; decontamination systems and methods; physical properties of WMD materials; signs and symptoms of WMD exposure; treatment of exposure to WMD materials; toxicology information; federal response assets; and applicable laws and regulations. For reporting actual or potential acts of terrorism, health care facilities should contact their local or state health departments. The National Response Center (1-800-424-8802) can link callers to technical experts.

See Annex D for publications relating to WMD preparedness for health systems.

B.12.4 Continuing Operations Plan and Recovery. It has been well documented that a community cannot recover without the health care facilities recovering simultaneously or beforehand. If at all possible, a health care facility needs to remain operational throughout a disaster to care for its patients, as well as for those who are injured during the disaster.

It is important to advertise that the facility is open for business as soon as it is able to operate.

As part of disaster recovery, health care facilities should consider the following:

(1) Know the sources of funding, such as insurance and FEMA, and request loans from those sources to initiate cash flow as soon as possible.
(2) Activate lines of credit with vendors and banks.
(3) Use stock and other investments as collateral for loans and lines of credit.
(4) Have the finance section chief of the Incident Command System work with other section chiefs to keep precise records of disaster-related expenses for reimbursement following the disaster.
(5) Ensure that doctors' offices open simultaneously with the opening of the hospital to provide services to patients. Provide office support as soon as possible for physicians, with the priority being emergency department physicians, general practitioners, orthopedic surgeons, and cardiovascular surgeons.
(6) Activate billing and payroll as soon as possible.
(7) Consider setting up a bank within the hospital for staff.

Credits:

Educational Fact Finding and On-site Research in Houston, Texas, following Tropical Storm Allison, 2001.

National Fire Protection Association.

Russell Phillips & Associates, LLC.

Also see "Atmospheric Pressure," *Fire Journal*, July/August, 2002.

Educational Fact Finding and On-site Research for Hurricane Katrina, Louisiana, Mississippi, 2005.

American Society of Healthcare Engineers: Dale Woodin.

Russell Phillips & Associates, LLC: Russell Phillips & Scott Aronson.

B.13 Reserved.

B.14 Additional Information on Chapter 14.

B.14.1 Nature of Hazards.

B.14.1.1 Fire and Explosion.

B.14.1.1.1 The occurrence of a fire requires the presence of combustible or flammable materials, an atmosphere containing oxygen or other oxidizing agent(s), and heat or energy source of ignition.

Note that certain substances such as acetylenic hydrocarbons can propagate flame in the absence of oxygen.

B.14.1.1.2 Under hyperbaric conditions utilizing compressed air, the partial pressure of oxygen is increased. Leakage of oxygen into the atmosphere of the chamber (for example, from improper application of respiratory therapy apparatus) can further increase markedly the oxygen partial pressure.

B.14.1.1.2.1 The flammability or combustibility of materials generally increases as the partial pressure of oxygen increases, even when the percentage of oxygen in the gas mixture remains constant. Materials that are nonflammable or noncombustible under normal atmospheric conditions can become flammable or combustible under such circumstances.

B.14.1.1.3 Sources of Fuel.

B.14.1.1.3.1 Materials that might not ignite in air at atmospheric pressure or require relatively high temperatures for their ignition but that burn vigorously in 100 percent oxygen include, but are not necessarily limited to, the following: tricresyl phosphate (lubricant); certain types of flame-resistant fabrics; silicone rubber; polyvinyl chloride; asbestos-containing paint; glass fiber-sheathed silicone rubber-insulated wire; polyvinyl chloride-insulated asbestos-covered wire and sheet; polyamides; epoxy compounds; and certain asbestos blankets.

Note that flammable lubricants are used widely in equipment designed for conventional use, including shafts, gear boxes, pulleys and casters, and threaded joints, which are coupled and uncoupled.

B.14.1.1.3.2 The flammability of certain volatile liquids and gases containing carbon and hydrogen is well known. Hazards and safeguards for their use in oxygen-enriched atmospheres at ambient pressure are well-documented in the NFPA *Fire Protection Guide to Hazardous Materials* and NFPA 53.

B.14.1.1.3.3 Human tissues will burn in an atmosphere of 100 percent oxygen. Body oils and fats, as well as hair, will burn readily under such circumstances.

B.14.1.1.3.4 When a conventional loose cotton outer garment, such as scrub suits, dresses, and gowns employed in hospital operating suites, is ignited in an atmosphere of pure oxygen, the garment will become engulfed in flame rapidly and will be totally destroyed within 20 seconds or less.

If such a garment is ignited in a compressed air atmosphere, the flame spread is increased. When oxygen concentration exceeds 23.5 percent at elevated total pressure, flame spread is much more rapid, and at 6 ATA, is comparable to 95 ± 5 percent at 1 ATA. Flame spread in air (21 percent oxygen) is somewhat increased at 6 ATA, but not to the level of 95 ± 5 percent at 1 ATA.

Combustible fabrics have tiny air spaces that become filled with oxygen when exposed to oxygen-enriched environments. Once removed to atmospheric air (e.g., room air outside the chamber), the fabric will burn, if ignited, almost as rapidly as if it were still in the oxygen environment. This hazard will remain until the oxygen trapped in the air spaces in the fabric has had time to diffuse out and be replaced by air.

B.14.1.1.3.5 Oil-based or volatile cosmetics (facial creams, body oils, hair sprays, and the like) constitute a source of fuel that is highly flammable in an oxygen-enriched atmosphere.

B.14.1.1.4 Sources of Ignition.

B.14.1.1.4.1 Sources of ignition that might be encountered in a hyperbaric chamber include, but are not necessarily limited to, the following: defective electrical equipment, including failure of high-voltage components of radiological or monitoring equipment; heated surfaces in broken vacuum tubes or broken lamps used for general illumination, spot illumination, or illumination of diagnostic instruments; the hot-wire cautery or high-frequency electrocautery; open or arcing switches, including motor switches; bare defibrillator paddles; overheated motors; and electrical thermostats.

B.14.1.1.4.2 Sources of ignition that should not be encountered in a hyperbaric facility, but that might be introduced by inept practice, include the following: lighted matches or tobacco, static sparks from improper use of personal attire, electrical wiring not complying with 14.2.9, cigarette lighters, and any oil-contaminated materials that present a spontaneous heating hazard.

B.14.1.1.4.3 In oxygen-enriched atmospheres, the minimum energy necessary to ignite flammable or combustible materials is reduced in most instances below the energy required in atmospheres of ambient air.

B.14.1.2 Mechanical Hazards.

B.14.1.2.1 General.

B.14.1.2.1.1 A large amount of potential energy is stored in even a small volume of compressed gas. In hyperbaric chambers of moderate or large size, the potential energy of the chamber's compressed atmosphere, if released suddenly, can produce devastating destruction to adjacent structures and personnel, as well as to structures and personnel remote from the site of the chamber. Such sudden release could result from failure of the vessel structure, its parts, or its piping.

B.14.1.2.1.2 A particular hazard can be created if individuals attempt to drill, cut, or weld the vessel in a manner contrary to ASME's *Boiler and Pressure Vessel Code.*

B.14.1.2.2 The restriction on escape and the impedance to rescue and firefighting efforts posed by the chamber create a significant hazard to life in case of fire or other emergency.

B.14.1.2.2.1 A particular hazard exists to chamber personnel in the event of a fire within the structure housing the chamber. Inability to escape from the chamber and loss of services of the chamber operator would pose serious threats to the lives of all occupants of the chamber.

B.14.1.2.2.2 All personnel involved in hyperbaric chamber operation and therapy, including patients and family, have to be made aware of the risks and hazards involved. Fire prevention is essential. Extinguishment of a fire within a Class B chamber is impossible. Extinguishment of a fire within a Class A chamber is only possible utilizing equipment already installed in such a chamber, and then often only by the efforts of the occupants of such a chamber or the chamber operator.

B.14.1.2.3 The necessity for restricting viewing ports to small size limits the vision of chamber operators and other observers, reducing their effectiveness as safety monitors.

B.14.1.2.4 Containers and enclosures can be subjected to collapse or rupture as a consequence of the changing pressures of the hyperbaric chamber. Items containing entrained gas include, but are not necessarily limited to, the following: ampuls, partially filled syringes, stoppered or capped bottles, cuffed endotracheal tubes, and pneumatic cushions employed for breathing masks or aids in positioning patients. The rupture of such containers having combustible or flammable liquids would also constitute a severe fire or explosion hazard.

B.14.1.2.4.1 The sudden collapse of containers from high external pressures will result in adiabatic heating of the contents. Therefore the collapse of a container of flammable liquid would constitute a severe fire or explosion hazard both from heating and from a spill of the liquid. *(See 14.3.1.6.2 and B.14.1.1.3.2.)*

B.14.1.2.5 Other mechanical hazards relate to the malfunction, disruption, or inoperativeness of many standard items when placed in service under pressurized atmospheres. Hazards that might be encountered in this regard are implosion of illuminating lamps and vacuum tubes; overloading of fans driving gas at higher density; and inaccurate operation of standard flowmeters, pressure gauges, and pressure-reducing regulators.

Note that illuminating lamps or vacuum tubes, which implode, or overloaded fans, are sources of ignition.

B.14.1.3 Pathophysiological, Medical, and Other Related Hazards.

B.14.1.3.1 Exposure of pregnant chamber occupants to hyperbaric atmospheres might result in fetal risk.

B.14.1.3.2 Medical hazards that can be encountered routinely include compression problems, nitrogen narcosis, oxygen toxicity, and the direct effects of sudden pressure changes.

B.14.1.3.2.1 Inability to equalize pressure differentials between nasopharynx (nose) and nasal sinuses or the middle ear can result in excruciating pain and might cause rupture of the eardrum or hemorrhage into the ear cavity or nasal sinus.

B.14.1.3.2.2 The breathing of air (78 percent nitrogen) under significant pressures (as by chamber personnel breathing chamber atmosphere) can result in nitrogen narcosis, which resembles alcoholic inebriation. The degree of narcosis is directly related to the amount of pressurization. Nitrogen narcosis results in impairment of mental functions, loss of manual dexterity, and interference with alertness and ability to think clearly and act quickly and intelligently in an emergency.

B.14.1.3.2.3 Oxygen toxicity can develop from breathing oxygen at partial pressures above 0.50 atmospheres absolute for a significant length of time. Oxygen toxicity can affect the lungs (pain in the chest, rapid shallow breathing, coughing), nervous system (impaired consciousness and convulsions), or other tissues and organs, or combinations thereof.

B.14.1.3.2.4 Direct effects of reduction in pressure can include inability to equalize pressures between the nasopharynx and sinuses or middle ear, expansion of gas pockets in the gastrointestinal tract, and expansion of trapped gas in the lungs.

B.14.1.3.2.5 The presence of personnel within the cramped confines of the hyperbaric chamber in close proximity to grounded metallic structures on all sides creates a definite shock hazard if accidental contact is made with a live electrical conductor or a defective piece of electrical equipment. Such accidental contact also could be a source of ignition of flammable or combustible materials. *(See B.14.1.1.4.)*

B.14.1.3.3 Medical hazards that are not ordinarily encountered during hyperbaric oxygen therapy, but that might arise during malfunction, fire, or other emergency conditions, include electric shock and fouling of the atmosphere of the chamber with oxygen, nitrous oxide, carbon dioxide, carbon monoxide, pyrolysis products from overheated materials, or the toxic products of combustion from any fire.

B.14.1.3.3.1 Increased concentrations of carbon dioxide within the chamber, as might result from malfunction of the systems responsible for monitoring or removal thereof, can be toxic under increased pressures.

B.14.1.3.3.2 The development of combustion products or gases evolved from heated nonmetallics within the closed space of the hyperbaric chamber can be extremely toxic to life because of the confining nature of the chamber and the increased hazards of breathing such products under elevated pressure.

Note that extreme pressure rises have accompanied catastrophic fires in confined atmospheres. These pressures have driven hot, toxic gases into the lungs of victims as well as exceeding the structural limits of the vessel in at least one case.

B.14.1.3.4 Physiological hazards include exposure to high noise levels and decompression sickness. Rapid release of pressurized gases can produce shock waves and loss of visibility.

B.14.1.3.4.1 During hyperbaric therapy, and especially during compression, the noise level within the chamber becomes quite high. Such a level can be hazardous because it is distractive, interferes with communication, and can produce permanent sensory-neural deafness.

B.14.1.3.4.2 Decompression sickness (bends, caisson worker's disease) results from the elution into the bloodstream or extravascular tissues of bubbles of inert gas (mainly nitrogen) that becomes dissolved in the blood and tissue fluids while breathing air at elevated pressures for a significant period of time.

Note that rapid decompression of the chamber can occur if the pressure relief valve is damaged from exposure to a fire external to the chamber or from the venting of hot products of combustion from within the chamber.

B.14.1.3.4.3 The use of decompression procedures will prevent immediate escape from the Class A chamber by occupants during emergency situations.

Note that these procedures are not followed if chamber occupants are exposed to a "no-decompression exposure" [compression to less than 2 atmospheres absolute (ATA) air], or when compressed to 2 ATA or higher pressures and breathing 100 percent oxygen.

B.14.1.3.4.4 The sudden release of gas, whether by rupture of a container or operation of a device such as used in firefighting, will produce noise, possible shock waves, reduced or obscured visibility, and temperature changes. The initial effect might be to cool the air, but resulting pressure rises will cause adiabatic heating.

B.14.1.3.5 In summary, the hazards of fire and related problems in hyperbaric systems are real. By the very nature of the hyperbaric atmosphere, increased partial pressures of oxygen are present routinely. Flammability and combustibility of materials are increased. Ignition energy is lowered. Both immediate escape and ready entry for rescue are impeded. Finally, attendants within the chamber, through effects of the elevated noise level and nitrogen pressure, might be unable to respond to emergencies quickly and accurately.

B.14.2 Suggested Procedures to Follow in Event of Fire in Class A Chambers.

B.14.2.1 Fire Inside Chamber. For fire inside the chamber, the following procedures should be performed:

(1) The actions of the inside observer should be as follows:

   (a) Don breathing air device immediately.
   (b) Activate fire suppression system and/or handheld hoses.
   (c) Advise outside.

(2) The actions of the chamber operator should be as follows:

   (a) Activate the fire suppression system, if needed.
   (b) Switch breathing gas to air.
   (c) Decompress the chamber as rapidly as possible.
   (d) Deactivate all unnecessary electrical equipment.

(3) The actions of the medical personnel (outside) should be as follows:

   (a) Direct operations and assist crew members wherever necessary.
   (b) Provide medical support as required.

(4) The actions of the other personnel (outside) should be as follows:

   (a) Notify the fire department by activating fire signaling device.
   (b) Stand by with a fire extinguisher.
   (c) Assist in unloading chamber occupants.

B.14.2.2 Fire Outside Chamber. For fire outside the chamber, the following procedures should be performed:

(1) The actions of the chamber operator should be as follows:

   (a) Notify the inside observer to stand by for emergency return to normal atmospheric pressure.
   (b) Notify the fire department by activating fire signaling device.
   (c) Switch breathing gas to air.
   (d) Don the operator's breathing device, if applicable.

(2) The actions of the medical personnel (outside) should be as follows:

   (a) Determine whether procedure should be terminated.
   (b) Provide medical support as required.

B.14.3 Suggested Fire Procedures for Facilities with Class B Chambers.

B.14.3.1 For fires within the facility not involving the chamber, the following procedure should be performed:

(1) Don the operator's means for respiratory and eye protection, if applicable (*see 14.2.5.4*).
(2) Decompress the chamber. The urgency of decompression should be determined by the location of the fire.
(3) Remove the patient and evacuate to a safe area.
(4) Turn off the oxygen zone valve to the chamber room and close any smoke/fire barrier doors. These steps are consistent with the rescue and confine elements of the rescue, alarm, confine, extinguish (R.A.C.E.) procedure. It is assumed that other personnel will evacuate other patients and visitors from the area and activate a fire alarm signaling device (if not already activated).

B.14.3.2 For fire within the chamber, the following procedure should be performed:

(1) Stop oxygen from flowing into the chamber by switching off the chamber (if the chamber is compressed with oxygen) or switching the supply gas of a breathing device from oxygen to air (if the chamber is compressed with air).
(2) Decompress the chamber as rapidly as possible in accordance with the emergency decompression procedures.
(3) Stand by with a handheld fire extinguisher and spray into the chamber (if necessary) when the chamber door is opened.
(4) Remove the patient and evacuate to a safe area.
(5) Turn off the oxygen zone valve to the chamber room and close any smoke/fire barrier doors.

These steps are consistent with the rescue and confine elements of the rescue, alarm, confine, extinguish (R.A.C.E.) procedure. It is assumed that other personnel will evacuate other patients and visitors from the area and activate a fire alarm signaling device (if not already activated). The injured patient should have appropriate medical attention immediately after evacuation to a safe area. Many Class B chambers require oxygen supply pressure to operate a rapid decompression feature. If this is the case, do not turn off the oxygen zone valve or any inline oxygen supply shutoff valve until all patients have been removed from the chamber(s).

B.14.4 See Table B.14.4.

B.14.5 Gas Purging. Inert gas or air purging is a means to mitigate the risk of fire from an electrical device brought into the chamber. The three main objectives to inert gas or air purging are to lower the oxygen level, to purge increased heat from the device and to help prevent dust accumulation inside the device.

Fire research has demonstrated that under normal conditions combustion will not take place when the oxygen level is at 6 percent or less. This is regardless of the treatment pressure and is related to the ratio of oxygen to the inert gas. With an oxygen level of 6 percent and the balancing inert gas level of 94 percent, the high percentage of inert gas will prevent combustion.

A clear policy and procedure should be written for an inert gas purging system. It should include the inert gas parameters for each device and instructions for the proper setup of the system.

Δ **Table B.14.4 Pressure Table**

Atmosphere Absolute (ATA)	mm Hg	psia	psig	Equivalent Depth in Seawater		mm Hg Oxygen Pressure of Compressed Air	mm Hg Oxygen Pressure of Oxygen-Enriched Air (23.5%)
				ft	m		
1	760	14.7	0	0	0	160	179
1.5	1140	22	7.35	16.5	5.07	240	268
2.0	1520	29.4	14.7	33.1	10.13	320	357
2.5	1900	36.7	22.0	49.7	15.20	400	447
3.0	2280	44.1	29.4	66.2	20.26	480	536
3.5	2660	51.4	36.7	82.7	25.33	560	625
4.0	3040	58.8	44.1	99.2	30.40	640	714
5.0	3800	73.5	58.8	132.3	40.53	800	893

Notes:

(1) The oxygen percentage in the chamber environment, not the oxygen partial pressure, is of principal concern, as concentrations above 23.5 percent oxygen increase the rate of flame spread. Thirty percent oxygen in nitrogen at 1 ATA (228 mm Hg pO$_2$) increases burning rate. However, 6 percent oxygen in nitrogen will not support combustion, regardless of oxygen partial pressure (at 5 ATA, 6 percent oxygen gives 228 mm Hg pO$_2$).

(2) The Subcommittee on Hyperbaric and Hypobaric Facilities recommends that one unit of pressure measurement be employed. Since a variety of different units are now in use, and since chamber operators have not settled upon one single unit, the above table includes the five units most commonly employed in chamber practice.

All testing to determine the proper inert gas or air flow should be well documented. At a minimum, approval signatures have to be obtained from the medical director and the hyperbaric safety coordinator. Other signatures should include the department manager and biomedical representatives.

Startup and shutdown checklists should include purge gas parameters with visual checks and verifications of inside devices, purge gas equipment, and alarms.

Where gas purging is used, the following should be considered:

(1) Each electrical device should comply with 14.2.9.3.17. Gas purging is only one element of the essential risk assessment and management that is critical to safely managing any electrical device that is introduced into the chamber. A comprehensive risk assessment with approved safety procedures and mitigation orders needs to be documented and signed by the medical director, hyperbaric safety coordinator and all who are directly involved, prior to the device being used in the chamber.

(2) Each gas purge device should have its own dedicated purging line and flowmeter with each flowmeter clearly labeled identifying the gas used. Splitting a purge line to supply two or more devices can create a disparity of flow between the multiple gas lines depending on the length and resistance of each line. One device might be well protected with high flow and the other device inadequately protected with very little flow. A single line with a single flowmeter will prevent this and will provide a measurable way to verify the correct flow to the device. A gas flowmeter can be mistaken for an oxygen flowmeter.

(3) When using an inert gas, oxygen should be maintained at less than or equal to 6 percent within the electrical compartment(s) of the device at all treatment levels. For initial testing and, to establish the proper inert gas flow, oxygen levels in the electrical compartments of the device should be tested at all treatment pressures.

(4) The manufacturer's safe operating temperature range should be maintained at all treatment levels. Gas purging is useful for purging increased heat from the device. For initial testing and, to establish the proper inert gas

flow, temperature levels in the electrical compartments of the device should be tested at all treatment pressures.

(5) Supply pressure for gas purging should be supplied from a regulator system that will maintain the surface pressure over the chamber's treatment pressure, or over-bottom pressure. Maintaining purge gas pressure at all treatment levels can be accomplished by means of a tracking type regulator outside the chamber or by placing the regulator inside the chamber with an adequate supply pressure for all treatment pressures.

(6) An audio and visual alarm system should activate at the operator's console if there is a loss of sufficient pressure to maintain set flowrates to the gas purging system during any pressurization of the chamber. The chamber operator needs to be alerted to a loss of purge gas flow.

(7) Chamber operations should be aborted if there is a loss of sufficient pressure to the gas purging system as noted in (6). Loss of purge gas pressure creates risks to patients and staff.

(8) When using inert gas, oxygen monitoring of the chamber's atmosphere should have a low-level alarm limit set at no lower than 19.5 percent. Normal gas purging is unlikely to lower the oxygen level of the chamber atmosphere during hyperbaric oxygen treatments. However, because inert gas is being introduced into the chamber, an oxygen low-level alarm limit of 19.5 percent should be set.

(9) Electrical devices that are enclosed, such as TV monitors placed in acrylic boxes, should have some means of extinguishing the device with water from the deluge system or the handheld hose. Acrylic boxes/enclosures are sometimes used to make gas purging easier. In the event of a fire or smoke inside this box there should be some means of drenching the device inside with water.

(10) The doors to chambers with gas purging systems using inert gas should be kept open during nonoperational hours. Chambers are made to be airtight. If the chamber doors are closed, (e.g., overnight), and the inert gas is inadvertently left on, the inert gas could potentially accumulate inside the chamber to a dangerous level. This would deplete the oxygen level and create a hazard for anyone entering the chamber.

Annex C Sample Ordinance Adopting NFPA 99

This annex is not a part of the requirements of this NFPA document but is included for informational purposes only.

C.1 The following sample ordinance is provided to assist a jurisdiction in the adoption of this code and is not part of this code.

ORDINANCE NO. _____

An ordinance of the *[jurisdiction]* adopting the 2024 edition of NFPA 99, *Health Care Facilities Code*, and documents listed in Chapter 2 of that code; prescribing regulations governing conditions hazardous to life and property from fire or explosion; providing for the issuance of permits and collection of fees; repealing Ordinance No. _____ of the *[jurisdiction]* and all other ordinances and parts of ordinances in conflict therewith; providing a penalty; providing a severability clause; and providing for publication; and providing an effective date.

BE IT ORDAINED BY THE *[health care facility's governing body]* OF THE *[jurisdiction]*:

SECTION 1 That the *Health Care Facilities Code* and documents adopted by Chapter 2, three (3) copies of which are on file and are open to inspection by the public in the office of the *[jurisdiction's keeper of records]* of the *[jurisdiction]*, are hereby adopted and incorporated into this ordinance as fully as if set out at length herein, and from the date on which this ordinance shall take effect, the provisions thereof shall be controlling within the limits of the *[jurisdiction]*. The same are hereby adopted as the code of the *[jurisdiction]* for the purpose of prescribing regulations governing conditions hazardous to life and property from fire or explosion and providing for issuance of permits and collection of fees.

SECTION 2 Any person who shall violate any provision of this code or standard hereby adopted or fail to comply therewith; or who shall violate or fail to comply with any order made thereunder; or who shall build in violation of any detailed statement of specifications or plans submitted and approved thereunder; or fail to operate in accordance with any certificate or permit issued thereunder; and from which no appeal has been taken; or who shall fail to comply with such an order as affirmed or modified by a court of competent jurisdiction, within the time fixed herein, shall severally for each and every

such violation and noncompliance, respectively, be guilty of a misdemeanor, punishable by a fine of not less than $ _____ nor more than $_____ or by imprisonment for not less than _____ days nor more than _____ days or by both such fine and imprisonment. The imposition of one penalty for any violation shall not excuse the violation or permit it to continue; and all such persons shall be required to correct or remedy such violations or defects within a reasonable time; and when not otherwise specified the application of the above penalty shall not be held to prevent the enforced removal of prohibited conditions. Each day that prohibited conditions are maintained shall constitute a separate offense.

SECTION 3 Additions, insertions, and changes — that the 2024 edition of NFPA 99, *Health Care Facilities Code*, is amended and changed in the following respects:

List Amendments

SECTION 4 That ordinance No. _____ of *[jurisdiction]* entitled *[fill in the title of the ordinance or ordinances in effect at the present time]* and all other ordinances or parts of ordinances in conflict herewith are hereby repealed.

SECTION 5 That if any section, subsection, sentence, clause, or phrase of this ordinance is, for any reason, held to be invalid or unconstitutional, such decision shall not affect the validity or constitutionality of the remaining portions of this ordinance. The *[health care facility's governing body]* hereby declares that it would have passed this ordinance, and each section, subsection, clause, or phrase hereof, irrespective of the fact that any one or more sections, subsections, sentences, clauses, and phrases be declared unconstitutional.

SECTION 6 That the *[jurisdiction's keeper of records]* is hereby ordered and directed to cause this ordinance to be published. [NOTE: An additional provision may be required to direct the number of times the ordinance is to be published and to specify that it is to be in a newspaper in general circulation. Posting may also be required.]

SECTION 7 That this ordinance and the rules, regulations, provisions, requirements, orders, and matters established and adopted hereby shall take effect and be in full force and effect *[time period]* from and after the date of its final passage and adoption.

Annex D Informational References

D.1 Referenced Publications. The documents or portions thereof listed in this annex are referenced within the informational sections of this code and are not part of the requirements of this document unless also listed in Chapter 2 for other reasons.

△ **D.1.1 NFPA Publications.** National Fire Protection Association, 1 Batterymarch Park, Quincy, MA 02169-7471.

NFPA 10, *Standard for Portable Fire Extinguishers*, 2022 edition.

NFPA 13, *Standard for the Installation of Sprinkler Systems*, 2022 edition.

NFPA 30, *Flammable and Combustible Liquids Code*, 2024 edition.

NFPA 53, *Recommended Practice on Materials, Equipment, and Systems Used in Oxygen-Enriched Atmospheres*, 2021 edition.

NFPA 55, *Compressed Gases and Cryogenic Fluids Code*, 2023 edition.

NFPA 56D, *Standard for Hyperbaric Facilities*, 1982 edition (withdrawn).

NFPA 58, *Liquefied Petroleum Gas Code*, 2024 edition.

NFPA 70®, National Electrical Code®, 2023 edition.

NFPA 70B, *Recommended Practice for Electrical Equipment Maintenance*, 2019 edition.

NFPA 72®, National Fire Alarm and Signaling Code®, 2022 edition.

NFPA 77, *Recommended Practice on Static Electricity*, 2024 edition.

NFPA 90B, *Standard for the Installation of Warm Air Heating and Air-Conditioning Systems*, 2024 edition.

NFPA 99B, *Standard for Hypobaric Facilities*, 2024 edition.

NFPA 101®, *Life Safety Code®*, 2024 edition.

NFPA 110, *Standard for Emergency and Standby Power Systems*, 2022 edition.

NFPA 111, *Standard on Stored Electrical Energy Emergency and Standby Power Systems*, 2022 edition.

NFPA 170, *Standard for Fire Safety and Emergency Symbols*, 2021 edition.

NFPA 220, *Standard on Types of Building Construction*, 2024 edition.

NFPA 252, *Standard Methods of Fire Tests of Door Assemblies*, 2022 edition.

NFPA 259, *Standard Test Method for Potential Heat of Building Materials*, 2018 edition.

NFPA 551, *Guide for the Evaluation of Fire Risk Assessments*, 2022 edition.

NFPA 730, *Guide for Premises Security*, 2020 edition.

NFPA 1660, *Standard for Emergency, Continuity, and Crisis Management: Preparedness, Response, and Recovery*, 2024 edition.

Fire Protection Guide to Hazardous Materials, 2010 edition.

D.1.2 Other Publications.

D.1.2.1 AAMI Publications. Association for the Advancement of Medical Instrumentation, 901 N. Glebe Road, Suite 300, Arlington, VA 22203.

ANSI/AAMI ES60601-1, *Medical electrical equipment — Part 1: General requirements for basic safety and essential performance*, 2005, revised 2012.

ANSI/AAMI ES60601-2, *Medical electrical equipment — Part 2: Collateral standard: Electromagnetic disturbances — Requirements and tests*, 2014.

ANSI/AAMI ES60601-8, *Medical electrical equipment — Part 8: Collateral standard: Alarm systems — General requirements, tests and guidance for alarm systems in medical electrical equipment and medical electrical systems*, 2006.

D.1.2.2 ASHE Publications. American Society for Health Care Engineering of the American Hospital Association, 155 N. Wacker Drive, Suite 400, Chicago, IL 60606.

Maintenance Management for Health Care Facilities, 2009.

D.1.2.3 ASHRAE Publications. American Society of Heating, Refrigerating and Air Conditioning Engineers, Inc., 180 Technology Parkway NW, Peachtree Corners, GA 30092.

ASHRAE Guideline 0, *The Commissioning Process*, 2019.

ASHRAE Guideline 1.1, *HVAC&R Technical Requirements for the Commissioning Process*, 2007, errata 2012.

ASHRAE Handbook — Fundamentals, 2021.

ASHRAE Standard 202, *Commissioning Process for Buildings and Systems*, 2018.

D.1.2.4 ASME Publications. The American Society of Mechanical Engineers, Two Park Avenue, New York, NY 10016-5990.

ASME B16.22, *Wrought Copper and Copper Alloy Solder-Joint Pressure Fittings*, 2021.

ANSI/ASME B16.50, *Wrought Copper and Copper Alloy Braze-Joint Pressure Fittings*, 2021.

ASME PVHO-1, *Safety Standard for Pressure Vessels for Human Occupancy*, 2019.

Boiler and Pressure Vessel Code, 2021.

D.1.2.5 ASSE Publications. ASSE International, 18927 Hickory Creek Drive, Suite 220, Mokena, IL 60448.

ASSE/IAPMO/ANSI Series 6000, *Professional Qualifications Standard for Medical Gas Systems Personnel*, 2021.

D.1.2.6 ASTM Publications. ASTM International, 100 Barr Harbor Drive, P.O. Box C700, West Conshohocken, PA 19428-2959.

ASTM E119, *Standard Test Methods for Fire Tests of Building Construction and Materials*, 2020.

ASTM F2213, *Standard Test Method for Measurement of Magnetically Induced Torque on Medical Devices in the Magnetic Resonance Environment*, 2017.

ASTM F2503, *Standard Practice for Marking Medical Devices and Other Items for Safety in the Magnetic Resonance Environment*, 2020.

ASTM G63, *Standard Guide for Evaluating Nonmetallic Materials for Oxygen Service*, 2015.

ASTM G72/G72M, *Standard Test Method for Autogenous Ignition Temperature of Liquids and Solids in a High-Pressure Oxygen-Enriched Environment*, 2015.

ASTM G88, *Standard Guide for Designing Systems for Oxygen Service*, 2021.

ASTM G93/G93M, *Standard Guide for Cleanliness Levels and Cleaning Methods for Materials and Equipment Used in Oxygen-Enriched Environments*, 2019.

ASTM G94, *Standard Guide for Evaluating Metals for Oxygen Service*, 2005, reapproved 2014.

D.1.2.7 CGA Publications. Compressed Gas Association, 8484 Westpark Drive, Suite 220, McLean, VA 22102.

CGA E-7, *Standard for Medical Gas Pressure Regulators, Flowmeters, and Orifice Flow Selectors*, 2018.

CGA G-8.1, *Standard for Nitrous Oxide Systems at Customer Sites*, 2013, reaffirmed 2018.

CGA P-2.5, *Standard for Transfilling of High Pressure Gaseous Oxygen Used for Respiration*, 2018.

CGA P-2.6, *Standard for Transfilling of Liquid Oxygen Used for Respiration*, 2018.

CGA P-2.7, *Guideline for the Safe Storage, Handling, and Use of Small Portable Liquid Oxygen Systems in Health Care Facilities*, 2018.

CGA P-50, *Standard for Site Security*, 2021.

CGA V-1, *Standard for Compressed Gas Cylinder Valve Outlet and Inlet Connections* (ANSI B57.1), 2021.

N **D.1.2.8 CSA Group Publications.** CSA Group, 178 Rexdale Blvd., Etobicoke, ON M9W 1R3, Canada.

CSA Z305.13, *Plume Scavenging in Surgical, Diagnostic, Therapeutic, and Aesthetic Settings*, 2013, reaffirmed 2020.

D.1.2.9 FGI Publications. Facility Guidelines Institute, 9750 Fall Ridge Trail, St. Louis, MO 63127.

Guidelines for Design and Construction of Hospitals, 2022.

Guidelines for Design and Construction of Outpatient Facilities, 2022.

Guidelines for Design and Construction of Residential Health, Care, and Support Facilities, 2022.

D.1.2.10 IEC Publications. International Electrotechnical Commission, 3, rue de Varembé, P.O. Box 131, CH-1211 Geneva 20, Switzerland.

ANSI/AAMI/IEC 80001-1, *Application of Risk Management for IT Networks Incorporating Medical Devices — Part 1: Roles, Responsibilities and Activities*, 2010.

ANSI/IEC/ISO 80001-1-1, *Application of Risk Management for IT Networks Incorporating Medical Devices — Part 1-1: Risk Management of Medical IT Networks*, 2010.

ANSI/IEC/ISO 80001-2-5, *Application of Risk Management for IT Networks Incorporating Medical Devices — Part 2-5: Application Guidance — Guidance for Distributed Alarm Systems*, 2014.

ISO/IEC 31010, *Risk Management — Risk Assessment Techniques*, 2019.

N **D.1.2.11 ISO Publications.** International Organization for Standardization, ISO Central Secretariat, BIBC II, Chemin de Blandonnet 8, CP 401, 1214 Vernier, Geneva, Switzerland.

ISO 16571, *Systems for evacuation of plume generated by medical devices*, 2014.

D.1.2.12 IEEE Publications. IEEE, 3 Park Avenue, 17th Floor, New York, NY 10016-5997.

ANSI/IEEE 493, *Recommended Practice for the Design of Reliable Industrial and Commercial Power Systems*, 2007.

IEEE 602, *Recommended Practice for Electric Systems in Health Care Facilities*, 2007.

N **D.1.2.13 NIOSH Publications.** National Institute for Occupational Safety and Health, Centers for Disease Control and Prevention, 1600 Clifton Road, Atlanta, GA 30329.

NIOSH 96-128, "Control of Smoke From Laser/Electric Surgical Procedures," Department of Health and Human Services (DHHS), 1996.

Δ **D.1.2.14 NEMA Publications.** National Electrical Manufacturers Association, 1300 17th Street N, Suite 900, Arlington, VA 22209.

ANSI/NEMA PB 1.1, *General Instructions for Proper Installation, Operation and Maintenance of Panelboards Rated 600 V or Less*, 2013.

ANSI/NEMA WD 6, *Wiring Devices — Dimensional Specifications*, 2016.

NEMA ICS 2.3, *Instructions for the Handling, Installation, Operation and Maintenance of Motor Control Centers Rated Not More than 600 V*, 2019.

D.1.2.15 NETA Publications. InterNational Electrical Testing Association, 3050 Old Centre Road, Suite 101, Portage, MI 49024.

ANSI/NETA ATS, *Standard for Acceptance Testing Specifications for Electrical Power Equipment and Systems*, 2021.

Δ **D.1.2.16 Ocean Systems, Inc., Publications.** Ocean Systems, Inc., Research and Development Laboratory, Tarrytown, NY 10591.

T. C. Schmidt, V. A. Dorr, and R. W. Hamilton, Jr., "Technical Memorandum UCRI-721, Chamber Fire Safety." *(Figure A.3.3.12.2 is adapted from Figure 4 of this memorandum.)* Work carried out under US Office of Naval Research, Washington DC, Contract No. N00014-67-A-0214-0013.

D.1.2.17 SFPE Publications. Society of Fire Protection Engineers, 9711 Washingtonian Blvd, Suite 380, Gaithersburg, MD 20878.

Engineering Guide to Fire Risk Assessment, 2006.

D.1.2.18 TIA Publications. Telecommunications Industry Association, 1310 North Courthouse Road, Suite 890, Arlington, VA 22201.

ANSI/TIA 569-D, *Telecommunications Pathways and Spaces*, 2015.

△ **D.1.2.19 UL Publications.** Underwriters Laboratories Inc., 333 Pfingsten Road, Northbrook, IL 60062-2096.

UL 263, *Fire Tests of Building Construction and Materials*, 2011, revised 2022.

UL 498, *Attachment Plugs and Receptacles*, 2017, revised 2021.

UL 943, *Ground-Fault Circuit-Interrupters*, 2016, revised 2018.

UL 1069, *Hospital Signaling and Nurse Call Equipment*, 2007, revised 2022.

UL 1363A, *Outline of Investigation for Special Purpose Relocatable Power Taps*, 2010.

D.1.2.20 US Government Publications. US Government Publishing Office, 732 North Capitol Street, NW, Washington, DC 20401-0001.

Crisis Standards of Care: A Systems Framework for Catastrophic Disaster Response, Institute of Medicine (IOM) Report, 2012.

Title 21, United States Code, Part 321(g)(1), "Federal Food, Drug, and Cosmetic Act."

Title 49, Code of Federal Regulations, Subchapter C, "Hazardous Materials Regulations," and Part 190, "Pipeline Safety Enforcement and Regulatory Procedures."

US Government Publication 3152, *Hospitals and Community Emergency Response — What You Need to Know*, 1997.

D.1.2.21 USP Publications. US Pharmacopeia, 12601 Twinbrook Parkway, Rockville, MD 20852-1790.

United States Pharmacopeia and National Formulary (USP-NF).

D.1.2.22 Other Publications.

2017-2022 Health Care Preparedness and Response Capabilities, Assistant Secretary for Preparedness and Response (ASPR), November 2016.

Hoeltge, G.A., A. Miller, B.R. Klein, W.B. Hamlin. "Accidental Fires in Clinical Laboratories." *Archives of Pathology & Laboratory Medicine* 117, no. 12 (1993): 1200-4.

Publication 1132, *Diesel Engines for Use with Generators to Supply Emergency and Short-Term Electric Power*, National Academy of Sciences — National Research Council, 1963.

SEMI S10-0307E, *Safety Guideline for Risk Assessment and Risk Evaluation Process*.

"Atmospheric Pressure," *Fire Journal* July/August 2002.

D.2 Informational References. The following documents or portions thereof are listed here as informational resources only. They are not a part of the requirements of this document.

D.2.1 Published Articles on Fire Involving Respiratory Therapy Equipment and Related Incidents.

Benson, D. M., and C. H. Wecht. "Conflagration in an ambulance oxygen system." *Journal of Trauma* 15, no. 6 (1975):536–649.

Dillon, J. J. "Cry fire!" *Respiratory Care* 21, no. 11 (1976):1139–1140.

Gjerde, G. E., and R. Kraemer. "An oxygen therapy fire." *Respiratory Care* 25, no. 3 (1980):362–363.

Walter, C. W. "Fire in an oxygen-powered respirator." *JAMA* 197 (1960):44–46.

Webre, D. E., R. Leon, and N. W. Larson. "Case History; Fire in a nebulizer." *Anesthesia and Analgesia* 52 (1973):843–848.

N **D.2.2 Reference for A.3.3.12.2.**

G. A. Cook, R. E. Meierer, and B. M. Shields, "Screening of Flame-Resistant Materials and Comparison of Helium with Nitrogen for Use in Dividing Atmospheres." First summary report under ONR Contract No. 0014-66-C-0149. Tonawanda, NY: Union Carbide, 31 March 1967. DDC No. Ad-651583.

D.2.3 References for A.14.3.1.6.4.3.

NASA BMS Document GRC-M8300.001. 2005. Chapter 5, Paragraph 5.6.3.

Raleigh, G., et al. "Air-Activated Chemical Warming Devices: Effects of Oxygen and Pressure." *Undersea & Hyperbaric Medicine* 32, no. 6 (2005): 445–449.

Workman, W. T. 1999. *Hyperbaric Facility Safety: A Practical Guide*, p. 531. Flagstaff, AZ: Best Publishing.

Kindwall, E. P., and H. T. Whelan. 2004. *Hyperbaric Medicine Practice*, p. 86. Flagstaff, AZ: Best Publishing.

Burman, F. 2015. *Risk Assessment Guide for the Installation and Operation of Clinical Hyperbaric Facilities*. San Antonio, TX: International ATMO.

D.2.4 Other Organizations that Publish Standards or Guidelines.

American Conference of Governmental Industrial Hygienists, 1330 Kemper Meadow Drive, Cincinnati, OH 45240-1634.

American Industrial Hygiene Association, 3141 Fairview Park Dr., Suite 777, Falls Church, VA 22042.

US Department of Health and Human Services, Office of the Assistant for Preparedness and Response (ASPR), National Disaster Medical System (NDMS).

National Emergency Management Association, Council of State Governments, Emergency Management Assistance Compact, 2760 Research Park Drive, Lexington, KY.

Laboratory Products Association, 1114 Fairfax Place, Box 12, White Post, VA 22663.

Natural Hazards Center (University of Colorado), 483 UCB, Boulder, CO 80309-0483.

Disaster Research Center (University of Delaware), 166 Graham Hall, 111 Academy Street, Newark, DE 19716.

American Society for Healthcare Engineering, 155 North Wacker Drive, Suite 400, Chicago, IL 60606.

△ **D.2.5 Addresses of Organizations and Agencies That Provide Health Care Emergency Preparedness Educational Materials.**

D.2.5.1 Publications.

National Fire Protection Association, 1 Batterymarch Park, Quincy, MA 02169-7471.

American Health Care Association, 1201 L Street, NW, Washington, DC 20005.

American Hospital Association, 155 North Wacker Drive, Chicago, IL 60606.

American Medical Association, AMA Plaza, 330 North Wabash Ave, Suite 39300, Chicago, IL 60611-5885.

American Nurses' Association, 8515 Georgia Avenue, Suite 400, Silver Spring, MD 20910-3492.

American Red Cross, National Headquarters, 431 18th Street, NW, Washington, DC 20006.

Association of American Railroads, 425 3rd Street, SW, Washington, DC 20024.

Charles C. Thomas Publisher, 2600 South First Street, Springfield, IL 62704-4730.

Federal Emergency Management Agency, 500 C Street, SW, Washington, DC 20472.

Florida Health Care Association, 307 W. Park Avenue, P.O. Box 1459, Tallahassee, FL 32301.

Helicopter Association International, 1920 Ballenger Avenue, 4th floor, Alexandria, VA 22314-2898.

Hospital Emergency Incident Command System, State of California Emergency Medical Services Authority, 10901 Gold Center Drive, Suite 400, Rancho Cordova, CA 95670.

International Association of Fire Chiefs, 4025 Fair Ridge Drive, Suite 300, Fairfax, VA 22033-2868.

The Joint Commission (TJC), One Renaissance Blvd., Oakbrook Terrace, IL 60181.

National Interagency Fire Center, 3833 Development Avenue, Boise, ID 83705-5354.

Pan American Health Organization, 525 23rd Street, NW, Washington, DC 20037.

Standardized Emergency Management System, State of California Governor's Office of Emergency Services, 3650 Schriever Avenue, Mather, CA 95655-4203.

Disaster Research Center (University of Delaware), 166 Graham Hall, 111 Academy Street, Newark, DE 19716.

US Department of Transportation, available from the US Government Publishing Office, 732 North Capitol Street, NW, Washington, DC 20401-0001.

D.2.5.2 Audiovisual Materials.

National Fire Protection Association, 1 Batterymarch Park, Quincy, MA 02169-7471.

Abbott Laboratories (Corporate Headquarters), 100 Abbott Park Road, Abbott Park, IL 60064-6500.

Federal Emergency Management Agency, 500 C Street, SW, Washington, DC 20472.

National Audiovisual Center, General Services Administration, 1800 F Street, NW, Washington, DC 20405.

Helicopter Association International, 1920 Ballenger Avenue, 4th floor, Alexandria, VA 22314-2898.

Pyramid Media, 3200 Airport Ave, Ste 19, Santa Monica, CA 90405.

University of Illinois Hospital and Health Sciences System, 1740 West Taylor Street, Chicago, IL 60612.

D.2.6 Additional US Government Informational Sources.

Kidney Community Emergency Response Coalition, 3000 Bayport Dr., Suite 300, Tampa, FL 33607.

"National Response Framework," June 2016, Federal Emergency Management Agency, 500 C Street, SW, Washington, DC 20472.

"National Disaster Recovery Framework" January 2017, Federal Emergency Management Agency, 500 C Street, SW, Washington, DC 20472.

(The following is available from the US Government Publishing Office, 725 North Capitol Street, NW, Washington, DC 20401-0001.)

Title 29, Code of Federal Regulations, Part 1910.1030, "Bloodborne Pathogens."

Title 29, Code of Federal Regulations, Part 1910.1450, "Occupational Exposure to Hazardous Chemicals in Laboratories."

Title 49, Code of Federal Regulations, Subchapter C and Part 190 (US Dept. of Transportation, Specifications for Transportation of Explosives and Dangerous Articles). (In Canada, the regulations of the Board of Transport Commissioners, Union Station, Ottawa, Canada, apply.)

Title 49, Code of Federal Regulations, Part 173, "Shippers — General Requirements for Shipments and Packagings."

Commercial Standard 223-59, *Casters, Wheels, and Glides for Hospital Equipment.*

Environmental Protection Agency, Chemical Emergency Preparedness and Prevention.

National Research Council Publication 1132, *Diesel Engines for Use with Generators to Supply Emergency and Short Term Electric Power.* (Also available as Order No. O.P.52870 from University Microfilms, P.O. Box 1366, Ann Arbor, MI 48106.)

(The following is available from the US Department of Health and Human Services, 200 Independence Avenue, SW, Washington, DC 20201.)

HHS Publication No. 93–8395, *Biosafety in Microbiological and Biomedical Laboratories,* Centers for Disease Control and Prevention.

"Public Health Preparedness and Response for Bioterrorism Program," Centers for Disease Control and Prevention.

"Emergency Response Resources: Personal Protection Equipment," National Institute for Occupational Safety and Health (NIOSH).

"Protecting Building Environments from Airborne Chemical, Biologic, or Radiologic Attacks," CDC's *Morbidity and Mortality Weekly Report* 51, no. 3 (6 September 2002): 9.

(The following is available from the US Department of Homeland Security, 3801 Nebraska Ave NW, Washington, DC 20016.)

IS-120.C: An Introduction to Exercises" (interactive web-based course).

Guide for All-Hazard Emergency Operations Planning, September 1996.

"National Health Security Strategy," Office of the Assistant Secretary for Preparedness and Response (ASPR).

Health Professional Pre-Disaster Identification (ESAR-VHP), Office of the Assistant Secretary for Preparedness and Response (ASPR).

"Hospital Preparedness Program," Office of the Assistant Secretary for Preparedness and Response (ASPR).

"National Disaster Medical System," Office of the Assistant Secretary for Preparedness and Response (ASPR).

"Strategic National Stockpile," Office of the Assistant Secretary for Preparedness and Response (ASPR).

Publications Library, Office of Domestic Preparedness, US Department of Justice.

(The following is available from the US Department of Labor, 200 Constitution Ave, NW, Washington, DC 20210.)

Title 29, Code of Federal Regulations, Part 1910.38, "Emergency Action Plans."

Title 29, Code of Federal Regulations, Subpart H, "Hazardous Materials," specifically Part 1910.120, "Hazardous Waste Operations and Emergency Response" (HAZWOPER).

Title 29, Code of Federal Regulations, Subpart I, "Personal Protective Equipment," specifically Part 1910.132, "General Requirements," Part 1910.133, "Eye and Face Protection," Part 1910.134, "Respiratory Protection," Part 1910.136, "Foot Protection," Part 1910.138, "Hand Protection," and Appendices A–D.

Title 29, Code of Federal Regulations, Subpart Z, "Toxic and Hazardous Substances," specifically Part 1910.1200, "Hazard Communication" (including Appendices A–E).

Publication 3114, *Hazardous Waste Operations and Emergency Response*.

Publication 3152, *Hospitals and Community Emergency Response – What You Need to Know*.

D.2.7 Additional Resources for Emergency Management.

Barbera, J. *Emergency Management Principles and Practices for Healthcare Systems*, Institute of Crisis, Disaster and Risk Management, 2010, George Washington University, for the Veterans Health Administration, Washington, DC.

Barbera, J. A., and A. G. Macintyre. 2007. *Medical Surge Capacity and Capability Handbook: A Management System for Integrating Medical and Health Resources During Large-Scale Emergencies*, Contract No. 233-03-0028, Department of Health and Human Services, Washington, DC.

NFPA 3000™ (PS), *Standard for an Active Shooter/Hostile Event Response (ASHER) Program*, 2018 edition.

D.2.8 Other Publications.

Barbera, J. and A. G. Macintyre. 2002. *Medical and Health Incident Management (MaHIM) System: A Comprehensive Functional System Descriptions for Mass Casualty Medical and Health Incident Management*, George Washington University, School of Engineering and Applied Sciences, Institute for Crisis, Disaster and Risk Management.

DuPont Safety News, June 14, 1965.

Dasler and Bauer, *Ind. Eng. Chem. Anal*, Ed. 18, 52 (1964).

IEEE 3001.2, *Recommended Practice for Evaluating the Electrical Service Requirements of Industrial and Commercial Power Systems*, 2017.

IEEE 3001.5, *Recommended Practice for the Application of Power Distribution Apparatus in Industrial and Commercial Power Systems*, 2013.

IEEE 3003.2, *Recommended Practice for Equipment Grounding and Bonding in Industrial and Commercial Power Systems*, 2014.

IEEE 3006.2, *Recommended Practice for Evaluating the Reliability of Existing Industrial and Commercial Power Systems*, 2016.

IEEE 3006.3, *Recommended Practice for Determining the Impact of Preventative Maintenance on the Reliability of Industrial and Commercial Power Systems*, 2017.

IEEE 3006.5, *Recommended Practice for the Use of Probability Methods for Conducting a Reliability Analysis of Industrial and Commercial Power Systems*, 2014.

IEEE 3006.7, *Recommended Practice for Determining the Reliability of 7x24 Continuous Power Systems in Industrial and Commercial Facilities*, 2013.

IEEE 3006.9, *Recommended Practice for Collecting Data for Use in Reliability, Availability, and Maintainability Assessments of Industrial and Commercial Power Systems*, 2013.

IEEE 3007.1, *Recommended Practice for the Operation and Management of Industrial and Commercial Power Systems*, 2010.

IEEE 3007.2, *Recommended Practice for the Maintenance of Industrial and Commercial Power Systems*, 2010.

IEEE P3007.3, *Recommended Practice for Electrical Safety in Industrial and Commercial Power Systems*, 2017.

D.3 References for Extracts in Informational Sections.

NFPA 55, *Compressed Gases and Cryogenic Fluids Code*, 2023 edition.

NFPA 70®, National Electrical Code®, 2023 edition.

NFPA 70B, *Standard for Electrical Equipment Maintenance*, 2023 edition.

NFPA *101®, Life Safety Code®*, 2024 edition.

NFPA 110, *Standard for Emergency and Standby Power Systems*, 2022 edition.

NFPA 5000®, Building Construction and Safety Code®, 2024 edition.

Index

-A-

Absolute atmosphere (ATA), B.14.1.3.4.3, Table B.14.4
  Definition, 3.3.12.1
Absolute pressure, A.5.1.12.2.6.5
  Definition, 3.3.156.1
Access, 13.6, A.13.6.3.1
Adapters, 10.2.4, 10.5.2.3
Adiabatic heating, B.14.1.2.4.1, B.14.1.3.4.4
  Definition, 3.3.1
Aerosols, 11.5.1.2.1, 16.14.3.1
  Definition, 3.3.2
Aftercoolers, 5.1.3.6.3.5, 5.1.3.6.3.9(C), 5.1.3.6.3.9(H), 5.1.13.3.7.9(1), 5.2.3.5(1), 15.3.2.1.5(1)
Air
  Compressors, *see also* Dental air compressors; Medical air compressors
    Hyperbaric chambers, 14.2.4.2
    Instrument air, 5.1.13.3.7.12
    Starting devices, 6.7.1.3.6
  Dental, *see* Dental air
  Medical, *see* Medical air
  Monitoring, hyperbaric chamber, 14.2.10.6, A.14.2.10.6, A.14.2.10.6.1
  Nonmedical compressed air, 8.3.5
Air conditioning, *see* Heating, ventilating, and air conditioning (HVAC) systems
Air dryers, 5.1.3.6.3.3, 5.1.3.6.3.7, 5.1.3.6.3.9(E), 5.1.3.6.3.9(F), 5.1.3.6.3.9(I), 5.1.13.3.7.9(3), 5.2.3.5(1), A.5.1.3.6.3.9(F)
Alarm systems, 16.7, A.16.7.1 to A.16.7.4.3.5; *see also* Nurse call systems
  Annunciator, remote, 6.7.1.2.7, A.6.7.1.2.7.2(B), A.6.7.1.2.7.2(H)
  Area, 5.1.8.1.6, 5.1.9.1, 5.1.9.4, 5.1.12.4.5.3, 5.1.13.9.3, 15.3.2.7, 15.4.3.4.3, A.5.1.9.4
    Definition, 3.3.3.1
  Category 1, 5.1.3.10.12, 5.1.8.1.6, 5.1.9, 5.1.14.7.11, 15.3.2.7, A.5.1.3.10.12, A.5.1.14.7.11, B.5.2.9 to B.5.2.13, B.5.2.15, B.5.2.16; *see also subheads:* Area, Local, Master
    Instrument air, 5.1.13.3.7.11
    Medical air compressors, *see* Medical air compressors
    Support gases, 5.1.13.9
    Tests, 5.1.12.4.5, 5.1.14.7.8
    Waste anesthetic gas disposal (WAGD), *see* Waste anesthetic gas disposal (WAGD) systems
  Category 2, 5.2.9, 15.4.2.10, 15.4.3.4
  Category 3, 5.3.9
    Definition, 3.3.3.2
  Changeover signals, 5.1.9.2.4(1), B.5.2.10
  Cryogenic liquid withdrawal systems, 5.4.6.8
  Essential electrical systems, 6.7.5.1.2.2(7), 6.7.6.2.1.5(A)(3)

  Generator sets, 6.7.1.3.8.1, 6.7.1.3.8.3
  Hyperbaric chambers, 14.2.1.4.6, 14.2.6.1.4, 14.2.6.3.8, 14.2.8.2, 14.2.9.3.15, A.14.2.9.3.15.1
  Labeling, 5.1.11.4, A.5.1.11.4.2
  Local, 5.1.3.5.8, 5.1.3.6.3.12, 5.1.3.7.8, 5.1.3.9.5, 5.1.9.1, 5.1.9.5, 5.1.13.3.6.7, 5.1.13.9.4, 15.3.2.7, 15.4.3.4.4, A.5.1.9.5; *see also* Local signal
    Definition, 3.3.3.3
  Master, 5.1.3.6.3.14(C)(9), 5.1.3.9.5.1(3), 5.1.3.9.5.3, 5.1.8.1.6, 5.1.9.1, 5.1.9.2, 5.1.12.4.5.2, 5.1.13.9.2, 15.3.2.7, 15.4.3.4.2, A.5.1.3.6.3.14(C)(9)
    Computer systems as substitutes for, 5.1.9.3
    Definition, 3.3.3.4
  Occupant notification, 16.7.4
  Remote control, 6.7.1.2.7, A.6.7.1.2.7.2(B), A.6.7.1.2.7.2(H)
  Signal initiation, 16.7.2, A.16.7.2.4
  Silencing means, 6.7.1.2.7.2(E), 6.7.1.2.7.2(F)
Alternate power sources, 6.7.1.2, A.6.7.1.2.2.2 to A.6.7.1.2.4; *see also* Generator sets
  Connection to, 6.7.5.1.4.2
  Failure of, 6.7.3.6
  Maintenance and testing of, 6.7.4.1.1, 6.9.4.2, A.6.7.4.1.1.5(A), A.6.9.4.2
  Transfer to, *see* Transfer switches
Alternative equipment maintenance (AEM) program, 6.9.4.2, A.6.9.4.2
Ambient atmosphere, *see* Atmosphere
Ambient pressure, *see* Pressure
Ambient temperature, *see* Temperature
Ambulatory health care occupancies, 16.7.4.3.2
  Definition, 3.3.4
Ampacity, 10.2.3.1.1, 10.2.3.6
  Definition, 3.3.5
Anesthetic apparatus, 11.4.1.1, A.11.4.1.1
Anesthetics, *see also specific gases*
  Definition, 3.3.6
  Flammable, 5.1.14.3.1, A.5.1.14.3.1
  Nonflammable anesthetic agent (definition), 3.3.129
  Waste, *see* Waste anesthetic gas disposal (WAGD) systems
Anesthetizing locations, 1.3.4.2, 16.14.3, A.16.14.3.2; *see also* Waste anesthetic gas disposal (WAGD) systems
  Definition, 3.3.7
Animal chambers, 14.1.2.2(3), 14.2.2.3, 14.2.2.4
Antiseptics, 16.14.3, A.16.14.3.2
Apparatus, *see* Anesthetic apparatus; Equipment
Appliances, *see also* Electrical equipment; Equipment
  Battery-powered, 14.2.9.3.16.4
  Definition, 3.3.8
  Double-insulated, 10.2.2.1.2, 10.4.2.3
    Definition, 3.3.46, A.3.3.46
Applicable code (definition), 3.3.9

Application of standard, 1.3, A.1.3.1.3

Applicator, 16.14.3.2, A.16.14.3.2
Definition, 3.3.10, A.3.3.10

Approved (definition), 3.2.1, A.3.2.1

Area of administration, 11.5.1.1.3, 11.5.1.1.4, A.11.5.1.1.2
Definition, 3.3.11

Atmosphere
Absolute (ATA), B.14.1.3.4.3, Table B.14.4
Definition, 3.3.12.1
Ambient, 5.1.10.4.5.5, 14.2.4.3.1, B.14.1.1.4.3; *see also* Temperature, Ambient
Chamber, 14.2.4.1.3, 14.2.4.2, 14.2.9.2.4, 14.2.10.3.1, 14.2.10.4.3, 14.3.1.6.2.2, 14.3.2.6.1, A.14.2.9.3, A.14.3.1.6.2.2(2), B.14.1.3.2.2
Definition, 3.3.12.3
Definition, 3.3.12, A.3.3.12
Of increased burning rate (definition), 3.3.12.2, A.3.3.12.2
Oxygen-enriched, *see* Oxygen-enriched atmosphere (OEA)

Attachment plugs, *see* Plugs (attachment plugs, caps)

Authority having jurisdiction
Definition, 3.2.2, A.3.2.2
Emergency planning responsibilities, 12.2.1, A.12.2.1

Automatic (definition), 3.3.13

Automatic sprinklers, *see* Sprinklers, automatic

Auxiliary source connections, 5.1.3.5.12, 5.1.3.9.3(12), 5.1.4.10, 5.3.3.5.7
Definition, 3.3.14

-B-

Basic care rooms, *see* Patient care spaces

Bathrooms
Definition, 3.3.15
Electrical receptacles, 6.3.2.2.1(D), 6.3.2.2.2(D)
Nurse and staff emergency assistance calls, 7.3.3.1.2.5, 7.3.3.1.8.2
Wet procedure locations, 6.3.2.3.3

Batteries
Appliances, battery-powered, 14.2.9.3.16.4
Automatic detection system, for, 14.2.6.6.3
Cranking, 6.7.1.3.5
Maintenance, 6.7.4.1.2.2

Battery-powered lighting units, 6.3.2.6
Definition, 3.3.16

Bends, B.14.1.3.4.2
Definition, 3.3.17

Bilge, hyperbaric facilities, 14.2.2.5.2

Branch circuits
Definition, 3.3.18
Patient bed locations, 6.3.2.4.1, 6.3.2.4.2, A.6.3.2.4

Branch (lateral) lines, piping, *see* Pipe and piping, gas

Brazing, 5.1.6.11, 5.1.7.8, 5.1.10.3.1(1), 5.1.10.3.3, 5.1.10.4, 5.1.10.11.11, 15.3.3.7.2.4, 15.4.2.1.3, 15.4.4.2.3.2, 15.4.4.2.4.1, 15.4.6, 15.5.5.2.3, 15.5.5.2.4, 15.5.5.3.2.2, 15.5.5.3.2.3

Breathing apparatus, hyperbaric chambers, 14.2.4.1.3, 14.2.4.4.3

Building system categories
Application, 4.3
Plumbing system, 8.2, A.8.2.1

Bulk systems, 5.1.3.6.1(1)

Cryogenic liquids, *see* Cryogenic liquids, Bulk systems
Definition, 3.3.20, A.3.3.20.3
Inert gas, 5.1.3.3.1.10, A.5.1.3.3.1.10
Definition, 3.3.20.1
Nitrous oxide (definition), 3.3.20.2
Oxygen (definition), 3.3.20.3, A.3.3.20.3; *see also* Cryogenic liquids, Bulk systems

Bypass-isolation switch, 6.7.2.1.6, A.6.7.2.1.6.3

-C-

Cannula, nasal, *see* Nasal cannula

Carbon dioxide
Designation colors/operating pressures, Table 5.1.11
Monitoring, 14.2.10.5
Supply systems, 5.1.1.2, 5.1.3.3.1.8, 5.1.3.3.1.9, 5.1.3.5.2, 5.1.3.10.2.8, A.5.1.1.3; *see also* Medical gas systems

Carbon monoxide monitors, 5.1.14.7.7(2)

Cardiac defibrillators, *see* Defibrillators

Carts, for cylinders, 11.4.3.1

Casters, 14.3.4.5.2, 14.3.4.5.3

Category 1 emergency management requirements, 12.3, 12.5, A.12.5.3.1.2 to A.12.5.3.5

Category 2 emergency management requirements, 12.3, 12.5, A.12.5.3.1.2 to A.12.5.3.5

Category 1 information technology and communications systems, 7.3
Infrastructure, 7.3.1
Cabling pathways and raceway requirements, 7.3.1.2.4
Entrance facility (EF), 7.3.1.2.1, A.7.3.1.2.1.4(C) to A.7.3.1.2.1.8(C)
Premises distribution system (fiber and copper), 7.3.1.1
Remote primary data center, 7.3.1.2.1.3
Telecommunications equipment room (TER), 7.3.1.2.1.1, 7.3.1.2.2, A.7.3.1.2.2.2
Telecommunications room (TR), 7.3.1.2.3
Telecommunications systems spaces and pathways, 7.3.1.2, A.7.3.1.2 to A.7.3.1.2.2.2
Nurse call systems, 7.3.3.1, A.7.3.3.1.1.1 to A.7.3.3.1.4.1

Category 2 information technology and communications systems, 7.4
Infrastructure, 7.4.1
Nurse call systems, 7.4.3.1

Category 3 information technology and communications systems, 7.5

Category 1 patient care spaces, *see* Patient care spaces, Category 1

Category 2 patient care spaces, *see* Patient care spaces, Category 2

Category 3 patient care spaces, 1.3.4.1, 6.6
Definition, 3.3.145.3, A.3.3.145.3

Category 4 patient care spaces, 1.3.4.1, 6.6
Definition, 3.3.145.4, A.3.3.145.4

Category 1 piped gas and vacuum systems, 5.1, A.5.1.1 to A.5.1.14.7.11(2)(a), B.5.1, B.5.2; *see also* Central supply systems; Medical-surgical vacuum systems; Waste anesthetic gas disposal (WAGD) systems
Alarms, *see* Alarm systems
Applicability of requirements, 5.1.1, A.5.1.1
Cross-connections, 5.1.12.2.4, 5.1.12.4.3, B.5.1
Dental air, 15.3.3, A.15.3.3.4, A.15.3.3.5
Dental gas and vacuum systems, 15.3, A.15.3.3.3.4, A.15.3.3.5

Designation colors/operating pressures, Table 5.1.11

Distribution, 5.1.10, 5.1.13.10, 15.3.2.8

Filtration, 5.1.3.7.4

Hazards, nature of, 5.1.2, 5.1.13.2

Labeling and identification, 5.1.11, 5.1.12.4.13, 5.1.13.11, 5.1.14.5, 15.3.2.9, A.5.1.11

Maintenance, 5.1.14.4, 5.1.14.7, 15.3.2.12, B.5.2

Manufactured assemblies, *see* Manufactured assemblies

Operation and management, 5.1.14, 15.3.2.12, 15.3.3.8.4, A.5.1.14

Performance criteria and tests, 5.1.6.1, 5.1.6.2, 5.1.12, 5.1.13.12, 15.3.2.10, A.5.1.12, B.5.1

Pressure and vacuum indicators, 5.1.8, 5.1.13.7, 15.3.2.6, B.5.2.5, B.5.2.14

Reserve supply, 5.1.9.2.4, B.5.2.10 to B.5.2.12

Sources, 5.1.3, A.5.1.3, B.5.2.6; *see also* Central supply systems

Dental air systems, 15.3.3.3

Dental-surgical vacuum supply systems, 15.3.2.1.7

Instrument air supply systems, *see* Instrument air, Supply systems

Medical air supply systems, 5.1.3.6, 15.3.2.1.5, A.5.1.3.6, B.5.2.6

Medical-surgical vacuum supply systems, 5.1.3.5(5), 5.1.3.7, 5.1.12.4.14.6, A.5.1.3.7

Reserve supply, *see* Reserve supply

Support gases, 5.1.13.3, A.5.1.13.3.7

Verification of equipment, 5.1.12.4.14, 5.1.14.7.6

Waste anesthetic gas disposal (WAGD), 5.1.3.8, A.5.1.3.8

Station inlets, *see* Station inlets

Station outlets, *see* Station outlets

Support gases, 5.1.13, 5.1.14.4, 15.3.2.11, A.5.1.13.1, A.5.1.13.1.2

Breaching or penetrating of medical gas piping, 5.1.10.11.12.1

Central supply system for, 5.1.3.5.3

Joints, 5.1.10.3.1

Surface-mounted medical gas rails, 5.1.7, 15.3.2.5, A.5.1.7

Tests

Maintenance program, 5.1.14.4.3, 5.1.14.7.1, 5.1.14.7.5 to 5.1.14.7.7, 15.3.3.8.5, A.5.1.14.4.3, B.5.2

Performance, *see subhead:* Performance criteria and tests

Retests, B.5.2

Valves, *see* Valves

Category 2 piped gas and vacuum systems, 5.2; *see also* Central supply systems

Alarms, 5.2.9, 15.4.2.10, 15.4.3.4

Applicability of requirements, 5.2.1, A.5.2.1

Dental air and piping systems, 15.4.3

Dental gas and vacuum systems, 15.4, 15.4.2, A.15.4.2.6.1

Distribution, 5.2.10

Hazards, nature of, 5.2.2

Installers, qualification of, 15.4.2.1, 15.4.7.3

Labeling and identification, 5.2.3.1, 5.2.11, 15.4.2.11

Manufactured assemblies, 5.2.6, 15.4.2.8

Operation and management, 5.2.3.2, 5.2.14, 15.4.9, A.5.2.14

Performance criteria and tests, 5.2.12, 15.4.7, 15.4.8

Piping, 15.4.4 to 15.4.9

Pressure and vacuum indicators, 5.2.8, 15.4.2.9

Source equipment, 15.4.2.5, 15.4.3.3

Sources, 5.2.3

Station outlets/inlets, 5.2.5, 15.4.2.7

Support gases, 5.2.13

Surface-mounted medical gas rails, 5.2.7

Valves, 5.2.4, 15.4.2.6, A.14.2.6.1.5

Category 3 piped gas and vacuum systems, 5.3; *see also* Category 3 vacuum systems; Central supply systems; Scavenging

Alarms, 5.3.9

Definition, 3.3.3.2

Applicability of requirements, 5.3.1, A.5.3.1

Dental gas and vacuum systems, 15.5

Distribution, 5.3.10

Hazards, nature of, 5.3.2

Labeling and identification, 5.3.3.1, 5.3.11

Manufactured assemblies, 5.3.6

Medical-surgical vacuum systems, 5.3.3.7

Operations and management, 5.3.3.2

Oxygen central supply systems using concentrators, 5.3.3.5.11

Performance criteria and tests, 5.3.12

Pressure and vacuum indicators, 5.3.8

Scavenging systems, *see* Scavenging

Sources, 5.3.3

Medical air supply systems, 5.3.3.6

Station inlets, 5.3.5

Station outlets, 5.3.5

Surface-mounted medical gas rail systems, 5.3.7

Tests, performance, 5.3.12

Valves, *see* Valves

Waste anesthetic gas disposal (WAGD) systems, 5.3.3.8, 5.3.12

Category 3 vacuum systems, *see also* Category 3 piped gas and vacuum systems

Management, 5.3.14

Operation, 5.3.14

Performance criteria and tests, 5.3.12

Source equipment, 5.3.3.7, 15.5.4

Support gases, 5.3.13

Central supply systems

Category 1

Components, 5.1.3.5, A.5.1.3.5

Control equipment, 5.1.3.4, 5.1.13.3.5, 5.1.13.3.6.4

Headers, *see* Headers

Labeling and identification, 5.1.3.1, 15.3.2.1.1, A.5.1.3.1.1, A.5.1.3.1.2

Locations, 5.1.3.3, 15.3.3.2, A.5.1.3.3

Operations, 5.1.3.2, 15.3.2.1.2

Reserve supply, *see* Reserve supply

Category 2, 5.2.3.1 to 5.2.3.4

Labeling and identification, 5.2.3.1, 15.4.2.2

Locations, 5.2.3.3, 15.4.2.4

Operations, 5.2.3.2, 15.4.2.3

Category 3, 5.3.3.5

Labeling and identification, 5.3.3.1

Locations, 5.3.3.3

Operations, 5.3.3.2

Definition, 3.3.21, A.3.3.21

Hyperbaric oxygen systems, 14.2.1.4.4.1, 14.2.1.4.5.1, 14.2.1.4.7.1

Chamber atmosphere, *see* Atmosphere

Check valves, 5.1.3.5.12.2(4), 5.1.4.9, 15.3.2.11(2)

Chutes, waste/linen, 16.6

Circuits
  Branch, *see* Branch circuits
  Maintenance and testing of, 6.7.4.1.2, 14.3.4.3.2.1
  Patient bed locations, 6.3.2.4.1
  Telecommunications facility, 7.3.1.2.1.7, 7.3.1.2.2.7, 7.3.1.2.3.7

Clean agent
  Definition, 3.3.22
  Extinguishers, A.14.2.1.2(3)

Cleaning, hyperbaric facilities, 14.3.4.7, A.14.3.4.7

Clinical IT network, 6.7.5.1.3.2(8), 7.3.3.5.1, 7.3.3.7, A.7.3.3.7.1 to A.7.3.3.7.5
  Definition, 3.3.23, A.3.3.23

Clinical support activities, emergency plan for, 12.5.3.3.6.4

Closets, sprinklers in, 16.9.1.4, A.16.9.1.4

Clothing in hyperbaric chambers, 14.3.1.6.5.1, 14.3.1.6.8, B.14.1.1.3.4

Code
  Adoption
    Requirements, 1.6
    Sample ordinance, Annex C
  Definition, 3.2.3, A.3.2.3
  Enforcement, 1.6.2

Code calls, 7.3.3.1.4, A.7.3.3.1.4, A.7.3.3.1.4.1

Combustible (definition), 3.3.24

Combustible liquids
  Definition, 3.3.25, A.3.3.25
  Use of, 11.5.1.2.3

Combustion (definition), 3.3.26, A.3.3.26

Communications, *see* Information technology and communications systems

Compact storage
  Definition, 3.3.27
  Fire protection, 16.11, 16.12, A.16.11, A.16.12.3
  Mobile, 16.12, A.16.12.3

Compartmentation of facility, 16.2

Compressed air starting devices, 6.7.1.3.6

Compressed medical gases (CMG), 5.1.3.10.1.1, 5.1.3.10.3.3, 5.1.3.10.5.1, 5.1.3.10.7.1, 5.1.3.10.7.3 to 5.1.3.10.7.5, A.5.1.3.10.1.1
  Definition, 3.3.28, A.3.3.28

Conductive accessories, 14.3.4.6.1

Conductive surfaces, exposed
  Definition, 3.3.57
  Tests, 6.3.3.1.1.2, 6.3.3.1.1.3

Conductors
  Isolated ungrounded systems, 6.3.2.9.4
  Isolation of neutral, 6.7.2.1.3.13, A.6.7.2.1.3.13

Connections, 15.4.1.5
  Exterior, 12.5.3.3.6.6
  Future, valves for, 5.1.4.8

Connectors, flexible, *see* Flexible connectors

Construction
  Central supply systems and storage, 5.1.3.3.2, A.5.1.3.3.2
  Health care facility, 16.2
  Hyperbaric facilities, 14.2, A.14.2.1.1.1 to A.14.2.1.3.3

Containers, *see also* Cylinders
  Connections, 11.6.3
  Definition, 3.3.29
  Filling, 11.7.3.5.3, 11.7.3.6.1, A.11.7.3.6.1.1
  Handling, 5.1.3.2.2, 5.1.3.2.12, 5.1.3.3.1.8, 5.1.3.3.1.9, 11.4.2.3, 11.5.2
  Labeling, 5.1.3.1, A.5.1.3.1.1, A.5.1.3.1.2
  Liquid oxygen base reservoir containers, 11.7, A.11.7.3.1 to A.11.7.3.6.1.1
    Definition, 3.3.29.1
  Liquid oxygen portable containers, 11.7, A.11.7.3.1 to A.11.7.3.6.1.1
    Definition, 3.3.29.2
  Safety mechanisms, 11.6.4
  Source, 11.2
  Storage, 5.1.3.2.3, 5.1.3.2.7, 5.1.3.2.11, 5.4.2.2, 11.3, 11.6.5

Controls
  Central supply system, 5.1.3.4, 5.1.13.3.5, 5.1.13.3.6.4
  Electrical equipment, 14.2.10.1.4(1)

Conveyors, 16.5.3

Cooking operations, 16.5.2.3

Cooling, essential electrical system generator sets, 6.7.1.2.6

Cords, *see* Power cords

Cover plates, 6.7.6.3.2

Cranking batteries, 6.7.1.3.5

Critical branch, 6.7.5.1.1(2), 6.7.5.1.3, 6.7.5.1.4.3(B), 7.3.1.2.3.7(B), 14.2.6.6.3, 14.2.9.2.3.2, A.6.7.5.1.3, A.6.7.5.1.3.2(6)
  Definition, 3.3.30

Critical care area (definition), *see* Patient care spaces, Category 1

Critical equipment
  Definition, 3.3.31

Cross-connections, tests, 5.1.12.2.4, 5.1.12.4.3, 15.4.7.4.3, 15.4.7.5.3, 15.4.8.1.4, B.5.1

Crowd control, 13.8, A.13.8

Cryogenic fluid central supply system
  Bulk, 5.1.3.3.2.4, 5.1.3.5.5.2, 5.1.3.5.8.1(4), 5.1.3.5.12, 5.1.3.10, A.5.1.3.10
  Bulk nitrous, 5.1.3.3.1.7
    Definition, 3.3.32.1
  Definition, 3.3.32

Cryogenic liquids, 5.1.3.1.4 to 5.1.3.1.6, 5.1.3.2.7, 5.1.3.2.8, 5.1.3.3.1.1, 5.1.3.3.1.2(2), 5.1.3.5(2), 5.1.3.5(3), 15.4.2.2.4 to 15.4.2.2.6, 15.4.2.3.7, 15.4.2.3.8
  Bulk systems, 5.1.3.3.3.1.10, 5.1.9.2.4, 5.1.14.7.2, 5.1.14.7.3, A.5.1.3.3.3.1.10, B.5.2.4
  Containers, 5.4.2
  Manifolds, cylinder, 5.1.3.5.8.1, 5.1.3.5.11, 5.4.6, A.5.1.3.5.11, A.5.4.6.2 to A.5.4.6.10(4)
  Storage or transfilling, ventilation for, 5.4.3, 9.3.6, A.5.4.5.2, A.5.4.6.2, A.9.3.6.3, A.9.3.6.5.1, A.9.3.6.5.2.1
  Withdrawal of, 5.4, A.5.4.1 to A.5.4.6.10(4)

Cylinders
  Connections, 11.2.1 to 11.2.3, 11.2.8, 11.2.9, 11.6.3
  Definition, 3.3.33
  Handling, 5.1.3.2.2, 5.1.3.2.8 to 5.1.3.2.10, 5.1.3.2.12, 11.4.2.3, 11.5.2, 11.6, 11.6.5.5
  Headers, *see* Headers
  Labeling, 5.1.3.1, A.5.1.3.1.1, A.5.1.3.1.2
  Management, 11.6, 11.6.5.5
  Manifolds for, *see* Manifolds
  Regulators, 11.2.4 to 11.2.6

Reserves, 5.1.9.2.4

Safety mechanisms, 11.6.4

Source, 11.2

Storage, 5.1.3.2.3 to 5.1.3.2.7, 5.1.3.2.9, 5.1.3.2.11, 5.1.3.2.12, 5.1.3.3.4, 11.3, 11.6.5, B.11.4

Supply systems, 5.1.3.6.1(1), 14.2.1.5.4.7(2)

Transfilling, 11.5.2.2, 11.5.2.3, 11.7.3.6, A.11.7.3.6.1.1

-D-

Debrief, 12.5.3.3.9.3, 12.5.3.3.9.4, A.12.5.3.3.9.4

Definition, 3.3.34

Decompression sickness, B.14.1.3.4.2

Definition, 3.3.35

Defend in place, 16.7.4.3, 16.9.1.3, A.16.9.1.3

Definition, 3.3.36, A.3.3.36

Defibrillators, 10.5.2.4, 10.5.4.6, A.10.5.4.6

Definitions, Chap. 3

Delayed-automatic connection, equipment for, 6.7.5.1.4.3, 6.7.5.1.4.4, 6.7.6.2.1.6(D), 6.7.6.2.1.6(E), A.6.7.5.1.4.3, A.6.7.5.1.4.4 to A.6.7.5.1.4.4(9), A.6.7.6.2.1.6(E)

Deluge systems, 14.2.6.2, A.14.2.6.2.3 to A.14.6.2.10

Demand check, 5.1.8.2.3, 5.1.8.2.4

Definition, 3.3.37

Dental air, 15.3.3.4, 15.5.4.2, A.15.3.3.4

Definition, 3.3.38

Piping systems, 15.3.3, 14.4.3, A.15.3.3.4, A.15.3.3.5

Source equipment, 15.4.3.3.2

Dental air compressors, 15.3.3.4.2, 15.4.3.3.2.2, 15.5.4.2.2

Dental gas and vacuum piping systems, Chap. 15

Applicability, 15.1

Category 1, 15.3, A.15.3.3.4, A.15.3.3.5

Dental air and vacuum piping systems, 15.3.3, A.15.3.3.4, A.15.3.3.5

Medical gas systems, 15.3.2

Category 2, 15.4

Category 3, 15.5

Hazards, 15.2

Operation and management, 15.5.8

Performance criteria and testing, 15.4.7, 15.5.7

Dental office (definition), 3.3.39

Dental-surgical vacuum, 15.3.3.5, 15.5.4.3, A.15.3.3.5; *see also* Dental gas and vacuum piping systems

Category 1, 15.3.2.1.7

Definition, 3.3.41

Tests, 15.4.8.1.8, 15.5.7.1.3.5

Dental vacuum/scavenging, 15.4.3.3.3, 15.4.3.3.4

Definition, 3.3.40

Dental vacuum systems, 15.5.2

Dental vacuum units, 15.5.4.3.2

Detonation (definition), 3.3.42

Direct electrical pathway to heart

Definition, 3.3.43, A.3.3.43

Protection of patients, 10.5.2.2, A.10.5.2.2

Disasters (definition), 3.3.44, A.3.3.44; *see also* Emergency management

D.I.S.S. connectors, 5.1.14.4.3.1(D)

Definition, 3.3.45

Distribution piping, 5.1.13.10

Documentation

Brazing procedure, 5.1.10.11.10.5, 5.1.10.11.11.4

Electrical equipment, records of, 10.2.3.6(5), 10.5.3.1, 10.5.3.2, 10.5.6, 14.2.9.3.2, 14.2.9.3.16.2, A.10.5.6.2

Electrical preventive maintenance program, 6.9.2, 6.9.3.1, A.6.9.3.1

Emergency management, 12.4.1, 12.5.3.3.2, 12.5.3.3.6.4(10), 14.3.1.5.4

Health care microgrid system commissioning report, 6.10.7.3

HVAC, 9.3.3.2, A.9.3.3.2

Installers, 5.1.10.1.8

Liquid oxygen, 11.7.2

Maintenance, 5.1.14.4.1, 5.1.14.7.2, 10.5.3.1, 10.5.3.2, 14.3.4.2, A.5.1.14.4.1

Manufacturers, 5.1.6.4, 10.5.3.1, 10.5.3.2

Test procedures, 5.1.12.1.1, 5.1.14.4.3.1(F), 6.3.4.1, A.6.3.4.1.1

Test records and reports, *see* Tests

Double-insulated appliances, 10.2.2.1.2, 10.4.2.3

Definition, 3.3.46, A.3.3.46

Drains, 8.3.12

Hyperbaric chamber wiring enclosures, 14.2.9.3.7

Drills

Emergency plans and operations, 12.5.3.3.8

Fire, 14.3.1.5.4, 16.14.3.10.3

Security management, 13.12.1, 13.12.2, A.13.12.1

-E-

Egress, 13.6, A.13.6.3.1

Electrical equipment, 5.1.3.3.2.2(11), 5.1.3.3.2.2(13), Chap. 10, A.5.1.3.3.2, A.5.1.3.3.2.2(7) to A.5.1.3.3.2.2(11); *see also* Patient-care-related electrical equipment

Administration, 10.5, A.10.5.2.2 to A.10.5.8.3

Cord- and plug-connected (portable), 10.2.2, 10.4.2, 14.2.9.3.16.5

Electrical preventive maintenance (EPM), 6.9, A.6.9.1.1 to A.6.9.4.2.2(4)

Emergency power supply systems (EPSSs), 6.11

Fire protection, 16.5.1.2

Hazards, 6.2, A.6.2.1

Health care microgrids, 6.10, A.6.10.1.2 to A.6.10.7.2(2)

Hyperbaric facilities, 14.2.10.1.1, 14.3.4.4

Instructions for, 10.5.3.1, 10.5.3.2, 10.5.6.1

Laboratory, 10.5.5, A.10.5.5.1

Life support

Definition, 3.3.47

Maintenance, 10.5.3

Nonpatient, 10.4

Not supplied by facility, 10.5.2.6

Performance criteria, 10.2, A.10.2.3.2.4 to A.10.2.3.6(2)

Permanently connected (fixed), 10.2.1

Portable, 10.2.2, 10.4.2, 14.2.9.3.16, A.10.3.1 to A.10.3.6, A.14.2.9.3.16

Protection, 6.3.2.8.1

Qualification and training of personnel, 10.5.8, A.10.5.8.1, A.10.5.8.3

Recordkeeping, 10.5.6, A.10.5.6.2

Respiratory therapy apparatus, B.11.3.4.1.1 to B.11.3.4.2

Site acceptance testing, 6.8, A.6.8.1, A.6.8.2

System demonstration, 10.5.2.5, A.10.5.2.5

Testing, 6.8, 10.3, 10.5.2.1, A.6.8.1, A.6.8.2, A.10.3.1 to A.10.3.6
Electrical equipment branch, 6.7.5.1.1(3), 6.7.5.1.4, A.6.7.5.1.4.3 to A.6.7.5.1.4.4(9)
Electrical hazards, 6.2, A.6.1 to A.6.10.7.2(2)
Electrical maintenance program (EMP)
  Definition, 3.3.48, A.3.3.48
Electrical preventive maintenance (EPM), 6.9, A.6.9.1.1 to A.6.9.4.2.2(4)
Electrical receptacles, *see* Receptacles
Electrical systems, 1.1.4, Chap. 6, A.6.1 to A.6.10.7.2(2); *see also* Essential electrical systems
  Administration of, 6.3.4, A.6.3.4.1.1
  Design considerations, 6.7.1.1, A.6.7.1.1
  Distribution, 6.3.2, A.6.3.2.1 to A.6.3.2.9.3.4
    Isolated power systems, *see* Isolated power systems
    Patient bed locations, 6.3.2.4, A.6.3.2.4
  Emergency plan, 12.5.3.3.6.5(1)
  Equipment branch, 6.7.5.1.1(3), 6.7.5.1.4, A.6.7.5.1.4.3 to A.6.7.5.1.4.4(9)
  Fire protection, 16.5.1.2, 16.5.1.3
  Hyperbaric facilities, 14.2.10.1.1
  Information technology and communications systems, 7.3.1.2.1.7, 7.3.1.2.2.7, 7.3.1.2.3.7, 7.5.1.1.2
  Instrument air supply systems, 5.1.13.3.7.12
  Isolated power systems, *see* Isolated power systems
  Medical air systems, 5.1.3.6.3.10
  Medical-surgical vacuum supply systems, 5.1.3.7.6
  Patient care spaces
    Grounding systems, 6.3.3.1, A.6.3.3.1.1 to A.6.3.3.1.4
    Instructions for appliances, 10.5.3.1, 10.5.3.2, 10.5.6.1
  Performance criteria and tests, 6.3.3, A.6.3.3.1.1 to A.6.3.3.1.4
    Grounding systems in patient care rooms, 6.3.3.1, A.6.3.3.1.1 to A.6.3.3.1.4
    Isolated power systems, 6.3.3.3
    Receptacle testing in patient care rooms, 6.3.3.2
  Sources of power, 6.3.1, 6.7.1, A.6.7.1.1 to A.6.7.1.3.5
    Alternate, *see* Alternate power sources
    Failure of, 6.7.3.3, 6.7.3.7
    Performance criteria and tests, 6.7.5.3.1, 6.7.6.4.1
    Power loss, emergency management of, B.12.3.2.5
    Transfer to, *see* Transfer switches
    Type 1 essential electrical systems, 6.7.1, A.6.7.1.1 to A.6.7.1.3.5
  Tests, 6.3.3, 6.3.4, A.6.3.3.1.1 to A.6.3.3.1.4, A.6.3.4.1.1
  Waste anesthetic gas disposal (WAGD) systems, 5.1.3.8.4
Electrical wiring, B.6.1
  Essential electrical systems, 6.7.5.2, 6.7.6.3, A.6.7.5.2.1, A.6.7.6.3.1, A.6.7.6.3.2
  Fire protection, 16.5.1.2
  Hyperbaric facilities, 14.2.9.3 to 14.2.9.6
  Isolated power systems, 6.3.2.9.2
Electrocautery equipment, 14.3.2.1.2(2), 16.14.3.2, 16.14.3.3, A.16.14.3.2
Electrode, 5.1.14.3.2, 6.3.2.9.3.7
  Definition, 3.3.49
Electrostatic safeguards, hyperbaric chambers, 14.3.4.6, A.14.3.4.6 to A.14.3.4.6.5
Electrosurgery, 16.14.3.2, 16.14.3.3, A.16.14.3.2
Elevators, 16.5.3, A.16.5.3.3, B.12.3.2.5(2)

  Alarm systems, 16.7.4.2.1
  Essential electrical systems, 6.7.5.1.2.2(5), 6.7.5.1.4.4(3), 6.7.6.2.1.5(A)(6)
  Temporary operation of, 6.7.6.2.1.6(E)(2), A.6.7.6.2.1.6(E)(2)
Emergency care, policies for, 1.3.3
Emergency generators, *see* Generator sets
Emergency management, 1.1.10, Chap. 12, A.1.1.10; *see also* Emergency procedures
  Administration, 12.5.3.6
  Category 1 and Category 2 requirements, 12.3, 12.5, A.12.5.3.1.2 to A.12.5.3.5
  Committee for, 12.2.3, A.12.2.3 to A.12.2.3.3, B.12.1.1.3, B.12.1.1.6, B.12.3.3.1
  Continuing operations plan and recovery, B.12.4
  Definition, 3.3.50
  General requirements, 12.4, A.12.4.1 to A.12.4.2
  Medical air, loss of, 5.2.3.5(2)
  Mitigation, 12.5.3.2, A.12.5.3.2.3(7), B.12.1.1.2
  Preparedness, 12.5.3.3, A.12.5.3.3.6.1(5) to A.12.5.3.3.9.8, B.12.1.1.2
  Program development, B.12.1
  Responsibilities, 12.2
    Authority having jurisdiction, A.12.2.1
    Emergency management committee, 12.2.3, A.12.2.3 to A.12.2.3.3, B.12.1.1.3, B.12.1.1.6, B.12.3.3.1
    Senior management, 12.2.2
  Safety and security, 12.5.3.3.6.3, A.12.5.3.3.6.3
  Special considerations and protocols, B.12.3
  Staff education, 12.5.3.3.7
  Surge capacity of victims, 12.5.3.3.8.5, 12.5.3.4.10, A.12.5.3.4.10.1
  Waste anesthetic gas disposal (WAGD), loss of, 5.2.3.8(2)
Emergency operations plan, 12.2.3.3, 12.5.3.3.5, 12.5.3.3.8, A.12.2.3.3, B.12.1.1.4
Emergency oxygen supply connection (EOSC), 5.1.3.5.12, A.5.1.3.5.12
  Definition, 3.3.51
Emergency power supply systems (EPSSs), 6.11
Emergency power system (EPS) room HVAC systems, 9.3.9
Emergency procedures, *see also* Emergency management
  Hyperbaric facilities, 14.3.1.4.3, 14.3.1.5, A.14.3.1.5.2, A.14.3.1.5.4, B.14.2, B.14.3
  Operating room, 16.14.3.9
Emergency recovery, 12.5.3.5, A.12.5.3.5
Emergency response, 12.5.3.4, A.12.5.3.4.1 to A.12.5.3.4.10.1, B.12.3
Emergency systems, *see* Critical branch; Equipment branch; Life safety branch
Employees
  Emergency roles, 12.5.3.3.6.7, 12.5.3.3.7, B.12.2, B.12.3.2.8
  Gas equipment cylinders and containers, handling of, 11.5.2.1, A.11.5.2.1.1
  Gas equipment servicing, 11.5.3.3.5, 11.6.1.2
  Hyperbaric chambers, 14.3.1.3, 14.3.1.6.3, 14.3.1.6.5, A.14.3.1.3.2 to A.14.3.1.3.5.4, A.14.3.1.6.3, B.14.1.1.3.3 to B.14.1.1.3.5, B.14.1.2.2, B.14.1.3, B.14.3
  Medical gas and vacuum systems, 5.1.10.11.10, 5.1.10.11.11, 5.1.12.2, 5.1.14.4.2.5, 5.1.14.7.4, B.5.1
  Operating rooms, 16.14.3.10
  Protection, 6.3.2.8.2

Respiratory therapy, B.11.1.1.1, B.11.1.1.2, B.11.3.5, B.11.3.6
Responsible facility authority, 5.1.14.1, 5.1.14.2, A.5.1.14.2.1, A.5.1.14.2.2(4)
Security management, 13.4, 13.10, 13.11, A.13.4.2(3)(c), A.13.10, A.13.11
Training, *see* Training, employee
Enclosures, gas system, 11.3.6.1, 11.4.2.2
Endotracheal tube, B.14.1.2.4
Definition, 3.3.189.1, A.3.3.189.1
Energy converters, 6.7.1.3.5, A.6.7.1.3.5
Equipment, *see also* Electrical equipment
Critical, 6.9.4.2.2, A.6.9.4.2.2(4)
Definition, 3.3.31
Hyperbaric, 14.2, 14.3.2, A.14.2.1.1.1 to A.14.2.1.3.3, A.14.3.2.2 to A.14.3.2.6
Portable
Electrical, *see* Electrical equipment
Patient care gas equipment, 11.4.1, A.11.4.1.1, A.11.4.1.3
Rack or cart, 11.4.3.1
Equipment branch, 6.7.6.2.1.2(2), 6.7.6.2.1.6, 7.3.1.2.2.8(B)
Definition, 3.3.52
Equipment grounding bus, 10.2.1
Definition, 3.3.53
Equivalency to standard, 1.4
Escalators, 16.5.3
Essential electrical systems, 5.1.3.3.2.2(11), A.5.1.3.3.2.2(11), B.6.2, B.6.3
Definition, 3.3.54, A.3.3.54
Information technology and communications systems, *see* Information technology and communications systems
Sources, 6.7.1, A.6.7.1.1 to A.6.7.1.3.5
Type 1, 6.7.5, A.6.7.5 to A.6.7.5.2.1
Administration, 6.7.4, A.6.7.4.1.1.5(A)
Alternate power sources, 6.7.1.2, 6.7.4.1.1, A.6.7.1.2.1 to A.6.7.1.2.7.2(H), A.6.7.4.1.1.5(A)
Branches, 6.7.2.2, A.6.7.2.2.5(B)
Distribution, 6.7.2, A.6.7.2, A.6.7.2 to A.6.7.2.2.5(B)
Generator sets, 6.7.1.3, A.6.7.1.3.4 to A.6.7.1.3.5
Maintenance and testing, 6.7.4.1, A.6.7.4.1.1.5(A)
Performance criteria and tests, 6.7.5.3
Sources, 6.7.1, A.6.7.1.1 to A.6.7.1.3.5
Type 2, 6.7, 6.7.6, A.6.7.6 to A.6.7.6.3.2
Distribution, 6.7.2, A.6.7.2, A.6.7.2 to A.6.7.2.2.5(B)
Performance criteria and tests, 6.7.6.4
Sources, 6.7.1, 6.7.6.4.1, A.6.7.1.1 to A.6.7.1.3.5
Evacuation, waste gas, *see* Waste anesthetic gas disposal (WAGD) systems
Evacuation of occupants
Emergency plan, B.12.3.2.11, B.12.3.3
Hyperbaric facilities, B.14.3.1
Natural disasters, due to, B.12.3.2.11
Oxygen-enriched atmosphere (OEA), B.11.3.2.1
Event, planned, 12.5.3.3.6.1, A.12.2.3.3
Definition, 3.3.152
Exercises, 12.5.3.3.8, 12.5.3.3.9, A.12.5.3.3.8 to A.12.5.3.3.9.8
Definition, 3.3.56
Exhaust systems, 6.7.5.1.4.3(A)(5), 6.7.5.1.4.3(A)(6), 6.7.5.1.4.4(4); *see also* Ventilation

Emergency systems, 6.7.5.1.4.4(4)
Hyperbaric facilities, 14.2.11.2, A.14.2.11.2, A.14.2.11.2.5
Medical gases storage or transfilling areas, 9.3.6.5.3
Vacuum or scavenging source, 5.1.3.7.7
Waste anesthetic gas disposal (WAGD) systems, 5.1.3.8.5
Exposed conductive surfaces
Definition, 3.3.57
Tests, 6.3.3.1.1.2, 6.3.3.1.1.3
Extension cords, 10.2.4, 10.5.2.3; *see also* Power cords
Exterior connections, 12.5.3.3.6.6
Extinguishers, portable fire, 14.2.6.1.5, 14.2.6.5, 16.10.1, A.14.2.6.1.5, A.16.10.1, B.11.3.4.2, B.14.2.1, B.14.3.2
Extinguishing systems, *see* Fire extinguishing systems and equipment

-F-

Facility fire plan, B.11.3.2.1(2), B.12.3.1; *see also* Emergency operations plan
Definition, 3.3.58, A.3.3.58
Failure
Power sources, 6.7.3.3, 6.7.3.7
Fault current, 6.3.2.3.2, 6.3.2.9.3.1, 6.7.2.1.1.1, 14.2.9.3.6.5, A.6.3.2.9.3.1
Definition, 3.3.59
Fault hazard current, 6.3.2.9.3.2, 6.3.2.9.3.4
Definition, 3.3.74.1
Feeders
From alternative source, 6.7.2.2.4
Definition, 3.3.60
Insulation resistance, 6.7.4.1.2.1
FGI guidelines, 8.3.1 to 8.3.3, 8.3.6, 8.3.8, 8.3.12, 9.3.10, A.5.1.5, A.7.1
Definition, 3.3.61, A.3.3.61
Filters, air
Instrument air, 5.1.13.3.7.8
Medical air, 5.1.3.6.3.8, 5.1.3.6.3.9(E), 5.1.3.6.3.9(F), 5.1.3.6.3.9(I), 5.2.3.5(1), A.5.1.3.6.3.9(F)
Final tie-in tests, 5.1.12.4.9, 15.4.7.5.7
Fire alarm systems, *see* Alarm systems
Fire blankets, 14.2.6.1.5, A.14.2.6.1.5
Fire dampers or shutters, 6.7.1.3.4.2(C), 6.7.1.3.4.5, 16.7.4.2.2
Fire detection systems, 16.7; *see also* Alarm systems; Smoke alarms/detectors
Hyperbaric facilities, 14.2.6.6, A.14.2.6.4.1
Fire extinguishing systems and equipment, 16.9, 16.10, 16.12.3, 16.13, A.16.10.1 to A.16.10.2.2, A.16.12.3, B.12.3.2.7; *see also* Fire protection
Hyperbaric chambers, 14.2.1.2, 14.2.6, B.14.2.1
Respiratory therapy apparatus, B.11.3.4
Telecommunications facilities, 7.3.1.2.1.8(D), 7.3.1.2.3.8(B)
Fire hazards
Dental gas and vacuum piping systems, 15.2
Electrical systems, 6.2.1, A.6.2.1
Gas systems, 5.1.2, 5.3.2
Hyperbaric facilities, B.14.1.1
Oxygen delivery equipment, 11.5.1.1.6, 11.5.1.2.2
Oxygen-enriched atmospheres (OEAs), 11.5.1.2.1
Respiratory therapy, 11.5.1.1, 11.5.1.2, A.11.5.1.1.2, A.11.5.1.1.3, B.11.3.1

Fire prevention
Hyperbaric facilities, 14.3.1.6, A.14.3.1.6.1.1, A.14.3.1.6.1.3
Operating rooms, 16.14, A.16.14.3.2
Fire protection, 12.5.3.3.6.5(6), Chap. 16
Construction and compartmentation, 16.2
Hyperbaric facilities, 14.2.6 to 14.2.8, B.14
Respiratory therapy, B.11.3
Firefighters' emergency operations (elevator), 16.5.3.2
Flammable (definition), 3.3.62, A.3.3.62
Flammable gases, 14.3.1.6.2; *see also* Cylinders; Gases
Definition, 3.3.63; *see also* Cylinders
Hyperbaric facilities, 14.3.2.6.1, 14.3.3.3, 14.3.4.1.4.1
Special hazard protection for, 16.3, A.16.3.2
Storage, 14.3.3.3, 14.3.4.1.4.1
Valves, 5.1.4.1.5
Flammable liquids, 16.14.3.2, A.16.14.3.2
Definition, 3.3.64
In hyperbaric chambers, 14.3.1.6.2, A.14.3.1.6.2.2(2)
Special hazard protection for, 16.3, A.16.3.2
Use of, 11.5.1.2.3
Flammable substances and agents, misuse of, 11.5.1.2
Flash point, 3.3.25
Definition, 3.3.65, A.3.3.65
Flexible connectors
Category 1, 5.1.6.5, 5.1.6.6, 5.1.6.9, 5.1.10.11.6, 5.1.14.4.3.1
Category 2, 15.4.5.10
Flexible cords, *see* Power cords
Flow-control valves, 11.5.3.3.1
Definition, 3.3.66
Flowmeters
Definition, 3.3.67, A.3.3.67
Labels on, 11.5.3.1.3
Footwear, nails in, 14.3.1.6.3.3
Frequency (definition), 3.3.68, A.3.3.68
Fuel supply or sources, 6.7.1.3.7, 12.5.3.3.2, 12.5.3.3.6.5, A.12.5.3.3.6.5, B.14.1.1.3
Fume hoods, 6.7.5.1.4.3(A)(6)
Definition, 3.3.69, A.3.3.69
Fundamentals, Chap. 4
Furniture, hyperbaric facilities, 14.3.4.5

-G-

Gas cylinders, *see* Cylinders
Gas equipment, Chap. 11
Administration, 11.5, A.11.5.1.1.2 to A.11.5.3.2
Cylinders and containers, 11.2, 11.6, 11.6.5
Fire protection, 16.5.1.1
Performance criteria and tests, 11.4, A.11.4.1.1, A.11.4.1.3
Qualification and training of personnel, 11.5.3.3.5
Source, 11.2
Transport, storage, and use, 11.5.3.3
Use, 11.5.3
Gases, *see also* Waste anesthetic gas disposal (WAGD) systems; *specific gases*
Flammable, *see* Flammable gases
Handling, 14.3.3, A.14.3.3.4
Medical, *see* Medical gases

Monitoring, hyperbaric chambers, 14.2.10.3 to 14.2.10.6
Nonflammable, 11.3.5; *see also* Medical gases
Oxidizing, *see* Oxidizing gas
Gasket material, 14.2.3.1(2)
Gas systems, *see* Medical gas systems
Gas tungsten arc welding (GTAW), 5.1.10.5.1, A.5.1.10.5.1.5
General anesthesia and levels of sedation/analgesia
Deep sedation/analgesia, 5.1.3.3.1.5(2), 5.1.9.4(1), 5.1.9.4.4(2), 6.3.2.6.1, 15.3.1, A.5.1.9.4(2)
Definition, 3.3.70.2
Definition, A.3.3.70
General anesthesia, 5.1.3.3.1.5(2), 5.1.9.4(1), 5.1.9.4.4(2), 6.3.2.6.1, 15.3.1, A.5.1.9.4(2)
Definition, 3.3.70.1
Minimal sedation (anxliolysis), 3.3.39, 3.3.114, 15.1.2, 15.4.1.1
Definition, 3.3.70.4
Moderate sedation/analgesia (conscious sedation), 5.1.3.3.1.5(2), 5.1.9.4(1), 5.1.9.4.4(2), A.5.1.9.4(2)
Definition, 3.3.70.3
Generator sets
Alarm annunciator, A.6.7.1.2.7.2(B), A.6.7.1.2.7.2(H)
Design considerations, 6.7.1.1, A.6.7.1.1
Fuel supply, 6.7.1.3.7
Hyperbaric chambers, 14.2.9.2.3.1
Installation, 6.7.1.2.3.2
Maintenance and testing, 6.7.4.1.1, A.6.7.4.1.1.5(A)
Power loss, emergency management of, B.12.3.2.5
Safety devices, 6.7.1.3.8
Type 1 essential electrical systems, 6.7.1.3, 6.7.2, A.6.7.1.3.4 to A.6.7.1.3.5, A.6.7.2, A.6.7.2 to A.6.7.2.2.5(B)
Germicides, 16.14.3, A.16.14.3.2
Governing body, 6.3.2.3.4, 6.3.2.3.5, 6.7.5.1.3.2(7), 8.2, 9.2, A.6.3.2.3.4, A.6.3.2.3.8
Grease interceptors, 8.3.7
Ground-fault circuit interrupters (GFCIs), 6.3.2.3.8, 6.3.2.3.9, 6.3.2.8.2
Definition, 3.3.71, A.3.3.71
Ground-fault protection, 6.3.2.8, 6.3.3.4, 14.2.9.4
Grounding, 6.3.2.2.5, A.6.3.2.2.5; *see also* Grounding systems
Appliances, 10.2.2.1, 10.4.2.3
Hyperbaric chambers, 14.2.2.5.3, 14.2.9.4, 14.2.11.1
Patient care spaces, 6.3.2.5, 6.3.3.1, A.6.3.2.5.1.5, A.6.3.2.5.3, A.6.3.3.1.1 to A.6.3.3.1.4
Piping system, 5.1.14.3.2
Special, 6.3.2.3.1, A.6.3.2.3.1
Grounding circuit integrity, 6.3.2.5.1.1
Grounding conductors, 10.2.3.2, A.10.2.3.2.4
Grounding point
Patient equipment, 6.3.2.5.2
Definition, 3.3.147
Reference, *see* Reference grounding point
Grounding systems
Definition, 3.3.73, A.3.3.73
Tests, 6.3.3.1.1, A.6.3.3.1.1
Guide (definition), 3.2.4

-H-

Handlines, 14.2.6.3

Hand trucks, 11.4.3.1

Hazard current

    Definition, 3.3.74

    Fault hazard current, *see* Fault hazard current

    Monitor, 6.3.2.9.3.4, A.6.3.2.9.3.4

        Definition, 3.3.74.2

    Total, 6.3.2.9.3.2, 6.3.2.9.3.4, 6.3.2.9.3.6

        Definition, 3.3.74.3

Hazards

    Fire, *see* Fire hazards

    Nature of

        Hyperbaric facilities, 14.3.1.2, 14.3.1.6, A.14.3.1.2,
            A.14.3.1.6.1.1, A.14.3.1.6.1.3, B.14.1

        Piped gas and vacuum systems, 5.1.2, 5.2.2, 5.3.2, 15.2

Hazard vulnerability analysis (HVA), 12.5.2, 12.5.3.1, A.12.5.3.1.2,
    A.12.5.3.1.3(1), B.12.1.1.1, B.12.3.2.1, B.12.3.3.1

Headers

    Instrument air, 5.1.3.5.9, 5.1.3.5.10.4 to 5.1.3.5.10.6, 5.1.3.5.11.2
        to 5.1.3.5.11.9, 5.1.13.3.6.8, 5.1.13.3.7.10,
        5.1.13.3.7.11(B), A.5.1.3.5.9

    Cryogenic liquid withdrawal manifolds, 5.4.6.3 to 5.4.6.7

    Local signals, 5.1.3.5.8.1(6)

    Reserve, 5.1.3.3.1.4, 5.1.3.3.4.2, 5.1.3.5.11.3, 5.1.3.5.11.4(2),
        5.1.3.5.11.8, 5.1.3.5.11.9, 5.1.9.2.4(4)

    Standby, 5.1.3.3.1.2(4)

    Medical air, 5.1.3.6.3.4(C), 14.2.1.5.4.7(2)

Health care facilities (definition), 3.3.75, A.3.3.75

Health care facility's governing body, 4.2.1 to 4.2.2, A.4.2.2

    Definition, 3.3.76, A.3.3.76

Health care microgrid, 6.7.1.4, 6.10, A.6.10.1.2 to A.6.10.7.2(2)

    Definition, 3.3.77, A.3.3.77

Health care microgrid control system, 6.10.6, A.6.10.6

    Definition, 3.3.78

Heart, direct electrical pathway to

    Definition, 3.3.43, A.3.3.43

    Protection of patients, 10.5.2.2, A.10.5.2.2

Heating, adiabatic, *see* Adiabatic heating

Heating, ventilating, and air conditioning (HVAC) systems, Chap. 9

    Commissioning, 9.3.3, A.9.3.3.2

    Ductwork, 9.3.5

    Emergency plan, 12.5.3.3.6.5(5), B.12.3.2.5(2)

    Emergency power system room, 9.3.9

    Energy conservation, 9.3.2

    Fire protection, 16.5.2, A.16.5.2.1

    Information technology and communications
        systems, 7.3.1.2.1.8(B), 7.3.1.2.2.8(B), 7.5.1.1.3,
        A.7.3.1.2.1.8(B)

    Medical plume evacuation, 9.3.8

    Piping, 9.3.4

    Smoke detectors, 16.7.4.2.2

    System category criteria, 9.2, A.9.2.1

    Waste gas, 9.3.7

Heating equipment

    Essential electrical system generator sets, 6.7.1.2.6, 6.7.1.3.4,
        6.7.6.2.1.6(E)(1), A.6.7.1.3.4, A.6.7.6.2.1.6(E)(1)(a)

    Water heating, 8.3.3

Heliports, 16.8, A.16.8

Helium, *See* Medical gas systems

High-energy devices, 14.3.2.1.2(3)

High pressure, *see* Pressure

Home care (definition), 3.3.79, A.3.3.79

Hoods

    Fume, 6.7.5.1.4.3(A)(6)

        Definition, 3.3.69, A.3.3.69

    Oxygen, A.11.5.1.1.5

        Definition, 3.3.138, A.3.3.138

Hose

    Gas and vacuum systems, 5.1.6.5, 5.1.6.6, 5.1.6.8 to 5.1.6.10,
        5.1.10.11.6

    Standpipe and hose systems, 16.10.2, 16.10.2.2, A.16.10.2.2

Hospitals

    Definition, 3.3.80

    Governing body, *see* Governing body

Humidification, 11.4.2.4, 14.2.4.3.3

Humidifiers, 11.4.2.5, 11.4.2.6

    Definition, 3.3.81

Humidity control, 7.3.1.2.1.8(A), 7.3.1.2.2.8(A), 7.3.1.2.3.8(A),
    14.2.4.3

Hydrostatic tests, 14.2.1.1.9.1

Hyperbaric facilities, 1.1.12, Chap. 14, A.1.1.12

    Administration and maintenance, 14.3, A.14.3.1.2 to A.14.3.1.6.9

    Air supply, monitoring of, 14.2.10.6, A.14.2.10.6, A.14.2.10.6.1

    Chambers, classification, 14.1.2

    Communications and monitoring equipment, 14.2.10

    Construction and equipment, 14.2, 14.3.2, A.14.2.1.1.1 to
        A.14.2.1.3.3, A.14.3.2.2 to A.14.3.2.6

    Definition, 3.3.82

    Electrical equipment, 14.3.4.4, A.10.5.4.5, A.10.5.4.6

    Electrical systems, 6.7.5.1.4.4(5), 14.2.9, A.14.2.9.2.1 to
        A.14.2.9.6.1.1

    Emergency depressurization capability, 14.2.5

    Emergency procedures, 14.3.1.4.3, 14.3.1.5, A.14.3.1.5.2,
        A.14.3.1.5.4, B.14.2, B.14.3

    Fabrication of chamber, 14.2.2, A.14.2.2.1 to A.14.2.2.7

    Fire prevention, 14.3.1.6, A.14.3.1.6.1.1, A.14.3.1.6.1.3

    Fire protection, 14.2.6 to 14.2.8, B.14

    Gases

        Handling of, 14.3.2.2 to 14.3.2.4, 14.3.3, A.14.3.3.4

        Monitoring of, 14.2.10.3 to 14.2.10.6

    Hazards, nature of, 14.3.1.2, 14.3.1.6, A.14.3.1.6.1.1,
        A.14.3.1.6.1.3, B.14.1

    Housing for, 14.2.1

    Ignition sources, 14.3.1.6.1, A.14.3.1.6.1.1, A.14.3.1.6.3

    Illumination, 14.2.3

    Intercommunications equipment, 14.2.10.2, A.14.2.10.2 to
        A.14.2.10.2.2

    Other fixtures and equipment, 14.2.11, 14.3.2, A.14.2.11.2,
        A.14.2.11.2.5, A.14.3.2.2 to A.14.3.2.6

    Personnel, 14.3.1.3, 14.3.1.6.3, 14.3.1.6.5, A.14.3.1.3.2 to
        A.14.3.1.3.5.4, A.14.3.1.6.3

    Rules and regulations, 14.3.1.4, A.14.3.1.4.1

    Ventilation of chambers, 14.2.4, 14.2.11.2, A.14.2.4.1.2 to
        A.14.2.4.4.1, A.14.2.11.2, A.14.2.11.2.5

    Viewports, 14.2.2.7, A.14.2.2.7, B.14.1.2.3

    Wiring and service equipment, 14.2.9.3 to 14.2.9.6

Hyperbaric operations (definition), 3.3.83, A.3.3.83
Hyperbaric stand-alone oxygen system, 14.2.1.4.5, 14.2.1.4.7, 14.2.1.5.4.3, 14.2.1.5.4.6
Definition, 3.3.84
Hypobaric facilities
Definition, 3.3.85
Electrical systems, 6.7.5.1.4.4(6)
Hypoxia (definition), 3.3.86, B.11.2.13

-I-

Identification, *see* Labeling and identification
Ignition sources, *see also* Fire hazards
Hyperbaric facilities, 14.3.1.6.1, A.14.3.1.6.1.1, A.14.3.1.6.3, B.14.1.1.4
Respiratory therapy locations, 11.5.1.1, A.11.5.1.1.2, A.11.5.1.1.4
Immediate restoration of service (definition), 3.3.87
Impedance
Definition, 3.3.88, A.3.3.88
Of isolated wiring, 6.3.2.9.2
Limit, 6.3.3.1.6.2
Measuring, 6.3.3.1.4
Incident, 12.5.3.3.8, 12.5.3.3.9
Definition, 3.3.89
Incident command system (ICS), 12.2.3.3, 12.5.3.3.7.3, 12.5.3.3.7.5, A.12.2.3.3, B.12.3.2.1
Definition, 3.3.90
Incinerators, 16.6
Inert gas bulk systems, 5.1.3.3.1.10, A.5.1.3.3.1.10
Definition, 3.3.20.1
Inert gases
Distribution of, A.5.1.1.3
Purging of, B.14.5
Information technology and communications systems, Chap. 7, 16.7; *see also* Alarm systems
Category 1, *see* Category 1 information technology and communications systems
Category 2, 7.4
Infrastructure, 7.4.1
Nurse call systems, 7.4.3.1
Category 3, 7.5
Clinical information systems, 7.3.3.7, A.7.3.3.7.1 to A.7.3.3.7.5
Emergency plan, 12.5.3.3.6.1, A.12.5.3.3.6.1(5), B.12.3.2.5(2), B.12.3.2.6
Essential electrical systems, 6.7.6.2.1.5(A)(4), 7.3.1.2.2.7(B), 7.3.1.2.2.8(B), A.6.7.6.2.1.5(A)(4)
Hyperbaric facilities, 14.2.10
Life safety branch, 6.7.5.1.2.2(3)
Wireless phone and paging integration, 7.3.3.5, A.7.3.3.5.2
Inhalation anesthetics, *see* Anesthetic apparatus; Anesthetics; Anesthetizing locations
Inlets, *see* Station inlets
In-line valves, 5.1.4.7, 5.1.4.9
Inspections
Category 1 piped gas and vacuum systems, 5.1.12.3, 5.1.14.4.2.2, 5.1.14.4.2.3, 5.1.14.4.3, 5.1.14.7.4, A.5.1.14.4.2.2, A.5.1.14.4.3
Category 2 piped gas and vacuum systems, 15.4.7
Health care microgrid system, 6.10.8

Instructions
Category 1 piped gas and vacuum systems, 5.1.3.5.1, 5.1.10.3.3, 5.1.10.6.2, 5.1.10.7.2, 5.1.10.11.8, 5.1.12.4.14.3(A), 5.1.12.4.14.5(B), 5.1.13.3.6.1(B), 15.3.3.8.4.3
Category 2 piped gas and vacuum systems, 15.4.9.3
Category 3 piped gas and vacuum systems, 15.5.8.2
Electrical equipment, 10.5.3.1, 10.5.3.2, 10.5.6.1
Liquid oxygen equipment, 11.7.2
Instrument air, *see also* Support gases
Definition, 3.3.91, A.3.3.91
Supply systems, 5.1.1.2, A.5.1.1.3; *see also* Medical gas systems
Category 1 piped gas and vacuum systems, 5.1.3.5(7), Table 5.1.11, 5.1.13.3.7
Alarms, 5.1.9.5, 5.1.13.3.7.11, A.5.1.9.5
Headers, 5.1.13.3.6.8, 5.1.13.3.7.10, 5.1.13.3.7.11(B)
Category 2 piped gas and vacuum systems, 5.2.3.9
Category 3 piped gas and vacuum systems, 5.3.3.9
Insulation resistance, circuitry, 6.7.4.1.2.1
Integrity tests, 10.3.1, A.10.3.1
Intentional expulsion, site of, *see* Site of intentional expulsion
Intermittent positive-pressure breathing (IPPB)
Definition, 3.3.92, B.11.2.15
Internal combustion engines, 6.7.1.3.8.1
Intrinsically safe
Circuits, hyperbaric chamber, 14.2.6.1.3.1, 14.2.9.3.6.6
Definition, 3.3.93, A.3.3.93
Invasive procedure (definition), 3.3.94
Isolated ground receptacles, 6.3.2.2.5, A.6.3.2.2.5
Isolated patient leads, 10.5.2.2, A.10.5.2.2
Definition, 3.3.95
Isolated power systems, 6.3.2.3.7, 6.3.2.3.8, 6.3.2.9, A.6.3.2.9 to A.6.3.2.9.3.4
Definition, 3.3.96, A.3.3.96
Tests, 6.3.3.3, 6.3.4.1.3
Isolation switch, bypass, 6.7.2.1.6, A.6.7.2.1.6.3
Isolation transformers, 6.3.2.9.1
Definition, 3.3.97

-J-

Joints, 5.1.10.3, 15.3.3.7.3.2(C), 15.4.4.2.4, 15.4.4.3.4, 15.4.4.4.2.3, A.5.1.10.3.1
Axially swaged, 5.1.10.3.1(4), 5.1.10.7, 15.4.4.2.3.1, 15.4.4.2.3.5
Brazed, 5.1.10.3.1(1), 5.1.10.4, 5.1.10.11.11, 15.3.3.7.2.4, 15.3.3.7.2.5, 15.3.3.7.3.2(B), 15.3.3.7.3.2(C), 15.4.4.2.3.1, 15.4.4.2.4.1, 15.4.6.2, 15.4.6.4, 15.4.6.7, 15.4.6.8, 15.5.5.2.3, 15.5.5.2.4, 15.5.5.3.2.2, 15.5.5.3.2.3
Memory metal, 5.1.10.3.1(3), 5.1.10.6, 15.4.4.2.3.1, 15.4.4.2.3.4
Prohibited, 5.1.10.10, 15.4.4.2.4.3
Special fittings, 5.1.10.9
Threaded, 5.1.10.3.1(5), 5.1.10.8, 15.4.4.2.4.2, 15.5.5.2.4(1), 15.5.5.3.2.3(1), A.5.1.10.8(3)
Welded, 5.1.10.3.1(2), 5.1.10.5

-L-

Labeled (definition), 3.2.5
Labeling and identification
Cylinders and containers, 5.1.3.1, 11.3.12, A.5.1.3.1.1, A.5.1.3.1.2
Gas equipment, 11.5.3.1, 11.5.3.2, A.11.5.3.2

Gas/vacuum systems, 5.1.11, 5.1.14.5, 5.2.3.1, 5.2.11, 5.3.3.1, 5.3.11, 15.3.2.9, 15.4.2.2, 15.4.2.11, A.5.1.11
    Alarm panels, 5.1.11.4, A.5.1.11.4.2
    Outlets and inlets, 5.1.11.3
    Pipes, 5.1.11.1, A.5.1.11
    Shutoff valves, 5.1.11.2
    Support gas, 5.1.13.11
    Verification of, 5.1.12.4.14
Hyperbaric facilities, 14.2.6.1.7, 14.2.8.1, A.14.2.8.1
Oxygen, 11.5.3.1, 11.5.3.2, A.11.5.3.2
Respiratory therapy, 11.5.3.1, 11.5.3.2, A.11.5.3.2
Valves, 5.1.4.1.3

Laboratories
Definition, 3.3.98, A.3.3.98
Electrical equipment and appliances, 10.5.5, A.10.5.5.1
Electrical outlets in, 6.3.2.2.7, A.6.3.2.2.7
Fire protection, 16.4, 16.5.2.4
Heating, ventilating, and air conditioning (HVAC) systems, 9.3.1.2
Ventilation, 16.5.2.4

Lasers, 14.3.2.1.4, 16.14.3.2, 16.14.3.3, A.16.14.3.2
Leakage current, *see also* Touch current
Fixed equipment, 10.3.4
Limits, 10.3.3.4, 10.3.6, A.10.3.6
Portable equipment, 10.3.6, A.10.3.6
Tests, 10.3.3, 10.3.4.1, 10.3.6, A.10.3.3, A.10.3.6

Leak detectant, 5.1.12.2.3.5, 5.1.12.4.9.2
Definition, 3.3.99

Life safety branch, 6.7.5.1.1(1), 6.7.5.1.2, 6.7.6.2.1.2(1), 6.7.6.2.1.5, A.6.7.5.1.2.2(3), A.6.7.6.2.1.5(A)(4)
Definition, 3.3.100

Life support equipment, electrical, B.12.3.2.5(1)
Definition, 3.3.47

Lighting, B.6.3
Hyperbaric chambers, 14.2.9.3.14, A.14.2.9.3.14
Photographic lighting equipment, 14.3.2.1.3

Limited-combustible material, 4.4.2, A.4.4.2
Definition, A.3.3.101

Line isolation monitor, 6.3.2.9.3
Definition, 3.3.102
Tests, 6.3.3.3.2

Linen chutes, 16.6

Liquids (definition), 3.3.103, A.3.3.103; *see also* Combustible liquids; Flammable liquids; Oxygen

Listed (definition), 3.2.6, A.3.2.6

Local signal
Definition, 3.3.104, A.3.3.104
Proportioning system for medical air, 5.1.3.6.3.14(C)(9), A.5.1.3.6.3.14(C)(9)

Lubricants, 14.3.2.3(4), 14.3.2.4, 14.3.4.5.3, 14.3.4.5.4

-M-

mA (definition), 3.3.105

Main lines, piping
Definition, 3.3.151.2
Valves, 5.1.4.3, 5.1.11.2.5, A.5.1.4.3

Maintenance
Electrical preventive maintenance (EPM) program, 6.9, A.6.9.1.1 to A.6.9.4.2.2(4)
Essential electrical systems, B.6.2
Fire protection systems, 16.13
Health care microgrid system, 6.10.8
Piped gas and vacuum systems, Category 1, *see* Category 1 piped gas and vacuum systems
Piped gas and vacuum systems, Category 2, 15.4.9.4
Piped gas and vacuum systems, Category 3, 15.5.8.3

Manifolds, 5.1.3.3.1.1, 5.1.3.3.1.2, 5.1.3.5(1), 5.1.3.5(2), 5.1.3.5.10, 5.1.9.2.4(1), 11.6.2, 15.3.2.11(2), A.5.1.3.5.10
Cryogenic liquid containers, 5.1.3.5.8.1(3), 5.1.3.5.11, 5.1.3.10.8, 5.1.13.3.6.9, 5.1.13.3.6.10, 5.3.3.5.12, 5.3.3.5.13, 5.4.6, 9.3.6.5, A.5.1.3.5.11, A.5.1.3.10.8.3, A.5.4.6.2 to A.5.4.6.10(4)
Cylinders without reserve supply, for, 5.1.3.5.8.1(1)
Definition, 3.3.106
Ventilation of manifold areas, 9.3.6.5

Manual extinguishing equipment, 16.10, A.16.10.1 to A.16.10.2.2

Manufactured assemblies
Category 1 piped gas and vacuum systems, 5.1.6, 5.1.13.6, 5.1.14.4.3.1, 15.3.2.4, A.5.1.6
Category 2 piped gas and vacuum systems, 5.2.6, 15.4.2.8
Category 3 piped gas and vacuum systems, 5.3.6
Definition, 3.3.107, A.3.3.107
Rough-in, 5.1.6.1, 5.1.12.2.2, 15.3.3.8.3.3(B), 15.4.7.4.2, 15.4.7.4.4.2, 15.4.8.1.5.2, 15.5.7.1.3.2(B), A.5.1.12.2.2
Definition, 3.3.108

Manufacturers
Documentation, 5.1.6.4, 10.5.3.1, 10.5.3.2
Instructions, *see* Instructions

Masks
Definition, 3.3.109
Oxygen mask microphones, 14.2.10.2.3

Measurement, units of, 1.5, A.1.5

Media control, 13.7, A.13.7 to A.13.7.2

Medical air, 5.1.1.2, A.5.1.1.3; *see also* Dental air; Medical gas systems
Alarms, 5.1.3.6.3.12
Category 1 supply systems, 5.1.3.5.2, 5.1.3.6, 15.3.2.1.5, A.5.1.3.6, B.5.2.6
Category 2 supply systems, 5.2.3.5
Definition, 3.3.110, A.3.3.110
Designation colors/operating pressures, Table 5.1.11
Dryers, 5.1.3.6.3.3, 5.1.3.6.3.7, 5.1.3.6.3.9(E), 5.1.3.6.3.9(F), 5.1.3.6.3.9(I), 5.2.3.5(1), 15.3.2.1.5(1), A.5.1.3.6.3.9(F)
Filters, 5.1.3.6.3.8, 5.1.3.6.3.9(E), 5.1.3.6.3.9(F), 5.1.3.6.3.9(I), 15.3.2.1.5(1), A.5.1.3.6.3.9(F)
Hyperbaric facilities, 14.2.1.5
Proportioning system for medical air (USP), 5.1.3.5(8), 5.1.3.6.3.14, A.5.1.3.6.3.14(A), A.5.1.3.6.3.14(C)(9)
    Components, 5.1.3.6.3.14(C), A.5.1.3.6.3.14(C)(9)
    Definition, 3.3.110.1
    Location, 5.1.3.6.3.14(B)
    Tests, 5.1.12.4.14.5
Purity test, 5.1.12.4.12
Quality monitoring, 5.1.3.6.3.13

Receivers, 5.1.3.6.3.6, 5.1.3.6.3.9(D), A.5.1.3.6.3.9(D)

Regulators, 5.1.3.6.3.9(E), 5.1.3.6.3.9(F), 5.1.3.6.3.9(I), 15.3.2.1.5(1), A.5.1.3.6.3.9(F)

Medical air compressors, *see also* Dental air compressors

Category 1, 5.1.3.5(4), 5.1.3.6.1(1), 5.1.3.6.3, 5.1.3.6.3.9(B), 5.1.14.7.7(1), 15.3.2.1.5(1), A.5.1.3.6.3

    Alarms, 5.1.3.6.3.12, 5.1.9.5, A.5.1.9.5

    Electrical power and control, 5.1.3.6.3.10

    Intake, 5.1.3.6.3.11

    Tests, 5.1.12.4.14.3

Category 2, 5.2.3.5(1)

Category 3, 5.3.3.6.1

Definition, 3.3.111

Electrical power and control, 6.7.5.1.4.3(A)(3)

Intake, 14.2.4.2.2

Medical devices not for patient care, 11.4.3.2

Medical gases, 5.1.1.2, A.5.1.1.3; *see also specific gases*

Concentration test, 5.1.12.4.11, 15.4.7.5.9, A.5.1.12.4.11(3)

Definition, 3.3.112

Patient medical gas, *see* Patient medical gas

Permitted locations, 5.1.3.5.2

Medical gas rails (MGRs), *see* Surface-mounted medical gas rail systems

Medical gas systems, Chap. 5; *see also* Cylinders; Gas equipment; Medical gases; Medical-surgical vacuum systems; Supply systems; Waste anesthetic gas disposal (WAGD) systems

Category 1, *see* Category 1 piped gas and vacuum systems

Category 2, *see* Category 2 piped gas and vacuum systems

Category 3, *see* Category 3 piped gas and vacuum systems

Definition, 3.3.113

Distribution, piped, *see* Piped distribution systems

Emergency plan, 12.5.3.3.6.5(9)

Manufactured assemblies to use with, *see* Manufactured assemblies

Storage or transfilling of gases, ventilation for, 9.3.6, A.9.3.6.3, A.9.3.6.5.1, A.9.3.6.5.2.1

Medical office (definition), 3.3.114, A.3.3.114

Medical plume evacuation, 9.3.8, A.9.3.8.1, A.9.3.8.1(1)

Medical-surgical vacuum

Category 1, 15.3.2.10

Definition, 3.3.116

Medical-surgical vacuum systems, Chap. 5

Alarms, 5.1.3.7.8

Category 1, 5.1.3.5(5), 5.1.3.7, 5.1.10.3.1 to 5.1.10.3.3, 5.1.12.4.14.6, 5.1.14.5, A.5.1.3.7

    Area alarms, 5.1.9.4, A.5.1.9.4

    Conversion to gas system, 5.1.10.11.9.2

    Designation colors, Table 5.1.11

    Electrical power and control, 5.1.3.7.6

    Filtration, 5.1.3.7.4

    Maintenance, 5.1.14.4, 5.1.14.7.7(3)

    Operating pressures, Table 5.1.11

    Piping, 5.1.3.7.5, 5.1.10.2, 5.1.14.7.7(3)

    Shutoff valves, 5.1.4.1.1

    Special precautions, 5.1.14.3, 5.1.14.3.3, A.5.1.14.3.3 to A.5.1.14.3.5

    Standard designation colors and operating pressures, Table 5.1.11

    Station outlets/inlets, 5.1.5, A.5.1.5, B.5.2.18

Category 2, 5.2.3.7

Category 3, 5.3.3.7, 5.3.10, 5.3.12

Definition, 3.3.117

Emergency plan, 12.5.3.3.6.5(9)

Exhaust, 5.1.3.7.7

Installers, qualification of, 5.1.10.11.10, 5.1.10.11.11

Labeling, 5.1.14.5

Manufactured assemblies to use with, *see* Manufactured assemblies

Tests, 5.3.12; *see also* Cross-connections, tests

    Source system, 5.1.12.4.14.6

    Standing vacuum tests, 5.1.12.2.7, 15.3.3.8.3.6, A.5.1.12.2.7.5

Microphones, oxygen mask, 14.2.10.2.3

Monitor hazard current, *see* Hazard current

Motor load transfer, 6.7.2.1.3.12

Multiple treatment facility, 15.4.2.5.13, 15.4.2.6.2

Definition, 3.3.118

mV (definition), 3.3.119

-N-

Nasal cannula, 11.5.1.1.2, A.11.5.1.1.2

Definition, 3.3.120

Natural disasters, B.12.3.2, B.12.3.7

Nebulizers, 11.4.2.5, 11.4.2.6

Definition, 3.3.121

Negative pressure, *see* Pressure

Nitrogen, 5.1.1.2, A.5.1.1.3; *see also* Medical gases; Medical gas systems; Support gases

Category 1 medical air proportioning system, 5.1.3.6.3.14, A.5.1.3.6.3.14(A), A.5.1.3.6.3.14(C)(9)

Category 1 medical air supply systems, 15.3.2.11

Definition, 3.3.123

Joints, purging of, 5.1.10.4.5, 15.4.6.6, A.5.1.10.4.5

NF (oil-free, dry)

    Category 1 medical air supply systems, 5.1.3.6.1(1), 5.1.13.3.6

    Definition, 3.3.123.1

    For purge, 5.1.10.4.5.1

    For tests, 5.1.12.2.1.2, 5.1.12.2.2, 5.1.12.3.1.2, 5.1.12.4.5.1(F), 5.1.12.4.7.5, 5.1.12.4.8.1, 15.4.7.4.1.2, 15.4.7.5.1.3

Piping, 15.4.4.5

Nitrogen narcosis, B.14.1.3.2

Definition, 3.3.124

Nitrous oxide, 15.4.1.2

Definition, 3.3.125

Scavenging, 15.3.3.6

Storage, 5.1.3.3.2.2(6), 11.3.6.2, 11.3.6.3

Nitrous oxide systems, 5.1.1.2, A.5.1.1.3; *see also* Medical gas systems

Bulk (definition), 3.3.20.2

Designation colors/operating pressures, Table 5.1.11

Locations for, 5.1.3.3.1.5, 15.4.2.4

Piping, 15.4.4.2

Supply systems, 5.1.3.3.1.7, 5.1.3.5.2, 5.1.3.5.4(2), 5.1.3.10.2.9, 15.4.2.3

Noncombustible material, 4.4.1, A.4.4.1

Nonessential electrical loads, 3.3.155

Definition, 3.3.127

Nonflammable (definition), 3.3.128

Nonflammable anesthetic agent (definition), 3.3.129; *see also* Anesthetics

Nonflammable anesthetizing location, *see* Anesthetizing locations

Nonflammable gases, 11.3.5, A.11.3.5 to A.11.3.6; *see also* Medical gases

Nonflammable medical gas systems, *see* Medical gas systems

Nonmedical compressed air, 8.3.5

    Definition, 3.3.131

Nurse call systems, 6.7.5.1.3.2(4), 7.3.3.1, 7.4.3.1, A.7.3.3.1.1 to A.7.3.3.1.4.1

Nursing homes (definition), 3.3.132

-O-

Occupant notification, 16.7.4

Odor, positive pressure outlets, 5.1.12.4.6.4, A.5.1.12.4.6.4

Operating rooms

    Electrical receptacles for, 6.3.2.2.1(C), 6.3.2.2.2(C)

    Emergency procedures, 16.14.3.9

    Fire loss prevention, 16.14, A.16.14.3.2

    Personnel orientation and training, 16.14.3.10

    Wet procedure locations, 6.3.2.3.4, 6.3.2.3.8, 6.3.2.3.9, A.6.3.2.3.8

Operating supply, 3.3.168, 5.1.9.2.4

    Definition, 3.3.183.1

Opportunity for improvement

    Definition, 3.3.133

Outlets, electrical, *see* Receptacles

Outlets, gas, *see* Station outlets

Overcurrent protection, 6.3.2.4.4, 6.7.2.1.1.1

Oxidizing gas, 11.3.6.2, 11.3.6.3; *see also* Nitrous oxide; Oxygen

    Definition, 3.3.134, A.3.3.134

Oxygen, 15.4.1.2; *see also* Medical air; Medical gases

    Ambulatory patients receiving, 11.5.2.5

    Compatibility, 14.3.2.3, 14.3.2.4

    Definition, 3.3.135, A.3.3.135

    Designation colors/operating pressures, Table 5.1.11

    Gaseous (definition), 3.3.135.1

    Handling, 11.6.2, 14.3.2.2 to 14.3.2.4

    Liquid, 14.3.3.2

        Definition, 3.3.135.2, A.3.3.135.2

        Equipment, 11.7, A.11.7.3.1 to A.11.7.3.6.1.1

        Transfilling, 11.5.2.3, 11.7.3.6, A.11.5.2.3.2, A.11.7.3.6.1.1

    Monitoring, 14.2.10.4, A.14.2.10.4.2.2, A.14.2.10.4.4

    Storage, 5.1.3.1.9, 5.1.3.3.2.2(6), 11.3.6.2, 11.3.6.3, 14.3.2.2, A.14.3.2.2

    Therapy, *see* Hyperbaric facilities

    Toxicity (hyperbaric), B.14.1.3.2

        Definition, 3.3.140, A.3.3.140

    Transfilling, 11.5.2.2, 11.5.2.3, 11.7.3.6, A.11.5.2.2.2, A.11.7.3.6.1.1

Oxygen concentrator units, 5.1.3.9, 5.1.12.4.14.4, 5.3.3.5.11, A.5.1.3.9 to A.5.1.3.9.2(5)

    Definition, 3.3.136

Oxygen cylinders, *see* Cylinders

Oxygen delivery equipment, 10.5.4.5, 15.4.2.5, A.10.5.4.5; *see also* Cylinders; Pipe and piping, gas

    Definition, 3.3.137, A.3.3.137

    Hazards, 11.5.1.1.6, 11.5.1.2.2

    Maintenance of, 11.5.1.3.3, A.11.5.1.3.3

Oxygen enclosures, 11.4.2.2

Oxygen-enriched atmosphere (OEA), *see also* Hyperbaric facilities

    Definition, 3.3.142

    Electrical appliances in, 10.5.4, A.10.5.4.5, A.10.5.4.6

    Equipment transport, storage, and use, 11.5.3.3

    Fire protection, B.11.3.1

    Hazards of, 11.5.1.2.1

    Labeling of equipment for use in, 11.5.3.1.1

Oxygen hoods, A.11.5.1.1.5

    Definition, 3.3.138, A.3.3.138

Oxygen systems, 5.1.1.2, A.5.1.1.3, B.5.3; *see also* Cylinders; Medical gas systems; Oxygen delivery equipment; Pipe and piping, gas

    Bulk (definition), 3.3.20.3, A.3.3.20.3; *see also* Cryogenic liquids, Bulk systems

    Hyperbaric facilities, 14.2.1.4

    Locations for, 5.1.3.3.1.5, 15.4.2.4

    Piping, 14.2.1.3, 15.4.4.2

    Supply systems, 5.1.3.3.1.6, 5.1.3.5.2, 5.1.3.5.4, 15.4.2.3, A.5.1.3.5.4

        Closing off supply, B.11.3.2.1(3), B.11.3.3, B.14.3.2(1)

        Emergency oxygen supply connection (EOSC), *see* Emergency oxygen supply connection (EOSC)

Oxygen USP

    Category 1 medical air proportioning system, 5.1.3.6.3.14, A.5.1.3.6.3.14(A), A.5.1.3.6.3.14(C)(9)

    Category 1 medical air supply systems, 5.1.3.6.1(1)

    Definition, 3.3.141

Oxygen 93 USP, 5.1.3.9.1.1, 5.1.12.4.11

    Definition, 3.3.139

-P-

Paper, 14.3.1.6.9, A.14.3.1.6.9

Partial pressure, *see* Pressure

Particulate test, piping, 5.1.12.4.7, 15.4.7.5.5

Patient area call stations, 7.3.3.1.2, A.7.3.3.1.2.1 to A.7.3.3.1.2.3

Patient bed locations

    Call station, 7.3.3.1.2.1, 7.3.3.1.2.3, A.7.3.3.1.2.1, A.7.3.3.1.2.3

    Definition, 3.3.143

    Electrical receptacles for, 6.3.2.2.1(C), 6.3.2.2.1(D), 6.3.2.2.2(A), 6.3.2.2.2(B)

    Electrical systems, 6.3.2.4.1

    Liquid oxygen storage, 11.7.4

Patient-care-related electrical equipment, 10.2, 10.3.2, 10.5.6, 14.2.9.3.16, A.10.2.3.2.4 to A.10.2.3.6(2), A.10.3.2, A.10.5.6.2, A.14.2.9.3.16

    Definition, 3.3.144

Patient care spaces, 1.3.4, 6.7.6.2.1.6(E)(1)

    Category 1, 1.3.4.1

        Definition, 3.3.145.1

        Electrical receptacles, 6.3.2.2.1(D), 6.3.2.2.2(B)

        Electrical systems, 6.4

    Category 2, 1.3.4.1

        Definition, 3.3.145.2

        Electrical receptacles, 6.3.2.2.1(D), 6.3.2.2.2(A)

        Electrical systems, 6.5

    Category 3, 1.3.4.1, 6.6

        Definition, 3.3.145.3

Category 4, 1.3.4.1, 6.6
  Definition, 3.3.145.4
Definition, 3.3.145, A.3.3.145
Electrical systems, 6.3.3.1, 6.3.3.2, 6.3.3.3.1, A.6.3.3.1.1 to
  A.6.3.3.1.4
Liquid oxygen storage, 11.7.4
Receptacles, 6.3.2.2.1(D)
Sprinklers, 16.9.1.4, A.16.9.1.4
Patient care vicinity
  Definition, 3.3.146
  Electrical equipment, testing of, 10.3.4.1
Patient equipment grounding point, 6.3.2.5.2
  Definition, 3.3.147
Patient leads, 10.3.6, A.10.3.6; *see also* Electrical wiring
  Definition, 3.3.148, A.3.3.148
  Isolated, 10.5.2.2, A.10.5.2.2
    Definition, 3.3.95
Patient medical gas, *see also* Medical air; Nitrous oxide; Oxygen
  Definition, 3.3.149
  Identification, 5.1.11.1.1
  Permitted locations for, 5.1.3.5.2
  Positive pressure piping, 5.1.10.11.12.1
Performance tests
  Category 1 piped gas and vacuum systems, 5.1.6.1, 5.1.6.2,
    5.1.12, 5.1.13.12, A.5.1.12, B.5.1
  Category 2 piped gas and vacuum systems, 5.2.12, 15.4.7, 15.4.8
  Category 3 piped gas and vacuum systems, 5.3.12, 15.5.7
Permit-to-work system, 5.1.14.2, A.5.1.14.2.1, A.5.1.14.2.2(4)
Photographic lighting equipment, 14.3.2.1.3
**Physicians, discretionary use of nonconforming
  materials**, 14.3.1.6.4.4
Pin-index safety system, A.11.4.1.1
Pipe and piping, gas
  Branch (lateral) line, 5.1.3.6.3.9(G), 5.1.4.5, 5.1.10.3.3,
    5.1.10.3.4, 5.1.10.11.1.3
    Definition, 3.3.151.1
  Breaching or penetrating, 5.1.10.11.12, 5.1.14.7.6
  Category 1, 5.1.3.6.3.9, A.5.1.3.6.3.9(D), A.5.1.3.6.3.9(F)
    Distribution, 5.1.10, 5.1.13.10
    Supply, 5.1.3.6.3.9, 5.1.3.7.5, A.5.1.3.6.3.9(D),
      A.5.1.3.6.3.9(F)
  Category 2 distribution piping, 5.2.10, 15.4.4
  Category 3 distribution piping, 5.3.10, 15.5.5
  Copper, 15.3.3.7.3.2, 15.4.4.4.2, 15.4.6, 15.5.5.2.2.1, 15.5.5.3.2
  Cryogenic liquid withdrawal systems, 5.4.6.9, A.5.4.6.9.1.3
  Definitions, 3.3.151
  Dental air and vacuum systems, 15.3.3.7, 15.4.4 to 15.4.6
  Dental air systems, 15.5.5.2
  Fire protection, 16.5.1.1
  Ground, use as, 5.1.14.3.2
  Hyperbaric facilities, 14.2.1.3, A.14.2.11.2, A.14.2.11.2.5
  Installation, 5.1.10.11, 15.4.5, 15.5.6
  Interconnections, prohibited, 5.1.10.11.7, 15.4.9.2
  Labeling, 5.1.11.1
  Main line, 5.1.4.3, 5.1.11.2.5
    Definition, 3.3.151.2
  Manufacturer's instructions, 5.1.10.11.8
  Materials, 5.1.10.1, 5.1.10.2, A.5.1.10.1.4

PVC plastic, 15.3.3.7.3.3, 15.3.3.7.3.4, 15.4.4.4.3, 15.4.4.4.4,
  15.5.5.3.3, 15.5.5.3.4
Special precautions, A.5.1.14
Support, 5.1.10.11.4, 15.4.5.6, 15.5.6.4, A.5.1.10.11.4.4
Tests
  Blowdown, 15.4.7.4.2
  Installer performed tests, 5.1.12.2, 15.4.7.4, 15.4.8.1.3,
    15.5.7.1.3, B.5.1
  System verification, 5.1.12.4, 5.1.14.7.6, 15.4.7.5, A.5.1.12.4.2
Underground piping outside of buildings, 5.1.10.11.5, 15.4.5.7,
  15.5.6.5
Underground piping within buildings/within floor
  slabs, 15.4.5.8, 15.5.6.6
Piped distribution systems, 5.1.10, 5.2.10, 5.3.10, 15.3.2.8; *see also*
  Central supply systems
  Definition, 3.3.150
Piped gas systems, *see* Medical gas systems
Piping, heating, cooling, ventilating, and process systems, 9.3.4
Planned event, 12.5.3.3.6.1, A.12.2.3.3
  Definition, 3.3.152
Plugs (attachment plugs, caps), 10.2.2.2, 14.2.9.3.16.5(3)
  Definition, 3.3.153
Plumbing, Chap. 8
  Building system categories, criteria for, 8.2, A.8.2.1
  Drainage systems, 8.3.12
  Fixtures, 8.3.8
  General requirements, 8.3
  Grease interceptors, 8.3.7
  Nonmedical compressed air, 8.3.5
  Potable and nonpotable water, 8.3.1, 8.3.2
  Special use water systems, 8.3.6
  Wastewater, 8.3.9 to 8.3.11
  Water conditioning, 8.3.4
  Water heating, 8.3.3
Plume (medical), 9.3.8.1
  Definition, 3.3.154
Portable equipment
  Electrical, *see* Electrical equipment
  Patient care gas equipment, 11.4.1, 11.4.2, A.11.4.1.1, A.11.4.1.3
Positive pressure
  Breaching or penetrating of medical gas piping, 5.1.10.11.12.1
  Change in system, 5.1.10.11.9.1
  Definition, 3.3.156.7
  Indicators, 5.1.8.1.3, A.5.1.8.1.3
  Joints for positive pressure gas systems, 5.1.10.3.1
  Labeling of systems, 5.1.11.1.2, 5.1.11.2.2
  Odor from outlets, 5.1.12.4.6.4, A.5.1.12.4.6.4
  Storage of positive-pressure gases, 5.1.3.3.2.2
  Telecommunications facilities, for, 7.3.1.2.1.8(C), 7.3.1.2.2.8(C),
    A.7.3.1.2.1.8(C)
Power cords, 10.2.3, 10.5.2.3
  Hyperbaric chambers, 14.2.9.3.8, 14.2.9.3.16.5
  Patient care spaces, 6.3.2.3.6
Power sources, 6.3.1
  Definition, 3.3.155
Power systems, *see* Electrical systems
Pressure
  Absolute, A.5.1.12.2.6.5

Definition, 3.3.156.1
Ambient, 14.2.5.1, 14.2.5.2, B.14.1.1.3.2
Definition, 3.3.156.2
Gauge (definition), 3.3.156.3
High
Definition, 3.3.156.4
Intermixing of gases, 11.2.7, A.11.2.7
Pressure reducing regulators and gauges, 11.2.4, 11.2.5, 11.5.3.3.4
Valve, 11.6.2.2(2)
Multiple, central supply system, 5.1.3.5.7, 5.1.13.3.6.6
Negative, 9.3.6.5.3.1, 9.3.7.1.1
Definition, 3.3.122
Operating, 5.1.12.2.3.4, 11.2.5, 11.6.3.1(6), 14.2.6.3.4
Definition, 3.3.156.5, A.3.3.156.5
Partial, B.14.1.1.2, B.14.1.3.2.3, B.14.1.3.5
Definition, 3.3.156.6, A.3.3.156.6
Positive, *see* Positive pressure
Standard operating pressures, gas and vacuum systems, Table 5.1.11
Working (rated), 5.1.3.5.6.1(3), 14.2.9.3.14.1
Definition, 3.3.156.8
Pressure indicators, 5.1.8, 5.1.13.7, 5.2.8, 5.3.8, 15.3.2.6, 15.4.2.9, B.5.2.5, B.5.2.14
Pressure-reducing regulators, 11.2.4 to 11.2.6, 11.5.3.1.2, 11.5.3.1.3, 11.5.3.3.4, 15.3.2.11
Definition, 3.3.157, A.3.3.157
Pressure regulators, 5.1.12.4.3.2(F); *see also* Pressure-reducing regulators
Final line, 5.1.3.5.5, 5.1.3.5.10.4(1), 5.1.3.5.11.4, 5.1.3.6.3.9(K), 5.1.3.6.3.14(C)(10), A.5.1.3.5.5.1
Headers, 5.1.3.5.9(8), 5.1.3.5.10.4, 5.1.3.5.11.4
Nitrogen purge, 5.1.10.4.5.3
Pressure relief valves, 14.3.4.1.1.1
Central supply systems, 5.1.3.3.3.2, 5.1.3.5.6, 5.1.3.10.10, 5.1.13.3.6.5
Emergency oxygen supply connection (EOSC), 5.1.3.5.12.2(5)
Liquid withdrawal systems, 5.4.5, A.5.4.5.2
Medical air supply systems, 5.1.3.6.3.9(J), 5.1.3.6.3.14(C)(8)
Pressure tests
Individual pressurization, 5.1.12.4.3.1
Initial pressure, 5.1.12.2.3, 15.4.7.4.4, 15.4.8.1.5, 15.5.7.1.3.2, A.5.1.12.2.3.5, A.15.4.7.4.4.5
Operational pressure, 5.1.12.4.10, 15.4.7.5.8, A.5.1.12.4.10.6
Pressure differential, 5.1.12.4.3.2
Standing pressure, 5.1.6.2, 5.1.12.2.6, 5.1.12.4.2, 15.3.3.8.3.5, 15.4.7.4.6, 15.4.7.5.2, 15.4.8.1.7, 15.5.7.1.3.4, A.5.1.12.2.6.1, A.5.1.12.2.6.5, A.5.1.12.4.2
Pressure vessels, *see* Hyperbaric facilities
Procedure room, 16.7.4.3.7
Definition, 3.3.158
Producers, 5.1.3.5, 5.1.3.8
Definition, 3.3.159, A.3.3.159
Psia (pounds per square inch absolute) (definition), 3.3.160
Psig (pounds per square inch gauge) (definition), 3.3.161, A.3.3.161
Pumps, vacuum, *see* Vacuum pumps
Purge test, piping, 5.1.12.2.5, 5.1.12.4.6, 15.4.7.4.5, 15.4.7.5.4, 15.4.8.1.6, 15.5.7.1.3.3, A.5.1.12.4.6.4

Purity test
Medical air, 5.1.12.4.12
Piping, 5.1.12.4.8, 15.4.7.4.5, 15.4.7.5.6, A.5.1.12.4.8
Purpose of standard, 1.2

-Q-

Qualified person (definition), 3.3.162

-R-

Radiation equipment, hyperbaric chambers, 14.3.2.6, A.14.3.2.6
Reactance (definition), 3.3.163
Receptacles, 6.3.2.2, A.6.3.2.2.1, B.6.3
Definition, 3.3.164, A.3.3.164
Grounding of, 6.3.2.2.5, 6.3.2.5, A.6.3.2.2.5, A.6.3.2.5.1.5, A.6.3.2.5.3
Hyperbaric chambers, 14.2.9.3.9, A.14.2.9.3.9
Life safety and equipment branches, 6.7.6.3.2, A.6.7.6.3.2
Number of, 6.3.2.2.2
Other services, for, 6.3.2.2.4
Polarity of, 6.3.2.2.3
Retractable power taps, 10.2.3.6, A.10.2.3.6 to A.10.2.3.6(2)
Selected (definition), 3.3.171
Special-purpose outlets, 6.3.2.2.6
Telecommunications facilities, 7.3.1.2.1.7(C), 7.3.1.2.3.7(C)
Tests, 6.3.3.2
Types of, 6.3.2.2.1, A.6.3.2.2.1
Wet procedure locations, 6.3.2.3.6, 6.3.2.3.9
Reference grounding point, 6.3.2.9.2.1, 6.3.2.9.3.6, 6.3.3.1.2(1)
Definition, 3.3.165
Reference point, 6.3.3.1.2, 6.3.3.1.4.1, 6.3.3.1.4.2
References, Chap. 2, A.2.1, Annex D
Refrigerating equipment, B.12.3.2.7
Regulators
Cylinders, 11.2.4 to 11.2.6
Medical air, 5.1.3.6.3.9(E), 5.1.3.6.3.9(F), 5.1.3.6.3.9(I), 5.2.3.5(1), 15.3.2.1.5(1), A.5.1.3.6.3.9(F)
Pressure-reducing, *see* Pressure-reducing regulators
Relocatable power tap (RPT), 10.2.3.6
Definition, 3.3.166
Remote (Level 3 supply source), 15.4.2.5.12, 15.4.2.6.4
Definition, 3.3.167, A.3.3.167
Reserve supply
Category 1
Bulk cryogenic liquid systems, 5.1.3.10.5
In-building emergency reserves, 5.1.3.5.8.1(5), 5.1.3.5.13
Warning signals, 5.1.9.2.4, B.5.2.10 to B.5.2.12
Definition, 3.3.168
Reservoir jars, 11.4.2.4
Resistance tests, 10.3.2, 10.3.3.2, A.10.3.2
Respiratory therapy, B.11; *see also* Oxygen-enriched atmosphere (OEA)
Administration and maintenance, 11.5, A.11.5.1.1.2 to A.11.5.3.2
Apparatus for, 11.4.2
Equipment labeling, 11.5.3.1
Equipment servicing and maintenance, 11.5.1.3
Equipment transport, storage, and use, 11.5.3.3
Fire hazards, 11.5.1.1, 11.5.1.2, A.11.5.1.1.2, A.11.5.1.1.4, B.11.3.1

Responsible facility authority (RFA), 5.1.14.1, 5.1.14.2, A.5.1.14.2.1, A.5.1.14.2.2(4)

Risers, piping, 15.4.2.7
    Definition, 3.3.151.3
    Valves, 5.1.4.4, 5.1.11.2.6

Risk assessment, 4.2, A.4.2

Risk categories, 4.1, A.4.1
    Category 1, 4.1.1, A.4.1, A.4.1.1
        Definition, 3.3.169.1
    Category 2, 4.1.2, A.4.1, A.4.1.2
        Definition, 3.3.169.2
    Category 3, 4.1.3, A.4.1
        Definition, 3.3.169.3
    Category 4, 4.1.4, A.4.1
        Definition, 3.3.169.4
    Risk assessment procedure, determination using, 4.2, A.4.2

-S-

Safety mechanisms, 11.6.4

Scavenging, *see also* Waste anesthetic gas disposal (WAGD) systems
    Category 3 systems
        Piping, 15.5.5.3
    Definition, 3.3.170
    Dental air and vacuum piping systems, 15.3.3.6, 15.3.3.7.3, 15.4.3.3.4, 15.4.4.4
    Ventilation system, 9.3.7
        Passive systems, 9.3.7.1.2
        Semi-active system, 9.3.7.1.1

Scope of standard, 1.1, A.1.1.10, A.1.1.12

Security management, Chap. 13
    Access control equipment, 13.9, A.13.9.4
    Emergency, 12.5.3.3.6.3, A.12.5.3.3.6.3
    Information technology and communications systems, 7.3.1.2.2.6, 7.3.1.2.3.6
    Operations, 13.11, A.13.11, A.13.11.1
    Plan, 13.2, 13.12.3 to 13.12.5, A.13.2, A.13.2.2
    Program evaluation, 13.12, A.13.12.1
    Responsible person, 13.4, A.13.4.2(3)(c)
    Security-sensitive areas, 13.5, A.13.5.2(1) to A.13.5.7(1)
    Security vulnerability assessment, 13.3, A.13.3.1

Selected receptacles (definition), 3.3.171

Self-extinguishing (definition), 3.3.172

Semipermanent connection (definition), 3.3.173

Sensors, inside hyperbaric chambers, 14.2.10.1.2

Service inlets, A.15.3.3.5
    Definition, 3.3.174

Service outlets
    Definition, 3.3.175

Service outlets (definition), 3.3.175

Service valves, 5.1.4.5, 5.1.11.2.7

Shall (definition), 3.2.7

Should (definition), 3.2.8

Shutoff valves
    Emergency oxygen supply connection (EOSC), 5.1.3.5.12.2(3), 15.4.2.6, A.14.2.6.1.5
    Gas, 5.1.4.1.1, 5.1.4.2.1, 5.1.4.3.1, 5.1.4.4, 5.1.4.7, 15.4.9.1.2, A.5.1.4.3
    Hyperbaric facilities, 14.2.1.3.2

    Labeling and identification, 5.1.11.2
    Vacuum, 5.1.4.1.1

Signs, *see* Labeling and identification

Single treatment facilities, 15.4.2.5.12, 15.4.2.5.14
    Definition, 3.3.176, A.3.3.176

Site of intentional expulsion, 10.5.4.1, 10.5.4.2, 11.5.1.1.6, 11.5.1.2.3
    Definition, 3.3.177, A.3.3.177

Sleep lab, 5.1.11.3.1.1, A.5.1.12.4.10.6
    Definition, 3.3.178

Smoke alarms/detectors, 16.7.3, 16.7.4.2.1, 16.7.4.2.2, 16.12.2

Smoke compartments, 16.7.4.3.1, 16.9.1.3, A.16.9.1.3

Smoke control, 6.7.5.1.4.3(A)(4), 6.7.6.2.1.6(D)(4)

Smoke zones, 16.7.4.3.3

Smoking, 11.5.1.1.1, 11.5.2.5, 11.5.3.2, 14.3.1.6.1.1(1), A.11.5.3.2

Sound-deadening materials, 14.2.2.6.4, A.14.2.2.6.4

Source valves, 5.1.4.2, 5.1.11.2.3, 5.1.11.2.4, A.5.1.11.2.3

Spaces (definition), 3.3.179; *see also* Patient care spaces

Sprinklers, automatic, 7.3.1.2.1.8(D), 7.3.1.2.3.8(B), 16.9, 16.11, 16.12.3, A.16.11, A.16.12.3
    Hyperbaric facilities, 14.2.1.2, A.14.2.1.2 to A.14.2.1.2(3)

Staff, *see* Employees

Staff emergency calls, 7.3.1.3, A.7.3.3.1.3.1

Standard (definition), 3.2.9

Standard cubic feet per minute (SCFM) (definition), 3.3.180

Standpipe and hose systems, 16.10.2, 16.10.2.2, A.16.10.2.2

Station inlets
    Category 1, 5.1.4.6.1, 5.1.5, 5.1.6.9, 5.1.6.11, 5.1.7.5 to 5.1.7.7, 5.1.10.10(1), 5.1.11.3, 5.1.12.1.2, 5.1.12.1.10, 5.1.12.2.1.3(3), 5.1.12.2.4.6, 5.1.12.4.3.1(D), 5.1.12.4.3.2(E), 5.1.12.4.10, 5.1.12.4.13, 5.1.14.7.9, 15.3.2.3, A.5.1.5, A.5.1.12.4.10.6
    Category 2, 5.2.5
    Category 3, 5.3.5
    Definition, 3.3.181

Station outlets
    Category 1, 5.1.4.6.1, 5.1.5, 5.1.6.9, 5.1.6.11, 5.1.7.5 to 5.1.7.7, 5.1.10.1.1, 5.1.10.10(1), 5.1.11.3, 5.1.12.1.2, 5.1.12.1.10, 5.1.12.2.1.3(3), 5.1.12.2.4.6, 5.1.12.2.6.1, 5.1.12.4.3.1(D), 5.1.12.4.3.2(E), 5.1.12.4.3.2(G), 5.1.12.4.6.1, 5.1.12.4.6.3, 5.1.12.4.6.4, 5.1.12.4.7.2 to 5.1.12.4.7.4, 5.1.12.4.8.2, 5.1.12.4.8.6, 5.1.12.4.10, 5.1.12.4.13, 15.3.2.3, 15.3.3.4.1.2, A.5.1.3.6.3.10, A.5.1.5, A.5.1.12.2.6.1, A.5.1.12.4.6.4, A.5.1.12.4.10.6, B.5.2.18
    Category 2, 5.2.5, 15.4.1.6, 15.4.2.7
    Category 3, 5.3.5
    Definition, 3.3.182

Storage
    Compact, *see* Compact storage
    Containers, *see* Containers
    Cryogenic liquids, ventilation for storage of, 9.3.6, A.9.3.6.3, A.9.3.6.5.1, A.9.3.6.5.2.1
    Cylinders, *see* Cylinders
    Flammable and combustible liquids, 16.3, A.16.3.2
    Flammable gases, 14.3.3.3, 14.3.4.1.4.1, 16.3, A.16.3.2
    Gas equipment, 11.5.3.3
    Hyperbaric facilities, 14.2.1.6, 14.3.2.2, 14.3.3.3, 14.3.4.1.4, A.14.3.2.2
    Nonflammable gases, 11.3.5, 11.3.6, A.11.3.5 to A.11.3.6
    Oxygen, 5.1.3.1.9, 14.3.2.2, A.14.3.2.2

Ventilation for medical gas storage, 9.3.6, A.9.3.6.3, A.9.3.6.5.1, A.9.3.6.5.2.1

Stored electrical energy systems, 16.5.1.3

Supply source, *see also* Category 1 piped gas and vacuum systems, Sources; Category 3 piped gas and vacuum systems, Sources

    Category 2 piped gas and vacuum systems, 5.2.3

    Definition, 3.3.183

    Operating supply, 3.3.168, 5.1.9.2.4

        Definition, 3.3.183.1

    Portable, 11.4.1, A.11.4.1.1, A.11.4.1.3

    Primary supply, 5.1.3.6.3.14(C)(6)

        Definition, 3.3.183.2

    Reserve supply (definition), 3.3.183.3; *see also* Reserve supply

    Secondary supply, 5.1.12.4.14.2

        Definition, 3.3.183.4

Supply systems, *see also* Category 1 piped gas and vacuum systems; Category 2 piped gas and vacuum systems; Category 3 piped gas and vacuum systems; Central supply systems; Pipe and piping, gas; Piped distribution systems

    Hyperbaric facilities, 14.2.4.1.3.2

Support gases, *see also* Instrument air; Nitrogen

    Category 1 piped gas and vacuum systems, *see* Category 1 piped gas and vacuum systems

    Category 2 piped gas and vacuum systems, 5.2.13

    Category 3 piped gas and vacuum systems, 5.3.13

    Medical, 5.1.1.2, 5.3.12, A.5.1.1.3

        Central supply system, 5.1.13.3

        Definition, 3.3.115

Surface-mounted medical gas rail systems, 5.1.7, 5.2.7, 5.3.7, 15.3.2.5, A.5.1.7

    Definition, 3.3.184, A.3.3.184

Switches, *see also* Transfer switches

    Essential electrical systems, 6.7.2.1.2.1, 6.7.2.1.6, 6.7.2.2.1, A.6.7.2.1.3.1(A) to A.6.7.2.1.3.17

    Hyperbaric facilities, 14.2.9.3.10, A.14.2.9.3.10.1

    Isolation switch, bypass, 6.7.2.1.6, A.6.7.2.1.6.3

    Test, 6.7.2.1.3.10

Synthetic materials, *see* Textiles, hyperbaric chamber use

-T-

Task illumination, 6.7.5.1.2.2(4), 6.7.5.1.3.2, 6.7.6.2.1.5(A)(5), 6.7.6.2.1.6(D)(1), A.6.7.5.1.3.2(6)

    Definition, 3.3.185

Telecommunications entrance facility (EF), 7.3.1.2.1, 7.5.1.1.1 to 7.5.1.1.3, A.7.3.1.2.1.4(C) to A.7.3.1.2.1.8(C)

    Definition, 3.4.1

Telecommunications equipment room (TER), 7.3.1.2.1.1, 7.3.1.2.2, 7.5.1.1.2, A.7.3.1.2.2.2

    Definition, 3.4.2

Telecommunications room (TR), 7.3.1.2.3, 7.5.1.1.2, 7.5.1.1.3

    Definition, 3.4.3

Temperature

    Ambient, 5.1.3.6.3.1(3), 5.1.3.7.1(3), 5.1.3.8.1.3(4), 5.1.3.8.1.4(2), 5.1.10.11.3.3, 5.1.12.2.6.5, 5.1.12.2.7.5, 6.7.1.3.4, 6.7.1.3.4.6, A.5.1.12.2.6.5, A.5.1.12.2.7.5

    Generator sets and, 6.7.1.3.3

    Hyperbaric chambers, 14.2.4.3, 14.2.9.3.11, A.14.2.9.3.11

Temperature control, 7.3.1.2.1.8(A), 7.3.1.2.2.8(A), 7.3.1.2.3.8(A), 14.2.4.3

Terminals

    Definition, 3.3.186

    Inlets, *see* Station inlets

Test equipment, 6.3.3.1.5

Tests, *see also* Performance tests

    Cryogenic liquid withdrawal systems, 5.4.6.10, A.5.4.6.10(4)

    Dental gas and vacuum systems, 15.3.3.8, 15.4.7, 15.4.8, 15.4.9.5, 15.5.7

    Elevators, 16.5.3.4

    Emergency plans and operations, 12.5.3.3.8

    Fire protection systems, 16.13

    Health care microgrid system, 6.10.8

    Hyperbaric chambers, electrical equipment for, 14.2.9.3.2, 14.3.4.3.2 to 14.3.4.3.5

    Maintenance program

        Gas and vacuum systems, 5.1.14.4.3, 5.1.14.7.1, 5.1.14.7.5 to 5.1.14.7.7, A.5.1.14.4.3, B.5.2

    Records and reports, 5.1.12.1.6 to 5.1.12.1.9, 5.1.12.1.12, 5.1.12.2.1.1, 5.1.14.4.3.1(F), 5.1.14.7.1, 6.3.4.1, 6.7.4.2, 6.8.3, 10.5.6.2, 10.5.6.3, 15.4.7.1.1.2 to 15.4.7.1.1.5, 15.4.8.1.1.2 to 15.4.8.1.1.5, A.6.3.4.1.1, A.10.5.6.2

    Retests, B.5.2

    Site acceptance, 6.8, A.6.8.1, A.6.8.2

Test switches, 6.7.2.1.3.10

Textiles, hyperbaric chamber use, 14.3.1.6.4, A.14.3.1.6.4 to A.14.3.1.6.4.3

Total hazard current, *see* Hazard current

Touch current

    Definition, 3.3.187

    Limits, 10.3.3.4

    Portable equipment, 10.3.5

    Test procedure, 10.3.5.3

Training, employee

    Electrical equipment, 10.5.8, A.10.5.8.1, A.10.5.8.3

    Emergency management, 12.5.3.3.6.7(B), 12.5.3.3.7

    Gas equipment and systems, 11.5.2.1, 11.6.1.2, A.11.5.2.1.1

    Hyperbaric facilities, 14.3.1.4.3, 14.3.1.5.2, 14.3.1.5.3, 14.3.4.7.1, A.14.3.1.5.2

    Operating rooms, 16.14.3.10

    Security personnel, 13.11.2

Transfer switches, 6.7.2.1.2.1, 6.7.2.1.3, 6.7.2.2.1, 6.7.2.2.3, A.6.7.2.1.3.1(A) to A.6.7.2.1.3.17, B.6.1, B.12.3.2.5; *see also* Switches

    Automatic, 6.7.2.1.2.1, 6.7.2.1.3.16, 6.7.3.5, A.6.7.2.1.3.1(A) to A.6.7.2.1.3.17

    Isolating, 6.7.2.1.6, A.6.7.2.1.6.3

    Nonautomatic, 6.7.2.1.3.17, 6.7.2.1.4, 6.7.2.1.5, 6.7.2.1.6, 6.7.3.7, A.6.7.2.1.3.17, A.6.7.2.1.6.3

    Performance criteria and tests, 6.7.3.1, 6.7.4.1.1, A.6.7.4.1.1.5(A)

    Rating, 6.7.2.1.3.15

Transfilling, 9.3.6, 11.5.2.2, 11.5.2.3, 11.7.3.6, A.9.3.6.3, A.9.3.6.5.1, A.9.3.6.5.2.1, A.11.5.2.2.2, A.11.7.3.6.1.1

    Definition, 3.3.188

Transformers, isolation, 6.3.2.9.1

    Definition, 3.3.97

Tube (pipe), *see* Pipe and piping, gas

Tube, endotracheal, B.14.1.2.4

Definition, 3.3.189.1, A.3.3.189.1

-U-

Units of measurement, 1.5, A.1.5
Use points, 3.3.176, 15.4.2.4.9, 15.4.2.6.1, 15.4.2.6.2
  Definition, 3.3.190
Utilities
  Emergency plan for, 12.5.3.3.6.5, 12.5.3.3.6.6, A.12.5.3.3.6.5, B.12.3.4
  Fire protection for, 16.5, A.16.5.3.3

-V-

Vacuum, dental-surgical, *see* Dental-surgical vacuum
Vacuum indicators, 5.1.8, 5.2.8, 5.3.8, 15.3.2.6, 15.4.2.9
Vacuum pumps
  Alarms, 5.1.9.5, A.5.1.9.5
  Category 1 systems, 5.1.3.7.2, 5.1.3.7.5.1(3)
Vacuum receivers, 5.1.3.7.3, 5.1.3.7.5.2
Vacuum systems, *see* Medical-surgical vacuum systems
Vacuum terminals, *see* Station inlets
Valves, *See also* Check valves; Pressure relief valves; Shutoff valves; Zone valves
  Accessibility, 5.1.4.1.4
  Category 1, 5.1.3.2.10, 5.1.3.3.3.2, 5.1.3.5.6, 5.1.3.5.12.2, 5.1.3.6.3.9(G), 5.1.3.6.3.9(J), 5.1.3.6.3.14(C)(8), 5.1.3.10.11, 5.1.4, 5.1.8.2.3.1, 5.1.11.2, 5.1.12.1.2, 5.1.12.2.5.2, 5.1.12.4.2(1), 5.1.12.4.4, 5.1.13.4, 15.3.2.2, 15.3.2.11(2), A.5.1.3.10.11.4(A), A.5.1.4, B.5.2.17
  Category 2, 5.2.4
  Category 3, 5.3.4
  Flow-control, 11.5.3.3.1
    Definition, 3.3.66
  Future connections, for, 5.1.4.8
  Gas equipment, cylinder and container sources for, 11.2.1, 11.2.8, 11.2.9, 11.6.2.2
  High pressure, 11.6.2.2(2)
  Hyperbaric facilities, 14.3.2.2(2), 14.3.2.3(1), 14.3.4.1.1.1
  In-line, 5.1.4.7, 5.1.4.9
  Labeling, 5.1.4.1.3
  Protection caps, 5.1.3.2.10
  Security, 5.1.4.1.2
  Service, 5.1.4.5, 5.1.11.2.7
  Source, 5.1.4.2, 5.1.11.2.3, 5.1.11.2.4, A.5.1.11.2.3
  Types, 5.1.4.1.6
Vaporizers, 5.1.3.10.7, 5.1.10.4.1.8
  Definition, 3.3.191
Ventilation, 6.7.5.1.4.4(4); *see also* Exhaust systems; Heating, ventilating, and air conditioning (HVAC) systems
  Alternate power sources, 6.7.1.2.6, 6.7.1.3.4, 6.7.5.1.4.3(A)(6), 6.7.5.1.4.3(B), A.6.7.1.3.4
  Central supply systems and storage, gas, 5.1.3.3.3, 5.1.13.3.3
  Construction, during, 9.3.10
  Cryogenic liquids, storage or transfilling of, 5.4.3, 9.3.6, A.5.4.5.2, A.5.4.6.2, A.9.3.6.3, A.9.3.6.5.1, A.9.3.6.5.2.1
  Definition, 3.3.192
  Dental air and vacuum piping systems, 15.3.3.2.3, 15.5.3.3
  Emergency systems, 6.7.5.1.4.4(4)

Hyperbaric chambers, 14.2.4, 14.2.11.2, A.14.2.4.1.2 to A.14.2.4.4.1, A.14.2.11.2, A.14.2.11.2.5
Laboratories, 16.5.2.4
Medical gas, storage or transfilling of, 9.3.6, A.9.3.6.3, A.9.3.6.5.1, A.9.3.6.5.2.1
Waste gas, 9.3.7
Venting, *see* Ventilation
Voltages
  Limit, 6.3.3.1.6.1
  Measuring, 6.3.3.1.2 to 6.3.3.1.3.3
Voltage sensing equipment, 6.7.2.1.3.1(B)

-W-

Warning signs, *see* Labeling and identification
Warning systems, *see* Alarm systems
Waste anesthetic gas disposal (WAGD) systems
  Alarms, 5.1.3.8.3
    Area, 5.1.9.4, A.5.1.9.4
    Local, 5.1.9.5, A.5.1.9.5
    Master, 5.1.9.2.4(12)
  Category 1 piped gas and vacuum systems, 5.1.3.3.1.3(3), 5.1.3.5(6), 5.1.3.8, 5.1.10.2.3, 5.1.10.3.3, 5.1.14.3, 5.1.14.4, 5.1.14.7.7(4), 15.3.2.1.8, 15.3.2.10, A.5.1.3.8, A.5.1.10.2.3.2
  Category 2 piped gas and vacuum systems, 5.2.3.8
  Category 3 piped gas and vacuum systems, 5.3.3.8, 5.3.12
  Definition, 3.3.193
  Designation colors, Table 5.1.11
  Electrical power and control, 5.1.3.8.4
  Exhaust, 5.1.3.8.5
  Maintenance, 5.1.14.4, 5.1.14.7.7(4)
  Operating pressures, Table 5.1.11
  Producers, 5.1.3.8.1.1, 5.1.3.8.2
  Sources, 5.1.3.8.1, A.5.1.3.8.1
  Special precautions, 5.1.14.3
  Ventilation system, 9.3.7
Waste chutes, 16.6
Waste water, 8.3.9 to 8.3.11
  Black, 8.3.9
    Definition, 3.3.194.1
  Clear, 8.3.11
    Definition, 3.3.194.2
  Gray, 8.3.10
    Definition, 3.3.194.3
Water, potable and nonpotable, 8.3.1, 8.3.2, 12.5.3.3.6.5, A.12.5.3.3.6.5, B.12.3.2.5(2), B.12.3.2.7
Water conditioning, 8.3.4
Water heating, 8.3.3
Welded joints, 5.1.10.3.1(2), 5.1.10.5
Wet procedure locations, 1.3.4.3, 6.3.2.3, A.6.3.2.3.1 to A.6.3.2.3.8
  Definition, 3.3.195, A.3.3.195
Wiring, *see* Electrical wiring
Working pressure, *see* Pressure
Work space or room
  Telecommunications facility, 7.3.1.2.2.5, 7.3.1.2.3.5

-X-

X-ray equipment, 14.3.2.1.2(1)

-Z-

Zone valves

Category 1, 5.1.4.1.4, 5.1.4.1.5, 5.1.4.6, 5.1.8.2.2(3), 5.1.8.2.3.1,
5.1.11.2.8, 5.1.12.1.2, 5.1.12.2.5.2, 5.1.12.4.2(1),
A.5.1.4.6.1(2), A.5.1.4.6.1(3), A.5.1.11.2.8

Gas equipment, B.11.3.3.1

Hyperbaric facilities, B.14.3.1, B.14.3.2

Submitting Public Input / Public Comment Through the Online Submission System

Following publication of the current edition of an NFPA standard, the development of the next edition begins and the standard is open for Public Input.

Submit a Public Input

NFPA accepts Public Input on documents through our online submission system at www.nfpa.org. To use the online submission system:

- Choose a document from the List of NFPA codes & standards or filter by Development Stage for "codes accepting public input."
- Once you are on the document page, select the "Next Edition" tab.
- Choose the link "The next edition of this standard is now open for Public Input." You will be asked to sign in or create a free online account with NFPA before using this system.
- Follow the online instructions to submit your Public Input (see www.nfpa.org/publicinput for detailed instructions).
- Once a Public Input is saved or submitted in the system, it can be located on the "My Profile" page by selecting the "My Public Inputs/Comments/NITMAMs" section.

Submit a Public Comment

Once the First Draft Report becomes available there is a Public Comment period. Any objections or further related changes to the content of the First Draft must be submitted at the Comment Stage. To submit a Public Comment follow the same steps as previously explained for the submission of Public Input.

Other Resources Available on the Document Information Pages

Header: View document title and scope, access to our codes and standards or NFCSS subscription, and sign up to receive email alerts.

Current & Prior Editions	Research current and previous edition information.
Next Edition	Follow the committee's progress in the processing of a standard in its next revision cycle.
Technical Committee	View current committee rosters or apply to a committee.
Ask a Technical Question	For members, officials, and AHJs to submit standards questions to NFPA staff. Our Technical Questions Service provides a convenient way to receive timely and consistent technical assistance when you need to know more about NFPA standards relevant to your work.
News	Provides links to available articles and research and statistical reports related to our standards.
Purchase Products & Training	Discover and purchase the latest products and training.
Related Products	View related publications, training, and other resources available for purchase.